Human Services Administration

PUBLIC ADMINISTRATION AND PUBLIC POLICY

A Comprehensive Publication Program

Executive Editor

JACK RABIN
Graduate Program in
Human Services Administration
School of Education
Rider College
Lawrenceville, New Jersey

1. Public Administration as a Developing Discipline (in two parts), *by Robert T. Golembiewski*
2. Comparative National Policies on Health Care, *by Milton I. Roemer, M.D.*
3. Exclusionary Injustice: The Problem of Illegally Obtained Evidence, *by Steven R. Schlesinger*
4. Personnel Management in Government: Politics and Process, *by Jay M. Shafritz, Walter L. Balk, Albert C. Hyde, and David H. Rosenbloom* (out of print)
5. Organization Development in Public Administration (in two parts), *edited by Robert T. Golembiewski and William B. Eddy* (Part two out of print)
6. Public Administration: A Comparative Perspective. Second Edition, Revised and Expanded, *by Ferrel Heady*
7. Approaches to Planned Change (in two parts), *by Robert T. Golembiewski*
8. Program Evaluation at HEW (in three parts), *edited by James G. Abert*
9. The States and the Metropolis, *by Patricia S. Florestano and Vincent L. Marando*
10. Personnel Management in Government: Politics and Process. Second Edition, Revised and Expanded, *by Jay M. Shafritz, Albert C. Hyde, and David H. Rosenbloom*
11. Changing Bureaucracies: Understanding the Organization Before Selecting the Approach, *by William A. Medina*
12. Handbook on Public Budgeting and Financial Management, *edited by Jack Rabin and Thomas D. Lynch*

13. Encyclopedia of Policy Studies, *edited by Stuart S. Nagel*
14. Public Administration and Law: Bench v. Bureau in the United States, *by David H. Rosenbloom*
15. Handbook on Public Personnel Administration and Labor Relations, *edited by Jack Rabin, Thomas Vocino, W. Bartley Hildreth, and Gerald J. Miller*
16. Public Budgeting and Finance: Behavioral, Theoretical and Technical Perspectives, *edited by Robert T. Golembiewski and Jack Rabin*
17. Organizational Behavior and Public Management, *by Debra W. Stewart and G. David Garson*
18. The Politics of Terrorism. Second Edition, Revised and Expanded, *edited by Michael Stohl*
19. Handbook of Organization Management, *edited by William B. Eddy*
20. Organization Theory and Management, *edited by Thomas D. Lynch*
21. Labor Relations in the Public Sector, *by Richard C. Kearney*
22. Politics and Administration: Woodrow Wilson and American Public Administration, *edited by Jack Rabin and James S. Bowman*
23. Making and Managing Policy: Formulation, Analysis, Evaluation, *edited by G. Ronald Gilbert*
24. Public Administration: A Comparative Perspective. Third Edition, Revised, *by Ferrel Heady*
25. Decision Making in the Public Sector, *edited by Lloyd G. Nigro*
26. Managing Administration, *edited by Jack Rabin, Samuel Humes, and Brian S. Morgan*
27. Public Personnel Update, *edited by Michael Cohen and Robert T. Golembiewski*
28. State and Local Government Administration, *edited by Jack Rabin and Don Dodd*
29. Public Administration: A Bibliographic Guide to the Literature, *by Howard E. McCurdy*
30. Personnel Management in Government: Politics and Process, Third Edition, Revised and Expanded, *by Jay M. Shafritz, Albert C. Hyde, and David H. Rosenbloom*
31. Handbook of Information Resource Management, *edited by Jack Rabin and Edward M. Jackowski*
32. Public Administration in Developed Democracies: A Comparative Study, *edited by Donald C. Rowat*
33. The Politics of Terrorism, Third Edition, Revised and Expanded, *edited by Michael Stohl*
34. Handbook on Human Services Administration, *edited by Jack Rabin and Marcia B. Steinhauer*

Other volumes in preparation

Handbook of Public Administration, *edited by Jack Rabin, W. Bartley Hildreth, and Gerald J. Miller*

HANDBOOK ON

Human Services Administration

edited by

JACK RABIN
MARCIA B. STEINHAUER
Graduate Program in
Human Services Administration
School of Education
Rider College
Lawrenceville, New Jersey

MARCEL DEKKER, INC. New York and Basel

Library of Congress Cataloging-in-Publication Data

Handbook of human services administration / edited by Jack Rabin,
Marcia B. Steinhauer.
p. cm. -- (Public administration and public policy ; 34)
Includes bibliographies and index.
ISBN 0-8247-7924-X
1. Human services--United States--Management--Handbook, manuals,
etc. 2. Health services administration--United States--Handbooks,
manuals, etc. I. Rabin, Jack. II. Steinhauer, Marcia B. III. Series.
HV91.H27 1988
361'.0068--dc 19 88-7009

MARCEL DEKKER, INC.
270 Madison Avenue, New York, New York 10016

Current printing (last digit):
10 9 8 7 6 5 4 3 2 1

PRINTED IN THE UNITED STATES OF AMERICA

To

Philip, Susan, Joshua, and Benjamin Rabin

Lillian D. Buan--Mother and Ever-Ready Source of Encouragement

and

Students of Administration--
Individuals Who Combine Abstract Theory with the Realities of
Application in Order to Make Organizations More Humane

Preface

The *Handbook on Human Services Administration* is designed so that a reader may obtain an encyclopedic view of the subject matter. It is organized in a unique way: Each unit begins with a chapter introducing the reader to theories and concepts of a general nature. Thus, units on human services organization theory and management, budgeting and financial management, personnel administration and labor relations, law and regulation, innovation and change, and data administration and information systems start with introductory chapters dealing with theories and concepts which frame the subject matter of each unit. The reader can obtain a grounding in basic administrative theory through these introductory chapters.

Each unit of the *Handbook* also contains one or more chapters of a more specific nature relating the unit's subject matter directly to the human services field. For example, the organization theory and management unit contains a chapter on organizational structure and service delivery arrangements; the budgeting and financial management unit has specific chapters on internal financial planning, marketing and the financial impact of government policies on human services administration.

The personnel and labor relations unit presents specific chapters on supervisory issues and employee organizations, while the law and regulation unit puts forth chapters on health and human services law and regulation, and legal and ethical dilemmas of modern medical technology.

The unit on innovation and change also has a chapter on innovation and change in the delivery of drug services, while the unit on data administration and information systems contains chapters on new technological advances in computer hardware and software, and the implementing of medical information systems.

We want to thank the many contributors to this volume; we feel that a basic understanding of administration, as well as human services administration, may be obtained through the use of this *Handbook*.

Jack Rabin
Marcia B. Steinhauer

Contents

Contributors

Andrea Camerlingo-Aluisi Coordinator, Department of Epidemiology, United Hospitals Medical Center, Newark, New Jersey

Robert W. Broyles Professor of Health Administration, Department of Health and Medical Services Administration, School of Management, Widener University, Chester, Pennsylvania

William H. Campbell Professor and Chair, Department of Pharmacy Practice, University of Washington School of Pharmacy, Seattle, Washington

Dale B. Christensen Associate Professor, Department of Pharmacy Practice, University of Washington School of Pharmacy, Seattle, Washington

Michael A. Counte Associate Director, Center for Health Management Studies, and Assistant Chair and Associate Professor, Department of Health Systems Management, Rush-Presbyterian-St. Luke's Medical Center, Chicago, Illinois

Paul E. Fitzgerald, Jr.* Associate Professor, Health Services Administration, University of Arkansas at Little Rock, Little Rock, Arkansas

Robert T. Golembiewski Research Professor, Department of Political Science, University of Georgia, Athens, Georgia

Kyle L. Grazier† Associate Professor, Epidemiology and Public Health, School of Medicine, Yale University, New Haven, Connecticut

**Present Affiliation*: Director, Marketing and Strategic Planning, Arkansas Children's Hospital, Little Rock, Arkansas

†*Present Affiliation*: Department of Social and Administrative Health Sciences, School of Public Health, University of California, Berkeley, California

Rodger P. Hildreth Department of Political Science, Jackson State University, Jackson, Mississippi

W. Bartley Hildreth Associate Professor, Public Administration Institute, Louisiana State University, Baton Rouge, Louisiana

Marc D. Hiller Assocaite Professor, Department of Health Management and Policy University of New Hampshire, Durham, New Hampshire

John F. Hough Coordinator, Division of Community Health and Patient Advocacy, California Medical Association, San Francisco, California

Edward M. Jackowski Assistant Professor, Graduate Program in Human Services Administration, School of Education, Rider College, Lawrence, New Jersey

Kristen H. Kjerulff Assistant Professor, Center for Nursing and Health Services Research, School of Nursing, University of Maryland at Baltimore, Baltimore, Maryland

Donald E. Klingner Professor and Coordinator of Doctoral Studies, Department of Public Administration, Florida International University, North Miami, Florida

Joel M. Lee Professor, Department of Community Health, College of Allied Health Professions, University of Kentucky Medical Center, Lexington, Kentucky

Norman Metzger Guggenheim Professor and Vice President, Department of Health Care Management, The Mount Sinai Medical Center, New York, New York

William J. Page Professor, Department of Public Administration and School of Social Work, Florida State University, Tallahassee, Florida

David H. Rosenbloom Professor, Department of Public Administration, The Maxwell School of Citizenship and Public Affairs, Syracuse University, Syracuse, New York

Michael D. Rosko Associate Professor, Department of Health and Medical Services Administration, School of Management, Widener University, Chester, Pennsylvania

Jeffrey Colman Salloway Associate Professor, Department of Psychology and Social Sciences, Rush Medical College of Rush University, Chicago, Illinois

Winsor C. Schmidt Associate Professor, Department of Political Science, Memphis State University, Memphis, Tennessee

Marcia B. Steinhauer Associate Professor, Graduate Program in Human Services Administration, School of Education, Rider College, Lawrence, New Jersey

Barbara Stevens New Jersey Department of Corrections, Trenton, New Jersey

James D. Suver Professor of Accounting and Health Administration, Graduate School of Business Administration, University of Colorado, Denver, Colorado

John Abbott Worthley Professor of Public Service Management, Center for Public Service, Seton Hall University, South Orange, New Jersey

Human Services Administration

Unit I

Organizational Theory and Management in Human Services Administration

1

Organization Theory

Robert T. Golembiewski Department of Political Science, University of Georgia, Athens, Georgia

I. ORGANIZATION THEORY: INTRODUCTION

Broad characterizations often are hazardous, but—substantially more than less—the theory and practice of organizing have required and have experienced major consciousness-raising over the past several decades. Principles and practices that seemed basically secure for long periods of time are being subjected to corrosive criticism. Not only have constants become galloping variables, but "organizing" has had to sharply expand its field of vision to encompass what had generally been undervalued, if not abjectly neglected, as well as to magnify its focus so as to highlight details that often went unnoticed in the past.

Organization studies have had to become both broader and deeper, as it were, because practice has faced an expanding range of choices and dilemmas, which this essay expresses in three basic thrusts. This essay draws attention to some of the major developments that resulted from this ongoing ferment; it seeks to illustrate why changes were required; and it sketches the character and quality of major examples of ongoing changes.

The millenium is not yet with us, of course. Thus, we are still better at prescribing in general what should be done when organizing than we are at translating those general requirements into concrete proposals tailored to specific organization settings. Moreover, overall, the lines of the development of theory and practice are jagged and broken, rather than an even wave of progress that sweeps all before it. Specifically, for complex reasons, developments in public-sector organizing have lagged far behind pioneering profit-sector counterparts (Golembiewski, 1985, 1987). And major segments of business and industry have just begun to get their feet wet in the analytic and applied waves of our apparently new future, and this several decades after the leaders had made their fateful decision to innovate organizational forms and systems (Chandler, 1962).

This chapter adopts a direct approach to outlining these developments in practice and theory. Since there is no way to easily and evenly characterize this area of research and application, this essay must be suggestive and illustrative rather than definitive and comprehensive. Moreover, applications to specific health care settings fall well beyond the scope of this chapter. Readers are invited to examine the selective overview below.

II. THE PRESENT PATCH IN THE "MANAGEMENT THEORY JUNGLE"

Even if in a preliminary way, let us try to be more specific about the place of this chapter in the variegated literature in which it generally rests, and from which it specifically springs (March, 1965; Nystrom and Starbuck, 1981). The metaphors commonly applied to that literature give us a strong, if general, sense of how selective this chapter must be. Some have called organization theory an "elephantine problem" (Waldo, 1961); others see it as a "jungle," rich and luxuriant, but also treacherous (Koontz, 1961); others see it in terms bordering on methodological despair as seeing selectively because of the limiting ways that the literature looks at its conceptual targets (Miller and Friesen, 1984, especially pp. 12-25); and some see the literature as fundamentally confused about its empirical and normative aspects, and, hence, as a tragically unguided missile in great need of tethering by our values lest we become unwitting servants of the technocratic biases in an "organizational imperative" (Scott and Hart, 1979).

All of these foci, and many more, have much to recommend them. But we will focus here on the "jungle" metaphor, in both describing the scope of this chapter and sketching the dimensions of the broader literature which the chapter summarizes.

As for the broad literature, the term "jungle" does nicely to suggest the variety of ideas and concepts that have grown in the managerial and organizational gardens—sometimes growing straight and tall, and other times being bent into curious shapes, if not being choked, by antagonistic notions occupying the same conceptual spaces.

Details are useful here, lest the "jungle" metaphor get out of hand. Usefully, Koontz (1961) isolates the main traditions of inquiry that have variously dominated or coexisted in thought about organizations. Five will be introduced here briefly.

1. The Management Process School

This may be considered the classical, or traditional, approach, and it regards management as involving universal processes—regardless of the type of enterprise or the hierarchical level. Basically, if these processes are identified and understood, principles for their constant application will become manifest to the careful observer. Frederick Taylor (1911) was no doubt the most celebrated practitioner in this tradition at the level of everyday labor, and he pushed his ideas toward a specific theory for organizing work, which will get detailed attention later. At upper management levels, Henri Fayol (1925) and others labored to isolate processes and to elucidate their interaction in complex systems. Doubtless, the most familiar expression of this focus was the mnemonic POSDCORB, which proposed to identify the key managerial functions or processes—planning, organizing, staffing, directing, coordinating, reporting, and budgeting (Gulick and Urwick, 1937).

2. The Empirical School

Basically, this second cluster of managerial students proposed that the Process School looked with too little care, and often in the wrong places. Perhaps the case study approach reflected the most common early effort to learn from experience, and that approach is represented by studies of individual organizations (Kaufman, 1949; Roethlisberger and Dickson, 1939; Selznick, 1949) as well as in collections of cases (Glover and Howar, 1957; Stein, 1948). The conclusions encouraged by this case literature often gave little comfort to those focusing on functions or processes. At best, functions constituted useful labels for some of the things that managers do, but these labels stop very far short of providing principles to guide action. Indeed, case studies often showed the principles to be sharply limited, in describing both what does exist and what should exist in effective organized activity (Golembiewski, 1962; Kaufman, 1949; Selznick, 1949).

A variety of critical analyses both inspired the Empirical School and derived momentum from it. For example, a long tradition of scholarship (Simon, 1946) highlighted the logical inconsistencies in the traditional organization theory associated with the Process School. And an even longer tradition of inquiry explained that the problem was less in the prescriptions of the Process School than it was in the often-implicit starting points of that kind of effort—as in assumptions about human nature that were at least debatable, as well as in values and attitudes about authority which were rooted in minds rather than in nature (Coker, 1922; Golembiewski, 1965).

3. The Human Behavior School

This third school focused on, and hoped to deepen, the effort to learn from experience. The focus owed much to psychology and social psychology, and was reflected in such general emphases as human relations (Davis, 1957, 1962) and in more specific and related areas of work, such as group dynamics (Cartwright and Zander, 1953), leadership styles (Lewin, Lipitt, and White, 1939), and features of work settings (Roethlisberger and Dickson, 1939).

In a variety of ways, this third orientation had a profound impact on the Process School. The latter tended to assume an economic view of employees, while the Human Behavior School was strong on a broader range of individual needs (Argyris, 1957; McGregor, 1960). The third approach also focused on group properties, such as norms and climates, more than on the individual. Moreover, students of the Human Behavior approach also tended to focus on microphenomena rather than on managerial functions or processes (Roethlisberger and Dickson, 1939). Unlike the Process School, in addition, Human Behavior focused on elaborating a contingency theory, rather than on seeking universal principles—the former guideline was "it all depends," while the latter goal focused on simple and sovereign principles that were said to apply everywhere.

4. The Social System School

This fourth emphasis has a strong sociological flavor, and in a basic way extends the Human Behavior approach. The latter has a micro focus, especially on small groups and leadership. The Social System view seeks to be more comprehensive and, as Koontz notes (1961, p. 179), "identifies the nature of the cultural relationships of various social groups and attempts to show these as a related, and usually an integrated, system."

The Social System School appears in many forms. At the macro level, the approach is perhaps the best represented by the early work of Barnard (1938). Also representative are powerful syntheses that dot the literature (Drucker, 1954; March and Simon, 1958; Thompson, 1967). See also the "interorganization analysis" that has recently appeared (e.g., Miles, 1980; Nystrom and Starbuck, 1981, Vol. 2, pp. 409-527). At low levels of organization, "sociotechnical systems" also represent the genre (Miller, 1975).

5. The Decision Theory School

The focus here is on a rational approach to decision making, and has often been seen as a conceptual linchpin for thought about management, which patently involves decision making in intimate and persisting ways. Simon (1947, 1957) provides a classic general statement, and the focus has inspired a range of statistical-mathematical and more qualitative offshoots. At the social level, for example, the "public choice" literature has recently attracted much attention (Buchanan and Tullock, 1962). At micro levels, decision making provides a conceptual home for a huge array of orientations and technologies in inventory control, forecasting, transportation, and so on.

As for this chapter, the "jungle" metaphor poses no great problems. The chapter may be seen as but a patch in a very large and exotic tangle of flora and fauna. But this chapter is a special kind of "patch in the jungle." Thus, it seeks to direct attention to all of the schools sketched above. Directly, the several schools came to exist because they touch aspects central to the phenomena of collective activity. And the focus below will variously illustrate how the integration of these multiple perspectives has much to recommend it.

III. SPECIFIC FEATURES OF THIS PATCH IN THE JUNGLE

What follows amounts to doing one's best in a summary way, with little attention to qualifications, while acknowledging the need for analysis that often varies dramatically from detail to detail. Hence the need to emphasize here what is always true of summary efforts—that this chapter is not the territory. Rather, this essay provides one map to a territory whose often subtle contours and qualities cannot be expressed by a mere map—not even a very detailed map. Thus, this essay will introduce readers to some central issues and developments in organization analysis and practice, but the readers must skillfully—and sometimes laboriously—adapt these generalities to the specific histories and environments of their individual organization settings.

We settle here for the essentials of some recent developments relating to organization analysis and action, while recognizing that some details concerning even major developments are far out of reach. What constitute some recent developments? Three basic questions get attention, albeit briefly. Essentially, they ask:

1. What certainties about organizing guided most thought and practice, with little effective challenge, until recently?
2. What kinds of issues have shaken those certainties, and what challenges do these issues pose for emerging principles and practices?
3. Where are these emerging and burgeoning challenges carrying thought about organizing, and how will the emerging ideas influence practice?

Attention gets directed to each question in turn.

IV. WHENCE COME TRADITIONAL PRINCIPLES FOR ORGANIZING?

Even those with poor historical perspective and sensitivities will have no trouble tracking our initial quarry. The basic sense of traditional principles for organizing has been expressed across the entire span of recorded history.

The real historical bloodhounds can trace the scent all the way back to biblical times, when Jethro was the first management consultant and Moses the first client. Recall that Moses had for years been guiding his followers around some very inhospitable territory, and he apparently found that his personal charisma was no longer up to the task of seeing that the needed things got done when they needed doing. Moses sank into despair, but Jethro did not prescribe therapy; rather, he proposed a familiar model for organizing Moses' now-and-again followers. Oversimply, Moses had fallen into the habit of making all decisions–great and small–and while he decided, his people dawdled. As a result, the exodus was going poorly. Jethro gave some advice to Moses, on which the latter acted. The Bible notes:

> Moses picked out able men from all Israel and put them in charge of the people as officers over groups of thousands, of hundreds, of fifties, and of tens. They rendered decisions for the people in all ordinary cases. The more difficult cases they rendered to Moses, but all the lesser cases they settled themselves.

For those with more myopic historical perspective, the source for traditional organizing principles might be the work of the theoretician Max Weber, or such avowed practitioners as Frederick W. Taylor. The latter had his heyday in the Scientific Management movement that dominated the first two decades or so of this century (Taylor, 1911) and still has potent impact. Weber may be more vivid to many of today's readers, and he gained popularity through the English translations made around 1940 of his earlier work, which was written in German (Gerth and Mills, 1946).

But the particular source of the traditional principles matters not. Their multiple varieties have major commonalities that span the dates between the three possible wellsprings of our traditional principles for organizing noted above, and resemble numerous other dated sources as well (Golembiewski, 1985, pp. 151-170).

Moreover, picturing this hardy approach to organizing people and resources poses no great problems, although some observers prefer a variety of pictorialization that others find unrevealing. For present purposes, Fig. 1 sketches the kind of organization structure consistent with what will here be called the traditional principles. Figure 1 also details some major prescriptive rules of thumb for how work should be patterned, if one follows the traditional model.

The work to be organized in Fig. 1 is deliberately simplified, with only three activities being involved–A, B, and C. The reader may want to think of these activities in conventional terms. Thus, most of the organization literature labels activities common toward the top of organizations as functions–e.g., operations, finance, quality control, and personnel. Activities at workaday levels are usually called processes, and these can include typing, filing, and so on. Whether function or process, however, only the other relation needs to be specified for our example. Directly, A + B + C yields some product or service.

More differentiated schemes exist (Golembiewski, 1984, 1987; Mintzberg, 1979), but they come to pretty much the same point. So the following analysis can be bold, even though it is not the only way to go and certainly does not pretend to be the most detailed way to go.

There were significant challenges to these principles–first in business (Chandler, 1962), and later in government (Golembiewski, 1962; Simon, 1946)–but until recently, these challenges for the most part disturbed the principles rather than displaced them. In business, for example, major efforts beginning in the 1920s successfully replaced Fig. 1

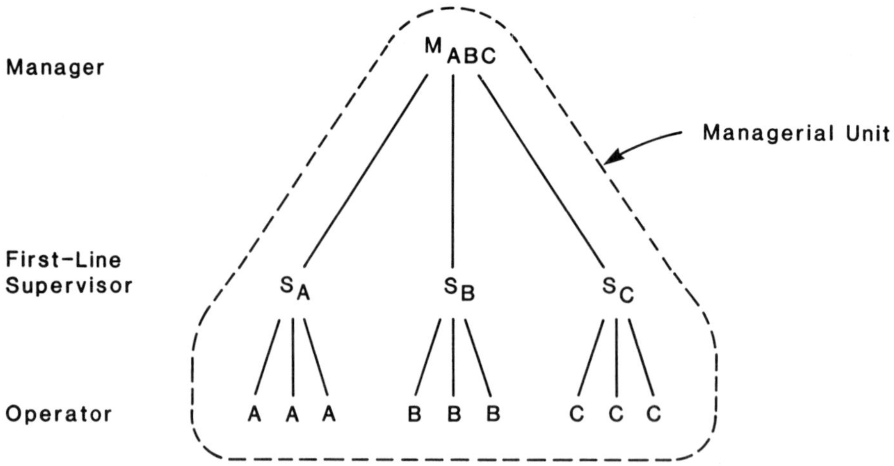

FIGURE 1 Traditional principles for organizing:

1. Structure has a dominant vertical bias.
2. Departments aggregate the same or similar jobs or operations.
3. Specialization by function or process dominates.
4. Each superior manages a small number of subordinates, each of whom reports to one and only one superior.

structures, but this victory was partial only. To explain, this organizational innovation began at the very highest levels and, even in organizations with innovative structures at top levels, Fig. 1 still dominated at lower levels. Indeed, only the last decade or so has seen determined, but still-infrequent efforts to replace the principles at, for example, the plant level (Perkins, Nieva, and Lawler, 1983; Zager and Rosow, 1982). Public-sector experience is similar, if delayed by perhaps a decade or more. More will be written about such innovations in the third section of this essay.

By and large, Fig. 1 sketches the kind of structure that one will likely encounter in practice today, then, in both public and business sectors, but especially in the former. Perhaps even more remarkably, that kind of structure also dominates worldwide, despite basic differences from country to country, such as those in forms of government or in economic philosophy (Golembiewski, 1985, pp. 151-170). Capitalist or socialist, in sum, the world became bureaucratized, and far faster and more thoroughly than it became pasteurized, Sanforized, or IBM-ized.

V. ORGANIZING PRINCIPLES FOR WHAT?

Perhaps most remarkably, the traditional principles have persisted despite their neglect of two aspects of the central question: Organizing for what? That is, the principles were never much concerned with this general question. Indeed, proponents often implied that the question was nonsensical, because its very asking implied one might organize differently for different "whats." To the contrary, proponents often preferred to think of a "one best way"—of the traditional principles as universal to all situations and conditions. Why this position was so common is not easy to explain, but that it was common cannot be denied or even doubted.

In any case, it would not have sufficed to have simply asked that key question—Organizing for what?—and then to have closed the books with a working answer good enough for one day and time. No mystery shrouds this point. Satisfactory working answers to that central question have changed over time, and for two distinct, but interacting, reasons. Thus, not only have existing conditions changed substantially, but common views about what conditions are desired, or at least are tolerable, also have undergone profound transformations. Put another way, both empirical and normative issues are relevant to the key question, Organizing for what? What exists can change, and so can our views about the desirable.

These empirical and normative changes have profound implications for the traditional principles for organizing. In sum, even if those traditional principles were congruent with early answers to the central questions, that congruence sharply decreased in later versions of reasonable working answers to *the* question: Organizing principles for what?

Subsequent analysis will, in due time, provide specifics about some of the hows and whys of this increasingly poor fit between the traditional principles and reasonable working answers to what existed and to what was normatively valued. But one point requires elaboration now, because it helps explain the staying power of the traditional principles in the face of their unresponsiveness to changes in what exists and is valued. Despite its centrality, as noted, the key question had not received the attention it deserved. This often was no oversight, please note. For a long time, indeed, a long line of students of organization sought to finesse this question—as via the common opinions that the principles had scientific status and, hence, were of universal applicability. This may seem a weak association, as it was. Even if the first descriptor obtained—and it certainly did not in the heyday of those opinions—the second would not follow. But many drew comfort from the convenient linkage, invoking it for a long time, often, and emphatically. Even capitalist and communist thinkers shared that view, in fact. Marxist doctrine emphasized the following view, for example, and the description could have applied equally to the basic position of the National Association of Manufacturers (NAM), the chamber of commerce, or various do-gooder political traditions. Ebenstein (1956, pp. 657-658), characterizes the dominant Marxist position in these terms:

> The *administration of things* is a matter of technical *knowledge* and not of political will. Government as an agency of settling disputes between men by force will be replaced in the classless society by administration as a scientific method of using resources in the best way in accordance with verifiable procedures of science and technology.

Of course, the NAM and Marxist doctrines do not share the goal of a classless society, even as they share a view of management as science. But such basic differences somehow managed to avoid getting in the way of the general adoption of the traditional principles, even in countries with opposed philosophies of government.

Let's get somewhat more specific. The traditional principles get a very mixed review when the central question—Organizing principles for what?—gets even a little attention. Seven points serve here to illustrate the fuller analysis, and they combine both empirical and normative issues—that is, they combine concerns about what is and what should be. The general form of the analysis is simple and arbitrary, and should serve tolerably if not pushed too far. That is, each of the seven points will relate to general polarities, or continua, such as certainty $\leftrightarrow$ uncertainty. In the present analytical shorthand, these continua represent the range of some partial answers to the question "Organizing for what?" Specifically, one could organize for two different portions of the continuum from, for example, certainty to uncertainty, and the resulting organizations might be similar only in the qualified senses that two reptiles are similar—let's say, eastern diamondback rattlesnakes and seagoing turtles. To illustrate, organizations structured for certainty would have many different properties than those focusing on high degrees of uncertainty. Decision making could be leisurely under certainty, but that would be counterproductive, if not dangerous, under conditions of uncertainty. Organizations suited to uncertainty would have to march to a spritely drumbeat, as well as more complicated rhythms. Organizations under uncertainty would require numerous and different channels of communication to permit cross-checking, the capacity for quick tests and psychological commitment, and for even quicker withdrawal when initial tests implied inadequate information.

In addition to suggesting the possible range of answers to our central question, the following analysis will do two things. It will try to generally identify portions of the several continua that seem the special targets of the traditional principles for organizing. Moreover, the analysis will seek to assess whether any major changes occurred in the portions of these continua that constitute reasonable targets for the structuring of today's organizations.

The purpose is transparent. If traditional principles seem targeted to one portion of any continuum, and if a major change has occurred in what is empirically necessary or normatively desirable, that implies that those principles are based on awkward working answers to our central question: Organizing for what? Illustratively, if—as is the case—the traditional principles are designed for certainty, and if—as also seems the case—uncertainty is today far more the name of the game, the principles would poorly suit present conditions, or at best would do so only by accident.

But enough of these general comments. Seven specific points will help illustrate how the traditional principles in Fig. 1 provide less-than-sensitive guidance under emerging conditions and preferences.

First, organizing principles should relate to what is often called the causal texture of the environment within which organizations exist. Many operational indicators could be cited, but the favorites emphasize such polarities as these:

certainty ↔ uncertainty
placidity ↔ turbulence

The leftward portions of such continua imply a simple and stable technology, a limited product line, and a long half-life for products. Those leftward portions also imply a slow pace of social and technological change or development.

More or less clearly, recent developments have definitely shifted rightward on such continua, and this has profound implications for an appropriate organization structure. Moreover, as even a little reflection will establish, the traditional principles are better designed for certainty and placidity. So adherence to those principles will complicate adaptations to any changes in environmental conditions. In those organizations with certain and placid environments, of course, the traditional principles should apply better.

This distinction is the heart of the seminal demonstration by Lawrence and Lorsch (1967), who compared firms in different environments—for example, firms in plastics, which typically face dynamic and uncertain markets, with cardboard-carton makers, which are in relatively certain and placid markets. They suggest that four orientations will differ in such firms:

1. The period of useful feedback, or the time interval between perception and action, will vary from short to very long
2. The kind of interaction between people and groups will vary: from constant and intense, to infrequent and variable but generally of low intensity
3. Goal certainty will vary: from low and hard to measure, to definite and easy to measure
4. The structure required will vary: from the informal and spontaneous, to highly formalized and specific statements of policies, roles, and relationships

Lawrence and Lorsch permit analysis at several levels. Their four orientations not only will be reflected in the policies and structures guiding organization members, for example, but they will tend to be reflected in individual attitudes and values as well as behaviors. The latter may prove very resistant to change when conditions dictate changing the former. Moreover, the orientations may be used to characterize different activities within the same organization—for example, research and development vs. routine operations.

Clearly, the kind of hyperspecialization reflected in Fig. 1 structures will heighten any differences in organizational and personal orientations, which should contribute to the potential for interpersonal and interunit conflict in such structures. Just as clearly, conflict can arise when intraorganization differences in orientations exist.

But let us return to the more general point. We deal with issues of great practical and theoretic importance when we make the simple statement that the traditional principles are tailored to certainty and placidity. For example, even general metaphors suggest the conclusion. Organizations traditionally were thought of as well-oiled machines, or precise clocks, which, once wound and set running, would reliably duplicate certain processes with little loss in efficiency. Turbulent environments reject such metaphors.

More complex analysis leads to the same conclusion about the compatibility of the traditional principles with certainty and placidity. Consider the impact on information systems of any rightward movement on the two polarities above, relying on analyses such as that of Galbraith (1973, 1977) for detail and nuance beyond the scope of this chapter. In elemental and profound ways, uncertainty and turbulence imply serious problems for the information systems consistent with Fig. 1 structures. Thus, such structures grow tall very rapidly as organizations move beyond even smallish size, and the distance between action and decision levels tends to increase quickly and sharply. What are the common cumulative effects? Among other consequences, Fig. 1 structures tend to induce sluggish communication—even if organizations avoid the common sweetening of upward-bound messages, and even when those at managerial levels have a clear concept of the diverse conditions current at the multiple operating sites. However, sweetening often will occur as messages wend their way up through hierarchies; and the bird's-eye view of the worm often differs dramatically from the worm's-eye view of the bird. Hence, far from ideal conditions for communication typically exist, and this accentuates the poorness of fit of the traditional principles to emerging conditions.

Consider that we live in an organizational age, of big and growing aggregates of capital and labor. This pattern affects Fig. 1 structures at one of their weak points, since communication tends to get chancy very fast, as Fig. 1 systems grow larger by even modest increments. The limited span of control dictates this sensitivity to smallish increments in size, for which the traditional principles prescribe additional levels of hierarchy. That is why such organizations quickly grow tall. The readers can test this for themselves. Assume a span of control of three to one—three subordinates to each superior—and see what happens to the number of levels of organization as you increase the number of members—by doubling them, then tripling, and so on.

In any case, the consequences of this escalating tallness can be profound, as in inducing and reinforcing low estimates of mutual competence by those at different hierarchical levels, which can cycle into low levels of trust. Thus, organizational underdogs will complain, "They just don't understand what we have to face everyday." Moreover, over-dogs will complain, "They don't have the big picture; they see only their limited self-interest." And in-between dogs will lament, "Boy, is our job tough in getting those two levels together." And all three can be correct. In turn, lack of trust often generates high levels of risk, which can both reinforce and lower estimates of mutual competence. And the cycle is in such ways triggered to build on and heighten itself.

In brief contrast, uncertainty and turbulence place a clear premium on organization features different from those characteristic of Fig. 1 structures. These include flat organizations, with less distance between points of decision and action, and quick-reacting systems, characterized by high trust. A following section will detail principles more appropriate for such a structure than the traditional principles.

But first we need to deepen and broaden this initial analytic perspective on Fig. 1 structures. One key element in such awkward effects of the traditional principles is the kind of managerial unit (MU) they require. The MU concept is not in the common vocabulary, but refers to that portion of an organization that is monitored by some authoritative decision maker—a singular or plural—in a position to make reasonable decisions about a total flow of work. In Fig. 1, only M_{ABC} is in such a position. Hence, the information flow there, perforce, will be centralized. The good news is that centralization can permit the application of uniform standards and perhaps direct superior expertise to local problems. A real potential for bad news also exists, however. Among other features, a kind of decisional gridlock can occur, featuring an overloaded decision-making center, which can serve at once as tormentor and victim of operating officials, who have to secure overhead clearance before acting, or who are subject to regular ex post facto second-guessing after having acted. This condition can intimidate lower levels, where personnel may exaggerate any personal tendency to wait to be told what to do. Or this condition may inspire innovations to do what requires doing, in spite of overhead controls, even if this requires creative bookkeeping or variously massaging the truth. Of course, both kinds of tactics can occur in bewildering combinations.

Decision making under such conditions often will have an offputting quality, for both clients and organization members, and especially for professionals or other skilled employees. Thus, such organizations may appear to be slow-moving and even ponderous, overall, but with fits and starts of activity—as in "hurry up and wait." Or employees will be leery about taking personal initiatives, and will "hunker down" and let "the system" make decisions, except when the point at issue is so critical or so convenient that extreme risk taking occurs on the general principle that it is easier to say "I'm sorry" than to face rejection of the request "May I?" Or decisions may be quite reasonable overall, while they apply poorly or not at all at specific sites or on specific issues. Lower level officials in such cases must mentally or physically shrug their shoulders when berated by some client distressed about why some apparently reasonable thing cannot be done. "Beats the hell out of me why not," they may commiserate in their mutual disempoweredness. This is the essence of what people usually mean by bureaucracy, and few respond positively to it, including those most instrumental in creating the condition.

An obvious point should be made, for the record. To the degree that an organization's causal texture features uncertainty and turbulence, the traditional principles are suspect as guides for organizing. Those conditions often exist nowadays in substantial degree, of course, or at least substantially more so than during the earlier days, when those principles were elaborated and identification with them grew.

Second, organizing principles need to be rooted in a clear concept of the basic exchange process that is involved, and this process depends vitally on a normative view of the person at work. What is this basic exchange process? Simply, it refers to the concept of what gets the work done, what motivates people, what energizes action. Various polarities can express the general sense of the present point:

Limited economic contract: "We do X work for Y dollars."	↔	Complicated psychological and economic contract
The person as basically responsive to economic stimuli	↔	The person as responsive to a broad range of psychologic, social, and economic stimuli

Details about these polarities can be provided in various ways. No doubt the most common approach has been to contrast the simple stimulus → response assumption of "economic man"—dollars motivate work—with the various needs models of Argyris, Herzberg, Maslow, and others. These needs models have a mixed record. They have proved elusive targets for rigorous research, even as they provide useful conceptual handles for dealing with the kinds of realities generated by people in collective settings.

Exhibit 1 reflects the detailed sense of Argyris's early version of a model of human needs (1957, pp. 49-53), which he viewed as the basic predisposition for individuals as they seek self-actualization, or the attainment of what they might become. Individuals acting consistent with their predispositions will experience feelings of potency and essentiality. For example, such individuals will see themselves as making a difference on things that really matter to themselves.

Such needs models have clear implications for practice. Organize work so that people can act on their predispositions, in short, and to that degree, work will be seen as freeing individuals to pursue their own ends at work, as empowering individuals to become more than they are. Such a work setting will reduce coercion and, hence, resistance, with greater energy being available to do the task and with less effort required because the individual needs to contend with less resistance.

Note that Exhibit 1 also details several major implications for organizing work consistent with Argyris's view that people need to be viewed as "economic persons, plus." The alternative seems somber. One can choose deliberately to diminish what people may become, and one can then become reconciled to dealing with the negative reactions of those who sense their own diminution.

Exhibit 1 helps make some major points directly, in sum. Readers may well be motivated to generate a long list of such implications for organizing, but two points will suffice for the present written record. Significantly, the needs model highlights normative as well as empirical issues. That is, the needs model not only purports to describe reality—how most people are "wired," which has clear implications for the organizational features that will energize and engage that internal motivational apparatus. Needs models typically

Exhibit 1.

A Loose Interpretation of Argyris'
Dimensions for Self-Actualization, with Associated Operating Rules for Organizing Work

I. Individuals seem predisposed to move along such dimensions*	II. Consequently, work structures should be so designed as to permit -- even encourage -- individuals to:
o passivity ——>increasing activity	o epxerience increasing segments of the organization
o dependence ——>growing independence and interdependence	o increase self-responsibility, self-discipline, and self-motivation
o limited behaviors ——>widening repertoire of behaviors	o decrease compulsive and defensive behaviors
o erratic, casual interests ——>abidding interests	o increase control over the worksite
o short time perspective ——>lengthening time perspective	o utilize an increasing range of abilities, especially cognitive and interpersonal abilities
o subordinate position ——>aspiration to equality or superiority	o increase their time perspective
o lack of awareness and control ——>growing awareness and control	

* Based on Argyris (1957), pp. 49-53.

also propose that failure to be sensitive to such human properties will have serious costs in organizations, at least over the long run. People whose needs are not met, the models imply, will be dissatisfied and frustrated, and these conditions can lead to high productivity only under quite special circumstances (Golembiewski, 1962, pp. 131-138). Put another way, managements that design structures so as to frustrate human needs play a dangerous game, including a disaffection from work that can convert even objective success into perceived failure. If your work forces you into doing "dumb things"—with "dumb" being defined as acting against one's predispositions—then even being successful at work implies failure as a human being. Social and psychological dynamite obviously inheres in equating success at work with failure as a human being.

In addition, moreover, the needs models like Argyris's imply "shoulds" or "oughts," and this feature can be neglected only at great peril. Viewed from one perspective, the needs models draw attention to the crucial question "How should organizations treat their members?" This is a vital reminder. Organizing always is a moral problem, for the structuring of behavior implies choice, and choices often are consequential in moral or value senses. And make no mistake about it. Since significantly different alternatives to organizing typically exist in each case, as we will suggest later, conscious processes should dominate in choices between them. The two following sections will provide some detail about a structural model that is a commonly available alternative to structuring much work which permits—indeed, forces—such a normative choice. Empirical considerations can provide insight about the consequences of various normative choices, but what is can never define what should be.

In multiple senses, Fig. 1 structures are not very sensitive to the several empirical and normative richnesses to which the needs models draw attention. The classic disregard of structural options is reflected in the once-comfortable assurance that there is a "one-best way to organize," which the traditional principles just happen to prescribe. For the present, this analysis will content itself with illustrating that—whatever else—the traditional principles do not provide easy guidance to energizing and engaging the motivational forces of the person consistent with Argyris's dimensions for self-actualization. For example, those principles encourage specialization and departmentalization by specialties, and this encourages the tunnel vision which inhibits being aware of the totality of an organization.

Readers can generate for themselves multiple illustrations of such insensitivities of the traditional principles from Exhibit 1, of course, but additional pump-primers may be helpful. Consider the issue of self-discipline, for example. This could be increased only with difficulty in Fig. 1 structures, which neither encourage nor reinforce that effort, even when they avoid triggering the resistance or the withdrawal and passivity that may be induced by psychological failure when one succeeds at doing a job poorly attuned to meeting a broad range of human needs. In contrast to meeting this range of individual needs, indeed, the traditional principles consistently emphasize ways of enhancing hierarchical power of a few over most others. Thus, flows of work are fragmented into specialized jobs, to suggest the point, one of whose consequences is to reduce the ability of individuals to influence their work site. Replaceable cogs in a big machine, of course, are far more acted upon than acting.

Whence comes the motivation for such reductionist specialization? Technical arguments will stress its several advantages, as in low requirements for training and, hence, for skills, and this argument has some merit as well as, beyond some point, substantial costs. At another level, reductionist specialization implies a pessimism about people, if not a positive distrust. In Fig. 1 structures, no single person controls an entire transaction, and this limits some kinds of errors of commission—easy fraud, for example. But the same strategy also can result in many errors of omission or noncaring, as well as in a loss of opportunities to heighten motivational states.

On the latter point, an extended example helps highlight how the traditional principles do not encourage self-discipline, or even tolerate it, often at substantial costs to both manager and the managed. Consider the issue of increasing efficiency or productivity. In Fig. 1 structures, no single unit can increase productivity, for only cooperative effort by all units can accomplish that end. On the other hand, any single unit supervised by an S might reduce productivity. S_C probably is in the most advantageous position to do so, and—by adamantly proposing that "C is harder to do than A or B"—might well either serve to reduce A's or B's productivity, or gain additional resources at C which in effect would punish A and B for their industry. The tactical advantage of S_C will be greatest in those cases where A + B will somehow degrade, or spoil, without C, as in treating rubber in conventional manufacturing. In all cases, lacking C, A + B never can generate a good or service in the simplified flow of work emphasized throughout this essay. Such potentialities do not go unremarked in organizations, and effective effort consequently shifts toward the lowest level.

I propose a general law of human conduct. Indeed, I have often thought of calling it Golembiewski's First Law of Social Dynamics. Whatever it is called, the law has a simple and sovereign significance. Specifically: That will occur most frequently which is easiest or more convenient. If this law holds, the traditional principles shoot themselves in the foot, as it were. Reductions in productivity, being easiest or most convenient in Fig. 1 structures, are more likely to occur there than are increases in productivity.

Alert managers in traditional structures consequently will be inhibited about providing opportunities for self-discipline, even when they want very badly to do so. Indeed, those managers even may be inveigled into gross approaches to blunting the effects of Golembiewski's First Law in Fig. 1 structures, as by energizing the "fink factor" via informants to provide bypasses around the formal structure (Dalton, 1959). In more technical terms, such managers will be conflicted about enhancing employee cohesiveness, or the balance of forces attracting an individual to a group, minus those forces encouraging that individual to leave the group.

Heightened cohesiveness is a source of human comfort and support valued by most or all employees (House, 1981), but it might also well serve to reinforce the awkward potential in traditional structures for reducing output as one expression of any heightened cohesiveness. A highly cohesive supervisory unit should be more equipped to exploit that potential of the traditional structure, by definition. Since cohesiveness implies control over member behavior, highly cohesive units would be most successful in acting on the First Law to reduce output in Fig. 1 structures.

Hence, managers might paradoxically be encouraged by the traditional principles to try to monopolize influence—even though as individuals, they might personally not like that when done to either self or others, and even though we have known for quite a while that the self-defeating consequences of that effort seem common enough (Trannenbaum, 1966, especially pp. 84-102). The dangers of not monopolizing in Fig. 1 structures, sadly, may be great enough to overwhelm both personal preference and the knowledge of what is forfeited thereby. The other side of the coin is even more ironic. Under the Fig. 1 structure, precisely those supervisors put themselves in greatest jeopardy who contribute most to meeting individual needs, as by enhancing work group cohesiveness.

The present point of how the traditional principles do not encourage self-discipline or self-motivation has numerous other expressions. For example, vertical cliques tend to dominate in Fig. 1 structures, and for good reasons. Thus, promotions and career advancement most often involve moving up one's specialized ladder, and such factors encourage vertical identification and loyalty. However, work flows horizontally in traditional structures, and enhancing the cohesiveness of any vertical clique might only enhance its ability to exert influence without a corresponding potential to increase productivity. Horizontal cliques are necessary to raise productivity in Fig. 1 structures—as via a cohesive group including S_A, S_B, and S_C—but such cliques are rare and short-lived, apparently because the convenient relationships in traditional structures are so pervasively up and down rather than across. Dalton (1959, especially pp. 58-64) provides the classic statement of this pervasive bias, which Exhibit 2 briefly describes. Dalton distinguishes three kinds of cliques, in sum, with vertical cliques dominating and exacerbating the divisiveness encouraged by Fig. 1 structures.

Third, all organizing principles need to be quite explicit about what is being contracted for. Simply, structures might differ very markedly, given differences in this one particular. And what is the possible range of choices? They might fall anywhere along such polarities:

Employee possession of limited abilities or skills, e.g., as hired hands	↔	Employee capacity and willingness for continual retraining in probably changing and perhaps even unanticipated abilities or skills

Here again, the traditional principles can be located in the leftward reaches of this polarity, and that can be awkward in today's world. Patently, the awkwardness would be greatest under empirical conditions of environmental uncertainty and turbulence. Moreover, a strong normative commitment to personal growth and development would exacerbate the awkwardness of the traditional principles.

Consider here a simple illustration of how, in this particular polarity, Fig. 1 structures are damned for what they do, cursed because of what they don't, and often in trouble because they can't motivate effective action. The focus will be on job rotation and enlargement. For our introductory purposes, "job rotation" refers simply to periodic switching of activities, as when air traffic controllers come down from being on the radar scope by performing different and less-demanding duties. "Job enrichment" refers to building jobs with more scope that permit greater individual control over some related sets of activities. Both, in effect, but in different ways, reject the hyperspecialization prescribed by the traditional principles.

The cases for job rotation and enlargement have compelling qualities, in both instrumental senses as well as broader psychological, social, and, even, political senses. To illustrate, the two approaches are often associated with higher employee satisfaction and productivity (Zager and Rosow, 1982), and this provides powerful practical motivation. Others emphasize the normative attractions of rotation/enrichment (Golembiewski, 1965), as well as their consistency with needs models such as that in Exhibit 1. Management also may see multiple attractions in job rotation and enrichment, especially in turbulent environments. Thus, work force flexibility may be enhanced, which reduces staffing and scheduling problems. Moreover, the need for close supervision may be reduced sharply, not to mention the employee motivation and experience that may become available at the work site.

Exhibit 2.

Three Kinds of Organizational Cliques.

---

1. Vertical cliques. This type of clique is based upon an exchange of services. For example, a supervisor may aid and protect his subordinates, in return for which they keep him posted concerning conditions at work or threats to the supervisor's position, and so on.

Dalton concludes of the main kind of vertical clique -- the "symbiotic" -- that it "is the most common and enduring clique in large structures . . . the real power [center which] is essential for a given department to compete on a par with other departments for favors from higherups and to set up workable arrangements with other departments."

2. Horizontal cliques. Horizontal cliques may be "defensive" or "aggressive." These cliques cut across departments, in contrast to the vertical cliques. Defensive cliques are usually formed in response to threat or crisis, e.g., reorganization, which affects several functions. Aggressive cliques are interested in bringing off a change rather than resisting it.

Horizontal cliques, of course, reduce interdepartmental and interfunction tension and they ameliorate the particularism of vertical cliques in serving as a mutual-aid bloc for the several departments or functions.

However, horizontal cliques are strong only as long as the threat or crisis exists. Consequently, they disturb the primacy of the vertical cliques only temporarily, disappearing as a particular crisis or threat abates.

3. Random cliques. The random clique is based upon friendship and social satisfaction. This differentiates it from the other types of cliques, in which (according to Dalton) "Friendship is not [the] end and may be hardly present."

In comparison to the vertical or horizontal cliques, random clique's members "may come from any part of the personnel, managers and managed, [and] do not anticipate important consequences of their association."

Although random cliques may be long-lived, various factors limit their incidence, persistence, and influence in organizations. Primarily, they lack . . . continuing and compelling support. In contrast, vertical cliques receive such support from the . . . strong tendency to organize by major function or process, as prescribed by the "principles."

From Golembiewski (1967), pp. 94-95, based on Dalton (1959).

These and other attractions of job rotation/enrichment hold more or less, of course, and not absolutely. Thus, failures of both job rotation and enrichment have been reported (Locke, Sirota, and Wolfson, 1976), although they seem in a very definite minority (Alber, 1978). And we are beginning to learn about the various conditions supporting success or failure in specific cases—as in factors that distinguish mere enlargement from true enrichment (Chung and Ross, 1977), which knowledge presumably will increase the probability of successful applications.

So let us return to the general point, now sufficiently qualified for present purposes. For employees, job rotation/enrichment can counter tedium and boredom, and even encourage a growing sense of mastery and control (Ford, 1969; Herzberg, et al., 1959). For management, job rotation can provide the cross-training that permits flexibilities in scheduling and hiring, and might even lead to an economic and philosophic investment in the changes in job content called job enrichment. In a broader sense, such techniques also might reduce a sense of stuckness which can not only reach flash points in low morale and later in strikes, but which also can erode the sense of the dignity of work that provides basic support for doing well the many things that just and efficient societies need to do. So much for the supporting case, which would easily be extended in many ways (Bernstein, 1980; Elden, 1977; Golembiewski, 1985).

Figure 1 structures provide little comfort for efforts at job rotation or enlargement, despite their several attractions to both employees and management. In fact, job rotation and enlargement were first touted as ways of relieving common problems induced by the traditional principles. Curiously, this elemental fact has been neglected by those who continue their basic support of those principles even as they recommend rotation and enrichment.

Why this paradox often exists will have to remain unexplored, while we draw attention to only a few elements of the uncongenial field of forces for job rotation and enrichment generated by traditional structures. To begin, consider that the two approaches have awkward reward/punishment features in a Fig. 1 structure. Basically, perhaps, the major rewards of successful rotation or enlargement programs will accrue to M_{ABC} and to the total organization, and also to employees. All well and good, as far as a first reaction goes, but more subtle and subversive issues are involved. However, the basic day-to-day pains will be experienced by the several supervisors (S). Motivating consistent supervisory attention to enrichment/enlargement programs may constitute a major problem, consequently. If nothing else, the basic Fig. 1 structure mandates S_A to focus on A, and not on job rotation or enrichment, which are clearly A+.

This description of reward/punishment features implies numerous unfortunate and multiple imbalances, which Fig. 1 structures tend to create or, at least, aggravate. Consider that the several supervisory units in Fig. 1 structures often will have interests in opposition, even major ones, while a successful rotation/enrichment program will require the harmonious participation of all units. As many observers have made plain (Golembiewski, 1986), traditional structures encourage—and may even require—"throwing dead cats into the backyards" of others in budgetary squabbles, or in guerrilla warfare about cost allocations in contention. The classic formulation of this crucial point (Lawrence and Lorsch, 1967) emphasizes that functionally organized structures have strong tendencies toward differentiation. These need to be countered in all effective organizations—especially those operating in turbulent environments—by managerial techniques or structures that encourage integration. Job rotation and, especially, enrichment have integrative thrusts, patently.

The sincerity of efforts in Fig. 1 structures to transcend such organizational warfare may be highly variable, as a consequence, with good intentions in effect succumbing to differentiating and fragmenting forces. Consider all the good and humanistic reasons for job rotation and enrichment, for example, and contrast these with practical exigencies that can impact decisions about which A should be cross-trained in B or C. Supervisors might be pardoned for nominating their dispensables, if not their organizationally halt and lame. For S_A is paid so that A is done well, elementally. Hence, even the temporary loss of an effective A has to be of some concern to S_A. Moreover, what happens to an A newly versed in B and C? Will A return, or be snapped up by some S_B or S_C who knows talent when they see it? Worse still, perhaps, is a kind of digging of one's own grave, as supervisors may see the issue. In Fig. 1 structures, only a single convenient job exists for individuals having experienced successful job rotation or enrichment–that of supervisor. The prospect of nourishing one's possible competitors, or even successors–and at some personal cost–might well induce the kind of mixed motivations in supervisors that get reflected in what the French call one-buttock performance.

Again, an obvious point needs to be made. The traditional principles are awkward to the degree that urgencies–whether practical or normative–require emphasis on broad or unknown factors in the kind of basic contracting on which many organizations are becoming increasingly dependent. Consider only two brief illustrations. Work may be so complex or changeable that it is awkward to think as if the organization were contracting for some limited set of skills. That would put organization authorities in a deep dilemma: whether to periodically cull the misfits, or bump along with employees not aware from the start what demands would be made upon them and, perhaps worse still, identify with a limited set of skills/attitudes that heighten the obsolescence of employees. Alternatively or additionally, a society could make a commitment to public education, and the resulting educated society–which reflects a basic value choice–also would poorly suit the traditional principles. As Exhibit 5 will show, in fact, both factors have simultaneously come to bear in growing segments of American industry. So the point is no mere hypothesis.

Fourth, to emphasize a point already made in passing at several points, useful organizing principles must provide a working balance between the whole and the parts, between the processes of integration and differentiation. Such continua reflect the kind of choices that might be made:

Emphasis on the parts–e.g., on differentiated functions or processes	↔	Emphasis on integrated wholes–e.g., broad purposes, products, flows of work

Generally, the working balance should move rightward under quite specific conditions–that is, as organizations exist in turbulent environments, as product lines grow more complicated, and as broad human needs are taken into greater account.

Figure 1 structures do not facilitate such attractive flexibility. On balance, indeed, the traditional principles focus on the parts rather than on the whole. Figure 1 structures build around separate functions or processes rather than an integrated flow of work, it should be obvious. The often cited rationale notes that this prohibits any one source from dominating a flow of work, and this creates a balancing of powers that enhances overhead influence and also might prevent the malfeasance possible when the work flow is not organizationally fragmented. At certain lower stages of organizational development, indeed, this feature can imply more benefit than cost. But the costs soon become onerous—as in complicated decision-making chains, slow decision processes, and the balkanization around the special interests of separate units contributing to a flow of work like A + B + C in Fig. 1. See also the discussion immediately following about stages of development.

Fifth, all of the evidence implies that organizing principles should be specific to developmental differences, as contrasted with being universal to all patterns and stages of development. This does not propose that "it all depends," which is a common position taken by some organizational "contingency theorists." All situations are ultimately unique, goes the present view, but some select sets of situations are enough alike to be considered as discrete phases or stages. We can only illustrate here with the notion of basic strategies for growth. As Chandler (1962) explains, organizations can increase in size in four basic ways, which tend to occur in this sequence:

1. Adding capacity at a central site for doing X, which is some product or service
2. Adding field units for doing X at several locations
3. Adding functions related to doing X
4. Diversifying product lines, or doing Q and Z, as well as X

In sum, all organizing principles have to be located somewhere along such continua:

Early stages of growth and development	↔	Advanced stages of growth and development

The choice will be consequential. Organizations utilizing the first two strategies are quite limited in their growth potential—although adding field units usually permits far more growth than adding capacity at a central site. Both tend to come early in an organization's history. The most leverage for growth derives from the diversification strategy. Readers may amuse themselves by applying the four strategies to a concern like McDonald's, which not so long ago had a limited product line—one kind of burger, fries, and two kinds of shakes. Those with racier preferences might consider applying the strategies for growth to a single house of ill repute with a determined amd ambitious management.

Details are beyond this summary, but Fig. 1 structures are most compatible with the first strategy. When field units are added, vexing issues of the balance of centralization/decentralization begin to surface that stress the traditional principles. Diversification creates the most challenge for any set of organizing principles, and, as is true of the four previous perspectives on organizing principles, the problems are greatest when the operating model is consistent with leftward positions on the fifth continuum, while environmental forces or value choices encourage rightward positions.

The notion of differential priority rosters illustrates the growing potential for mischief resulting from insensitivity about the several strategies for growth in an organization patterned after Fig. 1. Consider the experience in DuPont around World War I. The firm had essentially one product—gunpowder—and featured three functions related to producing and selling it. The firm's Fig. 1 structure had this basic character:

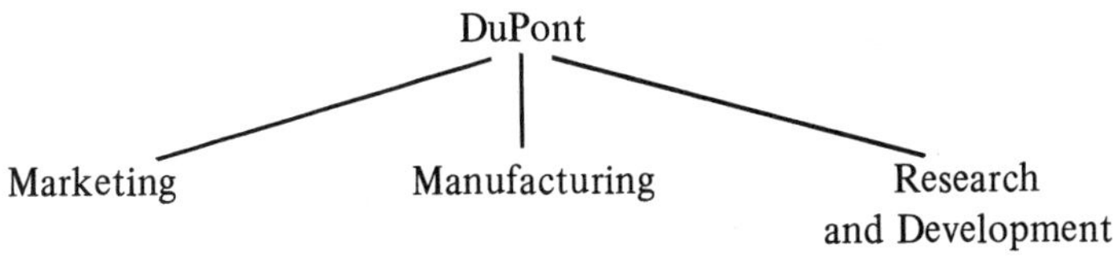

To simplify some, given one basic product, the three functions will have similar or identical priority rosters for what should get attention, in terms of dollars and time. This will be the case even in some very large single- or limited-product enterprises, since adding field units does not greatly complicate matters. Generally, adding functions and, especially, diversifying cause the major problems with differential priority rosters.

Diversification definitely created new organization challenges for DuPont after World War I. Gunpowder was joined by a range of products—paints and varnishes, celluloid collars, and so on—as DuPont sought to make some postwar use of its expanded physical plant and work force, even as the demand for gunpowder dropped sharply. Priorities quickly grew complicated, and conflict consequently developed between the three historic functions. Broadly, where 1 = highest preference for attention and N = some lower rank:

	Marketing		Manufacturing	Research and Development
Gunpowder	1	N	1	N
.	.	.	.	.
.	.	.	.	.
.	.	.	.	.
Celluloid collars	N	1	N	1

The implied dynamics can be sketched. Manufacturing ranked gunpowder highest on its priority roster: Manufacturing problems were well known; costs were predictable; and large runs could be counted on, with consequent economies. The new products posed variably chancy ventures for Manufacturing, in contrast, and consequently often got treated like intruders at a family picnic. Manufacturing officials reasonably tended to favor the easy way of looking good, as opposed to the probability of running into situations that posed interesting challenges, but whose potential for failure was high.

Research and development, in contrast, tended to see its future in the new products, and its priority roster tended to be the mirror-opposite of manufacturing's. Celluloid collars, in effect, dominated their priority roster.

Marketing was basically in conflict, to close this brief survey of problems with which the traditional principles coped poorly. Some marketers were pleased with the status quo, with gunpowder—even given the sharply reduced demand—with the type of salespersons required and their training, and so on. But some marketers were more sensitive to the limited market for gunpowder, now that the war to end all wars had ended. One marketing faction pushed for new products, consequently, while another was more willing to leave well enough alone. Marketing tended to have conflicting priority rosters, in short.

This analysis of differential priority rosters might well be elaborated in various ways. Thus, the four orientations of Lawrence and Lorsch (1967), introduced earlier, suggest the detailed dynamics generated by the strategy of diversification. The new products required quick and fluid feedback, while the previous massive preoccupation with gunpowder generated slow-moving channels of communication. Even for the willing, conflict was probable, if not inevitable.

But enough, already, on this point. Massive conflict resulted at DuPont, and it was moderated only by basic structural changes that permitted more flexible responses to differential priority rosters. Later, description will emphasize the properties of the structural innovations better adapted to dealing with differential priority rosters. But for now, the analysis will rest with the bare description of differential priority rosters and their potential for generating conflict in organizations patterned after the traditional principles.

Sixth, organizing principles must adopt a model person the principles both help create and must rely upon. Simply, such a model person might have basic attributes falling along such continua:

A high tolerance for command/obey situations, even a preference for them	↔	A high preference for independence and interdependence
A strong sense of duty or obligation rooted in collective concerns, with personal needs or concerns being less dominant	↔	A strong emphasis on personal needs or interests, with collective concerns being less dominant

Pretty clearly, the traditional principles are oriented toward the leftward portions of such continua, and this implies variable, but often significant, costs. Again, both empirical and normative factors can heighten these costs of the traditional principles and the often unrecognized assumptions underlying those principles.

Specifically, Fig. 1 structures imply a definite tendency toward autocratic or directive styles of supervision, which incline toward asymmetric and narrow distributions of influence, as well as toward unilateral control over both policy and its implementation. The managerial unit characteristic of Fig. 1 structures, to sketch an explanation of such effects, encourages a centralization of decision making, with information flowing upward and orders flowing downward. And this bias encourages autocratic or directive supervision, for substantial reasons suggested by brief reference to two alternative leadership styles—laissez-faire and supportive, or democratic. A laissez-faire style might generate tendencies counter to organization goals, as in a supervisory unit's developing norms of low output in the absence of vigilant supervision. The effects of a supportive or democratic, style of supervision are more difficult to predict in Fig. 1 structures. No single supervisory unit can turn the implied group forces toward high productivity, however, and that may discourage experiments with such nontraditional supervisory styles because of a fear that their consequences may get out of control. For reference, these three styles of supervision are briefly characterized in Exhibit 3, which describes the behavior of adult leaders in the famous research of Lippitt and White (1943) with children's groups.

Evidence and conjecture both imply some sharply expanding limits on this targeting of the traditional principles to the left portion of the sixth continuum, at least in developed countries. Basically, empirical evidence generally indicates that most organization members do not respond positively to an autocratic or directive style of supervision. On definite balance, they seem to prefer some degree of participation, an ability to influence work and work site, and so on (Golembiewski, 1962c, especially pp. 209-218). Why? Exhibit 1 provides one perspective on a working answer. To the extent that Argyris has correctly captured the predispositions of people, so also would individuals tend to reject autocratic styles of supervision. Such styles reduce self-responsibility, for example, and discourage fuller awareness and control.

Exhibit 3.

Leadership Styles in "Group Atmosphere" Studies with Children

Authoritarian	Democratic	Laissez faire
1. All determination of policy by leader	All policies a matter of group discussion and decision, encouraged and assisted by the leader	Complete freedom for group or individual decision, with a minimum of leader participation
2. Techniques and activity steps dictated by the authority, one at a time, so that future steps were uncertain to a large degree	Activity perspective gained during discussion period. General steps to group goal sketched, and when technical advice was needed the leader suggested two or more alternative procedures from which choice could be made	Various materials supplied by leader, who made it clear that he would supply information when asked. He took no other part in work discussion
3. Leader usually dictated the the task and companion of each member	Members were free to work with whomever they chose and division of tasks was left to the group.	Complete nonparticipation of the leader
4. Leader tended to be "personal" in his praise and criticism of each member's work; remained aloof from active group participation except when demonstrating how the work should be done and when issuing orders	Leader was "objective" in his praise and criticism, and tried to be regular group member in spirit without doing too much work	Leader did not comment on member activities unless questioned, did not attempt to appraise or regulate the course of events

The present point should not be pushed too far. The conclusions above should be read as "more or less" generalizations that might not apply at all in specific settings, or that might apply only in restricted senses. For example, as has been shown by early and contemporary research, preference for a leadership style will vary with the personality characteristics of members, the broad cultural setting in which individuals are embedded, the specific phases or stages of development of a group or an organization, and so on (Golembiewski, 1962c, pp. 209-218, 260-273). Consider a convenient example of these qualifiers. Most individuals, under quite general conditions, prefer to move rightward on the predispositions—toward greater activity, lengthening time perspective, and so on. But not all individuals start from the same point or are willing or equipped to go equally far. In sum, basic similarities should be accompanied by specific differences in how a batch of employees is likely to respond to any opportunity for movement along the predispositions toward self-actualization. Much the same may be said for the general attractions of supportive or democratic supervision, given that there will be occasions when an effective autocrat will get support, and when the license associated with laissez-faire will inspire adherents.

Ample reasons help us understand such general preferences for nonautocratic styles of supervision, as well as support for the educated guess that such effects probably will grow more pronounced, at least in the economically developed areas, if not everywhere. These reasons include greater educational opportunities, higher expectations about standards of living, safety nets of unemployment insurance and pay for strikers, managements which are variously unwilling or unable to assert counterbalancing claims, and the life-style changes characteristic to the "me and mine" generation, to merely sample from a very much longer possible list. In common, these factors suggest a work force that is less amenable to unilateral control, as well as one which at the same time is more oriented toward greater self-determination.

Counterforces to these "I want" or "I need" tendencies obviously exist, but the general trend implied above does not appear to have been stopped, let alone reversed, even by the ongoing high rates of unemployment in Western countries. To be sure, practically, the recent difficulties of finding any regular employment might diminish the enthusiasm of some demands for a fulfilling job, at least in the short run. And the attractions of Japanese employees have been widely touted in the last five years or so, precisely because they are said to have a strong sense of duty and discipline in the service of collective goals (Pascale and Athos, 1981). So not everyone is pleased with the tendencies sketched above, and some are energetically devoted to rolling back the years to some supposedly idyllic period in labor-management relationships. But the tendencies seem to exist nonetheless, and some argue that they also constitute desirable tendencies, on balance.

Seventh, and finally, but only for present purposes, organizing principles need to be tethered to a sense of basic purpose. "Basic purpose" is better illustrated than defined, as in this polarity:

Limited to efficient provision of goods or services, with loyalty cushioning any repression of employees, whether required or simply convenient	↔	Oriented toward continually increasing responsible freedom at work, for increasing proportions of the work force, while efficiently providing goods and services

The focus here is on what is often called the quality of working life, or, conveniently for present purposes, QWL. Essentially, the broadest QWL issues relate to powerful questions: What is the relevance of the structuring of work to other spheres of individual, social, and (perhaps especially) political life? What should be the relevance?

For a long time, QWL seemed to be no big issue, even a nonissue. Thus, some observers were always worried about the traditional principles for organizing work, because of their autocratic and unilateral character, and their poor fit with representative political institutions and ideals (Coker, 1922). But these were isolated concerns, or at least expressions of concerns that definitely did not bowl over the traditional principles.

What was mainstream concerning the values to be reflected in work or embodied in managerial techniques or theories? Note that in the early days, significantly, these techniques or theories were largely borrowed from experiences in Germany and Prussia, which had a broad reputation for efficiency and thoroughness. Woodrow Wilson was warier than most, but he was still optimistic that such borrowing could be accomplished without compromising American representative ideas and institutions. Management approaches like the traditional principles for organizing derived largely from Germanic experiences, he recognized, and as such, they certainly were infused with "foreign gases." However, Wilson (1887, p. 205) saw no need for great concern. The "fires" of republican institutions would "distill" these gases, he explained vaguely, leaving only the solid scientific core. Most other observers were even less concerned about the possible dilemmas of putting autocratic means in the service of republican ideals. Thus, one common rationale noted bluntly: "Autocracy [at work] is the price of democracy after hours" (quoted by Waldo, 1980, p. 91).

These cavalier views have faded, both rapidly and substantially. Elden (1981) well represents the growing and pro-active position on the theme that—since work and politics interact, and since one's experiences at work possibly are crucial in determining the quality of our political life—forceful attention has to be directed at inducing work sites that have characteristics that reinforce our political ideals. Earlier views, as in Marxism, usually proposed that political experience would dominate economic forms. But nowadays, that point is far from clear.

The traditional principles fare poorly in the context of this revisionist thinking about what is horse and what is cart. To illustrate, our representative political ideals would be well served by a work site that induced such experiences for organizing members:

1. Heightened personal potency, as in reducing the sense to which a person feels powerless and acted upon
2. Increased political efficacy, as in a positive attitude that one can influence authoritative figures in constructive ways, without resort to violence or other extreme expressions of discontent
3. Improved skills and attitudes centering on participation, which constitute the primary vehicles for attaining greater personal potency and political efficacy

The research literature is far from complete on such crucial consequences of the traditional principles (Witte, 1980), but the bottom line seems to be clear enough (Bernstein, 1980; Mason, 1982). The general conclusion may be phrased in these stark terms: "Some power over one's work covaries with one's attitudes toward taking up participative opportunities [in politics, in community service, and so on]" (Elden, 1981,

p. 48). In short, the features of work seem to induce a very broad range of effects. Given the early stage of research, Elden concludes (1981, p. 48):

> Democratized authority structures [at work] are likely to benefit individual workers (more work satisfaction, personal development, and skills acquisition); their organization (increased identification and contribution as reflected, for example, in better quality, less absenteeism and turnover); and their social class or society as a whole (increased political resources more widely diffused, and decreased alienation).

If these emerging emphases are anywhere near the mark, the traditional principles imply substantial costs. Refer to Exhibit 1. That structure is not oriented toward increasing participation, but rather toward concentrating control, as narrowly defined, among hierarchical elites. Moreover, that structure is not designed around heightening individual senses of efficacy, but rather focuses on filtering higher-level skills upward in the hierarchy. In addition, that structure emphasizes the reduction of personal potency, as in simplifying work routines and in narrowing one's channels of information. Pointedly, one observer described one of the more impressive traditional organizations—a military one—in such terms: "It was designed by geniuses to be implemented by idiots."

VI. WHERE ARE INNOVATIVE ORGANIZING PRINCIPLES HEADED?

All crystal balls concerning the future of organization theory are cloudy when it comes to details, but at least three main lines of broad development seem clear enough. They relate to:

1. Change in the basic structural model sketched in Fig. 1
2. Elaborating various tactics, typically at higher levels of organization, to moderate common consequences of Fig. 1 structures under two general circumstances: where basic structural change is inconvenient or impossible, or during the usually extended period in which transitions from the traditional model are occurring at specific sites
3. Extending the lively progress in creating high-involvement work sites, typically at the department and plant levels, which efforts blend innovation in both the basic structural model and the supporting tactics

Each theme gets summary attention below.

By way of introduction, note that the three themes focus on both hierarchical and nonhierarchical approaches, but with emphasis on the former. Hence, this treatment does not go as far as those observers calling for an end to all hierarchies (e.g., Thayer, 1973), even as it agrees that all alternatives to hierarchy deserve attention (e.g., Kraus, 1984). Here, the basic views may be sketched in one long sentence. Although they will be with us for a long while, conventional hierarchies have a variety of awkward features that can be moderated or eliminated—either by unconventional hierarchies alone, or by various nonhierarchical approaches alone or in complex combinations with innovative hierarchical approaches.

1. Basic Structural Change

In broad outline, the challenges to the traditional principles have encouraged the development of various integrative structures which organize around comprehensive flows of work rather than separate functions or processes. Details about such specific forms of these integrative structures as the matrix are available elsewhere (e.g., Baber, 1983; Davis and Lawrence, 1977); and summaries of a variety of these structural forms exist elsewhere (Golembiewski, 1980, 1986). Here, the focus will be on the generic structural model.

What is the pedigree of this alternative model? A few details must suffice. Such innovations occurred first at high levels of organization (Chandler, 1962), and then only in a few large business firms, beginning in the 1920s and gaining later momentum in the postwar period. In the public sector, attention was directed to the alternative model somewhat later (Golembiewski, 1962b), and a growing volume of theoretical efforts have focused on the properties of such a model (Gawthrop, 1984; Golembiewski, 1984, 1987). More recently, the generic model has begun to influence efforts at the plant or operator level (Zager and Rosow, 1982), again basically in business, but with a growing number of public-sector cases in point (Carew, et al., 1977; Locke, Sirota, and Wolfson, 1976; Rainney, 1985).

Figure 2 sketches such a generic structure, whose basic departmentation focuses on purposes or products at high levels of organization. See the departmentation in General Motors: Cadillac, Chevrolet, and so on. At lower levels, Fig. 2 structures permit job enrichment or organizing around autonomous teams responsible for some related cluster of operations. Note that Fig. 2 structures at the top hierarchical levels often have been coupled with Fig. 1 structures at operating levels. Figure 1 structures do not easily admit such flexibility when they constitute the model for the top-level structure.

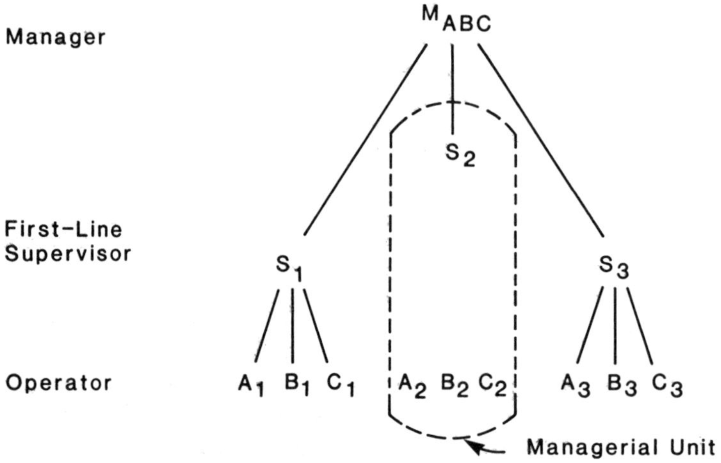

FIGURE 2 Alternative principles for organizing:

1. Structure combines vertical linkages in the chain of command with horizontal linkages of social and psychological forces.
2. Departments aggregate related activities necessary for some flow of work.
3. The flow of work dominates, although it may be served by functions or processes at high levels and by particularistic specializations at other levels.
4. Superiors can manage very large numbers of subordinates, and authoritative direction can come from multiple formal, informal, and personal sources.

Note that Fig. 2 relates to the same three activities as Fig. 1—that is A, B, and C. Just as there, moreover, A + B + C generate some product or service.

There is no need here to review the full briefing about the seven continua as they apply to Fig. 2 structures, but readers might well take on that challenge, whose bottom line has direct features, in general. The alternative structure is more responsive in numerous particulars to the rightward portions of all of the continua detailed above. This section will illustrate the senses in which this bottom-line conclusion is a reasonable one, but without depriving the reader of the fun of developing the fuller analysis—whether alone or in study groups of fellow students.

Three illustrations will provide the reader with a model for the fuller scale analysis of Fig. 2 structures, using concepts earlier applied to the traditional principles and to Fig. 1 structures. The illustrations deal with, in turn:

1. A needs model for self-actualization
2. The tongue-in-cheek First Law of Social Dynamics
3. Differential priority rosters

The approach seems robust enough to support a variety of other emphases common in organization analysis, be it noted. Thus, the reader might choose to apply the details of Lawrence's and Lorsch's (1967) integration/differentiation model. Or the energetic reader might test the summary below by applying to it the major themes of such excellent texts as that of Bolman and Deal (1984). However, also note that the model is not specific enough to encompass some work in organizational analysis such as the promising initial efforts with archetypes (Miller and Friessen, 1984).

First, Fig. 2 structures are responsive to the needs model of individual development sketched in Exhibit 1. How can this point be demonstrated, and without patronizing the reader who has understood and internalized the earlier discussion? Many approaches could do the job, but here consider only the several advantages that the alternative model provides for job rotation and enrichment efforts. This brief demonstration will build on, while transcending, the earlier details concerning the several senses in which job rotation and enrichment suit the needs model. Thus, both emphasize increased activity as well as greater awareness and control, among many other common features, as readers will recall.

And what of the linkages between Fig. 2 structures, job rotation/enrichment, and human needs models? A two-track approach will highlight the prominence of such linkages. Overall, the key feature of the alternative model in meeting individual needs derives from its small managerial unit—each supervisory unit is now an MU, since its supervisor monitors an entire flow of work about which she or he can make reasonable decisions. This feature permits a safe energizing of various social and psychological forces that are at least more chancy in Fig. 1 structures, in general, while avoiding the potential in the traditional principles for units to express their influence over work only or mostly by limiting output.

What specific advantages does the alternative structure offer for job rotation and enrichment? Several illustrations may be listed, in no particular order of significance:

1. Any single S can activate such programs, extending them to a range of activities that would have required the cooperation of all three Ss in Figure 1 structures. This feature reduces the scale of the start-up, no doubt increases self-choice, and, hence, decreases manipulative "selling," or coercion, reduces the risk and cost of such efforts, and respects the real possibility that the several Ss will have different interests

in the programs—ranging from great to none at all, depending upon such variable features as the experience levels of their employees, their specific life stages, their personality characteristics, and so on.

2. Success of the programs might inspire nonparticipants to get on board, and failure would rightly reinforce their original decision not to be involved. The alternative model permits a useful emphasis on testing and comparison, in contrast to command and even coercion. Some have referred to such a feature as respecting the law of the situation, which not only brings immediate experience to bear on decision making, but also avoids charges of arbitrariness and permits mutual empowerment of both management and employees, especially when different conditions encourage or permit variable adaptations.
3. Any advantages deriving from rotation or enrichment directly impact the S who is paying the basic costs, and they also impact the operators in S's unit who are attempting to stretch their competencies. Any failure also will be paid for directly by the actors risking-for-reward. This condition implies a clear motivational setting with no cross-cutting or undermining features.
4. Operators can learn and do new activities without leaving their unit, all of whose members have a common stake in the success of the programs. This suggests multiple advantages in start-up, among them being the avoidance of several awkward features of many rotation/enrichment programs in conventional structures. These usefully avoided consequences include the need to join a "them" with which "we" have had organizational problems, as a prerequisite for a development experience; stereotyping participants as so upwardly mobile that they would leave their old buddies; and resistance to sharing knowledge with outsiders.
5. Operators learning new skills could be rewarded for their effort, without any necessary promotions, and while enhancing a unit's flexibility of response. For example, a mini-career ladder for operators might be developed on this model:

Competency	Pay Grade
A or B or C	I
A + B, or B + C, or A + C	II
A + B + C	III

Individuals could experience a sense of real progress via increasing pay grades rooted in greater skills, in short, while providing a pool of resources that could respond flexibly to fluctuations in the need for specific skills. At the same time, their progress would not necessarily raise troublesome issues of moving to other MUs for training or for promotion.

6. Unlike Fig. 1 structures, job rotation and, especially, enrichment can be activated within any single MU and without disturbing basic policies, procedures, and structures of other MUs. Innovations can be highly targeted in Fig. 2 structures, in short, which facilitates trial and error, as well as local responsiveness to particular conditions, possibilities, or, even, personal preferences.

Second, Fig. 2 structures permit such useful responses to rotation/enrichment programs—and, hence, to individual needs—because of a subtle feature that relates to the previously introduced First Law of Social Dynamics. Any single MU can now raise output directly, but only all of them operating together can lower it. Recall the Golembiewski

First Law of Social Dynamics: The easiest or most convenient thing tends to happen. A powerful reinforcer of the implied potential for self-discipline and self-control requires emphasis. Productivity can be meaningfully compared in Fig. 2 supervisory units, in short, and this permits greater responsible freedom for the units. That is, the performance of units supervised by S_1, S_2, and S_3 can be directly compared. In contrast, the comparison of performance in Fig. 1 structures has to deal with a difficult and often arbitrary judgment: How many As = how many Bs = how many Cs? So close and detailed oversight dominates in traditional structures.

Extended chains of attractive consequences derive from the field of forces surrounding such possibilities for self-discipline and self-control in Fig. 2 structures. For example, a basic change can occur in the role of supervision—from a basic role of detailed monitor or watchdog, to a role with substantial potential for the attitudes and behaviors of the skilled helper. Generally, in turn, autocratic or directive supervision would be less frequent—because it is less encouraged or made less necessary than by the traditional principles. Note the obvious connection. Generally, individuals do not prefer autocratic or directive supervision because (among other reasons) it inhibits meeting the human needs of both the supervisor and the supervised. Illustratively, directive supervision inhibits interdependent and independent behaviors on the parts of both parties, to refer to Exhibit 1. Consequently, with regard to style of supervision, Fig. 2 structures allow both the supervised and the supervisor to utilize high-preference behaviors more often than would be the general case in Fig. 1 structures. Such a potential contributes to making work more rewarding in social and psychological ways and, hence, generates less resistance to personal commitment to work and requires less coercion or manipulation to motivate what needs doing.

Note that this represents no argument for passive or flaccid supervision. Rather, Fig. 2 structures reduce some onerous demands on supervisors and, consequently, can make available energies and, often, goodwill that frequently are dissipated by reasonable efforts to anticipate or to manage the awkward outcomes encouraged by Fig. 1 structures.

Third, relatedly, the priority rosters in the MUs in Fig. 2 structures tend to induce cooperation rather than conflict. Why? Note that each MU will still have a priority roster, and the rosters may well differ between MUs. But that difference is of no particular consequence, because several ways to achieve comparable performance may exist, and, in the bargain, the comparative measures of the performance by the several MUs permit facile judgments about relative performance. The real resolution of differences in priority rosters in Fig. 2 structures, moreover, is within the MU. Major social and psychological forces thus can be mobilized for problem solving in Fig. 2 structures. Indeed, it is in the immediate interests of the members of each MU to develop the necessary skills and energies, for failure to do so would no doubt show up in comparisons of performance with the other MUs. In Fig. 1 structures, in contrast, win/lose conflict between supervisory units often will exist, and this consumes energies that become unavailable for application to the total flow of work.

These general comments might well profit from some reinforcing details. The alternative structuring of DuPont illustrates a Fig. 2 structure and implies the new character and role of the MU. Basically, each product line becomes an MU, as Fig. 3 shows.

In short, members of any unit may succeed in enhancing a flow of work, while all other units also may do so, but in separate and even diverse ways.

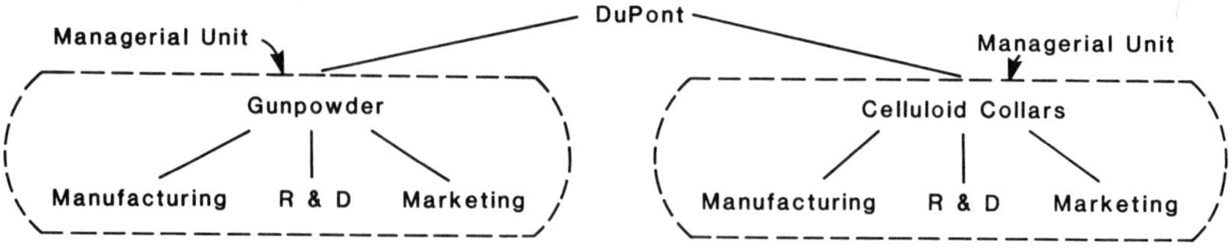

FIGURE 3 Managerial unit in alternative structure.

Figure 1 structures imply very different force fields. Creating high energy levels in Fig. 1 structures might contribute more to conflict than to problem solving, for example, for no single supervisory unit can itself raise productivity, and because multiple reasons support attitudes of every unit for itself. In Fig. 1 structures, to repeat a crucial point, a unit often succeeds at the expense of other units, which, in turn, implies relationships unlikely to support an effective flow of work. This is an awkward combination, and it suggests why authorities in Fig. 1 structures seem to tolerate low energy levels or may even prefer them, because high energy levels can lead to consequences which Fig. 1 structures are poorly configured to contain. These consequences include unilateral and forcing/power modes of handling differences between people and units.

This general point may gain impact from greater detail concerning the modes of conflict resolution likely to be induced by the two basic models for organizing work outlined here in Figs. 1 and 2 with the latter getting an assist from Fig. 3. Usefully, consider six possible modes of dealing with conflicting relationships, which owe most to the work of Thomas (1975), but are also similar to the approaches of others. Thus, organization actors in responses to actual or anticipated differences with other persons or units might adopt these modes of approaching the situation:

1. Confronting other persons or units, which here means openly raising and discussing the issues, tensions and all, with the intent of seeking mutual solutions
2. Unilateral action, where actors decide unilaterally with basic concern for own needs
3. Forcing, or power, which implies the kind of unilateral action where a dominant person or coalition employs power plays and so on with the intent of gaining own ends with little or no thought to a mutual solution
4. Bargaining, or log rolling, in which two or more actors agree to negotiate with minimal openness and without direct concern to solve a problem, but, rather, with an orientation to split the difference or to trade-off so that each side gets some of what it wants by risking other aspects of what it wants
5. Avoiding, which refers to a public neglect of real differences, and which may also be accompanied by private insensitivity to and unawareness of real issues
6. Smoothing, which refers to a special kind of semiavoidance where people seek to minimize differences–a kind of mutual agreement not to take notice of differences

Now what modes seem more likely in Figs. 2 and 3? That is not the best question to ask. Better framed, what modes might be expected within an MU, and what kind between two or more MUs? The key relationships in Figs. 2 and 3 will occur within an MU, and there, one might well expect to see most of confronting and perhaps smoothing. Why? All three activities in each unit–each of which is an MU–share responsibility for a complete flow of work, and their performance is quite directly comparable to each other unit in our illustration. Such features encourage recognizing differences and solving problems, especially when things go poorly. When things are going well, smoothing also may be generally acceptable.

Other modes might well dominate between the units/MUs in Figs. 2 and 3, but they have less potential for fragmenting a flow of work. Indeed, on balance, any unresolved differences between units/MUs in the alternative structure might well heighten the performance of each!

In Fig. 1 structures, no supervisory unit constitutes an MU, and degenerative interaction might well dominate in relationships between units (Golembiewski, 1979, vol. 1, pp. 48-72). This encourages the view that confronting would be less frequent than the other modes. Some Fig. 1 organizations might emphasize unilateral action or forcing. Most probably, however, the softer and nonconfronting modes would be common–log rolling, smoothing, and avoiding. Relatively few organizations seem to be characterized by the tougher, nonconfronting modes (Harrison, 1972)–unilateral action and forcing/power.

The description of features of Figs. 2 and 3 also can be enriched in terms of the vocabulary about cliques introduced earlier. In Fig. 1 structures, vertical cliques dominate. Awkwardly, this helps fragment the flow of work, which has important horizontal features. So work units S_A, S_B, and S_C will have no particular structural reason for integrating their efforts, and practical or political issues often will put them in the role of adversaries or even enemies. Hence, if total productivity is low, A, B, and C will tend to point an accusing finger outward: "What *we* did was good. *They* make the problems." M_{ABC} will be put in uncomfortable situations, as a consequence, being obliged to act like Solomon but with an often dull and unreliable sword for dealing with some very ugly babies which no one will claim as their own, and rightly so, because of the specialization of each unit in only one of the activities required for a flow of work.

In Fig. 2 structures, such divisive human responses are discouraged. Cliques will still be dominantly vertical, in that they will involve superiors and subordinates, but–since each unit is manned by As, Bs, and Cs–relocating blame is a limited strategy. For example, if A_1, B_1, and C_1 get into a squabble about assigning blame–as opposed to solving a problem–their performance will suffer in comparison to the units supervised by S_2 and S_3. That direct feature encourages more problem solving than finger pointing. Golembiewski (1967) observes that Fig. 2 structures preserve vertical cliques, but–because of their basic departmentalization around the flow of work–those cliques serve to horizontally integrate the several activities required for producing the product or service A + B + C. This feature captures much of the character and quality of a Fig. 2 structure. In contrast, similar cliques formed around supervisory units in Fig. 1 structures would tend to fragment a flow of work.

2. Integrative Approaches at Middle and Executive Levels

On occasion, it may not be possible to realize structural changes like those prescribed by Fig. 2–as when distant legislatures mandate Fig. 1 structures–while it remains attractive or even necessary to approach the essence of Fig. 2 outcomes. In fact, substantial experience exists with just such situations (Golembiewski and Kiepper, 1983; 1983b; Sapolsky, 1972; Sayles and Chandler, 1972), often in government agencies.

Exhibit 4 conveniently summarizes the sense of several comprehensive efforts that seek to transcend some of the common awkward consequences of the traditional

Exhibit 4.

Value Overlays of Conventional Structures: Features, Advantages, and Disadvantages

A. Typical Features

-- Value overlays seek to increase

1. the use of multiple ways of generating valid and reliable knowledge of the several worlds of actual and potential organizational collaborators

2. a sense of an organization that seeks excellence, as in being "problem-solving" in contrast with being hierarchy-serving or role bound.

3. the sense and reality of "creative redundancy," as in alternative centers of initiative and responsibility that complement or on occasion supplement functional responsibilities

4. the degree to which progress and problems gain visibility among numerous publics

5. the senses in which hiding an error is viewed as the major organizational transgression

6. the development of norms and rewards that promote interdependence

B. Advantages

* seeks to normatively reinforce the integration of structurally-segregated activities

* some well-known examples exist

* preserves the functional model while seeking to moderate its awkward features

* may be a reasonable "next step", an intermediate phase in a later movement to basic structural change

* may be perceived as less threatening than basic structural change

* does not directly challenge policies and procedures commonly in place -- e.g., traditional position classification, specialist career ladders, and so on

* law or tradition often mandate functional structures, which are thus givens, perhaps especially but not solely in the public sector

-- Value overlays seek to decrease

1. the reliance on formal authority -- indeed to look on the need to rely on formal authority as signalling a managerial failure, as in formal termination unexpected by the individual

2. "throwing of dead cats in the backyards of others," as in avoiding or seeking to relocate responsibility

3. the fragmentation or balkanization of organization units, line from staff, and so on

4. "tunnel vision," both individual and organizational, as by encouraging actors to "take the role of the other"

C. Disadvantages

* specialties remain structurally separated even as exhortation supports integration

* the value-loaded culture may be vulnerable during crises or managerial successions

* the value-infusing process often depends on a chraismatic leader, whose success at one site may lead to quick promotion which, ironically, may threaten that process in direct proportion to its success

* values may inhibit convenient actions, reducing the flexibility of key actors and their motivation to support the values

* value-driven organizations may not satisfy personal needs of key actors -- for style or even flair, dominance, arbitrariness, and so on

* stress on participants may be high

From Golembiewski (1986).

principles, while still relying on those principles to structure the work. That exhibit uses the term "value overlays," which relates to the development of normative agreements among organization members that, in effect, fill in the gaps often induced by the traditional principles. These value overlays moderate or inhibit the separations of Fig. 1 structures, to put the point oversimply.

How is such organizational cement, or solidarity, created in the face of the fragmentation characteristic of the traditional principles? The general answer is—with care, at some cost, and with no certainty of success. This general answer applies even when—as has often been the case—the mission has compelling attractions, time constraints are very tight, and standard operations would mean, in effect, that the mission could not be accomplished. Public-sector examples include our space program (Sayles and Chandler, 1971), a crucial weapons system (Sapolsky, 1972), and a mass urban transit system which had to be built quickly or, in all probability, not at all (Golembiewski and Kiepper, 1983a,b). Commonly, organizations used team building (Dyer, 1977) or various other organization development interventions to build understanding and norms that swim against the strong separatist tides often induced by the traditional principles (Golembiewski and Kiepper, 1983a,b).

Exhibit 4 reflects the essence of several comprehensive and wide-ranging efforts, with a special locus in NASA (Sayles and Chandler, 1971) and the U.S. Navy's POLARIS program (Sapolsky, 1972). The tactics for integration can cover a very broad range, but their normative goals typically seek basic improvement in the relationships between organization members from different units. These relationships between people, in effect, become human counterbalances to the fragmentation characteristic of Fig. 1 models. Specifically, the traditional principles tend to induce degenerative relationships between actors: low openness, low owning of thoughts or feelings, high risk, and low trust. The desired value overlay is regenerative and stresses high openness, high owning, low risk, and high trust. For details about how regenerative models can be approached and maintained, see Golembiewski (1979, vol. 1, especially pp. 48-72).

The rationale for inducing regenerative relationships is direct. Fast-paced projects cannot tolerate degenerative interaction. The belief-cum-evidence is that people who really get to know one another will induce one of two effects. In most cases, they will generate regenerative interaction—people will "get it together." In a few cases, individuals will demonstrate early to self and to others that they simply cannot function in the required ways, and changes can be made before the mission is jeopardized.

The tactics for approaching regenerative relationships can be humble and direct, or complicated and subtle. Consider one case of the former type, which illustrates only one aspect of a multifaceted thrust. Hostile proponents of two alternative approaches from different units are sent on a long trip in side-by-side airline seats—not so much that both are needed at the destination, but because the long coming and going will permit the pair (indeed, will challenge them) to develop that greater understanding of one another that will improve the quality of their relationship or (as happens occasionally) that indicates forcefully to both that "there ain't no way." This sending of two for one illustrates one variety of the creative redundancy mentioned in Exhibit 4, as well as suggests how organization members could go about developing a sense of the multiple worlds of the people with whom they have to work intensively and (it is hoped) effectively.

To a similar point, but in less direct ways, an organization might publicly mandate several different units to work on some common project. The hook? A later public comparison between their several products is intended to motivate the creativity of each unit. The approach adds yet another wrinkle. It provides an opportunity for competitors to learn how to learn from others by requiring an eventual amalgamation of the strongest points of two or more designs. In some cases, moreover, two or more of the designers will know that they will implement the design together. This adds further motivation to develop the best design possible, within two basic conditioning features. Thus, a good design will give due attention to implementation, as opposed to mere technical elegance. In addition, the approach helps eliminate any tendency to gold-plate projects, were the designer to be the sole implementer.

The format of Exhibit 4 is direct, despite the diversity of forms in which its spirit might become manifest in practice. It describes typical features of "value overlays" that can reinforce conventional structures, which features refer both to things that should be increased as well as to things that should be avoided. Typically, the exhibit also illustrates how these increases or decreases can be approached. Moreover, Exhibit 4 also details several advantages and disadvantages of such efforts to transcend the tendencies of the traditional principles.

3. High-Involvement Settings at Plant or Department Levels

In sum, the sections above sketch two ways of dealing with the problems of the traditional principles: by basic structural innovation, or by trying to infuse conventionally organized structures with the spirit and values which can help integrate people and units.

How about combinations of the two? They exist. Indeed, no doubt the sharpest and most detailed examples of what is being done to deal with both structure and spirit or values come from relatively low levels of organization. There, avowed efforts to improve performance by comprehensively enhancing the quality of working life have been reflected in plant designs. Exhibit 5 sketches some major structural and tactical aspects of those innovative efforts.

Basically, Exhibit 5 deals with efforts to develop work cultures as well as rational-technical features that are consistent with Fig. 2 structures, as well as with the spirit or philosophy underlying them. Directly, Exhibit 5 seeks to blend both hierarchical and nonhierarchical contributors to high involvement, which in turn contributes to a quick-reacting system and, thus, superior performance over the long haul. For example, Exhibit 5 reflects Fig. 2 features in the sections labeled "Organization Structure" and "Job Design," and these have hierarchical aspects, as do the "participative employee councils." At the same time, the heavy involvement of peers in selection, socialization, training, rewarding, and directing—see points III, V, VI, VII, and VIII in Exhibit 5—reflects a strong nonhierarchical thrust intended to complement and reinforce these basic structural features.

How much is required to help the reader develop a real sense of this intended association of culture and structure, of hierarchy as well as social-psychological features? It is hoped that not much more than the guiding comments already made is required. For the reader can see numerous points at which high-involvement settings depart from the traditional structure. See "Organization Structure" in Exhibit 5, for example, which variously departs from the traditional principles. This departure is perhaps most marked in the use of employee councils or similar forums to meet several objectives: to get a broad range of input; to share information widely; and to develop understanding and agreement, or even consensus.

Exhibit 5.

Characteristics of High-Involvement Settings at Plant or Department Levels.

I. Organization Structure

- o Designed around teams handling a flow of work vs. departmentation around separate tasks
- o Oriented toward low-cost performance on a flow of work ("lean") vs. gaining authorization of large cadres of separate functional/processual specialists ("fat")
- o Few hierarchical levels and supervisors
- o Little reliance on conventions such as "line" and "staff"
- o Uses participative council or other similar decision-making bodies often at plant as well as lower levels

II. Job Design

- o Emphasis is on challenging and motivating jobs
- o Jobs are enriched
- o Autonomous teams are utilized
- o Oriented around increasing employee/team control over work

III. Information System

- o Has open, multi-lateral, and multi-channel features
- o Carries broad range of data re many topics related to jobs
- o Deliberately seeks to stimulate upward as well as downward communication

IV. Career System

- o Provides several tracks for employee growth and development with counselling available
- o Rests on mobility-enhancing features -- e.g., open job posting and active training efforts

V. Selection

- o Based on realistic preview of job responsibilities, with an emphasis on helping potential employees to ascertain the degree of "fit" between organization and personal skills/preferences
- o Strong team input, as in interviewing as well as in decision to hire
- o Emphasizes potential for learning and interpersonal process skills
- o Heavy commitment of resources

Exhibit 5. (continued)

VI. Training

- o Involves peers and intact teams
- o Emphasizes economic education and interpersonal skills
- o Heavy commitment of resources

VII. Reward System

- o Has strong egalitarian features, as in having all salaried employees as opposed to white-collar vs. blue-collar
- o Based on skills possessed, rather than specific tasks actually performed
- o Encourages skill development, even far beyond task currently performed
- o Includes gain-sharing, ownership, or other features to enhance motivation by tying rewards to performance

VIII. Authority System

- o Has major participative features, in cases extending to substantial employee control over production processes and other central aspects of work
- o Reflects strong bias toward "law of the situation" rather than toward hierarchy, toward who has the skills or information rather than the rank
- o Relies on clear and shared measures of performance and goals, which changes the quality of management and supervision from monitoring behavior to facilitating performance, from ordering to coaching, from exerting influence to respecting a common discipline

IX. Physical Lay-out

- o Reduces or eliminates invidious status distinctions
- o Is safe and pleasant
- o Is defined in accordance with flow of work and organization structure, e.g., decision-making rooms near several worksites

---

Nine of the 10 categories come from Perkins, Nieva, and Lawler, 1983, esp. p. 14. The several characteristics are conflated from personal observation and several sources: Perkins, Nieva, and Lawler, 1983, pp. 5-15; Golembiewski, 1965; Walton, 1977, pp. 422-433; and Zager and Rosow, 1982.

Exhibit 5 also variously reflects the intent to meet a broad range of individual needs at work. For example, the reader might well focus on "Selection and Training" in that exhibit. Clearly, employees are encouraged more than permitted to "utilize an increasing range of abilities, especially cognitive and interpersonal abilities," to quote some of the language of Exhibit 1.

The details of Exhibit 5 could preoccupy this essay for a long time, and I hope readers will give those details the scrupulous attention they can bear. But the essence of it is transparent. For example, Walton (1985) describes the movement from Fig. 1 structures to Exhibit 5 as a movement from basic reliance on control in the former case to commitment in the latter. Thus, Fig. 1 structures propose to fragment work into its elemental pieces, and then to control those pieces by autocratic hierarchical controls. Such work seems to demand little of the employee who is willing to alienate self from work, but in fact it sacrifices much in terms of concern for quality and for the continual fine-tuning based on experience that has proved so advantageous to the Japanese. Psychologically, this association with work can imply very high costs for many employees; and in the long run, the approach can prove a costly way to run any enterprise, and especially an enterprise with a demanding technology in a turbulent environment. Hence the growing emphasis on commitment to replace reliance on control. Walton observes (1985, p. 79):

> In this new commitment-based approach to the work force, jobs are designed to be broader than before, to combine planning and implementation, and to include efforts to upgrade operations, not just maintain them. Individual responsibilities are expected to change as conditions change, and teams, not individuals, often are the organizational units accountable for performance. With management hierarchies relatively flat and differences in status minimized, control and lateral coordination depend on shared goals and expertise.

The transition from control to commitment often will not occur in one smooth jump, as Walton cautions. But one common crucial element is involved in that transition—a replacement of Fig. 1 thinking by the spirit and structure associated with Fig. 2. That change in consciousness both underlies and will facilitate that transition. This elemental, but critical, fact motivates the structure of this essay, which intends just such a change in the reader's consciousness.

The last comment has the clear ring of advocacy about it, but there is no need to be concerned about conscious and intelligent advocacy. What motivates championing such high-involvement systems? For some, normative issues are dominant. These high-involvement systems give more to their employees as a matter of philosophy. Probably, for most people involved in their development, high-involvement systems are more necessary—to do work better than before, less expensively, and with better quality. From this perspective, work gives more to individuals in exchange for getting more from them.

VII. CONCLUSION

Despite its detail, then, the basic flow here is direct. For various reasons, one approach to organizing work not only was developed early in our history, but it has persisted in the face of considerable adverse evidence. That persistence is both impressive and troublesome, and as deriving from the unavailability during critical periods of an alternative model for organizing work (Golembiewski, 1984, 1987). Now we can do somewhat better, and we have substantial experience that can ease the attempt.

Hence, the bare bones of this essay. The traditional principles for organizing are detailed and illustrated, to review the flow of this argument. Moreover, selective challenges to them are elaborated. Finally, three new directions for thought and theory about organizing more sensitively to those challenges are broadly circumscribed and briefly discussed.

A final question may suggest itself to the inquiring mind. Why, given such features, are not Fig. 2 structures omnipresent, or at least far more common than appears the case? I shall let the readers mull that one, at their leisure. A few clues may help. Thus, readers may doubt the basic argument here, which is fair enough, providing that they attempt to support their concerns by wide-ranging reading. Any such suspicion, if reinforced by evidence, would provide reason aplenty for sharp limits on the diffusion of the organizational innovations introduced above. Or one can propose that skills are now lacking for Fig. 2-ship, and that a developmental lag exists between what we are coming to know and our ability to orient systems to the knowledge.

For me, this final question is inept. Why does not Fig. 2 exist almost everywhere, or at least in more places? That question approximates asking, for example, why cholera ravaged so much of mankind for so long. One can specify reasons, of course: ignorance, sloth, willingness to accept what is, and so on. We are forever in flux. Sometimes things get worse; on balance, I judge, organizational matters have improved substantially and more or less continuously since early big project days—as when the pyramids were built. So my preferred strategy is to assess the desirability of what exists, and to seek to reduce the undesirable or less desirable, with no great concern about why the undesirable or less desirable existed in the first place.

The undesirable always will exist, in short, and two human challenges inhere in our fallibility-cum-progress. We need to isolate the undesirable at the earliest possible opportunity; and we need to change the undesirable when we have reasonable guides as to how to go about doing that with reasonable probability of success.

REFERENCES

Alber, A. F. (1978). Job enrichment programs seen improving employee performance, but benefits not without cost, *World of Work Report,* 3: 8.

Argyris, C. (1957). *Personality and Organization*, Harper, New York.

Baber, W. F. (1983). *Organizing the Future*, University of Alabama Press, University, Alabama.

Bernstein, P. (1980). *Workplace Democratization*, Transaction Books, New Brunswick, New Jersey.

Bolman, L. G., and Deal, T. E. (1984). *Modern Approaches to Understanding and Managing Organizations*, Jossey-Bass, San Francisco.

Buchanan, J. M., and Tullock, G. (1962). *The Calculus of Consent*, University of Michigan Press, Ann Arbor.

Carew, D. K., Carter, S. I., Gamache, J. M., Hardiman, R., Jackson, B., III, and Parisi, E. M. (1977). New York State Division of Youth: A collaborative approach to the implementation of social change in a public bureaucracy, *Journal of Applied Behavioral Science*, 13: 327.

Cartwright, D., and Zander, A., eds. (1953). *Group Dynamics*, Row, Peterson, Evanston, Illinois.

Chandler, A. D. (1962). *Strategy and Structure*, The M.I.T. Press, Cambridge, Massachusetts.

Chung, K. H., and Ross, M. F. (1977). Differences in motivational properties between job enlargement and job enrichment, *Academy of Management Review*, 2: 113.
Coker, F. W. (1922). Dogmas of administrative reform, *American Political Science Review*, 16: 399.
Dalton, M. (1959). *Men Who Manage*, Wiley, New York.
Davis, K. (1957, 1962). *Human Relations at Work*, McGraw-Hill, New York.
Davis, S., and Lawrence, P. R. (1977). *Matrix*, Addison-Wesley, Reading, Massachusetts.
Drucker, P. F. (1954). *The Practice of Management*, Harper, New York.
Dyer, W. G. (1977). *Team-Building*, Addison-Wesley, Reading, Massachusetts.
Ebenstein, W. (1956). *Great Political Thinkers*, Rinehart, New York.
Elden, J. M. (1981). Political efficacy at work, *American Political Science Review*, 75: 43.
Fayol, H. (1925). *Administratif Industrielle et Général*, Dunod, Paris.
Ford, R. N. (1969). *Motivation Through the Work Itself*, American Management Association, New York.
Galbraith, J. R. (1973). *Designing Complex Organizations*, Addison-Wesley, Reading, Massachusetts.
Galbraith, J. R. (1977). *Organization Design*, Addison-Wesley, Reading, Massachusetts.
Gawthrop, L. C. (1984). *Public Sector Management, Systems, and Ethics*, Indiana University Press, Bloomington, Indiana.
Gerth, H. H., and Mills, C. W. (1946). *From Max Weber: Essays in Sociology*, Oxford University Press, New York.
Glover, J. D., and Hower, R. M., eds. (1957). *The Administrator*, Irwin, Homewood, Illinois.
Golembiewski, R. T. (1962a). *Behavior and Organization*, Rand McNally, Chicago.
Golembiewski, R. T. (1962b). Civil service and managing work, *American Political Science Review*, 56: 961.
Golembiewski, R. T. (1962c). *The Small Group*, University of Chicago Press, Chicago.
Golembiewski, R. T. (1965). *Men, Management, and Morality*, McGraw-Hill, New York.
Golembiewski, R. T. (1967). *Organizing Men and Power*, Rand McNally, Chicago.
Golembiewski, R. T. (1979). *Approaches to Planned Change*, vols. 1 and 2, Marcel Dekker, New York.
Golembiewski, R. T. (1980). Infusing organizations with OD values: Public-sector approaches to structural change, *Southern Review of Public Administration*, 4: 269.
Golembiewski, R. T. (1983). Structuring the public organization, *Handbook of Organization Management* (W. B. Eddy, ed.), Marcel Dekker, New York.
Golembiewski, R. T. (1984). Organizing public work, round three: Toward a new balance between political agendas and management perspectives, *The Costs of Federalism* (R T. Golembiewski and A. Wildavsky, eds.), Transaction, New Brunswick, New Jersey.
Golembiewski, R. T. (1985). *Humanizing Public Organizations*, Lomond Publications, Mt. Airy, Maryland.
Golembiewski, R. T. (1987). Public sector organization: Why theory and practice should emphasize purpose, and how to do so, *A Centennial History of the American Administrative State* (R. C. Chander, ed.), Macmillan, New York.
Golembiewski, R. T., and Kiepper, A. (1983a). Lessons from a fast-paced public project, *Public Administration Review*, 43: 547.
Golembiewski, R. T., and Kiepper, A. (1983b). Organizational transition in a fast-paced public project: Personal perspectives of MARTA executives, *Public Administration Review*, 43: 246.
Gulick, L., and Urwick, L., eds. (1937). *Papers on the Science of Administration*, Institute of Public Administration, New York.

Harrison, R. (1972). Understanding your organization's character, *Harvard Business Review*, 50: 121.
Herzberg, F., et al. (1959). *The Motivation to Work*, Wiley, New York.
House, J. S. (1981). *Work Stress and Social Support*, Addison-Wesley, Reading, Massachusetts.
Jennergren, P. (1981). Decentralization in organizations, *Handbook in Organizational Design*, vol. 1 (P. C. Nystrom and W. Starbuck, eds.), Oxford University Press, New York.
Kaufman, H. (1949). *The Forest Ranger*, Johns Hopkins Press, Baltimore.
Kaufman, H. (1985). *Time, Chance, and Organizations*, Chatham House Publishers, Chatham, New Jersey.
Koontz, H. (1961). The management theory jungle, *Academy of Management Journal*, 4: 174.
Kraus, W. A. (1984). *Collaboration in Organizations: Alternatives to Hierarchy*, Human Sciences Press, New York.
Lawrence, P. R., and Lorsch, J. W. (1967). *Organization and Environment*, Harvard Graduate School of Business Administration, Boston.
Lewin, K., Lippitt, R., and White, R. K. (1939). Patterns of aggressive behavior in experimentally created "social climates," *Journal of Social Psychology*, 10: 271.
Lippitt, R., and White, R. H. (1943). The "social climate" of children's groups, *Child Behavior and Development* (R. G. Barker, J. S. Kounnin, and H. F. Wright eds.), McGraw-Hill, New York.
Locke, E. A., Sirota, D., and Wolfson, A. D. (1976). An experimental case study of successes and failures of job enrichment in a government agency, *Journal of Applied Psychology*, 61: 701.
McGregor, D (1960). *The Human Side of Enterprise*, McGraw-Hill, New York.
March, J. G., ed. (1965). *Handbook of Organizations*, Rand McNally, Chicago.
March, J. G., and Simon, H. A. (1958). *Organizations*, Wiley, New York.
Mason, R. M. (1982). *Participatory and Workplace Democracy*, Southern Illinois University Press, Carbondale, Illinois.
Miles, R. H. (1980). *Macro Organizational Behavior*, Goodyear, Santa Monica, California.
Miller, D., and Friesen, and P. H. (1984). *Organizations: A Quantum View*, Prentice-Hall, Englewood Cliffs, New Jersey.
Miller, E. (1975). Socio-technical systems in weaving, *Human Relations*, 28: 348.
Mintzberg, H. (1979). *The Structuring of Organizations*, Prentice-Hall, Englewood Cliffs, New Jersey.
Nystrom, P. C., and Starbuck, W. H. eds. (1981). *Handbook of Organizational Design*, vols. 1 and 2. Oxford University Press, New York.
Pascale, R. T., and Athos, A. G. (1981). *The Art of Japanese Management*, Simon and Schuster, New York.
Perkins, D. N. T., Nieva, V. F., and Lawler, E. E., III. (1983). *Managing Creation*, John Wiley and Sons, New York.
Rainney, G. W., Jr., and Rainney, H. G. (1985). Organizational decentralization in the public sector: Modularization of the social security claims process vs. the hierarchical imperative. Unpublished.
Roethlisberger, F. F., and Dickson, W. J. (1939). *Management and the Worker*, Harvard University Press, Cambridge, Massachusetts.
Sapolsky, H. M. (1972). *POLARIS*, Harvard University Press, Cambridge, Massachusetts.
Sayles, L. R., and Chandler, M. (1971). *Managing Large Systems*, Harper & Row, New York.
Scott, W. G., and Hart, D. K. (1979). *Organizational America*, Houghton Mifflin, Boston.

Selznick, P. (1979). *TVA and the Grass Roots*, University of California Press, Berkeley.
Simon, H. A. (1946). The proverbs of administration, *Public Administration Review*, 6: 53.
Simon, H. A. (1947, 1957). *Administrative Behavior*, Macmillan, New York.
Stein, H., ed. (1948). *Public Administration and Policy Development*, Harcourt, Brace, New York.
Tannenbaum, A. S. (1966). *Social Psychology of the Work Organization*, Wadsworth, Belmont, California
Taylor, F. W. (1911). *The Principles of Scientific Management*, Harper, New York.
Thayer, F. C. (1973). *An End to Hierarchy! An End to Competition!* Franklin Watts, New York.
Thomas, K. W. (1976). Conflict and conflict management, *Handbook of Industrial and Organizational Psychology* (M. D. Dunnette, ed.), Rand McNally, Chicago.
Thompson, J. D. (1967). *Organizations in Action*, McGraw-Hill, New York.
Waldo, D. (1961). Organization theory: An elephantine problem, *Public Administration Review*, 21: 210.
Waldo, D. (1980). *The Enterprise of Public Administration*, Chandler and Sharp, Novato, California.
Walton, R. (1977). Work innovations at Topeka, *Journal of Applied Behavioral Science*, 13: 422.
Walton, R. E. (1985). From control to commitment in the workplace, *Harvard Business Review*, 64: 85.
Wilson, W. (1887). The study of administration, *Political Science Quarterly*, 2: 197.
Witte, J. F. (1980). *Democracy, Authority, and Alienation in Work*, University of Chicago Press, Chicago.
Zager, R., and Rosow, M. P., eds. (1982). *The Innovative Organization*, Pergamon, New York.

2

Organizational Structure and Service Delivery Arrangements in Human Services

William J. Page Department of Public Administration and School of Social Work, Florida State University, Tallahassee, Florida

I. INTRODUCTION

This chapter explores and interprets certain aspects of organizational structure and service delivery arrangements in human services. The primary focus is public organizations in the state segment of the federal-state-local human services of the United States. Major objectives are more practical than theoretic:

1. To identify and explain environmental and other variables that influence structure
2. To provide and interpret models of different types of structures and to explain advantages and disadvantages of each type
3. To suggest criteria for service delivery arrangements

The surge of changes in national human services policy during the 1960s and 1970s was matched by extensive changes in state and local organizations. Although the national revisions substantially altered the policy environment of the federal-state partnership, changes in structures of state organizations were not federally mandated. Instead, they were state initiatives or cooperative intergovernmental projects intended to improve management, policy formation, accountability, and delivery of services. Federal and state policy changes figured importantly in shaping state structures for imlementation. Many existing programs were greatly expanded during the 1960s and 1970s. New provisions were made for extending services to millions of additional persons and to population groups who had not received services in the past. Medicaid and social service titles of the Social Security Act are examples of major expansions. Increments of staff were required to provide the expanded services. New service and informational technologies were developed, old methods were changed, and state and local appropriations for fixed capital increments created more places to serve more people.

The cumulative effect of programmatic expansions and additions was a substantial increase in complexity of national, state, and local human service establishments. New and revised structural forms were developed to accommodate an expanded and more differentiated collection of programs.

Changes also occurred in the politics and technology of human services. Greater size and increased funding increased visibility of organizations. New technologies required or permitted new types of workers, particularly in information handling and other aspects of management. Bigger budgets were simultaneously a cause and an effect of greater expectations by politicians, clientele groups, and contractual service providers. Priorities were debated. Competition for greater, but still insufficient, resources produced an exceedingly turbulent human service arena. Doubts were raised concerning the efficacy of new programs and larger appropriations in solving social problems. Forceful demands were made for evaluation of results and for improved management.

Excepting wars and technological developments, scientific and practical gains in human service were arguably the most outstanding features of life in the United States during the past five decades. Increased size and greater complexity frequently were followed by changes in organizational structures.

This chapter deals with selected organizational and service delivery facets of the revolution in human services. It is concerned primarily with public organizational structures and systems created or changed to provide a broad range of complex human services. Special attention to state structures is warranted by the middle position of states in the federal system of government. The states implement federal policy, generate their own policies and service delivery structures, and control a vast array of local public and private policy-making and service delivery arrangements. States are the agents for financing and operating the total system. Interdependence is the outstanding characteristic of the tremendously varied components of the intergovernmental system.

Organizational structure must be placed in perspective. Structure alone does not assure success or guarantee failure. On the other hand, structure is a necessary and possibly important aspect of organizations that are expected to accomplish goals in human services. Goals may be sharply defined or ambiguous, formal or informal. Goals may be conveniently ignored or changed, but they are an essential part of conventional expectations of public and private human service systems. Regardless of the characteristics of goals, the administrative pragmatist utilizes them as a driving force in managing human service organizations. In this context organizational structure is the formal arrangement of people and functions necessary to achieve desired results.

Administrators alone are not the determiners of goals or organizational structures. Legislators and elected executives, guided by their own concepts and responding to influential constituencies, are important participants in determining and legitimizing goals and structure. Fortunately, the concept of equifinality suggests the possibility of different means of accomplishing an end. Any of several organizational structures might serve equally well in a given situation. Among the thousands of governmental entities and private organizations providing human services in the United States, structural variability is the rule, rather than the exception—even within the crude typology examined in this chapter.

Recent scholarly works (Meyer and Rowan, 1983), while acknowledging the necessity of structure, suggest that observable forms are based on the myths and ritualized behaviors of institutions, or professional domains, in the general environment. Specialized professions, each having its own belief system, knowledge base, and societal niche, attempt to codify these properties in human service organizations. In other words, given the lack of a reality to which all participants can subscribe in structuring and operating an organization, one should expect two things: each profession will attempt to realize its values and norms in configuring the human service organization, and each profession will to some extent ignore, circumvent, or possibly challenge structural variance that conflicts with professional beliefs and domain. It may be expected that individuals and groups, as members of organizations, will use clientele, professional organizations, or other political forces in the organizational environment to influence organizational structure and behavior.

It is not possible here to examine all possible definitions and meanings of "organizational structure." Organizational structure for present purposes is defined as the formal positional distribution and role relations of persons in a human service organization (Hall, 1982, p. 53).

This chapter now proceeds to explore selected aspects of variance in human service structures, especially environmental influences and complexity, then presents a typology of complex human service organizations and, finally, shifts to a focus on service delivery arrangements.

II. VARIABLES IN HUMAN SERVICE STRUCTURES

Tens of thousands of human service organizations exist in the public and private sectors. These organizations originate and operate in a great variety of settings, perform an impressive range of services and have not been adequately characterized, analyzed, or classified. Structural differences are the rule, rather than the exception.

The intention here is not to analyze comprehensively or describe in detail the tremendous variety of human service organizations and their structural configurations. Instead, the objective is to identify some of the various conceptions of organizations which appear to be relevant to human services, and to identify phenomena that apparently influence organizational structure.

A. Notes on Organizational Theory

Organization theory changes, as most bodies of knowledge change, over time and with new learning from research and practice. Scott (1981) identifies different concepts of organization, associates concepts with their originators and followers, and identifies time frames in which various concepts gained currency. Theoretic themes are nearly as variable as the structures they purport to explain and, similarly, are adapted over time. Gleanings from a wealth of evolving theory consistently register the importance of systems concepts, including the general concept of environmental influence on organizational structure and functions.

By "environment" we mean the set of phenomena which influence and are influenced by an organization. In their creation, operation, and adaptation, human service organizations demonstrate the utility of different perspectives of organizations as rational, natural, or open systems—or a combination of all three perspectives. The human service practitioner may be best served by the notion that open and natural systems attempt to achieve some measure of rationality in organizational structure. Probably more important is the reality that workers and other participants in service delivery frequently create their own informal structures, sometimes called networks, which may vary according to the needs of a particular client or situation. Thus, opportunism may be a significant determinant of actual structure at the supremely important point of service delivery. However, it is clear that several sets of environmental variables may systematically influence strategic and operational choices of persons who design and deliver human services.

B. Environmental Influences

1. Values

Social service managers and workers own some values that are frequently ascribed to the whole society. The value attached to human dignity and worth is a ready example. The major differences between the value sets found in human services, compared to the whole society, are attributable to influences such as professional education and training, the conditioning effect of advocating the interests of clients, organizational climates, and organizational cultures. These influences tend to prioritize certain values and to differentiate classes of human service workers.

Given hundreds of occupational titles in a large human service organization, the priority ranking of values understandably varies among classes of workers. The managerial class is heavily influenced by external and personal expectations of efficiency, effectiveness, and orderly administration. Values of this sort do not displace, but may affect, the comparative managerial ranking of independence and total satisfaction of the needs of clients. In contrast, the front-line social workers may place higher value on social adjustment, familial relations, independence, and self-esteem of the client. The public health nurse might maximize the value of physical health to a greater extent than either the manager or the social worker.

Any or all of the values owned by members of human service disciplines can influence organizational structure. Each member wants and attempts to realize a structure that facilitates or enhances the performance of his or her own work. The perceived importance of the overall configuration of an organization is inversely related to the positional location of the worker, unless structure is a significant barrier to service delivery. Unhampered opportunity to apply appropriate technology in accordance with professional values transcends structure as a daily concern of most human service workers. Whatever the symbolic value (for example, structural visibility of a professional specialization) to the worker, structural subdivision may be of greater importance to external persons who have strong ideological or institutional commitment to a particular structural form.

2. Technology

Human service organizational structure is influenced significantly by technology. Two types of technological influences are apparent: knowledge and methods which are institutionalized through education, training, practices, and organization of specialized professions; and technology from other fields, such as information handling, which creates interdependence of professions and organizational units. These certainly are not the only technological concerns of human service establishments, but they are sources of influence on the organizational structures in which human service managers and specialists practice.

Each of the human services depends on its knowledge base and methodology for its legitimacy, relative status, and effectiveness. The methods used by most human service specializations are indeterminate in character (Hasenfeld, 1983). As an example, it is not easy to prove that counseling of a drug abuser or medication given to a sick person causes that person to overcome his or her problem. Either person might have recovered without the methodological intervention, given other known and unknown variables. Demonstration of cause-effect relationships often is not possible in individuals or classes of individuals, because the disciplines of knowledge and practice are not supported by the types of knowledge base that is available in the physical sciences, which is the realm in which scientific methods were developed.

The social scientist or practitioner, striving to develop and use knowledge and methods in the manner required by the hard sciences, places special importance on organizational structure which recognizes domain and technology. Health service practitioners often make compelling demands for distinction and visibility in policy-making, programming, and structuring their work environments. Similarly, social workers as individuals or primary work groups sometimes appear to be preoccupied with domain. Practicing in a health setting, such as a large medical center, the social worker often experiences social disadvantage, structural obscurity, and organizational powerlessness. The public health nurse mentioned in an earlier example might have similar experience if placed in an organizational unit, such as a protective services unit, whose primary charge is social services.

Technology and corresponding specialization are difficult enough without structural implications. Professional and technical differentiation is institutionalized and politicized, thus gaining significant influence on organizational structure. This is not a local phenomenon. National legislation in extreme cases—vocational rehabilitation is such a case—not only requires a single state organizational unit, but prescribes state structural relationships within state agencies for a specific program and group of workers. Only a vocational rehabilitationist can supervise another of the same occupational kind if a state is to comply with federal law. Thus, specific programmatic and structural identity and separatism are assured at the cost of state and local discretion and flexibility in organizational design and service delivery. This pattern of categorical structuring is part of the history of many intergovernmentally financed and managed programmatic entities in human services.

3. Politics and Policy

Politics and policy pervasively influence human service structures. The literature of human service policy and administration suggests that structural revision is an easy alternative for politicians wishing to avoid difficult, fundamental reform of human service policy (Radin, 1987). This assertion might be valid in some instances, but it does not give appropriate credence to other possible motivations for structural change. Lynn (1976, 1980) and Agranoff (1977) observe and report ideological, rational, social and other strong motivations of various policy actors and managers who take considerable risks and spend enormous amounts of energy in reorganizing human service systems—for purposes of higher order rather than "show and tell."

Elliot Richardson (1976), who served in a variety of state and federal elected and appointed positions, strongly believed that local governmental and citizens' involvement in policy formation is requisite to improvement of the quality of community life in a democracy. He repeatedly proposed national policy changes and sponsored dozens of experiments in design and delivery of human services. The strategy of governmental and organizational learning implicit in his efforts transcended simplistic issues of structure and fragmented implementation of existing policies. Richardson's active pressure for policy and operational changes preceded, suffused, and postdated his policy role as secretary of the U.S. Department of Health, Education, and Welfare. His persistence and extensive experimentation are especially remarkable when one considers multiple countervailing pressures from political and administrative environments. Certain members of Congress, federal program directors and staff, organizations representing human service specialists, and other special interest lobbies were among the staunch defenders of the prevailing categorical structure of human service organization. That model and its accompanying set of values best express the values of specialization and domain, which are consistently associated with professionalism. Policymakers seeking change bear a special burden of changing multiple professional subcultures.

State legislators and elected executives have initiated most of the structural revisions in state and local human service organizations. These principal actors in the policy process normally have taken action because it is not usually expected that state agency heads, as peers, can meet and agree to abolish structure or transfer major functions to or from a proposed or existing organization. Institutionalized dominions strongly inhibit such actions. Appointed administrators may participate in policy planning and formation after the issues are defined, but their major role has been implementation of policy which mandates reorganization.

The policy-related sets of reasons for structural change include control of the political environment (Curtis and Yessian, 1979; Imershein et al., 1983); desire to improve service delivery (Gans, 1976); and gains in citizen and other local participation through decentralization (Richardson, 1976). The traditional categorical pattern of organization, a series of separate structures, was infinitely expandable and not feasible for policymakers to control satisfactorily. As a specific social problem was recognized and gained space on the national policy agenda, legislation was enacted and appropriations were made to provide one or more services to reduce or eliminate the problem. State and local governments were offered and usually accepted financial incentives to create mirror-image structures. Coalitions of program administrators, specialized professionals, and, in some instances, persons adversely affected by a specific problem perennially returned to federal, state, and local policymakers, making persuasive arguments for program expansions. The increase in the number of categorical programs outstripped information and available time for overall policy review and evaluation.

Narrowly bounded programs and proliferated organizational structures made it practically impossible for legislators and chief executives to hold categorical programs, administrators, specialized professionals, or anyone accountable for achieving statutory intent or broad policy commitments. High mortality rates among children, as an example, was an issue. Categorically structured prenatal and infant health services could respond only to limited possibilities for prevention of infant mortality. Malnutrition, as a contributing problem, frequently was beyond the remedies available through traditional public health programs. Provision of food stamps was the job of the public assistance agency, but this program was administered nationally by the U.S. Department of Agriculture, whose major mission had no direct relation to state public assistance functions. Child abuse and neglect were factors in childhood mortality, but these difficult problems traditionally were within the province of the Children's Bureau nationally and separate child welfare commissions or other structures in the states. The broader the scope of the policy problem, the more intractable it became for legislators, governors of states, and narrowly specialized administrative agencies.

Quantitatively and qualitatively adequate information resources might have informed the policy process. Categorical agencies are intrinsically limited, even if included, in managing information on human problems which involve more than one agency. Further, they are more inclined toward delivering service than toward highly technical informational performances. Laudable policy depends on the capacity of principal actors to perceive problems and performances in context. Categorical structures and programming force policymakers, program managers, and specialized service providers to function in a pattern of extreme, dysfunctional reductionism.

Reductionism in organizational design forces or permits elaborate structural identity of minute functional bits. The effects are equally observable in a large, multifunction state agency which provides a box in its organizational chart for each activity and in a state or local government which can include 50 or more departments and agencies. The normal collection of dozens of operating human service programs alone can require more separate agencies than any elected chief executive can lead effectively. Legislatures are similarly overburdened and unable to perform responsible oversight of dozens of discrete human service organizations. Clock time is only one of the important considerations. More significant problems are associated with the difficulty of perceiving issues, policies, and service delivery in a holistic way or understanding their interrelation. To take a reductionist approach to structural design in human service is to build in failure of elected officials, agency managers, and clients whose problems do not coincide with narrowly defined categorical functions and organizational structures.

4. Leadership and Resistance to Change

Changes are easier for some organizations than others. Quality of leadership and the culture of a particular organization are the major variable sets. A prominent scholar integrates leadership and organizational culture in the assertion that management of the culture of an organization may be the most important performance of any leader (Schein, 1985). Lynn (1980) gave specific attention to appointed and elected leadership in his landmark studies of state agencies affected by policy and structural changes. Literature and a vast amount of unpublished practical experience provide some insight which can enable understanding and ease the traumatic effects of major organizational change. An organization with recent experience of successful management of change probably has had recent imposition of leadership from outside. Attitudes favorable to change can be inculcated into the culture of an organization. The climate of such an organization encourages open discussion of ideas, proposals, or actions of structural revision. Successful management of change indicates that leaders and staff have a clear vision of the desired form and intended effects of proposals or options for revision. Additional requirements of leadership are ability to articulate the vision well enough to be understood and persistence, leavened with patience, in achievement of change. An ordinary leader can mandate and control the process of change. An excellent leader can enable acceptance of change and minimize adverse effects. No leader can succeed in changing a human service organization without cooperation of staff.

Schon (1971) makes it clear that resistance to change is normal behavior in organizations. He outlines a predictable sequence of reactions to a major structural or functional revision. The initial response is to ignore the possibility of change. If it becomes impossible to ignore the proposed change, a fighting response is predictable. Absent a successful fight, acceptance begins. Concurrently, one should expect efforts of compromise and cooperation. Significant resistance or subversive efforts should be confronted, but not handled punitively. Punishment creates martyrs. Martyrdom adversely affects organizational climate and culture, but rarely eliminates variant behaviors.

Potentially the most difficult change situation for leaders and other members of an organization occurs when neither the organization nor its leadership has changed significantly for a decade or longer. Given the estimated average tenure of less than two years for leadership of large national and state human service organizations, long tenure usually is not a realistic expectation for leaders of such organizations. No major sector of the private corporate realm has—or would tolerate—the turnover rate in executives experienced by large, complex human service organizations.

5. Special Interest Groups

Special interest groups have a long record of influence in human services. The traditional pattern is advocacy by groups for enacting authorizing legislation, advice and other participation in structural design, advisory involvement in recruitment and selection of key appointees, informal or formal monitoring of service quality and delivery, and perennial support in resource extraction and other transactions with the organizational environment. Interest groups, particularly in human services, tend to develop strong identification with and a sense of ownership of public and private organizations operating in their realms. Most influential are the interest groups whose members are highly successful in securing appropriations or donated resources and who are identified with a single categorical program.

It is normal, though not always agreeable, for interest groups to seek the highest possible organizational placement in the existing organizational structure and to insist on maximum autonomy for "their" organizational entity. It is not uncommon for special interest advocates to prefer a completely autonomous agency, despite known costs of beneficial interorganizational support and services. The characterization of these propensities as normal merely indicates the prevalent illusion that autonomous authority is efficacious and visibility is generally beneficial. On the deficit side, the reality is that governors and mayors do not have the time and usually lack the information required for consistent and effective day-to-day leadership of program development and operations. Additionally, elected chief executives are seldom willing to expend significant amounts of political capital for limited functional purposes.

Special interest groups closely related to an organizational entity always should be provided full information and easy access to leaders who propose or manage organizational change. Openness does not necessarily equate with easy compromise. Openness does reduce vulnerability to destructive criticism and organizational subversion during a major structural change.

C. Organizational Complexity

The known elements of organizational complexity are vertical differentiation, horizontal differentiation, and spatial dispersion (Hall, 1982, pp. 78-83). That short list of factors could disappoint persons who prefer to believe that size consistently correlates with complexity. Each of these variables will be discussed briefly in relation to design and articulation of structure.

1. Vertical Differentiation

Vertical differentiation is the least complicated and most easily documented dimension of organizational complexity. Vertical differentiation also evokes subjective criticism of "layering" and "bureaucracy," especially in conflictual environments. Simplistic counting of levels provides an index of vertical complexity, although the process is about as useful as counting the boards used in constructing a house. Occasional differences may arise about apparently redundant staffing of supervisory components. As an example, is an additional layer created when a full deputy reviews all information directed by subentities to the head of an organizational unit? The answer may be affirmative if all contacts with and information to be received by the chief are subject to control by the deputy. The answer may be negative if the deputy can decide any issue or take any other action that the chief is authorized to take, but only when the chief is absent or is overloaded with work. This is more than a theoretical matter; it has practical implications. The person who manages all field operations for a complex human service organization in a large state might understandably choose to spend a significant portion of his or her time in multiple, widely dispersed field offices. That pattern would be highly compatible with a "walking-around" style of management. The manager's being away from his or her own office for several consecutive days might not be an unusual occurrence. To avoid delays, the deputy might handle matters which need to be disposed of promptly and might also substitute for the chief in a continuing special assignment—for example, as a member of the organization's planning team. The arrangement would not constitute two layers of management for the entity and would not amount to unnecessary structural elaboration.

2. Horizontal Differentiation

Human service organizations, being relatively high on a professionalization scale, are prime examples of the organizational effects of dividing work in an age of expanding knowledge and specialization. Horizontal differentiation is the structural consequence of dividing tasks in an organization according to specialized knowledge and skills. An indicator of such differentiation might be the number of different occupational titles or the number of major and minor structural subdivisions.

The number and distribution of subdivisions are not the only, and certainly not the most important, aspect of horizontal differentiation. A major factor is the requirement of coordination. Coordination is exceedingly costly in terms of executive time, as well as the time of the persons being coordinated. The process costs so much time that staff assistants frequently are assigned to coordinative duties. It is axiomatic that coordination is a good thing or a bad thing, depending on whether it is being done to others or to oneself. Status-conscious professional persons often do not respond well to the coordinative interventions of staff assistants.

Coordination connotes something more than voluntary behavior. The process requires sufficient directive power in the coordinator to resolve deadlocks and meet deadlines. Cooperation occurs without the directive power involved in coordination. Therefore, to the extent that cooperation increases, investment in coordination can and should be reduced. It is possible to achieve an understanding among organizational units and specialized professionals that third-party involvement can be reduced markedly through their own efforts to collaborate and cooperate. Perceptive persons will understand and value the difference as an increment of freedom and autonomy. Gains in satisfaction from work can be substantial and can have the effect of reducing negative perceptions and feelings associated with working in a complex organization.

The tasks remaining for top management are to articulate clear expectations of cooperation, to participate responsibly in necessary coordinative processes, and, of course, to find useful work for the former coordinators.

3. Spatial Dispersion

Spatial dispersion can be achieved with any of several types of human service structures. Although measuring dispersion might not be quite as simple as counting the number of different workplaces, it is largely a quantitative and geographic dimension of complexity. A human service organization comprising largely autonomous categorical entities may be extensively dispersed geographically. Without coordinated or unified direction of field staff, coterminous regional boundaries, and collocated service units, field subsystems are disaggregated fragments affording no significant whole-agency identity and low potential for interunit collaboration.

Spatial dispersion also has important political significance. Special interest groups, elected officials, and local entities are sensitive to actual or apparent differences in allocations of staff and service facilities between their geographic areas or political subdivisions and other jurisdictions. This problem is exacerbated by quantitatively inadequate staffing to perform the agency's work. Commitments to geographic decentralization without first obtaining adequate staff can evoke specific criticism and opportunistic sniping at the organization.

D. Notes on Size and Structure

Given the earlier dismissal of size as a variable in complexity, it is now appropriate to put size into appropriate perspective and deal with it as an important influence on organizational structure. There is no generally accepted measure of size. Useful characterization of an organization might be derived from consideration of several different elements of size (Hall, 1982, pp. 56-63). Number of staff is frequently used as the sole indicator of size. Counting employees can be misleading. Organization A has 5,000 employees; organization B has 7,000 employees. Organization A staffs heavily for direct provision of services, while B contracts extensively with other organizations to provide services. It is possible that B directly and indirectly uses more personnel than A, although B has fewer in-house staff.

The number of clients served is another indicator of size. But if A provides a greater number of services than B, or provides a higher quality of services, the number of clients loses utility as a comparative indicator of size. Size of budget is similarly flawed as an indicator of organizational size. Differences in salaries, rent, travel costs, and countless other variables must be taken into account if one attempts to make valid comparisons. The exhaustive work required to achieve valid and reliable budgetary comparison is yet to be done in human services.

Questions arise relative to the manageability of large human service organizations. At what size does an organization become too big to manage? Lacking an acceptable measure of size, the question is impossible to answer. If one counts employees, the largest human service organizations are smaller than many corporate entities or military establishments. Diversified private corporations may have more functions, or lines of business, than the most comprehensive public organizations providing human services. Retail merchandising chains may serve more customers than large human service organizations serve clients. Issues about the size of public organizations usually are more political than managerial in character, deriving from the American societal aversion to accretion of power at any governmental locus.

Size is relative. Valid comparisons can be made only if compared organizations are similar in the factors used for comparison. The size of a primary work group is much more meaningful than the overall size of an organization to a human service worker. Secondary importance is attached to the size of the internal and external networks on which the worker relies for providing services or in which the manager is involved. Direct service workers and managers have similar experiences of organizational size. Each can work intensively with perhaps 10 other persons and can interact frequently, but less intensively, with approximately 20 persons. It is possible for a service worker or manager to know the names and general functional responsibilities of a few hundred people. No person can be aware of all persons and all details of structure or operations of a large public or private organization. Fortunately, comprehensive knowledge of an organization's structure, staff, and technology are not requisite to performance of properly designed managerial or service delivery jobs. Concern about the size of human service organizations probably derives from the traditional American aversion to accretion of power by administrators in the public sector and the questionable assumption that organizational size is an indicator of administrative power. Another possibility is that the aggregate of budget or staff in a particular organization might exceed a critic's notion of appropriate allocation for services to the number or classes of clients being served.

III. TYPOLOGY OF STRUCTURES

The great prevalence of human service organizations is not matched by extensive descriptive or analytical information on their structural configurations. The Council of State Governments (COSG) collected fairly extensive data on state organizations in the early 1970s as part of a larger study of the "services integration" movement. COSG's attention was focused on the states' organizational changes which were intended to improve human service management and service delivery. COSG's report of its study quickly was recognized as the most authoritative work on state actions to integrate and improve the functioning of scattered human servives.

The council gave particular attention to organizations in the 26 states found to have "comprehensive human resource departments" (COSG, 1974, p. 1), commonly called umbrella agencies. Comprehensiveness was defined as including public assistance and related social services and at least three other major human service programs, such as public health or employment services. The extreme variability among state organizational structures and functions made it desirable to create several categories of organizational forms. Four categories of state agencies were established by the COSG study and remain today as the closest approximation of a typology of state human service structures. The council recently resurveyed the states and reported its findings, again using the classifications established in 1974 (Chi, 1987). Thus, a by-product of an inquiry into state efforts of services integration became an authoritative reference on organizational forms and is the only work of its kind which has been updated in the 1980s. The council's four types of state structures are used as a framework for this chapter because no subsequent research has produced models or definitive information of better quality. The four structural types are (1) no comprehensive human service agency: structural design and articulation follow the traditional *categorical* mode; (2) *confederated* agency, which aggregates functions but does not unify their policies or management; (3) *consolidated* agency, which unifies supportive services and some executive authorities; and (4) *integrated* agency, which unifies policy management and service delivery arrangements.

Each of these four types of agencies is discussed below.

A. State Categorical Agency

The categorical structure is one which comprises one major function or a limited array of closely related functions. A public welfare agency of the categorical type might include only public assistance and food stamps, or it might include other economic service functions.

The two structural designs shown in Fig. 1 represent two models of a large, traditional public welfare department which is established as a separate, multifunctional categorical agency. A state or local area with this type of organizational pattern would have separate, additional agencies for corrections, employment services, developmental services, public health, mental health, aging, and so on.

Figure 1a depicts a state-operated human service system. Figure 1b depicts a county-operated, state-supervised system. Another variant of this model might cluster the entitlement programs—public assistance, food stamps, and Medicaid—in one major subdivision, possibly headed by a deputy or assistant director, and place the other programs in a second major subdivision, thus dichotomizing economic assistance and services within a categorical agency.

The categorical model, according to conventional wisdom, simplifies the tasks of executive leadership, permits superior fiscal and programmatic accountability, and enhances the interaction of the agency and its clientele. The categorical arrangement indisputably mirrors the categorical pattern of federal organization, whether it contains one or multiple categorical functions. This intergovernmental arrangement gives rise to the characterization "picket-fence federalism," because it creates separate programmatic lines vertically linking federal, state, and local governments.

The COSG (1974, 1987) studies indicate that 24 states organize their agencies to some degree according to the separate categorical authorizations which are prevalent in federal and state statutes. Some of these states have placed two or three major categorical agencies—for example, health and welfare—in a single structure, but the major components in such cases usually operate separately in policy formation and service delivery. None fits the COSG criterion of integration, which requires unified policy, executive direction and service delivery. In the categorical context, "social services" usually refers to provisions of Title XX the Social Security Act and does not include, as examples, vocational rehabilitation, corrections, employment services, aging, youth services, and mental health. Categorical structures were the prevailing pattern in states prior to the increases in number, size, cost, and complexity of human service programs in the 1960s and 1970s.

Critics of the categorical structural configuration refute some of the benefits claimed by categorical advocates and add other objections. Lynn (1976, 1980) has documented serious objections of policymakers and others: insularity and cost of

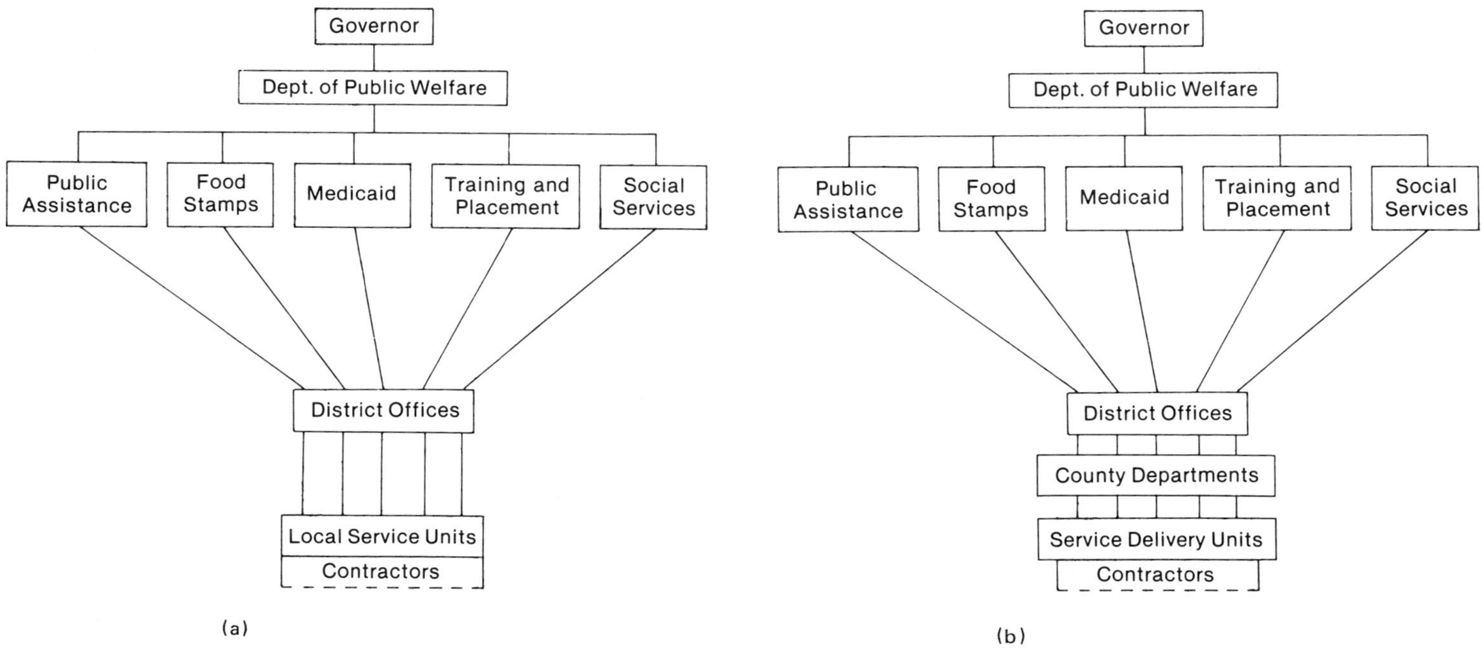

FIGURE 1 Two models of state categorical agencies: (a) a state-operated human service system; (b) a county-operated, state-supervised systems.

coordinating proliferated bureaucracies; lack of responsiveness to policies made by elected officials and to complaints from clientele; inefficient use of information-handling technology, facilities, and staff; excessive burdens of legislative hearings and lobbying; inadequate coordination with other human services; ineffective referral of clients among separate and functionally limited organizations. Perhaps the greatest precipitant of change toward more unitary organizational forms was (and is) state policymakers' sense of inability to communicate and control human service policy among an extensive array of specialized and nearly autonomous organizations. Stated positively, elected officials frequently prefer to delegate public functions to one or a few, rather than many, administrators.

Depending on one's perspective, it might be advantageous or disadvantageous to manage or provide services in the categorical structural arrangement, which corresponds most closely to existing domains of specialized professions. More certain is the fact that initiatives to consolidate or unify human service structures consistently elicit opposition from professional organizations. Increased size or complexity is the complaint usually expressed, but the core of the objection is threatened or compromised professional domain.

Two characteristics of the categorical organizational form make it vulnerable to initiatives for consolidative change. First, coordination of human service policy management is exceedingly difficult and costly for general government and agency executives. The worst case in coordination involves a situation remarkably similar to international diplomacy: structural separatism; language barriers; low levels of trust; costly competition; and disparity of goals and organizational cultures. Top-level interaction of agencies, as with most nations, tends to be relatively infrequent. Interagency contracts and agreements, if they exist, are frequently violated with impunity and without effective remedy.

The second major flaw of the traditional categorical arrangement is best perceived by clients and service delivery staff. The multiproblem client—as an individual, family, or group—must coordinate the service delivery system in order to receive needed services. Each agency has separate facilities, usually in different locations, a situation which creates problems with client transportation. The client who telephones the wrong agency must make one or more additional calls to locate the appropriate service entity. Making appointments with multiple agencies is time-consuming and difficult for many clients. The professional staff must negotiate with an external entity to arrange for supplementary services or services not provided by his or her specialized agency. Frequently, interagency negotiations of services involve one or more supervisory levels in addition to the direct service worker, particularly when costs are shared. Transportation is a frequent problem for clients, and the problem is exacerbated by disconnected scattering of service delivery units of multiple agencies.

Complicated analysis is not required to conclude that human service delivery, as labor-intensive activity, is more costly and uncertain of achievement when organizationally separate and remote entities attempt to coordinate their work. There is a surprising lack of research effort on the comparative dollar and qualitative costs of services provided, and failures to provide needed services that are available, under various structural arrangements.

B. Confederated Agency

The confederated agency modeled in Fig. 2 is one step away from the catgeorical pattern toward an integral structure. The structural features of the confederated agency, except

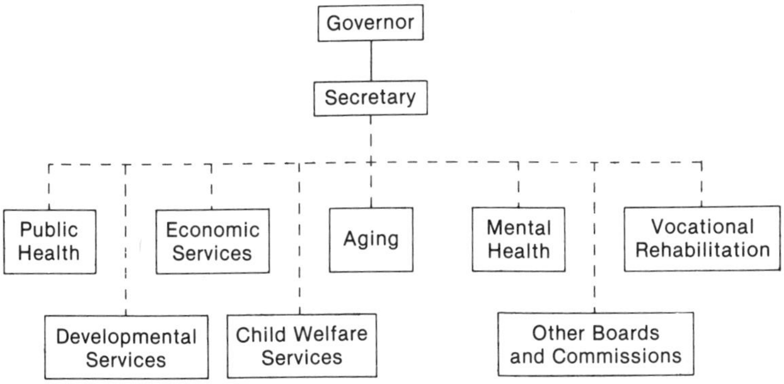

FIGURE 2 Confederated state human service agencies.

the top layer, bear close resemblance to the categorical form. Each programmatic entity has a separate unit for its own planning, evaluation, budgeting, and other administrative support; each major categorical service has its own separate field structure for service delivery; and each categorical entity has its own set of external relations with interest groups, legislative bodies, and overhead administrative units. The model expressed in Fig. 2 shows the familiar dotted-line relationship between the agency head and the program director, the latter having comparatively strong directive roles.

The top layer usually consists of an appointed secretary, director, or commissioner with minimal staff support and, at best, a weak coordinative role. Heading such an agency is not an appealing prospect for persons with strong leadership tendencies.

The confederated arrangement provides a focal point of communication for external policymakers, mass media, and agencies with related missions—particularly for response to requests for information. Neither the creative statute nor the organizational design for a consolidated agency provides significant directive power for the agency head. Categorical domains are protected. Policy management for the whole agency is not possible, and a unified budget for all entities is not expected. Planning, evaluation, and personnel administration are functions of the major programmatic units. Coordination depends entirely on persuasion in this situation of weak executive authority and loosely coupled, parallel service delivery arrangements.

A question arises: Why would a state choose to create a confederated structure, which appears to have so few advantages over the categorical form? A plausible answer is that this initial, nearly cosmetic step toward systematization might be all that the political environment allows. Some elected officials, special interest groups, and professional organizations become anxious about vesting broad executive authority in a single executive appointee. This anxiety, which is deeply ingrained in citizens of the United States, can easily be transformed into opposition to organizational proposals which call for a strong executive performance. Conversely, a failure to discern the operative differences between a coordinative role and an executive role can produce unreasonable expectations of performance in a coordinative situation. Five states—Hawaii, Massachusetts, Nevada, Oregon, and Wyoming—have created comprehensive human service organiations of the coordinative type. In contrast, 13 states use a consolidated model for structuring their comprehensive agencies.

C. Consolidated Agency

Proceeding from a base of separate categorical agencies, a consolidated agency is created by transferring most or all programmatic functions and administrative authorities to a new, more unified organization. The structural configuration of a consolidated agency is shown in Fig. 3. Thirteen states and the District of Columbia have adopted one or another version of this structural form.

The distinguishing feature of a consolidated human service structure is statutory provision for consolidation of all or most program and administrative authority in a single agency. This arrangement permits unified policy management, administrative services, and agency-wide planning and evaluation. Providing policy development capability that is superior to that of the categorical or confederated model, the consolidated agency preserves programmatic identity at the second (bureau or division) level of structure. The divisional array normally bears close resemblance to the traditional categorical structure. Specialized substate district offices and local service units are directed by the respective headquarters program divisions. Local service facilities of the several divisions may or may not be collocated. The major difference between the consolidated and integrated structural forms is unified direction of all service delivery under the integrated model. In other words, the prominence and power of the consolidated agency's program offices at headquarters and in the districts are enhanced by their ownership of technical expertise and by management of service delivery operations. From the overall agency perspective, a diffusion of authority for service delivery occurs in the field.

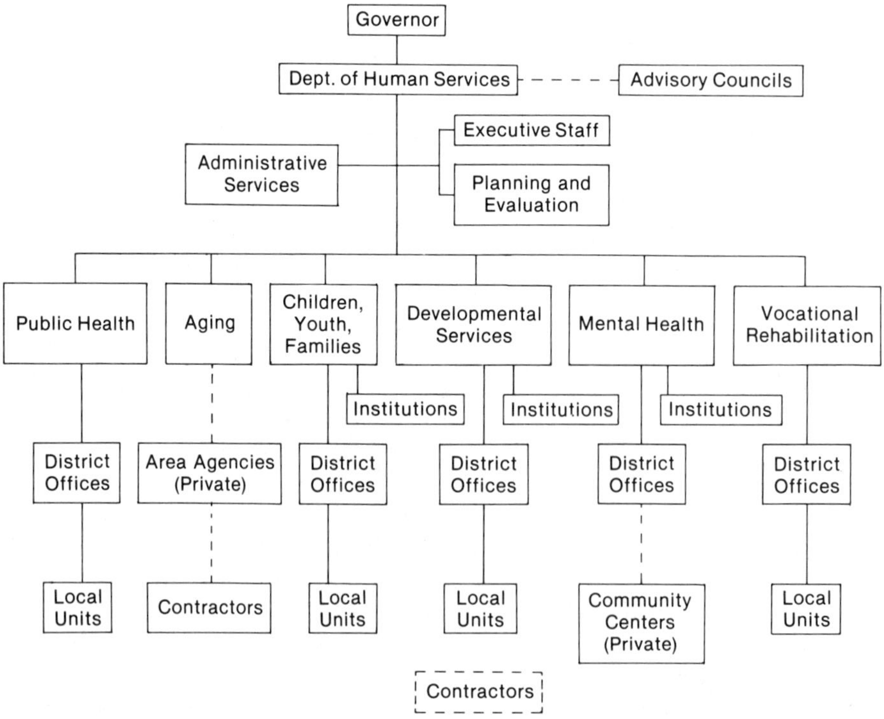

FIGURE 3 State human service agency: consolidated model.

The prevalence of consolidated structures (13 states and the District of Columbia) suggests that political agreement is easier and parochial turf guarding by special interest groups, especially professional organizations, is less vigorous when program units control their respective service operations. On the other hand, a consolidated structure requires an enormous investment of time and energy by the overall organization for coordination of internal and external activities at all levels of the organization. Some states have attempted, without notable success, to use a "lead agency" for department-wide coordination in substate districts, perhaps designating different agencies in different districts. Possibly the most unrewarding role is that of a district person whose sole or major role is coordination of several independent field subsystems. This administrative role is characterized by intensive coordinative effort and insufficient power to achieve the desired effect. Frustration can overwhelm a district manager who lacks authority over human and fiscal resources, physical facilities, and administrative services in this type of field system.

The consolidated structural form, compared to the less unified models, eases the coordinative and other interactive burdens of elected and appointed officials. A governor has a single point of contact in the person of the secretary or commissioner. An appropriations committee can get information without having to contact multiple organizational units. Legislators, as individuals or committees, can expect accountability from a single source for a broad range of functions. Clients, as individuals or groups, who receive services from more than one specialized program can gain access and seek resolution of their problems from a single agency head.

The consolidated design simultaneously reduces complexity for top management through unification of policy management and support functions and contributes complexity through horizontal (divisional) differentiation. The unfortunate lack of pertinent research prevents conclusive statements on the comparative efficacy of the consolidated and other structural models. A prudent agency head will establish and maintain staff capability for extensive and direct monitoring and evaluation of field operations. Diffuse authority for service delivery is the weakest structural feature of the consolidated agency model.

D. Integrated State Human Service Agency

The symbolic appeal of services integration is a mixed blessing (or liability) for scholars and practitioners in the human service sector. Positive connotations of the expression are associated with structural and functional (process) characteristics of systems, especially the following:

A system comprises components, which in human service organizations translate into organizational units and programs.
A system has common goals to which all components' activities are related.
Components of a system are linked by communication and are interdependent in the performance of their functions.
A system is integrated, functions as a whole entity, and is contained by its environment.

Criticisms of general systems theory are abundant and interesting, but are not to be explored in this chapter. Flawed or not, systems theory provides a considerable portion of the conceptual base for changes made in complex human service organizations since the 1950s. This body of theoretic formulations is useful in interpreting the myths and facts about the structure and functions of human service organizations. One of the myths created by opponents of unified organizations is that specific programs and specialized professionals are invalidated, or lose identity, through the integration of traditional programs and technologies. An extensively specialized work force can be acutely disturbed by a rumor that workers in an integrated human service organization might be required or permitted to perform a wide variety of services for which they are not trained. An important fact is that integration of services does not alter requirements for technical knowledge and expertise and that prenatal services should continue to be provided by appropriate health professionals, child welfare services by qualified social workers, and mental health services by persons with specific knowledge and skills. If inadequate job classifications and qualifications compromise quality of service, the causes invariably can be found in the political and economic environment, not in the integrative process or structure.

In contrast to minimal effects on service technology, integration of previously separate categorical entities profoundly changes the social dimension of an organization. The power structure is radically altered by organizational redesign. Regular communication with formerly remote persons and disciplines may be required in a collocated service arrangement and, especially, in an integrated planning or budgetary process which involves senior professionals and managers. Midlevel and higher managers may be charged with achieving interprogram objectives and consequently are dependent on staff whose technologies are different from those in which the manager is trained. Specialized workers may object to and resist the influence of a manager whose professional preparation is different from their own training. Solving these problems depends on sensitively designed training, and not on structural design.

These problems and possibilities are just a few of the realities associated with profound organizational change. The important fact here is that organizational movement from a categorical to a consolidated or integrated arrangement of human service functions is profound in character and consequences. Formerly intact organizational entities must depend on a shared administrative support system. Their program plans and budgetary proposals are reviewed and may be changed prior to submittal to a governor or legislature. Collaborative and other interaction with related programs or organizational entities may be required, rather than elective. Monitoring of service operations may be required, but changes may depend on negotiations with a unified service delivery subsystem rather than autonomous action of program experts. Evaluation of program performance may be carried out by former professional associates who are now organizationally placed in a consolidated evaluation unit concerned with all programs. All of these effects are implicit in the simple model presented in Fig. 4.

The structural configuration of an integrated and decentralized organization, shown in Fig. 4, is sufficient to reveal differences between the integrated organization and categorical, confederated, and consolidated agencies. The distinguishing features are as follows:

All programmatic and administrative authorities are vested in one executive, who delegates to a few deputies or assistants.

Three major subdivisions—administrative services, service delivery operations, and program development—serve the whole organization; each of these subdivisions may be further subdivided, providing program offices for specific functional clusters under one assistant secretary, administrative services reporting to another assistant secretary, and the service delivery subsystem reporting to the third assistant secretary.

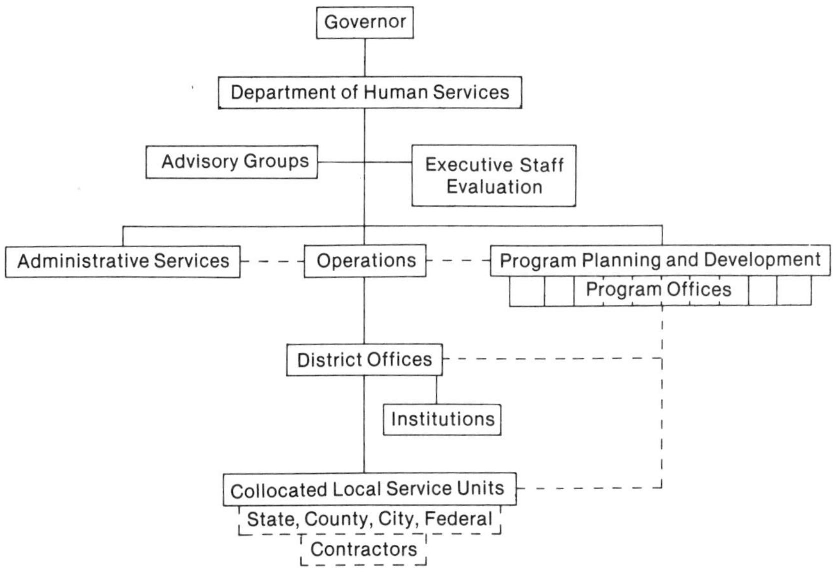

FIGURE 4 Integrated state human service agency.

Unified management of policy development and implementation is feasible in the integrated structure.

Program offices are relieved of operational mangement; they concentrate on program development, technical assistance to program specialists and managers in the districts, and monitoring program implementation.

Authority to manage programs, institutions, and administrative functions is delegated to district administrators; district personnel rely on program offices at headquarters for specialized expertise and consultation; institutions managed by a district office can serve a substate region or a whole state.

The utility of the integrated structure is enhanced by collocation of service delivery units, which are the pivotal points in service networks. Further enhancements include a case management process for individuals or families who have multiple or highly complex problems, district participation in policy and budgetary development, and use of the integrated district units for concerted planning and other interaction with local governments.

Legislators and officials of local governments in all areas of the state have ready access to a district administrator who represents the whole agency. Informational needs of public officials, mass communication media, citizens, and interest groups usually can be satisfied by the district offices. This convenience saves time for external entities, the agency head, and other persons at headquarters. Most operational problems can be solved by service delivery networks or district offices.

The integrative model has distinctive problems as well as advantages. Program specialists at headquarters experience moderate to severe role deprivation when their direct service responsibilities are assigned to the unitary service delivery subsystem. Having been accustomed to managing all aspects of programs from design to service delivery, they feel a loss of power and can be quite unhappy about dependence on others for operational management. If their behaviors in relation to field staff are excessively directive, specialists in the program offices can create conflict with the service delivery system. In the integrated agency the greatest source of power for the program offices derives from ownership of substantive program knowledge and skills and use of these resources in policy formation and consultation.

The integrated agency is not suitable for indiscriminate application to all states or other jurisdictions. The policy studies of Lynn (1976, 1980) and others clearly show that certain conditions are necessary for successful application of this model. The political environment must be strongly supportive at the time of proposal to achieve enactment and for sufficient time after establishment to achieve a modicum of organizational stability. Managerial leadership of high quality and total commitment to the integrative concept is necessary for wholehearted engagement by staff and maintenance of external support. Technology appropriate to modern management must be acquired and used. As an example, capital investment and training for effective management of informational resources should be an early and unalterable commitment. Manual data collection, processing, storage, and retrieval generate unwanted, unnecessary, and inefficient paperwork burdens. Finally, expectations of an integrated system must be realistic. Revisions of structure and process will not cure inadequate resources, vacuous promises of dollar savings, or a turbulent environment. Reorganizing several small agencies into one department may produce some economies of scale. However, if the new department is extensively decentralized into several districts, replication of the agency in each district might require administrative outlays as great as or greater than the preexisting arrangement.

Attention now turns to the ultimate objective of all structural designs and efforts: the actual delivery of services to clients.

IV. SERVICE DELIVERY ARRANGEMENTS

Service delivery arrangements are an integral part of human service organizational configuration. There is no universal pattern of human service delivery in the United States. Features of the delivery components of any human service system are shaped by a great variety of factors, including, but not limited to, constitutional and statutory roles of state and local governments; technologies employed in providing services; resources; demography; and geography.

State constitutional and statutory provisions for distribution of powers between state and local governments determine the general characteristics of their respective service systems. A state may place heavy or light responsibility on local government and may provide a small or large share of the fiscal resources used by local entities. Constitutional and statutory provisions for taxation and assessment of fees determine the resources available for human services and other functions. Power to design and control the performance of services frequently follows the dollar.

Just as governmental powers vary among and within states, actual provision of service may vary by type of service and demography of clientele. Immunization of children may be accomplished in a variety of settings by different types of workers. Complex cardiac surgery requires hospitalization and highly skilled professional performance. An urban area might afford multiple choices of facilities for a multiservice center. Choices of service facilities in a sparsely populated area might be severely limited.

Fiscal capacity, fiscal effort, characteristics of the population, and economic conditions are only a few of the interdependent factors that influence human service policies and delivery arrangements.

This section on service delivery arrangements necessarily is limited to a few selected aspects. The content is focused on important concerns of participants in most service delivery situations, different governmental settings, and variable management patterns.

A. Participants and Roles

One may concentrate on structure and methods for human service without apology if it is understood that the overriding concern in any arrangement for service delivery is for clients. To serve appropriately is to be constantly aware that administrative and professional practices are means to secure well-being of clients, however service operations may be situationally defined. Establishment and maintenance of this ideological fixation are special responsibilities of managerial and other leaders of human service organizations. The ideology is most effective when it is inculcated into the organizational culture of a whole human service system.

Beyond clients, participants are divided into classes: state human service agencies, with central and local actors; local governments, with variable roles; private providers of service, with contractual and noncontractual relations to the system; other state agencies; federal agencies; and volunteers.

1. State Human Service Agency

State roles in human service delivery vary with constitutional provisions and statutes. An important feature of relevant statutory law is prescriptive or permissive provisions for intergovernmental allocation of authority and tasks in human services. The tradition, as reflected in the literature of human services, is to classify state human service systems as either state-supervised, locally administered or state-administered. This characterization is flawed, as are most simple dichotomies. Some states—Virginia and Minnesota are examples—allow local jurisdictions options of local or state administration alone or in combination. Accordingly, some states have a mixed pattern of state and local administration of services, depending on local choices. Another variant is the situation in which counties administer some programs, while the state retains administrative authority for some functions, such as Medicaid and regulatory activities. Even in a state-administered system, local governments may provide facilities for offices and service centers, with or without compensation. This chapter does not deal with all possible variants. Instead, it attends to two types of situations that generally, but imperfectly, are characterized as state-administered and state-supervised, locally administered. Fig. 5 is an effort to portray the principal institutional actors, major functions, and interactions in a way that comprehends both types of administrative situations. Fortunately for clients and others who are involved, state and local human service activities are characterized more by cooperation than by continuous conflict. As one approaches the terminal point of a human service system, where the client is served, the greater is the propensity for different professions and organizational units to cooperate in their efforts to meet the client's needs. Collaboration and cooperation occur more readily at this level of organization, because participants in direct service delivery normally are relatively free of an obligation which is immediate, continuous, and powerful at the apex of an organization. That obligation is to promote the organization, protect its boundaries, and eliminate

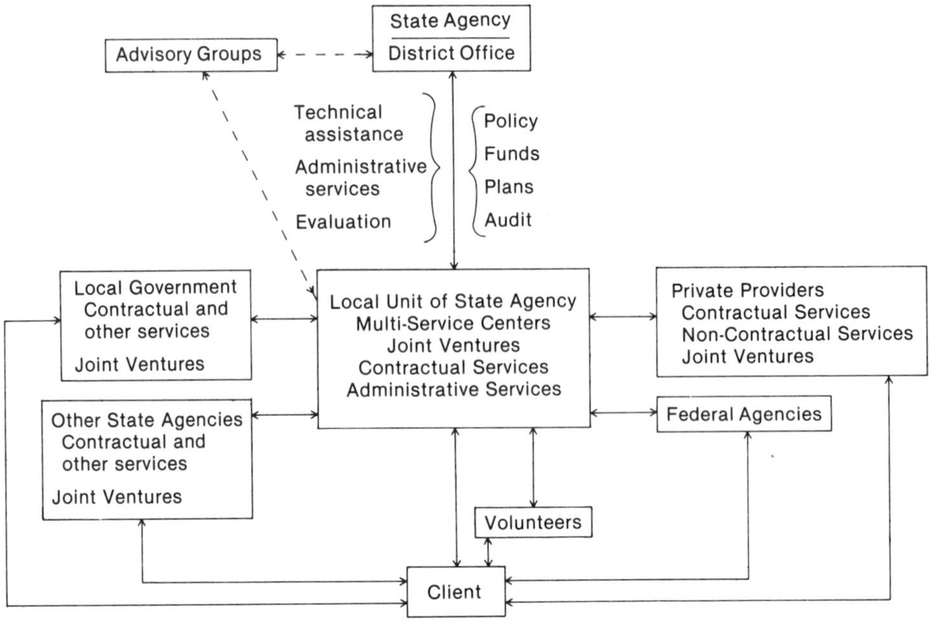

FIGURE 5 Local service delivery network (integrated system).

alien or intrusive behaviors. Service delivery workers can concentrate on providing services to a human being who is in need of assistance without excessive concern for institutional and structural artifacts.

This section of the chapter identifies the classes of participants in service delivery, selected influences on their work, and the complex tasks involved in service delivery management. If a skeptic doubts that organizational structures and arrangements can substantially help in service delivery, perhaps he or she could agree that such devices ought, at least, to avoid hindrance of service.

The service delivery arrangement modeled in Fig. 5 is one which comprises a state-administered integrated system, a secondary role for local government, nonprofit and for-profit providers, other state and federal agencies as sources of service, and volunteers. Joint ventures may involve participation from two or more of these participants. The entire arrangement is called a network, although the connective lines, as drawn, show only a few of the linkages among participants.

If the arrangement were changed to fit the situation of a locally administered, state-supervised system, the local human service agency would become the organizational center of the model. The state role would consist mainly of making or transmitting policy and supplying resources, technical assistance, and administrative oversight of the local service delivery arrangement.

Joint ventures are activities in which two or more types of participants invest financial or human resources to provide a service. An example occurs in mental health when a private nonprofit foundation and a state agency jointly commit capital resources to construct a facility for treatment of severely emotionally disturbed children. The agreement between the state and the foundation specifies that the foundation will own and operate the facility, which will accept clients referred by local public and private organizations or individuals. Services normally would be purchased by the state through a contract, which would be managed by the local or district unit of the state agency in the integrated model.

2. Local Government

Local governments provide direct services—such as adult education, job training, and placement—or other services to state public assistance clients under a contractual arrangement. The physical facility for a multiservice center might be provided by the state or local government, or through a joint venture.

Another example of state-local-private-public interaction occurs when the state contracts with local government to manage local child day-care arrangements. Through its local service unit, the state might negotiate a local per diem rate, or pay a fixed statewide rate to the local government, as contractor. The local government would subcontract with private providers for a stipulated number of days of child care and would oversee their operations. The state might retain or delegate to local government the licensure and inspection tasks, according to provisions of state law.

A county or city general hospital frequently is a key component of local service networks. Social services and food service to elderly persons are provided mainly by private agencies, using predominantly public funds and organized as substate regional and local units. Federal, state, and local public funds are added to local private funds for support of these services. Local governments and private organizations (for example, churches) usually provide facilities under rental or contributional arrangements stipulated in purchase-of-service contracts.

More recent and less extensive are capitation (prepaid) arrangements between states and local health units, some of which are outside the integrated state human service agency for medical and other health care of Medicaid and other clients.

3. Private Providers

Billions of dollars worth of contractual services for public agencies' clients are purchased from private persons and organizations. An important stimulus for contracting is the prevalent aversion of elected public officials to increases in public payrolls. Purchased services range from hospital care to total management of correctional facilities to group homes for different types of clients. Some state statutes mandate purchase of services from private providers unless state agencies can prove that public services are cheaper. Emphasis on controlling costs and concern for quality of private services are two of many reasons for developing contractual instruments of high quality and generating expertise in contract management among public employees.

A rash of literature has appeared to inform public purchasers and private providers of contractual human services. Publications reflect ideological conflicts, concern for quality and effectiveness of services, and great need for learning the intricacies of contract law and management by human service personnel, whose curricular preparation usually does not include the law of contracts. Short (1987) and the Council of State Governments have produced a "cookbook" on contracting for services to fill this important cognitive gap among human service personnel.

Whether the trend toward purchase of services will continue or subside in the future, possibly varying with changes in the dominant political ideology, is a topic for conjecture. The importance of skilled contract management is a certainty which faces private providers and public agencies as prudent buyers. State and national policies favoring purchase of services frequently fail to take into account the scarcity of providers in sparsely populated areas. Private providers often avoid such areas because of a low volume of business and scarcity of professional staff.

4. Other State Agencies

From the state human service agency's perspective, whether functions are integrally or separately established in other state agencies depends on constitutional or statutory provisions. Employment services and adult corrections appear to be most frequently allocated to state departments other than the primary human service organization. A unified policy management process established in the executive office of a governor is probably the best instrument for coordinating interdepartmental policy development and implementation, especially if this process includes strategic and operational planning and budgeting.

Service delivery arrangements among departments can be formalized through letters of agreement, contracts, or a combination of these instruments, statutory provisions, and other legislative expressions of intent. Financial support for services involving two or more state agencies may be provided through legislative allocation to the department that is obligated to provide a service or through administrative transfer of funds to the providing agency from an agency responsible for the client. Interdepartmental arrangements are prevalent in physical and mental health, environmental protection, data processing, training, and employment services. Construction and maintenance of facilities used by two or more state agencies may be handled as any other joint venture, usually under oversight from the state's department of general services or an equivalent agency.

5. Federal Agencies

District or local units of federal agencies participate in local human service networks. Referrals of clients to district and local offices of the Social Security Administration occur frequently. Medicare or survivor benefits may be outcomes of these referrals. Less frequent, but important, are interactions between state human service units and federal law enforcement agencies or Veterans Administration hospitals. Intergovernmental linkages may produce wilderness camps for services to delinquent children or a great variety of informational exchanges. The greater the variety of functions included in a local human service network, the greater is the volume of such intergovernmental traffic.

6. Volunteers

Possibly the greatest unrealized potential resource for human service is assistance from uncompensated volunteers. Figure 5 shows volunteers as an integral component of an integrated service network. Increased numbers of retirees and part-time jobs, lower average age at retirement, and the valuable competences of retired or other volunteers are characteristics of the underutilized human resource. Participation in local service activities has beneficial effects for volunteers, clients, and agencies. Volunteers gain understanding of public agencies which may produce mutual advantages. Clients may receive more services and the psychic benefit of more contact time with the agency. The agency supplements predictably scarce resources and gains valuable community ownership through participation.

The two most important criteria for appropriate volunteers are full-time professional management and optimal interaction of volunteers with clients. Although volunteers may assist in the administration of voluntary service arrangements, a paid professional with specific training should manage the overall arrangement to assure quality, continuity, and organizational integration. Most volunteers get greatest satisfaction from working directly with clients. Unfortunately, there is a tendency among using agencies to "dump" on volunteers the unwanted paperwork burdens of impersonal administrative and maintenance tasks. Successful volunteer programs emphasize sharing the more rewarding tasks with appropriately trained, professionally managed volunteers.

B. Policy Development and Implementation

1. Policy Mandates and Limitations

Policy often does more than legitimate the provision of services. Policy expressed in statutory language can include criteria for structuring and operating a human service system. These provisions usually are written in general terms, often without defining terms or detailing the implementation process. A statutory mandate to "integrate services" or "decentralize administrative authority" can pervasively influence organizational design and service delivery arrangement. The service network modeled in Fig. 5 closely approximates Florida's local service delivery arrangement, yet the network concept or configuration is not prescribed in the authorizing statute. In contrast, specific tasks and authorities of principal headquarters and district administrators are spelled out in the same statute. Clear intent without prescriptive operational mandates is administratively advantageous, because it allows administrators to determine deployment of staff, to choose sites and facilities for service delivery, to establish or change internal and external linkages, and to take other actions to adapt to fluctuations in resources or other conditions. Administrative discretion in these matters is especially important in human service delivery because the work cannot be routinized. Considerable discretion for the service provider is necessary for fitting agency and network responses to the needs of particular clients. The point to be made in this respect is that excessively rigid structure and rules of procedure which limit initiative and discretionary action can defeat efforts to achieve statutory purpose.

2. Excessive Regulation and Controls

Entitlement programs, such as public assistance and food stamps, are among the most extensively regulated activities of government. Problems of excessive formalism begin with narrowly categorical prescriptive federal law and regulations and are exacerbated by additional sets of state constraints. Penalties are levied by the federal government for errors in some programs even when errors are caused by inaccurate information provided by clients. These situations are troublesome to administrators. They are devastating to service delivery workers. Policies need fixing when desired results are thwarted by excessive controls and penalties on service delivery workers.

The broad functions to be performed, the boundaries of major substate areas, and general provisions for centralized or decentralized authority in a system are entirely appropriate issues for policymakers. Prescriptions beyond these general mandates can cause frequent statutory revisions, reduced initiatives of field-workers and administrators, low productivity, and frequent violations of unreasonable constraints.

3. Collocation as Policy

The policy base of a local service network should require collocation of staff and facilities, wherever feasible, but this policy does not necessarily mean planning all functions in one facility. The desirable effects of collocation are possible to achieve if service sites are clustered in an area which permits convenient interaction among staff and access to multiple services by clients. Collocation is overvalued when excessive costs are incurred or when dilapidated physical facilities are chosen simply because they will house all or most service activities. Here, as in other matters, sensible policy and responsible administration are key elements in successful service delivery.

4. Resources

Human services are similar to most other public and private activities in that they require money, people, and materials. Policy determines the supply of resources and, consequently, largely determines the quantity and quality of services delivered to clients. The structure and performance of a human service organization may be adversely affected if direct service personnel and midlevel staff are severely reduced during fiscal cutbacks. Sharply reduced funding for immunization against preventable diseases creates high risk of epidemics—which cost more than immunization. Reduction or discontinuance of training due to lack of funds can produce disastrous consequences in critically important activities, such as protective services for children and elderly clients.

Coordination of services is often and properly mentioned as a way of optimizing utilization of scarce resources. But coordination has limits in offsetting resource scarcity. Effective coordination presumes the availability of public or private providers. When potentially helpful agencies are understaffed or underfunded, or both, coordinative effort is not productive. Even the most skilled coordination of a service network is neither a substitute nor a significant offset for inadequate resources. Coordinative efforts under conditions of resource scarcity may generate conflict and frustration rather than service response.

Block grants for social services and other purposes are more fungible than resources from categorical sources. Flexibility in possible uses of these funds will not cure a generally deficient resource situation. However, these funds have high utility in enabling transfers to meet emergencies and other critical needs during acute shortages of resources. The advantages of block grants can be fully realized only if a human service system is fully integrated from top to bottom—that is, from policy formation to service delivery.

C. Management of Complexity

Effective management of a human service delivery arrangement is contingent on multiple and interrelated sets of variables. Among the more important of many possible sets are policy, comprehensiveness of functions, structural adequacy, adequate or better human and other resources, and suitable technology. The managerial variables are interactive with each of these other sets. The importance and interrelation of managerial concerns—policy and operational management, including human factors—are discussed below.

1. Policy

Activism in policy is one of the hallmarks of effective human service management. Most policies are imperfect and, therefore, can be improved. Working collaboratively with professional specialists, client organizations, and myriad others who are involved, managers are in a key position to propose policy initiatives, revisions, and terminations. Legislators and elected executives, being concerned with a broader range of policy issues, are entitled to expect initiative and expertise from the full-time human service managers to whom they entrust human service functions. This expectation should include responsible, sensitive policy proposals, as well as the traditional implementation role. Advocacy of policy changes, both increments and revisions of existing policy, adds job satisfaction that is unattainable in any other aspect of managerial practice. Creative or innovative ideas about policy may be stimulated by direct observation and analysis of data from operations, careful consideration of information provided by contractors and other participants, and occasionally by persons who are outside the system. Managers who are open to ideas and information from outside of the system are likely to have a repertoire of policy proposals to fit a great variety of opportunities.

The question for managers is not whether human service policies will change. Policy in this sector has not been and is not likely to be static. The practical question is how best to influence the provisions, feasibility, equity, and outcomes of policy. An active role is more satisfactory than a passive one to the effective manager.

2. Operational Management

Operational management which succeeds in service delivery is attentive to policy goals and operational objectives, highly skilled in leadership and coordination, appropriately informed of operational successes and failures, and resistant to excessive formalization. Excessive rules and procedural controls are possibly the greatest hazards for organizational performance and individual job satisfaction.

It is common knowledge that, second only to the value of the work itself, freedom to exercise one's own judgment in performing the work is the greatest source of motivation and job satisfaction. The highly generalized societal ambivalence about human service is a probable source of fetishes concerning fiscal integrity, detailed procedural rules, copious recording, and review of all activity steps in serving clients. Managers at any level who allow themselves to be trapped by excessive formalism are engaged in fantasy. The bulk of the activity in human service organizations occurs between workers and clients at the point of service delivery. It is impossible to supervise the countless interactions that occur daily between workers and clients, often in a confidential relationship. Some managers are able to accept the infeasibility and undesirability of knowing and controlling all activities. Others delude themselves by laying on futile efforts to accomplish a level of process control which is neither appropriate nor possible. A more realistic approach is to establish standards of work and measure the results of work against such standards. If performance standards do not exist for human service programs and workers, managerial energy is more appropriately turned to that deficiency than to excessive control of process.

Federal statutes and regulations often are the initial forces that generate excessive controls and attendant paperwork. State and local governments tend to increase the volume and specificity of written rules and reporting requirements. Managers at all levels have a professional and ethical obligation to resist formalism when excessive costs are incurred in productivity and job satisfaction of workers. The formalism fetish may be the greatest cause of inefficiency in human service delivery.

Productivity in service delivery can also be enhanced by allowing field staff to spend most of their time doing what they do best—providing services. Application of existing technology can reduce the time lost to paperwork and delays of responses to service network requests for information or action on cases. A corollary effect is reduction of dissatisfaction associated with searching files and performing related clerical tasks. Automated client information and tracking arrangements are far superior to manual data collection, storage, retrieval, and reporting. These technologies are known to human service systems, but are far from universally applied. An inhibiting factor is the tendency of policymakers and administrators invariably to prioritize services and neglect possibilities for service gains through improved technology. That tendency can be counterproductive in achieving service goals or improving administrative support systems. Managers are in a better position than network staff to secure policy commitments for, and general use of, information-handling technology.

Possibly the greatest challenge in human service management is the development of a distinctive organizational culture and mutually supportive climate for workers among disparate professions. In this regard, the integrated organizational model provides the most rigorous test of managerial leadership. Bennis and Nanus (1985) report their findings from a study of 90 leaders of major corporations. Four strategies of leadership discovered in their research appear to be applicable to leadership of large, complex human service organizations. First, leaders must have a vision of the future into which they lead an organization. That vision attracts and energizes followers. Second, leaders must be able to communicate the vision to persons being led. Third, the leader must earn and build trust among the members of an organization. Fourth, leaders must learn to use and improve themselves in an organizational context. They become more effective as they gain positive self-regard.

As indicated earlier in this chapter, human service organizations that are comprised of dozens of different programs, hundreds of occupations, and mediating structures to serve a widely dispersed work force are as complex as any private corporation. Managers must be able to derive satisfaction from complexity. They must be able to lead an organization in an environment characterized more by flux than by stability, more by uncertainty than by certainty. Effective leadership of a complex human service organization seeks to turn the entire organization into a self-confident learning system with shared values. Leadership of that order effectively removes the threat from uncertainty about the future.

V. SUMMARY AND CONCLUSIONS

This chapter has considered human service organizational structure and delivery arrangements within a context of environmental influences and complexity. Distinctive values are a significant environmental force, while disparate values and traditional domains are conflictual internal forces in complex human service organizations. Elements of complexity are vertical differentiation, horizontal differentiation, and spatial dispersion. Size is not considered to be consistently related to complexity.

No organizational model fits all state and local situations. Conceptual models of four types or organizational structures are provided. The models are derived from categories of state human service organizations reported by the Council of State Governments, first in the 1970s and again in 1987. The models represent traditional categorical structures (state-operated and state-supervised), a confederated agency, a consolidated agency and an integrated agency. Attributes of each model are discussed.

Characterization of human service delivery arrangements focuses on the structure of an integrated local service network and participants in service delivery. Public agencies, private agencies, and clients are considered to be integral components of the network. Selected variables in service delivery are identified and discussed briefly. Emphasis is placed on the operational and human costs of excessive formalism.

Leadership is perceived as a key factor in the success or failure of management in complex human service systems.

BIBLIOGRAPHY

Agranoff, R., ed. (1977). "Coping with the Demands for Change within Human Services Administration," Proceedings of a Workshop, American Society for Public Administration, Washington, D.C.

Agranoff, R. (1987). "Managing Policy, Program, and Structure at the Local Level," Paper presented to the Conference on Human Services Administration, Suffolk University, March 28.

Anderson, W., Frieden, B. J., and Murphy, M. J., eds. (1977). *Managing Human Services*, International City Management Association, Washington, D.C.

Bell, G. A., and Howard, D. (1975). Human services integration, *State Government 48*(2): 99.

Bennis, W., and Nanus, B. (1985). *Leaders: The Strategies for Taking Charge*, Harper & Row, New York.

Baumheier, E. C., and Agranoff, R. (1979). *Models for Coordinated Health and Human Services*, U.S. Department of Health, Education, and Welfare, Health Resources Administration, Hyattsville, Maryland.

Buntz, C. G., ed. (1976). *Human Resource Administration: Papers from the 1976 ASPA Conference*, American Society for Public Administration, Washington, D.C.

Chi, K. S. (1987). Umbrella human services not ubiquitous, *State Government News, 30*: 22. This report is based on a more extensive paper, "The Status of State Human Resources Agencies," presented to the Conference on Human Services Administration, Suffolk University, March 28, 1987.

Council of State Governments (1974). *Human Services Integration*, Lexington, Kentucky.

Curtis, R., and Yessian, M. (1979). *State Management of Human Services*, Council of State Governments, Lexington, Kentucky.

Dye, T. R. (1984). *Understanding Public Policy*, fifth ed., Prentice-Hall, Englewood Cliffs, New Jersey.

Emery, K. J., and Mamerow, D. C. (1986). Making services integration work at the local level: The partnership in Dayton, Ohio, *New England Journal of Human Services, 6*(2): 12.

Frumkin, M., Imershein, A., Chackerian, R., and Martin, P. (1983). Evaluating state level integration of human services, *Administration in Social Work, 7*(1): 13.

Gage, R. W. (1976). Integration of services delivery system, *Public Welfare, 34*(1): 27.

Gans, S. P., and Horton, G. T. (1976). *Integration of Human Services*, Praeger, New York.

Goodman, P. S., Pennings, J. M., and Associates (1977). *New Perspectives on Organizational Effectiveness*, Jossey-Bass, San Francisco.

Gruber, M. L. ed. (1981). *Management Systems in the Human Services*, Temple University Press, Philadelphia.

Hagan, H., and Hansan, J. E. (1978). How the states put the programs together, *Public Welfare, 36*(3): 44.

Hagebak, B. R. (1982). The forgiveness factor: Taking the risk out of efforts to integrate services, *Public Administration Review, 42*(1): 72.

Hall, R. H. (1982). *Organizations: Structure and Process*, third ed., Prentice-Hall, Englewood Cliffs, New Jersey, pp. 53, 56–63, 78–83.
Hamilton, D. (1985). The negotiated investment strategy, *New England Journal of Human Services, 5*(4): 22.
Hasenfeld, Y. (1983). *Human Service Organizations*, Prentice-Hall, Englewood Cliffs, New Jersey, pp. 9–10.
Horton, G. T., Carr, V. M. E., and Corcoran, G. J. (1976). *Illustrating Services Integration from Categorical Bases*, Project SHARE, Rockville, Maryland.
Howard, D. (1975). *Human Resource Agencies: Creating a Regional Structure*, Council of State Governments, Lexington, Kentucky.
Imershein, A. W., Chackerian, R., Martin, P., and Frumkin, M. (1983). Measuring organizational change in human services, *New England Journal of Human Services, 3*(4): 21.
Imershein, A. W., Polivka, L., Gordon-Girvin, S., Chackerian, R., and Martin, P. (1986). Service networks in Florida: Administrative decentralization and its effects on service delivery, *Public Administration Review, 47*(2): 161.
Jones, T. (1975). Some thoughts on coordination of services, *Social Work, 20*: 375.
Kettner, P., Daley, J. M., and Nichols, A. W. (1985). *Initiating Change in Organizations and Communities*, Brooks/Cole, Monterey, California.
Kettner, P. M., and Martin, L. L. (1986). Making decisions about purchase of service contracting, *Public Welfare, 44*(4): 30.
Lowi, T. J. (1979). *The End of Liberalism*, second ed., W. W. Norton, New York.
Lynn, L. E., Jr. (1976). Organizing human services in Florida, *Evaluation, 3*: 58.
Lynn, L. E., Jr. (1980). *The State and Human Services*, MIT Press, Cambridge, Massachusetts.
Meyer, J. W., and Rowan, B. (1983). Institutionalized organizations: Formal structure as myth and ceremony, *Organizational Environments* (J. W. Meyer and W. R. Scott, eds.), Sage, Beverly Hills, p. 21.
Mickulecky, T. J. ed. (1974). *Human Services Integration*, Council of State Governments, Lexington, Kentucky.
Morris, R. and Lescohier, I. H. (1978). Services integration: Real versus illusory solutions to welfare dilemmas, *The Management of Human Services* (R. Sarri and Y. Hasenfeld, eds.), Columbia University Press, New York.
National Academy of Public Administration (1977). *Reorganization in Florida: How is Services Integration Working?* Washington, D.C.
Orlans, H., ed. (1980). *Nonprofit Organizations: A Government Management Tool*, Praeger, New York.
Patti, R. J. (1983). *Social Welfare Administration*, Prentice-Hall, Englewood Cliffs, New Jersey.
Polivka, L., Imershein, A. W., White, J. W., and Stivers, L. E. Human service reorganization and its effects: A preliminary assessment of Florida's services integration experiment, *Public Administration Review, 41*(3): 359.
Price, I. (1978). What's happening to federally aided health programs under state departments of human resources, *Public Health Reports, 93*: 221.
Radin, B. A. (1987). "Why Do We Care about Organizational Structure?" Paper presented to the Conference on Human Services Administration, Suffolk University, March 28.
Redburn, F. S. (1977). On human services integration, *Public Administration Review, 37*: 264.
Richardson, E. (1976). *The Creative Balance: Government, Politics, and the Individual in America's Third Century*, Holt, Rinehart and Winston, New York. (See, especially, chapters 4–6.)
Sauber, S. R. (1983). *The Human Services Delivery System*, Columbia University Press, New York.

Schein, E. H. (1985). *Organizational Culture and Leadership*, Jossey-Bass, San Francisco.
Schon, Donald (1971). *Beyond the Stable State*, Random House, New York.
Scott, W. R. (1981). *Organizations: Rational, Natural, and Open Systems*, Prentice-Hall, Englewood Cliffs, New Jersey.
Short, J. (1987). *The Contract Cookbook for Purchase of Services*, Council of State Governments, Lexington, Kentucky.
Steiner, R. (1977). *Managing the Human Service Organization*, Sage, Beverly Hills.
Terrell, P. and Kramer, R. M. (1984). Contracting with nonprofits, *Public Welfare, 42*(1): 31.
Weiner, M. E. (1982). *Human Services Management: Analysis and Applications*, Dorsey, Homewood, Illinois.
Weiner, M. E. (1983). Strategic thinking: An imperative for the human services field, *New England Journal of Human Services, 3*(3): 15.
Wholey, J. S., Abramson, M. A., and Bellavita, C., eds. (1986). *Performance and Credibility*, D. C. Heath, Lexington, Massachusetts.
Wineburg, R. J. (1985). Pulling together, *Public Welfare, 43*(4): 37.

Unit II

Budgeting and Financial Management in Human Services Administration

3

Budgeting and Financial Management

W. Bartley Hildreth Public Administration Institute, Louisiana State University, Baton Rouge, Louisiana

Rodger P. Hildreth Department of Political Science, Jackson State University, Jackson, Mississippi

I. INTRODUCTION

As a rule, the management of an organization's financial resources greatly determines the relative success or failure of the management team as well as of the organization itself. Health and human service organizations have historically not paid much attention to the rule. This has been the case because most of these organizations have been able to rely on government or philanthropic funding and near market monopoly as their financial bases.

Hospitals are the largest, most complex and financially significant organizational component of the health and human service sector of the economy. However, hospitals and their management, until recently, have been substantially insulated from paying for the consequences of lackadaisical or even poor financial management. The growth of the private sector, the emergence of competition, and the shift away from cost-based reimbursement require financial performance and viability to be the criteria for assessing organizational and managerial effectiveness.

The definition of financial management, then, must be expanded beyond accounting practices into operations and strategic planning. All of management must be involved in the financial management of the organization, even though a single division and a particular individual are usually tasked with the responsibilities of financial management.

Finance—an essential part of organizational decisions—must be integrated with the organization's professional clinicians. The synergism is irrefutable. A health or human service organization must strive toward economic or financial efficiency to be viable over time, and clinicians associated with the organization require a viable practice modality to deliver services meeting professional and community standards for quality. Although finance is narrowly defined as obtaining and managing funds, it is essential that managers consciously weave the various aspects of the organization's mission and activities into a defined financial agenda.

A. Financial Management

Health and human service financial managers have the designated responsibility to see that financing for their organizations is both available and managed in an appropriate manner. Financing requirements which must be assessed and dealt with are generally differentiated as either capital financing or operational financing. Acquiring, or collecting, funds for these two purposes, allocating, disbursing the funds, and accounting for every transaction are fundamental job responsibilities for financial managers.

Each organization has limits on its financing options. A responsibility of management is to recognize these limits while meeting the organization's short- and long-term fund requirements (Wildavsky, 1985). Health and human service organizations are associated with all three economic sectors—government, corporate, and voluntary (not-for-profit). It is necessary, then, to present a short discussion of the basic differences these sectors present the financial manager.

For the government, or public, sector, financial limits generally relate to the revenue available through taxation. Some public-sector organizations, like hospitals, have the ability to bill directly for services rendered; but there are usually large portions of their clientele which must be served at the general public's expense, that is, through taxes. Long-term financing, or borrowing, is used for capital expenditures rather than operational ones, except for the federal government, which borrows for operating expenditures, too.

The contemporary attitude that taxation levels have been too high has begun to affect the spending for services. California's Proposition 13, in 1978, and Massachusetts' Proposition 2½, in 1980, provide evidence of taxpayers' insistence on placing limits on government's taxing capability (Straussman, 1979). At the federal level, income tax rates have been driven down from a high in 1981 of seventy percent to a high in 1988 of twenty-eight percent, and the deficits created by these tax reductions are being dealt with by funding cuts, program terminations, interim congressional guidelines, like Gramm-Rudman, and talk of a constitutional amendment to require a balanced federal budget (Abramson and Salamon, 1986).

For the corporate, or private, sector, operational financing is derived from collecting fees for services delivered. Factors such as demand for services, pricing of services, collection rates from payers, and return on investment to owners affect operational financing. Business firms attempt to sell a sufficient quantity of goods and services at prices so that a profit is returned to the firm's owners. The firm can also borrow money or use equity (or ownership) to generate more funds for either operating or long-term financing. These financing opportunities are limited by the firm's credit quality, stockholder support, and customers' acceptance (Jensen and Smith, 1984).

Organizations in the voluntary, or nonprofit, sector can have the responsibility of providing the same services as private- or public-sector organizations, but different fiscal realities control their behavior. Voluntary organizations legally must have a social purpose—research, education, service, religious, or charity—to permit their activities to receive special legal and tax treatment. And voluntary organizations are not permitted to have individual investors or owners. The community is the owner as a quid pro quo for the organization to be allowed to function under special tax treatment (Lohmann, 1980; Wacht, 1984).

Financial managers must take the differences between organizations in the three sectors into account. While many of the financial aspects of day-to-day operations are indistinguishable from one sector to the other, there are enough fundamental distinctions to require the financial manager's concern. Inadequate or poor financial management results as much from failure to acknowledge and understand these points as from inattention or neglect. This essay attempts to take this into account, while addressing many transferable features of financial management which are often thought to be the basics of "doing" finance.

B. Overview

This chapter is the introduction to the unit on budgeting and financial management of health and human service organizations. The purpose of this chapter is specifically to deal with the generic, and perhaps overly mundane, aspects of the topic. These aspects are the very foundation for managerial finance, and they are important and significant for their fundamental nature.

The primary areas of discussion are budgeting, financial operations, and managing finances. Budgeting refers to the allocation of resources. As such, it involves unit managers as well as the chief executive officer. Since budget formats relate to allocation questions, alternative types of budgets are introduced as are certain analytic techniques. Both capital budgeting and operational budgeting are included in the first section.

The second section is financial operations. Major financing issues are reviewed. They are working capital, long-term financing, and equity financing.

An organization's working capital is the first operational financing issue. Working capital places an emphasis on the organization's current assets—such as cash, marketable securities, receivables, inventory, and credit—which normally can be converted, or liquidated, into cash within a year. These assets, therefore, can be made available to cover developing needs.

The other operational financing issues are long-term financing, typically of over one year in length, and equity financing. Bond and stock financing is viewed from the manager's perspective. Major issues are reviewed. And related to long-term financing is the orderly acquisition of long-term assets.

Once acquired, financial resources must be managed and controlled. Therefore, the third section of this essay focuses on accounting, financial reporting, auditing, and risk management. The language of financial management—accounting—consists of financial and managerial accounting. Financial reporting to management and other users flows from accounting and, therefore, receives attention. It is through financial reporting that managers (and others) learn the details of the organization's resources and their uses. Armed with timely and accurate financial information, managers can strive to improve decisions. Auditing serves to help verify the accuracy of financial records, and it is reviewed here as well.

The final financial control issue discussed is risk management. Risk management refers to the planned (or unplanned) approach taken to protect the organization from the risks of loss due to fire, storm, liability suit, revenue interruption, and other exposures. Inadequate attention to this area can result in large payments to insurance companies to handle risks which could be managed and financed more economically and effectively by the organization itself.

By understanding these critical financing and control issues, managers have an opportunity to use the organization's financial system to help accomplish organizational goals and objectives. With such a background, managers may diminish or avoid the likelihood of program failure, organizational bankruptcy, default, and interruption of work due to insufficient resources.

II. BUDGETING

To predict the demand for health and human services is extremely difficult. But an organization engaged in providing these services must attempt to project the quantity of services it will render so that adequate resources will be available to meet the demand. Even with this apparent conundrum, financial managers in health and human service organizations must engage in fiscal foresight. And the manifestations of fiscal foresight are the budgets—capital, and operating.

The operating budget has a short-term focus. It provides a rational process for allocating resources for the upcoming fiscal year. The capital budget is the reflection of the financial decisions to acquire capital assets in order to pursue the short- and long-term goals of the organization. Except for some low-cost items, capital assets are items such as equipment, buildings, and property which have a useful life longer than one fiscal operating period, usually one year. Since the usefulness of these assets is expected in future operating periods, it is necessary to plan fiscally for the future, at least over a reasonable time horizon of three to five years.

This section examines in some detail the purposes and uses of the operating budget. Then, the capital allocation process is discussed. The purpose of this extended discussion of budgeting is to convey the importance of the allocation of resources and the interconnections between the budget and individual behavior, program planning, and an organization's financial viability.

A. Operating Budget

The operating budget is a one-year financial plan for allocating resources necessary to implement organizational goals. As such, it is an integral part of management and is effective only to the degree management is interested in influencing the financial status and future of the organization (Edwards, 1981). An operating budget is a management tool to implement program plans. Program planning involves the determination of organizational goals and objectives and the programs which most effectively help achieve them. The budget helps link program planning to the available resources (Herkimer, 1986; Lohmann, 1980).

Additionally, the budget helps managers direct and control operations. Changes in operations may be required. The more the budget can help guide the choice of priorities under dwindling resources, escalating expenses, and fluctuations in service demands, the better the manager will control operations instead of being controlled by them.

The budget addresses control, planning, and management concerns (Anthony, 1965). Some organizations use the budget merely to guarantee fiscal responsibility, or control. That is, the budget is used to account for how resources are expected to be used and are used. Little more is asked of the budget.

The budget can add power to a goal of efficient and economical delivery of services, a management orientation. Under such an approach, the budget is used to focus attention on the costs of services. For the budget to help in planning, it must facilitate the comparison of planned and actual consumption of resources and the relative accomplishment of stated goals. This requires a concern for the identification of program goals and objectives, alternatives for accomplishing them, and the evaluation of the effectiveness of the various means of accomplishing desired programs. As might be expected, as the budget moves beyond a control orientation, budget complexity arises (Schick, 1966).

Fundamentally, an operating budget is often a requirement, not just a need. Agencies soliciting United Way or government funds are required to submit a budget of how the requested funds would be utilized. The boards of directors of hospitals and some third-party intermediaries, which set reimbursement rates prospectively, typically require the hospital administration to submit a budget for the upcoming fiscal period. And, of course, human service agencies of federal, state, and local governments must follow a legal process of budgeting if public funds are utilized. Unfortunately, operating budgets are often pro forma and do not adequately reflect the fiscal operation of the organization during the upcoming fiscal period.

1. Operating Revenue

There are different types of operating revenues. The four major payment systems are charges for specific services, cost reimbursement, prospective payment, and negotiated bids (Cleverley, 1986, p. 16). Charges for specific services are the most understood method. This is where the provider sets a fee and users are obligated to pay the fee if they desire that provider's services. More operating revenue is likely to come from other sources, however. For example, hospitals receive most of their operating revenue from public sources (such as Medicare and Medicaid) and commercial insurance (Blue Cross and other group and individual insurance programs).

The dependency of health and human service organizations on Medicare and Medicaid funding opens up two additional funding sources. Medicaid is a cost reimbursement program, or one where a payer (in this case, the state government) reimburses the health care provider (for example, the hospital, nursing home, or physician) for reasonable expenses incurred by providing a covered service to a covered individual. In such cases, the provider has an incentive to get the payer to accept as reasonable as much costs as possible, however much it might prevent economical service delivery.

Medicare has been a prospective payment system since 1983. Under this payment system, the provider knows prior to providing a given service to a covered patient how much the government will subsidize (or pay) the costs of that service. Each patient's diagnosis is assigned to one or more of the 467 diagnosis-related categories (DRGs). The federal government specifies how much it will pay for each DRG. The provider has an incentive to keep its costs at or below the amount to be paid by the government. All profits stay with the provider; all costs in excess of the government's pay level are borne by the provider.

An increasingly important source of funding for health and human service care comes from negotiated-priced services. Under this form of payment system, the hospital negotiates to provide certain services to a client. One arrangement is called a preferred provider organization (PPO), where in return for a provider's services at a price discount, an employer agrees to steer its employees to the preferred provider (for example, a hospital) when covered services are needed. The employer steers the employee by offering to pay a higher percentage of the total service costs if the employee utilizes the preferred provider; otherwise, the employee bears more of the service cost. A PPO offers an employer discounted service costs (for instance, lower group hospital charges), while the preferred provider gains access to a volume of clients important for steady use of its facilities and services. The provider assumes the risk that the costs of services can be maintained within the negotiated prices.

Another form of negotiated-priced service is the health maintenance organization (HMO). The HMO offers a wide range of services for a fixed charge, instead of the uncertain charges received from an uncertain number of actual service units. Again, the service provider gains access to a volume of clients by assuming more of the risks that cost control and service utilization will follow their forecasted levels. The HMO concept also provides an incentive to treat clients in a preventive mode instead of during critical care episodes because the latter approach is more costly.

After revenue has been considered, the task facing the financial manager is to consider the expenditures necessary to produce those revenues. It would be an optimum budget circumstance if each revenue source were linked to a single identifiable cost center, but in health and human services organizations, this circumstance does not exist. Therefore, it is necessary to define units of analysis for budgeting purposes, and these can be termed the budget units.

2. Budget Unit

Most organizations are divided into subdivisions, usually called departments. Larger departments may be further subdivided into smaller units around particular tasks. Programs may cross departmental lines and include the services of individuals and equipment in various units. For budget purposes, the key concern is which level should constitute a budget unit? Is it the subdivision of a department, or is it the program with its cross-cutting function? While in accounting terminology this is called a responsibility center or cost (profit) center, a budget unit is defined here as the lowest level organizational unit over which management plans to exercise control. The use of this definition of a budget unit does not prevent later emphasis on functions which cross departmental lines.

3. Procedures

The budget is a regular and recurring aspect of most organizations. The routinization of the budget is achieved through a budget process (Vinter and Kish, 1984). The process moves from preparation to adoption to implementation (Rabin, Hildreth, and Miller, 1983). The preparation stage includes the development of statistical support material, including spending and receipt histories, as well as forecasts about the future year's volume of services, rate changes, and spending needs based upon various assumptions. While most of this information may be generated by a staff unit—such as budget, finance, or planning—the individual budget units throughout the organization usually are knowledgeable about most factors affecting the volume of services.

The individual budget units have to develop spending estimates for the upcoming fiscal period based on the assumed level of services, or demand; central management guidance concerning general resource availability; policy changes; and cost control initiatives. Each budget unit manager, then, has to submit the unit's budget to the next higher level of supervision in a format mandated by central management. At successively higher levels of management, individual budget units are compared and incorporated into larger and larger aggregates.

The chief executive of the organization has the responsibility in most organizations to finalize a budget based upon the allocation of resources among the various budget units. Since the budget reflects policy choices, the chief executive typically tries to convey organizational goals and the specific ways the budget seeks to meet those goals.

Budget adoption varies by type of organization. For nongovernmental agencies, a board of directors is generally empowered to review, modify, and adopt the budget. Often, however, the board accepts most, if not all, of the chief executive officer's proposed budget.

Budget implementation includes the formal notification to the budget units of their respective budget allocations and the drawdown of the budgeted resources as expected spending requirements materialize. If a budget unit's performance is effectively monitored, the budget unit will have to address any material variances which might occur in the dollars received or spent, or threats to the budget assumptions, such as the volume of services rendered.

4. Budget Unit Management

The manager of a budget unit benefits from involvement in the budget process. The budget serves as an operational objective. Relative success (or failure) can be adjudged from a manager's ability to forecast accurately spending requirements for the upcoming fiscal period. This requires attention to expected levels of service. If the budget unit is a social service unit of a hospital or agency, the service question may be framed: what types of services will be offered, how many clients are expected for each service, and what degree of contact intensity will each service entail? Only by such questioning can the unit manager determine the appropriate staffing pattern and related service expenses. All too commonly, the past staffing pattern and the number of past clients are projected into the future as if no change is warranted or possible. Thus, the budget is more of a confirmation of past spending levels than a management tool to help assess future service plans.

An operating budget allows the organization and its informed observers to understand better key aspects of the management of budget units. First, the budget conveys who is responsible and accountable for performing certain work in a specific budget unit and at a specific funding level.

Second, the budget conveys what work is to be performed. Some budgets are more detailed than others on this point. Basically, the budget conveys that for the allocated dollars, the budget unit will provide certain services.

Third, the budget identifies the basic inputs and outputs of the budget unit. The inputs are the sources and amounts of funds available for use by the budget unit. The outputs are the amounts of dollars expended, their uses, the time spent by employees, and the number of production units of service handled during the time period.

Fourth, the budget can tell where the funds are derived from. If a restrictive funding source is expected, perhaps a federal grant, then the budget handles that source separately from sources of unrestrictive funds. This is critical when the budget unit is subject to fluctuations in services based on the receipt of such funds. For an organization to charge for its services, it should base the service charge on the cost of producing the service. Thus, expected expenses for a period help determine what to charge, based on a given number of expected clients.

At a bare minimum, the budget conveys that the budget unit is staffed with *x* staff members who will be available during certain work schedules (for example, 7:00 A.M. to 3:00 P.M.) to provide a range of services appropriate to their skill levels (Cascio, 1982).

5. Behavioral Aspects of the Budget

Budgets not only are financial plans, they guide individual and organizational behavior. Lest we forget, individuals react to behavioral stimuli. The budget, therefore, can influence individual behavior in both positive and negative ways. Also, individual behavior can influence the budget (Argyris, 1975).

Budgets cause stress due to the fear of inequitable or inadequate distribution of resources. One reaction to stress is in overstating needs, known as padding the budget or budget slack (Merchant, 1981, 1985). Budget slack is a waste of scarce resources and represents a lost opportunity for their use in alternative areas (Bourgeois, 1981; Onsi, 1973; Young, 1985).

Budget stress in managers arises in part from their lack of involvement in budgeting. One solution is to let them have a more effective role in budget making (Rose, 1977). This option is grounded on the research finding that when individuals perceive they are participating in a decision, goal commitment is higher (Tosi, 1974). Also, when managers have specific objectives, such as budget allocations, they are more likely to do better than when they have very general or nonspecific ones. The objectives must be demanding but doable, says the research. If the required services cannot possibly be provided within a given budget allocation, stress becomes counterproductive, but if there is too much slack, individuals have little incentive to produce the services in an economical manner. Thus, demanding objectives, expressed in quantitative terms and understood by team members, are the foundation for a high-performing budget unit.

6. Budget Roles

The manager of a budget unit is inherently the strongest advocate for allocating resources to the unit. In health and human service organizations, it is common to find budget units with separate professional orientations (for example, social work, psychology, medicine, nursing). Each profession and, therefore, each budget unit has certain professional norms about the quality of services to be delivered. In all likelihood, a different interpretation of service delivery issues is manifested as an operating budget is reviewed by successively higher levels of management, even when those at higher levels have similar professional backgrounds. Certainly this problem can easily occur when the reviewers have different professional backgrounds. Often the reason for the resulting disharmony is benign, since it may occur because of such reasons as a wider scope of responsibilities or a different vantage point.

A unit manager prepares a budget for submission to a higher level manager, who incorporates that budget with several other units. The integrated budget is submitted to still a higher level in the organization. This process may be repeated several times, depending upon the vertical dimensions of the organization. At each level of budget review, it is examined for accuracy and comprehensiveness, as well as the degree of fit between it and organizational goals. Thus, there are two basic roles in budgeting: advocate and reviewer.

The advocate decides what to request in a budget for a given budget level. The conventional theory of budgeting is called incrementalism (Davis, Dempster, and Wildavsky, 1966; Wildavsky, 1964). That is to say, the advocate typically has to look only at the last year's budget to determine the basic needs for the upcoming period (Gist, 1977). An implicit assumption is that the components of service and the production of services will not be significantly changed; little attention is given to quality of services or to the possibility that particular services or programs should be discontinued completely or redesigned.

For an understanding of incremental theory, it is necessary to recognize the difference between the base and the increment (Wanat, 1974). There are three theoretical components to the base. First, there is the so-called uncontrollable part of the base, which reflects budget items fixed from one year to the next because of law, contract, or policy. While such items are not truly uncontrollable, to change them would require dramatic departures from past decisions. Incrementalism posits that fundamental change is not highly probable (Lindblom, 1959). The clearest examples are debt payments, office leases, and equipment leases. Also included are items which reflect policy, such as current staffing patterns and the normal commodity expenses, required for the provision of expected services (for example, office supplies, medical supplies).

Second, an inflationary part is included in the base. This is an item to keep up with inflation and other cost of service increases. To the past funding level is added enough to cover expected cost increases for roughly the same items of expense (for example, phone charge increases, rental charge escalations, inflationary increases in office supplies and other work commodities).

Third, the base includes a discretionary part. This part of the base allows the budget unit to carry out service options which are not directly required but which have become standard practice. Of course, in times of scarce resources or changes in management policy, the discretionary elements are likely candidates for severe reduction or elimination.

An increment is considered any addition to the base. Additional resources or major shifts in allocations allow for expansions, changes or additions to programs or services. For so long, the major budget strategy of advocates was to get as big an increment as possible. A corollary approach was to seek at least a "fair share" of any additional funds. Thus, a fair share strategy is basically competition between budget units within an organization. It often has more to do with successful internal politics than with actual service delivery efficiency or effectiveness (Collins, Munter, and Finn, 1983).

A fair share or even a disproportionate share, is gained by assertive budget strategies (LeLoup and Moreland, 1978). Instead of waiting for the budget unit's service needs to achieve a high degree of organizational consensus, some budget unit managers are quite adept at choosing strategies to enhance their unit's propensity for incremental (or larger) allocations. One strategy is for the advocate to request more than the base and a fair share of an increment. By requesting more than a fair share, the advocate has a chance to end up with something less than requested but more than the level in the most recently adopted budget. A fair share funding level may result once expected cuts are made. While not the optimum allocation method from the standpoint of organizational goals, such strategies represent individual strategies (LeLoup, 1978).

The power of an advocate arises from his or her position relative to that of others in the organization. Advocates have the closest ties to their service recipients or clients. The advocates are also best able to translate plans into actions, given their substantive expertise. In a more perverse view, advocates enjoy an ability to alter, subvert, or ignore organizational plans by manipulating dimensions of service delivery such as quality, timeliness, cooperation, and coordination.

The second major role is the reviewer. A budget is presented by an advocate to a reviewer. To guard against assertive spenders, budget reviewers attempt to identify the slack in budget proposals (Davis and Ripley, 1967). Special staff persons are often assigned a review function. At a minimum, reviewers check for accuracy and comprehensiveness in budget preparation. Also, reviewers look at budget specifications, that is, the degree of compliance with budget procedures and formats (Sundelson, 1935).

Budget reviewers are not prone to reexamine de novo all budget unit assumptions and service choices (Fenno, 1966). Instead, budget reviewers adopt budget simplification strategies (Barber, 1975). The main one follows incremental theory: The more the proposed budget mirrors the most recently adopted budget, the less scrutiny is needed. Review focus may be placed merely on large dollar or large percentage increases over past levels of funding. High visibility areas, such as requests for new employees or the purchase of operating equipment, are also vulnerable to examination.

7. Budget Formats

The theory of budget formats is that the design of the budget influences budget deliberations, which, in turn, influences budget outcomes, or allocations (Grizzle, 1986). If the budget is designed to show the cost of every pencil purchased, the theory of budget formating would suggest that the deliberations will focus on such items instead of broader goals. Thus, management policy is reflected in the types of budget utilized (Pyhrr, 1973).

The oldest budget is called a "lump sum" budget. Under this approach, the advocate provides little detail on how the requested money will be spent, and the reviewer exerts little inquiry into anything other than the basic purpose and aggregate level, since little else is revealed in the budget. This budget type is unlikely to exist today, given the need for accountability over spending. Little or no management control is needed if lump sum budgeting is desired. To meet various management needs, three basic types of budgets have evolved: the line-item, performance, and program budgets.

The budget system which imposes the most control is the line-item budget, as demonstrated by the pencil example. Some form of line-item budgeting will always be used, because all accounting and reporting systems record each expense transaction against an assigned line item—for example, a purchase of pencils, or payment of a bill (Wildavsky, 1978).

One improvement in budgeting is to group certain line items into budget categories of like items. Thus, all line items related to salaries, wages, overtime, employee health insurance, and other benefits are collapsed into a "personal services" category for budget format purposes. Similarly, all office expense items which entail the purchase of commodities are grouped into the "supplies" category. While a categorical budget is an improvement over pure line-item budgeting, it still leaves the budget in a very weak position to confront questions about economy and efficiency.

The budgeting system with the most emphasis on efficiency and productivity is performance budgeting. A performance budget focuses attention on issues such as the cost per client served, cost per inspection made, cost per census day in the hospital, and so on. These are all essentially production questions, which ask how much it costs per unit of production.

Performance budgets rely upon a degree of sophistication in determining the total costs of a service, not just the amounts spent by a budget unit. First, it is hard to define a unit of service. Is the unit one client, one hour, one bed, or some other measure? Furthermore, service operations have an inherent problem in making each unit equal. One client may require more attention or level of skill involvement than another. Thus, instead of defining its basic service unit as a client, an organization such as a hospital may define the service as a "bed" (as in an intensive care bed, nursing home bed, etc.) and set different prices for each to reflect the various cost structures. In other cases, the practice of professionals to use time as the unit may make more sense.

Second, the cost for a service may defy easy determination. While the budget unit's direct costs are an easy start, there are additional costs for an organization's services, or indirect costs. Thus, total costs include direct and indirect costs associated with a given budget unit (Arnstein and Gilabert, 1980). For instance, a social service unit of a hospital would not normally have a budget item for debt service or electrical utilities. Instead, these costs would more likely be included in other hospital budget units, since one small budget unit (office) within a much larger organization (building) has little control over the cost of such items. That is not to say that in day-to-day operations the social service department, as in this example, apparently does not affect building costs as represented in the budget.

Should the social service department conduct weekend programs to help achieve more effective marketing of the hospital to the community, the costs for such services might best reflect total costs, not just the marginal costs associated with the overtime wages paid to the staff member serving as instructor. Instead, the unit's total cost should be used to determine true unit costs. One benefit of using total costs is that an appropriate service fee can be considered by dividing the number of expected attendees by the total costs. If the service is designed, instead, to be free to the public, the total cost approach allows the organization to know the implicit subsidy involved in the community program.

In summary, performance budgeting offers an opportunity to make each budget unit consider the efficiency of its activities. Efficiency is measured by determining a production value. Management gains by having a highly visible linkage between the volume of services and costs. This is important, since health and human service organizations are more and more vulnerable to faulty volume assumptions. Thus, performance budgeting forces advocates and reviewers alike to think in terms of production issues. The key missing ingredient is that performance budgeting does not incorporate effectiveness measures.

Program budgeting focuses on effectiveness. The most renowned approach is the so-called Planning, Programming, Budgeting System, or PPBS, a device of the early 1960s (Lyden and Miller, 1972; Rabin, 1975). It asks the questions "What are we actually accomplishing? What impact are we having?"

The planning component deals with the definition of problems, development of goals and objectives, consideration of alternative activities capable of leading to accomplishment of objectives, and estimation of costs and benefits of the alternatives (Mishan, 1976). Programming refers to the selection of the alternative method of delivery that appears to most clearly meet stated goals and objectives, given favorable benefits over costs. Budgeting, then, is the assignment of sufficient resources to each activity so as reasonably to expect accomplishment of the identified program objectives (Lyden and Miller, 1978; Wright, 1969).

8. Performance Measurement

"Productivity" is a key management term meaning the return received for the money spent. Management asserts control to achieve favorable productivity returns. For example, to what degree has the organization met its goals and objectives, and at what price? Is there room for improvement in the delivery of services? These and other questions frame the management drive for productivity. To judge relative success, however, requires the measurement of performance within discrete organizational units—often called responsibility centers in cost accounting, but referred to here as budget units.

The performance of a budget unit is subject to different types of measurement. The simplest approach is to measure effort, such as volume (that is, the number of services performed). While this information is helpful, it offers little clue to real productivity.

Efficiency measures seek to draw a relationship between output and input, a form of productivity. Costs per service unit provided or units provided per hour of work are frequently employed efficiency measures.

Of more use is measurement aimed at the effectiveness of a budget unit. Examples of indicators include response time and percentage of target population served. It should be noted that effectiveness measures imply the appropriateness of the output for meeting the stated goals, which may not always be the case.

To generate effort, effectiveness, or efficiency measures, it is important first to collect and organize the requisite data. Within a budget unit, all work elements, or tasks, have to be enumerated. For example, within a social service department, a listing of tasks might include referrals, inspection of appropriate referral sites, and so on. For each task, the work unit has to be determined. A work unit is the physical unit of work accomplished which describes the activity—for example, phone calls. The next step is to generate a workload measure, simply by linking a verb with the work unit, as in "calls received" or "inspections conducted." By following this logical sequence, workload costs can be generated. This requires the assessing of costs to each work unit, as in "it costs $12 per inspection" (State of Rhode Island, 1983).

Management control revolves around the generation of workload costs both as an aid in budget preparation and, later, as a comparison to actual costs. The variance between budgeted and actual workload costs can provide information for management decision making. Furthermore, the targeted workload costs can be assessed against historical levels (What did it cost us last year?), comparable organizations (What is it costing our competitors?), and improvement goals (How well have we achieved our goal of providing more services at less cost?)

In summary, the purpose of performance evaluation is to ensure proper implementation of organizational goals. Budgeting can facilitate performance evaluation by casting the budget to help emphasize past and targeted performances. When effectively followed, a performance evaluation system helps match budget performance to organizational expectations.

9. Fixed versus Flexible Budgets

The two basic budget types are fixed and flexible. The fixed budget is a budget which is established prior to a fiscal period based on certain up-front assumptions. It is not subject to change, except by special supplemental methods. Government budgets are the most clear examples of fixed budgets. In contrast, a flexible budget is one that is based on a given volume of services and is designed to adjust as volume changes. As the number of clients served increases, expenses increase. Thus, flexible budgets recognize this cost behavior by allowing the budget unit to expand to meet the service demands, and in a corresponding manner budget allocations are increased, especially if clients pay for their services.

While most health and human service organizations follow a fixed budget, flexible budgeting is gaining more adherents. Since the volume of services affects revenues and expenses, a flexible budget offers management a more dynamic approach to budgeting than is offered by the more static fixed budget. The flexible budget is by design vulnerable to volume fluctuations, but it copes by contracting or expanding as the need arises. In contrast, the fixed budget is built on the assumption that volume has little bearing on expenses. In fact, midyear budget cuts or increases may occur to accommodate budget variances.

10. Budget Variances

The difference between the budgeted and actual results is called a variance. In health and human service organizations, variances are due to volume, price, and usage (Cleverley, 1986). As the volume of services changes, both receipts and expenses are affected. If a budget is based on rates charged for services, then the expected volume times the rate equals the yield. Thus, a change in rates affects the yield. Usage is a broad term which encompasses patient/client mix, service utilization, and efficiency of operations. The patient/client mix refers to the different funding sources associated with patients or clients (for example, Medicare, Medicaid, commercial insurance, private payment).

The degree to which available services are utilized is best illustrated by the bed census of nursing homes and hospitals. If the budget is premised on a certain percentage of beds to be utilized by Medicare-funded patients, and the actual bed utilization and patient mix is different, then the budget is likely to be off. Fundamentally, the ability of a budget unit to produce services in an economical manner also affects the budget bottom line. Unsupervised spending within the budget unit can lead to budget variances.

B. Capital Budgeting

Most organizations have to make capital investments in order to produce operating revenue. The investment of capital in a new building, an improvement to an existing facility, or even a major piece of equipment is not a decision which can be taken lightly. Nearly all capital investments require a high level of financial commitment, and a long time span between the decision to purchase an item and its effective use. A capital investment decision has the quality, as well, of an almost irreversible decision, because once purchased or built, the item is not an easy commodity to sell and move.

The large financial commitments of most capital investments make them too expensive to pay for out of one year's working capital. It may take several years to save for the item; this, of course, does nothing to satisfy service needs or demands during the interim. To accommodate current demands, the pay-as-you-go plan may have to be replaced with one based on the borrowing of sufficient funds to acquire and place the capital item into more immediate service. By borrowing, the organization typically agrees to pay an amount in installments (or debt service) over several years. These periodic payments include repayment of the principal and interest, the fee for using another's funds.

The debt service payment is paid out of working capital, unless a capital grant, or bequest, or an earmarked revenue source is available. Whether through savings or borrowing, capital budgeting requires planning and judicious use of working capital and borrowing capacity. Too much debt can place the organization in a weak position to deal with severe revenue reductions, since debt service would comprise an increasingly larger share of all revenues.

A profit-seeking organization has to analyze capital expenditure proposals in terms of their impact on cash flow and profitability. For example, what resources are required to build and equip a proposed facility in comparison with the expected cash to be generated from the project? Will the project return the investment costs? Are there alternative uses of the scarce dollars which could provide a higher return for a similar investment? In seeking to answer these basic questions, management has to make assumptions. Faulty assumptions about a facility's operating potential can ruin an organization if the forecasts do not have a high probability of conforming with actual experience. Thus, assumptions about projected operating potential require serious management inquiry and investigation (Wacht, 1984).

An organization often has competing needs for scarce investment dollars. Choices have to be made between highly desirable projects. Basically, the organization has to ration its investments in capital projects. To assist in this decision-making process, several analytic approaches are available which fall under the category of either a qualitative or quantitative approach. The qualitative approach rests on bargaining or ranking systems. The bargaining approach is best illustrated by the age-old political image of one politician's obtaining commitments from fellow officials for one project in return for promises to support their needs later. This is called "pork-barrel politics" (Ferejohn, 1974).

The ranking system is a marked improvement in which all projects are ranked according to a standard set of criteria. The criteria might range from "necessary to comply with law" down to a mere "comfort improvement," with points assigned from high to low. Under a point system, the capital projects with the highest points are more likely to receive funding than those with lower points.

Analytic techniques have evolved to help in the capital rationing process. The payback period is one technique. It is a measure of the time required to recover the investment through net cash inflows. The initial investment cost is divided by the annual net cash flow savings (yearly gross savings less yearly costs). This yields the number of years before the investment is recovered from the savings. A problem with this technique is that it does not address the fact that a dollar invested today is not equal to a dollar received tomorrow.

The value of a dollar changes over time. This is important in capital budgeting because investments are made in a project during one or more fiscal periods, but may not produce any tangible benefits until a subsequent fiscal period. Thus, there is the need to find out how much a dollar realizable in a future year is worth today, or the dollar's present value, as it is called. The formula for determining present value is:

$$PV = p\,(1/1{+}i)^n$$

Where "PV" is the present value, "p" equals the principal, "i" is the discount rate (or interest rate), and "n" is the number of years. For example, if a project is expected to generate $100 of net cash flow savings in the year following an investment, what would be the present value of the future savings? To arrive at an answer, a discount rate must be determined. Often this is considered the cost of capital, alternatively called the opportunity cost, and is measured by either the rate of return that would have been received if the funds were left to earn interest or the cost to borrow funds. Both portray the cost of alternative uses of funds. If, for example, the organization had to pay ten percent for borrowed funds, then that figure could serve as the discount rate. Then, the formula as filled out would show:

$$PV = 100(1/1{+}.10)^1 \text{ or } PV = \$90.91$$

If $100 was expected for each of two years, then the present value of the two years would be equal to $82.65. There are tables which make the calculations easier, especially when it is necessary to consider longer time periods (Brigham, 1979). The formula can be used to convert any flow of dollars in future time periods to an equivalent single present value. The selection of the discount rate is the key decision, because the selected figure can significantly influence the results. By inserting a nine percent discount rate in the above example, the present value would be $91.74 for one year and $84.17 for two years. Thus, it is important to insert into the formula various discount rates to test the sensitivity of the results to a given rate. This is called sensitivity analysis.

Benefit-cost analysis flows from an understanding of the present value technique. In it, both the benefits and the costs of a project are calculated, however difficult it might be to quantify all benefits (for example, improved quality of life). Following the establishment of benefits and costs for each year of the project's life, the future stream of benefits and costs are discounted to present value. When the sum of the discounted benefits exceeds the sum of the discounted costs, a project is viable.

In summary, capital budgeting represents a specialized decision-making sequence for making major allocations of organizational resources.

III. FINANCING OPERATIONS

A portfolio of financing options exists for most organizations. Two major components include working capital, basically financing of current operations, and long-term financing, including equity financing for private businesses. Each will be reviewed. Long-term financing influences the organization for many years into the future, and it must be considered within the capital budgeting and strategic planning processes.

While all of these issues (except equity financing) affect all organizations—whether government, not-for-profit, or profit-seeking—the impact is not the same across all organizations. Government jurisdictions contend with tax dollars which do not fit easily the traditional definition of working capital management. Profit-seeking endeavors must consider the income tax implications of the handling of their funds. And not-for-profit entities must perform in a manner so as not to surrender their tax-exempt status.

Working capital includes cash and marketable securities, plus other assets, which can be liquidated within one year to cover current liabilities. This definition is not quite absolute, however. Tax receipts can be used to cover the succeeding year's needs, if necessary, and accrual accounting for nongovernmental organizations permits the shifting of cash receipts and expenditures into other fiscal years, somewhat. For our purposes, tax receipts will be categorized as cash, despite the difficulties with this definition.

A. Working Capital

Financial viability demands management attention to current assets and liabilities. Basically, working capital management attempts to plan and control an organization's flow of money to ensure sufficient liquidity. Thus, working capital management involves attention to cash and marketable securities, accounts receivable, inventory, and short-term credit (Goodman, 1975a,b).

1. Cash and Marketable Securities

Cash provides organizations with the capability to finance current operations. Yet, to have cash in accounts not drawing interest is poor financial management. The reason is that "idle cash" can yield significant interest earnings. The extent to which idle cash is available for short-term interest investment is a management decision.

How does the organization acquire cash? Business firms sell products and services for a price. Governments receive tax receipts, fines, fees, and intergovernmental aid. Many not-for-profit organizations depend upon contributions and government aid. In each case, organizations are paid either in cash or in some form convertible into cash.

What purpose does cash serve? Cash is needed to meet current payment obligations, as well as to serve as a precaution against unpredictable circumstances (Donaldson, 1969). Furthermore, cash allows organizations to take advantage of reduced prices on needed goods and services which might be offered at bargain prices or may be discounted with prompt payment. Finally, minimal cash reserves in a bank account sometimes are required by the bank to compensate the bank for its servicing of normal banking operations (such as check handling) or outstanding loans. These cash reserves are termed compensating balances (Broyles, 1981).

The optimum approach is to place idle cash in interest-drawing investments, including interest-earning checking accounts and marketable securities. The purpose is to produce interest earnings, while maximizing safety (protection of principal) and liquidity (ease of withdrawal, without penalty). For government units, the safety of public funds limits investment options. In fact, public funds, typically, must be secured with one hundred percent collateral by the depository institutions, like banks.

A cash budget is a necessity if an organization wants to achieve the optimum benefits from its cash. A cash budget provides a way to chart cash inflows with cash outflows for a given time period (daily, weekly, monthly, quarterly, or yearly). The cash budget compares a forecast of revenues (from sales, taxpayers, service recipients, or whatever the case may be) with expenses/expenditures. Therefore, the cash budget allows management to identify when additional cash will be needed to cover outlays and when there should be opportunities to invest idle cash (Loscalzo, 1982). Some enterprising financial executives take advantage of the ability to make investments of idle cash over weekends.

When forecasted outflows exceed inflows, several options can be considered: Reduce expenses; increase revenues (raise prices, increase taxes, etc.); or, perhaps, use short-term borrowing to get over a temporary cash deficit. Advance notice of impending cash deficits or cash investment opportunities allows management to utilize the organization's cash assets better.

Cash management involves the steps of collecting, mobilizing, and disbursing cash. Furthermore, cash management demands the determination of cash balances. The investment of a cash flow surplus in a marketable security allows the principal and interest earnings to be used to deal with expected cash flow shortages later in the fiscal period. The following sections review the basic considerations of the cash management function (Smith, 1979:72).

a. Collecting Cash

Most organizations extend credit instead of receiving cash payments. That is, a service or good is produced and delivered prior to payment, sometimes weeks or months ahead of payment. Many local governments, for example, provide services using property tax receipts paid or due in the prior year. While government services are provided sometimes without regard to who pays for them, businesses and not-for-profits cannot operate the same way. They must try to change the payment behavior of those receiving credit.

The customer or client might be given an incentive or opportunity to pay sooner. Utilities, for example, typically require payment within a week from the billing date before interest or service charges are added. Another approach is to offer discounts to customers who pay bills earlier than bills normally are due. This works especially well for distributors and suppliers, but it also could work for others.

To collect cash effectively also requires the processing of customer checks as soon as possible, sometimes faster than normal mail delivery might allow. Thus, well-designed cash management systems avoid mail delays. For example, utility customers usually can pay a bill at any of several local banks. The money then is deposited by the bank into the utility's bank account. This reduces the amount of time the check otherwise might be floating in the mail or in the bank's processing and handling system.

An organization with dispersed customers can employ a lockbox system to achieve cash management advantages. The lockbox is a post office box rented by the organization but entrusted to a bank. The bank has the responsibility to monitor constantly the letters received in the lockbox. The bank processes all checks received and deposits the money into the company's account. Thus, cash is available to the company much more quickly than would be possible through mail delivery and handling at the company's offices. More recently, electronic transfer of cash between banks and organizations has achieved even more time efficiencies.

b. Mobilizing Cash

Poor financial management occurs when a single organization has a cash-poor unit borrowing money at a higher rate of interest than another organizational unit actually earns on its idle cash. Organizations with operations at several different locations find it important to mobilize cash among and between units through a "unified cash management system." For example, a health care management company with several divisions and many facilities could find it beneficial to coordinate the cash deposits and payments of each unit to achieve an optimal cash position for the entire company.

c. Disbursing Cash

An organization can use cash disbursement to its advantage. This involves a deliberate attempt to delay payment to creditors. Thus, money is made available for a few more days (or weeks) for investment opportunities at the expense of the creditor (the person to whom payment is owed), who will receive late payment. A major problem with this no-interest credit, as it is called, is the intentional effort to delay payment of a legitimate bill.

d. Cash Balance

It is necessary for an organization to determine the appropriate cash balance it needs to retain at a given time. To do this, the organization must first chart, on a daily basis, all cash inflows and outflows. When cash outflows exceed inflows, a cash balance is required. This can be handled by building up cash reserves to offset the expected cash deficit. Changes have to be made to reflect revised policies and procedures concerning cash collection, mobilization, and disbursement. Any remaining cash shortages, or cash imbalances, would have to be remedied, primarily by obtaining borrowed money or by liquidating existing investments, or a combination of the two.

e. Marketable Securities

Marketable securities provide organizations with a means to invest currently idle cash. If used carefully, marketable securities stand as cash substitutes, plus have the bonus of earned interest, for marketable securities are investments which enjoy a secondary market permitting liquidation by the original holder. For example, organization X invests in marketable security A, using its excess cash. A month later, organization X needs to liquidate marketable security A to cover a planned cash need. Another buyer (Y) is located for security A, since the security is marketable. Organization A receives its proceeds in time to cover the projected cash needs, while buyer Y invests excess cash until the security normally matures, or until another buyer is found to liquidate buyer Y's investment.

There are many types of marketable securities. U.S. Treasury bills (T-bills) are a relatively risk-free investment, since they are issued by the U.S. government, and the securities are traded in an active secondary market producing high liquidity. Securities issued by other federal agencies, such as the Government National Mortgage Association (Ginnie Mae), also are almost risk-free and highly liquid (Miller, 1982, pp. 78-79).

Two marketable securities often used are certificates of deposit (CDs) and repurchase agreements. A CD is an agreement by a bank to offer, in return for a deposit of a stated amount and period, a stated rate of return. The maturity period ranges from less than a month to over a year. Premature redemption, however, can result in interest penalties. Thus, these instruments are not highly liquid. There is a high degree of risk associated with CDs exceeding the federal deposit insurance limits of $100,000.

Repurchase agreements (repos) enjoy widespread use. Repos work the following way. An organization purchases a U.S. T-bill from a financial institution or investment banking firm. An agreement between the bank and the purchasing organization states that the selling bank will repurchase the T-bill on a specified date at a stated price. The T-bill itself serves as collateral. This investment vehicle commonly is used for overnight or weekend investments, although a repurchase agreement can be acquired for longer periods. While repos are highly liquid, it is important for the organization purchasing a repo to know the specific collateral it is agreeing to buy. The repurchase market has suffered in recent years due to poor attention by some major repo purchasers as to the collateral for their investments. Furthermore, repurchase agreements are not covered by federal deposit insurance.

2. Accounts Receivable

Most health and human service organizations have one thing in common: They issue credit to customers or clients. The amount owed is an account receivable. To manage its accounts receivable, an organization's credit policy and collection process deserve management attention.

To develop a credit policy requires attention to several issues. Who is to be extended credit? What criteria will be used to judge credit quality? Some organizations extend credit to all customers or clients. Others are more selective, basing their decisions on ability to pay, collateral offered, default risk, etc. Some not-for-profit health care providers have responsibilities under their organizational charters or law to provide care for the indigent; thus, credit quality is not a deciding factor in some cases of care giving.

Whatever the credit policy, the cost of extending credit should be considered. What impact will credit policy have on sales or good will? What are the costs of implementing the credit policy? It is important to consider these questions when designing a credit policy.

The collection process for accounts receivable focuses on the payment pattern and how the organization uses the information. An "aging schedule" helps examine the payment pattern. Basically, this requires an analysis of the time accounts are still open. It shows the number, amount, and percentage of all open accounts for different time intervals. Basically, an aging schedule helps pinpoint the size and magnitude of outstanding accounts receivable. An organization gains from an aggressive accounts receivable collection policy (Smith, 1979).

3. Inventory

Inventories represent a major asset, which, if necessary, could be liquidated to cover cash needs. Supplies needed to produce a certain product or service can accumulate to such a point that the costs of financing the inventory outweigh the potential sales or service receipts (Smith, 1979). For example, a pharmacist must keep a variety of supplies and equipment in preparation for a customer who needs only one small, unique prescription.

Organizations attempt to reduce inventories to the bare minimum. To do so, however, calls for a well-planned system to link inventory needs with supplies and to reduce the time lag between the order, the delivery, and the use of the inventory (for example, a sale). For hospitals, the cost of carrying a large supply inventory needs to be calculated against the price of supplies, because often in metropolitan areas one or more supply firms can provide immediate delivery. Thus, even a premium price paid to a local supplier may be a net savings to a hospital which otherwise would elect to carry a large inventory.

Holding more inventory than is needed limits the funds which could go for more productive uses, including earning interest on funds placed in marketable securities. Of course, inventory purchased at bargain prices might offset this concern. That is, even if held for a longer time period, bargain purchases might still be beneficial.

4. Financing Working Capital

To this point, the discussion has focused on different current assets, including inventory, accounts receivable, cash, and marketable securities. Several options are available to finance current assets. Long-term debt (or debt outstanding for longer than a year) is not a recommended way to finance current needs. Rather, short-term debt financing, or better management of payables and accruals, offers more advantages. This section first examines payables and accruals, then presents an overview of short-term borrowing.

a. Payables and Accruals

Part of an organization's debt is free from interest. Wages and taxes are paid after work is performed. Thus, the organization gains the interest income on the funds until the wages and taxes must be paid. A decision on when to pay employees should therefore consider the benefits (and costs) associated with added investment income which might be generated by elongating the payment period. Of course, contracts, employee preferences, and payment customs help render many options unworkable.

Another financing method is accounts payable. Accounts payable occur when supplies, parts, and materials are purchased by an organization but the payments on these items are delayed for weeks or months. Meanwhile, funds are available to draw interest. The delay between acquisition and payment of a debt is considered a "trade credit."

While some organizations deliberately delay payments, especially when there are no penalties for tardy payment, managers should consider the propriety of such actions. Unfortunately, some government and other organizations employ payment delays as a way to overcome cash deficits. More effective cash-flow planning would contribute to better buyer-seller relations. Otherwise, critical suppliers might decide to terminate business with late-paying customers.

b. Short-Term Bank Borrowing

Organizations sometimes have to resort to loans from banks (and others) to cover cash deficits. Short-term borrowing represents a financing method used mainly to overcome temporary cash-flow problems.

Managers strive to obtain short-term financing at the lowest possible costs. If the borrowing capacity or lender interest is absent, some operations might have to be curtailed or other steps taken to bring cash inflows more in line with cash outflows.

Many organizations try to plan ahead by arranging with a bank a line of credit. A line of credit is an agreement by a bank to provide a borrower with a preset loan amount which is made available for use at the borrower's discretion within a certain time period (for example, one year). The agreement establishes the collateral (if any) and the rate of interest due the bank. In addition, the borrowing organization often has to pay a commitment fee up front to compensate the bank for arranging to have the necessary funds available anytime within the contract period to meet the terms of the agreement.

Government units face a more complicated process in obtaining short-term financing. They have to issue Tax Anticipation Notes (TANs) and Revenue Anticipation Notes (RANs), both exempt from federal income tax for the holder of the note. TANs are issued to cover cash-flow problems prior to receipt of certain collateral taxes (such as local property tax). RANs are used mainly by government enterprise operations (such as public hospitals) to borrow against anticipated accounts receivable. The issuance procedures for TANs and RANs are expressed in state law. Typically, these debt instruments can be placed with a bank by negotiation, not by competitive, public bid. Also, most state laws require all TANs and RANs to be paid within the same year (Public Securities Association, 1981).

B. Long-Term Financing

Organizations use long-term financing to provide the basic capital needed to finance major fixed asset purchases (such as key facilities or major equipment) or, in the case of business firms, to expand operations. Long-term financing is basically debt which requires repayment after one year or more, according to an established schedule of principal and interest payments. Prior to entering into any long-term financing plan, management should exercise caution, since the decision binds the organization for years into the future.

An early consideration in any long-term financing program has to be an examination of the organization's future. Is the organization facing a stable flow of funds—whether from taxpayers, contributions, or sales? An organization's debt capacity relates to its actual and potential cash inflow. For example, most state laws limit local governments from issuing debt in excess of a stated legal limit, usually a percentage of taxable property (Moak, 1982).

While enjoying a more flexible debt capacity, business firms confront debt limits imposed by the judgment of lenders as to the firm's creditworthiness. Basically, the more profitable the business firm, the more debt capacity. Organizations with assets which have high resale value or revenue-generating capacity (if effectively managed) also may be better able to carry higher debt levels by pledging assets as collateral, or security, for loans.

A debt issuer's credit has an impact on (1) the capacity to borrow, and (2) the cost of debt. If a lender views the issuing organization as a poor credit risk, either the credit will not be extended at all, or what credit is extended will be so poor as to make the interest due on such borrowing quite onerous. To aid lenders in making credit assessments, several independent credit rating services conduct extensive research on the credit character of borrowing organizations. Such services rate the credit quality of business firms, government units, and sovereign governments (for example, Canada, Third World countries) in their issuance of long-term debt. Moody's Investors Service and Standard & Poor's Corporation are the two best-known rating firms.

Credit analysis takes into consideration the nature of the organization and its financial viability. A business firm is examined partly as to its past and current operation (that is, profitability) and its past use of debt (the debt currently carried).

There are two basic types of long-term financing: term loans and bonds. The term loan is a debt instrument negotiated between the lender and the borrower. The loan agreement establishes the conditions (such as interest rate and repayment schedule) under which the loaned funds will be repaid. The term loan is a flexible method of borrowing. First, additional funds can be borrowed under certain conditions (for instance, adequate credit quality, display of need). Furthermore, the loan agreement can be modified if the parties agree. (For example, the loan repayment schedule could be extended.)

A bond is a more formalized long-term financing instrument than a term loan. Bonds have to follow more exacting issuance guidelines. The reason is that bonds are made available to a wider set of investors, not just a single lender, as could be the case for a term loan. Typically, bonds are purchased by investment firms and then sold to potential investors, either individuals or institutions (such as insurance companies, pension funds). The Securities and Exchange Commission oversees the bond issuance process and market, except for tax-exempt securities.

In addition to bonds issued by corporations, there are U.S. government bonds and municipal bonds. U.S. government bonds are different from other instruments—they are almost risk-free from default. Municipal bonds enjoy a separate, special characteristic—they are exempt from U.S. income tax laws. Municipal bonds are issued by state governments, special state agencies (such as hospital construction authorities), and municipalities (for example, hospital and clinic industrial development boards) (Lamb and Rappaport, 1980).

C. Equity Financing

Business firms can raise capital by issuing stock. A share of stock—or equity—does not carry with it the legal contract for repayment of the amount of investment, as is the case for a bond. Under a corporate bankruptcy, stockholders have a right to the firm's proceeds only after payment of all legal contracts (such as accounts payable and bonds). Thus, equity financing has risks for investors. For the corporation, however, equity financing offers one way to obtain needed capital for expansion (Franks, Broyles and Carleton, 1985).

Firms anticipate paying dividends to stockholders as a way to compete against fixed-income securities—such as bonds which pay out interest and principal according to a preestablished schedule. Neither a dividend's size nor its regularity is guaranteed. Yet, firms make every effort to continue paying the same, or higher, dividends each year as a way to retain shareholders and share prices.

In summary, equity financing is a sound method of obtaining capital if consistent with organizational needs. However, dilution of ownership can result, as can buy-outs by more financially capable firms, if stock is publicly owned.

IV. MANAGING FINANCES

Financial management is an essential, routinized exercise in managerial coordination and control. It integrates accounting, financial reporting, auditing, and, increasingly, risk management into the organizational system.

A. Accounting

Accounting is the language of finance. While financial managers do not have to be certified accountants, managers are likely to be ineffective without a basic understanding of accounting. Accounting is not just "number crunching" or "green eyeshade" work. Rather, accounting is a standardized method of classifying, recording, summarizing, and interpreting financial transactions.

There are two accounting approaches: financial and managerial accounting. Financial accounting focuses on the more traditional bookkeeping functions of classifying, recording, and summarizing financial transactions. Managerial accounting concentrates on making accounting data more useful for managerial decision making by aiding in the interpretation of financial activities (Anthony and Herzlinger, 1980).

Accounting principles provide managers with benchmarks to judge the degree of completeness of an organization's system. The Financial Accounting Standards Board provides authoritative statements on what constitutes generally accepted accounting principles, or GAAP (Anthony, 1978).

Corporations that have public shareholders or have to deal with the financial community must have accounting records developed in accordance with GAAP. Small, unincorporated firms have little need for GAAP-based accounting, although keeping accounting records on a true GAAP-based system is advised to permit comparison with similar firms.

Government and not-for-profit institutions are increasingly meeting GAAP, but in slightly different forms, to allow GAAP to adjust to their different conditions. For example, governments employ funds to separate different activities, many of which are mandated by law. In this context, funds are separate accounting entities which have their own self-balancing set of accounts, or assets and liabilities (Hay, 1980; Henke, 1980).

Financial accounting concerns the way the organization relates receipts or revenues (depending on the type of organization) to expenditures for a given time period. The accounting cycle includes data recording, trial balances, adjusting entries, and closing procedures. Trial balances are used to check on the accuracy of the initial entries. Prior to being closed for reporting purposes, accounts have to be adjusted (for example, accrued), to make sure appropriate receipts and expenses are included within the reporting period (Ameiss and Kargas, 1977).

Accounting for business firms indicates expenses required to produce a good or service, along with the revenues (sales) emanating therefrom, all within the period of time the good or service is manufactured, prepared, or delivered. Thus, under this system, all earned revenues are accrued to permit matching of revenues with the expenses incurred to produce the revenues. This accounting system is called the accrual approach.

Governments use a modified accrual system (Herzlinger and Sherman, 1980). Since government expenses are not related directly to a given product or service, revenues are accrued when they are measurable and quantifiable. For example, a government unit does not know for sure how many dollars will be collected in fees in a twelve-month period (a fiscal year), but the government must budget for the delivery of services nevertheless. These public services are usually provided as a government duty or an earned entitlement, and as such, all reasonable costs usually will be funded (Vargo, 1977).

The form of accounting familiar to most people is cash-based accounting. For instance, receipts of income and expenditures for deductions are mostly computed on a cash basis for individual income tax purposes. In this accounting approach, both expenses and revenues are recognized when cash transactions occur—expenses paid and revenues received. A cash basis of accounting is not recommended for any organization. Even individuals, say the experts, set aside (or accrue) funds to pay outstanding bills.

Managerial accounting is the use of accounting data for managerial decision making. This is achieved substantially by following the performance measurement approach to budgeting, with the focus on the delineation of budget units (or responsibility centers, in accounting terminology) and, for each budget unit, the calculation of total costs of operation, including both direct and indirect costs (Moore and Jaedicke, 1980).

Cost accounting helps in establishing prices for goods and services, comparing alternative operations, and, for organizations doing business with the federal government, recovering all contract costs, not just direct costs. Government units, universities, and hospitals receiving federal financial assistance have developed elaborate cost recovery programs to show the federal government the total costs of performing government-sponsored work.

Financial accounting and managerial accounting offer systematic ways to use financial data. Managerial decision making benefits from accurate and consistent financial data, maintained in such a way as to facilitate comparisons among and between operating units both inside and outside the organization.

B. Financial Reporting

The financial condition of an organization interests many people. Owners of a firm (stockholders), directors of a hospital, and citizens who "own" a government unit all represent users of financial information. An organization's management team requires timely and authoritative financial information to enable it to make informed decisions regarding the organization's future. Sometimes, employees and employee unions have an interest in knowing the organization's financial health (Hulpke and Watne, 1976). Also, investors and creditors have an almost insatiable appetite for financial information.

Financial reporting is the systematic approach taken to provide reports on the organization's financial operation to different users, both inside and outside the organization.

Accounting and auditing standards guide financial reporting practice. Financial transactions should be handled according to GAAP. Auditors will use generally accepted auditing standards (GAAS) in their reporting of financial results and condition. Three financial statements, which should follow these standards, are the balance sheet, the income statement and the statement of changes in financial position.

The balance sheet shows the financial condition at a given point in time. It serves a as a financial snapshot. Usually prepared at the beginning and again at the end of the fiscal period, it reflects the organization's assets, liabilities, and owner's equity (or fund balance, in government accounting). It follows the accounting equation: Assets = Liabilities + Owner's Equity.

The income statement reports revenues, expenses, and net income or earnings for a stated period of time, usually one year. It helps explain the differences between starting and ending year balance sheets. The income statement is the most important financial statement for profit-oriented organizations, because it indicates net worth (income or loss).

The statement of changes in financial position reflects sources and uses of funds for a stated fiscal period. Fund sources include earnings from current operations, sale of assets, long-term borrowing, new stock, etc. Fund uses include asset purchases, long-term debt repayment, cash dividend payout, etc. Thus, this statement helps explain the changes between starting and ending year balance sheets.

In summary, the balance sheet provides a view of financial condition at a given point in time, such as at the start and at the end of a year. In contrast, the income statement and the statement of changes in financial position provide two ways of determining what acutally transpired between balance sheets.

More frequent financial statements or reports typically are desired by management. For example, a daily cash budget report helps isolate idle cash which deserves investment consideration and permits early revision in the cash budget to reflect changing conditions. During the year, special income statements might be needed to provide bankers or other investors. Also, line-item expense reports can help control troublesome responsibility centers or items of expense.

Standardized financial reports permit managers to conduct financial analysis. Ratio analysis helps relate segments of financial operations. Ratios are the result of dividing one financial element by another; the value comes from the interpretation. For example, a key ratio on the liquidity of an organization is the current ratio, current assets divided by current liabilities. For the result to mean anything, it helps to relate it to industry standards. In the case of hospitals, for example, there are industry norms (Cleverley, 1986). Additionally, it is useful to plot ratios over time for the same organization.

Basically, management has to weigh the need for more financial information with the potential of reaching information overload. The myth that more information improves management decisions is just that, a myth. Yet, too little financial information can lead to inadequate or ill-conceived consideration of the financial consequences of management decisions.

C. Auditing

The purpose of auditing is to ensure that reliable and accurate information about an organization's financial operations is made available to interested parties. Auditing primarily concerns financial accountability, including a concern with detecting misappropriation of funds, embezzlement, and other financial chicanery. Auditors attempt to make an examination of accounting records and practices to such an extent as to be able to express an informed opinion as to whether the organization's financial statements present fairly its financial position (Meigs, Larsen, and Meigs, 1977).

Auditing has expanded in scope to include a concern with the organization's economy and efficiency. For example, improved ways for handling the operation of an outpatient center now are included with traditional issues of how to improve the internal control over funds handled by an organization such as a hospital (Bolandis, 1982). Especially for governments and service organizations, auditing concepts serve as useful ways to evaluate program efficiency and effectiveness.

Auditing must be both an internal and an external function. Internal auditors have the responsibility to advise management on ways to improve the efficiency, effectiveness, and results of organizational activities (Mosher, 1979). External auditors, who do many of the same functions as internal auditors, offer a more detached assessment. Many organizations use internal auditors to provide daily advice and guidance, supplemented by external auditors who assess the financial statements at the end of the year, or as needed.

There are two basic approaches to financial auditing. One is called the "tick and turn" method. Under this traditional approach, all financial transactions are examined exhaustively to make sure that each entry conforms to the expected practice.

Development of computerized accounting systems has led to more refined auditing approaches. Sampling of transactions and tests of the accounting system's integrity have replaced the traditional tick and turn approach. Under the improved approach, an auditor makes sure the accounting system generates the right numbers in the right places following data entry; then, a random sample of transactions is reviewed, and their postings are checked. Furthermore, internal controls over cash and securities are reviewed. If no problems exist, the auditor attests to the financial statements in a form similar to the following:

> The examination was made in accordance with generally accepted auditing standards and, accordingly, included such tests of the accounting records and other auditing procedures as we considered necessary in the circumstances.

The American Institute of Certified Public Accountants establishes GAAS. Certified public accountants who deviate from the GAAS may have to justify their actions to their peers. One result of violating professional standards is professional censure.

D. Risk Management

Organizations face a plethora of potential losses. A listing of losses might include liability judgments (including medical malpractice); work-related injuries to employees; employee health care off the job; fire damage to a major operational facility; damage to business automobiles; employee dishonesty; and interruption of operations due to destroyed facilities. Typically, organizations try to protect against loss by purchasing different insurance coverages. Yet, insurance premiums continue to rise even with few, if any, claims.

The current economic environment demands that management carefully scrutinize insurance programs to ensure that losses are prevented or minimized and that alternative financing is explored for the losses which cannot be prevented. Risk management offers a comprehensive agenda for management action (Brown, 1979).

An effective risk management program rests on the identification, measurement, and evaluation of loss exposures. Plus, it includes efforts to reduce and to control hazards leading to potential losses. Equally important, decisions must be made about the actual funding of an organization's risks. Is insurance the best way to finance losses? Should the organization use self-insurance?

Self-insurance is a planned program undertaken by the organization to take more responsibility for loss control and prevention, and includes direct payment of most small or middle-size claims and the use of insurance only for the most catastrophic situations. One result is the opportunity to invest the organization's self-insurance reserves, or funds set aside to offset expected losses.

The investment potential can be substantial, since most claims against a given type of insurance coverage—such as workers' compensation, employee group health insurance, or general liability—are not paid out within the policy year. While claims are incurred during the year, they might not be reported for several years, or the claims might be contested, and the final disposition left unresolved for several years. In fact, fewer than twenty percent of claims under an organization's automobile liability, workers' compensation, and general liability policies are likely to be paid during the policy year. The last claims under these types of policies typically remain outstanding for up to eight or nine years after the policy year. Thus, insurance companies earn interest during the intervening years on the one-half to two-thirds of a premium used to pay valid claims.

Financial officers, in particular, question why insurance firms should be paid to invest the organization's funds (and retain the earned interest) until such time that the money might be used to pay for losses (claims). The result has been a movement toward more effective risk management and the funded retention of risks. The need is not eliminated even when the law is structured to place upper limits on liability exposures, as in dollar caps on medical malpractice exposures.

V. SUMMARY

Financial resources provide organizations with the capability to operate. The acquisition and allocation of adequate financing is the first finance element facing an organization. The constant, almost never-ending quest for adequate financing demands informed leadership. Since few organizations have a pay-as-you-go capability, most have to contend with a portfolio of financing elements, including long-term debt. The allocation of scarce funds is a real test of a manager's ability to balance competing interests.

Funds have to be used to develop more resources. Governments invest in their capital infrastructure in an effort to promote the area's economic development.

Business firms find that returning all profits to shareholders through dividends eventually retards the firm's future. Therefore, the firm's growth is enhanced by reinvesting funds into research and development, acquisition of profitable new lines of business, or capital expansion of existing lines of work.

Hospitals view the acquisition of advanced technology in medical diagnosis and treatment as means of retaining (or acquiring) a health care reputation, patient census, and medical staff. Thus, a combination of effective working capital management practices and the judicious use of long-term financing offers an organization the means for financing today's demands and future needs.

A second element of finance concerns the multifaceted management of acquired resources. Financial transactions require standardized treatment; the accounting system achieves this requirement. Managers, and other users of financial information, need accurate and informative financial reports. Periodic reviews, or audits, of finance-related activities serve to assure interested parties that the actual financial condition is consistent with the stated position as expressed by the organization and its officers.

Another management issue which has gained much attention is risk management. Risk management offers guidance on when and how to transfer loss exposures to insurance companies and when and how to keep the funds operating to the direct advantage of the organization.

Financial management affects the entire organization and its activities. To be most effective, the financial system requires top management attention. Sloppy financial management or inattention to the financial consequences of organizational activities can only raise questions about the organization's continued viability and the resulting loss to the community of the health and human services being delivered.

REFERENCES

Abramson, A. J., and Salamon, L. M. (1986). *The Nonprofit Sector and the New Federal Budget*, The Urban Institute Press, Washington, D.C.

Ameiss, A. P., and Kargas, N. A. (1977). *Accountant's Desk Handbook*, Prentice-Hall, Englewood Cliffs, New Jersey.

Anthony, R. N. (1965). *Planning and Control Systems: Framework for Analysis*, Division of Research, Graduate School of Business Administration, Harvard University, Boston.

Anthony, R. N. (1978). *Financial Accounting in Nonbusiness Organizations*, Financial Accounting Standards Board, Stanford, Connecticut.

Anthony, R. N., and Herzlinger, R. E. (1980). *Management Control in Nonprofit Organizations*, revised edition, Richard D. Irwin, Homewood, Illinois.

Argyris, C. (1975). Budget Pressure: Some Causes and Consequences, *Public Budgeting and Finance*, second edition (R. T. Golembiewski and J. Rabin, eds.) F. E. Peacock Publishers, Itasca, Illinois, pp. 321–327.

Arnstein, W. E., and Gilabert, F. (1980). *Direct Costing*, American Management Association, New York.

Barber, J. D. (1975). Complexity, Synopticism, Incrementalism, and the Real Questions, *Public Budgeting and Finance*, second edition (R. T. Golembiewski and J. Rabin, eds.), F. E. Peacock Publishers, Itasca, Illinois, pp. 137–148.

Bolandis, J. L. (1982). *Hospital Finance*, Aspen Systems Corporation, Rockville, Maryland.

Bourgeois, L. J. (1981). On the measurement of organizational slack, *Academy of Management Review, 6*: 29–39.

Brigham, E. F. (1979). *Financial Management Theory and Practice*, second edition, The Dryden Press, Hinsdale, Illinois.

Brown, B. L. (1979). *Risk Management for Hospitals*, Aspen Systems Corporation, Germantown, Maryland.

Broyles, R. W. (1981). *The Management of Working Capital in Hospitals*, Aspen Systems Corporation, Rockville, Maryland.

Cascio, W. F. (1982). *Costing Human Resources: The Financial Impact of Behavior in Organizations*, Kent Publishing Company, Boston.

Cleverley, W. O. (1986). *Essentials of Health Care Finance*, Aspen Publishers, Rockville, Maryland.

Collins, F., Munter, P., and Finn, D. (1983). Do managers play games with their budgets?, *Management Planning, 32*: 28–34.

Davis, J. W., and Ripley, R. B. (1967). The Bureau of the Budget and executive branch agencies: Notes on their interaction, *Journal of Politics, 29*: 749-769.

Davis, O. A., Dempster, A. H., and Wildavsky, A. (1966). A theory of the budgetary process, *American Political Science Review, 60*: 529-547.

Donaldson, G. (1969). *Strategy for Financial Mobility*, Harvard Business School Press, Boston.

Edwards, A. B. (1981). Managing in the era of limits, *Topics in Health Care Financing, 7*: 1-93.

Fenno, R. (1966). *The Power of the Purse*, Little, Brown & Company, Boston.

Ferejohn, J. (1974). *Pork Barrel Politics*, University of California Press, Berkeley.

Franks, J. R., Broyles, J. E., and Carleton, W. T. (1985). *Corporate Finance*, Wadsworth, Belmont, California.

Gist, J. R. (1977). "Increment" and "base" in the congressional appropriations process, *American Journal of Political Science, 21*: 341-352.

Goodman, S. R. (1975a). *Corporate Treasurer's and Controller's Encyclopedia*, revised, volume 1, Prentice-Hall, Englewood Cliffs, New Jersey.

Goodman, S. R. (1975b). *Corporate Treasurer's and Controller's Encyclopedia*, revised, volume 2, Prentice-Hall, Englewood Cliffs, New Jersey.

Grizzle, G. (1986). Does Budget Format Really Govern the Actions of Budgetmakers? *Public Budgeting and Finance, 6*: 60-70.

Hay, L. E. (1980). *Accounting for Governmental and Nonprofit Entities*, sixth edition, Richard D. Irwin, Homewood, Illinois.

Henke, E. O. (1980). *Introduction to Nonprofit Organization Accounting*, Kent Publishing Company, Boston.

Herkimer, A. G. (1986). *Understanding Hospital Financial Management*, second edition, Aspen Publishers, Rockville, Maryland.

Herzlinger, R. E., and Sherman, H. D. (1980). Advantages of Fund Accounting in Non-Profits, *Harvard Business Review, 58*: 94-105.

Hulpke, J. F., and Watne, D. A. (1976). Budgeting behavior: If, when and how selected school districts hide money, *Public Administration Review, 36*: 667-674.

Jensen, M. C., and Smith, C. W. (1984). *The Modern Theory of Corporate Finance*, McGraw-Hill, New York.

Lamb, R., and Rappaport, S. P. (1980). *Municipal Bonds*, McGraw-Hill, New York.

LeLoup, L. (1978). The myth of incrementalism, *Polity, 10*:488-509.

LeLoup, L., and Moreland, W. (1978). Agency strategies and executive review: The hidden politics of budgeting, *Public Administration Review, 38*: 180-192.

Lindblom, C. (1959). The science of "muddling through," *Public Administration Review, 19*: 78-88.

Lohmann, R. A. (1980). *Breaking Even: Financial Management in Human Service Organizations*, Temple University Press, Philadelphia.

Loscalzo, W. (1982). *Cash Flow Forecasting*, McGraw-Hill, New York.

Lyden, F. J., and Miller, E. G., eds. (1972). *Planning Programming Budgeting: A Systems Approach to Management*, second edition, Markham, Chicago.

Lyden, F. J., and Miller, E. G., eds. (1978). *Public Budgeting, Program Planning and Evaluating*, third edition, Rand McNally, Skokie, Illinois.

Meigs, W. B., Larsen, E. J., and Meigs, R. F. (1977). *Principles of Auditing*, sixth edition, Richard D. Irwin, Homewood, Illinois.

Merchant, K. A. (1981). The design of the corporate budgeting system: Influences on managerial behavior and performance, *Accounting Review, 56*: 813-829.

Merchant, K. A. (1985). Budgeting and the propensity to create budgetary slack, *Accounting, Organizations and Society, 10*: 201-210.

Miller, G. (1982). *A Public Investor's Guide to Money Market Instruments*, Municipal Finance Officers Association, Chicago.

Mishan, E. J. (1976). *Cost-Benefit Analysis*, Praeger, New York.
Moak, L. L. (1982). *Municipal Bonds*, Municipal Finance Officers Association, Chicago.
Moore, C. L., and Jaedicke, R. K. (1980). *Managerial Accounting*, fifth edition, South-Western Publishing Company, Cincinnati.
Mosher, F. C. (1979). *The GAO: The Quest for Accountability in American Government*, Westview Press, Boulder, Colorado.
Onsi, M. (1973). Factor analysis of behavioral variables affecting budgetary slack, *Accounting Review, 48*: 535-548.
Pyhrr, P. A. (1973). *Zero-Base Budgeting: A Practical Management Tool for Evaluating Expenses*, John Wiley and Sons, New York.
Public Securities Association (1981). *Fundamentals of Municipal Bonds*, Public Securities Association, New York.
Rabin, J. (1975). State and local PPBS, *Public Budgeting and Finance*, second edition (R. T. Golembiewski and J. Rabin, eds.), F. E. Peacock Publishers, Itasca, Illinois, pp. 427–446.
Rabin, J., Hildreth, W. B., and Miller, G. J. (1983). *Budget Management*, Institute of Government, University of Georgia, Athens.
Rose, R. (1977). Implementation and evaporation: The record of MBO, *Public Administration Review, 37*: 64–71.
Schick, A. (1966). The road to PPB: The stages of budget reform, *Public Administration Review, 26*: 243-258.
Smith, K. V. (1979). *Guide to Working Capital Management*, McGraw-Hill, New York.
State of Rhode Island (1983). Monitoring performance, *Budget Management* (J. Rabin, W. B. Hildreth, and G. J. Miller, eds.), Institute of Government, University of Georgia, Athens.
Straussman, J. D. (1979). A typology of budgetary environments: Notes on the prospect for reform, *Administration and Society, 11*: 216–226.
Straussman, J. D., and Hahn, G. E. (1978). Budget 'reform' as a technique of managerial assertiveness, *Public Administration Review, 38*: 584–588.
Sundelson, J. W. (1935). Budgetary principles, *Political Science Quarterly, 50*: 236–263.
Tosi, H. L. (1974). The human effects of budgeting systems on management, *MSU Business Topics, 22*: 53–63.
Vargo, R. J. (1977). *Readings in Governmental and Nonprofit Accounting*, Wadsworth Publishing Company, Belmont, California.
Vinter, R. D., and Kish, R. K. (1984). *Budgeting for Not-For-Profit Organizations*, The Free Press, New York.
Wacht, R. F. (1984). *Financial Management in Non-Profit Organizations*, Business Publishing Division, Georgia State University, Atlanta.
Wanat, J. (1974). Bases of budgetary incrementalism, *American Political Science Review, 68*: 1221–1228.
Wildavsky, A. (1964). *The Politics of the Budgetary Process*, Little, Brown & Company, New York.
Wildavsky, A. (1978). A budget for all seasons? Why the traditional budget lasts, *Public Administration Review, 38*: 501–509.
Wildavsky, A. (1985). *Budgeting: A Comparative Theory of Budgetary Processes*, revised edition, Transaction Books, New Brunswick, New Jersey.
Wright, C. (1969). The Concept of a Program Budget, *Program Budgeting and Benefit-Cost Analysis* (H. H. Hinrich and G. M. Taylor, eds.), Goodyear, Santa Monica, pp. 23–32.
Young, S. M. (1985). Participative budgeting: The effects of risk aversion and asymmetric information on budgetary slack, *Journal of Accounting Research, 23*: 829–842.

4

Financial Management in Health Care Organizations

James D. Suver Graduate School of Business Administration, University of Colorado, Denver, Colorado

Kyle L. Grazier* Department of Epidemiology and Public Health, School of Medicine, Yale University, New Haven, Connecticut

I. INTRODUCTION

This chapter focuses on the decisions faced by the organization's financial manager and planner and the techniques available to assist in those decisions. While position titles and the scope of responsibility vary among institutions, the decisions are similar. They involve the effective and efficient allocation of the existing and potential resources of the organization. The resources of interest here are those which can be represented over time by dollars, such as tangible assets, services, and wages for labor. Understanding the past behavior of these resources, and the potential for better use or for substitutability among them provides the basis for short- and long-term budgeting, financing and investment decisions.

The health care industry, when taken as a whole, is extremely diverse in mission, complexity, sophistication, size and age: for example, pharmaceutical companies, medical supply companies, hospitals, clinics, and home care agencies. For purposes of this chapter, emphasis will be on the institution-based service delivery portion of the industry: primarily hospitals and health maintenance organizations (HMOs), regardless of their tax status.

Relative to other industries, managing in this subsector is in many ways unique. Its institutions are subject to a wide array of pricing and payment-related regulations imposed by state, federal, and private agencies, subject to rapidly changing political and legislative environments. In addition, health care institutions differ from many other organizations in that a much higher proportion of their direct costs are labor-related. Many of the institutions are also not for profit, which can affect the recording, use, and sources of funds for operation and investment.

**Present affiliation*: Department of Social and Administrative Health Sciences, School of Public Health, University of California, Berkeley, California.

Sound internal financial planning and management in these health care institutions is based on internally and externally generated information. This is defined, collected, and collated to assist the decision makers to anticipate and respond appropriately to internal needs and externally imposed constraints, which may affect the choice of services to be offered, their prices, expansion of facilities, and even returns on investments.

The chapter provides description and case studies of many of the techniques available to the financial manager and planner. While one chapter cannot provide sufficient detail to make the inexperienced manager proficient, it can expose the reader to financial concepts and the associated translation into the appropriate mechanics.

II. TECHNIQUES TO SUPPORT MANAGEMENT DECISIONS

A. Organizational Analysis

Understanding the organization is crucial to the effective and efficient allocation of resources by the financial manager. The informal as well as the formal organization of responsibility and decision making must be examined. The long-range goals and mission of the organization as stated in the bylaws and as reflected in the attitudes and culture of the organization help inform the manager and planner as to the choice of financial techniques and their efficient application.

One indication of the decision structure and process is the flow of information throughout the organization. Careful study of the decisions made by managers and the managers' perception of the type and timing of the data needed for those decisions can aid in the understanding of the short- and long-range goals of the institution. Knowledge of these goals helps the financial manager in evaluating internally and externally generated alternatives for the institution's resources.

B. Financial Statements

Financial statements represent a vital factor in the administrator's decision-making process. Collectively, they present the financial condition of the organization to management, stockholders, lenders, regulators, and other interested parties. Because typically they are prepared in accordance with generally accepted accounting principles, the information can be analyzed and compared with previous years and, in some cases, with similar institutions. A thorough and continuing analysis of the financial statements can highlight potential problem areas and aid in determining corrective action.

1. Basic Financial Statements

The three primary types of financial statements are the balance sheet, the income statement, and the statement of changes in financial position. Each of these statements has particular strengths and weaknesses for determining the financial condition of the organization. The balance sheet shows the financial position of the organization at any point in time. This can be the end of the year, the end of the month, or any other time desired by the administrator. Its reliability is determined by the accuracy of the accounting information and the appropriateness of generally accepted accounting principles and regulations. The Financial Accounting Standards Board (FASB) and other professional accounting organizations issue guidance through pronouncements and opinions on appropriate accounting practices for presenting fair financial statements. For example, the physical assets of the organizationare typically carried at their initial acquisition costs, while the amounts carried in inventory and accounts receivable are a function of the accuracy of the record-keeping system and the time selected for the report. Some facilities will use the calendar year, January 1 through December 31, as their reported period. Others may use another fiscal period which is more appropriate in terms of patient services and census. For example, a December 31 cutoff date for the balance sheet may have been selected more as a matter of tradition than because it is the proper time to analyze the financial position. December may typically be a low census month, and some other time may be more representative. A typical balance sheet format and the types of accounts are shown in Fig. 1.

The components of the balance sheet are typically classified into definite groupings. For example, current assets include the assets that are expected to be converted into cash or expenses within the current operating period, or within one year. Fixed assets are usually the physical plant and equipment, which are expected to benefit more than one time period. Fixed assets are converted into current expenses through depreciation techniques. The choice of depreciation methods can have major impact on the reported income and tax liability.

Offsetting the asset accounts are the liabilities and equity accounts of the organization. Liabilities consist of both short-term (current liabilities) and long-term debt (payable over more than one year). Equity accounts are composed of the initial capital investment of the owners and the earnings retained in the organization from providing services. Balance sheet accounts are usually considered to be permanent accounts; that is, they do not close at the end of each accounting period.

The income statement measures the results of providing services over a period of time. It, too, is prepared in accordance with generally accepted accounting principles. The accrual method (matching of revenues and expenses), the depreciation method (straight line, accelerated), and the inventory valuation method can have a decided impact on the reported income. Under the accrual method of accounting, and where noncash expenses such as depreciation are included, the income reported on the income statement is not the same as cash; in fact, using this method it is possible to report high income and still experience a serious cash shortage. (This problem will be discussed in greater detail later in this section.) A typical income statement for an HMO is shown in Fig. 2.

The major components of the income statement are the revenue account and the expense account.

Expenses are typically presented on a functional basis and reflect the amounts expended to provide the services responsible for the revenues shown in the income statement.

Income statement accounts are considered to be temporary accounts because they are zeroed out at the end of each accounting period to prepare them for the next accounting period.

2. Statement of Changes in Financial Position

This statement, more commonly known as a source and use of funds statement, provides information on how funds in the organization were obtained, and for what purpose they were used, between two points in time. A comparison of changes in balance sheet accounts between two annual statements provides a basis for preparing the

Consolidated Balance Sheet — December 31, 1985 and 1984

Assets

	1985	1984
Current Assets		
Cash, including short term cash investments of $15,974,000 in 1985 and $18,176,000 in 1984	$18,961,522	$19,139,887
Receivables:		
Group and individual premiums	2,029,613	1,380,549
Interest	231,326	308,417
Overpayment of income tax	423,493	
Officers and shareholders		140,302
Affiliates	253,999	232,183
Other	655,023	320,410
Marketable equity securities (4)	1,538,679	2,374,991
Prepaid expenses	1,176,388	1,062,430
Inventories	481,604	279,689
Restricted cash deposits	970,500	125,000
Total Current Assets	$26,722,147	$25,363,858
Investments		
Marketable equity securities (4)	$2,310,073	$2,529,999
Long term cash investments		2,400,000
Total Investments	$2,310,073	$4,929,999
Equipment and furniture, at cost less accumulated depreciation	$2,721,021	$1,019,572
Notes receivable	681,902	
Organizational costs, less accumulated amortization (1)	1,581,383	742,616
Excess of costs over values assigned to net assets of acquired businesses, less accumulated amortization (10)	2,799,789	3,447,460
Other	169,473	48,875
	$36,985,788	$35,552,380

(See accompanying notes.)

FIGURE 1 A typical consolidated balance sheet. The notes referred to in the footnote are reproduced in Appendix 1.

source-and-use-of-funds or changes-in-financial-position statement. Sources of funds include the net income received from resident care (shown in retained earnings account), an increase in liability accounts, and a decrease in fixed assets accounts. Uses of funds include increases in assets (buying equipment) and decreases in liability accounts (paying of a loan). The sources and uses of funds will be equal over a period of time; the balance sheet accounts reflect this equality. An example of a statement of changes in financial position is shown in Fig. 3.

Consolidated Balance Sheet December 31, 1985 and 1984

Liabilities and Stockholders' Equity

	1985	1984
Current Liabilities		
Accounts payable:		
Hospital claims	$2,584,865	$2,104,262
Capitation fees	552,411	81,000
Other	687,538	537,240
Pending and estimated unreported claims	864,767	1,041,319
Income taxes payable		664,020
Accrued liabilities	559,013	314,322
Unearned premium income	814,987	809,413
Current portion of long term debt (7)	112,064	110,021
Total Current Liabilities	$6,175,645	$5,661,597
Long term debt due after one year (7)	$1,704,443	$1,988,459
Deferred income taxes (10)	368,492	
Commitments (9)		
Minority interest in consolidated subsidiaries and partnerships	943,724	847,849
Stockholders' equity (8 & 10)		
Preferred stock without par value; 1,000,000 shares authorized, none outstanding		
Common stock, without par value -Stated value $.01; 10,000,000 shares authorized 5,435,491 Shares issued (5,435,451 in 1984)	54,355	54,355
Capital in excess of stated value	22,731,162	22,730,694
Retained earnings	8,025,098	4,711,427
	$30,810,615	$27,496,476
Less:		
226,261 Shares (18,761 shares in 1984) common stock held in treasury, at cost	(2,978,405)	(281,842)
Unrealized loss on noncurrent marketable equity securities (4)	(38,726)	(160,159)
Total Stockholders' Equity	$27,793,484	$27,054,475
	$36,985,788	$35,552,380

(See accompanying notes.)

(In addition to the statements in Figs. 1-3, much additional information is available from the footnotes accompanying a statement. Appendix 1 presents some sample footnotes which clarify information contained in this financial statement.)

3. Financial Statement Analysis

An analysis of the financial statements can be accomplished by several methods. Single-point estimates can be obtained for comparison with other institutions, or external standards or a trend can be established to identify possible problem areas. Both point and

Consolidated Statement of Income Years ended December 31, 1985, 1984, 1983

	1985	1984	1983
Revenues:			
Premium income	$56,812,716	$39,951,037	$16,506,941
Pharmaceutical sales	2,531,019	811,241	286,454
Other (principally management and contractual service)	337,073	424,616	664,445
	$59,680,808	$41,186,894	$17,457,840
Expenses:			
Medical	$39,830,916	$28,723,334	$12,101,904
Cost of pharmaceutical sales	1,989,957	734,120	275,866
Compensation and fringe benefits	6,899,753	3,114,372	1,481,019
Contractual services	865,961	455,801	195,687
Facilities	1,360,712	466,445	137,293
General and administrative	4,323,518	2,198,431	542,840
	$55,270,817	$35,692,503	$14,734,609
Operating income	$4,409,991	$5,494,391	$2,723,231
Other income (expense):			
Interest and dividend income	2,438,664	1,725,498	314,652
Interest expense	(242,106)	(197,818)	(51,527)
Net realized and unrealized gain (loss) on marketable equity securities (4)	167,094	(154,240)	
Gain on sale of management contract (2)		263,622	
Income before income taxes and minority	$6,773,643	$7,131,453	$2,986,356
Provision for income taxes (10)			
Current	$2,361,508	$3,020,000	$1,089,200
Deferred	368,492		
	$2,730,000	$3,020,000	$1,089,200
Income before minority interests	$4,043,643	$4,111,453	$1,897,156
Minority interests in consolidated subsidiaries and partnership	729,972	629,375	731,330
Net income	$3,313,671	$3,482,078	$1,165,826
Net income per common share	$0.62	$0.72	$0.35
Weighted average common shares outstanding	5,384,796	4,805,071	3,357,243

(See accompanying notes.)

FIGURE 2 A typical consolidated statement of income.

trend analysis are important for management information, but trend analysis has the added benefit of not requiring external comparison data. Due to the dissimilarity of many institutions, point comparisons can be very misleading. The accounts in the balance sheet and the income statements can be analyzed on a percentage basis. Common-size and vertical analyses provide information on changes in the structure of the statements in terms of percentages. These composition ratios can indicate when profit margins are shrinking and what is causing the decrease—for example, when certain asset categories are increasing in relationship to the total asset structure. An analysis of two statements is generally more effective than single estimates.

Fig. 4 presents a vertical analysis of the income statement, while Fig. 5 presents a common-size analysis of a balance sheet.

Another commonly used analytic technique is the computation and comparison of ratios. Ratios can be grouped into specific management areas to aid in analysis. Four key management areas are as follows:

Liquidity: Can the organization meet its current obligations?
Turnover: Are the organization's assets being used effectively?
Performance: Are the organization's assets being used efficiently?
Capitalization: How are the assets being financed?

A summary of the ratios is included in Table 1.

In addition to the normal financial ratios, there are several performance indicators that can help the administrator manage his or her institution. They are used primarily for internal analysis. Table 2 illustrates a few of the more important areas. Table 3 illustrates the calculation of these ratios using data provided by the financial statements for the HMO (Figs. 1-3). Analysis of these ratios should include comparisons with industry norms and comparisons of the institution's ratios over time.

C. Overview of Budgets

The organizational analysis, the study of the mission and goals of the institution, and the review of the financial statements provide a view of the expected and actual performance of the hospital or HMO over time. Based in part on the information gained from these analyses, the manager can proceed to build a plan for the operation, coordination, evaluation, and control of the many components of the firm which are responsible for short- and long-term viability.

A budget is essentially this plan expressed quantitatively. There are several types of budgets, depending on the function, timing, user needs, and goals of the organization or part of the organization.

Most organizations have or need to have a master budget, the purpose of which is to provide to all managers an overall picture of the needs of the organization. Part of the master budget is the operating budget, which provides detail on the expected revenues and expenses, usually over the next year. The capital budget, a component of the master budget, provides financial information on future needs for capital resources with lives of over one year. The purpose of the capital budget is to force the organization's planners to evaluate carefully the investment choices as to quality of and need for the investment relative to the firm's goals and present and future resources.

Cash budgets, another part of the master budget, are prepared by the manager to ensure that the cash position of the organization is sound at any point in time. Especially

Consolidated Statement of Changes in Financial Position
Years ended December 31, 1985, 1984 and 1983

	1985	1984	1983
Financial resources provided by:			
Operations			
Net income:	$3,313,671	$3,482,078	$1,165,826
Items not affecting working capital:			
Amortization and depreciation	794,201	292,840	65,331
Retirement of equipment and furniture	153,350	11,233	2,119
Write-off of deferred loan costs	--	--	28,750
Working capital provided by operations	4,261,222	3,786,151	1,262,026
Decrease in investments	2,741,359	--	--
Issuance of long term debt	--	2,036,918	--
Increase in deferred income taxes	368,492	--	--
Issuance of common stock	468	14,201,830	8,530,911
Increase in minority interests (net)	95,875	516,753	331,096
Income tax benefit from utilization of prior years' net operating losses used to reduce excess of cost over values assigned to net assets of acquired businesses (Note 10)	750,255	--	--
Consolidation of The Plan, Ltd.	--	--	580,864
Other	6,760	--	--
	8,224,431	20,541,652	10,704,897
Financial resources applied to:			
Purchase of investments	--	5,090,158	--
Increase in organizational and deferred loan costs	1,059,573	733,489	824
Issuance of notes receivable to officers	681,902	--	--
Purchase of equipment and furniture	2,295,605	1,070,053	164,079
Acquisition of minority interests in consolidated subsidiaries	86,625	--	69,487
Excess of cost over values assigned to net assets of acquired businesses	96,752	2,251,799	1,276,756
Decrease in long term debt	342,572	48,459	450,000
Net additions to other assets	120,598	48,875	--
Acquisition of common stock for treasury	2,696,563	281,842	--
Net noncurrent assets of acquired subsidiaries	--	--	72,726
	7,380,190	9,524,675	2,033,872
Increase in working capital	$844,241	$11,016,977	$8,671,025

See page 2 for changes in components of working capital.
See notes in Exhibit IV.

FIGURE 3 Typical consolidated statement of changes in financial position.

Years ended December 31, 1985, 1984 and 1983

	1985	1984	1983
Changes in components of working capital:			
Increase (decrease) in current assets:			
Cash and short term cash investments	$(178,365)	$8,204,942	$10,680,694
Receivables	1,211,593	2,041,717	198,443
Marketable equity securities	(836,312)	2,374,991	--
Prepaid expenses and other	113,958	976,646	74,207
Inventories	201,915	231,262	25,163
Restricted cash deposits	845,500	(7,996)	132,996
	1,358,289	13,821,562	11,111,503
Increase (decrease) in current liabilities:			
Accounts payable	1,102,312	1,876,485	790,677
Pending and estimated unreported claims	(176,552)	657,846	383,473
Income taxes payable	(664,020)	(454,080)	1,054,612
Accrued liabilities	244,691	223,169	40,018
Unearned premium income	5,574	606,144	203,269
Current portion of long term debt	2,043	(104,979)	215,000
Other	--	--	(246,571)
	514,048	2,804,585	2,440,478
Increase in working capital	$844,241	$11,016,977	$8,671,025

(See accompanying notes.)

in health care, receipt of payment from the many third-party payers may not coincide with the need to meet weekly or monthly payrolls or pay for equipment or contractual services from another organization. Planning for these needs through the cash budget minimizes the dangers from cash crises.

Program budgets are often prepared by planners in organizations in which many of the services are program-based, such as home care programs or primary care programs Often these special programs require services or resources from several different parts of the organization, and special budgetary efforts are expended to ensure coordination of fiscal needs.

Each of these budgets can be prepared and revised at any time the manager or planner chooses, since the budgets are tools for effective management and should therefore meet the specific decision-making needs of the manager. Most budgeting is done at least on an annual basis, although continuous budgeting is used in some hospitals and long-range budgets are often prepared only once every five years. The choice of timing should, however, be fine-tuned to the organization, and variations in timing should be adopted as needed.

Once the master budget has been prepared, pro forma financial statements can be constructed to express the impact on the financial condition of the organization if the plan is followed.

Income Statement Vertical Analysis

Revenues			
Premium income	56,812,716		95%
Sales	2,531,019		4%
Contractual service	337,073		1%
		59,680,808	100%
Expenses			
Medical	39,830,916		72%
Cost of pharmaceutical sales	1,989,957		4%
Compensation	6,899,753		12%
Facilities	1,360,712		2%
General and administrative	4,323,518		8%
Contractual services	865,961		2%
		55,270,817	100%
Operating income		4,409,991	
Other income (expense)			
Interest and dividend income	2,438,661		
Interest expense	(242,106)		
Net realized and unrealized gain on securities	167,094		
Income before income taxes and minority interests		6,773,643	
Provision for income taxes			
Current	2,361,508		
Deferred	368,492		
Income before minority interests		4,043,643	
Net income		3,313,671	

FIGURE 4

D. Budgeting for Operations

Preparing the operating budget requires the commitment and cooperation of top management and decision makers throughout the organization. Substantial revenue and expense data, statistical data which permit longitudinal and cross-sectional analysis of the operational indicators, and a determination of the appropriate inflation indicators for salaries, equipment, food, supplies, and so on are needed to achieve an effective, useful operating budget. Also required is a basic understanding of the behavior of costs within the organization.

1. Cost Behavior

Costs can be expressed as they relate to changes in activities such as occupancy rates, patient-days, patient mix, services provided, and meals served. A fixed cost is a cost that does not change with the level of activity. For example, the administrator's salary will not change with the number of residents. This does not mean it cannot be changed, but it

Balance Sheet Common Size Analysis

Current assets		
Cash	18,961,522	
Receivables	3,593,454	
Marketable securities	1,538,679	
Prepared expenses	1,176,388	
Inventories	481,604	
Restricted cash deposits	970,500	
Total current assets	26,722,147	72%
Investments		
Total investments	2,310,073	6%
Equipment and furniture	2,721,021	7%
Other assets	5,232,547	14%
total assets	36,985,788	
Current liabilities		
Accounts payable	3,824,814	
Pending claims	864,767	
Income taxes payable	--	
Accrued liabilities	559,013	
Unearned premium income	814,987	
Current portion long term debt	112,064	
Total current liabilities	6,175,645	17%
Long term debt due after one year	1,704,443	5%
Deferred income tax	368,492	
Minority interests	943,724	
Stockholders equity	27,793,484	
Total liabilities	36,985,788	

FIGURE 5

changes as a function of management decision rather than of occupancy level. Variable costs, on the other hand, are costs that vary directly with volume. For example, raw food costs will vary with the number of meals served; the costs of drugs and pharmacy items can vary with the number of patients served. Fixed and variable costs are illustrated graphically in Fig. 6.

In addition to the total cost approach displayed in Fig. 6, the administrator must also make the per-unit comparisons. The cost per individual service is usually expressed a as a per-unit basis for reimbursement rate setting and billing activities. Variable costs are the same for each individual unit of service. For example, the cost for one type of test is \$10.00; for two tests, \$20.00; for three tests, \$30.00. This cost relationship can be expressed graphically, as shown in Fig. 7.

In determining the per-unit cost, the allocation of the fixed-cost component present a difficult challenge. Since per-unit modalities are obtained by dividing total fixed costs by the level of activity provided, the more units provided, the lower the per-unit costs. As most experienced institutional administrators have determined, the level of occupancy is of vital concern for financial well-being. This is caused by the heavy fixed-cost nature of most health care facilities. The per-unit fixed costs are illustrated in Fig. 8.

TABLE 1 Summary of Ratios

I. Liquidity

Current ratio $= \dfrac{\text{Current assets}}{\text{Current liabilities}}$

Quick ratio $= \dfrac{\text{Current assets} - \text{inventories} - \text{outdated accounts receivable}}{\text{Current liabilities}}$

Acid test $= \dfrac{\text{Cash}}{\text{Current liabilities}}$

Daily cash flow $= \dfrac{\text{Operating expenses} - \text{depreciation} + \text{debt payments} \quad \text{purchases of fixed assets}}{\text{Days in period}}$

Days of cash flow available $= \dfrac{\text{Cash}}{\text{Daily cash flow}}$

Days of cash available $= \dfrac{\text{Cash (in banks)}}{\text{Daily cash flow}}$

Times fixed charges $= \dfrac{\text{Revenues in excess of expenses from operations} + \text{fixed charges}}{\text{Fixed charges}}$

Debt service ratio $= \dfrac{\text{Revenues in excess of expenses from operation} + \text{interest} + \text{depreciation} + \text{annual debt service requirements}}{\text{Annual debt service}}$

Working capital per bed $= \dfrac{\text{Working capital}}{\text{Available beds}}$

II. Turnover Ratios

Asset turnover $= \dfrac{\text{Net operating revenue}}{\text{Total assets}}$

Fixed asset turnover $= \dfrac{\text{Net operating revenue}}{\text{Fixed assets}}$

Current asset turnover $= \dfrac{\text{Net operation revenue}}{\text{Current assets}}$

Cash turnover $= \dfrac{\text{Net operating revenue}}{\text{Cash}}$

Accounts receivable turnover $= \dfrac{\text{Net operating revenue}}{\text{Accounts receivable}}$

Inventory turnover $= \dfrac{\text{Net operating revenue}}{\text{Inventory}}$

TABLE 1 *(continued)*

$$\text{Average daily patient revenue} = \frac{\text{Net operating revenue}}{\text{Number of days}}$$

$$\text{Average collection period} = \frac{\text{Net accounts receivable}}{\text{Average daily patient revenue}}$$

$$\text{Average daily operating expenses} = \frac{\text{Operating expenses}}{\text{Number of days}}$$

$$\text{Accounts payable payment period} = \frac{\text{Current liabilities}}{\text{Average daily operating expenses}}$$

III. Performance Ratios

$$\text{Operating margin} = \frac{\text{Revenues in excess of expenses from operations}}{\text{Gross revenues}}$$

$$\text{Return on assets} = \frac{\text{Revenues in excess of expenses from operations}}{\text{Total assets}}$$

$$\text{Return on equity} = \frac{\text{Revenues in excess of expenses from operations}}{\text{Total equities}}$$

$$\text{Prefinancing return on assets} = \frac{\text{Revenues in excess of expenses from operations + interest}}{\text{Total assets}}$$

$$\text{Prefinancing return on equity and long-term debt} = \frac{\text{Revenues in excess of expenses from operations + interest}}{\text{Total equities - long-term debt}}$$

IV. Capitalization Ratios

$$\text{Total debt to net worth} = \frac{\text{Total debt}}{\text{Net worth}}$$

$$\text{Long-term debt to net worth} = \frac{\text{Long-term debt}}{\text{Net worth and long-term debt}}$$

$$\text{Total debt to total capitalization} = \frac{\text{Total debt}}{\text{Net worth and liabilities}}$$

*Adapted from Suver, J. D., and Neumann, B. R. (1981). *Management Accounting for Health Care Organizations*, HFMA, Oakbrook, Illinois, ch. 11.

TABLE 2 Key Performance Indicators

Laundry per pound	=	$\frac{\text{Laundry expenses}}{\text{Pounds processes (wet or dry)}}$
Dietary per meal	=	$\frac{\text{Dietary expenses}}{\text{Meals served}}$
Wages per man-hour	=	$\frac{\text{Payroll expenses}}{\text{Total man-hours}}$ or $\frac{\text{Payroll expenses - salaries}}{\text{Total hours reported by hourly employees}}$
Nursing wages per bed	=	$\frac{\text{Nursing salaries}}{\text{Nursing hours}}$
Revenue per bed	=	$\frac{\text{Net operating revenues}}{\text{Licensed beds}}$
Total assets per bed	=	$\frac{\text{Total beds}}{\text{Licensed beds}}$
Long-term debt per bed	=	$\frac{\text{Total long-term debt}}{\text{Licensed beds}}$
FTE per bed	=	$\frac{\text{Total full-time equivalent employees}}{\text{Licensed beds}}$
Revenue per FTE	=	$\frac{\text{Net operating revenues}}{\text{FTE employees}}$
Total assets per FTE	=	$\frac{\text{Total assets}}{\text{FTE employees}}$
Payroll per FTE employee	=	$\frac{\text{Payroll expenses}}{\text{FTE employees}}$

*Adapted from Suver, J. D., and Neumann, B. R. (1981). *Management Accounting for Health Care Organizations*, HFMA, Oakbrook, Illinois, ch. 11.

2. Related Cost Definitions

In addition to the fixed and variable cost behavior dichotomy, the administrator must also be aware of other cost classifications. One of the more useful categorizations is direct and indirect costs. Direct costs are costs that can be traced directly to the cost objective being measured. For example, the cost of the food, the cost of the dietitian, the cost of the cooks and servers, and the cost of the equipment used in preparing the meal are all direct costs of the meal. Conversely, costs that are necessary but are not directly involved with the meal preparation are indirect costs. Indirect costs include the administrator's salary, the business office, and the housekeepers. These are part of the total cost of preparing the meal, but since they cannot be traced directly to meal preparation, they must be allocated through some subjective means. The distinction between direct and indirect costs is vital in responsibility accounting and reporting. By separating costs into direct and indirect categories, supervisors can be held accountable for costs they can control. An example of this type of report is illustrated in Fig. 9.

Incremental costs are particularly useful for management decision making. Under this concept, only the costs that change with a decision being considered are relevant to the decision. For example, for an administrator deciding between two new stoves for the dietary department, the cost of the food and the cost of the preparers would not be factors—unless they varied between the two alternatives. Similarly, the salary of the dietitian and other administrative costs would not be considered.

The concept of opportunity costs can pose difficulties for the inexperienced administrator because this type of cost does not appear in the financial records. Basically, opportunity costs are the benefits that would be received from other alternatives to the course of action being recommended. For example, converting a resident room into a supply area results in the opportunity costs being the revenues forgone by the removal of the bed.

Sunk costs are costs that have been capitalized and cannot be changed by new decisions. Capitalized costs are assets which cannot be completely written off in the year of purchase. Typically, these assets are items of equipment that benefit more than one operating period (a bed, a stove, a typewriter). These assets are converted to expenses by the means of periodic depreciation charges. Over the useful life of the assets, depreciation charges result in the recovery of the purchase price of the asset as a noncash expense against the revenue of the facility. The amount of the asset that is undepreciated is shown on the balance sheet as an asset minus the accumulated depreciation charges. This net amount is called the book value of the asset. For example, the replacement of the stoves in the dietary department will result in the removal of the old stoves. If the stoves still have an undepreciated book value of $2,000, this $2,000 should not be considered in the purchase decision. The $2,000 cost will be the same under either alternative, replaced or not. For tax purposes, the $2,000 book value will be written off either as a depreciation expense (if not replaced) or, in most cases, as a capital loss (if it is replaced). In either case, the $2,000 cost remains the same. The timing impact on taxes to be paid would be an incremental cost to the decision and should be considered due to the time value of money.

3. Overhead Costs

Overhead, or indirect, costs can represent a significant part of the total costs of the institution. Costs that cannot be traced directly to the provision of patient services typically fall into the "overhead" area. For example, the salaries of the administrator, the clerical staff, the accounting staff, and the housekeeping staff, as well as general housekeeping costs, are overhead costs. These costs are difficult to control because, while they are necessary, they are typically not directly related to the provision of a resident service. Thus, they do not directly provide revenues to the institution.

In addition, because there is no direct relationship between revenues and costs, it is difficult to determine what should be the "correct" amount of these costs—that is, when they should be expanded and when they should be cut. For example, what should be the size of a business office? How many accountants, clerks, and so on are needed? What type of equipment do they require? How much space should be allotted to them?

TABLE 3

I. Liquidity

Current ratio	= Current assets / Current liabilities	= $26,722,147 / $6,175,645	= 4.19
Quick ratio	= (Current assets − inventories − outdated accounts receivable[a]) / Current liabilities	= ($26,722,147 (481,604) (359,345)) / $6,175,645	= 4.19
Acid test	= Cash / Current liabilities	= $18,961,522 / $6,175,645	= 3.07
Daily cash flow	= (Operating expenses − depreciation[b] + debt payments[c] + purchases of fixed assets[d]) / Days in period	= ($55,270,817 (440,806) 1,816,507 2,295,605) / 365	= $161,485

II. Turnover Ratios

Asset turnover	= Net operating revenue / Total assets	= $4,409,991 / $36,985,788	= 0.12
Fixed asset turnover	= Net operating expense / Fixed assets	= $4,409,991 / $2,721,021	= 1.62
Current asset turnover	= Net operating revenue / Current assets	= $4,409,991 / $26,722,147	= 0.17
Accounts receivable turnover	= Net operating revenue / Accounts receivable	= $4,409,991 / $3,593,454	= 1.23
Inventory turnover	= Net operating revenue / Inventory	= $4,409,991 / $481,604	= 9.16
Average daily patient revenue	= Net operating revenue / Number of days	= $4,409,991 / 365	= $12,082
Average collection period	= Net accounts receivable / Average daily patient revenue	= $3,593,454 / $12,082	= 297.42 days
Average daily operating expense	= Operating expense / Number of days	= $55,270,817 / 365	= $151,427
Accounts payable payment period	= Current liabilities / Average daily operating expense	= $6,175,645 / $151,427	= 40.78 days

TABLE 3 *(continued)*

III. Performance Ratios

Operating margin	=	Revenues in excess of expenses from operations[e] / Gross revenues	=	\$4,409,991 / \$59,680,808	=	0.07
Return on assets	=	Revenues in excess of expenses from operations[a] / Total assets	=	\$4,409,991 / \$36,985,788	=	0.12
Return on equity	=	Revenues in excess of expenses from operations + interest[f] / Total equity	=	\$6,848,655 / \$27,793,484	=	0.25
Prefinancing return on and long-term debt	=	Revenues in excess of expenses from operations + interest[b] / Total equities + long-term debt[g]	=	\$6,848,655 / \$30,810,143	=	0.22
Prefinancing return on assets	=	Revenues in excess of expenses from operations + interest[b] / Total assets	=	\$6,848,655 / \$36,985,788	=	0.19

IV. Capitalization Ratios

Total debt to net worth	=	Total debt[h] / Net worth	=	\$9,192,304 / \$30,810,615	=	0.30
Long-term debt to total capitalization	=	Long-term debt[j] / Net worth and long-term debt	=	\$3,016,659 / \$33,827,724	=	0.09
Total debt to capitalization	=	Total debt / Net worth and liabilities	=	\$9,192,304 / \$36,986,260	=	0.25

[a]Outdated accounts receivable were calculated as 10% of total accounts receivable for that year.

[b]Depreciation has been calculated by:

Balance 1984	\$1,019,572
Purchase 1985	\$2,295,605
Retirement	(\$153,350)
Balance 1985	(\$2,721,021)
Expense due to depreciation	\$440,806

All entries are taken from the changes in financial statement.

[c]Debt payments include long-term debt after one year and current portion due.

[d]Purchases of fixed assets was taken from the changes in financial statement.

[e]Operating income.

[f]Operating income plus interest and dividend income.

[g]The difference between (total liabilities and stockholders' equity) minus total current liabilities.

[h](Total liabilities and stockholders' equity) minus total stockholders' equity.

[i]Stockholders' equity plus capital in excess of stated value and retained earnings.

[j]Long-term debt plus deferred income taxes, commitments and minority interests.

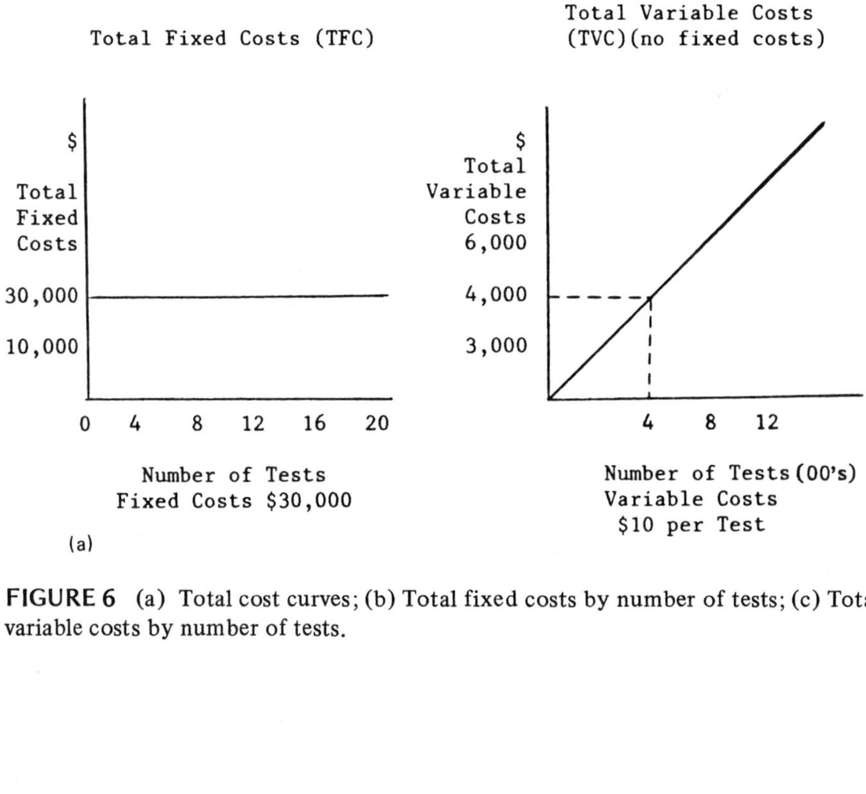

FIGURE 6 (a) Total cost curves; (b) Total fixed costs by number of tests; (c) Total variable costs by number of tests.

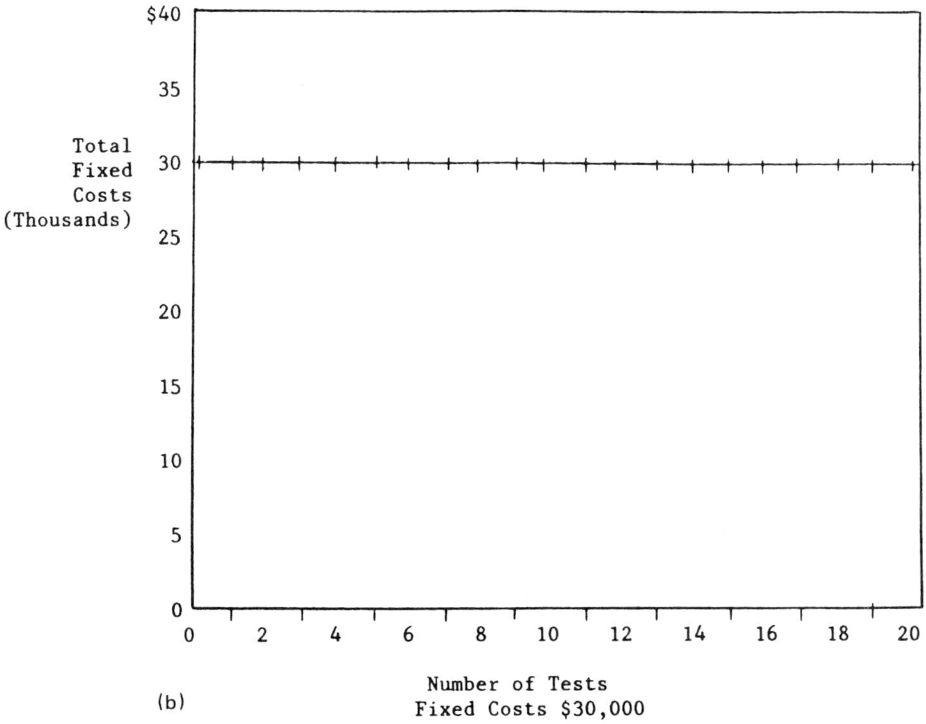

(b)

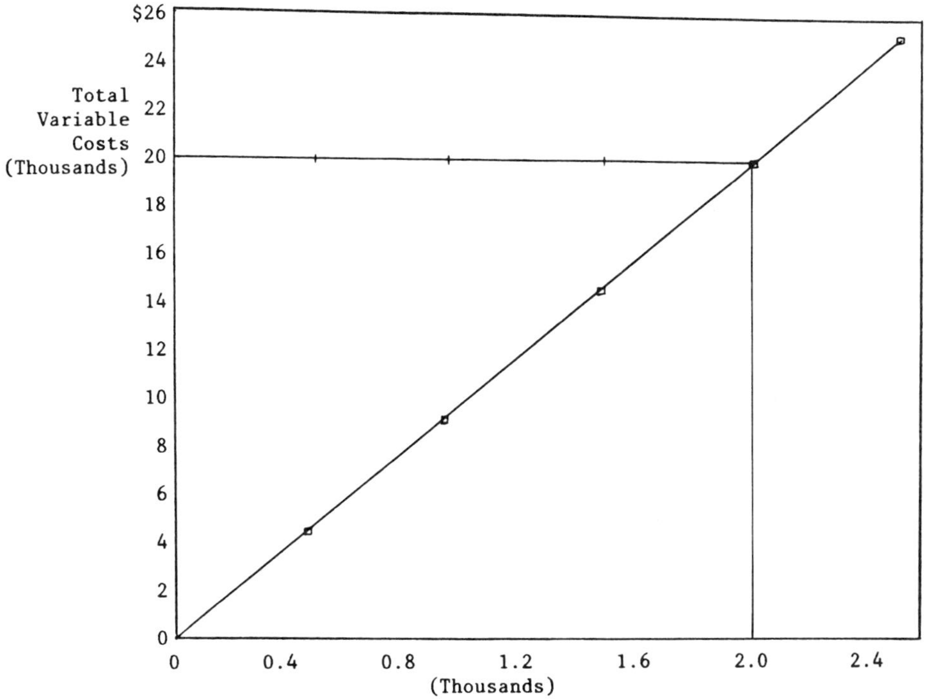

(c)

FIGURE 6 *(continued)*

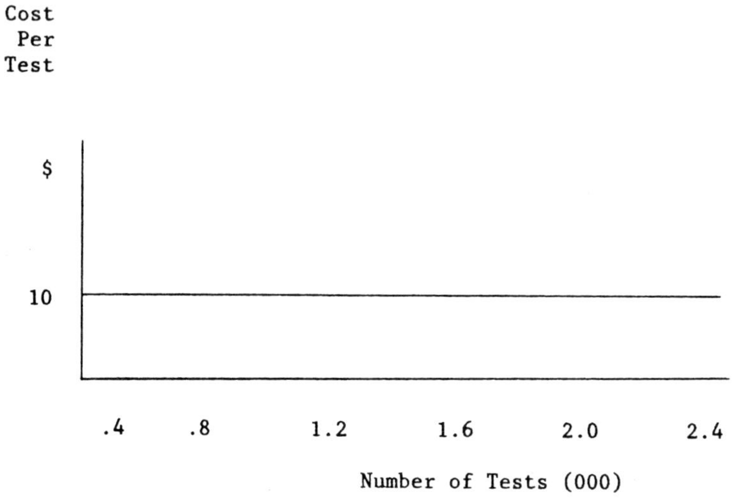

FIGURE 7 Per test variable cost curve.

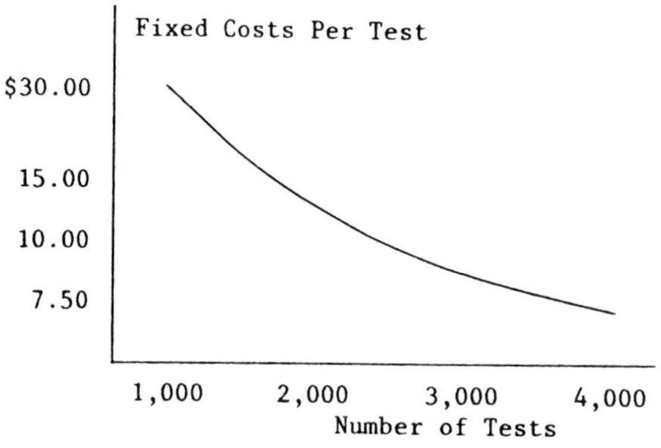

Total Fixed Costs $30,000
Average Fixed Cost Per Test

(1) Number of Tests	(2) Average Fixed Costs	(3) Total Fixed Cost (1 x 2 = 3)
1,000	$30.00	$30,000
2,000	$15.00	$30,000
3,000	$10.00	$30,000
4,000	$ 7.50	$30,000

FIGURE 8 Per test fixed cost curve.

Responsibility Center Reporting

Activities Department for the Month of May, 198X	$	%
Gross operating revenues	$3,300	110
Deduct allowances	300	10
Net revenues	$3,000	100
Controllable operating expenses		
Variable costs	450	15
Contribution margin	$2,550	85
Controllable fixed costs	2,280	76
Controllable operating margin	$270	09
Allocated costs	1,500	50
Net operating margin (loss)	($1,230)	(41)

Census Days			Occupancy %		
Budgeted	Actual	Volume	Budgeted	Actual	Volume
100	90	10	94%	85%	9%

FIGURE 9

These decisions–and their resultant costs–are not directly related to the number of patient-days, number of procedures performed, and so forth, but they are in essential part of providing quality service to clients or patients. In order to determine the full cost of providing such services, therefore, it is necessary to devise some method of allocating a "fair" share of the overhead costs to each activity being performed.

4. Allocation Methods

The allocation of overhead costs to the various activities of the organization requires the development of an overhead charge per unit of service. Overhead charges are basically average shares of the total overhead costs which can be applied to the service performed. The total overhead costs can be determined from the budget before the period of operation and from the accounting system at the end of the period. These total overhead costs are divided by the activity base selected to obtain the overhead charge (total overhead costs divided by volume). Each unit of service receives an estimated share of the overhead cost through this average rate. For example, the business office costs could be allocated on the basis of the number of employees in each section. Facility administration costs could be allocated according to the number of users or patients. Recreational center costs could be allocated according to the number of users or the total number of residents.

In hospitals and HMOs that rely on federal or state monies for payment of services or for programs, the allocation method is determined by regulation. Medicaid programs have often modeled their requirements on federal Medicare program allocation methods, and although the federal payment system has changed for hospitals and HMOs, many state programs still reimburse hospitals in traditional ways.

Medicare has traditionally required a cost finding and allocation method which attributed indirect and direct costs only to Medicare beneficiaries. The regulations specify the total methodology, including the allocation bases, such as square footage or pounds of laundry, and the step-down allocation order.

Institutional managers are finding other methods of cost finding and allocation more useful for internal decision making, costing, and budgeting. The introduction of computer packages into finance departments has simplified use of more sophisticated methods, such as the algebraic method, as it is called. Under this method algebraic equations are defined to represent the relative proportions of costs borne or contributed by each support and service department, and then solved simultaneously to provide a more accurate allocation formula. These types of alternatives to the traditional step-down methods will grow in use as their value is realized and as computer packages make their manipulation more time-efficient.

5. Pricing Services

Often, the allocation and depreciation methods are not the only items determined by third-party reimbursers. Frequently specified is the charge or rate an institution must charge for a particular service. In other instances, competition determines the charge to the patient. And in others, internal managers set a price based on the volume of services expected or realized.

While there are many ways to determine the fair price for services, the most common method seems to be to use the estimate of the full cost of providing the service, which includes the variable costs of providing the service, allocation of the appropriate overhead, and the addition of a profit margin. Obviously, the volume of services projected and actually delivered is a critical factor in this pricing determination. Modeling the cost, volume, and profit relationship can assist the accuracy of our efforts.

6. Cost/Volume/Profit Models

Based on our understanding of cost behavior, a management accounting tool can be developed which will enable the administrator to make better estimates of what the rate or the volume should be, or to assess the impact of changes in variable or fixed costs. To review our understanding of cost behavior, the following definitions are presented:

Variable costs are assumed to vary directly in proportion to the volume of services provided.

Fixed costs are assumed not to vary with volume changes.

Given these two basic assumptions, the cost structure for the facility can be expressed as follows:

1. Total costs (TC) = total variable costs (TVC) + total fixed costs (TFC), or TC = TVC + TFC.
2. Total variable costs (TVC) = variable costs per unit of service (VCU) × volume of service (Q), or TVC = VCU × Q.* Therefore, equation one can be also expressed as TC = TFC + (VCU × Q).

*Total variable costs can also be expressed as a percentage of total revenues (TR). For example: $\frac{TVC}{TR}$ or $\frac{40{,}000}{100{,}000} = .4\ TR$.

3. Average cost per unit of service

$$\frac{TC}{Q} = \frac{TFC}{Q} + \frac{TVC}{Q}$$

$$\frac{TC}{Q} = ATC$$

$$\frac{TFC}{Q} = AFC$$

$$\frac{TVC}{Q} \text{ or } \frac{(VCU)(Q)}{Q} = AVC$$

The first three equations can be expressed as the following model when revenues and profits requirements are introduced.

4. Total revenues = Rate per service (R) × quantity of service (Q).
5. Desired profit (I) can be expressed as a dollar requirement or as a percentage of total revenue requirement and on a before- or after-tax basis.

After-tax dollar requirement $= I$

Before-tax dollar requirement $= \dfrac{I}{(1 - \text{rax rate})}$

After-tax percentage $= \%\,TR$

Before-tax percentage requirement $= \dfrac{\%\,TR}{(1 - \text{tax rate})}$

6. The summary and complete model can be expressed as

TR = TC + I

or

$$R \times Q = TFC + (VCU)(Q) + \frac{I}{1 - \text{tax rate}}$$

Some examples of how this can be used are shown below:

(A) Determine the number of tests that must be offered to obtain a desired level of profit. Given

R = \$30 per test
TFC = \$30,000
VCU = \$10.00
I = \$5,000 (after taxes)
Tax rate = 34%
Q = unknown quantity of tests
R × Q = TFC + (VCU × Q) + I/(1 - rax rate)
\$30 × Q = \$30,000 + (\$10.00 × Q) + \$5,000/(1 -0.34)
Q = 1,879 tests

Therefore, 1,879 tests would have to be accomplished given the rate, cost, and desired profit constraints. If this is not a reasonable number of tests to be performed, the constraints will need to be changed to meet the environment.

(B) For example, assume, in the following problem, only 2,000 tests could be performed due to physical constraints of staff and equipment. What rate would have to be established to meet the cost and profit requirements? Given

R = unknown rate per test
TFC = \$30,000
VCU = \$10.00
I = \$5,000 (after taxes)
Tax rate = 34%
Q = 2,000 tests

$$R \times Q = TFC + (VCU \times Q) + I/(1 - \text{tax rate})$$

$$R = (TFC + (VCU \times Q + I/[1 - \text{rax rate}])/Q$$

$$R = \frac{\$30{,}000 + (\$10.00 \times 2{,}000) + \$5{,}000/(1 - 0.34)}{2{,}000}$$

$$R = \$28.79 \text{ per test}$$

Any of the answers in these examples can be verified by completing a simplified income statement.

Total revenue	2,000 x \$28.79	=	\$57,580
Variable costs	2,000 x \$10.00	=	20,000
Contribution margin	2,000 x \$18.79	=	\$37,580
TFC	\$30,000	=	30,000
Income before taxes		=	\$7,580
Tax rate 34%		=	2,580
Income after taxes		=	\$5,000

E. Capital Budgeting

Capital investment requirements should be derived from the organization's objectives. These objectives should be based on community needs, the competitive market, and the profit requirements of the owners. Properly motivated department supervisors are usually the best source of capital investment proposals. It becomes the task of the administrator and the financial management team to evaluate and prioritize the proposals.

1. Framework for Analysis

There are two major aspects in the analysis of capital investment proposals: qualitative and quantitative. The first and most important is typically the qualitative issue. Such factors as quality of care, improved employee morale, and other intangible benefits are usually decided on subjective issues. However, most proposals also have a quantitative side. It is in the analysis of quantitative factors that considerable improvement can be made.

Every capital investment proposal requires information on five quantitative factors:

1. The cash outflow
2. The cash inflow
3. The economic life
4. The opportunity cost for funds
5. The impact of taxation or cost-based reimbursement

Graphically, these factors can be diagrammed as shown in Fig. 10.

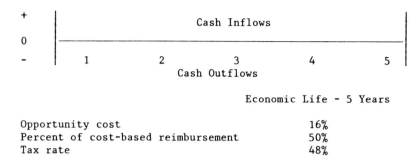

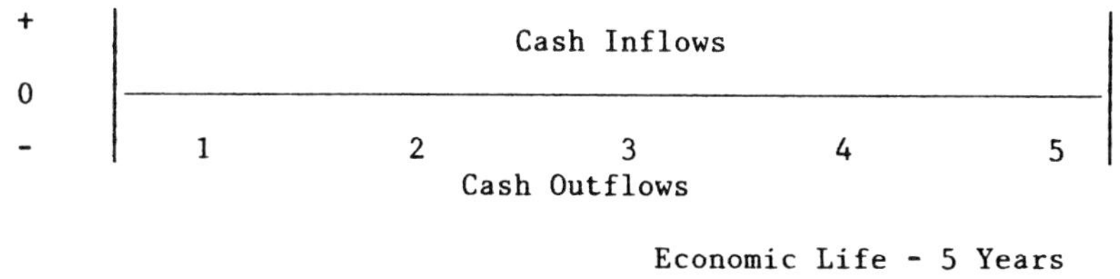

Opportunity cost	16%
Percent of cost-based reimbursement	50%
Tax rate	48%

FIGURE 10 The capital investment framework.

Each of these factors is explained in greater detail below. Cash outflows represent the amount of cash required for the investment proposal. This amount should include the purchase cost, any installation costs, and any other out-of-pocket costs that are associated with this decision.

Cash inflows consist of any additional revenues associated with the decision, including any personnel or material savings and other types of negative cash outflows.

The economic life can be defined as the period of time during which the facility is expected to receive the benefits. It should not be confused with the physical life (although it does set the upper limit on benefits) or the depreciation period established by the Internal Revenue Service (IRS) or third-party payers. The economic life of the proposal should be consistent with the cash outflows and inflow analysis.

The opportunity cost refers to the benefits received from the next best alternative use of the investment funds. Some facilities use the interest rate on invested funds or a weighted average cost of available funds (the cost-of-capital concept). No matter what technique is used, it is, in the end, a subjective estimate by management on what rate to use.

In the case of proprietary institutions, the tax rate will reduce any savings realized from the investment proposal. Similarly, the percentage of cost-based payers will also reduce any savings achieved through the investment decision. Cost-based payers will also fund their share of the depreciation and interest expense, which will add to the cash flow.

2. Methods of Analysis

Once the estimates have been made of the major factors discussed above, the evaluation process can begin. There are two problems in evaluating capital investment decisions. The first is a screening problem: Does the investment meet the minimum return on investment criteria of the organization? The second is a ranking problem: Given the number of investment proposals, how do we prioritize them? This is particularly sensitive when you have a capital rationing problem or more projects than you have funds available.

Several techniques are currently in use.

1. The accounting rate of return (sometimes called the unadjusted rate of return)
2. The payback method
3. The present-value and time-adjusted rates of return methods

Each of these has its strengths and weaknesses, and all of them should be thoroughly understood if they are to be used effectively.

1. The accounting rate of return was used exclusively in part (if any technique was used at all) because it closely approximates the normal reporting of financial information. The increase in income as reported on the Statement of Revenue and Expenses is divided by either the total or the average investment. The resulting rate of return is considered in determining whether or not to make the investment. This technique, although easy to understand, has a serious conceptual weakness in that it does not consider the time value of money: It considers the value of a dollar at some point in the future to be the same as its value today.

The accounting rate of return can be computed by using the following formula:

$$\frac{I_a \text{ (average increase in income)}}{O_t \text{ or } O_a \text{ (either the total or the average investment required to obtain the increase in income)}} = \text{Accounting rate of return}$$

2. The payback method refers to the amount of time it takes to recover the cash outflow for the investment from the cash inflows. This method is quite easy to compute and understand, but it has two weaknesses: It ignores the time value of money, and it disregards the cash inflows after the payback period.

$$\frac{O_t \text{ (cash outflow)}}{I_o \text{ (cash inflow)}} = \text{Payback period}$$

Both of the first two methods ignore the time value of money. That is, they treat dollars equally at different points in time. This can be particularly troublesome in the capital investment process when the cash outflows occur early in the investment time frame, while the cash inflows occur later. The time value of money attempts to correct this deficiency by using discount techniques to put all dollar amounts on an equal basis.

3. Discounting can be better understood if we consider the normal compounding techniques with which most individuals are familiar. Banks and savings and loan companies use this technique to compute future value of an investment. For example, if you were to set aside $10,000 today in a ten percent savings account to pay for a future replacement of equipment, what would the account balance be in five years? This can be computed using the normal compound formula of $(1 + i)^n$ where n equals the period of time and i equals the interest paid by the savings and loan. For managers who do not want to calculate the amount, tables are available which solve the compounding equation. Following is the methodology for this approach.

Compounding of a single sum

Amount of investment today	$10,000
Compounding factor, five years, ten percent	1.611
Future value of $10,000 after five years at 10 percent	$16,110

The relationship of compounding to discounting can be illustrated in the following manner. Assume that administrators want to replace a piece of equipment in five years, and that it will then cost $16,110. How much should they invest today to have $16,110 in five years? We are now interested in the present value of a future sum, which is very different from the first problem, of determining the future value of a present sum. The formula for computing the present value of a future sum is $1/(1 + i)^n$, or the reciprocal of the compound formula. Tables have also been constructed to facilitate this type of computation. This approach is illustrated as follows:

Present value of future amount

Amount needed at the end of the fifth year	$16,110
Present-value factor, ten percent, five years	.621
Present amount that must be invested	$10,004.31 (Slight difference due to rounding)

The relationship between compounding and discounting should now be clear. The same relationship exists when you must consider the type of problem where annual sums are to be invested or received. For example, instead of a $10,000 initial investment, suppose we plan on investing $2,500 a year for five years. What will be the amount in the savings account if we can earn ten percent on the investment?

Amount invested annually for five years	$2,500
Compounding factor, ten percent, five years	6.105
Future value of savings account	$15,263

To consider a similar problem involving the concept of present value, we can ask what would we pay today for the right to receive $2,500 a year for five years if our opportunity cost for investment is ten percent.

Amount to be received for four years	$2,500
Discount factor, ten percent, five years	3.79
Present value of $2,500 a year for five years	$9,475

In other words, the right to receive $2,500 a year for five years in the future is worth $9,475 if our opportunity cost is ten percent. Since the present-value concept is most appropriate to the capital investment process, we will focus our attention on this technique.

The present-value approach to evaluating capital investment decisions compares the discounted cash outflows and the discounted cash inflows. The difference between the two is the present value of the decision. This amount can be either negative or positive. A positive net present value indicates that the investment returns a higher discount rate than the one selected for the analysis. A negative net present value indicates the opposite.

3. Case Example

Assume that as financial planner for a not-for-profit HMO in the Northeast, you are considering requests from two of the unit managers in the ancillary services department for new equipment: a diagnostic imaging machine for radiology and a gas chromatograph for the laboratory. The operating budgets for the department and the cast budget have noted the need for the equipment.

Radiology machine:	
Cost, including installation	$110,000
Estimated additional revenue and cost savings from the machine	$25,000/year
Estimated economic life	Five years
Laboratory equipment:	
Cost, including installation	$95,000
Estimated additional revenue and cost average	$20,000/year
Estimated economic life	Five years

The authorized method of depreciation in the year this is to be analyzed is the straight-line method. The discount rate or the opportunity cost of capital for analyzing this investment choice is ten percent.

ANALYSIS

Radiology		Laboratory
	Accounting rate of return	
$25,000/year	Additional income	$20,000/year
$22{,}000 = \frac{110{,}000}{5 \text{ years}}$	Depreciation expenses	$\frac{95{,}000}{5 \text{ years}} = 19{,}000$
3,000	Net income change	1,000
$\frac{3{,}000}{110{,}000} = .027$	Rate of return based on total investment	$.01 = \frac{1{,}000}{95{,}000}$
$\frac{3{,}000}{55{,}000} = .055$	Rate of return based on average investment	$.02 = \frac{1{,}000}{47{,}500}$
	Payback method	
$\frac{110{,}000}{25{,}000} = 4.4$ years		4.75 years $= \frac{95{,}000}{20{,}000}$
	Net present value	
(15,164)		(19,129)

Using the four methods of analysis described above, the following outcome is derived. Using the accounting rates of return and the payback method, it appears that the radiology equipment is a better investment for the HMO: rates of return are higher and the initial investment is recovered in a shorter time (4.4 years versus 4.75 years). However, the net present net value is negative in both cases, meaning that neither investment contributes positively to the HMO's investment return. The financial planner would then have to reevaluate the necessity of the equipment and the alternative uses for those funds.

Discounted cash-flow techniques require that care be taken along several dimensions in order to assure that the technique is accurate. Only cash flows are important, not income or accounting earnings. In addition, all cash flows and only cash flows or changes in cash flows which are a direct result of the project or projects should be considered. Finally, the analyst must be consistent in her handling of inflation. Both interest rates and cash flows over time must be adjusted or not adjusted for inflation. If cash flows are adjusted for inflation, then the discount rate should reflect the effect of inflation (approximately discount or interest rate minus inflation rate = real interest rate). If nominal interest rates are used, then the cash flows should not be adjusted for the effects of inflation.

F. The Cash Budget

While the master budget includes detailed budgets for the firm's investment in capital projects and other interest-bearing instruments, it also includes a plan for the active management of cash. The cost of credit and good relations with suppliers and clients require an accurate projection of cash needs, excesses, and shortfalls on a month-to-month or, in some cases, a day-to-day basis. Without a sound, up-to-date accounting of the cash balance, institutions are unable to pay bills on time, take advantage of cash discounts, or invest in short-term securities at times of cash excess.

The first step is to estimate minimum cash requirements. To do this, a cash budget must be developed based on institutional policies, third-party payment records, and anticipated changes. A typical cash budget is presented in Fig. 11. This can be done for

Cashflow Forecast - Month of ________, 19XX

Projected resident days -	
Beginning cash balance	$________
Cash inflows	
Medicare	
Medicaid	
Commercial ins.	
Self pay	
Endowment income	
Bank loans	
Miscellaneous	
Total cash inflows	$________
Cash outflows	
Payroll	
Accounts payable	
Taxes	
Dividends	
Repayment of debt	
Miscellaneous	
Total cash outflows	$________
Ending cash balance	$________
Desired minimum cash balance	$________
Excess or shortage of cash	$________

FIGURE 11

any time period required by management, but the maximum time frame should be one month. (To effectively manage cash balances, some larger organizations may want to do a weekly forecast in this area.)

For overall monitoring purposes, all of the monthly forecasts are combined to provide the cash budget for the year. Each month, the actual inflow and outflow can be compared with the forecasted budget, and variances explored when necessary. If conditions change significantly, forecasts can be revised for succeeding months.

The importance of taking into account the seasonal nature of cash inflow and outflow should be emphasized. Most administrators have experienced the slowing of payments from government agencies toward the end of each fiscal period. Also, the time allowance for bank float is influenced by the season, by technological improvements, and by the type of bank (local, regional, or national). All of these factors should be considered in order to make the cash-budget forecast as accurate as possible.

Cash budgeting also allows the administrator to plan capital investments to occur when excesses of cash will occur. This can prevent the borrowing of funds in one month, and having excess funds the next period. The shifting of expenses and the payment patterns of the third-party payers are also highlighted by the preparation of the cash-budget forecast.

Accounts receivable can be controlled by maintaining accounts records on the patients, promptly submitting statements to the payers, and aggressively following up on nonpayments of statements. Accounts receivable management requires an internal accounting system that will accurately collect charges for the patients and ensure prompt preparation of the billing statement. It may be necessary to observe mail pickup times at the post office, to hand-deliver statements to major third-party reimbursers who are located nearby, and to pick up payments for prompt deposit in the bank. Some organizations may want to have a "lock box" agreement with their bank—where the bank picks up the mail, credits the institution's bank account, and then forwards the documentation to the facility's accounting department.

G. Working Capital Management

Planning for cash needs is only part of the planning required for efficient working capital management in an organization. Working capital consists of the current assets of the organization, which include the cash, temporary or short-term investments, accounts receivable, and inventories. They can be manipulated quickly to respond to the current needs of the organization; as such, they require active management.

1. The Operating Cycle

Working capital is the input necessary to make the physical assets productive. For example, cash is used to purchase supply items, pay rent and salaries, and provide other services. This cash is not returned until the services are paid. Thus, accounts receivable are created. When they are paid, cash is returned to the organization. This describes the operating cycle of the institution, which is related to, but should not be confused with, the type of accounting system used—cash or accrual. A cash accounting system operates on the basis of cash received and disbursed. Revenues are not earned until received in cash, and expenses are not recognized until paid. The cash basis of accounting may be the most appropriate for the administrator of a small facility to use in day-to-day management decisions. Under an accrual system, revenues are recognized when the service has been provided, regardless of whether cash payment has been received. Similarly, expenses are recognized when the obligation is owed—not when actual payment is made. Current accounting principles require that financial statements be prepared on the accrual basis. (For the smaller facility this conversion from cash to accrual could be made at the year-end adjustment.) Working capital management utilizes both the cash and the accrual aspects of accounting, since it involves both types of current asset accounts—cash and receivables.

The outflow and inflow of cash constitutes the operating cycle of the institution. It can be decidedly influenced by management action and therefore varies among health care institutions. The operating cycle for a typical small HMO is illustrated in Fig. 12.

The operating cycle time frame can be reduced by close control over cash balances, inventory levels, and accounts receivable follow-up. In addition, bill preparation time, bill mailing time, crediting, and depositing of payment are all areas in which improved techniques can lead to significant reductions in the operating cycle. (These techniques will be discussed in greater detail later in this section.)

The delay between the outflow and inflow of cash creates the need for working capital. As the volume of services changes, as more efficient management control of the operating cycle occurs, then the cost of working capital can be minimized.

Two types of working capital are required in an institution: permanent working capital and temporary working capital.

Permanent working capital represents the current assets required on a continuing basis throughout the year—that is, the minimum level of working capital required to maintain operations. This type of working capital is financed through long-term debt or equity capital. The long-term debt is repaid through the excess of revenue over expenses in providing the service.

Temporary working capital represents the additional working capital required to accommodate seasonal factors during the year. These amounts are usually acquired through short-term loans, which are repaid by the release of current assets as the demand is reduced.

2. Net Working Capital

The current liabilities of the institution constitute a major offset to working capital. Current liabilities consist of amounts owed to interest-free trade credit suppliers, payments for utilities, and salaries to employees. Personnel paid after they perform the service

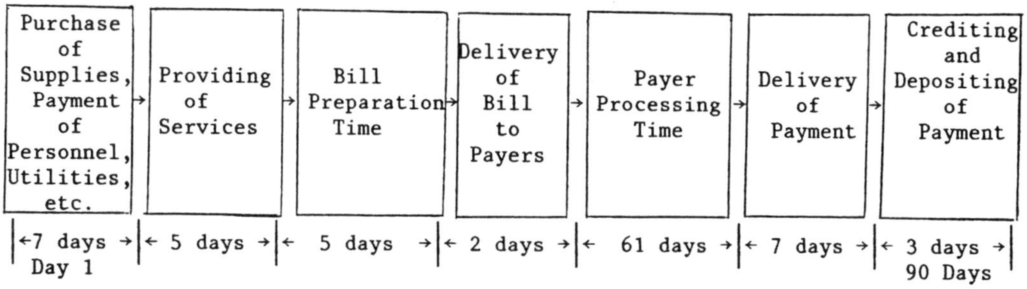

FIGURE 12 The operating cycle.

in effect provide interest-free loans to the institution for the pay period. Thus, a one-month salary payment plan is better than a two-week schedule.

After interest-free lines are considered, short-term lines of credit or bank loans can be used to meet the remainder of the temporary working capital needs. By using short-term loans for temporary needs, the institution minimizes the cost of working capital. Short-term loans can be obtained for only the time period needed, thereby reducing interest costs. Prompt repayment establishes better credit ratings.

The difference between current assets and current liabilities is called net working capital. The need for net working capital should be met through long-term debt or equity sources. Long-term sources for net working capital reduce risk, since the debt is typically repaid through net income and the danger of not having the funds available is lessened. Long-term sources also provide stability to the operations because of the long time frame involved before the debt must be repaid.

3. Current Liabilities

Short-term liabilities, primarily accounts payable and short-term bank loans, are another important aspect of working capital management, and offer additional opportunities for the administrator to reduce the costs of providing service. For example, accounts payable are, in effect, interest-free loans being provided by the supplier to encourage you to buy its products. Thus, where payment is requested "in 30 days" or "10 days after receipt of merchandise," it is not financially prudent to pay for these items until the due date. The accounts payable system should ensure that bills are paid on time–not early or late.

Some suppliers offer a cash discount for prompt payment. Terms of "1% 10, net 30," for example, indicate that a one percent discount can be taken if payment is made within 10 days. The objective is to minimize the cost of obtaining the supplies; thus, it is important to pay the bill at either the end of the discount period or the end of the net period.

It is useful to consider the effective cost to the facility of not paying within the discount period. For example, a one percent cash discount means the facility will pay $990 to settle a $1,000 invoice on the tenth day. If payment is delayed to the thirtieth day (the right to borrow the $1,000 for twenty days), the effective interest rate could be determined as follows:

Effective Cost of Trade Credit

$$\frac{\text{365 days per year}}{\text{25 days in nondiscount period}} = \text{14.6 time periods per year}$$

$$\frac{\text{1\% cash discount}}{\text{1\%} \times \text{14.6\%}} = \text{14.6\% effective cost}$$

$$\frac{\text{2\% cash discount}}{\text{2\%} \times \text{14.6\%}} = \text{29.2\% effective cost}$$

It is usually cheaper to borrow the funds from short-term lenders than to not take the cash discount. However, other factors must be considered, including the absolute amount paid for the credit, not just the determination of the annual interest rate.

4. Temporary Investments

The management of working capital also requires the investing of temporary excess cash. Excess cash may be built up in anticipation of purchasing new equipment, seasonal factors, or retirement of debt. Typically, the administrator should consult financial experts in this area, but there are certain options that the administrator or financial management team should consider. For example, with very little administrative effort, the investment of $1,000,000 over a four-day weekend at twelve percent could return $1,315. The key, of course, is safety of principal and liquidity for short-term investments.

Some possible options are the following:

Treasury securities
Commercial paper
Repurchase agreements
Certificates of deposit

Idle cash in today's market represents a source of income that should not be overlooked.

5. Inventory

The dollar amount of the inventory represents an investment in the institution (similar to accounts receivable, although usually considerably less in dollar amounts). Inventories are necessary to provide quality medical care and service to patients. Overstocking inventory items leads to opportunity costs from tying up cash, storage costs, additional taxes, and obsolescence costs; it also presents more opportunities for loss from pilferage and theft. Understocking inventory items leads to rush resupply orders (which are more costly), a reduction in the quality of care, and a general lack of control over purchases. The effective inventory policy makes trade-offs between the two types of costs and minimizes the total cost of carrying inventory.

Many facilities minimize their investment in inventories by ordering on a daily basis. This offers an excellent way to minimize costs—if suppliers are available to provide adequate service to ensure quality of care. A purchase order system that monitors and controls inventory levels and quality of care represents effective management. In larger institutions where higher inventory levels must be maintained, more formal inventory control techniques may be required.

Determining when and how much to order is a management function. Several techniques are available to assist the administrator. These range from quantitative models for high-cost items to visual aids for low-cost or frequently used items. One of the most common methods is to separate inventory items into categories reflecting a percentage of total inventory value. In a typical facility, Category A items would be those high-cost items representing from sixty to seventy percent of total inventory value (perhaps ten to fifteen percent of items carried in inventory); thus, they should receive the most attention. Category B items represent another twenty to thirty percent of inventory value (and ten to fifteen percent of inventory items). Finally, Category C, represents the largest category in terms of number of items (seventy to eighty percent), but accounts for only ten to twenty percent of total inventory value. This last category can be controlled by subjective estimates and items ordered at regularly scheduled intervals. Many facilities use markings on the storage bins to indicate the supply level of Category C items. This "red line" approach allows the supply supervisor to determine by a simple visual check which supplies should be reordered.

6. Managing Working Capital

Three major processes are involved in the management of working capital:

1. *Identifying what is needed.* This requires forecasting outflows and inflows based on predicted supply basis, wage levels, and volume of services. Cash budgeting can be a vital tool for this purpose.
2. *Identifying the best way to obtain the required funds.* When the needs have been determined, the administrator must determine the best source in terms of cost, time frame, and impact on future availability.
3. *Monitoring the levels of working capital.* Because of the volatile nature of the working capital estimation process, constant management attention is needed to identify shortages and excesses in working capital. The liquidity and turnover ratios discussed earlier provide useful clues to potential problem areas. By comparing such ratios with past trends and industry norms, areas to investigate can be identified early.

A shortage of working capital will quickly show up in the institution's inability to pay bills when they are due. An excess of working capital is not so readily identified, but the opportunity cost it represents to the institution can be substantial. Investing excess funds in areas with profit potential or using them to pay off existing loans or to pay dividends to stockholders is potentially more profitable to the institution than maintaining large current ratios or cash in the bank.

III. FINANCING VERSUS INVESTMENT DECISIONS

A. Sources of Funds

Effective financial management requires that the organization have sufficient funds to maintain operations, provide an adequate return to the owners, and allow for unanticipated requirements in the future. Basically, funds for long-term care institutions come from the following sources:

1. Net revenues
2. Conversion of assets
3. Debt financing and amortization
4. Equity financing

Each of the sources has particular advantages and disadvantages, and the financial manager must determine the proper mix to reduce the total cost of obtaining funds for the organization.

1. Net Revenues

Net income or profit, plus noncash expenses such as depreciation, provides a source for meeting the financial requirements of the institution. Given government restrictions on reimbursement and the cost/price squeeze for most institutions, this source does not usually provide sufficient capital for long-term requirements. In addition, as assets become fully depreciated, the amount from this source can be significantly reduced unless a continual replacement or expansion of depreciable assets is planned. In many cases, this is not economically feasible for facility owners.

2. Conversion of Assets

The conversion of assets can provide a one-shot approach to meeting capital requirements. However, once these assets are expended (for example, by selling investments or securities), they are not available for future needs. The selling of fixed assets can also promote capital on a onetime basis. Again they would not be available to provide service or funds in the future. The conversion of assets is basically a liquidating approach for meeting immediate financial requirements and can be detrimental to long-term survival.

3. Debt Financing and Amortization

Debt can be used by the long-term care institution to meet financial requirements. Debt is usually classified as either short- or long-term depending upon its repayment characteristics. Short-term debt is usually scheduled for repayment within one year.

All other debt falls into the long-term classification. The maturity structure of the institution's debt can have an impact on the risks and profits of the facility. Typically, the larger the percentage of funds obtained from long-term sources, the more conservative the debt policy of the firm. Short-term debt is usually more expensive than long-term, and decidedly more volatile. During 1980, the prime interest rate varied from ten to twenty-one percent. Being forced into the borrowing market at the high end of the interest rates would significantly reduce returns to the owners. In some cases, the owners may not be able to obtain funds at any price, thereby greatly increasing the risk of bankruptcy to the smaller owners with no additional source of funds.

Short-term debt, however, in spite of the risk, can offer more flexibility to the facility administrator, because the debt can be designed to match the seasonal or cyclical nature of the requirement. It also offers the ability to take advantage of temporary changes in interest rates. Some facility owners may not want to use long-term debt due to the lack of flexibility and return to the owner. Cash flow and capital budgeting are vital aspects of financial planning.

a. Short-Term Debt Sources

A facility often buys its supplies and materials on trade credit from other firms. This accounts payable category represents an interest-free loan by the supplier. The facility must be cognizant of the need to pay these creditors on time if future credit is to be assured. Many of these suppliers offer cash and quantity discounts. Quantity discounts should be taken into account in inventory policy, and these should be a trade-off between larger carrying costs and lower per-unit costs. Cash discounts represent a reduction in price based on payment within a specified period of time. The costs of not taking cash discounts can be quite high, as the following table indicates.

COST OF CREDIT (if cash discounts are not taken)

Credit Terms*	Approximate Cost of Credit
1/10, net 20	36%
1/10, net 30	18%
2/10, net 20	73%
2/10, net 30	37%

*Credit terms are typically expressed in this manner. One percent discount if paid within 10 days, with full payment required within 20 days. If the discount is not taken, the borrower is paying one percent for the use of the money for 10 days. There are 36 20-day periods in a year (360÷10); therefore, the cost is 36× 1%, or approximately 36%.

b. Short-Term Financing by Commercial Banks

Short-term requirements are typically met by borrowing from commercial banks. These loans may take the form of a single negotiated loan or a line of credit based on formal understanding as to the maximum amount the bank will lend to the owner. Line-of-credit short-term loans are typically negotiated in advance; an effective cash budgeting procedure can usually identify short-term needs early enough to allow maximum flexibility and lowest cost. The cost of these short-term loans is not only the regular or stated interest rate. The bank may also require compensating balances, which effectively reduce the amount the borrower can use and thereby increases the net cost. In addition, some banks may require that the borrower be free of debt for part of the year. If the facility is unable to pay off all its short-term debts for part of the year, it may indicate that short-term debt is being substituted for long-term capital requirements.

Determining the true, or effective, rate of interest on the loan depends on the stated rate of interest and the bank's method of charging interest. For example, if interest is paid at maturity of the loan, the stated rate of interest is the effective rate of interest. The interest at ten percent on a $10,000 note would be $1,000. If this interest is deducted in advance (or discounted) the borrower only receives $9,000. The effective interest rate would be $1,000 divided by $9,000, or eleven percent. If the loan is to be repaid in installments, the effective interest rate is even higher. For example, if the $10,000 note above is to be repaid in 12 monthly installments, the borrower has the $10,000 only for the first month. The loan balance is reduced as payments are made, and the borrower has on the average only one-half of the original loan outstanding over the course of the year.

If interest is charged on the original balance, the effective rate becomes $1,000 divided by 10,000/2, or twenty percent. If the loan was discounted, the rate becomes 1,000 divided by 9,000/2, or twenty-two percent.

Because of the different lending policies of banks, it is advisable for the administrator to develop a continuing relationship with banks that meet the basic financial requirements of their institutions—for example, lending policies, consulting services, loan specialization. Will they support you in bad times?

c. Other Sources

Some large facilities may be able to issue commercial paper as their own promissory notes to individual investors. Other institutions may pledge their accounts receivable or other assets to secure loans. These forms of financing require specialized treatment.

d. Long-Term Debt Sources

In most cases, both public and private sources of long-term debt can be available to the long-term care organization. Private sources are probably the most prevalent, and include conventional mortgages, taxable mortgage bonds, tax-exempt bonds, wraparound mortgages, and other creative options. Public sources include state and local authority financing, mortgages insured by the Federal Housing Administration, loans, and Government National Mortgage Association mortgage-backed securities. Other public options may be available from time to time, based on government policies and determination of need. The nonprofit facility should seek advice from local government authorities on the possibility of issuing tax-exempt securities, as the interest rate needed to sell the bonds may be considerably less than with taxable bonds. As in most cases with a dynamic environment, expert help from your banker or investment broker can be invaluable at this time. Fig. 13(a) provides basic definitions of debt instruments, and Fig. 13(b) provides a comparison of the instruments and their primary characteristics. Further information is found in Appendices 2A and 2B.

4. Leasing Alternatives for Capital Financing

In some instances it may be more appropriate to lease facilities or equipment rather than incurring debt by purchasing them. Leases usually fall into two categories, with different accounting and IRS treatment for each. See Appendices 2B, 2C, and 2D for information.

Operating leases include both financing and maintenance service. Such a lease is usually written for less than the full life of the equipment, and includes a cancellation clause. Also, the value of the lease payments is typically less than the full cost of the equipment. Operating leases do not have to be capitalized on the balance sheet under FASB-13 (Financial Accounting Standard Board), and the lease payments are chargeable to operating expense over the lease term.

Under *financial* or *capital leases*, maintenance services are not provided, the lease is not cancellable, and the lease payment will equal the full price of the leased equipment.

Specific accounting treatment under FASB-13 establishes the following criteria:

The lease transfers ownership to the lessee at the end of the lease term.

The lease term is equal to seventy-five percent or more of the estimated economic life of the property.

The present value of the minimum lease payments exceeds ninety percent of the fair value of the property at the inception of the lease.

The lease gives the lessee the option to purchase the property at a price sufficiently below the expected fair value of the property that the exercise of the option is highly profitable.

If a lease falls into the category of a capital lease, then the obligation must be capitalized on the asset side of the balance sheet, with a related lease payment obligation on the liability side.

In all cases, it is important that the lease contract be written in a form acceptable to the IRS. Otherwise, it may be treated simply as an installment loan, and full tax benefits may not be gained, as the full amount of annual lease payments will not be deductible for income tax purposes.

Basic Terminology for Debt Instruments

Bond	-	a long term promissory note.
Mortgage Bond	-	a bond secured by real property.
Debenture	-	a bond that is not secured by a pledge of specific property.
Sinking Fund	-	a provision that provides for the systematic retirement of bonds. Funds are set aside to purchase and return a certain number of the bonds each year as required by the terms of the debt instrument.

(a)

FIGURE 13 (a) Basic terminology for debt instruments. (b) Comparison of debt instruments.

Major Concerns	Method of Financing: FHA-242 (with GNMA)	Public Taxable Bonds	Private Placements	Tax-Exempt (Authority)	Tax-Exempt (IRS 63-20)
1. Ownership of assets	Yes	Yes	Yes	Yes	Not after retirement
2. Timing of application	4-6 months	1-3 months	1-2 months	3-6 months	3-6 months
3. Feasibility study required	(H.E.W.)	No	No	Yes	Yes
4. Sole source underwriter	No	No	No	Yes	No
5. Programmatic approval	Yes	No	No	No	No
6. 100% financing allowed	Yes	Yes	Not usually	Yes	Yes
7. Maximum term of loan	25 years	15 years	15 years	30 years	30 years
8. Pledge of gross revenues	No	Unsecured notes	Yes	Yes	Yes
9. First mortgage required	Yes	No	Possibly	Yes	Yes
10. Debt service reserve fund required	No	No	No	Yes	Yes
11. Coverage requirements	Funding provision test	Loan-to-value test	Loan-to-value test	1.5-1.7	1.5-1.7
12. Prepayment	Less restrictive	Less restrictive	Restrictive	Restrictive	Restrictive
13. Interest rate	Lower than current market, but discount points may be required to approximate market	Varies with market conditions - usually higher than other types of financing	Varies with market conditions - usually higher than other types of financing	1½-3% lower than taxable loans	1½-3% lower than taxable loans
14. Financing costs	FHA application and commitment fees FHA inspection fee (0.8%) servicing and placement fee (1-2%) Mortgage interest premium (½ of 1%)	Placement fee (usually) 1-2% of the loan amount May require a commitment fee	Placement fee (usually) 1-2% of the loan amount May require a commitment fee	Underwriter's fee (bond discount), usually 1½-2 3/4% Capitalized debt service Reserve funds Legal and other expenses 1-2%	Underwriter's fee (bond discount), usually 1½-2 3/4% Capitalized debt service Reserve funds Legal and other expenses 1-2%
15. Time required	6-9 months	2-4 months	2-4 months	6-7 months	6-7 months

(b)

B. Capital Structure and Cost of Capital

The underlying determinants of the cost of the instruments chosen—whether debt or equity—are based on the theories of risk and return. Implied in the preceding discussions is a capital structure for the organization determined intentionally or by default. The optimal degree of financial leverage or the optimal mix of financing is determined by the financial manager by evaluating the cost of capital to the organization. As will be seen below, this cost of capital determination informs the organizational analysis in terms of market position of the organization, budgeting techniques, especially capital budgeting, and even working capital management.

The cost of capital is, as its name implies, the costs of the market values of debt and equity. The market values of instruments can be determined at any point in time by examining the average interest rates and yields attached to various instruments of debt and equity in the marketplace. What is not so easy to determine is the specific relationship between these market instruments and the orgnization itself. How does the true cost of capital change as the firm's capital structure changes due to a financing or investment decision? The cost of capital can be recalculated to reflect the specific capital structure of the firm, including the relative amount from each source of capital used by the firm; this new weighted average cost of capital then reflects the return on assets that the organization must earn, given its leverage level, in order to maximize the profitability of the organization.

While the actual calculations for weighted average cost of capital are somewhat complex, the financial manager can estimate the return required on his investments and the organization's ability to finance the investments being considered. The cost of capital is related to the organization's debt-to-equity ratio, which influences the cost of the debt a lender is willing to provide, and the value of the stocks, since shareholders might require a higher rate of return on their investment in the firm to compensate for increasing riskiness from increased debt. In addition, the cost of capital is a function of the tax status of the hospital or HMO. The tax benefits from different forms of debt and equity need to be incorporated into the analysis of choice of funds and in valuing the long- and short-term benefits to the firm of those funds.

As an example of an estimate of a health care organization's cost of capital, assume that a not-for-profit hospital financial manager has determined that there will be no changes in the debt structure of his firm or in the market interest rates over the near term. In this case, the current interest costs may be used to compute the cost of debt capital. However, interest costs on debt are institution-specific and thus very sensitive to the existing debt capacity of the hospital. If the hospital is near its debt capacity or over its debt capacity, then the manager should adjust upward the estimates for interest costs on debt to his firm. He can determine this by talking to investment bankers or lending institution officers or by inserting a somwhat arbitrary but conservative interest level in the analysis (such as doubling the current rates).

Because the hospital is not taxed as a for-profit institution, incorporating the tax burden of each form of debt is less crucial than for a for-profit firm; nonetheless, tax consequences of many instruments exist and need to be investigated before a final cost of debt is determined.

The relationship of interest costs and reimbursement methods to which the hospital is subject can also be an important one for consideration. Whether interest costs are reimbursable by the various payers strongly affects the actual cost of capital to the hospital. Depending on the proportion of the hospital's payers that reimburse interest costs and the timing of this reimbursement, debt can be a very low-cost option for securing needed funds.

In addition to the cost of debt which the manager must evaluate, the opportunity cost of the fund balances must be determined. A theoretically sound approach is to consider what rate could be earned on the funds if invested in instruments which reflected the degree of risk the manager was willing to assume with the monies. For a minimal risk, the risk of default by the federal government, the funds could be invested in Treasury bills or bonds, which currently pay interest at rates of five to eight percent, depending on their term. However, the manager may decide that investing the balance internally in service programs generates a higher return on the investment than bills or bonds, in which case the opportunity cost of capital would be higher.

The basic opportunity cost for retained earnings could be considered the interest rate that could be earned by investing the funds externally, as in the Treasury bill example, or internally, as in the program example. Regardless of the method used, the key point is that retained earnings are a potential source of capital and have an associated cost which must be incorporated in the firm's average cost of capital determination.

IV. CONTROL AND EVALUATION

The role of the financial manager and planner requires short- and long-range decision making under varying levels of uncertainty and with varying amounts of information to inform those decisions. Consequently, an evaluation framework to aid that manager must be incorporated into the decision-making structures. The earlier in the process that evaluation and control are discussed, the more likely that the organization will be able to cope with variations and uncertainty in the plan.

Many of the techniques described in Sec. II provide feedback mechanisms by their very form. For instance, cash budgets require an analysis of the status of cash accounts almost on a weekly basis. Seldom are there surprises with such a schedule of review. Not so automatic, however, are the comparisons which should take place between the cash budget and perhaps the master budget, or even the institution's long-range plan and its mission statement.

Control and evaluation mechanisms are particularly important for the capital budgeting process. Capital investment decisions require ongoing performance measurement, postaudits to check the accuracy of the forecasting methods and results, and an analysis after the construction or installation is complete to assess the extent and impact of serious cost or timing overruns or breaches of contract.

Any evaluation or control mechanism requires the identification, collection, and feedback of information deemed critical to understanding the progress of a project. To be determined by the financial manager or planner are answers to questions of who should collect this information, what information is needed and at what frequency. Individuals within the organization most involved or affected by the project should be consulted frequently. Often, a complex computerized information system is not required; analysis of appropriate accounting entries, monitoring carefully formulated contract specifications on timing and costs, and evaluating the additional changes in cash flows due to the project can be performed by the financial planning staff without the aid of computers.

Evaluation and control mechanisms not only can contribute to the success of the projects at hand; they also can provide valuable information for the next round of planning and budgeting by the institution. Comparing actual figures with forecast figures can inform the decision models used for similar projects.

One technique, known as variance analysis, provides a systematic analysis of how and why actual costs or expenses vary from the budgeted or expected costs. By disaggregating budget item variance into components which reflect volume of or variability in services, prices of services and quantity or use of services, the financial planner can identify which portion of the forecast was faulty and which part of the operations might deserve closer scrutiny.

Budgeting is, in and of itself, a method of control within an organization. But detailed and ongoing analysis of the assumptions and accuracy of the budget can make it a far more useful planning tool for the financial manager and planner.

V. CONCLUSIONS

Financial decisions require an in-depth knowledge of the organization: its goals, financial history, competition, operations, and potential. The techniques presented in this chapter provide some assistance in organizing this knowledge in ways that aid the manager in the short- and long-range decisions for which he or she is responsible.

BIBLIOGRAPHY

Beck, D. F. (1980). *Basic Hospital Financial Management*, Aspen Publications, Rockville, Maryland.

Bolandis, J. L. (1982). *Hospital Finance*, Aspen Publications, Rockville, Maryland.

Brealey, R., and Myers, S. (1984). *Principles of Corporate Finance*, second ed., McGraw-Hill, New York.

Broyles, R. W. (1981). *The Management of Working Capital in Hospitals*, Aspen Publications, Rockville, Maryland.

Broyles, R. W. (1982). *Hospital Accounting Practice: Volume 1, Financial Accounting*, Aspen Publications, Rockville, Maryland.

Broyles, R. W. (1982). *Hospital Accounting Practice: Volume 2, Managerial Accounting*, Aspen Publications, Rockville, Maryland.

Broyles, R. W., and Rosko, M. D. (1986). *Planning and Internal Control Under Prospective Payment*, Aspen Publications, Rockville, Maryland.

Cleverley, W. O. (1986). *Essentials of Health Care Finance*, second ed., Aspen Publications, Rockville, Maryland.

Cohodes, D. R., and Kinkead, B. M. (1984). *Hospital Capital Formation in the 1980s*, Johns Hopkins University Press, Baltimore.

Finkler, S. A. (1984). *Budgeting Concepts for Nurse Managers*, Grune and Stratton, New York.

Furst, R. W. (1981). *Financial Management for Health Care Institutions*, Allyn and Bacon.

Helfert, E. A. (1987). *Techniques of Financial Analysis*, sixth ed., Richard D. Irwin, Homewood, Illinois.

Herkimer, A. G., Jr. (1978). *Understanding Hospital Financial Management*, Aspen Publications, Germantown, Maryland.

Horngren, C. T. (1982). *Cost Accounting: A Managerial Emphasis*, fifth ed., Prentice-Hall, Englewood Cliffs, New Jersey.

Neumann, B. R., Suver, J. D., and Zelman, W. N. (1984). *Financial Management: Concepts and Applications for Health Care Providers*, National Health Publishing. Owings Mill, Maryland.

Schafer, E. L., Zulauf, D. J., and Gocke, M. E. (1985). *Management Accounting for Fee-For-Service/Prepaid Medical Groups*, Center for Research in Ambulatory Health Care Administration, Denver.

Shaffer, F. A., ed. (1985). *Casting Out Nursing: Pricing Our Product*, National League for Nursing, New York.

Shields, G. B. (1983). *Debt Financing and Capital Formation in Health Care Institutions*, Aspen Publications, Rockville, Maryland.

Smith, H. L., and Fottler, M. D. (1985). *Prospective Payment: Managing for Operational Effectiveness*, Aspen Publications, Rockville, Maryland.

Suver, J. D., and Neumann, B. R. (1985). *Management Accounting for Healthcare Organizations*, revised ed., Pluribus Press, and HFMA.

Warner, D. M., Holloway, D. C., and Grazier, K. L. (1984). *Decision Making and Control in Health Administration*, second ed., Health Administration Press, Ann Arbor, Michigan.

APPENDIX 1: NOTES TO CONSOLIDATED FINANCIAL STATEMENTS DECEMBER 31, 1985, 1984, AND 1983

1. Summary of Significant Accounting Policies

The Company owns and operates federally qualified Health Maintenance Organizations (HMOs), pharmacies, and an underwritten Preferred Provider Plan, all of which provide health care services to its members.

Principles of consolidation and organization:

The accompanying consolidated financial statements include the accounts of the Company and all of its wholly- and majority-owned subsidiaries and its majority-owned partnership.

Inventories:

Pharmaceutical inventories are carried at the lower of cost or market on the specific identity method.

Amortization:

Cost in excess of the values assigned to net assets of acquired businesses is being amortized from the date of acquisition over 40 years.

Organizational costs (which consist principally of the costs incurred commencing in 1984 of developing new health maintenance organizations prior to the commencement of operations) are amortized on a straight-line basis over five years, once operations commence. Prior to 1983, deferred loan costs were being amortized on a straight-line basis over six years (expected life of loan). During 1983, the related loan was paid off and the balance of deferred loan costs was charged against income.

Income taxes and investment tax credits:

Deferred income taxes result from the recognition of the income tax effect of timing differences in reporting transactions for financial and tax purposes.

Investment tax credits are accounted for as reductions of income tax expense in the year allowable for income tax purposes.

Equipment and furniture:

Equipment and furniture are stated at cost, with depreciation provided over the estimated useful lives of the respective assets, ranging from three to eight years, on straight-line and accelerated methods.

Premium income:

Premiums from members are recognized as income in the period to which health care coverage relates.

Premiums are billed in advance but are not recorded until they are paid or earned.

Medical expenses:

Medical expenses represent capitation fees from physician groups, charges by hospitals and other health care providers for health care services rendered to members during the period, which includes claims paid, claims in process, and estimated liability for pending and unreported claims.

2. Business Combinations

The Company was organized on September 20, 1982, and shortly thereafter, it exchanged 2,818,800 shares of its common stock for 60% of the outstanding common stock of Management, Inc. In 1983, the Company acquired the balance of the common stock outstanding for cash of $280,000. Management, Inc., is the general partner of The Plan, Ltd. The general partner's share of partnership income amounted to 20% prior to 1982 and 30% for subsequent periods. Management, Inc., also owns a 3-1/3% limited partnership interest in The Plan, Ltd.

In 1982, the Company acquired a 14% limited partnership interest in The Plan, Ltd., for $268,000 of cash. In 1983, in two separate transactions, the Company acquired an additional 3-1/3% limited partnership interest in The Plan, Ltd., for $65,000 of cash and 32-2/3% limited partnership interest in exchange for 147,804 shares of its common stock value at $1,345,000 and cash of $125,000. The combined general and limited partnership interests owned by the Company and Management, Inc., amounts to 83-1/3%.

In 1983, the Company purchased the minority interest (26% of the outstanding common stock) in TLC Management, Inc. (TLC), in exchange for 15,385 shares of its common stock valued at $140,000. TLC managed under contract TLC Health Plan, Ltd., a health maintenance organization, located in the Florida area. In July 1984, the Company terminated its management contract in exchange for cash of $19,000 and 15,385 shares of the Company's stock valued at $244,622.

On September 12, 1983, the Company acquired all of the outstanding common stock of Pharmaceutical Associates, Inc. (PAI), which was formed in 1982, in exchange for 5,769 shares of its common stock. This transaction was accounted for as a pooling of interests. In 1984, PAI purchased the assets of three pharmacies for a combined price of $282,000, composed of cash and notes. Also, PAI purchased in 1985 the assets of one pharmacy and the outstanding common stock of another pharmacy for a combined purchased price of $204,000 cash.

In August 1984, the Company exercised its option to purchase 800 shares of common stock (84.2% of the outstanding common stock) of the newly established Ohio HMO Corp. (Ohio HMO) at $71.43 per share, or a total of $57,144. In December 1985, the Company purchased an additional 140 shares of common stock of Ohio HMO at $618.75 per share or a total of $86,625 cash, which increased the Company's ownership interest to 95%.

In June 1985, the Company acquired all of the outstanding common stock of Health Providers, a California HMO, in exchange for 580,993 shares of its common stock. This business combination has been accounted for as a pooling of interests. Accordingly, the consolidated financial statements of the Company have been restated to include the operations of Health Providers since April 1, 1984, the date HP became a for-profit corporation. Separate results of operations of the combined entities for the year ended December 31, 1984, and for the six months ended June 30, 1985, are as follows:

	The Plan	HP	Total
1984:			
Revenues	$26,379,406	$14,807,488	$41,186,894
Net income	3,099,550	382,528	3,482,078
Net income per common share	$0.71	$0.01	$0.72
Six months ended June 30, 1985:			
Revenues	$17,454,924	$11,403,201	$28,858,125
Net income	1,606,260	370,276	1,976,536
Net income per common share	$0.30	$0.07	$0,37

The acquisition of HMI, TLC, the limited partnership interests in The Plan, Ltd., Ohio HMO, and the pharmacies described above have been accounted for as purchases. The financial statements for 1983 reflect their operations for the entire year with preacquisition income deducted as part of minority interest.

Had the acquisitions described above occurred at the beginning of each period presented, the pro forma revenues, net income, and net income per share for the year ended December 31, 1983, would have been as follows (1985 and 1984 revenues, net income, and net income per share would not have been materially different):

	1983
Revenues	$17,457,840
Net income	1,302,846
Net income per share	$0.37

The pro forma amounts reflect estimated adjustments for goodwill amortization over 40 years and interest expense on the indebtedness assumed to have been incurred to finance the cash portions of such business combinations.

3. Related Party Transactions

Certain limited partners of The Plan, Ltd. (the partnership), and stockholders of the Company are physicians of the Medical Groups under contract to the partnership and Health Providers to provide noninstitutional professional health care to their enrolled members.

The amounts incurred by the partnership and Health Providers for these services amounted to $15,315,000, $12,334,000, and $5,825,000 for the years ended December 31, 1985, 1984, and 1983, respectively.

The Company leased certain office facilities from P & Q Properties, a partnership consisting of the principal officers and stockholders of the Company for rentals of $86,000 in 1985, $78,000 in 1984, and $63,000 in 1983. This lease was terminated on December 31, 1985, when the offices were moved to larger facility.

4. Marketable Equity Securities

At December 31, 1985, the current and noncurrent marketable equity securities are each carried at the lower of cost or market. Marketable equity securities included in current and noncurrent assets had a cost of $1,563,291 ($2,431,953 in 1984) and $2,348,799 ($3,090,158 in 1984), respectively, at December 31, 1985.

To reduce the carrying amount of the current marketable equity securities to market, which was lower than cost at December 31, 1985, a valuation allowance in the amount of $24,614 ($56,692 in 1984) was established with a corresponding charge to net income at the date and to reduce the carrying amount of the noncurrent marketable equity securities to market, which was also lower than cost at December 31, 1985, a valuation allowance representing the unrealized loss of $38,726 ($160,159 in 1984) was established by a charge to stockholders' equity.

At December 31, 1985, and 1984, there were no gross unrealized gains, whereas the gross unrealized losses pertaining to the marketable equity securities in the portfolios amounted to the following:

	1985	1984
Current	$24,612	$56,692
Noncurrent	$38,726	$160,159

A net realized gain of $191,697 on the sale of marketable equity securities was included in the determination of net income for 1985, whereas a loss of $97,548 was included in determining net income for 1984. The cost of the securities sold was based on the average cost of all the shares of each such security held at the time of sale.

5. Reinsurance

The Company purchases, on a premium basis, reinsurance coverage from an insurance company which limits the Company's exposure on individual claims for institutional services incurred in excess of $100,000 (in excess of $55,000 from November 1, 1983, to October 31, 1984, and $50,000 from November 1, 1982, to October 31, 1983). Individual claims between $100,000 and $1,000,000 are covered by the reinsurance agreement in varying amounts up to a maximum of $1,000,000. The Company self-insures for individual claims in excess of $1,000,000. Reinsurance premiums incurred, net of related reinsurance recoveries, are classified as medical expense in the financial statements. Reinsurance recoveries on paid claims are classified as current receivables at the balance sheet date.

Reinsurance premiums, net of recoveries, were $105,229, $247,527, and $177,237 for the years ended December 31, 1985, 1984, and 1983, respectively.

6. Restricted Cash Deposits

The Company and its subsidiaries are required to maintain a cash deposit with the Insurance Commissioner in the states of California, Ohio, and Florida (see also Note 7) for unpaid claims.

7. Long-term Debt

Long-term debt consists of the following:

	1985	1984
$1,000,000 line of credit, expiring July 20, 1986, interest at 1% over prime (10.5% at December 31, 1985)	$ –	$ –
10% note payable, interest payable monthly, principal balance due $37,500 annually through January 1986	37,500	75,000
9% subordinated notes payable, to HHS (see below), interest payable semiannually, principal balance due $64,000 annually increasing each year by $6,000 through 1988; $7,000 through 1990; $8,000 through 1991; $10,000 through 1994; $12,000 through 1996; $14,000 through 1997; $15,000 through 1998 and decreasing by $9,000 in 1999, discounted $479,725 and $531,521 at December 31, 1985 and 1984, to reflect interest rate of 17%	1,158,276	1,165,479
9%-20% notes payable to affiliates, subordinated to all all present and future creditors of Health Providers	593,125	589,582
Other notes payable due in varying amounts to 1988	27,606	23,216
8% subordinated note payable paid in 1985	–	245,203
	1,816,507	2,098,480
Less current portion	112,064	110,021
Long-term debt due after one year	$1,704,443	$1,988,459

The aggregate annual maturities of long-term debt for the four years subsequent to 1986 are 1987–$42,420; 1988–$45,580; 1989–$50,464, and 1990–$60,393.

Health Providers has entered into an Operating Cost Assistance Agreement with the Secretary of Health and Human Services (HHS) under Title XIII, Section 1306, of the Public Health Service Act. Under this agreement, HHS loaned them a total of $1,800,000. The promissory notes issued under the agreement are secured by liens on all revenues, funds, and accounts; however, the liens are subordinated to all claims of normal trade creditors, short-term indebtedness, and any future funded indebtedness approved by the Secretary. It is prohibited from incurring any future funded indebtedness including lease agreements, mortgages, and other assistance loans without prior approval from the Secretary of Health and Human Services. Events of default under the loan agreement include noncompliance with the requirements of the Act.

A restricted reserve account is required to be established to accumulate an amount equal to one year's payment of principal and interest by 1991. The reserve account amounted to $35,000 and $20,000 at December 31, 1985, and 1984, respectively, and is included in restricted cash deposits (see Note 6) in the accompanying financial statements. In addition, each month it is required to deposit in a sinking fund 1/6 of the amount of interest due at the next succeeding interest payment due date and 1/12 of the next principal due. Amounts held in the sinking fund as of December 31, 1985, and 1984, amounted to $105,700 and $105,900, respectively, and are included in cash in the accompanying financial statements.

8. Stock Options

In 1982, the Company issued stock options to two officers/employees under a nonqualified plan for the purchase of 226,800 shares of its common stock at $0.12 per share, or a total of $28,000. The options were exercised, 1983.

On September 9, 1983, the Company adopted an incentive stock option plan under which options to purchase 250,000 shares of common stock may be granted to eligible employees. The options may be granted for a term not to exceed 10 years (5 years with respect to a 10% stockholder), and the exercise price must be at least equal to the fair market value of the common stock on the date of the grant (110% of fair market value with respect to a 10% stockholder). The status of the plan at December 31, 1985, is as follows:

	Options granted	Exercise price	Exercise value
Exercisable	4,720	$10.00–$22.25	$ 60,922
Not exercisable	99,097	$10.00–$22.25	1,248,808
Outstanding	103,817	$10.00–$22.25	$1,309,730

During the year ended December 31, 1985, options for 40 shares were exercised for $11.69 per share, or a total of $468.

9. Commitments

The Company and its subsidiaries are committed under various operating leases for buildings and equipment for the following minimum rental payments at December 31, 1985:

1986	$1,093,000
1987	830,000
1988	740,000
1989	690,000
1990	598,000

Rent expense was approximately $593,000, $396,500, and $103,300 in 1985, 1984, and 1983 respectively.

10. Income Taxes

The provision for income taxes for the years ended December 31, 1985, 1984, and 1983 is comprised of the following:

	1985	1984	1983
Current:			
Federal	$2,024,899	$2,675,000	$969,604
State	336,609	345,000	199,596
	2,361,508	3,020,000	10,089,200
Deferred:			
Excess of tax over book depreciation	81,102	–	–
Organizational costs, net of amortization, which have been deducted for tax	193,304	–	–
Investment tax credit basis reduction	46,950	–	–
Other, net	47,136	–	–
	368,492	–	–
	$2,730,000	$3,020,000	$1,089,200

A reconciliation between the provision for current income taxes at expected and effective rates is as follows:

	Years ended December 31		
	1985	1984	1983
Provision computed at statutory rate on income before income taxes	$3,115,875	$3,280,468	$1,373,724
Increase (decrease) in taxes resulting from:			
State income taxes, net of federal tax benefit	181,769	186,429	64,582
Investment tax credits	(156,052)	(72,068)	–
Tax effect of minority interests in partnership	(341,288)	(289,513)	(336,412)
Dividend exclusion	(155,333)	(117,126)	–
Other, net	85,029	31,810	(12,694)
	$2,730,000	$3,020,000	$1,089,200

The income tax benefit from utilization of Health Providers' prior years net operating losses of $750,255 has been used to reduce excess of cost over values assigned to net assets of acquired businesses. These operating losses were generated prior to the time Protective was acquired.

11. Common Stock Transactions

On November 16, 1983, the Company completed a public offering for the sale of 795,500 shares of its common stock. Proceeds of $7,017,889 (net of expenses of the offering of approximately $937,000) were credited to common stock and capital in excess of stated value.

On September 18, 1984, the Company completed a second public offering for the sale of 650,000 shares of its common stock. Proceeds of $14,151,830 (net of expenses of approximately $954,000) were credited to common stock and capital in excess of stated value.

12. Quarterly Financial Data (unaudited)

Summarized quarterly financial data for 1985 and 1984 are as follows:

	Three months ended			
	March 31	June 30	September 30	December 31
1985				
Revenues	$14,153,605	$14,704,520	$15,181,614	$15,641,069
Operating income	1,762,576	777,037	1,215,076	655,302
Net income	1,184,106	792,430	852,454	484,681
Net income per common share	$0.22	$0.15	$0.15	$0.10
1984				
Revenues	$6,051,954	$11,218,755	$11,306,829	$12,609,356
Operating income	1,230,876	1,282,791	1,378,715	1,602,009
Net income	688,676	760,167	1,011,387	1,021,848
Net income per common share	$0.16	$0.16	$0.21	$0.19

The information for the quarter ended March 31, 1985, and the last three quarters for 1984 include the operations of Health Providers, which was acquired in a transaction accounted for as a pooling of interests.

APPENDIX 2A: Benefits of Equipment Financing Instruments as Compared With Term Loan Financing and Cash Purchases, Using Accounting Definitions

Benefits / Type of Purchase or Financing	Equipment/Mortgage Conditional Sale	Capital Lease with Bargain Purchase Option	Capital Lease with Fair Market Value Option	Operating Lease	Unsecured Bank Credit Term Loan	Cash Purchase
Conserve working capital Little or no down payment	Yes: 100% financing available payments usually in arrears	Yes: 100% financing available	Yes: 100% financing available	Yes, no down payment required	Partially, 20% down payment usually required	No
Extended terms, terms comparable to equipment life	Yes	Yes	Yes	No, but renewable	No	No
Fixed rate financing	Yes	Yes	Yes	Yes	Usually floats	N/A
Flexible payment structure	Yes	Yes	Yes	No	Usually equals amortization	N/A
Title to equipment	Yes	At lease expiration	No, unless purchase	No, unless purchase	Yes	Yes
Capitalize debt	Yes	Yes	Yes	No	Yes	N/A
Protection from technological obsolescence	No	No	Yes	Yes	No	No
Reimbursement through depreciation and interest	Yes	Yes	Yes	No, through rental expense	Yes	Yes depreciation
Off balance sheet financing	No	No	No	Yes	No	N/A
Availability of investment tax credit	Yes	Yes	Yes, if passed through by lessor	Yes	Yes	Yes

Source: Adapted from Touche Ross presentation (Denver office), Colorado Springs, Colorado, October 22, 1980.

APPENDIX 2B: EXCERPTS FROM FINANCIAL ANALYSIS REPORT – TOUCHE ROSS AND COMPANY

Summary

Qualitative Analysis

Tax-Exempt Financing
- Authority source
- Required debt service coverage test
- Timing considerations
- Limited flexibility
- Refinancing of existing debt
- Rates currently high
- Third-party treatment of "funding"
- Underwriting/marketing risk

Tax-Exempt Financing (IRS 63-20)
- Loss of ownership of assets

Hill Burton Direct Loans
- Currently not available to voluntary private non-profit except in combination with IRS 63-20

Hill Burton Loan Guarantee and Interest Subsidy Program
- Least effective interest rate
- Currently not available
- Programmatic review and approval

FHA-242 Program
- Highly available
- Time constraint
- Refinancing existing debt
- H.H.S. programmatic review and approval
- Limited marketability without GNMA pass through security
- Potential for discount points to market yield
- Underwriter commitment may be required

Public Taxable Bonds
- Minimum processing time
- Generally higher coupon rate than tax exempt
- Flexible terms
- Less restrictive refinancing
- Minimum financial test
- No programmatic review or approval
- Commitment required

Private Placements
- Highest interest rate
- Equity required (loan-to-value ratio) – 60/40
- Interim (construction) financing normally required

Lease Financing
- Highest interest rates (third-party prudent buyer)
- Usually involves design-build concept
- May involve management contract

FINANCING ALTERNATIVES: FHA-242 PROGRAM

Parameter	Consideration to (Facility)	Potential Impact or Comment(s)
1. Interest rates and the possibility of discount points	1. The maximum rate on FHA mortgages is set by the FHA and is typically set independent of marketing environment at the time of issue. If this rate happens to be less than current market rates, it has to provide front end discount points in order to make up the difference to provide the effective yield required to attract an investor.	1. This discount amount is paid at the time of closing (cash) and cannot be generally financed over the term of the term of the borrowings. This requires careful timing and certainly impacts the selection of the appropriate underwriter. Negotiation of the underwriter discount financing.
2. Timing of applications process	2. Since this requires processing through more than one government agency, the time varies accordingly.	2. Early application and use of an experienced financial agent can substantially improve the time constraint.
3. Refinancing of existing debt	3. Under this program, refinancing of existing debt is required as FHA will not take a secondary position.	3. This, of course, depends on the market rate at the time of issue, in contrast to current fixed agreements as well as those that may be fluctuating with the prime rate. Must be evaluated.
4. Government National Mortgage Association (GNMA)	4. Very often used in combination with FHA-242 Program as an added guarantee and security to the investor plus the aspect of liquidity. GNMA involves the sale of securities and in the event of default, the investor receives cash. FHA on the other hand simply mortgages and in the event of default FHA-242 pays off in debentures typically lower than current market yield.	4. While the underwriter discount for the sale of FHA mortgages is typically less than in GNMA securities, FHA mortgages can be much harder to sell and the fact that a secondary market doesn't exist could mean a higher rate and a larger discount.

EXAMPLE

Assume that, at the present time, the FHA coupon rate is 8.00%. To market this mortgage may require a yield to the investor of 9.00% and require that (facility) make up the difference of 100 basis points, or if this were a 25 year issue:

1 discount point	=	12.5 basis points/25 years
100 basis points	-	12.5 basis points = 8% discount
8% x ($8,500,000 loan)	=	$680,000 to be paid by (facility)

If (facility) were to utilize the FHA-242 Program in combination with the GNMA pass through security and guarantee, GNMA would take a 20 basis point discount yielding a rate 7.8%. However, the lender would require a yield of something less than 9.00% rate for the added guarantee and liquidity aspects. Assuming an 8.6% market rate for GNMA's (facility) would have to make up 80 basis points in discount (8.6% - 7.8%) or 80 - 12.5 = 6.4% discount x $8,500,000 = $544,000 in front end discount. While this is an oversimplified example and does not reflect underwriter discount and other associated fees, it illustrates the FHA-242/GNMA concept and its sensitivity to the FHA rate and market conditions at the time of issue.

APPENDIX 2C: (Facility) Outline of Major Qualitative Parameters: Method of Potential Financing

Major Parameter	Tax-exempt	Tax-exempt (IRS 63-20)	FHA-242 (with GNMA)	Public Taxable Bonds	Private Placements	Impact on (Facility) Favorable	Impact on (Facility) Unfavorable
1. Represent a pledge of gross revenues	Yes	Yes	No	Unsecured notes	Yes	–	x
2. First mortgage required	Most always	Most always	Yes	No	Possible	–	x
3. Debt service reserve fund required	Yes	Yes	No	No	No	–	x
4. Sole source underwriter	Yes	No	No	No	No	–	–
5. Underwriting fees	2–3%	2–3%	2–3½% + fees	3–4½%	0.5–3.0%	–	–
6. Feasibility study required	Yes	Yes	(H.E.W.)	No	No	–	x
7. Call provisions	Restrictive	Restrictive	N/A	Less restrictive	Restrictive	–	x
8. Interest rate	7.5 (approx.)	7.5 (approx.)	9.0 (approx.) fluctuate with FHA rate	9.5	10–11%	–	–
9. Level debt service allowed	Normally equal Amortization	Normally equal Amortization	Yes	Flexible	Yes	x	–
10. Maximum term of loan	30 years	30 years	25 years	15 + 5 years	15–20 years	–	–
11. Investment provisions	Restrictive	Restrictive	Less restrictive	Less restrictive	Less restrictive	–	–
12. Refinancing existing debt	Normally required	Normally required	Yes	Less restrictive	Usually	–	–
13. 100% financing allowed	Yes	Yes	Yes	Yes	Not usually	x	x
14. Coverage requirements	1.5–1.7	1.5–1.7	Funding provision tests	Loan-to-value test	Loan-to-value test	–	x
15. Programmatic approval	No	No	Yes	No	No	–	x
16. Prepayment	Restrictive	Restrictive	Less restrictive	Less restrictive	Restrictive	–	x
17. Timing of application	3–6 months	3–6 months	4–6 months	1–3 months	1–2 months	–	x
18. Discount points to market	N/A	N/A	Possibility	N/A	N/A	–	x
19. Construction standards	Local	Local	H.E.W.	Local	Local	–	x
20. Separate construction financing	No	No	Possibly	Possibly	Usually	–	–
21. Availability	Low	Low	High	High	Limited	–	–
22. Hospital ownership of assets	Yes	Not after	Yes	Yes	Yes	x	–
23. Annual fees	Yes	No	Yes	No	No	x	x

APPENDIX 2D: (Facility) Capital Financing Evaluation Summary of Cash Flows (Equal Amortization Payback)

Phase No.	Financing Vehicle	Project Cost ($ Millions)	Interest Rate (1)	Fund-raising Contribution Assumed	(1) 1983 Depreciation/ Amortization	(2) 1983 Principal Payment
I	Tax exempt (1)	$3,486	7.5	$ —	$320,000	$186,000
I	Tax-exempt (3)	3,486	7.5	500,000	317,000	168,000
II	Tax-exempt (11)	3,933	7.5	—	335,000	206,000
II	Tax-exempt (13)	3,933	7.5	500,000	332,000	184,000 . . . . .
III	Tax-exempt (16)	6,677	7.5	—	443,000	323,000
III	Tax-exempt (18)	6,677	7.5	500,000	441,000	301,000
III	Tax-exempt (19)	6,677	8.5	—	450,000	334,000
I	Private Placement (1)	3,486	10.0	—	318,000	248,000
II	Private Placement (4)	3,933	10.0	—	333,000	274,000
II	Private Placement (5)	3,933	10.0	250,000	331,000	259,000
III	Private Placement (11)	6,677	9.0	250,000	438,000	417,000
III	Private Placement (8)	6,677	10.0	250,000	443,000	424,000
III	Private Placement (9)	6,677	10.0	500,000	441,000	409,000 . . . . .
I	Private Placement (3)	3,486	10.0	500,000	314,000	218,000
III	Private Placement (10)	6,667	9.0	—	439,000	431,000
I	FHA-242 (1)	3,486	9.0	—	324,000	213,000
I	FHA-242 (3)	3,486	9.0	500,000	320,000	189,000
II	FHA-242 (4)	3,933	9.0	—	339,000	235,000
II	FHA-242 (6)	3,933	9.0	500,000	335,000	211,000
III	FHA-242 (7)	6,677	9.0	—	448,000	367,000 . . . . .
III	FHA-242 (10)	6,677	9.0	800,000	443,000	329,000
I	PTB-BCZ (4)	3,486	9.5	—	324,000	264,000
II	PTB-BCZ (9)	3,933	9.5	—	341,000	292,000
III	PTB-BCZ (11)	6,677	9.5	—	454,000	457,000
III	PTB-BCZ (14)	6,677	9.5	800,000	446,000	407,000
I	PTB-BCZ (5)	3,486	9.5	250,000	322,000	249,000
I	PTB-BCZ (6)	3,486	9.5	500,000	320,000	233,000
II	PTB-BCZ (10)	3,933	9.5	500,000	336,000	261,000 . . . . .

Working Capital Requirements

Accounts Receivable	$30,000	-	$50,000
Inventories	5,000	-	10,000
Capital Additions	50,000	-	75,000
	$85,000	-	$135,000

Avg: $100,000

	(3) Excess Deficiency Depr. – Princ. (1) (2)	(4) Pro Forma Excess of Revenues Over Expenses	(5) Positive Cash Flow (3) + (4)	(6) Less: Avg. Working Capital Requirement	(7) Net Cash Flow (5) – (6)	(8) Less Funded Depreciation Avg. Est.	(9) Available for Additional Investment, Debt Retirement or Other Capital Requirements
	$134,000	$597,000	$731,000	$110,000	$621,000	$160,000	$461,000
	149,000	623,000	772,000	110,000	662,000	160,000	502,000
	129,000	510,000	639,000	110,000	529,000	170,000	359,000
.....	148,000	560,000	708,000	110,000	598,000	220,000	378,000
	120,000	467,000	587,000	110,000	477,000	220,000	257,000
	140,000	515,000	655,000	110,000	545,000	220,000	325,000
	116,000	373,000	489,000	110,000	379,000	225,000	154,000
	70,000	573,000	643,000	110,000	533,000	160,000	373,000
	59,000	479,000	538,000	110,000	428,000	170,000	258,000
	72,000	508,000	580,000	110,000	470,000	170,000	300,000
	21,000	491,000	512,000	110,000	402,000	220,000	182,000
	19,000	441,000	460,000	110,000	350,000	220,000	130,000
.....	32,000	440,000	472,000	110,000	362,000	220,000	142,000
	96,000	681,000	727,000	110,000	617,000	160,000	457,000
	8,000	466,000	474,000	110,000	364,000	220,000	144,000
	110,000	577,000	688,000	110,000	578,000	160,000	418,000
	131,000	597,000	728,000	110,000	618,000	160,000	458,000
	140,000	487,000	591,000	110,000	481,000	170,000	311,000
	124,000	541,000	665,000	110,000	555,000	170,000	385,000
.....	81,000	414,000	495,000	110,000	385,000	220,000	165,000
	114,000	500,000	614,000	110,000	504,000	220,000	284,000
	60,000	504,000	564,000	110,000	454,000	160,000	294,000
	49,000	410,000	459,000	110,000	349,000	170,000	179,000
	(3,000)	326,000	323,000	110,000	213,000	220,000	(7,000)
	39,000	419,000	458,000	110,000	348,000	220,000	128,000
	73,000	532,000	605,000	110,000	495,000	160,000	335,000
	87,000	561,000	648,000	110,000	538,000	160,000	378,000
.....	75,000	468,000	543,000	110,000	433,000	160,000	273,000

5

An Introduction to Health Care Marketing

Joel M. Lee Department of Community Health, College of Allied Health Professions, University of Kentucky Medical Center, Lexington, Kentucky

I. INTRODUCTION

Health and human services planning has become a well established component of the management process. Concurrently, over the past decade, marketing of these services has received increasing attention. In the 1960s, professional books and journals frequently addressed the function of public health planning; over the last ten years a transition has occurred, placing increased emphasis upon institutional and strategic planning, and most recently, upon the marketing of services. While planning has been almost universally accepted as an appropriate organizational function, the appropriateness of marketing activities for health services has been subject to considerable debate.

The transition from planning to marketing activities is a response to changes in the external environmental context in which services are provided. Ireland (1977) states that the key to both present and future success lies in the ability to accurately assess the needs of the various groups of people an organization seeks to serve, and the opportunities available to do so. These opportunities and needs are influenced by the health care environment in the United States, which is experiencing a variety of changes including significant variations in technology, communication, characteristics of the population served, competition, and cost. Fisk (1986) predicts a variety of additional changes for the future of health care. The following trends assist in understanding the future concerning marketing and planning activities for health care services:

1. More health care services will be available
2. Demand for services will increase
3. There will be an increase in the number of suppliers of health services
4. Competition will be greater
5. Spending for services will continue to increase
6. Greater regulation of services will occur

7. Greater market segmentation will occur in the population served
8. The market will experience greater consumerism
9. Advertising directed at services for older Americans will increase
10. Advertising will become more informative
11. There will be greater diversity in the media used for advertising
12. Patients' insight into advertising strategies will increase.

Each of these trends results in change and uncertainty for providers of health care services. Presently health care organizations use marketing and planning activity to maintain the status quo. It is important to note that neither planning or marketing is a panacea to provide an immediate solution to the problems a provider faces (Beckham, 1984a). Responding to external trends will not result in immediate changes; time is required to respond and facilitate change.

The purpose of this chapter is to review the structure and process associated with marketing-specific topics including the relationship between marketing and other disciplines, current attitudes toward marketing, key concepts, and development of a marketing plan including health care-related data sources. In view of the complexity and rapid growth of health care marketing activity, this chapter will serve as an overview of important concepts. A more complete review will be possible through examination of pertinent materials listed in the bibliography at the end of this chapter.

II. DEFINITION OF MARKETING

Marketing is defined in a variety of ways, beginning with the simple explanation that marketing is listening (Mages, 1985b) or good communication (Carman, 1985). Frequently, marketing is presumed to be a subset of another discipline such as planning or public relations. Many authors refer to marketing as an exchange. Hemmes (1985) refers to marketing as the set of all human activities designed to facilitate an exchange of valuables (services and money) between two or more parties. Ireland (1977) notes that marketing is an exchange designed to achieve the satisfaction of wants, and states that the basis for an exchange is dependent upon an explanation of what the organization is "really selling," identifying the customer and what he or she is buying. Ireland notes that the primary purpose of a marketing program is to direct the purpose and resource of the organization toward the needs, interests, and expectations of people in the various markets it opts to serve.

III. INTRODUCTION TO HEALTH CARE MARKETING

In contrast to the well etablished marketing efforts in commercial product markets, the concept of marketing is relatively new in the health care sector. O'Connor (1982) reports that the earliest articles concerning marketing in nonprofit organizations did not appear until 1975, and publications concerning hospitals did not emerge until 1977. In addition to professional values concerning the propriety of marketing human services, the American Hospital Association (1982) states that health care programs could not be effectively marketed until consumers were ready to accept responsibility for their own health. Concurrently, turbulence and competition in the health care sector have resulted in excess capacity and reduced utilization of facilities and services. As a consequence, health care providers have become more accepting and interested in health care marketing. Review of special articles, regular market-related columns in professional journals, and development of new marketing-specific health care journals, as well as observation of the marketing efforts of health care providers demonstrates the current evolution of health care marketing.

Recognizing that health care marketing differs from traditional product marketing, review of new definitions is a useful method to gain insight concerning application of the technique in the health care setting. Cooper (1985) describes health care marketing as a dynamic process, referring to the constant state of change of the wants and needs of the patient/consumer. As a result, a process is needed to focus on these changes. Cooper continues defining health care marketing as the process of understanding the needs and wants of a target market. Marketing provides a viewpoint to integrate the organization, research analysis, planning, implementation, and control of such a process. Ireland (1977) notes the basics of a good health care marketing program more precisely as determining what the needs of the consumer are, devising strategies to make the consumer aware of these needs, developing services to meet these needs, developing a program to communicate the availability of services, delivering high-quality care, and then evaluating the care provided.

IV. COMPARISON OF HEALTH CARE MARKETING TO GENERAL MARKETING

In an effort to understand the unique nature and difficulties associated with marketing of health and human services, it is helpful to compare its characteristics to traditional marketing efforts. Most health literature focuses on new product development and market research, and is frequently tied to planning activities. O'Connor (1982) notes that very little work has been done on how the general marketing topics of sales management, channels, promotion, and pricing strategy apply to hospitals and other health care institutions. This is at least in part due to the fact that many of these concepts are not applicable to the health care environment. Additionally, O'Connor states that the market-driven strategies of large consumer products companies focus upon low price, frequent use, low technology, and automated processes offering economies of scale. In contrast, medical and hospital services are seldom-purchased, high-priced, high-technology services that patients find difficult to differentiate. Finally, some health care professionals presume efforts encouraging the use of services to be socially irresponsible. Anderson and Near (1983) cite that while health care marketing does differ from traditional product marketing, problems can be resolved and marketing can be successfully applied to services. In an effort to explain why marketing is misunderstood and misapplied in the health services setting, Brown (1985b) makes five observations:

1. The discipline of marketing is viewed and implemented too narrowly by health and medical services organizations, and fails to include employers, third party payers, health-related agencies and government representatives as well as clinical personnel in the process
2. Health care marketers are frequently undertrained and inexperienced, and a need for additional education exists
3. Health care marketing retains a negative connotation to both providers and consumers
4. Marketing presents ill-conceived and poorly implemented programs to provide a "quick fix" for serious problems and oversimplifies and/or oversells in response to pressure
5. Marketing must be the business of all health care organizations in order to assure a change in attitude and success

Sanchez (1983), recognizing these differences in perspective, recommends a series of measures to achieve success in health care marketing:

1. Health care marketing must begin to develop its own coherent body of knowledge rather than relying on traditional for-profit marketing knowledge
2. Marketing must balance the short-run marketing efforts with long-range marketing plans. Marketing is not a panacea for problems, and current overuse will not ameliorate problems based on past poor decisions
3. The marketing function must be reorganized to integrate it into top-level decision making. Responsibilities may no longer reside with poorly prepared practitioners at lower organizational levels making decisions (a common argument for all disciplines)
4. Industry must support and promote education of health services/marketing professionals
5. To be successful, health care marketing policy must be adopted and implemented at a moderate price

As O'Connor, Brown, and Sanchez note, the application of marketing concepts to the health care setting requires the modification of various strategies; however, recent experience and specialized publications demonstrate a successful evolution of marketing practice.

V. SPECIALIZED SERVICE MARKETING

The literature contains a variety of citations focusing on specialized services. Bonnem (1985) notes that in the case of these services, marketing efforts may be less complicated and more effective. Due to their narrow focus, services or facilities that specialize in one type of care may be more easily marketed. Specific health services receiving marketing attention include hospital services such as womens' care units offering obstetric services, midwifery, and early discharge (Dearing et al., 1987; Rynne, 1986), mammary reconstruction (Dugas, 1984), wellness programs such as occupational health and lifestyle programs (American Hospital Association, 1982), radiology (Cryan, 1985a), pharmacy (Whaley, 1985), geriatric services (George, 1984), and emergency departments (Vestal, 1984). New specialized hospital services receiving marketing attention include home health care (Legg and Lamb, 1986; Pappas, 1985a; Trotter, 1985), continuing care retirement communities (Evashwick, 1984; Rohrer and Bibb, 1986), nutritional services (Foltz, 1985, 1986), alternative delivery systems (Neilson, 1985), and mental health (George, 1984). Additional specialized marketing activity has focused on specific professional health services including medicine (Korneluk, 1985), optometry (Miller, 1983), dental services (Sanchez, 1983; Wallace, 1983), nursing (Brown, 1985), and social work (Genkins, 1985).

VI. A SURVEY OF HOSPITAL MARKETING ACTIVITIES

An understanding of hospitals, as the largest and possibly most experienced sector of health care field marketing, is of use to evaluate trends in marketing of human services. In 1985, the American Hospital Association, Society for Hospital Planning and Marketing (1986) commissioned a survey of the marketing efforts of community hospitals in the United States (Clarke and Neiman, 1986). Significant findings of the analysis address organizational and administrative characteristics, and performance of hospital marketing units. The poll conducted by SRI Gallop reports marketing departments are most common among proprietary or investor-owned hospitals (61 percent) with fifty percent of not-for-profit hospitals and forty-three percent of non-federal government hospitals establishing similar functions. Marketing activities are most frequently consolidated in a single department with planning and public relations (37.5 percent), although establishment of independent marketing departments is increasingly common, particularly in larger hospitals. Responsibility for marketing is most frequently noted as a primary function of twenty-three percent of hospital chief executive officers, and this is often the case in small hospitals. In other settings, marketing is the responsibility of a vice president or department director or the assistant or associate administrator. Other staff members involved in marketing activities were identified as the chief operating officer, vice president or director of nursing, chief of staff, and chair of the governing board.

In assessing budget and staffing, the AHA survey reports that marketing department dimensions and full-time equivalent personnel increase with hospital size. However, budgets also differ with departmental organization; marketing departments report average budgets of $103,250 per year and 1.7 staff members, public relations departments report a $125,100 budget and 1.9 staff members, while planning departments report budgets of $80,520 and 1.5 employees. Marketing budgets were allocated to a variety of purposes, principally media advertising (30 percent), professional and staff salaries (22 percent), market research (12 percent), clerical and other support services (11 percent), and direct mail (11 percent).

The survey also compared responses of the chief executive officers and marketing professionals concerning marketing activities. Both parties share the perception that marketing activities include media advertising and market research. The administrators also discern marketing efforts in public relations, image management, health maintenance organization and preferred provider activities, and joint ventures. A variety of other activities including physician recruitment and medical staff relations, analysis of past and present patient and marketing data, and the facility's strengths and weaknesses were identified by less than five percent of administrator respondents. In contrast, marketers cited strategic planning, news media relations, medical staff relations, analysis of marketing and competitive data, and direct mail as principal endeavors. A final component of the survey assessed the effectiveness of marketing efforts in five areas. Areas jointly perceived as most successful by executives and marketers were public relations, and analysis and modification of the existing product lines. Rated lower were media advertising, physician recruitment and placement, and data analysis and market research techniques. However, marketers evaluated effectiveness to be greater in these areas than did chief executive officers. These findings are interesting for a number of reasons; noteworthy is the lack of agreement internally and externally in defining the role of and performance of hospital marketing functions.

VII. THE RELATIONSHIP OF HEALTH CARE MARKETING TO PLANNING

As marketing functions are frequently associated with planning, an understanding of this concept is also important. Sweeney (1985c) notes that planning is the process of making current decisions in light of their future effects. More specific is the definition of Steiner (1979), citing four specific characteristics of planning.

1. Planning addresses the futurity of current decisions explaining the relationship of cause and effect

2. Planning is a process setting organizational aims and defining strategies and policies to achieve them, and develops detailed plans for implementation
3. Planning is an attitude or philosophy
4. Planning is a structure linking strategic plans, medium-range programs, and short-range budgets and operating plans

Planning may be accomplished at three tiers within the organization. At the highest level is policy or institutional planning with the purpose of creating social institutions of the future. At the second level is managerial planning, creating operational value-oriented systems. At the lowest level is technical planning, task-specific efforts within the organization (Reeves et al., 1984). Craig (1983) defines long-range strategic planning by identifying the business and marketing goals an organization seeks to achieve over time to keep major clinical services and the hospital viable in light of external constraints and internal resources. Reeves et al. (1984) suggest two methods to formulate strategic plans for the future. The first is "intuitive-anticipatory," basing decisions upon the judgment of one individual. While this method may be successful, since it is dependent upon the intuition or reflective thinking of one individual and tends to be unwritten, planning concepts are not shared by decision makers within the organization. An alternative approach is the use of formal strategic planning. The method is based upon a set of procedures, research and data, participation of many actors, and is written and well documented.

Planning is defined as a continuous and unending process. Reeves et al. describe a series of steps for rational planning as:

1. Identifying the resources that will be available to bring about changes toward the desired state
2. Determining the discrepancy between the desired state and conditions that might occur if no action is taken
3. Identifying the resources that will be available to bring about changes toward the desired state
4. Developing feasible alternatives and selecting those most likely to achieve the desired result within the limits imposed by resources
5. Evaluating the alternatives and selecting those most likely to achieve the desired result within resource limitations
6. Implementing selected alternatives
7. Appraising performance of alternatives and adjusting them to achieve the desired objectives

Health planning, in contrast to health marketing, has received considerable attention in the development of government policy, and its evolution is well documented. Key federal legislation addressing health planning activities includes Public Law 79-725, the Hospital Survey and Construction Act (Hill Burton Act of 1946); Public Law 89-239, The Heart Center and Stroke Amendments of 1965; Public Law 89-749, Comprehensive Health Planning and Public Health Services Amendment Act of 1966 (Partnership for Health), and Public Law 93-641, the National Health Planning and Resources Development Act (1974). The initial legislation promoted growth of health resources with subsequent legislation establishing a network of community, state, and federal panels responsible for health plan development and review of proposed projects.

Although the legislative efforts have been reduced to a minimal level, at least in part as a result of these public health planning efforts, health care organizations have developed institutional planning functions. In addition to efforts to interact with the public planning process, institutional planning departments have assumed responsibility for strategic planning efforts. In response to the rapid changes in the environment many planning units have recently assumed responsibility for marketing efforts, or have been reorganized into marketing or public relations units.

MacStravic (1977) notes that marketing and planning are closely related both conceptually and operationally. Planning presents a method for design and management of change while marketing offers design and management of exchange relations with important publics. MacStravic states that planning and marketing share functions; however, planning extends beyond exchange relationships and includes three perspectives of planning and marketing. The first perspective is planning, which suggests marketing is a tool to achieve desired change. The second perspective is marketing, viewing planning as a tool for a systematic and thorough approach to address change. The third perspective is organizational, and presents planning and marketing as coordinated if not integrated to achieve optimal effectiveness.

VIII. THE RELATIONSHIP OF HEALTH CARE MARKETING TO PUBLIC RELATIONS

In a fashion similar to the association between marketing and planning, marketing and public relations are interrelated in some settings. Although these functions may be independent, Sweeney (1985c) notes that planning and marketing are inextricably intertwined as they relate to health and health services. Kotler and Mindak (1978) note this growing confusion and observe that marketing people are increasingly interested in incorporating publicity as a tool within the marketing mix, although the publicity function is normally controlled by public relations departments. Public relations personnel are becoming increasingly concerned with marketing practices, and they concur with social responsibilities. As a result, it is suggested that public relations seeks to increase its influence over marketing practices. Kotler and Mindak state that the relationship between marketing and public relations varies from two independent departments to a single unit equally responsible for both sets of activities. A variety of intermediate steps exists where one component is subsumed by the other. Therefore, the relationship between these functions and the professional training of practitioners varies and is situational.

IX. BASIC CONCEPTS OF HEALTH CARE MARKETING

Many references to marketing refer to the "four P's" of traditional product marketing, product, place, price, and promotion (Hemmes, 1985; Keith, 1981; McLeod, 1985b) as the elements of the exchange process. Product refers to the commodity or service offered or being explored as a potential offering by the provider organization. Place addresses the location or locations offering the product or service, and price refers to the amount or fee charged for the product. Promotion concerns the advancement of publicity to inform users and potential users of the product or service.

Keith (1981) cites Cooper's modification of the four P's to shift marketing from the traditional product to health care services. The model transfers the concept of product to health care services. In the case of health care organizations, services may range from elective to medical emergency. In the case of health care facilities, while providers such as technicians and nurses may be employees, physicians and other professionals working in the facility normally are independent practitioners billing separately for their services. The concept of place is redefined as access, focusing not only on one geographic location, but also considering operating hours, barriers to patient access, and transportation. A significant consideration is the shift from the traditional delivery of a product to the customer to the alternative of patient access at a fixed facility location. The element of price is expanded to include consideration of anything of value offered by the consumer in exchange for services. Further complicating consideration is the complex third-party reimbursement system associated with health care services. Promotion, the final component is augmented to include an expanded role for health education and public relations associated with the delivery of complex health and medical services.

An alternative revision of the four P's for the health care setting is suggested by Shea and Shea (1985b). In addition to the four P's, six additional P's are added: (1) planning; (2) profiling; (3) patience; (4) patients; (5) professionals; and (6) people. The first three elements address evaluation, record keeping, and perseverance, while the remaining three elements focus attention on the individual participants in the health care marketing process. Shea and Shea state that implementation of the ten P's will serve as a means to identify needs and then design, develop, and deliver services to meet those needs. Although the health services organization differs from the traditional business setting, use of the four P's or a variation will assist in assessing the components of marketing.

In contrast to the traditional tangible product, health care organizations offer a service. In observing the difference between products and services, two distinctions are noted. First, services are intangible, resulting in difficulties in consumer perceptions. Second, there is a problem of simultaneous production and acceptance of services when dealing with receipts (Carman, 1986). In the delivery of health care services, the traditional service concept assumes that the consumer will react favorably to good services and facilities, and that very little marketing effort is required to obtain utilization. Prospective consumers must be made aware that a health service exists. Ireland (1977) states that promoting service is a result of determining the needs of consumers by market segment or characteristics, and it requires establishment of the correct mix of services, establishing a price structure, and implementing a strategy for access. In the current environment, many health care organizations are shifting their orientation to assume that consumers will normally not utilize their facilities enough unless they are approached with a substantial selling and promotional effort (Cooper, 1985).

Historically, the price of health care services has been perceived differently when compared to other consumer products and services. In contrast to other settings, in health care normally the consumer defers judgment of needed services to the clinically trained provider. Concurrently, the existence of private health insurance, health maintenance organizations, Medicare, Medicaid, and other government programs results in a party other than the actual consumer paying for services. In this unique environment, Nimer (1985) notes that hospital and health care providers do not price services, they cost them out. As a result, the relationship and positioning of price has not been given adequate consideration as an element in the marketing plan.

In the present environment, pricing of health services needs to be driven by demand and competition as well as cost (Carman, 1985). In developing a marketing plan, a pricing plan must be included. Pricing strategy must be based on the target market served, and the image the facility wishes to present as well as the balance between supply and demand (Lee, 1986a). Korneluk (1985) concurs, stating that while pricing strategies may not previously have been a factor in health care marketing, they are currently becoming important. In the effort to develop an appropriate pricing strategy, Nimer (1985) suggests four methods:

1. Increase the price of services to restore profitability, assuming there will be little impact on demand
2. Modify the nature and extent of the service to reduce costs assuming patients' needs will still be met
3. Reduce the price of service, assuming the demand for the service is fairly elastic and the expansion of use will reduce the unit costs
4. Increase the advertising and public relations budgets in an attempt to shift the demand curve upward, assuming that these expenditures will have the desired impact.

Recent changes in health care delivery such as the health maintenance organization have offered the option of prepayment for services as an alternative to fee-for-service medical care. In addressing prepaid care Korneluk (1985) suggests several creative approaches to pricing including:

1. Establishing a fixed base price for services and offering extra related services for additional fees
2. Discounting fees
3. Establishing a price differential for amenities.

As a result, the provider has a variety of options to consider in establishing prices for health care services.

Another useful component in understanding the marketing process is defining the market served. Edwards (1984) describes a market as a group with similar needs, a group that can generally be defined in sociodemographic terms. McMillan (1981) is more proactive, stating that in defining a market, you must find out what people want and give them more of it, while simultaneously learning what people do not want and giving them less of it. While the concept of human services marketing might focus more appropriately on offering those services that are professionally determined as necessary to the population served, McMillan suggests a "modest definition" which focuses upon listening, communication, openness, and an understanding of cohorts of the population. Marketers refer to a target market while planners discuss the population served. In both cases, organizations seek to identify the public groups they interact with. In developing a plan, the initial group under consideration is the public at large which may be subdivided into groups with specific needs (i.e., patients). Additional groups include the providers of health care services, with an emphasis upon physicians, employees, labor unions, and other groups representing the public, government, and regulatory agencies (Bonnem, 1985; Simon, 1978). In defining the population, providers may seek to change the behavior of an audience. As a component of the marketing plan, the market must be segmented to identify particular subgroups of the population that the organization wishes to serve. Cooper (1985) identifies three propositions to assist in segmentation of the target market. Cooper observes that (1) consumers of services are different, (2) differences between consumers are related to differences in market behavior, and (3) segments of consumers can be isolated within the overall market. A model for market segmentation must include division of the public by geographic, demographic, psychographic, and behavioristic criteria. Collection and analysis of data will then enable an understanding of the population served. Analysis of current experience and behavior may then be used to forecast future behavior. Concurrently the market environment may be analyzed and evaluated. Specific aspects of the environment appropriate to appraisal include competition and technology, as well as legal, economic, and cultural factors. As a result, the population may be partitioned by identifying the primary or core market, people who want a human service because it is correct for them, and a secondary or fringe market, those individuals wanting to use a service such as the one being offered, but have not decided from whom to purchase it.

Concerning promotion, health care professionals frequently assume that marketing and advertising are synonymous. They assume the sole function of marketing is to promote the use of health care services through newspaper advertisements and television commercials. Many professional associations have historically taken positions firmly in opposition to their members advertising, although recent trends clearly show reversal of this pattern. Darling and Bergial (1983) report the results of two surveys of professionals, including physicians and dentists. In reporting their findings they note a shift in attitudes favoring the general value of advertising and stating that advertising increases price, and that the absence of advertising decreases competition. The surveys report a decreasing concern for the negative effect of advertising upon the public image of respondent's professions, that it is difficult to advertise either competence and quality, and that advertising would not benefit respondents personally. Furthermore, the professionals agreed that advertising restrictions may be necessary to protect the public interest, and it is here to stay. Advertising is clearly a subset of the promotion available to the marketer, and decisions concerning the use of advertising will be contingent upon the defined objections. Fisk (1986) notes that advertising is a method to shift decision making from sellers to buyers of services. When properly executed, advertising is the least costly method to communicate with members of the general public unknown to you, and to motivate potential consumers to use your services. Fisk further notes that advertising allows the service to offer a controlled message on a repetitive basis to a mass audience. Marketing through use of advertised messages is becoming increasingly common in a variety of forms including, but not limited to, printed and electronic advertising, direct mail announcements and newsletters, listings in the yellow pages, patient information brochures, and sponsorship of community events.

X. MARKETING PLANS

Both marketing and planning activities depend upon a written document specifying desired outcomes, and a specific work program to achieve the specified outcomes. The principal difference in types of plans concerns the lengths of the time period covered, and the degree of specificity in objectives and programs. A typical planning model utilizes research and develops an organizational mission, assesses needs, sets specific outcome and measurable goals and objectives, develops strategies to achieve these outcomes, implements programs and offers services, and evaluates performance. Following evaluation Beckham (1984a) states that a marketing plan will also define strategies to achieve objectives include pricing, marketing, communication, distribution, and product development tactics that will ensure successful execution of strategies. In developing a successful marketing plan, Miaoulis et al. (1985) suggest the following guidelines for marketing plan implementation:

1. The plan must have visible support from senior administrators
2. The responsible party should have a background in both health care and marketing
3. In consideration of the plan's objectives, a realistic budget should be developed
4. The plan should be directed to internal as well as external audiences
5. Short- and long-term market recommendations should be developed
6. The implications of marketing decisions must be fully integrated into managerial decisions
7. Marketing knowledge must be merged with functional product expertise
8. The threat the marketing plan presents to some people should be anticipated and responded to.

A vital element in decision making is information. Miaoulis et al. present a model for understanding the marketing process identifying three components: data inputs, decision structures, and marketing outputs. Each of the components consists of two functional areas (1) marketing research and (2) planning information, where raw data is collected and transformed into useful information for decision making. In an effort to make informed decisions data is required. MacMillan and Rosenbaum (1986) note that market research is a powerful management tool for this purpose.

Market research becomes the basis for collection of required data. The research process includes two components. The first develops an analytical strategy to define the actual and potential consumers, and their needs and wants. The second function develops a steady flow of reliable information about the market. Chapman (1986) describes external environmental assessment as evaluation of community, health service practice patterns, the effects of external pressures, and signs of significant change to explain what has happened and predict the future of these events. Information describing the external environment would include data enumerating socioeconomic and demographic characteristics of the population served, community characteristics, and assessment of the quantity and characteristics of competitive health resources. A concurrent internal organizational review must be conducted. Sweeney (1985) defines a market audit as the systematic, impartial, critical review and appraisal of the total organization, its structure, and operations. Five specific objectives are identified for a market audit of an organization:

1. Evaluation of the quality and responsiveness of services
2. Evaluation of the soundness, relevance, and practicality of objectives and policies
3. Evaluation of the marketing opportunity in relation to the current service mix and market share
4. Identification of organizational weaknesses
5. Prevention or resolution of marketing problems

The market research profile is designed to identify the strengths and weaknesses concerning new or potential markets, changes in the environment, research for effective marketing, and strategic planning (Hillestadt and Berkowitz, 1984; Simon, 1978).

Dearing et al. (1987) report that as a result of market analysis, a series of research outcomes may be generated. These outcomes offer provision of an objective basis for decision making between alternative services, along with a comprehensive and shared understanding of the market place. Research outcomes will additionally provide an understanding of a health care organization's position in the community in regard to other facilities offering competitive services.

The analysis will also provide specific details concerning the prospective population to be served and should identify potential barriers to the establishment of new programs. Although this information is extremely beneficial to the decision making process, research analysis does not offer strategies; it does offer information to assist in making decisions. Although marketing research is a useful tool in decision making, Clarke and Shyavitz (1983) report the application of market research to this process is limited, and it is essential to have realistic expectations concerning application. These authors report that it is not possible to learn answers to all questions through research; particularly inaccessible are sensitive, complex, and costly issues. Additionally, experimental research findings need to be statistically significant, explaining a difference; equivocal findings may be of a timely nature, as attitudes, opinions, and perceptions are dynamic and will change with time. In summarizing the use of market research, MacMillan and Rosenbaum (1986) note that users of market research are probably leaders or innovators, and that process often leads to success through problem identification, establishing objectives, collecting and interpreting data, and action. Finally, research may be a consensus builder and enable action to be taken with confidence.

XI. SOURCES OF DATA FOR MARKET RESEARCH

In an effort to collect information an organization may obtain data directly or contract with a private research firm. A variety of private firms offer consultation services varying from simple data collection and analysis to customized data collection and computerized mapping. While these applications may be appropriate in specialized cases, baseline data may be obtained easily from a variety of primary and secondary data sources at relatively low cost. Primary data source information includes use of previously compiled internal cost, utilization, and managerial data. Concurrently new data may be collected concerning attitudes, knowledge, or satisfaction. Survey research in the form of interviews or mail questionnaires may also be collected. The process would include sample selection, development of a survey instrument, pretesting, interviewer selection and training, and analysis (MacMillan and Rosenbaum, 1986). As an alternative to currently available data, survey research may be both more specific to needs, and more costly in time and money.

A less costly alternative is the use of secondary data descriptive of the organization's service area. Following collection of data, a variety of techniques may be used for analysis. Future trends may be forecast based upon the collected information. Qualitative and quantitative techniques including extrapolation and statistical methods such as regression analysis may be applied. Comparison to standards or other reference data, use of standardized formulas and models may also be used to assess current and future requirements.

The key resource in assessing characteristics of population of the United States is the decennial census. Article I, Section 2 of the Constitution stipulates that for the purposes of taxation and appointment of seats in Congress an enumeration of the population shall be conducted every ten years (Kaplan and Van Valey, 1980). Although the census initially focused upon a simple count of the population, the process has become increasingly sophisticated over time. In addition to enumeration by state, the U.S. Census uses other legal geographic entities including counties and cities. A variety of statistical geographic areas have been developed to respond to the changing needs of census users. These include large physical regions and divisions of the U.S., metropolitan areas, urbanized areas, central and extended cities, metropolitan statistical areas (formerly standard metropolitan statistical areas), and urban and rural areas. In development of these areas, geography, total population, population density, and social and economic interdependencies were considered (Kaplan and Van Valey, 1980).

While the Bureau of the Census publishes a variety of publications, several basic publications will meet the needs of most users. A primary source is *The County and City Data Book* (U.S. Department of Commerce, 1983), which provides 1980 census data for the United States, the 50 individual states and the District of Columbia, census regions and divisions, counties (or their equivalent), incorporated cities, towns, boroughs, and villages with a population greater than 25,000 places and minor civil divisions with 2,500 or more residents, and unincorporated census-designated places. A reference table is also provided to convert data to standard metropolitan areas. The volume reports 216 variables for the nation; individual states and counties, and selected variables for other divisions. The data include:

1. Characteristics of the area and population including age, sex, race, ethnicity, and migration and household characteristics
2. Vital statistics including births, deaths, marriages, and divorces
3. Health care data summarizing information concerning physicians, dentists, nurses, hospitals, and nursing homes
4. Social welfare programs such as Medicare benefits, Social Security benefits, and Supplemental Security Income
5. Serious crimes including all reported crimes
6. Housing including private housing, total housing, and housing characteristics
7. Journey to work data concerning location and transportation
8. Education, current school enrollment, and years of school completed
9. Labor force information including labor force, unemployment, employment, and income by category
10. Money income by household, family, and individual
11. Local government finance
12. Employment by business sector
13. Characteristics of agriculture

Reported data in this volume is well defined and documented, and state maps by county are provided. Additional documents of importance include the *Current Population Reports: Population Estimates, Projections, and Special Censuses Reports* containing population estimates and projections, and special censuses; *Current Population Reports: Population Characteristics, Special Studies, and Income Series* reporting on population characteristics, special studies, farm population, and consumer income; *Statistical Abstracts of the United States;* and the *State and Metropolitan Area Data Book.*

Similarly, vital statistics may be obtained from a variety of sources. An essential source of this information is the U.S. Department of Health and Human Services' National Center for Health Statistics (NCHS) Vital Health Statistics Series. Among the publications of NCHS are over 500 individual volumes including:

1. Results of a continuing national (household health) interview survey of the U.S. population

2. Results of a direct health and nutrition examination of a sample of the U.S. population
3. Data concerning utilization of health professionals and facilities
4. Statistics concerning distribution and characteristics of health professionals and facilities
5. Data on natality, marriage, and divorce
6. Data concerning family growth

An additional series, *Advance Data From Vital and Health Statistics* provides early announcement of significant findings of the NCHS, while *Morbidity and Mortality Weekly Report, Monthly Vital Statistics Reports*, and *Vital Statistics of the United States* report incidence of specified notifiable diseases, births, deaths, marriages, divorces and other statistics on a regular basis.

In addition to the previously cited information, current detailed health resources data are available from a variety of professional association publications. *The American Hospital Association Guide to the Health Care Field*, 1987 (also known as the *AHA Guide*) is a well documented annual publication of data compiled through a survey of U.S. hospitals. The volume reports all hospitals in the United States by city, county, address, and telephone number, identifying acceptance by any of 13 approving bodies, reporting the presence of available medical services from 54 specified categories, identification of ownership and control, and characteristics of lengths of stay. Inpatient data reported include the total number of beds, the number of patients admitted, average daily inpatient census, percentage occupancy rate, newborn data, total and payroll budget expenses, and total personnel employed. An important consideration is the self-reporting of this data. As a result, in some cases data are absent or may be erroneous. The *Guide to the Health Care Field* also includes a series of directories, and beginning with the 1987 issue, presents individual state maps. A companion volume, *Hospital Statistics* (American Hospital Association, 1987), presents statistical tabulations of the individual hospital data by the above listed hospital organizational characteristics, and reports trends over time.

Similar efforts in reporting exist for other health care organizations. *The Directory of Nursing Homes* (Mongeau, 1982) presents information concerning 15,272 licensed long-term care facilities in the United States obtained from state licensure agencies. Geographically organized, the volume reports address, administrator's name, categories of licensure, and beds by category (intermediate care, skilled nursing, and personal care), and certification for Medicaid and Medicare reimbursement. Health Maintenance Organizations (HMOs) are reported by several sources, the most complete being *The National HMO Census, 1985* (InterStudy, 1985) listing facilities by name, total enrollment, Medicare and Medicaid membership, hospital utilization in days per 1,000 members, encounters per member, organizational model type, plan age, and for-profit/not-for-profit status. Hospice resources are reported in *The 1987 Guide to the Nation's Hospices* (National Hospice Organization, 1987). The guide identifies U.S. hospices by primary services offered, legal corporate status and ownership, type of organization, and specific program status characteristics (operational status, certificate of need requirements, licensure, accreditation, and certification). Specific services offered and counties included in the primary service area are also reported.

In similar fashion, health personnel data are reported in a variety of secondary sources. While directories exist for many professional groups, physicians will be used as an example. Information concerning medical doctors is important due to their key role in health care decision making and use of services. Also as a result of their primary role, greater detail is available for this group than for other health care professionals. The American Medical Association Physician Masterfile identifies physicians while they are in medical school and tracks them throughout their professional careers. Data from the Masterfile is printed in the *American Medical Directory*, also known as the *Directory of Physicians in the United States* (American Medical Association, 1986). The directory geographically lists all physicians (not simply AMA members) by professional mailing address and identifies medical school of graduation, for osteopathic physicians, year of licensure, primary and secondary specialties, type of practice (medical resident, direct patient care, teaching, research, other patient or nonpatient care, inactive, disabled, or retired), and American Specialty Board certification by code number are included. Although physician listings can be summarized by hand tabulation, the American Medical Association prepares a series of special publications similar to *Hospital Statistics*. These publications include *Medical Groups in the U.S., 1984; Socioeconomic Characteristics of Medical Practice, 1986*; and *Physician Characteristics and Distribution in the U.S., 1986 edition*. These volumes report *Directory* data tabulated for the United States as a whole, individual states and counties, demographic characteristics of physicians, and practice patterns. An adjunct to the American Medical Association sources is the *ABMS Compendium of Certified Medical Specialists* (American Board of Medical Specialties, 1987). The American Board of Medical Specialties, 1987). The American Board of Medical Specialties presents well documented geographic and alphabetical biographic listings for all members of a particular medical specialty by activity. As a result, specialists in anesthesiology in a specific geographic location can be identified. The volume reports certifications and dates, date and place of birth, medical school attended and date of graduation, internship, residency, and fellowship dates and locations, types of practice, current academic appointments, hospital staff appointments, professional associations, address, and telephone number.

The preceding data sources are presented as examples of available secondary data sources and were selected due to their high probability of use. Most recent publication years are cited, however earlier editions are available to assist in evaluating trends over time, and subsequent issues will be released as data become available. To expand on these citations, several directories are available describing citations, year of data, cost, and source. These publications, *A Guide to Health Data Resources* (Singer et al., 1985) and *Inventory of U.S. Health Care Data Bases, 1976-1983* (Mullner and Byre, 1984), identify both printed and machine-readable (computer) data sources concerning health care characteristics, status, determinants, facilities, personnel, programs, and expenditures. Additionally, the reference librarian staff in a large city library or university library is capable of assisting in locating these and other useful data sources. A final set of information sources are of a local nature. Regional and community data are frequently compiled and disseminated by state departments of commerce, university economic and business units, local chambers of commerce, real estate boards, and planning bodies. Sources and data vary with individual communities and should be explored for each project considered.

XII. MARKETING PLAN BUDGET

Implementation of a planning or marketing project will require financial resources. Therefore the magnitude of efforts will be tied to budget. Kotler (1986) states that the budget may be established based upon one of four methods:

1. The affordable method or what can be accomplished within the financial resources of the organization
2. The percentage of sales method where a predetermined portion of the total service charges are reinvested or reallocated to this function
3. The competitive parity method where an organization's budget is a direct response to the activities of other providers offering similar services in the community
4. The objective and tasks method where a budget is a direct product of the outcomes and actions specified in the organization's formal plans.

While the basis for allocation of financial resources is situational and may include a combination of these methods, the final budget should be based upon expectation for the funded programs.

XIII. ETHICAL CONSIDERATIONS

In concluding this discussion of health care marketing, the issue of ethical presentation of marketing efforts must be considered. Due to the nature of these services Walch and Tseng (1984) point out that although marketing can be appropriate, beneficial, and ethical, providers must be extremely careful as to how they market their services. In particular, when dealing with precious human services, it is inappropriate to proclaim the best, the lowest price, or the most personal or friendly service (Mages, 1986a). As an indicator of the change concerning ethics, the American Hospital Association Guidelines for Hospital Advertising are a useful example for review. The *Washington Report on Medicine and Health* (1985) cites that the 1977 guidelines state that "claims of being the best or most efficient are not necessary in making any point about the institution." By 1985, the American Hospital Association Guidelines were modified to refer to maintaining or increasing market share in an increasingly competitive and cost-conscious environment as a purpose of hospital advertising, stating that "direct comparisons should not be made unless they can be measured and substantiated."

XIV. WHY MARKETING FAILS

In developing a marketing program, it is useful to have an understanding of why marketing may be unsuccessful. Sweeney (1985a) succinctly enumerates the factors contributing to the failure of a health care marketing effort:

1. The failure to conduct proper internal preparation prior to beginning
2. The tendency to confuse marketing with advertising and solicitation and assume that efforts exclusively in these areas will result in success
3. Having unrealistic expectations for marketing and anticipating that accomplishment will be achieved in a shorter time or greater quantity than is possible
4. Inadequately staffing the marketing activities with personnel either unprepared for their responsibilities or in insufficient numbers.

An understanding of potential causes of failure in marketing will assist in preventing these errors.

As previously noted, health care marketing is a relatively young discipline, and is continuing to evolve. Additionally, the combination of external forces results in a variety of complex issues for health care organizations. Although these external factors may be considerable, conscientious development of a strategy for marketing remains important as a mechanism to achieve a successful outcome.

BIBLIOGRAPHY

Advertising: Is it integral to hospital marketing? (1984). *Cost Containment, 6*: 3-6.

Aguiar, A. V. (1984). The medical marketing audit: Technique for today's competitive extended care environment, *Health Marketing Quarterly, 1*: 45–50.

Albachten, D. R. (1985-1986). The direct marketing of physicians' services to the public, *Health Marketing Quarterly, 3*: 185–187.

Alexander, P. D., Anders, G. T., Beck, L. C., and Sweeney, D. R. (1983). Positioning your practice to best advantage, *Pennsylvania Medicine, 86*: 28, 32.

Alibrio, T. (1984). A fertile ground for marketing, *Food Management, 19*: 35-36.

Allcorn, S. (1985). Three dimensional strategic marketing analysis for hospitals, *Health Care Strategic Management, 3*: 9–12.

Allen, L. E. (1985). Competition in the marketplace of medical care, *Indiana Medicine, 78*: 46-48.

Almost everthing you need to know about HMOs but haven't had time to think about (1984). *Profiles in Hospital Marketing, 15*: 4-23.

Alpern, B. B. (1986). The next generation of healthcare advertising, marketing to women, *Healthcare Executive, 1*: 39–41.

Alward, R. R. (1983a). A marketing approach to nursing administration—Part I, *Journal of Nursing Administration, 13*: 9–12.

Alward, R. R. (1983b). A marketing approach to nursing administration—Part II, *Journal of Nursing Administration, 13*: 18–22.

American Board of Medical Specialists (1987). *ABMS Compendium of Certified Medical Specialists*, The Board, Evanston, IL.

American Hospital Association (1987a). *Guide to the Health Care Field*, The Association, Chicago.

American Hospital Association (1987b). *Hospital Statistics*, The Association, Chicago.

American Hospital Association (1982). *Planning Hospital Health Promotion Services for Business and Industry*, The Association, Chicago.

American Medical Association (1984). *Medical Groups in the U.S., 1984*, The Association, Chicago.

American Medical Association (1986). *Characteristics of Medical Practice*, The Association, Chicago.

American Medical Association (1986). *Directory of Physicians in the U.S., 1986*, The Association, Chicago.

American Medical Association (1986). *Physician Characteristics and Distribution in the U.S.*, The Association, Chicago.

American Medical Association (1986). *Socioeconomic Characteristics of Medical Practice, 1986*, The Association, Chicago.

Anderson, D. C. (1985-1986). What they see is what you get: Marketers perspective on hospital advertising, *Health Marketing Quarterly, 3*: 125–138.

Anderson, D. C., and Near, R. (1983). Something may not be working in the hospital—but is it marketing, *Journal of Health Care Marketing, 3*: 49–55.

Anderson, R. A. (1985). Products and product-line management in nursing, *Nursing Administration Quarterly, 10*: 65–72.

Andrews, A. H. (1984a). Marketing and the veterinary profession, *Veterinary Record, 115*: 191.

Andrews, A. H. (1984b). Strategy for marketing preventive medicine, *Veterinary Records, 115*: 305.

Andrus, D., and Kohout, F. J. (1984-1985). The effect of rural consumer satisfaction on outshopping for medical services, *Health Marketing Quarterly, 2*: 171-184.

Aquilina, D., and Johnson, A. N. (1985). The way to control hospital costs lies between regulation and competition, *Modern Healthcare, 15*: 152-154.

Archer, S. E. (1983). Marketing public health nursing services, *Nursing Outlook, 31*: 304-309.

Armstrong, D. M., Amo, E., Duer, A. L., Hanson, M., Hijeck, T., Karwoski, P., and Young, S. (1985). Marketing opportunities for a nursing department in a changing economic enrollment, *Nursing Administration Quarterly, 10*: 1-10.

Ascher, S. (1984). Incentive marketing can attract patients to your practice, *Dental Management, 24*: 48-49, 53.

Ascher, S. (1985). PR for the dental office, turning the public into patients, *Dental Management, 25*: 50-51, 54-55.

Ascher, S., and Ridgeway, K. (1984). Promotion for the professional, *Dental Economics, 74*: 75-76, 78.

Ascher, S. (1984). Smile! When you say advertising, *Dental Studies, 62*: 49-52.

Ashton, L. (1985). Marketing and health education units, *Health Education Journal, 44*: 155-156.

Asimus, A., and Hansburg, T. B. (1984). Marketing savvy, two hospitals share successful ideas, *Hospital Gift Shop Management, 2*: 34-37, 40.

A survey: Finance and marketing relationships in hospitals (1986). *Healthcare Financial Management, 40*: 54-58.

Austin, H. (1985). Hospital computer marketing to increase patient census, *Software in Healthcare, 3*: 66-68.

Autrey, P., and Thomas, D. (1986). Competitive strategy in the hospital industry, *Health Care Management Review, 11*: 7-14.

Baginski, Y. (1985). Marketing home care to the doctors, *Caring, 4*: 34-40.

Barlett, P. J., Schewe, C. D., and Allen, C. T. (1984). Marketing orientation, how do hospital administrators compare with marketing managers? *Health Care Management Review, 9*: 77-86.

Barnes, J. (1986). Good marketing takes a lot of strategic planning, *Health Care, 28*: 20-22.

Barnes, N. G. (1985). What Dewey didn't tell us, a closer look at our basic assumptions in marketing health services, *Journal of Health Care Marketing, 5*: 59-61.

Barnett, N. (1985a). Physicians and hospital marketing, *Southern Hospitals, 53*: 71-73.

Barnett, N. (1985b). Putting market research to work, *Southern Hospitals, 53*: 34-35.

Barney, D. R. (1985). Healthcare advertising, what you can and cannot say, *Healthspan Law and Business, 2*: 3-10.

Bassin, J. (1983). The DSSNY's marketing efforts on behalf of the membership, *New York State Dental Journal, 49*: 145-146.

Bassin, J., and Millman-Falk, N. I. (1984). DSSNY launches marketing workshops as new membership benefit, *New York State Dental Journal, 50*: 35-36.

Beck, C. (1985). Nursing administrator establishes marketing strategies, *Nursing Success Today, 2*: 26-30.

Beck, L. C., and Salmon, P. M. (1985). A checklist of practice marketing ideas, *North Carolina Medical Journal, 46*: 345-347.

Beck, L. C., and Sweeney, D. R. (1985). Marketing medical practice begins internally, *Pennsylvania Medicine, 88*: 32.

Beck, L. C., Anders, G. T., and Sweeney, D. R. (1984). Marketing ideas benefit patients, practice, *Pennsylvania Medicine, 87*: 20.

Beck, L. C., Anders, G. T., and Sweeney, D. R. (1985). Staff plays role in marketing practice, *Pennsylvania Medicine, 88*: 36.

Beckham, D. (1984a). Positioning marketing in the hospital's power structure, *Trustee, 37*: 22–26, 36.
Beckham, D. (1984b). Some marketing moves unique; others borrowed from industry, *Modern Healthcare, 14*: 104, 106.
Beckham, J. D. (1984). A strategic alternative for community hospitals, the principles of peripheral penetration, *Journal of Health Care Marketing, 4*: 37–40.
Beckham, J. D. (1985). New product development, *Hospital Forum, 28*: 59–61.
Bedrosian, J. (1985). One hospital chain's blueprint for survival, *Cost Containment, 7*: 3–8.
Bell, D. C. (1986). Make the newsletter a marketing strategy, *Journal of the American Health Care Association, 12*: 44–45.
Bellina, B. (1985). Internal marketing of material management, *Hospital Material Management Quarterly, 6*: 70–74.
Bellina, B. (1983). Marketing and materials management mix, *Hospitals, 57*: 52.
Bellino, B. S. (1985). Classic marketing principles for the modern dental laboratory, *Trends and Techniques in the Contemporary Dental Laboratory, 2*: 35–38.
Bentley, J. M., and Woodall, I. R. (1984). Networking. The private practitioner's key to quality and marketing, *Journal of Dental Practice Administration, 1*: 111–116.
Benz, P. D., and Burnham, J. (1985). Case study: Developing product lines using ICD-9-CM codes, *Healthcare Financial Management, 39*: 38–41.
Berger, A. (1985). The role of an agency in marketing a dental practice, *New York State Dental Journal, 51*: 586–587.
Berl, R., and Sweeney, R. E. (1985). What is strategic market planning, *Home Health Journal, 6*: 10–12.
Bernard, M. (1985). Overview of marketing for the pharmacist, *Topics in Hospital Pharmacy Management, 5*: 1–7.
Bills, S. S. (1984). In crowded market, hospital looks to wellness for competitive edge, *Promoting Health, 5*: 1–3.
Bittker, T. E. (1985). The industrialization of American psychiatry, *American Journal of Psychiatry, 142*: 149–154.
Blackburn, J. M. (1984). Marketing audit in group practice, *College Review, 1*: 97–108.
Blau, M. A. (1983). Marketing your practice, *Journal of Clinical Orthodontics, 17*: 519–528.
Bloch, P. H. (1984). The wellness movement: Imperatives for health care marketers, *Journal of Health Care Marketing, 4*: 9–16.
Block, L. F. (Ed.) (1981). Marketing for hospitals in hard times, *Teach 'em*, Chicago.
Block, L. F., and Press, C. E. (1985). Product line development by DRG builds market strength, *Healthcare Financial Management, 39*: 50–52.
Bonaguro, J. A., and Bonaguro, E. W. (1985). Use of benefit segmentation in designing family health programs, *Family and Community Health, 7*: 5–12.
Bonnem, S. (1985). Vox populi—or hearing the voices of your publics, *Health Care Marketing, Issues and Trends* (P. D. Cooper, ed.), Aspen Systems, Rockville, MD.
Bonner, P. (1985a). An overview of dental marketing, *Dental Economics, 75*: 37–38, 40–41.
Bonner, P. (1985b). Public relations as an ethical marketing tool, *Dental Economics, 75*: 77–78, 80–81.
Bourgeois, J. C., and Helm, B. (1985). Parenting and communication: A qualitative analysis key to marketing parenting services, *Health Marketing Quarterly, 2*: 131–143.

Bowers, M. R. (1986). Marketing for patient retention, *Medical Group Management, 33*: 40-41, 43.
Boyd, S. H. (1984). Fitness and health promotion: Big business and good business in Dallas. "What, where, why, and how," *Health Marketing Quarterly, 2*: 75-89.
Bradley, J. F. (1984). Key to multi advertising is finding the right channel, *Multis, 2*: M46, M48.
Bradt, M. E., and Allen, S. (1986). Marketing the image inside and out, *Provider, 12*: 33-35.
Brown, B. (1985). Marketing and image making, *Nursing Administration Quarterly, 10*: iv-vi.
Brown, B. S. (1983). What is business savvy? *Nursing Economics, 1*: 52-53, 72.
Brown, D. (1985). How to get in to see the dentist, *Lab Management Today, 1*: 22.
Brown, D. (1984). The case for direct mail marketing, *Lab Management Today, 1*: 44-45.
Brown, L. (1985a). Are you challenging your hygienist to sell needed treatment? *Dental Economics, 75*: 68, 70.
Brown, R. E. (1985b). Consumerism in health care delivery: The harbinger of opportunity, *Health Care Marketing, Issues and Trends* (P. D. Cooper, ed.), Aspen Systems, Rockville, MD.
Brown, R. H. (1986). Marketing yourself—the role of communication skills, *New Zealand Dental Journal, 82*: 7-9.
Brown, S. (1983). Dental marketing, from research to service, *Dental Economics, 73*: 34-40, 42-44.
Brown, S. W. (1985a). Future directions in health marketing, *Health Care Strategic Management, 3*: 23-26.
Brown, S. W. (1985b). Minding the store as competition intensifies, *Journal of Health Care Marketing, 5*: 65-67.
Bruce, G. (1985). On the scene: Stanford University. An evolution of marketing in nursing, *Nursing Administration Quarterly, 10*: 31-35.
Burnum, J. F. (1984). The unfortunate case of Dr. Z: How to succeed in medical practice in 1984, *New England Journal of Medicine, 310*: 729-730.
Burns, J. A. (1985-1986). Knowledge is power: How to develop effective market surveys, *Health Marketing Quarterly, 3*: 99-112.
Burns, K. (1986). Selling your hospital, *Volunteer Leader, 27*: 1-5.
Burton, M. E. (1985). Working smarter: Selling clinical pharmacy programs, *Topics in Hospital Pharmacy Management, 5*: 35-44.
Buschiazzo, L. (1985). Marketing the emergency department, *Nursing Management, 16*: 30B-30D.
Business and providers make competition the name of the game in Richmond, Va. (1984). *Review-Federation of American Hospitals, 17*: 52-54, 58.
Business outlook. 21% call marketing top priority (1984). *Modern Healthcare, 14*: 114.
Businesses join marketing fight against breast cancer (1984). *Plastic Surgical Nursing, 4*: 96-99.
Calderon, E. H. (1984). The marketing audit: The first step, *Texas Hospitals, 40*: 21-22.
Cameron, A. N., Jr. (1984). Hospital marketing: Now more than ever, *Southern Hospitals, 52*: 24-28.
Can marketing benefit your practice? (1983). *New York State Dental Journal, 49*: 586.
Caplan, C. M. (1984). Conversional marketing, *Journal of Dental Practice Administration, 1*: 175-178.
Carman, J. M. (1985). A conversation with Dr. James M. Carman on the continuing hospital struggle with marketing principles and methods, *Healthmarketing, 4*: 2-6.
Carter, J. (1986). Marketing a hospital: The specialty advantage, *Michigan Hospital, 22*: 19-22.

Carter, K. (1986). HCA corporate data center gives chain's hospitals a tool for research, *Modern Healthcare, 16*: 76, 82.
Case in point. St. Mary's Mountain View (1984). *Health Care Strategic Management, 2*: 26-28.
Case in point. The Affiliated Health System (1984). *Health Care Strategic Management, 2*: 27-28.
Case in point—the answer. The Affiliated Health System (1984). *Health Care Strategic Management, 2*: 28-29.
Case in point. Providence Hospital (1985). *Health Care Strategic Management, 3*: 31-32.
Chafee-Bahamon, C., and Lovejoy, F. H., Jr. (1984). Member hospital network for poison control, *Veterinary and Human Toxicology, 26*(Suppl. 2): 20-23.
Chapman, T. B. (1986). Organized competition and medical practice, opportunities and threats, *Topics in Health Records Management, 6*: 36-45.
Chaput, R., Pride, J., Tekavec, M., Press, B., and Roach, R. (1983). Dental marketing. ADA's program to assist members with practice development, *Journal of the American Dental Association, 23*: 160-166.
Chies, S. E. (1985). Being creative in your marketing, *Journal of the American Health Care Association, 11*: 26-29.
Cicatiello, J. S. (1985). Marketing: Competing through a holistic approach, *Nursing Administration Quarterly, 10*: 56-58.
Ciocci, G. (1984). Capitalizing on the hidden job market, *Nurse Practitioner, 9*: 31-33.
Clark, D. W. (1985). Retired executives link purchasers and providers in Greater Philadelphia, *Health Cost Management, 2*: 5-13.
Clarke, R. N., and Neiman, J. S. (1986). State-of-the-art of hospital marketing: Lessons from a national survey (xerographic), American Hospital Association, Society for Hospital Planning and Marketing, Chicago.
Clarke, R. N., and Shyavitz, L. (1983). Strategies for a crowded marketplace, *Health Care Management Review, 8*: 45-51.
Cohen, C. (1984). Operation: Patient awareness, *Contact Point, 62*: 24-26.
Cohen, D. M., Underly, N., Gentleman, C. A., and Salome, P. (1986). Marketing: Getting in the public eye, *Nursing Management, 17*: 79-80.
Cohn, J. P. (1985). Marketing medical care, *New Physician, 34*: 14-17.
Coile, R. C., Jr. (1985). The leading edge, *Hospital Forum, 28*: 6.
Colls, J. P. (1984). A business for profit can help the NP role, *Nurse Practitioner, 9*: 58, 60.
Colwell, W. B. (1984). A successful marketing campaign for individual hospitals in a health system, *Hospital Topics, 62*: 11-15.
Comport, W. J. (1984). Dental health is marketing, *Canadian Dental Association Journal, 12*: 44-45.
Conducting a marketing audit of your practice (1984). *New York State Dental Journal, 50*: 236, 238.
Connellan, T. K. (1984). Six steps for establishing a successful health promotion program, *Health Care Strategic Management, 2*: 35-38.
Contraceptive social marketing: Lessons from experience (1985). *Population Reports, Series 3*, (30): J773-812.
Conway, A. (1984). The key to successful psychiatric programs, *Southern Hospitals, 52*: 64-68.
Conway, J. B. (1985). AHRA Statistical/Resource Committee. Survey results: Programs, services and trends, *Radiology Management, 7*: 51-75.
Cooper, P. D. (1984). Marketing from the inside out. What does marketing have to do with orderlies? *Profiles in Hospital Marketing*, No. 16, 71-73.

Cooper, P. D., and King, K. K. (1985). Marketing ethics, functions, and content, a health education/marketing survey, *Health Values, 9*: 29-36.
Coppolillo, H. P. (1983). The marketplace, our language, and our values, *Hospital Practice, 18*: 64, 68.
Corrigan, A. (1986). From the President. The need for nurses to become involved in marketing, *National Intravenous Therapy Association, 9*: 175-176.
Costello, M. (1984). Discontinuing hospital services—questions to consider when deleting a program or service, *Healthmarketing, 3*: 11-12.
Costello, M. M. (1985). Marketing innovations, *Hospital Topics, 63*: 3, 38.
Craig, T. T. (1983). Integrating institutional long-range strategic planning, *Hospital and Health Services Administration, 28*: 16-26.
Cross, G. P. (1983). Marketing a dental practice, *Journal of the Oregon Dental Association, 52*: 31-32.
Cryan, T. V. (1985a). A marketing primer, *Radiology Management, 7*: 7-10.
Cryan, T. V. (1985b). Radiology managers apply marketing, *Radiology Management 7*: 38-42.
Cueny, D., Miller, K., and Elderidge, M. K. (1985-1986). The healthcare account executive—a sales approach to healthcare marketing, *Health Marketing Quarterly, 3*: 85-92.
Cunningham, D. (1985-1986). Community education as a marketing tool for your hospital, *Health Marketing Quarterly, 3*: 197-206.
Cunningham, L. (1985a). Focus groups. Everything you always wanted to know, *Profiles in Hospital Marketing*, No. 19: 83-85.
Cunningham, L., and York, K. P. (1985b). Getting the best from your ad agency, *Hospital Forum, 28*: 59-61.
Cunningham, R. M., Jr. (1984). Competition and health care's loss of innocence, *Hospitals, 58*: 65.
Curtin, L. L. (1985). Survival of the slickest, *Nursing Management, 16*: 7-8.
Curtin, L. L. (1986). Selling our wares in a not-so-open market, *Nursing Management, 17*: 7-8.
Cuscurida, J., and Shaw, E. M. (1985). St. Joseph Hospital's marketing strategy, in search of excellence, *Nursing Administration Quarterly, 10*: 47-52.
Darcey, R. C. (1985). Marketing: A tool for i.v. nurses, *National Intravenous Therapy Association, 8*: 421-425.
Darling, J. R., and Bergial, B. J. (1983). Health care advertising: A comparative analysis, *Journal of Health Care Marketing, 3*: 21-28.
David and Goliath. Small hospitals take on big competition (1984). *Profiles in Hospital Marketing*, No. 14: 62-69.
Davidson, J. P. (1985). Enhance your image and your patient flow with marketing, *Dental Studies, 63*: 14-15, 18-19, 44.
Day Surgery. Aggressive marketing secures success (1985). *Profiles in Hospital Marketing*, No. 18: 4-10.
Dearing, R. H., Gordon, H. A., Sohner, D. M., and Weidel, L. C. (1987). *Marketing Women's Health Care*, Aspen Publications, Rockville, MD.
Dedrick, S. C. (1985). Marketing outpatient pharmacy services, *Topics in Hospital Pharmacy Management, 5*: 73-77.
DeJoseph, J., and Swarts, M. (1985). On the scene: Stanford University. The development of a marketing plan for perinatal services, *Nursing Administration Quarterly, 10*: 41-43.
Delene, L. M., and Miller, C. M. (1984). The medical staff and the development of hospital marketing programs, *Journal of Health Care Marketing, 4*: 39-43.
Demby, N. A. (1985). Quality assurance and marketing, *Dental Clinics of North America, 29*: 605-614.

De-Monnin, J. L. (1984-1985). Promoting your practice, *Journal of the Oregon Dental Association, 54*: 27-28.
Desai, H. B., and New, J. R. (1985). Strategic development information for HMOs, *Medical Group Management, 32*: 48-52.
DeSalvo, C. P. (1986). Rural hospitals study the market, *Hospitals, 60*: 65.
DeSalvo, C. P., and Powills, S. (1986). More small, rurals begin using marketing, *Hospitals, 60*: 64, 66.
DeWitt, L. W. (1984). Physician contracting, *Minnesota Medicine, 67*: 647-649.
Dibble, K. C. (1984). Exploring new frontiers in advertising, *Medical Group Management, 31*: 60-62, 70.
Dickey, K. W. (1985). Market strategy–market analysis, *Illinois Dental Journal, 54*: 16–18.
DiGiulio, J. F. (1984). Marketing social services, *Social Casework, 65*: 227-234.
DiJulio, J., and Kniss, E. H. (1985). On the scene: Stanford University. Friends of nursing, a unique marketing approach for nursing, *Nursing Administration Quarterly, 10*: 27-30.
Dilenschneider, R. L. (1985). Ethics in health care marketing. Action now or trouble later, *Vital Speeches of the Day, 51*: 494-497.
Dockery, V. J. (1985-1986). Fostering organizational synergy for marketing: Practical issues and perspectives, *Health Marketing Quarterly, 3*: 19-26.
Dodge, W. G., Jr. (1985). Health care marketing, *Hawaii Medical Journal, 44*: 345-348.
Dodson, D. C. (1985). Health care marketing: Advancements but no cigar, *Health Marketing Quarterly, 2*: 13-23.
Doll birth certificates (1984). *Profiles in Hospital Marketing,* No. 14: 84-87.
Doll, R. J. (1984). The extra mile. Where do you go from here? *Ohio State Medical Journal, 80*: 451-453.
Donaldson, M. S., Nichlason, J. A., and Ott, J. E. (1985). Needs-based health promotion program serves as HMO marketing tool, *Public Health Representative, 100*: 270-277.
Donnelly, J. A. (1986). The potential for the introduction of the marketing concept into Australian public hospitals, *Australian Health Review, 9*: 52-58.
Doody, M. (1985). The financial manager as marketer, *Healthcare Financial Management, 39*: 12.
Dreyer, R. (1985). How to make successful sales calls, *Dental Laboratory Review, 60*: 8-10.
Drumwright, M. E., and Vernon, I. R. (1984). Synchromarketing, a new concept for hospital administrators, *Journal of Health Care Marketing, 4*: 45-50.
Dubuque, S. E. (1985). A case study of a successful ambulatory surgery marketing program, *Health Marketing Quarterly, 3*: 145-158.
Dugas, B. (1984). Marketing mammary reconstruction after radical mastectomy, *Plastic Surgery Nursing, 4*: 94-95.
Dunham, J. R. (1985). Marketing continuing education for nurses, *Nursing Administration Quarterly, 10*: 73-84.
Dunlap, B. J. (1986). Marketing in the health care arena: A preventive approach, *Journal of the American Dietetic Association, 86*: 29-30.
Dunlop, J. J. (1983). Developing a marketing orientation: Key to success, *National Library of Nursing Publication, 41*: 88-92.
Durham, J. D., and Hardin, S. B. (1983). Promoting private practice in a competitive market, *Nursing Economics, 1*: 24-28.
Durham, J. D., and Hardin, S. B. (1985). Promoting advanced nursing practice, *Nurse Practitioner, 10*: 59-62.
Dwight, M. B. (1985). Is your hospital ready to market geriatric services? *Health Management Quarterly, 2*: 7-11.

Early involvement of design team aids marketing success (1986). *Contemporary Longterm Care, 9*: 30-31.
Eckel, F. (1985). Are we successfully marketing our profession? *Topics in Hospital Pharmacy Management, 5*: 86-88.
Edwards, K. S. (1984). The pros and cons of marketing, *Ohio State Medical Journal, 80*: 793-795.
Edwardson, S. R. (1986). Shedding light on a shifting marketplace, competition in maternity care, *Nursing and Health Care, 7*: 72-77.
Effective marketing of veterinary services and products ((1986). *Veterinary Records, 118*: 83-84.
Eichhorn, S. (1985). A hospital humanizes patient care: New York's Mount Sinai—a case study, *Hospital Forum, 28*: 55-57.
Eliopoulos, C. (1985). Selling a positive image builds demand, *Nursing Management, 16*: 23-26.
Emergency game plans (1984). *Profiles in Hospital Marketing*, No. 14: 4-17.
Emery, K. R. (1986). Developing a new modified service analysis for decision making, *Health Care Supervisor, 4*: 30-38.
Enders, R. J. (1986). Understanding antitrust: Focus on the relevant market, *Healthcare Financial Management, 40*: 25-32.
Endress, R. (1984). Market strategies for private practice, *Journal of the Tennessee Medical Association, 77*: 522-528.
Engler, F., Jr. (1986). "We're better than they are"—a futile, wasteful game hospitals play, *Osteopathic Hospital Leadership, 30*: 24-25.
Erikson, G. M., and Fincler, S. A. (1985). Determinants of market share for a hospital's services, *Medical Care, 23*: 1003-1018.
Estes, C. L. (1986). The aging enterprise, in whose interests? *International Journal of Health Services, 16*: 243-251.
Evashwick, C. (1984). Marketing services for seniors, *Health Marketing Quarterly, 1*: 19-32.
Faber, M. (1983). Keep your research on target, *Dental Economics, 73*: 59-60, 62.
Faherty, V. E. (1985). First steps first: Developing a marketing plan. Case example, Senior Care Corporation, Inc., *Health Marketing Quarterly, 2*: 25-33.
Feldstein, P. J. (1984). How to cope in today's health care market, *Physicians' Management, 24*: 165, 168-169, 173-174.
Feldstein, P. J. (1986). The emergence of market competition in the U.S. health care system, *Health Policy, 6*: 1-20.
Feller, S. J. (1984). Research, the key to successfully marketing your practice, *Canadian Dental Association Journal, 50*: 745-746.
Fenton, D. (1986). Flow of clinical data for strategic planning and marketing, *Topics in Health Records Management, 6*: 46-52.
Festervand, T. A. (1984-1985). An introduction and application of focus group research to the health care industry, *Health Marketing Quarterly, 2*: 199-209.
Finding the fifth 'P' (1984). *Profiles in Hospital Marketing*, No. 15, 64-65.
Fine, R. B. (1985). Exchange behavior in administrative nursing marketing interactions, *Nursing Administration Quarterly, 10*: 53-55.
Fine, S. H. (1984). The health product: A social marketing perspective, *Hospitals, 58*: 66-68.
Finkler, S. A. (1983). The hospital as a sales-maximizing entity, *Health Services Research, 18*: 117-136.
Finn, M. (1986). Pastoral care: Marketing "high touch," *Health Progress, 67*: 50-51, 60.
Fisk, T. (1986). Advertising Health Services: What Works—What Fails? Pluribus Press, Chicago.
Fisk, T. A., and Brown, C. J. (1983). Target portion of marketing efforts to public, surveys, *Hospitals, 57*: 39.

Flexner, W. A. (1984). Evaluating a marketing consultant: A consultant's viewpoint, *Journal of Health Care Marketing, 4*: 55–58.

Flinton, J. (1985a). AMI's Flinton: Marketing mind takes hold, *Multis, 3*: M24.

Flinton, J. S. (1985b). Marketing research is crucial to ANI's strategy development, *Modern Healthcare, 15*: 88–91.

Flower, J. (1984). More on entrepreneurship: Thirteen questions for hospital CEO's, *Hospital Forum, 27*: 40-41.

Foden, J. P. (1985). Make marketing a team effort, *Dental Practice Management, 2*: 12–15.

Folland, S. T. (1985). The effects of health care advertising, *Journal of Health, Politics, Policy and the Law, 10*: 329–345.

Foltz, M. B., and Stephens, G. (1985). Marketing food and nutrition services, *Hospital Administration Currents, 29*: 7–12.

Foltz, M. B., and Stephens, G. (1986). Use of nutritional support systems to meet hospital marketing needs, *Hospital Materials Management Quarterly, 7*: 80–90.

Fontana, J. P. (1984). Hospital marketing is here to stay, *Hospital Topics, 62*: 12–13.

Fowler, S. (1983). Marketing: Is it magic? *Dental Assistant, 3*: 6–7.

Frank, B. G. (1983). Using talk show interviews as effective practice builders, *New York State Dental Journal, 49*: 164, 165.

Frank, I. C., and McGovern, F. (1983). Marketing one hospital's emergency department, *Journal of Emergency Nursing, 9*: 324-326.

Franz, J. (1984a). Albuquerque hospitals are even more competitive after suspension of regs, *Modern Healthcare, 14*: 64, 66.

Franz, J. (1984b). HMOs' aggressive marketing spurs leap in enrollment . . . and GAO probe, *Modern Healthcare, 14*: 64, 66.

Franz, J. (1984c). Hospital advertises cost comparisons to impress employers, physicians, *Modern Healthcare, 14*: 72.

Franz, J. (1984d). Joint ventures. Assign marketing to skilled partner, *Modern Healthcare, 14*: 76.

Fredrickson, T. L. (1984). The physician's role in health care marketing, *Minnesota Medicine, 67*: 497–498.

Free money from the Post Office (1985). *Hospital Topics, 63*: 46.

Friedman, J. (1983). Applying a marketing orientation to health care, *National Library of Nursing Publications,* No. 41-1935, 93–99.

Fullman, H. J. (1985). Bottom-line health care? *New England Journal of Medicine, 313*: 897.

Furgurson, J. (1986). Is your business card working for you? *Dental Economics, 76*: 85–86.

Gannon, K. R. (1985). Nursing's impact on a business venture, *Nursing Administration Quarterly, 10*: 90–96.

Garant, C. (1985). Interview: Carol Garant, RN, MSN, *Nursing Success Today, 2*: 34–38.

Gardner, S. F., and Paison, A. R. (1985). A survey on the current status of health care marketing, *Health Care Strategic Management, 3*: 26–27.

Garlington, D. (1984). How to turn down time into productive time in your OR, *Hospital Topics, 62*: 4–7.

Garlington, D. G. (1985-1986). Planning and executing a successful emergency medical care campaign, *Health Marketing Quarterly, 3*: 139–143.

Gary, D. L. (1984). Doctor, doctor, how does your garden grow!! *Journal of the Tennessee Dental Association, 64*: 20–23.

Gaudioso, L. (1985). Turning health-care trends to your advantage, *Medical Marketing Media, 20*: 66–72.

Gaylin, S. (1985). The coming of the corporation and the marketing of psychiatry, *Hospital and Community Psychiatry, 36*: 154-159.

Gaynes, N. L. (1985). Long term care marketing strategies, *Journal of the American Health Care Association, 11*: 22-25.

Genkins, M. (1985). Strategic planning for social work marketing, *Administration in Social Work, 9*: 35-46.

Gent, D. I. (1984). Hospitals embrace customer relations, *Modern Healthcare, 14*: 134-135.

George, S. (1984). Challenges in marketing mental health senior services, *Health Marketing Quarterly, 1*: 69-76.

George, W. R., and Compton, F. F. (1985). How to initiate a marketing perspective in a health services organization, *Journal of Health Care Marketing, 5*: 29-37.

Gerber, P.C. (1985). Should hospitals market themselves? *Physicians' Management, 25*: 94-95, 99-102, 107.

Gielisse, A. B. (1985a). How to market yourself, *Minnesota Nursing Accent, 57*: 52.

Gielisse, A. B. (1985b). Marketing your services, *Minnesota Nursing Accent, 57*: 64-65.

Gil, R. (1984). The role of the nurse in hospital marketing, *Health Care Strategic Management, 2*: 9-10.

Gillette, P. E. (1984). Marketing surveys, ads help suburban Atlanta facilities focus on strengths, *Modern Healthcare, 14*: 100, 102.

Gish, C. W. (1984). Marketing vs. National Children's Dental Health Month, *Journal of the Indiana Dental Association, 63*: 5.

Gitman, R. (1983). Plan ahead for profits, *Dental Laboratory Review, 58*: 19-20, 22.

Gleason, J. J., Jr. (1984). The marketing of pastoral care and counseling, chaplaincy, and clinical pastoral education, *Journal of Pastoral Care, 38*: 264-272.

Golaszewski, Y., and Prabhaker, P. (1984). Applying marketing strategies to worksite health promotion efforts, *Occupational Health Nursing, 32*: 188-192.

Goldman, E. F., and Morabito, C. P. (1984). Renovated hospital building provides housing alternative for the elderly, *Health Marketing Quarterly, 2*: 63-72.

Goldman, R. (1984-1985). Applying PPO theory in Maricopa County, *Health Marketing Quarterly, 2*: 135-144.

Goldman, R. L. (1984). Wanted, a practical approach to health care marketing ethics, *Health Marketing Quarterly, 3*: 7-10.

Goldsmith, J. C. (1984). Entrepreneurship, its place in health care, *Hospital Forum, 27*: 17, 19.

Goldsmith, M., and Leebov, W. (1986). Strengthening the hospital's marketing position through training, *Health Care Management Review, 11*: 83-93.

Gordon, L. (1985). Simplified marketing of your dental laboratory, establishing value, defining strategies, creating advertising promotions, using sales techniques, *Trends and Techniques in the Contemporary Dental Laboratory, 2*: 57-61.

Grauer, D. W., and Pathak, D. S. (1983). Marketing perspectives of hospital pharmacy directors, *American Journal of Hospital Pharmacy, 40*: 984-988.

Gray, J. (1986). The selling of medicine, 1986, *Medical Economics, 63*: 180-183, 186-194.

Graybill, M., Jones, E. E., Jr., and Rudnick, J. D. (1985). The time to sell "next time" is now! The planning and activation of a hospital guest relations program, *Hospital Topics, 63*: 3-5.

Great expectations, great results: Maternity marketing (1984). *Profiles in Hospital Marketing,* No. 16, 56-61.

Green, L. (1983). Newsletter helps keep practice healthy, *Dental Economics, 73*: 51-52, 54.

Greene, J. A. (1985). Building networks, what business are you really in? *Journal of the Tennessee Medical Association, 78*: 756-758.

Gregory, D. D. (1986). Building on your hospital's competitive image, *Trustee, 39*: 16–19.
Gregory, J. D. (1984). What marketing researchers expect from clients, *Journal of Health Care Marketing, 4*: 51–56.
Grier, J. D. (1983). Marketing of dental services (try utilizing auxiliaries more), *Canadian Dental Association Journal, 49*: 805-806.
Griff, S. L. (1984). Determining the need for home health services, *Caring, 3*: 15–19.
Griffith, M. J., and Baloff, N. (1984). Start-up analysis for marketing strategy, *Journal of Health Care Marketing, 4*: 17–26.
Grill, W. (1983). "Internal" marketing produces profits, *Dental Laboratory Review, 58*: 16, 18.
Gross, A. (1983a). How to get free publicity (and more new patients), *Dental Management, 23*: 30–32, 35–36.
Gross, A. (1983b). Locating your patients—present and potential, *Dental Economics, 73*: 40–46, 48, 50.
Gutterman, S. S. (1983). Marketing, the buzz word for the '80s, *Ohio Dental Journal, 57*: 43–45.
Haas, R., and Beideman, M. A. (1986). Marketing a hepatitis B vaccine program, *Infection Control, 7*: 339-341.
Hafer, J. C., and Joiner, C. (1984). Nurses as image emissaries, are role conflicts impinging on a potential assent for an internal marketing strategy? *Journal of Health Care Marketing, 4*: 25–35.
Hafer, J. C. (1984). "Telemarketing" hospital services, benefits, pitfalls, and the planning process, *Journal of Health Care Marketing, 4*: 29–35.
Hale, D. (1984). A path to success, *Dental Economics, 74*: 52–54, 56, 58.
Haley, M. (1985). Republic helps not-for-profit hospitals compete, *Multis, 3*: M27.
Halpern, K. G. (1984). The CEO's role in making marketing work, *Hospital Topics, 62*: 2-3.
Hammerle, R. L. (1985-1986). Hallmarketing patients, *Health Marketing Quarterly, 3*: 69–74.
Han, I. D. (1985). Rodeos to rock shows: A hospital covers spectator events, *Hospital Forum, 28*: 66–68.
Hanchey, K. (1984). The burgeoning home health care market, assessing your options, *Texas Hospitals, 40*: 19–21.
Hankin, R. A. (1986). "Targeting" campaigns, *Dental Management, 26*: 30, 32.
Hardy, T. (1986). St. Paul develops extensive alternative delivery systems, *Texas Hospitals, 41*: 14–19.
Harrell, G. D., and Fors, M. F. (1985). Marketing ambulatory care to women, a segmentation approach, *Journal of Health Care Marketing, 5*: 19–28.
Harris, J. P. (1985). Selling your concept: How to prepare and market an effective business plan, *Topics in Health Care Financing, 12*: 32–37.
Hartsfield, G. J. (1986). Planning and marketing: The sole community hospital, *Topics in Health Records Management, 6*: 35-45.
Haschke, M. B. (1984). Marketing in dietetics, *Journal of the American Dietetics Association, 84*: 933-935.
Hauser, L. J. (1984). 10 reasons hospital marketing programs fail, *Hospitals, 58*: 74–77.
Hauser, L. J. (1985). Hospitals beef up ad budgets; but lack sophisticated marketing, *Modern Healthcare, 15*: 170–171.
Hawes, J. M., and Rao, C. P. (1985). Using importance-performance analysis to develop health care marketing strategies, *Journal of Health Care Marketing, 5*: 19–25.
Hawken, P., and Mancuso, J. (1984). Brass tacks: Straight talk about the health care industry and the entrepreneurial spirit, *Hospital Forum, 27*: 35–37.

Haxton, R. S. (1983). The values of medicine and of the marketplace, *Hospital Practice, 18*: 24-26.
Hayes, T. J., and Mack, K. E. (1986). Commentary on: Making the hospital position successful, *Journal of Health Care Marketing, 6*: 65-70.
Hearne, T. (1984). Managing public opinion in a hostile environment, *Hospital Management Quarterly,* Spring, 7-11.
Hemmes, M. (1985). Using the four Ps of marketing to your advantage, *General Dentistry, 33*: 13, 16.
Henderson, T. M. (1985). No frills marketing of community-based primary care, *Journal of Health Care Marketing, 5*: 47-50.
Herbert, I. C. (1986). Know thy customer: Coca-Cola's Herbert (Interview), *Hospitals, 60*: 92-93.
Hernandez, L., and McNamara, E. J. (1984). Utilization of market research in managing hospital pharmacy resources, *Hospital Pharmacy, 19*: 677-679, 682-686.
Herring, M. (1984). Successfully marketing education program, *Texas Hospitals, 40*: 14-15.
Herrington, B. S. (1984). Sociologist Paul Starr warns of bad business–medicine mix, *Psychiatric News, 19*: 1, 8-9.
Herzog, T. P. (1985). Diversification, opportunity knocks at the nursing station, *Health Management Quarterly,* Fall-Winter, 18-20.
Hicks, N. J. (1986). Patients and other publics, *Public Relations Journal, 42*: 28-32.
Hillestand, S. G., and Berkowitz, E. N. (1984). Hospitals marshal sales forces, *Modern Healthcare, 14*: 122, 124.
Hites, A. (1985). To market is to grow, *Lab Management Today, 1*: 11-12.
Hoff, L. C. (1985). Marketing and distribution of pharmacueticals in the 21st century, two scenarios, *American Pharmacy,* NS25, 70-76.
Hoffman, S. E., and Fonteyn, M. E. (1986). Marketing the clinical nurse specialist, *Nursing Economics, 4*: 140-144.
Hogan, J. M. (1986). Compiling patient and clinical data for strategic planning, *Topics in Health Records Management, 6*: 61-75.
Holoweiko, M. (1984). Doctor entrepreneurs, are they hurting the profession? *Medical Economics, 61*: 116-124, 129, 133.
Holt, F. X. (1985). Nursing offers more marketing angles than you think, *Journal the American Health Care Association, 11*: 50-51.
Horty, J. (1986). Antitrust ruling may deter hospitals from challenging the market leader, *Modern Healthcare, 16*: 91-92.
Hostetler, D. (1985). Quality assurance activities should emphasize positive potential, *Journal of the American Medical Records Association, 56*: 50-52.
Housley, R. C. (1984). Marketing: Making a commitment to survival, *Computers in Healthcare, 5*: 56.
Housley, R. C. (1985). Developing auxiliary revenue sources, *Computers in Healthcare, 6*: 30-32.
How to use the yellow pages to attract new patients (1983). *Dental Management, 23*: 40-44.
Hudson, J. D. (1985). Radio: An effective way to market, *Dental Management, 25*: 46-49.
Huss, S. M. (1986). Profit-making opportunities in hospital pharmacy under prospective reimbursement, *Hospital Materials Management Quarterly, 7*: 36-40.
Huston, P. (1985). The pharmacist, key player in the home health market, *Medical Marketing Media, 20*: 8-9, 12-21.
Iglehart, J. K. (1984). The Twin Cities' medical marketplace, *New England Journal of Medicine, 311*: 343-348.

Imbrogno, S. (1985). A systems design developmental model for programs of deinstitutionalization, marketing base for follow-up care, *Health Marketing Quarterly, 2*: 145-157.
Ingram, T. N., and Hensel, P. J. (1985). Marketing in home health organization: Issues in implementation, *Family and Community Health, 8*: 22-32.
Inguanzo, J. M., and Harju, M. (1985a). Affluent consumers most discriminating survey, *Hospitals, 59*: 84, 86.
Inguanzo, J. M., and Harju, M. (1985b). Creating a market niche, *Hospitals, 59*: 62-64, 67.
Inguanzo, J. M., and Harju, M. (1985c). What's the market for outpatient surgery? *Hospitals, 59*: 55-57.
InterStudy (1986). National HMO Census 1985. InterStudy, Excelsior, MN.
Ireland, R. C. (1977). Using marketing strategies to put hospitals on target, *Hospitals, 51*: 54-58.
Israel, R. C. (1984). Recent developments in social marketing and their implications for international public health education, *Hygiene, 3*: 50-53.
Jackson, B., and Jensen, J. (1984). Majority of consumers support advertising of hospital services, *Modern Healthcare, 14*: 93-97.
Jackson, B., and Jensen, J. (1985). Strategic planning and marketing will be administrator's top concerns, *Modern Healthcare, 15*: 68, 70.
Jackson, M. K., and Strang, D. (1985). Marketing and public relations: A combined service, *Journal of the American Health Care Association, 11*: 30-31, 34-35.
Jacobs, D. B. (1985). Marketing the professional practice discreetly, *New York State Dental Journal, 51*: 582.
Jarboe, G. R., and McDaniel, C. D. (1985). Influence patterns and determinant attributes in nursing home choice situations, *Journal of Health Care Marketing, 5*: 19-30.
Jensen, J. (1986). Consumers who notice ads recall messages, *Modern Healthcare, 16*: 84-85.
Jensen, J., and Jackson, B. (1985). Planning, marketing are top priorities for administrators in next 12 months, *Modern Healthcare, 15*: 78-79.
Jensen, J., Jackson, B., and Miklovic, N. (1985). Two-thirds of hospitals relying on marketing research studies, *Modern Healthcare, 15*: 84-85.
Johnson, D. E. (1985). Marketers should be idea managers, *Modern Healthcare, 15*: 35.
Joint survey reveals best ways to capture dentists' attention (1986). *Lab Management Today, 2*: 6-13.
Jolson, M. A., and Blackman, R. (1985). Employee input as an aid in prepaid health care buying decisions, *Journal of Health Care Marketing, 5*: 39-46.
Jones, M. E. (1985). Marketing research: Assessing physician satisfaction, *Radiology Management, 7*: 24-29.
Jones, R. (1984). Marketing yourself in the I.V. nursing specialty, *National Intravenous Therapy Association, 7*: 430-431.
Jonsen, A. R. (1986). Ethics remain at the heart of medicine: Physicians and entrepreneurship, *Western Journal of Medicine, 144*: 480-483.
Josephson, R. V., Rupp, J. W., and Chambers, J. F. (1985). Needs assessment of enteral nutrition support products, *Journal of the American Dietetics Association, 85*: 1485-1487.
Kalman, S. H. (1984). Managing change, marketing and pharmacy, *American Pharmacy, NS24*: 41-43.
Kaplan, A. (1984-1985). Using the components of the marketing mix to market emergency services, *Health Marketing Quarterly, 2*: 53-62.
Kaplan, C. P., and Van Valey, T. L. (1980). *Census '80: Continuing the Fact Finding Tradition*, U.S. Government Printing Office, Washington, D.C.

Kasianuik, D. (1985). Let staff share in practice success, *Dental Practice Management,* Fall, *16*: 18–19.

Kaufman, N. (1984). Product integrity, the missing link in a hospital's marketing process, *Health Marketing Quarterly, 2*: 29–32.

Kaye, E. M. (1983). The delicate art of marketing, *New York State Dental Journal, 49*: 152–153.

Keamy, C., and Heckler, T. (1986). The rebirth of the elder market, *Healthcare Executive, 1*: 34-37.

Keckley, P. H. (1985). Using and misusing marketing research in the healthcare industry, *Healthcare Financial Management, 39*: 31–35.

Keefe, J. (1985). Joint ventures: The marketing function, *Radiology Management, 7*: 20–23.

Keele, R. L., and Delany, P. E. (1986). Should you consider a women's center, *Health Care Strategic Management, 4*: 9–12.

Keith, J. G. (1981). Marketing health care: What the recent literature is telling us, *Hospital and Health Services Administration, 26*(special issue II): 67–84.

Keith, J. G. (1985). Marketing concepts and strategies for ET nurses, *Journal Enterostomal Therapy, 12*: 99–103.

Keldaras, C. G. (1985). The salesmanship of social work, *Health Marketing Quarterly, 2*: 103–115.

Keller, M. H. (1984). Case study, St. David's Community Hospital, *Texas Hospitals, 40*: 37-39.

Kelly, J. R. (1984). Professional marketing for the pedodontic practice, *Dental Clinics of North America, 28*: 121-136.

Kenney, J. B. (1985). Using competition to develop a buyer driven market, *Business and Health, 3*: 39–42.

Kerkering, K. M., and Squires, D. (1986). Management information systems in a strategic planning process: A case study, *Topics in Health Records Management, 6*: 53–60.

Keyser, J. A. (1985–1986). Marketing medicine through a major event, *Health Marketing Quarterly, 3*: 159–174.

King, H. (1985). Increasing census with "phone-power," *Contemporary Longterm Care, 8*: 27-30.

Kingsley, V. H. (1986). Increasing market share through consumer marketing, a case study in obstetrics, *Health Care Strategic Management, 4*: 16–20.

Klann, S. S. (1984). Good news and bad news in the marketing age, *AORN Journal, 40*: 790-792.

Klegon, D. A., and Slubowski, M. A. (1985). Marketing ambulatory care centers: Assessment, implementation, evaluation, *Journal of Ambulatory Care Management, 8*: 18–27.

Kleisley, P. (1985). A marketing-orient staff is behind every successful practice, *Dental Economics, 75*: 89–94.

Kleisley, P. L. (1983). The direct approach: Get the most out of your mailings, *Dental Economics, 73*: 38–41, 43–44, 46.

Kneiser, M. R. (1986). Case history: One hospital's marketing success, *Medical Laboratory Observer, 18*: 51–54.

Knittig, M. J. (1984). Marketing and health care, *Journal of the Arkansas Medical Society, 81*: 267-268.

Kohlman, H. A. (1985). Physicians as business partners in healthcare marketing, *Healthcare Financial Management, 39*: 10.

Korneluk, G. N. (1983). Marketing: Borrowing a useful tool from business, *General Dentistry, 31*: 318–319.

Korneluk, G. M. (1985). *Practice Enhancement: The Physician's Guide to Success in Private Practice*, MacMillan Publishing, New York.
Korcok, M. (1984). Marketplace medicine in the United States, *Canadian Medical Association Journal, 130*: 785-788.
Kosterlitz, J. (1985). The hospital business, *National Journal, 17*: 2180-2187.
Kotler, P., and Mindak, W. (1984). Marketing and public relations, *Health Care Marketing: Issues and Trends* (P. D. Cooper, ed.), Aspen Systems, Rockville, MD.
Kotler, P. (1985). The role and development of marketing in today's health care institution, *Health Care Strategic Management, 3*: 21-24.
Kotler, P. (1986). How to set the hospital's marketing report, *Journal of Health Care Marketing, 6*: 7-12.
Kotler, P., and Clarke, R. N. (1986). Creating a responsive organization, *Healthcare Forum, 29*: 26-32.
Kragg, G. R. (1986). Pharmaceutical marketing practices, a victim's perspective, *Journal Rheumatology, 13*: 224.
Krampitz, S. D., and Coleman, J. R. (1985). Marketing–a must in a competitive health-care system, *Nursing Economics, 3*: 286-289.
Krauth, S. (1983). Target marketing brings new patients, *Dental Management, 23*: 14-17.
Kress, G. C., Jr., and Silversin, J. B. (1985). Internal marketing and quality assurance through patient feedback, *Journal of the American Dental Association, 110*: 29-34.
Kroeger, R. F. (1986). Marketing for the dental phobic: A neglected segment of the population, *Journal of Dental Practice Administration, 3*: 52-56.
Kuhn, P. J. (1984). Marketing a new product from your lab, *Medical Laboratory Observer, 16*: 72-76.
Kuhn, R. (1985). Marketing critical care nursing, the time is right, *Health and Lung, 14*: 19A-20A, 23A.
Kuntz, E. F. (1984). Marketing efforts yield profits for hospital wellness programs, *Modern Healthcare, 14*: 218-219.
Lageman, A. G. (1984). Marketing pastoral counseling, *Journal of Pastoral Care, 38*: 274-282.
Lambert, N., and Thanopoulos, J. (1985). A dynamic planning framework for nursing homes, *Nursing Homes, 34*: 39-42.
Lang, K. (1985). Those priceless giveaways, *Dental Economics, 75*: 61.
Langbaum, T. S., Rosenstein, B. J., and Rivest, J. A. (1986). Teaching facility learns marketing, *Hospitals, 60*: 72, 74.
Larkin, D. (1985-1986). Developing a marketing function in a multi-hospital system, how to define your job, *Health Marketing Quarterly, 3*: 37-45.
Larrick, B. (1985). Total marketing, the best way to build your practice, *Dental Mortgage, 25*: 30-32, 35, 38 passim.
Laskin, D. M. (1984). To market, to market, *Journal of Oral and Maxillofacial Surgery, 42*: 484.
LaTour, S. A. (1984). A plea for strategic marketing, *Journal of Health Care Marketing, 4*: 5-9.
Lee, J. M. (1984). What does a bar of soap have to do with health care marketing? *Health Care Strategic Management, 2*: 4-7.
Lee, J. R., Jr. (1986). Marketing your services, *Journal of Mental Health Administration, 13*: 34-37.
Lee, R. H. (1986). Marketing research for health authorities, *Hospital Health Services Review, 82*(2): 79-81.
Legett, B. J., Jr., and Wallace, C. J. (1983). Newspaper advertising by Louisiana dentists, *LDS Journal, 41*: 26-27.

Legg, D., and Lamb, C. W., Jr. (1986). The role of referral agents in the marketing of home health services, *Journal of Health Care Marketing, 6*: 51–56.

Leven, E. L. (1984). Price—a primer on the 2nd 'P' for marketers. *Health Marketing Quarterly, 2*: 33–42.

Levey, S., and Hesse, D. D. (1985). Bottom-line health care? *New England Journal of Medicine, 312*: 644–647.

Levin, R. (1985). Business promotions need to sell yourself, *Dental Student, 63*: 24, 28.

Levin, S. A. (1985). Retirement centers, opportunities for the astute hospital investor, *Health Care Strategic Management, 3*: 16–21.

LeVoy, B. (1985). Marketing means serving the needs of the patient, *Dental Management, 25*: 50, 53–54, 56 passim.

Light, D. W. (1983). Is competition bad? *New England Journal of Medicine, 309*: 1315–1319.

Lind, S. E. (1986). Fee-for-service research, *New England Journal of Medicine, 314*: 312–315.

Linden, R. (1986). Materials management's role in product line development, *Hospital Materials Management, 11*: 8–12.

Lipshultz, R. (1984). Newsletters: A tool for successfully marketing your dental practice, *Pennsylvania Dental Journal, 85*: 18–19.

Littlefield, J. E. (1984). Home health care, the opportunity for health care marketing, *Journal of Health Care Marketing, 4*: 51–55.

Long, J. (1984). Look who's helping build practices now! Hospitals have discovered that it makes good business sense to give attendings a boost, *Medical Economics, 61*: 75–76, 82–85.

Long, P. E. (1984). Community involvement as a marketing strategy, *Texas Hospitals, 40*: 24–25.

Loomis, L. M. (1984–1985). Marketing strategies for an ambulatory geriatric health care program, *Health Marketing Quarterly, 2*: 63–73.

Loomis, L. M., and Bufano, J. T. (1985). Marketing and social work—synergy in long-term care, *Health Care Strategic Management, 3*: 7–12.

Loubeau, P. R. (1984). Marketing as a health care concept, *Nursing Economics, 2*: 37–41.

Louden, T. (1984). Hospitals eager for a larger share of growing home healthcare marketing, *Modern Healthcare, 14*: 66, 68.

Louden, T. (1985a). How to select and support the hospital sales team, *Hospitals, 59*: 84–85.

Louden, T. (1985b). How to set up a hospital sales program, *Hospitals, 59*: 136, 140, 142.

Louden, T. L. (1985c). The how and why of hospital sales, *Health Management Quarterly*, Fall-Winter, 2–6.

Louden, T. L. (1986). Home care, six secrets to success, *Healthcare Executives, 1*: 45–48.

Louie, C., and Baxter, P. (1986). A new inexpensive marketing strategy, *Hospital Topics, 64*: 48.

Louie, C., and Baxter, P. (1985). How one hospital approaches marketing by being a good neighbor, *Hospital Topics, 63*: 2–3.

Luciano, D., and Darling, L. A. (1985). The physician as a nursing service customer, *Journal of Nursing Administration, 15*: 17–20.

Ludke, R. L., and Levitz, G. S. (1983). Referring physicians, the forgotten market, *Health Care Management Review, 8*: 13–22.

Lukacs, J. (1984). Marketing strategies for competitive advantage, *Nurse Practitioner, 9*: 37–38, 40.

Mack, K. E. (1985). Back to basics: Elements necessary to assure success to the hospital marketing function, *Journal of Health Care Marketing, 5*: 5–7.

Mack, K. E. (1985-1986). How to become local businesses' favorite hospital, *Health Marketing Quarterly, 3*: 189-195.

Mackesy, R. (1985). Marketing acceptance in small and medium sized hospitals, *Health Care Strategic Management, 3*: 19-22.

MacMillan, N. H., and Rosenbaum, G. (1986). *Managing Smart: Market Research for Hospital Decision Makers,* American Hospital Publishing, Chicago.

MacStravic, R. E. (1977). *Marketing Health Care*, Aspen Systems, Germantown, MD.

MacStravic, R. E., Mahn, E., and Reedal, D. C. (1983). Portfolio analysis for hospitals, *Health Care Management Review, 8*: 69-75.

MacStravic, R. S. (1984a). Being patients "personal" hospital is survival strategy in hard times, *Modern Healthcare, 14*: 182-184, 187.

MacStravic, R. S. (1984b). Marketing by managing relationships, *Health Progress, 65*: 49-51, 60.

MacStravic, R. S. (1984c). Marketing circles can help hospitals satisfy patients, boost staff morale, *Modern Healthcare, 14*: 192-194.

MacStravic, R. S. (1984d). Marketing health services: The engineering of satisfaction, *Health Progress, 65*: 35-37.

MacStravic, R. S. (1984e). Persuasive communication strategies for hospitals, *Health Care Management Review, 9*: 69-75.

MacStravic, R. S. (1985a). Cognitive commitments in health services marketing, *Health Care Management Review, 10*: 11-18.

MacStravic, R. S. (1985b). Promises, promises, *Hospital Forum, 28*: 31-32.

MacStravic, R. S. (1985c). Word-of-mouth communications in health marketing, *Health Progress, 66*: 25-29.

MacStravic, R. S. (1984-1985). Marketing medical care: The manufacturing of satisfaction, *Health Marketing Quarterly, 2*: 157-170.

MacStravic, R. S. (1986a). Hospital-physician relations: A marketing approach, *Health Care Management Review, 11*: 69-79.

MacStravic, R. S. (1986b). Product-line administration in hospitals, *Health Care Management Review, 11*: 35-43.

Magers, B. D. (1984a). Hospital advertising, a sign of the times, *Texas Hospitals, 40*: 28-30.

Magers, B. D. (1984b). Marketing, a survival strategy, *Texas Hospitals, 40*: 8-9.

Mages, P. (1984a). Like the Fortune 500 take your cues from the marketplace, *OH: Osteopathic Hospitals, 28*: 8-11.

Mages, P. M. (1984b). Implementing the results of survey research—a six-step model, *Healthmarketing, 3*: 3-5.

Mages, P. M. (1984c). Searching for the hospital sales department—where's the beef? *Healthmarketing, 3*: 5-7.

Mages, P. M. (1985a). A conversation with Dr. James M. Carman on the continuing hospital struggle with marketing principles and methods, *Healthmarketing, 4*: 2-6.

Mages, P. M. (1985b). Developing a marketing culture—the role of customer relations training, *Healthmarketing, 4*: 3-5.

Mages, P. M. (1985c). From the department of warm feelings to a major marketing function—the real role of the patient representative, *Healthmarketing, 4*: 11-14.

Mages, P. M. (1985d). Marketing is the art and science of listening, *Healthmarketing, 4*: 2-5.

Mages, P. M. (1986a). Commentary: Bad taste is timeless, *Healthmarketing, 5*: 5-6.

Mages, P. M. (1986b). CPR for hospital marketing, *Healthmarketing, 5*: 9-11.

Mahan, H. D. (1983). Marketing veterinary medicine, *Veterinary Clinics of North America (Small Animal Practice), 13*: 737-744.

Mammography awareness (1985). *Profiles in Hospital Marketing*, No. 19, 74–75.

Mangan, M. (1984). New health care strategy outgrowth of marketing focus, *Fund Raising Management, 14*: 46, 48–49.

Marketing an immediate care center (1985). *Profiles in Hospital Marketing,* No. 19, 4–10.

Marketing health promotion (1984). *Profiles in Hospital Marketing,* No. 13, 4–10.

Marketing hospital services: The time has really arrived for the industry to enter the arena (1984). *Cost Containment, 6*: 3–6.

Marketing is key to PR professional's roles (1985). *Hospitals, 59*: 60, 62.

Marketing OB services raises awareness (1984). *Profiles in Hospital Marketing,* No. 16, 38–45.

Marketing professional services to the patient and consumer (1983). *American Pharmacy, NS23*, 46–50.

Marsh, K. (1985). Increase your professional net worth *Nursing Success Today, 2*: 19–21.

Martin, L. Z. (1985). Marketing traps: 13 tips on how not to succeed, *Hospital Forum, 28*: 27–28.

Mason, S. A. (1984). Management implication of a shifting marketplace, *Hospital Health and Services Administration, 29*: 71–83.

Massey, R. U. (1986). Reflections on medicine: Marketing or humbug? *Connecticut Medicine, 50*: 347.

Maternity services literature (1984). *Profiles in Hospital Marketing,* No. 16, 46–51.

McBrien, M. (1986a). Health promotion–education or marketing strategy? *Nursing Success Today, 3*: 16–17.

McBrien, M. (1986b). Marketing your hospital, *Nursing Success Today, 3*: 17–19.

McCann, B. J. (1986). Spice up operations–diversity, *Computers in Healthcare, 7*: 56, 58.

McCarthy, J. B., and Hurlimann, L. L. (1984). Increasing competition will expand the healthcare marketer's role, *Health Marketing Quarterly, 1*: 33–44.

McDermott, D. R. (1984–1985). A market research analysis of an occupational health services program, *Health Marketing Quarterly, 2*: 91–97.

McDermott, D. R. (1985). A market research analysis of an occupational health services program, *Health Marketing Quarterly, 2*: 91–97.

McDevitt, P. K., and Shields, L. A. (1985). Tactical hospital marketing, a survey of the state of the art, *Journal of Health Care Marketing, 5*: 9–16.

McGann, B. (1985). Meeting the competitors, *Computers in Healthcare, 6*: 23–24.

McLaughlin, C. P., and Littlefield, J. E. (1983). Marketing in practice management, *North Carolina Medical Journal, 44*: 9–13.

McLeod, K. (1985a). The importance of research in marketing, *Journal of the American Health Care Association, 11*: 38–39.

McLeod, R. E. (1985b). Marketing: A tool for survival, *Radiology Management, 7*: 3–6.

McMillan, J. R., Younger, M. S., and DeWine, L. C. (1985). Marketing–results of a survey: Reasons patients select one hospital ER over another, *Hospital Topics, 63*: 38–40.

McMillan, N. H. (1981). *Marketing Your Hospital, A Strategy for Survival*, American Hospital Association, Chicago.

McMullin, D. (1986). Common financial problems encountered by CCRCs, *Contemporary Longterm Care, 9*: 50–51.

McNeill, G., and McNeill, M. (1985). The resident comes first a marketing philosophy that works, *Journal of the American Health Care Association, 11*: 8–9.

McWhorter, R. C. (1985). HCA's new president is familiar with change, *Multis, 3*: M25–26.

Meadors, A. C. (1984). Hospital information systems: A marketing resource, *Computers in Healthcare, 5*: 34.

Metz, E. N. (1986). Health services marketing accountability–tracking your marketing efforts, *Health Marketing Quarterly, 3*: 75–83.

Meyer, M., and Minch, D. (1984). Computerization and healthcare marketing, *Computers in Healthcare, 5*: 28–35.
Mezick, C. A., McCall, P. L., and Corder, R. M. (1986). Economic and marketing benefits of an air ambulance program, *Nursing Economics 4*: 122–127.
Miaoulis, G. (1984). Public relations: A marketing opportunity. What is it? *Profiles in Hospital Marketing,* No. 13, 82–83.
Miaoulis, G., Anderson, D. C., LaPlaca, P. J., Geduldig, J. P., Giesler, R. H., and West, S. (1985). A model for hospital marketing decision process and relationships, *Journal of Healthcare Marketing, 5*: 37–45.
Miaoulis, G., and Boyle, C. (1984). How can I use electronic advertising media more effectively? *Profiles in Hospital Marketing,* No. 15, 82–84.
Miaoulis, G., and O'Brien, V. (1984). How do I develop a new logo and slogan for my hospital? *Profiles in Hospital Marketing,* No. 14, 82–83.
Miaoulis, G., and O'Brien, V. (1985). A system approach to new service development for hospitals, *Health Care Strategies in Management, 3*: 14–19.
Midgett, M. (1984). Skilled nursing facility marketing: A better piece of pie, *Health Marketing Quarterly, 1*: 77–81.
Miller, J. (1985). On the scene: Stanford University. Development of a marketing committee, *Nursing Administration Quarterly, 10*: 43–46.
Miller, S. C. (1983). Professional marketing for optometry, *Journal of American Optometric Association, 54*: 819–822.
Millman-Falk, N. I. (1983). Marketing: Rx for your practice, *New York State Dental Journal, 49*: 148–150.
Milone, C. L., Blair, W. C., and Littlefield, J. E. (1982). *Marketing for the Dental Practice*, W. B. Saunders, Philadelphia.
Mindak, W. A. (1986). Myths and realities in health care marketing, *Physician Executives, 12*: 7–9.
Mistarz, J. E. (1984). The evolution of marketing in hospitals, *Hospitals, 58*: FB22, FB26, FB28.
Mistarz, J. E. (1985). Nationally branded products come to health care, *Hospitals, 59*: 64–67.
Mitchell, K. (1986). Courting the consumer, *Nursing Economics, 4*: 99.
Mitchell, W. T., Jr. (1984). Marketing: A dirty word? *Home Health Journal, 5*: 16.
Mongeau, S. (1982). *Directory of Nursing Homes: A State by State Listing of Facilities and Services*, Oryx Press, Phoenix, AZ.
Moody, T. (1984). Patient profiling, *Group Practice Journal, 33*: 39–40.
Moore, T. F. (1986). How military principles can help the hospital executive, *Hospital Topics, 64*: 2–5.
Morgan, R. A. (1985). Marketing in medicine, *Canadian Journal of Ophthalmology, 20*: 239–240.
Morrison, P. A. (1984). Tracking people, *Group Practice Journal, 33*: 47–53.
Moser, M., and Alpern, B. B. (1985). Creating a message for profit, *Medical Group Management, 32*: 52–57.
Moss, V., and Webster, J. A. (1986). Market yourself as a professional, *AORN Journal, 43*: 345–352.
Muller, A., and Sparkler, E. S. (1985). Marketing efforts of hospitals: Result of a sample survey, *Hospital Topics, 63*: 29–30.
Mullner, R. M., and Byre, C. S. (1984). Inventory of U.S. health care data bases, 1976–1983, U.S. Department of Health and Human Services, Bureau of Health Professions, Office of Data Analysis and Management, The Department, Washington, D.C.

Mullinax, C. W. (1984). A better mousetrap: 95 ways to market your practice, *Ohio State Medical Journal, 80*: 207-211.

Murphy, D. (1985). Marketing your nonprescription drug department, *American Pharmacy, NS25*, 38-41.

National Academy of Science, Institute of Medicine (1981). *Health Planning the United States Selected Policy Issues*, National Academy Press, Washington, D.C.

National Hospice Organization (1987). *The 1987 Guide to the Nation's Hospices*, The National Hospice Organization, Arlington, VA.

Neiman, J. S., and Mistarz, J. E. (1985). Planners and marketers see interests merge, *Hospitals, 59*: 95-97.

Nelson, G. D., and Barbaro, M. B. (1985a). Fighting the stigma: A unique approach to marketing mental health, *Health Marketing Quarterly, 2*: 89–101.

Nelson, G. D., and Barbaro, M. B. (1985b). Fighting the stigma: A unique approach to marketing mental health, *Journal of Mental Health Administration, 12*: 17–22.

Nevin, J. J. (1984). Expand your practice without print advertising, *CAL, 47*: 1, 3–7.

Newman, R. G. (1984). A conjoint analysis in outpatient clinic preferences, *Journal of Health Care Marketing, 4*: 41-49.

Nichols, P. (1986). Market oriented strategic planning, revisited, *Health Management Forum, 7*: 47–56.

Nicholson, M., Heagney, A., and Lucas, B. (1984). A successful physician marketing program, *Health Care Strategic Management, 2*: 8–10.

Nielson, D. (1985). Medical Center plots new strategies in alternative delivery, *Osteopathic Hospital Leadership, 29*: 14, 33.

Nielsen, R. P. (1984). How market piggy-backing affects your exempt status, *Fund Raising Management, 15*: 32–40, 102.

Nimer, D. A. (1985). Is pricing health care services a marketing decision? *Hospital Forum, 28*: 57–58.

Nimer, D. A. (1986). Everyone wants to go to heaven, but nobody wants to die, *Healthcare Forum, 29*: 74–75.

Noonan, B. (1985–1986). "Nothing happens unless someone buys something." Identifying and responding to your customers' communication style, *Health Marketing Quarterly, 3*: 27–35.

Norcross, D. R. (1985-1986). Developing effective public relations activities, *Health Marketing Quarterly, 3*: 207-224.

Norkett, B. (1985). The role of nursing in marketing health care, *Nursing Administration Quarterly, 10*: 85–89.

Nornhold, P. (1986). Power: It's changing hands and moving your way, *Nursing, 16*: 40–42.

O'Brien, V., and Miaoulis, G. (1984). Marketing the Health Protection Plan, *Journal of Health Care Marketing, 4*: 45–53.

O'Connor, C. P. (1982). Why marketing isn't working in the health care arena, *Health Care Marketing, 2*: 3-36.

O'Gara, N., and Hickey, K. F. (1984). Marketing the preferred provider organization, *Hospitals, 58*: 75–78.

Ohrt, D. (1983). Practice survival: MMA developing new marketing programs, *Minnesota Medicine, 66*: 735–737.

Oji-McNair, K. (1985). A cost analysis of hospice versus non-hospice care: Positioning characteristics for marketing a hospice, *Health Marketing Quarterly, 2*: 119–129.

Oliphant, C. A. (1984). How people treat the public: Bottom line in hospital marketing, *Healthmarketing, 3*: 2–4.

Olson, J. B., and Ekenstam, G. (1984). Marketing–a development opportunity, *Journal of National Association of Hospital Development*, 21–27.

O'Neal, P. (1984). Health care marketing: Has it lived up to its promises? *Southern Hospitals, 52*: 16–22.
Opening a new hospital (1985). *Profiles in Hospital Marketing,* No. 18, 20–25.
Oram, D. M. (1985). The challenge of marketing professional services, *Caring, 4*: 11-15.
Orme, D. V. (1985). Uncompensated care, *Healthcare Forum, 28*: 47–48, 51.
Ostrowski, M. (1984). Spotlight: Candace Allen, RRA, *Journal of American Medical Records Association, 55*: 48.
Ottensmeyer, D. J., Smith, H. L., and Piland, N. F. (1984). Hospital and physician advertising: Forging a constructive response, *Hospital Medical Staff, 13*: 7–14.
Owen, D. (1984). Medicine, morality and the market, *Lancet, 2*: 30–31.
Packa, J. J., and Guy, M. E. (1985). Marketing to survive: The challenge of the eighties for nonprofit organizations, *New England Journal of Human Services, 5*: 28-33.
Packman, R., and Gitman, R. (1985). A simple man's approach to marketing! *Trends and Techniques in Contemporary Dental Laboratories, 2*: 48–49.
Palma, L. (1985). Special needs programs: A unique niche for hospitals, *Michigan Hospitals, 21*: 17-23.
Papadopoulos, N. (1985). Health care marketing in Canada, *Health Management Forum, 6*: 26–39.
Pappas, J. P. (1985a). Marketing home care: Organizational posture and positioning, *Caring, 4*: 48–50.
Pappas, J. P. (1985b). The marketing audit and communications, *Caring, 4*: 54–59.
Paris, J. A. (1985). Small-area data resources for healthcare planners, *Computers in Healthcare, 6*: 26-28, 32-33.
Parks, P. (1984). For-profit health care, *Bulletin of the American College of Surgeons, 69*: 39–44.
Parks, S. C., and Moody, D. L. (1986a). A marketing model: Applications for dietetic professionals, *Journal of the American Dietetic Association, 86*: 37–40, 43.
Parks, S. C., and Moody, D. L. (1986b). Marketing: A survival tool for dietetic professionals in the 1990s, *Journal of the American Dietetic Association, 86*: 33-36.
Pathak, D. S. (1985). Integrating strategic planning and marketing for hospital pharmacy directors, *Topics in Hospital Pharmacy Management, 5*: 8–24.
Patzer, G. L. (1984). Uncontrollable variables in marketing, *Medical Group Management, 31*: 50–52.
Paul, D. T. (1985). *Building Marketing Effectiveness in Healthcare*, American Marketing Association, Chicago.
Paul, T., and Wong, J. (1984). The retailing of health care, *Journal of Health Care Marketing, 4*: 23–34.
Pegues, H. U. (1983). Doctors and patients in the new competitive market, *Journal of the Medical Association of the State of Alabama, 52*: 19–20, 23.
Perich, P. (1984). A guide to marketing your practice, *Journal of Dental Practice Administration, 1*: 50–57.
Perich, P. (1983). The ethical marketing of dentistry: Is it a misnomer? *Journal of American College of Dentists, 50*: 12–16.
Perspectives: Hospital advertising and marketing (1985). *Washington Report on Medicine and Health, 39*(suppl.): 1-42.
Peters, J. B. (1985). Using marketing to size up employer needs and sell hospital services, *Trustee, 38*: 20–21.
Peterson, K. E., and Orlikoff, J. E. (1985). Consumer oriented marketing, *Medical Group Management, 32*: 54–55, 58.
Petro, P. (1985a). Data and trends: Marketing orientation of hospitals, *Osteopathic Hospital Leadership, 29*: 31.

Petro, P. (1985b). Data and trends: Strategic planning and marketing, *Osteopathic Hospital Leadership, 29*: 13.
Piazza, C. J. (1985). Marketing of pharmaceutical services through matrix design analysis, *Topics in Hospital Pharmacy Management, 5*: 25-36.
Pickens, C. W., and Shanklin, C. W. (1985). State of the art in marketing hospital foodservice departments, *Journal of the American Dietetic Association, 85*: 1474-1478.
Pierce, J. S., and Barnett, N. (1986). The selling of a specialty program, *Southern Hospitals, 54*: 22, 24.
Pinto, J. (1984). The bottom line on advertising, *Health Marketing Quarterly, 2*: 73-81.
Porter, S. (1984a). Marketing mental health, *Ohio State Medical Journal, 80*: 112-113.
Porter, S. (1984b). Medicine's master marketeer, *Ohio State Medical Journal, 80*: 531-533, 535.
Potts, M. (1984). Cabbages and condoms: Packaging the channels of distribution, *Clinical Obstetrics and Gynecology, 11*: 799-809.
Powell, D. J. (1984). Nurses-"high touch" entrepreneurs, *Nursing Economics, 2*: 33-36.
Powills, S. (1985a). Hospital marketing, ad budgets triple, *Hospitals, 59*: 61.
Powills, S. (1985b). Hospital sales forces are here to stay, *Hospitals, 59*: FB30, FB36, FB40.
Powills, S. (1985c). Hospitals go international to increase market shares, *Hospitals, 59*: 50, 53.
Powills, S. (1986a). Banking industry sheds light on marketing, *Hospitals, 60*: 72, 74, 79.
Powills, S. (1986b). Contract management for marketing: A trend? *Hospitals, 60*: 60, 62.
Powills, S. (1986c). Creativity: A tool to combat competition, *Hospitals, 60*: 70, 72.
Powills, S. (1986d). Direct marketing prompts response, results, *Hospitals, 60*: 60, 62.
Powills, S. (1986e). Elderly market requires more than enlarged ad type, *Hospitals, 60*: 72, 74.
Powills, S. (1986f). Fitness centers: Profit centers? *Hospitals, 60*: 52-53.
Powills, S. (1986g). HMOs can teach hospitals the marketing game, *Hospitals, 60*: 52-53.
Powills, S. (1986h). Hospital advertising invisible to consumers, *Hospitals, 60*: 66.
Powills, S. (1986i). Hospitals call a marketing time-out, *Hospitals, 60*: 50-55.
Powills, S. (1986j). Immigrants: A new market segment? *Hospitals, 60*: 54.
Powills, S. (1986k). Marketing's essential P: Pricing, *Hospitals, 60*: 72.
Powills, S. (1986l). Market research: Learning the numbers game, *Hospitals, 60*: 57, 59.
Powills, S. (1986m). Market share: A valuable tool remains idle, *Hospitals, 60*: 68.
Powills, S. (1986n). Philly hospitals join in shared research project, *Hospitals, 60*: 62, 64.
Powills, S. (1986o). The elderly: A health marketer's challenge, *Hospitals, 60*: 70, 72.
Powills, S. (1986p). Travenol unveils profit analysis software package, *Hospitals, 60*: 64.
Powills, S. (1986q). Want return on capital investment? Market, *Hospitals, 60*: 58-59.
Powills, S. (1986r). What's in a name? Lawsuits, if you are not careful, *Hospitals, 60*: 59-60.
Preshing, W. A. (1986). Marketing management for dental students: An experience, *Canadian Dental Association Journal, 52*: 129-131.
Press, B. H. (1985). Former ADA president examines potential impact of marketing vote, *Dental Economics, 75*: 36-39, 41, 43.
Prezioso, F. C. (1983). Marketing in dentistry, *Pennsylvania Dental Journal, 84*: 29-30.
Pribilovics, R. M. (1985). Marketing mix case study: Family service agency of San Francisco, *Health Marketing Quarterly, 2*: 75-87.
Punch, L. (1984a). Alternative services: Urgent care centers seek niches, *Modern Healthcare, 14*: 108, 110, 112.
Punch, L. (1984b). Intermountain follows trend, adding alternative services to acute care base, *Modern Healthcare, 14*: 70-71.

Punch, L. (1984). New marketing strategies boost group practices' patient volume, *Modern Healthcare, 14*: 123–126.

Quinn, C. C. (1984). Health care regulation and market forces, *Nursing Economic, 2*: 204-209.

Radoszewski, P. H. (1985). Strategies to meet increased competition for outpatients, *AORN Journal, 42*: 666, 668–669.

Randolph, G. T., Baker, K. M., and Laubach, C. A., Jr. (1984). Involve physicians in marketing, *Medical Group Management, 31*: 16–18.

Ranelli, E. (1985-1986). Health care marketing–a service marketing approach, *Health Marketing Quarterly, 3*: 7–12.

Raphael, S. (1985). Two hospitals and HMO fight it out in Detroit medical advertising blitz, *Modern Healthcare, 15*: 88.

Rash, R. M. (1986). Decision support or support decision? *Computers in Healthcare, 7*: 24-26.

Rayner, G. (1984a). Selling of the private sector, *Health and Social Service Journal, 94*: 43-45.

Rayner, G. (1984b). US health care: Does the language of the marketplace speak with forked tongue? *Health and Social Service Journal, 94*: 622–623.

Razzouk, N. Y., and Brown, S. W. (1984). The distinctive marketing roles of physician office managers and staff, *Journal of Health Care Marketing, 4*: 9–18.

Reardon, M. G. (1985). Getting to market, *Health Care Strategies in Management, 3*: 14-16.

Reeves, P. N., Bergwall, D. F., and Woodside, N. B. (1984). *Introduction to Health Planning*, Information Resources Press, Washington, D.C.

Reif, R. A., Bickett, P. A., and Halbertstadt, D. E. (1985). Case study: Analyzing the market using DRGs and MDCs, *Healthcare Financial Management, 39*: 44–47.

Reynolds, J. (1984). Product manager must decide what products to market and how, *Modern Healthcare, 14*: 176–180.

Reinstein, A. (1985). Personalize your practice, *Dental Practice Management, 20*: 22, 25–27.

Reitz, G. D. (1983). The guide to Ohio's markets, *Ohio State Medical Journal, 79*: 117-119, 122.

Resnik, D. (1985). A special event can tell your story, *Texas Hospitals, 40*: 8–9.

Resource guide (1985). *Journal of Health Care Marketing, 5*: 51–58.

Resource guide: Publications, conferences, national associations, regional associations (1985). *Journal of Health Care Marketing, 5*: 49–58.

Rice, J. A., and Taylor, S. (1984). Assessing the market for long-term care services, *Healthcare Financial Management, 38*: 32–36, 42–46.

Riffer, J. (1984). The patient as guest: A competitive strategy, *Hospitals, 58*: 48, 51, 55.

Riggs, L. (1984a). Doctors in the marketplace: Help needed, *Healthmarketing, 3*: 6–7.

Riggs, L. (1984b). Public relations and marketing–partners in survival, *Healthmarketing, 3*: 7–8.

Riggs, L. (1984c). Targeting physicians for specialty service marketing, *Healthmarketing, 3*: 7–10.

Riggs, L. (1985a). Staffing the hospital public relations function, *Healthmarketing, 4*: 4–6.

Riggs, L. (1985b). The great Arizona shoot-out: Part II, *Health Marketing, 4*: 5–7.

Riggs, L. (1985c). What doctors want to know about marketing, *Healthmarketing, 4*: 5–7.

Roach, W. H., Jr., and Broccolo, B. M. (1984). Ambulatory and alternative services. How to dodge legal pitfalls of setting up primary care centers, *Modern Healthcare, 14*: 92–96.

Robbins, J. A. (1985). Cost containment in an equilibrium state, *American Journal of Medicine, 79*: 280–283.
Roberg, A. (1984). An interview with Adrian Roberg, RN, on his experience as a director of referral services, *Healthmarketing, 3*: 4–6.
Roberts, D. (1984). Marketing health promotion programs, *Southern Hospitals, 52*: 61-63.
Roberts, J., and Roberts, T. (1985). Taking the center to market, *Community Mental Health Journal, 21*: 264–281.
Robinson, E. (1983). Marketing as it applies to dentistry, *Journal of Michigan Dental Association, 65*: 420–421.
Roche, J. L. (1985). Marketing for long term care: Game plan for success, *Journal of American Health Care Association, 11*: 3–8.
Roda, C. (1985). A good marketing Rx may solve financial challenges, *Health Care, 27*: 42–45.
Rogers, B., and Enck, R. E. (1986). Toward a definition of community cancer centers: A theoretical marketing approach, *Progress in Clinical and Biological Research, 216*: 439–443.
Rogers, S. (1986). Retirement like planners building success in retirement housing, *Contemporary Longterm Care, 9*: 60–63.
Rohe, J., and Gelfant, B. B. (1985). Use a checklist for successful open house, *Today's OR Nurse, 7*: 24-26.
Rohrer, R. L., and Bibb, R. (1986). Marketing: The CCRC challenge, *Contemporary Longterm Care, 9*: 41-48, 51-58.
Roman, C. H. (1985). Marketing the mature facility, *Contemporary Longterm Care, 8*: 56, 58, 60.
Roselle, P. F. (1986). Women's health care services: An approach to exploring the market opportunity, *Health Care Strategies in Management, 4*: 4–8.
Rosenberg, J. C. (1984). Application of marketing to medical practice, *Michigan Medicine, 83*: 162-168.
Rosenstein, A. H. (1984–1985a). Ambulatory medicine: Opportunity analysis and strategy selection, *Health Marketing Quarterly, 2*: 35–50.
Rosenstein, A. H. (1984–1985b). The changing trends of medical care and its impact on traditional providers: Adaptation and survival via a marketing approach, *Health Marketing Quarterly, 2*: 11-34.
Rosko, M. D., and McKenna, W. (1983). Modeling consumer choices of health plans: A comparison of two techniques, *Social Science and Medicine, 17*: 421-429.
Rosko, M. D., DeVita, M., McKenna, W. F., and Walker, L. R. (1985). Strategic marketing applications of conjoint analysis: An HMO perspective, *Journal of Health Care Marketing, 5*: 27–38.
Ross, D. M. (1986). Organizational synergy in changing times, *National Intravenous Therapy Association, 9*: 127-129.
Ross, W. R. (1985). The impact of new media on medical marketing, *Medical Marketing Media, 20*: 20-22, 26–29, 32.
Rothman, E. P. (1985). Renovation: A tool for hospital commercialization, *Hospitals, 59*: 95-96, 99.
Rothman, H. (1984). Denver's access' to lower costs links homecare with new program, *Home Health Journal, 5*: 14.
Rower, J. A., and Bernstein, I. M. (1985). Presenting cosmetic dentistry to your community, *Dental Economics, 75*: 42–43, 46.
Rubin, J. S., and Salvo, B. J. (1984). Market-based strategic planning: The approach to success, *Texas Hospitals, 40*: 34-35.

Rubright, R., and MacDonald, D. (1981). *Marketing Health and Human Services*, Aspen Systems, Rockville, MD.

Rudnick, J. D., Jr. (1984). DRGs and marketing, *OH, 28*: 6-11.

Rudolph, B., and Densmore, M. L. (1984). Marketing medical services: How patients view physicians, *Health Marketing Quarterly, 3*: 19-27.

Ruffin, M. G., Jr. (1986). Entrepreneurship: Scorn or esteem? *Group Practice Journal, 35*: 43-45, 48.

Ruga, W. (1984). Environment design can strengthen a hospital's marketing campaign, *Health Marketing Quarterly, 2*: 43-61.

Rushinek, A., and Rushinek, S. F. (1984). Health marketing and sales distribution software related to computer user satisfaction, *Health Marketing Quarterly, 3*: 79-101.

Rusley, R. L. (1983). Ten non-advertising ways to attract and keep new patients, *Dental Management, 23*: 26-29.

Russell, B. (1986). How to pick up new accounts at the next dental meeting, *Dental Laboratory Review, 61*: 14-15.

Rutsohn, P. (1985). Market-based strategic planning for radiologic technology, *Radiologic Technology, 56*: 217-221.

Rynne, S. (1986). Women's health programming: It's more than mauve, *Healthcare Executive, 1*: 42-44.

Rynne, S. J. (1985a). Attracting women. Have you got what it takes? *Hospital Forum, 28*: 63-64.

Rynne, S. J. (1985b). The women's center: A bold strategy, *Health Management Quarterly*, Fall-Winter, 12-17.

Rynne, T. J. (1985c). Chairman's marketing flair helps scoop competition for hospital customers, *Trustee, 38*: 21-25.

Sanchez, P. M. (1983). Marketing in the health care arena: Some comments on O'Conner's evaluation of the discipline, *Journal of Health Care Marketing, 3*: 57-62.

Sauter, J. K. (1985). Pediatric dentistry and the marketplace, *Pediatric Dentistry, 7*: 66-71.

Scammon, D., and Kennard, L. (1984). Incorrect perception of public opinion may skew strategic planning, *Hospital Management Quarterly*, Spring, 14-15.

Schaeffer, L. D. (1985). Healthcare marketing: A model for HMO services to the elderly, *Healthspan, 2*: 8-10.

Schipske, G. (1984). Are your employees a marketing hazard? *Healthmarketing, 3*: 14-15.

Schipske, G. (1985). A primer for nurses: Marketing health care, *Nursing Success Today, 2*: 18-20.

Schlezinger, I. H. (1985). Marketing your medical staff, *Connecticut Medicine, 49*: 821-825.

Schmeling, D. G., and Schmeling, W. H. (1984-1985). The selling of an HMO: A field test of the questionnaire as marketing tool, *Health Marketing Quarterly, 2*: 101-113.

Schmeling, E. C. (1985). Identifying the salient outcomes of exercise: Application of marketing principles to preventive health behavior, *Public Health Nursing, 2*: 93-103.

Schmidt, D. A. (1986). The art of internal marketing, *Dental Economics, 76*: 58-60, 64, 67-69.

Scott, H. (1985). Want to expand? Hit the pavement, *Dental Laboratory Review, 61*: 12-13, 25.

Segal, R. (1985). Designing a pharmacy survey, *Topics in Hospital Pharmacy Management, 5*: 37-45.

Segal, R., and Smith, D. P. (1986). Pharmacists' beliefs and values about advertising patient oriented services, *Journal of Health Care Marketing, 6*: 35–41.
Sellers, K. G. (1984). To PPO or not to PPO? *Hospitals, 58*: 110–112.
Seymour, D. W. (1984). What PPS means for hospital marketing, *Hospitals, 58*: 70–72.
Shahoda, T. (1985a). Demand for certain rehab services in on the upswing, *Multis, 2*: M20, M22, M26.
Shahoda, T. (1985b). Psych services represent a double-edged sword, *Multis, 3*: M20–M23.
Shahoda, T. (1985c). The business of caring for industry, *Multis, 3*: M18–M19, M21.
Shahoda, T. (1986). Two Catholic hospitals team up to face HCA, *Hospitals, 60*: 40.
Share, S. H., Beck, L. C., Anders, G. T., and Alexander, P. D. (1985). Demographic analysis: A marketing must, *Connecticut Medicine, 49*: 302–308.
Share, S. H., and Pierce, A. (1985). How your hospital can help market your practice, *Hospital Physician, 21*: 27, 30.
Shavell, H. M. (1985). Today's marketing—cachet of disaster? *CDA Journal, 13*: 61–63.
Shaw, S. (1985). The changing marketplace: Market and program changes for the traditional intermittent provider, *Caring, 4*: 8–9, 79.
Shea, H. G., and Shea, B. (1985a). Health care marketing: What's ahead? *Physicians Management, 25*: 240, 243, 246-247.
Shea, H. G., and Shea, B. (1985b). Learn the basics of marketing a practice, *Physicians' Management, 25*: 372, 375, 378.
Shea, M. L. (1985). The dental assistant as marketing coordinator, *Dental Assisting, 4*: 40.
Shearer, M. H. (1984). Reconsidering the "market model" in obstetrics, Part I, *Birth, 11*: 213–214.
Shearer, M. H. (1985). Reconsidering the "market model" in obstetrics, Part III. Nursing, *Birth, 12*: 75–76.
Shelley, A. F. (1983). Health care marketing and the clinical laboratory, *American Journal of Medical Technology, 49*: 429–433.
Sheps, C. G., Chez, R. A., McCord, G., and McKay, S. (1985). Reconsidering the "market model," *Birth, 12*: 37–41.
Sherlock, J. F. (1984a). Development and marketing share similar characteristics, *Fund Raising Management, 14*: 73, 75.
Sherlock, J. F. (1984b). Institutions must routinely take market's pulse, *Fund Raising Management, 15*: 89.
Sherlock, J. F. (1984c). Physician support keyed to hospital marketing success, *Fund Raising Management, 15*: 80.
Sheridan, D. R. (1983). The health care industry in the marketplace: Implications for nursing, *Journal of Nursing Administration, 13*: 36–40.
Shugoll, M. S. (1984). Edging the competition with market research, *Contemporary Administration of Long-term Care, 7*: 37–38.
Sieverts, S. (1977). *Health Planning Issues and Public Law*, American Hospital Association, Chicago, pp. 93–641.
Simendinger, E. A., and Lekas, M. C. (1984). The referring physician: The key to a successful marketing analysis and program, *Health Care Strategic Management, 2*: 14-16.
Simon, J. K. (1978). Marketing the community hospital: A tool for the beleaguered administration, *Health Care Management Review, 3*: 11–23.
Singer, I. D., Meyerhoff, A. S., and Schiffman, S. B. (1985). *A Guide to Health Data Resources*, Center for Health Affairs, Project Hope, Millwood, VA.
Singer, J. L. (1983). The dental hygienist as a marketing agent, *Dental Hygiene, 57*: 14-17, 20-22.

Singer, J. L., and Romberg, E. (1985). Dental hygienists' attitudes toward marketing roles, *Dental Hygiene, 59*: 410-415.
Sinioris, M. E. (1985). Competitive marketing strategies: A challenge for academic practices, *Medical Group Management, 32*: 40-43, 57.
Sinioris, M. E., and Butler, P. W. (1983). Basic business strategy, *Hospitals, 57*: 68-73.
Smith, B. A. (1984). Toward a more profitable nursing image, *Nursing Success Today, 1*: 18-23.
Smith, B. F. (1984). Researching your market, *OH, 28*: 20-21.
Smith, D. B. (1984). Reflective listening as a marketing force, *New Zealand Dental Journal, 80*: 81-83.
Smith, F. E. (1985). Solve your hospital's marketing problems: Learn how to deploy the right components of a marketing grid, *Cost Containment, 7*: 3-6.
Smith, J. E. (1985). Expanding hospital pharmacy services to meet developing markets, *Topics in Hospital Pharmacy Management, 4*: 67-76.
Smith, J. E., and Sheafer, S. L. (1985). Marketing clinical pharmacy services, *Topics in Hospital Pharmacy Management, 5*: 53-62.
Smith, R. J. (1985-1986). Integrating the marketing function: A model for strategic management, *Health Marketing Quarterly, 3*: 13-17.
Smith, S., and Taylor, J. (1984). Market identification and hospital cost containment: A comparison of revenue contribution to utilization of strategic business units, *Journal of Health Care Marketing, 4*: 43-48.
Smith, T. (1986). Women's services—a product approach, *Health Care Strategic Management, 4*: 21-23.
Smyth, E. A. (1983). Internal Marketing: The first step to team success, *Dental Economics, 73*: 114-116, 119-120.
Smyth, T., and Smith, J. A. (1985). Internal marketing: The kindness approach, *Dental Economics, 75*: 102, 104.
Smythe, S. (1984). Marketing home health care, *Texas Hospitals, 40*: 22-24.
Social marketing of oral rehydration therapy (1985). *Population Reports*, Series 3: *Family Planning Programs*, July-August (30), J785-J786.
Solberg, L. I., Potter, A. C., and Flexner, W. A. (1985). Marketing research in medical practice: A case study of one practice's site survey, *Postgraduate Medicine, 77*: 317-319, 322, 326-327.
Sorce, P., Tyler, P. R., Minno, J. R. (1985). Marketing your organization to the health services volunteer, *Journal of Health Care Marketing, 5*: 55-63.
Special marketing wrap-up (1984). *Hospitals, 58*: 33-34, 38-46, 56-62.
Stahl, D. A. (1984). Developing and marketing ambulatory care programs, *Nursing Management, 15*: 20-24.
Stanberry, E., Jr., Rosenberg, L. J., and Rao, C. P. (1986). The use of consumer behavior analysis in marketing a dental practice, *Journal of the Alabama Dental Association, 70*: 34-37.
Stanton, M. P. (1985). Patient and health education: Lessons from the marketplace, *Nursing Management, 16*: 28-30.
Starr, A. (1986). The thoracic surgical industrial complex, *Annals of Thoracic Surgery, 42*: 124-133.
Steffire, V. (1986). *Developing and Implementing Marketing Strategies*, Praeger Scientific, New York.
Steiber, S. R., and Boscarino, J. A. (1984). A progress report on hospital marketing, *Hospitals, 58*: 98-102.
Steiber, S. R., and Jackson, E. D. (1985). Hospital marketing budgets in 1985: What will bigger budgets bring? *Health Care Strategic Management, 3*: 4-7.

Steiber, S. R., Boscarino, J. A., and Jackson, E. D. (1985). Hospital marketing more sophisticated: Survey, *Hospitals, 59*: 73, 76–77.

Stein, P. (1986). What is the most important activity in a dental laboratory? Answer: Sales, sales, sales!!! *Trends and Technology in the Contemporary Dental Laboratory, 3*: 16, 18, 20–22 passim.

Steiner, G. A. (1979). *Strategic Planning: What Every Manager Must Know*, The Free Press, New York.

Stevens, A. (1985). The Dos and Don'ts when building your marketing plan, *Dental Student, 63*: 21–23.

Stewart, N. (1985). Marketing tools and methods for small home health agencies, *Caring, 4*: 30–33.

Stier, R. D. (1986). Marketing strategies to consider in planning your campaign, *Hospital Topics, 64*: 6–9.

Stitt, V. J., Jr. (1985). Health care: Development of data for a marketing approach, *Journal of the National Medical Association, 77*: 485–488.

Strang, D. M. (1985). Marketing/public relations: A new dimension in long term care, *Journal of the American Health Care Association, 11*: 55–56.

Streety, M. (1984). The implementation of a specialty strategy (or how to win the young family market), *Hospital Topics, 62*: 17–19.

Strenski, J. (1985). Marketplace perceptions and the home care communications plan, *Caring, 4*: 18–19.

Strong, V. L. (1985). Nursing products: Primary components of health care, *Nursing Economics, 3*: 60.

Sturm, A. C., Jr. (1984a). Who's your target? The answer will help trigger effective ads, *Modern Healthcare, 14*: 98, 100, 102.

Sturm, A. C., Jr. (1984b). Selling the medical staff and hospital as a package, *Hospitals, 58*: 98–101.

Summers, J. (1985). Professional ethics in materials management and its impact on marketing, *Journal of Healthcare Materials Management, 3*: 56–60.

Super, K. (1985). Regional business publications vehicles for healthcare ads, *Modern Healthcare, 15*: 36, 38.

Super, K. (1986a). Hospitals will favor "hard-sell" in advertising, experts predict, *Modern Healthcare, 16*: 74, 76.

Super, K. E. (1986b). Chicago teaching hospital planning first comprehensive market program, *Modern Healthcare, 16*: 156, 158.

Super, K. E. (1986c). Hospital ad antagonizes competitor, *Modern Healthcare, 16*: 60.

Super, K. E. (1986d). Hospitals are beginning to focus on services for older patients, *Modern Healthcare, 16*: 80, 82.

Super, K. E. (1986e). Hospitals in Florida and Arizona bolster for battle with Mayo's clinics, *Modern Healthcare, 16*: 62, 64.

Super, K. E. (1986f). Hospitals try syndicated ad campaigns for commonly offered product lines, [news], *Modern Healthcare, 16*: 58–59.

Super, K. E. (1986g). Hospitals will demand results after big budget advertising, *Modern Healthcare, 16*: 69–70, 73.

Super, K. E. (1986h). Mississippi hospital uses campaign to keep awareness, patient days up, *Modern Healthcare, 16*: 55.

Super, K. E. (1986i). Private hospital bolsters its census with advertising, training program, *Modern Healthcare, 16*: 98, 100.

Super, K. E. (1986j). Products must be fully developed before they're advertised—experts, *Modern Healthcare, 16*: 30–31.

Super, K. E. (1986k). Tampa General changes image to attract private-pay patients, *Modern Healthcare, 16*: 52–56.

Swan, J. E., Sawyer, J. C., Van-Matre, J. G., and McGee, G. W. (1985). Deepening the understanding of hospital patient satisfaction: Fulfillment and equity effects, *Journal of Health Care Marketing, 5*: 7-18.

Sweeney, D. R., Beck, L. C., and Anders, G. T. (1984). Marketing–what does it mean to physicians? *Pennsylvania Medicine, 87*: 78.

Sweeney, R. E. (1985a). The power of a marketing audit, *Home Health Journal, 6*: 10-11.

Sweeney, R. E. (1985b). What is marketing? *Home Health Journal, 6*: 9-10.

Sweeney, R. E. (1985c). What is strategic market planning? *Home Health Journal, 6*: 10-12.

Sweeney, R. E. (1985-1986). The marketing audit–a strategic necessity: Marketing management for the mature non-profit, *Health Marketing Quarterly, 3*: 93-97.

Sweeney, R. E., and Rakowski, J. P. (1984-1985). Logistics considerations in the prepaid health industry: An exploratory analysis, *Health Marketing Quarterly, 2*: 115-133.

Suver, J. D., and Miller, J. A. (1984). Control of the marketing effort in health care organizations, *Health Marketing Quarterly, 1*: 83-100.

Swingle, K. M. (1983). Marketing midwifery, *Journal of Nurse Midwifery, 28*: 23-26.

Tanner, D. J. (1984). Assessing hospital entry into home care, *Caring, 3*: 41-48.

Tanner, D. J. (1985). Marketing considerations in home health care, *American Journal of Hospital Pharmacy, 42*: 2695-2701.

Tanner, S. E., and Klein, J. B. (1985). Market analysis reveals rehab program potential, *Hospitals, 59*: 65-66.

Tatge, M. (1985). The battle's on for Chicago customers as new entries offer low-cost plans, *Modern Healthcare, 15*: 37.

Taylor, R. B. (1984). What's in the future for doctor-hospital competition, *Physicians' Management, 24*: 152-160, 163, 166.

Telling the inside story. ASIM launches its public education (1984). *Internist, 25*: 33-36.

Reslow, P. A. (1984). Refining traditional behaviors for marketplace advantage, *Topics in Health Care Financing, 11*: 47-52.

Tetlow, K. (1985). New design for physical fitness, *Interiors, 145*: 168-173, 176.

Thanopoulos, J., and Kiser, G. E. (1984). Segmentation bases of the elderly health care consumer, *Health Marketing Quarterly, 2*: 129-138.

The market of the government (1985). *New England Journal of Medicine, 313*: 1663-1664.

Thorn, B. E. (1984). Marketing therapeutic recreation services, *Therapeutic Recreation Journal, 18*: 42-47.

Ting, H. M. (1984). New directions in nursing home and home healthcare marketing, *Healthcare Financial Management, 38*: 62-72.

Ting, H. M. (1985). Macro trends affecting long term care marketing, *Journal of the American Health Care Association, 11*: 10-14.

Tomiyama, A. S., and Cunningham, L. (1984). Multi treats advertising as board policy decision, *Multis, 2*: M53-M54.

Tootelian, D. H., and Gaedeke, R. M. (1986). The changing role of pharmacies in the 1990s, *Journal of Health Care Marketing, 6*: 57-63.

Tootelian, D. H., Gaedeke, R. M., and Gordon, C. L. (1984). Marketing to public-aid recipients: An examination of pharmacy profitability, *Journal of Health Care Marketing, 4*: 17-21.

Tracy, E. J. (1984). Cut-rate surgery is luring customers, *Fortune, 110*: 88.

Trandel-Korenchuk, K., and Trandel-Korenchuk, D. (1985). Alternative delivery systems, *Nursing Administration Quarterly, 10*: 61-64.

Traska, M. R. (1984). Hospital marketing came of age this year, *Hospitals, 58*: 65.

Trester, K. B. (1985). Hospital advertising: An interview with Patricia McCarthy of Henry Ford Hospital, *Healthmarketing, 4*: 6–9.

Trester, K. G. (1984a). The American Health Academy Association College and Society of Health Care Marketing and Planning and Public Relations, Inc.—Join now! *Healthmarketing, 3*: 9–10.

Trester, K. G. (1984c). The marketing budget: Dreams and reality, *Healthmarketing, 3*: 10-13.

Trester, K. G. (1985a). Marketing research tips: Keeping track of the competition—some practical tips, *Healthmarketing, 4*: 7–9.

Trester, K. G. (1985b). PLCLA—a new disease that afflicts aspiring marketers, *Healthmarketing, 4*: 7–9.

Trofino, J. (1985). Marketing nursing: A community medical center perspective, *Nursing Administration Quarterly, 10*: 58-61.

Trotter, J. (1985). The entrepreneur's approach: Business planning for home health agencies, *Caring, 4*: 20-24, 45.

Trusi, F. M. (1985). Hospitals take note: DO's can market and win, *Osteopathic Hospital Leadership, 29*: 8–9, 26.

Tyler, J. L. (1984). Locating a market director, *Southern Hospitals, 52*: 71.

U.S. Department of Commerce, Bureau of the Census (1983). *County and City Data Book—1983*, U.S. Government Printing Office, Washington, D.C.

Vander-Schaaf, D. J., and Jackson, E. D. (1986). Group purchasing marketing research: Is it competitive? *Hospitals, 60*: 114, 116.

Vargas, J. H., and Robertson, P. H. (1984). Plug into consumer thinking, *Group Practice Journal, 33*: 54-56, 60.

Venning, G. R. (1984). Priorities in the benefit-risk assessment of new drugs, *Adverse Drug Reactions and Acute Poisoning Reviews, 3*: 113–121.

Vestal, K. W. (1984). Marketing concepts for the emergency department, *Journal of Emergency Nursing, 10*: 274-276.

Walch, W. E., and Tseng, S. (1984). Marketing: Handle with care, *Trustee, 37*: 19–21.

Waldman, H. B. (1984a). Some potential targets for directed marketing of dental services, *Dental Economics, 74*: 47–48, 51–42.

Waldman, H. B. (1984b). Yesterday's dental market in the United States has changed in today's world, *New York Journal of Dentistry, 54*: 113–118.

Waldman, H. B. (1985). Targeted marketing helps find patients, *Dental Student, 63*: 30-32.

Walker, D. (1985). On the scene: Stanford University. Overview of marketing at Stanford University Hospital, *Nursing Administration Quarterly, 10*: 18-27.

Wallace, B. (1983). The dentist in the gray flannel suit: (Marketing in dentistry), *Contact-Point, 61*: 10–15.

Wallace, C. (1984). Presbyterian spins off new business, *Modern Healthcare, 14*: 68.

Wallace, C. (1985). Women's healthcare spending new target of hospitals' ads, *Modern Healthcare, 15*: 52, 56.

Wallace, C. (1986a). HMOs battle for market share throughout Southern California, *Modern Healthcare, 16*: 44–46.

Wallace, C. (1986b). HMO is targeting small employers to fuel expansion throughout state, *Modern Healthcare, 16*: 38.

Wallace, C. (1986c). Hospital's "personalized" care unit may boost share, patient satisfaction, *Modern Healthcare, 16*: 36, 38.

Walter, C. M. (1985). Auditing the hospital nursing market, *Nursing Management, 16*: 31-34.

Walters, M. J., and Ferrante-Wallace, J. (1985). Lessons from nonresponse in a consumer market survey, *Journal of Health Care Marketing, 5*: 17–28.

Ward, M. (1985). Selling to the business client: It's not easy—but it can be done, *Promoting Health, 6*: 1-4.

Washington Report on Medicine and Health (1985). *Hospital Advertising and Marketing, 39*(suppl.): 1-4.

Wassersug, J. D. (1986). From "patient" to "customer": A dangerous trend in healthcare, *Postgraduate Medicine, 79*: 255-257.

Webb, D. (1983). Medical marketing rampant, *New England Journal of Medicine, 309*: 1194.

Webster, N. E. (1984). Quality assurance as a market approach, *Topics in Health Records Management, 5*: 33-38.

Wehr, K. L. (1986). Where's the patient? or business as usual in health care—an internist's view, *Ohio State Medical Journal, 82*: 77-81.

Welch, W. P. (1984). HMO enrollment: A study of market forces and regulations, *Journal of Health Politics and Policy Law, 8*: 743-758.

Wells, J. B. (1985). Homecare marketing and product management, *Caring, 4*: 4-6, 9.

Whaley, F. D. (1985). A trend of the future: Marketing outpatient pharmacy services, *Hospital Materials Management Quarterly, 6*: 57-63.

Whitcomb, M. E., and Caswell, J. (1986). The market structure of residency training, *New England Journal of Medicine, 314*: 710-712.

White, E. (1985a). Columbia, MO, hospitals stage advertising blitz, *Modern Healthcare, 15*: 97-98.

White, E. C. (1985b). Centers refine their advertising as era of soft-peddling ends, *Modern Healthcare, 15*: 74-75.

White, E. C. (1985c). Competition for healthcare markets spurs race for demographic data, *Modern Healthcare, 15*: 79-82.

White, E. C. (1985d). Denver company trying to attract foreign patients to U.S. hospitals, *Modern Healthcare, 15*: 94.

White, E. C. (1985e). Microcomputer software helps hospital marketers, planners, *Modern Healthcare, 15*: 104-105.

Wiley, M. (1986). Hospitals learn key marketing lessons from banks, *Hospitals, 60*: 80-82.

Wilkinson, R. (1986a). Communication: Learning from the market, *Nursing Management, 17*: 42J, 42L.

Wilkinson, R. (1986b). Market with videos—your competition does, *Hospitals, 60*: 84.

Willenbrink, M. (1985). Use nursing medical knowledge for alternative careers, *Nursing Success Today, 2*: 12-15.

Wilson, A. L. (1986). Market research: Monitoring the public pulse, *Michigan Hospital, 22*: 26-28.

Wilson, V. J. (1984). Attitudes toward medical marketing in Maricopa County, *Arizona Medicine, 41*: 743-749.

Winning logos: How these labs did it (1986). *Lab Management Today, 2*: 19-21.

Winston, W. J. (1984a). Is the future of health marketing going to be directed by videotex systems? *Health Marketing Quarterly, 1*: 1-4.

Winston, W. J. (1984b). Positioning the long-term and senior care service in the minds of the medical provider and consumer, *Health Marketing Quarterly, 1*: 51-67.

Winston, W. J. (1984c). Public policy and hospital marketing, *Health Marketing Quarterly, 2*: 3-17.

Winston, W. J. (1984d). Why do the majority of marketing programs in hospitals fail? *Health Marketing Quarterly, 2*: xvii-xxi.

Winter, J. P. (1984). Getting your house in order with internal marketing: A marketing prerequisite, *Health Marketing Quarterly, 3*: 69-77.

Winters, P. A. (1985). Turn your ideas into profit, *Nursing Success Today, 2*: 20-23.

Wolfson, D. B., Bell, C. W., and Newbery, D. A. (1984). Fallon's Senior Plan: A summary of the three year marketing experience, *Group Health Journal, 5*: 4–7.

Wolinsky, H. (1986). Women's centers: Good medicine or good marketing? *Hospitals, 60*: 110.

Wood, J. (1984). Can the NHS be marketed like a detergent? *Health and Social Services Journal, 94*: 582–583.

Wotruba, T. R., Haas, R. W., and Oulhen, H. (1985). Marketing factors affecting physician choice as related to consumers' extent of use and predisposition toward use of physician services, *Journal of Health Care Marketing, 5*: 7–17.

Wright, R. A., and Allen, B. H. (1983). Marketing and medicine: Why advertising is not an issue, *Journal of the American Medical Association, 250*: 47–48.

Wunderman, L. (1984). Non-profit learns marketing techniques from ad agency, *Fund Raising Management, 42-48*: 76, 108.

Yanish, D. (1985a). Hospital council president takes job as head of for-profit research spinoff, *Modern Healthcare, 15*: 34.

Yanish, D. (1985b). Hospitals spending more money on advertising, market research, *Modern Healthcare, 15*: 49-50.

Yankey, J. A., Koury, N., and Young, D. (1985). Utilizing a marketing audit in developing a new services. Case examples: Breckenridge Village, *Health Marketing Quarterly, 2*: 37–50.

Yankey, J. A., Young, D., and Koury, N. (1985). Designing a promotional tool: Practical application of market targeting and research. Case example: Alcoholism Services of Cleveland, Inc., *Health Marketing Quarterly, 2*: 59–71.

Yenney, S. L. (1984). Capturing the small business market, *Promoting Health, 5*: 1–3.

Yoder, D. E. (1984). Presidential address: To market, *American Language/Hearing Association, 26*: 23-26.

Young, B. (1985). Market your hospital through health promotion, *Michigan Hospitals, 21*: 11-12.

Young, P. (1985). Marketing strategies in a competitive marketplace, *Emergency Medical Services, 14*: 90-92.

Zallocco, R. L., Joseph, W. B., and Doremus, H. (1984). Strategic market planning for hospitals, *Journal of Health Care Marketing, 4*: 19–28.

Zasa, R. J. (1984). Marketing health services, *College Review, 1*: 23–53.

Ziegler, E. F. (1983). Marketing, *Northwest Dentistry, 62*: 9–10.

Zufall, D. L. (1984). Health education expertise + strong "people skills"—marketing success, *Healthmarketing, 3*: 10–11.

Zurolo, G. (1985). The dental lab and the future: Dialing your way to new business, *Lab Management Today, 2*: 30–31.

6

The Financial Impact of Government on Health Services Administration: Prospective Payment Systems and Other Regulatory Programs

Michael D. Rosko and Robert W. Broyles Department of Health and Medical Services Administration, School of Management, Widener University, Chester, Pennsylvania

I. REVENUE REGULATION

Public- and private-sector initiatives to contain health care costs are as diverse as the theories of health care cost inflation. Government authorities have attempted to contain health care expenditures by (1) regulating revenues; (2) limiting utilization; (3) restricting capital expansion; and (4) fostering competition and creating market-like incentives. Approaches to regulate revenues include prospective payment, the Economic Stabilization Program, the Carter administration's Hospital Cost Containment Act, and the hospital industry's Voluntary Effort. Professional standards and review organizations and peer review organizations are examples of approaches designed to control utilization. Under capital controls are the federal review of capital expansion authorized by Section 1122 of Public Law (P.L.) 92-603 and state certificate of need laws. Among the most important of the competitive solutions to the problem of controlling costs are the formation of alternate delivery systems and patient cost sharing. The discussion in this chapter will be limited to the first three federal initiatives.

A. History of Prospective Payment

In the 1980s, prospective payment (PP) has emerged as the dominant federal strategy for hospital cost containment. On October 1, 1983, the Health Care Financing Administration began to replace a retrospective method of financing inpatient care for Medicare beneficiaries with a prospective payment system in which Diagnosis Related Groups (DRGs) are employed to establish hospital payment rates. As of February 1985, 13 states were using prospective payment to control the increase in hospital costs. Some PP programs have been developed in the private sector, mainly by Blue Cross plans (Hellinger, 1985).

There is a great amount of diversity among the PP systems. The establishment of rates in advance and the payment of these rates irrespective of actual costs is a characteristic common to all PP programs (Dowling, 1974). Traditionally, hospitals were reimbursed retrospectively for the costs incurred during the period. If expenditures increased, reimbursements were adjusted upward, implying that hospitals had little incentive to control costs. In contrast, under prospective payment, hospitals assume the financial risks of inflation and are forced to absorb unfavorable differences between the rate or amount of compensation and actual costs. It is thought that this threat to a hospitals' financial viability will motivate hospital executives to provide services in a more efficient and, hence, less costly manner.

Prospective payment did not receive widespread attention until the 1980s, when the Medicare PP system was being developed and implemented. However, since a prospective payment program was implemented in Indiana in 1960, the concept and practice of PP (or prospective reimbursement, as it was first termed) is not new. Although the program in Indiana was the first large-scale program that regulated revenue, it did not conform to the contemporary criteria of prospective payment, which stipulate that the program must be implemented by the government and compliance must be mandatory (Eby and Cohodes, 1985). The program was implemented by the Indiana Hospital Association and Blue Cross of Indiana, and compliance was voluntary (O'Donoghue, 1978).

The State of New York implemented the first "true" PP system in 1970 (Dowling, 1974). It is really three different programs: one for Blue Cross patients in the downstate area (New York City); one for upstate Blue Cross patients; and a statewide program for Medicaid patients. Although the rate-setting formula varied among the three programs, each considered allowable inpatient costs in the base year to determine prospective per diem rates. Allowable costs were established by comparing each hospital's costs with those of a peer group of hospitals. Base year allowable costs were adjusted upward to account for projected increases in factor input prices.

New York operated the only mandatory PP system until the mid-1970s, it was joined by seven other states which began to regulate hospital rates in either 1975 or 1976 (Biles, Schramm, and Atkinson, 1980).

Most of the evidence about the effects of hospital rate review comes from evaluations of the original eight prospective payment systems, the major features of which are presented in Table 1. There is a great deal of similarity among all of the early PP systems that were in use as of 1982 (see Table 1). For example, all of the programs had an appeals mechanism; and seven of the eight allowed retroactive adjustments to the prospective rate (usually on the basis of unanticipated changes in the input price inflation rate or in the volume of patients) and reviewed rates at least annually. There were also important differences among the programs. While in six states only a limited number of payers (usually Blue Cross and Medicaid) had their payments regulated, in two states—New Jersey and Maryland—payments of all payers were regulated. In half of the PP mechanisms, different units of payment were used for different payers: charges were used as a unit of payment in seven programs, and the patient-day (per diem) was used in four programs.

B. Recent Developments in Prospective Payment

1. Medicare Prospective Payment System

Effective October 1, 1983, the provisions of P.L. 98-21, the Social Security Amendments of 1983, replaced the traditional retrospective mechanism of financing the use of inpatient care by Medicare beneficiaries with a prospective payment system in which prices were established for each of 467 DRGs. With the exception of children's rehabilitation, psychiatric, and long-term hospitals, all hospitals have been subject to the provisions of P.L. 98-21 since October 1, 1983. Unlike the cost-per-case limit established by the Tax Equity and Fiscal Responsibility Act, the provisions of P.L. 98-21 do the following:

1. Sever the traditional relationship between actual costs and the revenues generated by providing inpatient care.
2. Constitute the basis for establishing prospective prices for each of 467 DRGs.
3. Assign the financial risk for unfavorable differences between the cost of providing care and the predetermined DRG prices to the hospital.
4. Permit the hospital to retain favorable differences between the cost of providing care and the corresponding predetermined DRG price.

Since the set of DRG prices is established prior to the operating period, the provisions of P.L. 98-21 were predicated on the assumption that rate regulation will contain costs, limit the financial risks assumed by the federal government, and enable hospitals to benefit financially from improved management.

Scheduled to be implemented during a three-year period, the prospective pricing system employs the patient and related diagnostic condition as the unit of payment. During each year of the implementation period, the payment for each Medicare beneficiary is determined by a composite price consisting of (1) the hospital-specific cost per case; (2) the average regional cost per case of the DRG to which the patient is assigned; and (3) the average national cost per case of the DRG to which the patient is assigned. Averages for the regional and national components are calculated separately for urban and rural hospitals.

The relative importance of the three components in determining the prospective prices changes during each year of the implementation period. During the first year, the prospective price for each Medicare discharge equaled the sum of seventy-five percent of the hospital-specific cost per case and twenty-five percent of the regional price for the DRG to which the patient was assigned. During the second year, the amount of payment for a Medicare discharge was determined by adding fifty percent of the hospital-specific cost per case, thirty-seven and one-half percent of the regional price, and twelve and one-half percent of the national price for the DRG to which the patient was assigned.

In the third year of the implementation period, the payment per discharge was scheduled to consist of twenty-five percent of the hospital-specific cost per case, thirty-seven and one-half percent of the national price, and thirty-seven and one-half percent of the regional price of the DRG to which the patient was assigned. After the implementation process is complete, the role of hospital-specific costs in the determination of prospective rates is to be eliminated, and the price structure is to be based solely on rural or urban national averages.

Concerning the hospital-specific component of the prospective prices, the base-year cost per case for each institution was determined by employing the costs recovered from Medicare during the period October 1, 1981, to September 30, 1982, after excluding capital costs, the direct cost of approved educational programs, and the indirect costs of medical education. Further, the cost per case prevailing during each year of the implementation period was derived by adjusting the base-year cost per case so as to compensate for trends in the prices of noncapital resources that hospitals use and by including an allowance for medical technology.

TABLE 1 State-Legislated Hospital Cost Containment Programs

State (year implemented)	Responsible agency	Payers covered	Revenue control method	Unit of payment	Frequency of review	Adjustments	Appeals
Connecticut (1976)	Commission on Hospitals and Health Care	Charge-based	Total revenue	Charges	Annually	Retroactive for volume, unforeseen and significant change in expense	Public hearing before commission
Maryland (1975)	Health Services Cost Review Commission	All payers	Total revenue; departmental revenue, guaranteed revenue per case, or maximum revenue per case	Rate-based charges	As necessary	Inflation, volume, cost beyond control	Public hearing before commission
Massachusetts (1976)	Massachusetts Rate Setting Commission	Charge-based	Total revenue with cost limit	Charges	Annually	Inflation, volume, cost beyond control	Division of Hearing Officers
		Blue Cross	Cost-based	Routine per diem, ancillary charges	Annually	Excess costs may be denied	Courts
		Medicaid	Cost-based with limits	Per diem	Annually	Uncontrollable costs associated with change in government regulations	Division of Hearing Officers
New Jersey (1975)	State Department of Health	Medicaid and Blue Cross	Cost-based	Per diem	Annually	Retroactive for volume, economic factor, pass-through items	Formal appeal before independent hearing officer

New Jersey DRG (1980–1982)	State Department of Health	All payers	Cost-based	Rate per case and controlled charges for outliers	Annually	Regional factor price differentials, retroactive for cost of capital, cost of medical education	Only for errors in rate calculations
New York (1970)	State Department of Health	Medicaid and Blue Cross	Cost-based	Per diem	Annually	Retroactive for actual economic factor and volume	Formal appeal before state hearing officer
		Charge-based	Charge increase	Charges	As necessary	Actual economic factor	Appeals board
Rhode Island (1975)	State Budget Office; Blue Cross of Rhode Island	Medicaid and Blue Cross	Total expenses	Percent of charges	Annually	Retroactive for volume	Binding arbitration before independent mediation
			Revenue				
Washington (1975)	Washington State Hospital Commission	Charge-based, including Blue Cross	Total revenue; rates per unit of service by revenue center	Charges	Annually	Volume	Formal hearing before commission or independent hearing officer
Wisconsin (1976)	State Department of Health; Rate Review Committee	Charge-based, including Blue Cross	Total revenue	Charges	Prior to any rate change, one a year at most	None	Hearing before independent appeals board
		Medicaid		Per diem			

TABLE 2 Case-Based Systems for Setting Hospital Rates

System	Period of operation	Payers covered	Rate setting-method
Maryland Guaranteed Inpatient Revenue Program	1976–present	All payers	Builds on original rate-setting system; covers 22 of state's 52 acute care hospitals; uses three- or four-digit ICD-9-CM codes, broad patient service categories, or DRGs; bases current year's rate on last year's rate, adjusted for volume and uncompensated care.
New Jersey	1980–present	All payers	Replaced two-payer program, uses DRGs to set rates; rates reflect combination of state and hospital-specific rates according to coefficient of variation of costs in DRG; adjusts for volume and uncompensated care; three-year phase-in period, 1980–1982.
California Medicaid (Medi-Cal)	1980–1982	Medicaid	Payments based on prior year's cost per case not adjusted for case mix; hospitals could appeal rates on grounds that case mix increased.
Georgia Medicaid	1980–1982	Medicaid	Used cluster analyses on several variables to define 10–12 groups; hospitals paid up to one hundred and thirty percent of group mean cost per case.
Utah Medicaid	July 1983–present	Medicaid	Uses same system as Medicare, except Medicare's rates are reduced by twenty percent.
Pennsylvania Medicaid	July 1984–present	Medicaid	Uses DRGs; defines eight peer groups based on complex formula that includes teaching status, medical assistance volume, environmental characteristics, and hospital costs; two-year phase-in period.
Ohio Medicaid	October 1984–present	Medicaid	Uses DRGs and 14 peer groups based on area wage rate and teaching status to set rates based on last year's costs; system phased in over two years.

TABLE 2 (continued)

System	Period of operation	Payers covered	Rate setting-method
Michigan Medicaid	February 1985 present	Medicaid	Rates set using DRGs, several peer groups, and adjustments to rates for area wage level, teaching status, capital costs, and outliers.
Washington State Medicaid	January 1985 present	Medicaid	Uses method similar to Medicare PPs; no plans to use peer groups.
Arizona Blue Cross and Blue Shield	November 1983-present	All insureds	Sets rates using DRGs for 10 peer groups of hospitals.
Kansas Blue Cross and Blue Shield	January 1984-present	All insureds	Sets rates using DRGs and five peer groups; billed charges are paid up to seventy-five percent of DRG rate.
Oklahoma Blue Cross and Blue Shield	January 1984-present	All insureds	Sets rates using DRGs and four peer groups defined using bed size.
Nebraska Blue Cross and Blue Shield	April 1985-present	All insureds	Rates to be set using DRGs; five or six peer groups.

Sources: Hellinger, 1985; Rosko, 1984a.

The regional DRG prices are based on the average cost per case in each of nine geographic divisions. Further, the regional averages are adjusted to reflect the level of wages in the state or standard metropolitan statistical area in which the institution is located, the rate of increase in actual costs during 1982, and the rate of increase in the hospital input price index. They also include an allowance for medical technology. Similarly, the national DRG prices used to calculate rates for urban and rural hospitals are based on the national average cost per case, as adjusted by employing techniques similar to those used to project regional prices. The Medicare program will continue to employ the cost-based retrospective system to reimburse the institution for the costs of capital—depreciation, interest, and lease expenses—until an acceptable prospective mechanism is developed.

2. State and Blue Cross Plan Prospective Payment Systems

Besides the implementation of the Medicare prospective payment system, the most significant developments in prospective payment in the 1980s have been the introduction of all-payer rate-setting programs and the increased reliance upon case-based payment mechanisms. During this period, all-payer hospital rate-regulation programs were operated in Maryland, Massachusetts, New Jersey, and New York. All-payer systems are able to prevent cost shifting and to provide for the equitable distribution of the burden of financing the cost of services provided to the indigent. The Medicare system has been criticized for not providing for these contingencies (Broyles and Rosko, 1985; Lave, 1984; Rosko, 1984b).

The state of Maryland implemented the first case-based hospital rate-regulation program in 1976. During the period 1980-1985, case-based prospective payment systems were implemented in 12 states, as Table 2 shows (Hellinger, 1985). Unlike per diem payment mechanisms, which create incentives to increase the duration of inpatient care, case-based payments encourage hospitals to discharge patients as soon as possible, resulting in a lower cost per admission (Rosko and Broyles, 1986).

Among the case-based systems in 13 states, seven regulated Medicaid payment rates, four regulated Blue Cross Plan payments, and two regulated all payers. With the exception of the programs in Maryland and California, all of these used DRGs to determine payment rates. Most of these programs divided hospitals into separate peer groups for which separate payment rates were calculated. Williams and colleagues (1984) demonstrated that peer groups used in conjunction with DRGs can control more of the interhospital variation in severity of illness than DRGs alone. Furthermore, the use of additional peer groups beyond those employed by Medicare (urban and rural) allows state and Blue Cross Plan payment systems to account for more exogenous, interhospital cost variations, resulting in a more equitable determination of payments (Rosko, 1986).

II. EVALUATIONS OF PROSPECTIVE PAYMENT

Although prospective payment of hospitals is intended to decrease costs by increasing efficiency, several policy analysts have expressed concern about unintended adverse consequences resulting from this form of rate regulation (Broyles and Rosko, 1985; Dowling, 1974; Lave, 1984; Newhouse, 1983). Two frameworks of analysis have been commonly used. One approach is to examine various dimensions of hospital performance under prospective payment. For example, Dowling (1974) examined 11 areas of hospital performance, which he called cost-influencing variables, in his analysis of the downstate New York prospective payment system. A second approach is to use normative criteria for payment systems. Cleverly (1979), in a qualitative evaluation of alternative payment strategies for hospitals, reported that a consensus of the literature (Dowling, 1974; Lave, Lave, and Silverman, 1973; Pauly, 1970) suggests that a payment system should promote efficiency, maintain provider viability, prevent differential pricing or payer cross-subsidization, and require minimal administrative cost. Broyles and Rosko (1985), in their qualitative assessment of the Medicare prospective payment system, added a fifth criterion, the prevention of behavior that might compromise the health status of beneficiaries.

Previous evaluations of PP programs can be placed into three groups: (1) early studies of individual programs; (2) univariate national studies, and (3) recent multivariate studies. The following sections will follow this trichotomy.

A. Evaluations of Individual Programs

In 1974, the Social Security Administration funded evaluations of PP programs in six areas: downstate New York, upstate New York, Indiana, New Jersey, Rhode Island, and western Pennsylvania. All of these studies suffer from similar defects. First, although all of these evaluations concluded that PP constrained cost increases, only the downstate New York and Indiana studies provided statistically significant evidence ($p < 0.05$) concerning individual programs. Second, the samples in western Pennsylvania (n=11) and Rhode Island (n=13) were very small, thus reducing the extent to which results are exportable to other settings. Third, in New York, the PP systems contained elements of voluntarism. The reaction of hospitals to a voluntary experiment is likely to be different from that to a mandatory program, an outcome that reduces the relevance of these studies to current policy considerations. Furthermore, in voluntary programs, self-selection may create a bias. Fourth, all of these evaluations ended by 1974, the year in which hospital wage and price controls under the federal Economic Stabilization Program (ESP) were lifted. As a consequence, it is difficult or impossible to separate the effects of ESP from those of PP on hospital costs. Fifth, most of the studies employed evaluation designs that are regarded as a "one-group, pretest-posttest" or a "static group comparison" (Campbell and Stanley, 1963). The weaknesses of these approaches are well known. Finally, all of the early studies evaluated new, rather than mature, programs. Recent evidence suggests that mature PP systems are better able to control hospital costs than are programs in their formative stage. Recognizing the fundamental defects in the evaluation techniques employed in early analysis and since, Rosko (1982) provided a summary of the impact of these mechanisms on 16 dimensions of hospital performance; the results, reported in studies of individual programs, will not be reviewed here.

B. Univariate National Studies

More recent studies by Biles, Schramm, and Atkinson (1980) and the General Accounting Office, or GAO, (1980) concluded that PP programs have constrained the rate of hospital cost increases. Both studies used the state as the unit of observation, and estimated cost savings by comparing the average annual rate of increase in the cost per admission in states with mandatory PP programs with the cost experience in all other states. The GAO study, which used data for the years 1975 through 1977, estimated annual cost savings of four percent. Biles and colleagues, whose evaluation period included the years 1970 through 1978, estimated savings of a similar magnitude for the years 1976 to 1978. Statistically significant savings ($p < 0.05$) were not found during the period 1970 to 1975. Both studies failed to control for the effects of changes in supply, demand, and regulatory conditions on hospital costs.

C. Recent Multivariate Studies

A comprehensive review of the methods used in the more recent PP evaluations by Eby and Cohodes (1985) obviates the need for a lengthy discussion of research design. In general, recent studies of prospective payment have used a research design which included data for study and comparison groups for periods before and after prospective payment was introduced. The estimated regression equations usually included a set of control variables used to isolate the impact of regional or state differences in market conditions which might affect hospital performance, and a set of regulatory variables representing the presence or absence of PP and other regulatory programs discussed in the introduction of this chapter. The features of the various PP programs have been measured by (1) the percentage of the population enrolled in insurance plans subject to rate setting (Sloan and Steinwald, 1980); (2) the percentage of hospital expenditures covered by new (that is, operating one or two years) rate-setting programs or mature rate-setting programs (Sloan, 1981, 1983); (3) the number of years or months that a state had a rate regulation program in effect as of any specific year (Joskow, 1981; Salkever, Steinwachs, and Rupp, 1986); (4) a single binary variable (Melnick, Wheeler, and Feldstein, 1981; Rosko, 1984b; Rosko and Broyles, 1986); (5) a set of binary variables representing individual programs (Coelen and Sullivan, 1981; Cromwell and Kanak, 1982; Morrisey, Sloan, and Mitchell, 1983; Worthington and Piro, 1982); and (6) the individual year effects of a single program (Rosko, 1984a). In the simplest specification, results pertain to the effects of PP averaged over time and across programs. Consequently, the average results may be biased by an outlier (a program which resulted in significantly different results from the group average). Although the more complex specifications attempted to account for some program differences, none estimated individual program effects for separate years. Because of statistical estimation problems (for example, multicollinearity), this level of specificity is difficult, if not impossible, to accomplish. Failure to capture the effects of individual programs is a serious deficiency, since the impact of different rate-setting mechanisms is likely to vary according to their underlying characteristics (Coelen and Sullivan, 1981; Cook et al., 1983; Morrisey et al., 1984). Although this argument is intuitively appealing, it has little empirical support. Despite this limitation, it is clear that because of superior research methods and increased relevance, the results of the studies in this group should be given more credence than the early studies.

Table 3 summarizes findings regarding the impact of prospective payment upon selected measures of hospital performance. Since the characteristics of rate regulation are likely to be important determinants of hospital performance, the summary should be viewed as a consensus of findings. Results contrary to those reported in Table 3 may be found in individual states or in individual studies.

Most of the recent studies concluded that prospective payment has constrained hospital costs. Rates of increase in expenditures per admission were estimated to have been reduced by 0.6 to 8.7 percent, cost per-patient day by 1.2 to 10.5 percent, and expenditures per capita by 2.0 to 7.6 percent (Coelen and Sullivan, 1981; Congressional Budget Office, 1979; Joskow, 1981; Melnick, Wheeler, and Feldstein, 1981; Sloan, 1981, 1983; Morrisey, Sloan, and Mitchell, 1983; Rosko, 1984a, 1984b; Rosko and Broyles, 1986).

There is concern that a portion of the savings in hospital costs that have been attributed to rate setting may have been shifted to nonhospital settings (Eby and Cohodes, 1985; Rosko and Broyles, 1986). Although this response has not been studied extensively, two studies have reported that, when Medicare Part A (inpatient hospital) expenditures are constrained, Medicare Part B (supplementary medical coverage) expenditures are also constrained (Coelen and Yaffe, 1983; Morrisey, Sloan, and Mitchell, 1983). However, since Medicare Part B expenditures do not represent all nonhospital costs, these results should not be viewed as conclusive.

Although an extensive body of empirical evidence suggests that state-mandated prospective payment systems have reduced the rate of growth of hospital expenditures, there is little evidence documenting how the savings were achieved. Thus, it is not clear that prospective payment has evoked desirable behavioral responses, such as increased efficiency, or less-desirable reactions, such as cost shifting or reducing the quality of care.

It is reasonable to suggest that hospitals will respond to rate regulation by increasing the efficiency with which resources are used and by acting to constrain increases in factor prices. Among the three major types of resources used by hospitals (labor, capital, and supplies), employee-related costs and labor productivity have received the most attention in previous evaluations of hospital rate regulation. The impact of PP on the costs of consumable supplies has been ignored. However, since supply expenses account for a much smaller percentage of hospital costs than the other two resources, this omission is not serious.

Focusing on 10 individual state PP programs and using data for the period 1969 to 1978, Kidder and Sullivan (1982) examined the impact of rate regulation on labor costs per unit of service, labor productivity, and payroll per employee. Their analysis suggested that PP reduced the rate of increase in payroll costs per adjusted patient-day in eight of 10 study states. They also reported that the growth in the number of full-time-equivalent employees (FTE) per adjusted patient-day (a measure of labor productivity) and payroll per FTE staff (a measure of factor price) was reduced in six of 10 states featuring PP.

Some corroboration of Kidder's and Sullivan's findings is reported in other studies. Adamache and Sloan (1982), who used data pertaining to 1979 collected from 781 hospitals which responded to a mailed questionnaire, reported that PP was associated with a reduction in the entry level of compensation paid to nonunion employees in five of six occupational groups. However, PP did not exert a significant effect ($p < 0.10$) on the rate of compensation paid to union employees in any occupational group. Rosko (1984b), employing multivariate analysis in a study of the New Jersey PP system for the period 1975 to 1978, reported that the rate of increase in the number of full-time equivalents per patient-day was inversely related to the introduction of rate regulation in hospitals that were located in inner-city catchment areas. However, statistically significant effects ($p < 0.10$) were not found for New Jersey hospitals located in other areas.

Evaluations of the impact of PP on capital assets is less conclusive. These studies focused on the growth of new services. Whether a reduction in the rate of adopting new services implies a more intense and, hence, more efficient use of existing plant assets or whether it implies that hospitals are not acquiring capital in which new technological developments are embodied is unclear. Ashby (1984) employed multivariate analysis on a set of pooled time-series data for the period 1971 to 1977. These results suggest that neither mandatory nor voluntary rate-setting programs had a significant effect on the percentage change in either hospital plant assets or the number of beds per capita.

Cromwell and Kanak (1982) examined the effects of PP on the adoption of new services. The estimates from their regression equations suggest that only two of 15 mandatory and voluntary PP programs studied reduced the growth of new hospital services. Romeo, Wagner, and Lee (1984) examined the effects of three PP programs (New York, Indiana, and Maryland) on the availability, extent, and speed of adopting three cost-raising technologies and two cost-reducing technologies. They report that the New York program, which is commonly regarded as the most stringent among the mandatory PP programs, showed consistent negative effects on the adoption of three cost-raising technologies and a positive effect on the adoption of one cost-reducing technology. The voluntary Indiana program appeared to stimulate the growth in both cost-reducing and cost-increasing technologies. Statistically significant effects were not found for any of the technologies in Maryland.

With regard to utilization, a number of studies have examined the impact of rate regulation on the length of stay, the number of cases treated, and the number of patient-days. Regarding length of stay, the hospitals' likely response to prospective payment is dramatically affected by the unit of payment employed by the rate regulators.

TABLE 3 Summary of Recent Multivariate Evaluations of Prospective Payment Programs

Study	Performance measures	Rate review variables	Level of aggregation	Findings
Coelen and Sullivan, 1981	Δ (expenses/adjusted patient-day) Δ (expenses/adjusted admission) Δ (expenses per capita) Log (expenses/adjusted patient-day) Log (expenses/adjusted admission) Log (expenses per capita)	Separate binary variable for each version of prospective payment in 15 states, of which eight featured mandatory compliance	Hospitals (expenditures per day and per admission) and counties (expenditures per capita); annual data, 1969–1978	Expenses per adjusted patient-day were contained by nine programs; savings ranged from 1.2 percent to 10.5 percent. Expenses per adjusted admission were contained by seven programs, savings ranged from 1.9 percent to 8.7 percent. Expenses per capita were contained in four programs, savings ranged from 3.1 percent to 7.6 percent. Estimated savings were consistently higher in log equations than in percentage change equations.
Kidder and Sullivan, 1982	Payroll per adjusted patient-day; FTE staff per adjusted patient-day; payroll per FTE staff	Same as Coelen and Sullivan	Hospitals, 1970–1977	Payroll per adjusted patient-day was contained by 10 programs, savings ranged from three percent to eleven percent. **PP** contains FTE staff per adjusted patient-day in six states, ranging from three percent to ten percent. **PP** contained payroll per FTE staff in six states, ranging from two percent to five percent.

Cromwell and Kanak, 1982	Percentage change in the total number of services classified as: quality-enhancing, complexity-expanding, community-oriented, supportive, competitive, diffusing, peaked, administrative shared services, and clinical shared services	Same as Coelen and Sullivan	Hospitals, 1969–1978	Ambiguous results were obtained. The rate-setting variables were significant ($p < 0.05$) in most equations. No program exerted significant effects in a majority of the equations.
Worthington and Piro, 1982	Admissions per bed; log length of stay; occupancy rate	Same as Coelen and Sullivan	Hospitals, 1969–1978	Increases in admissions per bed, ranging from 2.36 to 5.84, were associated with three rate-setting programs. Increases in length of stay, ranging from one percent to eight percent, were associated with five programs. A voluntary program in Nebraska caused a seven percent increase in length of stay. Occupancy rate increases, ranging from three percent to seven percent, were associated with five programs.
Sloan and Steinwald, 1980	Log (expenses/admission) Log (expenses/adjusted patient-day) Log (labor expenses/adjusted patient-day) Log (labor expenses/admission) Log (RNs/bed) Log (LPNs/bed)	Log (percent population) subject to formula prospective payment (Colorado, Massachusetts, New York)	Hospitals, cluster sample of hospitals located in 33 states and the District of Columbia; annual data, 1969–1975	Ambiguous results. Ordinary-least-squares (OLS) analysis found that formula programs reduced expenses per adjusted patient-day (2.6 percent) and per admission (1.4 percent), and reduced labor expenses per adjusted

TABLE 3 (continued)

Study	Performance measures	Rate review variables	Level of aggregation	Findings
Sloan and Steinwald, 1980 (continued)	Log (other employees/bed) Log (total beds) Log (assets/bed) Log (current nonlabor expenses/bed)	Log (percent population) subject to budget prospective payment (Arizona, Connecticut, Indiana, Kentucky, Maryland, New Jersey, North Carolina, Rhode Island, Wisconsin)		patient-day (1.7 percent) and per admission (0.6 percent). Time series analysis (TSA) found increased costs. Similar results were found for budget programs. Besides expense, significant effects were found only for LPNs per bed, which increased by 19 percent under formula programs.
Sloan, 1981	Cost per admission Cost per adjusted admission Cost per patient-day Cost per adjusted patient-day Total revenue/total cost	Separate variables for the fraction of hospital costs covered by new (in existence two years or less) and old PP programs	State; annual data, 1963–1978	Young PP programs did not have an impact upon hospital costs. Old PP programs reduced cost per day by 6.7 percent and cost per admission by 3.8 percent. Similar results were found for the profitability measure (total revenue/total costs).
Sloan, 1983	Expense/admission Expense/adjusted admission Expense/patient-day Length of stay Total revenue/total expense △ (expense/adjusted admission) △ (expense/adjusted patient-day) △ (adjusted admissions) △ (adjusted patient-day) △ (outpatient visits) △ (length of stay) △ (total revenue/total expense)	Percentage of hospital revenues regulated by each type of program (six variables): Mandatory regulatory, young Mandatory regulatory, old Voluntary regulatory, young Voluntary regulatory, old Mandatory advisory, young Mandatory advisory, old (Young = first two years of program)	State; annual data, 1963–1978	Mature mandatory PP programs contained cost per admission (4.8 percent) and cost per day (6.8 percent). Neither of these programs nor any of the other programs evaluated, had an impact on any of the other performance measures.

Ashby, 1984	% △ (total costs per capita) % △ (average length of stay) % △ (admissions per capita) % △ (plant assets) % △ (beds per capita)	Binary variables for voluntary rate-setting and mandatory PP programs	State; annual data, 1971–1977	The voluntary and mandatory rate-setting variables did not have a significant coefficient ($p \leqslant 0.10$) in any of the equations. (Note: using Sloan's criteria, most of the rate-setting study periods were new).
Joskow, 1981	% △ (total hospital expenses) Log (total hospital expenses) Log (FTE personnel per bed) Log (adjusted inpatient days) Log (average wage of FTE personnel)	Binary variable for mandatory PP programs, and number of years state had a PP program in effect	State; annual data, 1979	PP constrained growth of total hospital expenditures by two percent per year. No effect was found in the other equations.
Melnick, Wheeler, and Feldstein, 1981	% △ (total hospital expenses) % △ (total hospital expenses per admission) % △ (admissions) % △ (total hospital expenses per patient-day) % △ (average length of stay)	Binary variable for mandatory PP programs	State; annual data, 1975–1979	The existence of PP programs was associated with significant reductions in total expenses (1.7 percent), expenses per admission (1.3 percent), expense per patient-day (2.3 percent), and length of stay (0.9 percent).
Morrisey, Sloan, and Mitchell, 1983	Log (real expense/population) Log (real revenue/population) Log (real expense/adjusted admission) Log (real expense/adjusted patient-days) Log (total Medicare expense/Part A population) Log (Medicare Part A expense/Part A population) Log (Medicare Part B expense/Part A population)	Binary variables: First two years of program in Massachusetts, Maryland, New Jersey, New York, Washington, Wisconsin Mature New Jersey Mature New York (1972–1975) Refined New York (1976–1981) Mature Massachusetts Mature Maryland Mature Washington Mature Massachusetts or Maryland or Washington Mature Massachusetts or Maryland or New Jersey or New York or Washington	SMSA (34 geographic units were derived from 27 SMSAs by dividing multistate SMSAs into two or more groups); annual data, 1968–1981	State rate setting had no effect during first two years after implementation. Mature PP programs as a whole reduced expenses per adjusted patient-day (1.6 percent), per adjusted admission (1.7 percent), and per capita (2.0 percent). Insignificant results were found for some states, and significant savings were as high as 3.4 percent per adjusted patient-day, 4.9 percent per adjusted admission, and 5.6 percent per capita.

TABLE 3 (continued)

Study	Performance measures	Rate review variables	Level of aggregation	Findings
Romeo, Wagner, and Lee, 1984	Two measures (availability of technology and delay in adoption) were used for each of the following technologies: electronic fetal monitoring volumetric infusion pumps automated factual susceptibility testing centralized energy management systems	Variables for the proportion of patient-days covered by the PP programs in New York, Maryland, and Indiana	Hospitals (in six states), 1980	Significant estimates were found only for the equations for availability of technology. The New York program had a consistent negative effect on the adoption of three cost-raising technologies and a positive effect on one of two cost-reducing technologies. No effect was found in Maryland. Inconsistent results were found in Indiana.
Rosko, 1984a	Cost per admission Cost per patient-day	Binary variables for each year the New Jersey rate-setting program was in effect	Hospitals (in New Jersey and Pennsylvania); annual data, 1971–1978	No effects during first two years of rate setting. The New Jersey PP program contained annual increases in cost per patient-day (2.7 percent) and cost per admission (2.4 percent).
Rosko, 1984b	Cost per admission FTE personnel per 1,000 patient-days	Binary variable for years in which New Jersey regulated rates.	Hospitals (in New Jersey and Pennsylvania); annual data, 1971–1978	The New Jersey program resulted in savings for cost per admission amounting to $61.48 in inner-city hospitals and $25.19 in hospitals located in other areas. Reductions in personnel per 1,000 patient-days (0.098) were found only in inner-city hospitals.
Rosko and Broyles, 1986	Cost/admission Cost/patient-day Admissions Length of stay	Binary variable for all-payer DRG system	Hospitals (in New Jersey); annual data, 1979–1982	Relative to a two-payer, per diem PP program, the all-payer DRG system caused reductions in cost per admission ($71.16) and length of stay (0.28 days), and an increase in admissions per hospital (1,109.7).

Under a case-based payment mechanism (such as DRGs), hospitals are induced to contain expenditures per admission by reducing the length of stay. If all other factors remain unchanged, compressing the length of stay reduces the occupancy rate and forces the hospital to allocate fixed costs to fewer patient-days, an outcome that negates some of the savings resulting from the reduced use of stay-specific services. Therefore, it is likely that hospitals will attempt to increase the number of patients treated in response to a case-based payment system. Since total patient-days is the product of cases treated and the average length of stay, the impact of case-based rate regulation on the dimension of utilization is ambiguous.

In contrast to the incentives under case-based payment, hospitals are induced to increase length of stay under per diem-based prospective payment. For example, the hospital might attempt to subsidize those days of intensive care for which a loss is incurred by using the profits earned during days of convalescent care for which the hospital was paid an amount which exceeded actual costs. Further, if all else is equal, an increase in length of stay will increase the occupancy rate, thus reducing, but not eliminating, the need to increase the number of cases treated. Since the effects of per diem-based prospective payment on both length of stay and cases treated are positive, patient-days should increase if there is excess capacity.

Empirical results provide only slight support for these expectations. Focusing first on studies that examined per diem-based payment systems, Worthington and Piro (1982) conducted the most comprehensive analysis of utilization under rate regulation to date. They reported that in states where statistically significant results were found, prospective payment generally resulted in an increased average length of stay and number of admissions per bed. Melnick, Wheeler, and Feldstein (1981) reported similar results for the length of stay, but found no change in total admissions. Sloan (1981, 1983) found no statistically significant effects on changes in admissions, patient-days, or length of stay.

To date, only two multivariate studies of a case-based PP system have been published. Rosko and Broyles (1986) used data for New Jersey hospitals encompassing the years 1979 to 1982 to compare the responses of hospitals which were subject to an all-payer DRG system (see Table 2) with those of hospitals subject to a prospective payment program that set per diem rates for only two payers (see Table 1). Statistically significant results suggest that the all-payer DRG system was associated with a reduction in the average length of stay and an increase in admissions. Rosko and Broyles concluded that the decline in the cost per admission was attributable, in part, to the decrease in the length of stay. However, the savings in the cost per admission were offset by increases in the rate of admissions, resulting in only very small savings in total costs.

In the other published analysis of a case-based PP system, Salkever, Steinwachs, and Rupp (1986) examined the response of hospitals to two PP systems that operated concurrently in Maryland. One system used the number of cases treated to regulate revenue (see Table 2), while the other system based payments on services provided (see Table 1). Unlike the New Jersey PP system, which used DRGs to set rates, the Maryland system allowed hospitals to choose a case-mix index, consisting of either DRGs, three- or four-digit ICD-9-CM codes, or broad service categories (for instance, medicine, surgery, and obstetrics) which would be used to determine rates.

Using data for the period 1977 to 1981, Salkever, Steinwachs and Rupp found weak and generally statistically insignificant ($p < 0.05$) changes in the costs incurred by hospitals subject to per case payments relative to the performance of those that were compensated on a per service basis. They attributed the small impact on total costs to incentives embodied in the per case system to increase the rate of admissions.

Thus far, our evaluation of prospective payment systems has focused on performance measures. The remainder of this section will examine the impact of prospective payment from a normative framework, such as the ones developed by Cleverly (1979) or Broyles and Rosko (1985). Since many of the performance measures already discussed can be used as surrogates for normative criteria, we will emphasize measures which have not been previously discussed in this chapter.

It is commonly argued that PP systems should promote efficiency, a concept that refers to the relative costs of producing a desired level of output. Efficiency has been difficult to measure because of a number of conceptual difficulties, including the inability to define and precisely measure units of hospital output (Berki, 1972). Consequently, evaluations of the impact of PP upon efficiency have relied upon previously discussed performance measures, such as costs per unit of output, occupancy rate, FTEs per patient day, and input prices.

A second objective of a PP system should be to ensure the viability of efficient providers. Regulators face a difficult tradeoff between cost containment and financial solvency. If rates are set too high, there is little incentive for hospitals to contain costs. Conversely, if rates are set too low, the viability of hospitals is threatened. The goal of provider viability implies that hospitals should be paid at levels which are sufficient to meet their financial requirements. This presents a measurement and a data collection problem, because allowable financial requirements are normatively determined (Cleverly, 1979). In the absence of such a measure, profitability indicators have been used to measure viability.

Employing regression analysis in two studies, Sloan (1981, 1983) used total revenue divided by total cost as a measure of institutional viability. In both studies, Sloan concluded that PP did not affect hospital profits.

Morrisey, Sloan, and Mitchell (1983) compared the impact of PP upon revenues and costs during the period 1968 to 1981. They concluded that since costs were reduced more than revenue, hospital profits were not adversely affected by rate regulation. Applying tabular analysis on a set of data pertaining to standard financial ratios and encompassing the years 1975 to 1979, Rosko and Broyles (1984) concluded that the New Jersey PP system had a slight effect upon the financial status of the average New Jersey hospital. However, when disaggregated data were examined, they found that PP was associated with a serious deterioration of the financial position of teaching hospitals as well as hospitals located in inner-city areas. In contrast, PP exerted little or no impact on nonteaching hospitals and hospitals located in suburban areas.

A third criterion for PP systems is that they should promote equity among the purchasers of services. Cleverly (1979) identifies two concepts of equity: Different purchasers should pay the same price for the same services, and certain services should not be used to cross-subsidize others. Broyles and Rosko (1985) argued that the Medicare PP system creates an incentive for hospitals to use unregulated patients (especially those who are charge-based payers) to cross-subsidize losses accrued in the provision of services to Medicare beneficiaries. To the extent that hospitals succeed in shifting costs, the financial rigors of PP and, hence, incentives to improve efficiency are reduced.

A period of time sufficient to allow analysis of the impact of the Medicare PP system on cost shifting has not elapsed. However, there is a limited amount of information pertaining to the relationship between state PP programs and cost shifting.

A study of the New Jersey PP system, covering the period 1976 to 1979, estimated that unregulated charge-based purchasers paid as much as twenty-five percent more per patient-day than regulated purchasers (Worthington, Cromwell, and Kamens, 1979). Another evaluation of the New Jersey two-payer PP program indirectly examined the relationship between PP and cost shifting. Rosko (1984b) hypothesized that PP would have a greater impact on the costs of inner-city hospitals than of suburban hospitals, because the latter group typically have more patients who could be used for cross-subsidization purposes, thereby allowing them to avoid the rigors of PP. Employing cost-function analysis on a data set for the period 1971 to 1978, Rosko found that PP was associated with a reduction in the level of increase in cost per admission amounting to $61.48 in inner-city hospitals and $25.19 in suburban hospitals.

The last normative criterion requires that PP not reduce the role of health status in determining the use of health services. The dramatic reduction in length of stay associated with PP systems which rely upon DRGs as the unit of payment has prompted concerns that earlier patient discharges may be due to a reduction of needed services rather than to increased efficiency of patient management. Although some anecdotal evidence is available to support this concern (Walker, Broyles and Rosko, 1985), only preliminary empirical evidence is available.

III. PROSPECTIVE PAYMENT OF NURSING HOMES

Relatively little is known about the impact of prospective payment upon nursing homes. The research conducted in this area has focused upon prospective payment mechanisms developed by state Medicaid programs, which collectively paid for almost 50 percent of total nursing home costs in 1982 (Gibson, Waldo, and Levit, 1983).

Using the state as the level of aggregation, Harrington and Swan (1984) tested the hypothesis that the form of reimbursement had an impact upon Medicaid payment rates per day. Regression analysis was performed on a data set which included the years 1979 to 1982. The analysis compared the rate of increase of Medicaid payment rates to nursing homes under retrospective reimbursement with three types of alternative payment systems: prospective/facility-specific, prospective/class (a group rate), and a combination of prospective and retrospective methods. The alternative payment systems were analyzed as a group and individually. The authors reported that states with alternative payment systems in general, and facility-specific payment systems in particular, showed significantly lower increases in Medicaid payment rates for skilled nursing facilities (SNFs) than states which maintained retrospective payment systems. However, no such differences were found for rates set for intermediate care facilities (ICFs).

Buchanan (1983), who performed tabular analysis, also found support for the contention that prospective payment is associated with lower Medicaid payment rates for nursing homes. He reported that between 1975 and 1982, the average rate paid to SNFs rose by 90 percent and 120 percent in prospective and retrospective payment systems, respectively. Similar trends were found for ICFs during the same period. However, when differences in the rate of payment per patient-day between retrospective and prospective payment systems in individual years were considered, statistically significant ($p \leq 0.05$) results were found for SNFs in only one year, 1982. The analysis of ICFs found significant results in 1976 and 1982.

Buchanan also reported that compared with states with retrospective payment systems, states with prospective payment mechanisms had significantly greater ratios of

Medicaid patient-days per 1,000 elderly population, and Medicaid certified beds per 1,000 population. Thus, it was concluded that the use of prospective payment for Medicaid nursing home rates results in reduction of Medicaid expenditures without exerting adverse effects on the elderly's access to nursing home services.

The results of the studies conducted by Buchanan and by Harrington and Swan (1984) should be accepted with caution because of two serious methodological difficulties. First, both studies used the Medicaid payment rate as the dependent variable. Although Medicaid reimbursement levels may be related to costs, it is possible for nursing homes to avoid the fiscal rigors of prospective rate setting by shifting costs to nonregulated payers. Thus, if the real intent of the research is to evaluate the efficacy of prospective payment as an instrument for cost control, it would have been preferable to use expenditures per unit of service as the performance measure. Second, neither study controlled for interstate differences in factors which affect costs. This is an especially serious deficiency in light of the evidence reported by Harrington and Swan which suggested that, among states with retrospective reimbursement systems, those which experienced lower Medicaid payment rates in a given year were more likely to subsequently change to a prospective payment system. Accordingly, it is impossible to determine whether results of these studies are due to prospective payment or to interstate differences which were not adequately controlled for.

Holahan's (1985) study of nursing home responses to payment mechanisms attempted to rectify some of the weaknesses of earlier studies as described above. Unfortunately, since this study was limited to only 10 states, it is not possible to generalize reported findings. Holahan used the percentage change in total nursing home costs from 1978 to 1980 as the dependent variable in his regression analysis. Independent variables were used to control for the effects of changes in area wage levels, capacity utilization, and case mix. In addition to these variables, two separate specifications of binary variables were used to estimate the impact of reimbursement policy upon nursing home costs.

In one set of equations, a binary variable was entered for states with retrospective payment methods, and another binary variable was entered for states with a prospective payment formula which incorporates an adjustment for projected inflation plus approved base-year costs. The reference category in this equation was states with a prospective payment system in which flat rates were set at the projected median costs for each group, with facilities grouped by geographic area, size, and level of care. In the second specification, a binary variable was entered for each state except one, which served as the reference category. The results from this equation were analyzed by comparing the coefficients of the state variables which were grouped into the three types of reimbursement systems. This facilitated analysis of the disparate performance which occurred in the different states. The results suggest that in general, the two forms of prospective payment were associated with smaller percentage changes in nursing home costs from 1978 to 1980. However, these results should not be viewed as definitive, because of the small number of states that were examined and because only one variable, changes in area wages, was used to control for interstate differences that might affect nursing home costs.

IV. ECONOMIC STABILIZATION PROGRAM

The Nixon administration's Economic Stabilization Program (ESP) was developed to limit inflation by controlling prices in all sectors of the economy. The program was in effect from August 15, 1971, until April 30, 1974. The regulations enforced by the program were changed several times. Initially, wages and prices were frozen throughout the economy for 90 days. During this period, separate regulations were developed for different sectors of the economy. Because of the unique characteristics and problems of the health care industry, separate wage and price controls were developed by the Committee on the Health Services Industry for institutional and noninstitutional health service providers (Ginsburg, 1978). Following the recommendations of the committee, the Price Commission of the ESP imposed a six percent ceiling on the annual rate of increase in total hospital charges. Wage rate increases were limited to 5.5 percent per year, and nonlabor cost increases were restricted to 2.5 percent per year.

Multivariate studies of the impact of the ESP wage and price controls upon hospital behavior reported conflicting findings. Ginsburg reported a statistically insignificant impact of the program on hospital costs. Sloan and Steinwald (1980) found similar results when using ordinary-least-square regressions. However, statistically significant results were found in two studies which concluded that ESP exerted a negative effect upon hospital costs, ranging from 0.5 percent to 3.3 percent (Sloan, 1981; Sloan and Steinwald, 1980).

Several explanations have been offered for the ineffectiveness of ESP in the hospital sector. First, hospital executives may have perceived that their current performance may have been used to determine future cost ceilings. Thus, an incentive to overspend the budget in one year of the cost control program in order to receive a higher level of reimbursement in a future year may have existed. Second, it was difficult for hospitals to comply with a set of regulations that were very ambiguous. Finally, many hospital administrators believed that the controls would not be seriously enforced (Ginsburg, 1978).

V. THE VOLUNTARY EFFORT

The Carter administration's proposed Hospital Cost Containment Act of 1977 (S. 1391 and H.R. 6575) contained provisions that were designed to restrict the rate of increase in inpatient hospital revenues to 8.7 percent in 1978 (Dunn and Lefkowitz, 1978). Although this proposal was never enacted, the threat of increased government regulation caused the hospital industry to form the Voluntary Effort. This program was created jointly by the American Hospital Association, the Federation of American Hospitals, and the American Medical Association in November 1977. The Voluntary Effort proposed three major objectives: (1) a two percent reduction in hospital costs in 1978 and 1979; (2) no net increase in hospital beds in 1978; and (3) a reduction in the amount of total capital expenditures by twenty percent of the average hospital capital investment made during the period 1975 to 1977. Cost containment committees were developed by the hospital industry in each of the 50 states to help achieve the cost containment goals (Abernathy and Pearson, 1979).

Although the Voluntary Effort lasted only one year, it appears to have succeeded not only in postponing efforts by federal authorities to contain costs, but also in reducing the rate of increase in the cost per admission and cost per patient-day by about 2.8 to 4.9 percent, depending upon specification of the regression equation (Sloan, 1981). However, since this program was in effect for only one year, it was impossible to use time-series analysis to confirm that these results were actually due to the Voluntary Effort rather than to some anomaly which may have occurred in the economy in 1978.

VI. UTILIZATION REVIEW

Hospitals have been subject to utilization reveiw requirements, mandated by the federal government, since 1966. Concerned about the potential abuse of benefits provided under the Medicare, Medicaid, and Maternal and Child Care programs (respectively, Titles 18, 19, and 5 of the Social Security Amendments of 1965) the Social Security Administration developed utilization review (UR) requirements for hospitals participating in these programs. The federal government required that each hospital have a UR committee which reviewed, from the perspective of medical necessity and for the purpose of promoting the most efficient use of available health facilities and services, the admissions, the duration of stay, and the professional services rendered (Myers, 1970). The Senate Subcommittee Staff on Medicare/Medicaid (1970) concluded that UR had failed to act as an effective cost control mechanism, because of inadequate regulations and poor administrative control mechanisms.

Under the authority of P.L. 92-603, professional standards review organizations (PSROs) were established in 1972 with the goal of reviewing hospital utilization for quality and appropriateness. Review was limited to the use of hospital care that was the fiscal responsibility of the Medicare, Medicaid, and Maternal and Child Care programs (Blumstein, 1978). As a result of a political compromise, local physicians could establish PSROs, control their activity, and delegate much of the actual utilization review work to hospitals.

Implementation of the PSRO program was slow. As of 1977, 108 conditional PSROs were established, but none were fully operational. By 1980, only two-thirds of the hospitals in the United States were under PSRO review. From 1979 to 1983, the PSRO program received diminished support. Enacted in 1982, P.L. 97-248 repealed existing PSRO regulations and replaced them with provisions which created peer review organizations (PROs). PROs are performance-judged organizations which compete for government contracts rather than receive grants (Webber and Goldbeck, 1984).

Two factors make an evaluation of the PSRO program difficult. First, the program had two mandates (cost containment and quality assurance) which may have been in conflict. Second, there was a wide variation in the performance of individual PSROs (Deacon et al., 1979; Luft, 1985). Evaluations of the effects of the PSRO program can be grouped into two categories: studies that focused on PSROs and studies which examined other regulatory programs, but which statistically controlled and estimated the effects of PSROs. The research design for the latter group of studies is the same as that described in the section on recent multivariate studies of PP.

Mixed results were found in the former group of studies. The Department of Health, Education, and Welfare's Office of Planning, Evaluation, and Legislation study (1979) found that PSROs had no demonstrable effect on utilization. However, the PSRO program evaluation sponsored by the Health Care Financing Administration (1980) concluded that PSROs significantly reduced utilization rates in hospitals for Medicare beneficiaries. This study, limited to Medicare beneficiaries, reported that PSROs had a benefit-to-cost ratio ranging from 1.035 to 1.504, depending upon the assumptions used.

In national studies which focused primarily on hospital rate regulation, Worthington and Piro (1982) reported that PSROs resulted in a slight decrease in average length of stay, but an increase in admissions per bed and occupancy rate. Coelen and Sullivan (1981) found that PSROs were associated with increases in inpatient cost per day and hospital cost per capita. They reported insignificant results for the cost per admission.

Most studies suggest that the PSRO program failed to contain hospital costs. The ineffectiveness of this program can be attributed to many factors. First, PSROs relied upon peer review, which required the cooperation of physicians, even though the American Medical Association and many local medical societies opposed them. Second, government financial support never matched operating needs (Webber and Goldbeck, 1984). Third, PSROs did not attempt to address all dimensions of patient management which affect costs. In particular, utilization review conducted by PSROs focused upon unnecessary hospitalization and excessive length of stay, but ignored the need to control unnecessary diagnostic and therapeutic procedures provided to hospitalized patients. Further, PSROs emphasized the reduction of unproductive care rather than the promotion of more cost-effective patient management strategies (Blumstein, 1978).

VII. REGULATION OF CAPITAL FORMATION

Beginning in the mid-1960s, states and the federal government implemented various forms of capital formation regulation. Although there is a great amount of diversity among these programs, they can be dichotomized as exerting direct or indirect controls (Salkever and Bice, 1979). Direct controls typically are exercised under the authority of state certificate of need (CON) laws, which specify legal means designed to prohibit organizations from carrying out disapproved projects. Direct sanctions include the denial or suspension of operating licenses. Indirect controls use economic sanctions whereby third-party payers may refuse to reimburse providers for costs associated with investment projects or service changes that fail to receive prior approval from designated agencies (Lewin and Associates, Inc., 1974).

The first CON law was enacted by the state of New York in 1964. By 1974, 24 states operated some type of CON program (Salkever and Bice, 1979). Federal support for CON controls was provided by P.L. 93-641, the National Health Planning and Resources Development Act of 1974. This law had two important provisions. First, the law mandated states to enact CON legislation by 1980 or become ineligible for federal subsidies to support regional health planning. Only three states failed to enact CON legislation by 1980. Second, P.L. 92-603 created and subsidized a network of health systems agencies which were responsible to recommend approval or denial of CON applications to the state CON agency.

Section 1122 of P.L. 92-603, the Social Security Amendments of 1972, provided federal support for indirect control of capital formation. This section authorized states to designate agencies to review hospital plans for facility or service expansion for projects that cost more than $100,000. Reimbursement for the costs of unapproved capital projects can be withheld by federal payers (the Medicare, Medicaid, and Maternal and Child Care programs). However, hospitals are able to recover these lost payments from other sources, including other third-party payers which do not have conformance clauses in their reimbursement contracts. This clause links reimbursements for capital costs to project review and approval by designated agencies. As of July 1979, about one-half of the 72 Blue Cross plans had hospital contracts with conformance clauses (Salkever and Bice, 1979).

The methods used to estimate the effects of capital control programs on hospital performance were similar to those used in the prospective payment evaluations. In general, a binary variable was used to represent the presence or absence of a program designed to regulate capital formation. Some variations in specification of the regulatory variable exist in previous studies.

Sloan (1981) included separate binary variables for young and mature CON programs. In addition to these variables, Sloan and Steinwald (1980) used variables for comprehensive CON programs (those reviewing capital projects costing less than $100,000) and noncomprehensive programs (which review only capital projects that cost more than $100,000). Joskow (1981) used two specifications: a binary variable and a variable which was set at the number of years the CON program had been in operation.

Before presenting the empirical results, it is important to note that although some attempt was made by a few researchers to reflect the diversity of regulatory programs, a true depiction of their diversity was not accomplished. For example, although dimensions of maturity and comprehensiveness were included in some of the model specifications, no attempts were made to reflect the variations in criteria used to evaluate capital project proposals or the willingness of courts to reverse CON decisions. Therefore, it is possible that the effects of individual programs may be radically different from the average regression coefficients reported in the studies.

Virtually all of the empirical studies to date report that CON and Section 1122 reviews exerted little, if any, impact upon hospital expenditures (Coelen and Sullivan, 1981; Joskow, 1981; Policy Analysis and Urban Systems Engineering, 1980; Sloan, 1981; Sloan and Steinwald, 1980). One exception reported a statistically significant result and concluded that noncomprehensive CON programs were associated with increased hospital expenditures (Sloan and Steinwald, 1980). Other analyses suggest that capital formation controls exerted no influence on total assets or the diffusion of services (Cromwell and Kanak, 1982; Hellinger, 1976; Salkever and Bice, 1979). Salkever and Bice suggest that when regulation of capital succeeded in constraining the growth in the numbers of beds, hospitals substituted investment in new services for beds. Sloan and Steinwald (1980) corroborated these findings and also reported that Section 1122 review is positively associated with increases in the ratio of registered nurses per bed and licensed practical nurses per bed.

A likely explanation for the failure of regulatory agencies to control capital accumulation is industry capture. Noll (1975) points out several ways in which health systems agencies (HSAs) could fall prey to industry capture while carrying out their CON function. First, because of the high cost of acquiring specialized information, the regulator may rely on industry members for data and, thus, may become vulnerable to distorted information.

Second, members of the industry are usually more concerned about the regulatory agencies' decisions than is any individual member of the general public. Thus, the industry is more likely to sue the agency than is the general public. This threat of suit may create a proindustry bias on the part of the agency. Third, the legislation that created HSAs, P.L. 93-641, required authorities to ensure that the general public has access to health facilities. Thus, the HSA's charter implicitly charges the regulatory authority with the responsibility of ensuring the industry's health. A final force for industry capture is that the regulators' decisions can possess a life-or-death quality. For example, if doctors argue that certain equipment is necessary for the preservation of life, the regulatory agency will find it difficult to deny approval for installation of that equipment.

VIII. SUMMARY

Prospective payment of hospitals has been the only regulatory intervention in the United States for which a substantial body of evidence documenting cost control exists. Even though hospital rate regulation has succeeded in reducing the rate of increase in hospital expenditures, the efficacy of rate regulation is in doubt, because of its possible adverse consequences. Empirical studies have associated the introduction of prospective payment with consumer cross-subsidization, deterioration of the financial position of hospitals located in urban areas, and a greater level of dependence of patients upon discharge. Although these consequences have not been studied as extensively as hospital costs, the available evidence suggests further study before prospective payment can be endorsed unequivocally.

REFERENCES

Abernathy, D. S., and Pearson, D. A. (1979). *Regulating Hospital Costs: The Development of Public Policy*, AUPHA Press, Ann Arbor, Mich.

Adamache, K., and Sloan, F. (1982). Unions and hospitals: Some unresolved issues, *Journal of Health Economics, 1*: 81–102.

Ashby, J. (1984). The impact of hospital regulatory programs on per capita costs, utilization, and capital investment, *Inquiry, 21*: 45.

Berki, S. (1972). *Hospital Economics*, Lexington Books, Lexington.

Biles, B., Schramm, C. J., and Atkinson, G. J. (1980). Hospital cost inflation under state rate-setting programs, *New England Journal of Medicine, 303*: 664.

Blumstein, J. F. (1978). The role of PSROs in hospital cost containment, *Hospital Cost Containment* (M. Zubkoff, I. Raskin, and R. Hanft, eds.), Prodist, New York, p. 461.

Broyles, R. W., and Rosko, M. D. (1985). A qualitative assessment of the Medicare prospective payment system, *Social Science and Medicine, 10*: 1185.

Buchanan, R. J. (1983). Medicaid cost containment: Prospective reimbursement for long-term care, *Inquiry, 20*: 334.

Campbell, D., and Stanley, J. (1963). *Experimental and Quasi-Experimental Designs for Research*, Rand McNally, Chicago.

Cleverly, W. (1979). Evaluation of alternative payment strategies for hospitals; a conceptual approach, *Inquiry, 16*: 108–118.

Coelen, C., and Sullivan, D. (1981). An analysis of the effects of prospective reimbursement programs on hospital expenditures, *Health Care Financing Review, 2*: 1.

Coelen, C., and Yaffe, R. (1983). The national hospital rate-setting study: Summary of current findings on the effects of hospital prospective payment systems. Paper presented to the Labor-Management Health Care Cost Containment Conference, Atlantic City.

Congressional Budget Office (1979). *Controlling Rising Hospital Costs*, U.S. Government Printing Office, Washington, D.C.

Cook, K. S., Shortell, S. M., Conrad, D. A., and Morrisey, M. A. (1983). A theory of organizational response to regulation: The case of hospitals, *Academy of Management Review, 8*: 193.

Cromwell, J., and Kanak, J. R. (1982). The effects of prospective reimbursement programs on hospital adoption and service sharing, *Health Care Financing Review, 4*: 67.

Deacon, R. et al. (1979). Analysis of variations in hospital use by Medicare patients in PSRO areas, 1974–1977, *Health Care Financing Review, 1*: 79.

Dowling, W. (1974). Prospective reimbursement of hospitals, *Inquiry, 11*: 160.
Dunn, W., and Lefkowitz, B. (1978). Hospital Cost Containment Act of 1977: An analysis of the administration's proposal, *Hospital Cost Containment* (M. Zubkoff, I. Raskin, and R. Hanft, eds.), Prodist, New York, p. 166.
Eby, C. L., and Cohodes, D. R. (1985). What do we know about rate-setting? *Journal of Health Politics, Policy and Law, 10*: 299.
General Accounting Office (1980). Rising hospital costs can be restrained by regulating payments and improving management. U.S. Government Printing Office, Washington, D.C.
Gibson, R. M., Waldo, D. R., and Levit, K. R. (1983). National health expenditures, 1982, *Health Care Financing Review, 5*: 1.
Ginsburg, P. B. (1978). Impact of the Economic Stabilization Program on hospitals: An analysis with aggregate data, *Hospital Cost Containment* (M. Zubkoff, I. Raskin, and R. Hanft, eds.), Prodist, New York, p. 293.
Harrington, C., and Swan, J. H. (1984). Medicaid nursing home reimbursement policies, rates, and expenditures, *Health Care Financing Review, 6*: 39.
Hellinger, F. J. (1976). Prospective reimbursement through budget review: New Jersey, Rhode Island, and western Pennsylvania, *Inquiry, 13*: 269.
Hellinger, F. J. (1985). Recent evidence on case-based systems for setting hospital rates, *Inquiry, 22*: 78.
Holahan, J. (1985). State rate-setting and its effects on the cost of nursing-home care, *Journal of Health Politics, Policy and Law, 9*: 647.
Joskow, P. L. (1981). *Controlling Hospital Costs: The Role of Government Regulation*, MIT Press, Cambridge, Massachusetts, pp. 142–155.
Kidder, D., and Sullivan, D. (1982). Hospital payroll costs, productivity and employment under prospective reimbursement, *Health Care Financing Review, 4*: 89.
Lave, J. (1984). Hospital reimbursement under Medicare, *Health and Society, 62*: 251.
Lave, J., Lave, L., and Silverman, L. (1973). A proposal for incentive reimbursement for hospitals, *Medicare Care, 11*: 79.
Lewin and Associates (1975). An analysis of State and Regional Health Regulation. Final report submitted to the Health Care Financing Administration, contract no. HEW-05-73-212. Washington, D.C.
Luft, H. S. (1985). Competition and regulation, *Medical Care, 23*: 383.
Melnick, G. A., Wheeler, J., and Feldstein, P. J. (1981). Effects of rate regulation on selected components of hospital expenses, *Inquiry, 18*: 240.
Morrisey, M. A., Conrad, D. A., Shortell, S. M., and Cook, K. S. (1984). Hospital rate review: A theory and an empirical review, *Journal of Health Economics, 3*: 25.
Morrisey, M. A., Sloan, F. A., and Mitchell, S. A. (1983). State rate setting: An analysis of some unresolved issues, *Health Affairs, 2*: 36.
Myers, R. J. (1970). *Medicare*, Richard D. Irwin, Homewood, Illinois.
Newhouse, J. (1983). Two prospective difficulties with prospective payment of hospitals, *Journal of Health Economics, 2*: 269.
Noll, R. (1975). The consequences of public utility regulation of hospitals, *Controls on Health Care* (R. Hanft and P. Rettig, eds.), National Academy of Sciences, Washington, D.C.
O'Donoghue, P. (1978). Controlling hospital costs: The revealing case of Indiana, *Modern Healthcare, 8*: 42.
Pauly, M. (1970). Efficiency, incentives and reimbursement for health care, *Inquiry, 7*: 114.
Policy Analysis and Urban Systems Engineering (1980). Evaluation of the effects of certificate-of-need programs. Report to Department of Health, Education, and Welfare under contract no. HRA-230-7F-0165. Washington, D.C.
Romeo, A., Wagner, J., and Lee, H. (1984). Prospective reimbursement and the diffusion of new technologies in hospitals, *Journal of Health Economics, 3*: 1.

Rosko, M. D. (1982). Hospital responses to prospective rate setting. Unpublished doctoral dissertation. Temple University, Philadelphia.

Rosko, M. D. (1984a). The impact of prospective payment: A multidimensional analysis of New Jersey's SHARE Program, *Journal of Health Politics, Policy and Law, 9*: 81.

Rosko, M. D. (1984b). Differential impact of prospective payment on hospitals located in different catchment areas, *Journal of Health and Human Resources Administration, 7*: 61.

Rosko, M. D. (1986). Hospital rate regulation and market incentives: Complementary approaches to cost containment, *Journal of Health and Human Resources Administration, 8*: 320.

Rosko, M. D., and Broyles, R. W. (1984). Unintended consequences of prospective payment: Erosion of hospital financial position and cost shifting, *Health Care Management Review, 9*: 35.

Rosko, M. D., and Broyles, R. W. (1986). Impact of the New Jersey all-payer DRG system, *Inquiry, 23*: 67.

Salkever, D. S., and Bice, T. W. (1979). *Hospital Certificate-of-Need Controls: Impact on Investment Costs, and Use*, American Enterprise Institute, Washington, D.C.

Salkever, D. S., Steinwachs, D. M., and Rupp, A. (1986). Hospital cost and efficiency under per service and per case payment in Maryland: A tale of the carrot and the stick, *Inquiry, 23*: 56.

Sloan, F. (1981). Regulation and the rising cost of hospital care, *Review of Economics and Statistics, 63*: 479.

Sloan, F. (1983). Rate regulation as a strategy for cost control: Evidence from the last decade, *Health and Society, 61*: 195.

Sloan, F. A., and Steinwald, B. (1980). *Insurance Regulation and Hospital Costs*, D. C. Heath and Company, Lexington, Massachusetts.

U.S. Department of Health, Education and Welfare, Health Service Administration (1979). *PSRO: An Evaluation of Professional Standards Review Organization 1979 Program Evaluation*, Office of Planning, Evaluation and Legislation, Washington, D.C.

U.S. Senate (1970). *Medicare and Medicaid: Problems, Issues, and Alternatives*, Report of the Staff to the Committee on Finance. Washington, D.C.

U.S. Department of Health, Education and Welfare, Health Care Financing Administration (1980). Professional standards review organization program evaluation, *Health Care Financing Research Report*, Office of Research Demonstration and Statistics, Washington, D.C.

Walker, L., Broyles, R., and Rosko, M. (1985). Consequences of the DRG payment system on hospitalization for the elderly: The elderly at risk. Paper presented at the American Public Health Association Annual Meeting, November 20, 1985, Washington, D.C.

Webber, A., and Goldbeck, W. B. (1984). Utilization review, *Health Care Cost Management* (P. D. Fox, W. B. Goldbeck, and J. J. Spies, eds.), Health Administration Press, Ann Arbor, Michigan, p. 67.

Williams, S. V. et al. (1984). Methodological limitations in case-mix hospital reimbursement, with a proposal for change, *Inquiry, 21*: 17.

Worthington, N. L., Cromwell, J., and Kamens, G. (1979). Prospective payment in New Jersey, *Topics in Health Care Financing, 6*: 82.

Worthington, N. L., and Piro, K. A. (1982). The effects of hospital rate setting programs on volume of hospital services: A preliminary analysis, *Health Care Financing Review, 4*: 47.

Unit III

Personnel Administration and Labor Relations in Human Services Administration

7

Personnel Management

Donald E. Klingner Department of Public Administration, Florida International University, North Miami, Florida

I. INTRODUCTION

A. Personnel Management Functions and Tasks

Imagine that you are the personnel director of a new private, not-for-profit hospital corporation. Assuming that you have already received approval from the regional health planning council to begin operation, and that the building is already completed, what do you need to do to staff the facility and accomplish its mission? One of your first steps might be to hire new staff. But how do you know whom to hire, how many people to employ, and how much to pay them? Answering these questions would require you to make job descriptions, develop pay scales, and match these against your available budget and predetermined organizational structure.

Now you are ready to advertise vacancies, recruit applicants, and select them for available positions. But to do this, you must decide how you will determine their skills. Will you review their previous experience or education, give them written tests, establish probationary periods—or all of these? Who will interview applicants, and how much will the selection process cost?

Once employees are selected, they will need to be oriented to their new jobs and trained, and their performance will need to be assessed. Because it is important that employees be productive and content with their rewards in relation to the hospital's expectations of them, you must find ways of evaluating and developing them that meet their changing needs and those of the hospital.

Inevitably, some employees will fail to perform to your expectations. You will have to develop procedures for counseling and disciplinary action that protect the hospital's need for productivity, while also protecting good employees against poor supervisory practices.

TABLE 1 Essential Personnel Management Functions

Procurement	Advertise, recruit, select labor
Allocation	Divide and assign work; pay employees; promote, transfer, fire, lay off employees
Development	Train, assess, coach, motivate employees
Sanction	Discipline, negotiate and bargain with labor about working conditions; provide grievance and appeals procedure
Control and adaptation	Design personnel management system; establish role of personnel department and relationships with budget staff and line management; maintain information and forecasting systems relevant to other activities

Finally, it will be useful to organize the way you will accomplish these personnel management tasks in order that they not only will be carried out fairly and efficiently, but also will reflect changing conditions both inside and outside the department. This organization is reflected in Table 1.

These are the essential personnel activities that must be attended to in any organization. But you rarely carry them out directly in your role as personnel director. Rather, the personnel department is a staff department that (1) assists line departments by developing methods to conduct these activities and facilitate their accomplishment, and (2) monitors the way these activities are carried out to make sure they are performed fairly, according to their intent, and within policy and legal constraints (Dessler, 1978; Moore, 1985; Schuster, 1985).

B. Systems Theory and External Influences on Essential Personnel Functions

A system does not exist. It is an idea, a mental tool that helps us understand and learn. A system consists of a set of parts or components that relate to each other in some predictable fashion to produce some result. If one can isolate the components and draw a box around them, then the system will consist of three elements–inputs, throughputs, and outputs.

The human body is a natural system, which consists of several subsystems (such as respiratory, digestive, and reproductive) that work in conjunction with each other. The body is responsive to inputs from an external environment, and it produces outputs that affect that environment.

The systems concept was initially used to describe living and mechanical phenomena, but it has also been extended to include social phenomena, such as organizations, as well. Understandably, large organizations can be extremely complex, more so than many natural or mechanical systems. But the systems concept is very useful for describing or predicting the relationships between organizations and the external conditions, values, demands, and supports that constitute their environment. This is because organizations are extremely responsive to changes in their environment (Thompson, 1967).

For example, it is not possible to understand the contemporary role of hospitals without knowing a great deal about relevant social, economic, political, and technological conditions. These might include an aging population, technological advances in health care, and the economic resources to support expensive treatment and research activities. A second relevant environmental factor is societal values, which are not necessarily consistent with each other. For example, we are interested in having top-quality health care and in cost containment. These conditions and values result in choices by interest groups or consumers, and in government regulations intended to promote public policy objectives.

In sum, the value of systems theory is that it focuses on the critical relationship between agencies and their environment, and explains how organizations adjust to this dependency by being extremely responsive to changes in demands or supports provided by the environment (Elliott, 1985).

C. Conflicting Values and Conditions in Personnel Administration

It is commonly assumed that personnel functions can be carried out simply or routinely. This assumption is reinforced by the preceding description of functions, which was presented in an overly simplified and straightforward manner to make the major functions stand out clearly. In reality, the personnel director's job and personnel functions in general are full of conflict and change.

Here's why. Organizations fall into three categories—public, private for-profit, and private not-for-profit. And they fall into different functional areas, such as social services or manufacturing. In private agencies, the dominant value is efficiency, as shown by the profit motive and the bottom line. Public agencies are responsible for achieving other values as well, particularly social equity (affirmative action), employee rights, and political responsiveness. Not-for-profit corporations fall somewhere in between (Klingner and Nalbandian, 1978, 1985a).

II. PROCUREMENT OF HUMAN RESOURCES

A. Affirmative Action

Affirmative action represents one of the cutting edges of personnel management. It is a mediating variable that affects the way organizations recruit, hire, and promote employees. It supports the value of social equity by proposing that employees be hired, assigned, and promoted so that their percentage in the organization is proportionate to the percentage of their counterparts in the available labor market.

Affirmative action is a politically sensitive issue because it attacks widespread assumptions about hiring and promotion. For example, it implies that traditional selection criteria such as education, experience, and credentials may not be objective measures of ability; it diminishes the importance of seniority in determining eligibility for promotion; and it seeks to reduce the influence of personal favoritism in selection decisions (Mosher, 1982).

An initial point of confusion is that equal employment opportunity (EEO) and affirmative action (AA) are different principles. EEO prohibits discrimination on the basis of nonmerit factors (such as race, religion, age, sex, color, or national origin). AA requires that hospitals or agencies take positive steps to reduce historical patterns of discrimination by adopting preferential goals (or quotas) for selection and promotion. It is easy to see how an affirmative action plan might establish a goal of hiring more minorities or women until their percentage among employees in the organization equaled their percentage in the population, and how concern for protection of an applicant's or employee's rights for equal employment opportunity would prevent the establishment of hiring quotas (for example, four of the next ten employees hired must be black, Hispanic, or female). Also, under cutback conditions, it is difficult to achieve either goals or quotas because of the primacy of seniority as a retention criterion, or because of freezes on hiring or promotions.

1. Affirmative Action Laws

AA and EEO are implemented by a number of federal and state agencies, pursuant to various laws and executive orders (Klingner and Nalbandian, 1985a). A listing is found in Table 2.

EEO and AA laws, like all efforts to regulate behavior through law, are somewhat vague and conflicting (Ayton and Belohlav, 1982; Klingner, 1982). At the least, however, they require the personnel director of a health agency to do two things: (1) include a policy statement in personnel regulations emphasizing the nondiscriminatory nature of personnel policies and practices in the agency, and (2) prepare and implement a program that establishes the agency's plan for achieving affirmative action goals (*Equal Employment Opportunity Compliance Manual*, 1982).

The policy statement on nondiscrimination should read something like this: "In accordance with applicable federal and state law, the personnel policies and practices of [insert agency name here] prohibit employment discrimination on the basis of nonmerit factors such as age, race, religion, sex, color, national origin, or handicapped status." This statement or an abbreviated version ("The [insert agency name] is an AA/EEO employer") should be included in all vacancy announcements.

2. Compliance Procedures

Public agencies, and those that receive *any* public funds, are required to file an affirmative action plan with the EEOC or some other federal department to which the EEOC has delegated compliance responsibilities. An affirmative action plan consists of (a) a utilization analysis, (b) a self-assessment of the extent to which underutilization exists, and (c) a reasonable plan for ending underutilization. The utilization analysis is a summary of employees by racial and ethnic group (black, Hispanic, Native American, Asian or Pacific Islander, white) and sex. Underutilization exists if the percentage of employees from a particular group is significantly less in your agency than in the relevant labor market. Considerable confusion results from the fact that in reality, there is not one labor market, but several—geographic, occupational, health industry, etc. Substantial review of relevant labor statistics and negotiation with your compliance agency may be necessary before your percentage goals for representation can be agreed upon.

Finally, the agency is responsible for approving and implementing an affirmative action plan, which is a policy document comprising action items necessary to achieve full representation in such areas as recruitment, testing, selection, training, and promotion. While these personnel activities will be discussed in greater detail later in this section, some general areas of concern are included here:

Recruitment: *Do* advertise vacancies in media, locations, or schools targeted toward underrepresented groups; *do not* recruit by word of mouth.

TABLE 2 AA and EEO Laws and Compliance Agencies

Law	Practice covered	Compliance agency
Age Discrimination in Employment Act (1967, 1978)	Age discrimination against all employees aged 40–70	Department of Labor
Civil Rights Act of 1964, Title VII	Employment discrimination (particularly testing, selection, promotion, and training)	Equal Employment Opportunity Commission (EEOC); if conciliation fails, EEOC may file charges in federal court on behalf of plaintiffs
Equal Employment Opportunity Act (1972)	All employment practices that discriminate on the basis of nonmerit factors	EEOC
Vocational Rehabilitation Act of 1974	Employment discrimination against the physically handicapped (includes substance abusers undergoing treatment)	Department of Labor
Equal Pay Act (1963)	Equal pay for equal work regardless of sex	Wage and Hour Division, Department of Labor
E.O. 11246 E.O. 11375	Nonmerit discrimination (same as Title VII); affirmative action programs required for all federal contractors and subcontractors	Office of Federal Contract Compliance Programs, Department of Labor; delegates responsibility for health agencies to Department of Health and Human Services
1976 amendments to the Revenue Sharing Act of 1972	Nonmerit discrimination (same as Title VII)	Office of Revenue Sharing, Department of the Treasury

Testing: *Do* make sure that aptitude, ability, or performance tests measure skills, knowledge, or ability required on the job; *do not* use a test with a discriminatory impact if there are less-discriminatory alternatives that are equally job-related.

Selection: *Do* select on the basis of job-related experience, education, or ability; *do not* require degrees unless required by a credentialing agency, or height, weight, and age requirements unrelated to job performance.

Layoff and Promotion: *Do* publicize criteria and procedures for retention in a cutback situation and for promotion; *do not* promote or lay off strictly on a seniority basis without considering the impact on productivity or affirmative action.

Termination: *Do* establish policies and procedures for progressive disciplinary action that protect employee rights to due process; *do not* discharge employees undergoing treatment for substance abuse problems.

In a cutback situation, affirmative action and equal employment opportunity may come into conflict with each other. That is, requirements that the agency hire increasing proportions of underrepresented groups may conflict with a need to retain or promote existing employees on a seniority basis. In this situation, the most recent court cases have emphasized that agencies are not required to retain employees if they cannot afford to do so. Second, seniority-based layoffs are legitimate, even if they result in the discharge of disproportionately high numbers of underrepresented groups, provided that the seniority system itself is nondiscriminatory.

B. Recruitment

Recruitment is the process of attracting qualified applicants for available positions (Mangum, 1982). It assumes that the organization has completed a human resource forecast or needs survey (which defines the types of positions for which applicants must be recruited), and job analysis and evaluation (which determine the duties of each position, the qualifications applicants need to have, and the appropriate salary range).

Recruitment is a staffing function that is affected by economic and technological conditions, laws (particularly, affirmative action laws), and other political influences. For example, the growth of an industry can occur only in a society with available technology and money. Even given this favorable economic and technological climate, changes in the public laws and regulations that govern an agency cause changes in recruitment needs.

Economic conditions in a country, a region, or an industry affect recruitment. Under conditions of economic growth, there is a scarcity of qualified applicants. Agencies are likely to conduct open and continuous recruitment for a range of positions in response to high demand for vacancies that must be filled through internal promotion or external recruitment. During periods of economic decline, there is a surplus of qualified applicants. These same agencies are likely to recruit only for shortage-category occupations in response to low demand for both internal promotions and external recruitment.

1. Recruitment Procedures

Once human resource needs have been forecast and positions analyzed and evaluated, recruitment starts with a job announcement, issued by the personnel department, which formally notifies applicants that a job vacancy exists. To meet affirmative action laws and regulations, each job announcement must include the following information:

1. Job title, classification, and salary range
2. Duty location (geographic and organizational unit)
3. Description of job duties
4. Minimum qualifications
5. Starting date
6. Application procedures
7. Closing date for receipt of applications

The extent of recruitment efforts will depend upon several factors: the geographic area of consideration, the length of time during which applications are accepted, and the necessity for targeted recruitment efforts. Typically, professional and managerial positions have a larger geographic job market than do clerical or technical positions. While recruitment for the latter may be local (using state employment services, newspaper advertisements, or walk-in applicants), recruitment for the former may require regional or national efforts (through professional associations or recruiters).

2. Recruitment and Good Personnel Management

Good recruitment requires that the personnel director and other administrators agree on their respective roles and responsibilities in advance. Usually, a department cannot advertise a vacancy without the prior approval of the personnel department. This is necessary to ensure that the title, duties, and salary are consistent with other positions in the hospital. The administrator will normally interview the top candidates, particularly for a managerial or professional position, and no candidate can be hired by personnel without the written approval of the department in which the applicant will be working. If the personnel department continually sends candidates for interviews whom the department administrator considers unqualified, the administrator and the personnel director will need to get together and make sure that the minimum qualifications for the position, as established in the job description, are correct (Lubliner, 1981; Stoops, 1981; Wilheim, 1980).

Administrators often seek to place friends or acquaintances in positions. If these persons are qualified, and if they follow the normal application procedures, this practice can increase both productivity and loyalty. However, personal recruitment efforts by managers can sabotage the fairness of the selection process (even when managers seek to be objective), can create frustration and resentment among internal candidates for promotional vacancies, or can undercut the efforts of the personnel department to achieve affirmative action goals.

Lastly, it is important to remember that recruitment is but one facet of a cyclical process of acquiring, developing, and using human resources. Because poor development or utilization of existing employees will increase turnover, the personnel director may assume that the organization has a recruitment problem when in fact this is not the case. For example, budget cuts or changes in federal regulation may lead to a reduction in the number of staff nurse positions in a hospital. Increased workload for staff nurses may lead to increased turnover. On the surface, this turnover may appear to be desirable because it reduces personnel expenses by saving the money that would otherwise have been spent on occupied positions and allowing the hospital to fill any required positions at the bottom of the pay scale. But turnover of this nature may cause long-range problems in morale and the quality of patient care, leading to a potentially dangerous risk-management situation.

C. Selection and Promotion

Selection and promotion are the processes by which qualified employees are hired for available positions and moved from one position to another (Acuff, 1982). They reflect the conflict among several key values:

1. Administrative efficiency: Department directors want to fill vacancies as quickly as possible, since even a minimally qualified employee is more productive than a vacancy.
2. Employee rights: Current employees want maximum consideration for promotional vacancies—this usually translates to reassignment or promotion on the basis of seniority.

3. Social equity: Affirmative action advocates want vacancies filled by persons from underrepresented groups.
4. Political responsiveness: Managers are responsive to pressure from their own supervisors to hire a favorite designated person for available vacancies.

Naturally, the personnel department is the focus of all these conflicting pressures. It is supposed to hire quickly someone who meets affirmative action goals, can do the job well, and is acceptable to top management. It is not surprising that elements of this ideal combination are sometimes lacking.

1. Validation of Selection Criteria

The selection and promotion process begins with job analysis—the determination of what constitutes acceptable minimum qualifications for the position. The validation of minimum qualifications is called test validation, in that a test is considered to be any qualification (including review of education and experience, references, or other selection criteria not normally considered to be a test). The key to test validation is that it is perfectly legal to discriminate against applicants—indeed, hiring qualified rather than unqualified applicants is management's responsibility, and it is not possible to do this without discriminating against unqualified applicants. But in order for the discrimination to be legal, it must be based on job-related factors. Validation, in other words, is the process of determining that the minimum qualifications established for a position are job-related (Baker and Terpstra, 1982).

Through the *Uniform Guidelines on Employee Selection Procedures*, the Equal Employment Opportunity Commission has established three strategies by which employers may demonstrate the validity of minimum qualifications: empirical validation, construct validation, and content validation. Empirical validation requires that there be a statistically significant relationship between a preemployment test score and subsequent on-the-job performance. That is, higher test scores must correlate closely with higher performance appraisals, and lower test scores with lower appraisals, when regression analysis is used to measure the strength of the relationship between the two variables. Empirical validation is most suited to situations where large numbers of employees are hired into jobs for which objective performance standards can be easily developed and applied.

Construct validation involves both identifying psychological traits or aptitudes that relate to successful job performance and devising a test that measures these traits. For example, many insurance companies give psychological tests to applicants for sales positions in order to determine whether they have the same psychological profiles as the "ideal salesperson," which the company has previously determined by testing its top performing salespersons. The advantage of construct validation is that once job-related traits can be identified for a position, a test measuring those traits can be used to select employees for any organization. But it is often difficult to establish a link between personality traits and performance—someone with those traits might do a good job, but someone with different traits might also do well.

Content validation requires that minimum qualifications be logically related to the duties of the position for which they are required. For example, it is logical to assume that a business manager would need to have education or experience related to accounting, financial management, and thirty-party reimbursement. Or, a school bus driver would need to be able to qualify for a chauffeur's license, because this job requires transporting persons. The advantages of content validity are that it is relatively easy to explain to applicants or affirmative action compliance agencies, and it emphasizes the link between qualifications and job performance that health service agencies need to focus on the bottom line.

2. Selection Procedures

Once a department director has gotten management approval to establish a position, and job analysts have established the minimum qualifications for a position by using any of these three validation methods, the selection process occurs in the following steps (Carissimi, 1982; Dulewicz, 1982; Kravetz, 1982; Weiss, 1981; Witkin, 1981):

1. Recruitment of applicants through a vacancy announcement
2. Testing of applicants through any of these methods:
   a. review of education and experience, through resumes or standardized application forms
   b. written tests of personality, ability, or aptitude
   c. performance tests that measure actual job skills under simulated work conditions
   d. check of references (education, employment, or personal)
   e. previous performance evaluations (for a promotional vacancy)
   f. interviews with personnel or the department director
   g. assessment centers that systematically test candidates' performance under simulated job conditions

These selection methods are generally applied in the order listed above because they are arranged from the least costly to the most costly to administer. It is much easier and cheaper, for example, to screen out applicants on the basis of insufficient education or experience as shown by an application form than to interview all applicants to determine whether they have the minimum qualifications for a position. Yet each screening method has some potential flaws that must be guarded against. Minimum education requirements may screen out applicants who could do a job well. References may be biased in favor of the applicant, particularly one whom the current employer hopes will find another job. Unless panel interviews or structured interviews are used, interviews are prone to subjectivity and the hiring of applicants "just like us."

The personnel department plays multiple roles in the selection and promotion process. First, it must maintain productivity by assisting department directors to hire qualified employees. Second, it must protect the rights of current employees to be considered for promotional vacancies. Third, it must ensure that the organization complies with affirmative action guidelines in the selection or promotion process, and that its affirmative action goals for minority and female representation are achieved. Fourth, it must be sensitive to the hiring preferences of top management. As you might guess, it can be difficult to balance these objectives.

Once new employees are hired, they usually are placed in probationary status for six months or a year. Probationary appointments offer the highest validity of any screening method, for they ensure that the person can actually do the job. But they are the most costly, for the incumbent occupies a position for up to a year before a decision is made about keeping him or her. The use of the probationary period places upon supervisors the responsibility of weeding out unsatisfactory employees before they attain career status, and upon personnel managers the responsibility of developing valid probationary period evaluation systems.

The discussion of test validation methods and selection (and promotion) procedures may have raised fears that validation is a difficult and costly process. In many cases, it is. Given the current diminished political importance of affirmative action, is it necessary that we continue to validate minimum qualifications? It is. The most fundamental justification for test validation is not compliance with affirmative action laws, but maintenance of productivity by hiring only qualified applicants for available vacancies. Whether or not you are subject to affirmative action compliance pressure, the lack of validated qualifications means that you may be hiring unqualified people whose lack of qualifications place the organization or its clients at risk. To avoid this, develop a validation timetable that gives first priority to those positions that your experience indicates offer the greatest risk to clients or the agency, and those for which the largest numbers of employees are hired. In justifying the cost of validation to the director of administration, the personnel director might wish to emphasize that the cost of validation, though sometimes high, is invariably lower than the costs of litigation resulting from poor patient care, or workers' compensation claims arising from employee injuries.

III. ALLOCATION OF HUMAN RESOURCES

Allocation is the personnel activity that concerns dividing and assigning work, determining how much jobs are worth, and compensating employees through pay and benefit systems. Thus, it involves both the allocation of work to positions or units in the organization and the allocation of rewards to employees for work performance.

A. Human Resource Planning

Human resource planning is the personnel activity that mediates between an agency and its market or environmental conditions. As demand for services and availability of funds increases, human resource planning determines what positions should be added and which units shall receive them. As demand for services or funds decreases, human resource planning determines which positions shall be abolished in order to maintain solvency.

1. Environmental Influences

The market, or environmental, factors affecting public agencies are different in some respects from those affecting private employers. Public agency funding is determined partially by the level of revenue derived from user fees and partially by the priorities and allocations of the public budgeting process. For example, a major county hospital will derive some revenue from patients, some from third-party (insurance) reimbursement, and some from public appropriations by the county or state government. In addition, some specialized research activities or facilities may receive support from private foundations, private universities, or the federal government. Private hospital or health service agency funding is derived primarily from user fees and third-party reimbursement, though some revenue may be generated from other sources.

Both sectors are similarly subject to changes in federal or state regulations, which in turn reflect changing societal, economic, and technological conditions (Fallows, 1985; Levitan, Mangum, and Marshall, 1976; Spar, 1983).

2. Forecasting Techniques

The personnel department initiates human resource planning by asking departments to estimate the number and nature of the employees they will need, for the short term (next year) or farther in the future. The techniques managers use most often for forecasting their own human resource needs are collective opinion and incrementalism. That is, they determine the number of positions and type of positions they will need in the future on the basis of their needs in the past and their personal assessment of how perceived changes will affect human resource requirements.

In the private sector, this assessment might include changes in demand, available facilities, technology, or applicable regulations (Niehoff and Romans, 1982; Russ, 1982a,b; Scarborough and Zimmerer, 1982). In the public sector, it might include all of these, plus projected government revenues or budget allocations.

But the cost of equipment and facilities, and the need to avoid duplication of expensive facilities or equipment in a geographic area, has led to the development and utilization of more sophisticated planning techniques. Modeling (simulation) involves the creation of a computerized model that duplicates reality in those respects considered most relevant to future demand for services, or the ability to pay for them. This model might include population demographics, income, projected changes in technology, regulations, and other factors. These models can help planners determine the future needs of the industry by assessing how changes in one or more of those variables might be likely to alter aggregate demand for the organization's goods or services.

Is it better to use collective opinion or more rational forecasting techniques, such as modeling (Drandell, 1975)? Most agencies will continue to use the former, but the latter may be adopted fairly easily by many agencies, particularly those with adequate and competent staff, sufficient data on current resource requirements, receptive mangement, and access to computer facilities. The personnel administrator's skill and commitment to seeking the best solution determines the technique used and its effectiveness in forecasting.

Having used either technique to forecast the demand for human resources within the agency, personnel directors must also forecast the supply of qualified applicants—the potential labor market from which the agency can recruit. This forecast is influenced by a number of factors inside and outside the agency, including economic conditions, competition from other organizations, adequacy of educational and training facilities in shortage-category occupations, the number of vacancies, and the agency's recruitment practices.

By subtracting the aggregate supply of human resources from the aggregate demand for them, human resource planners compute the need for human resources. This figure is then used to develop programs for acquiring, developing, and using human resources.

3. Cutback Management

But what if the supply of available employees in an activity exceeds the demand? Increased public concern for the cost of services, changing demographics, or new federal regulations often affect the demand for services or the ability of users to pay for them. This can mean that a public agency will have to cut back employment to meet demand or resources. If cutbacks are drastic, the agency will have to abolish positions and lay employees off. When this occurs, the same value conflicts that affect the selection or promotion process arise, only worse. Employees want retention based on seniority;

management wants retention based on performance; affirmative action compliance agencies do not want layoffs to have a disproportionate effect on minorities and women; and managers want to keep favorite employees.

The best answer to this dilemma is to be prepared for a reduction in force (RIF) before it occurs. This means developing and publicizing retention criteria well in advance of the event, even before employees feel they may personally be affected by the choice of criteria. Personnel directors apply the criteria as equitably as possible, making sure that employees have adequate opportunity to challenge any cuts that affect them. The process is the same in both the public and the private sectors, since the constitutional protections that normally give public employees more job security do not apply in situations where their positions are being abolished because of lack of funds (Greenhalgh and McKersie, 1980; Levine, 1978).

While an RIF has the advantage of a quick reduction in payroll expenses, it has tremendous hidden costs resulting from decreases in employee morale and increases in self-protective behavior. In addition, it requires expenditures for lump-sum leave and retirement payouts, counseling, maintenance of a call-back system for employees affected by the RIF, increased unemployment compensation charge-backs, and other hidden costs. For these reasons, many health care agencies prefer to reduce costs gradually through hiring freezes and attrition. Yet, these have their costs as well. Turnover is normally among lower level service occupations, those most directly related to patient care or facility management; it is normally lowest among administrative and professional employees. Unless a hiring freeze is modified to permit the filling of lower level positions as they become vacant, or to permit contracting out for essential services, its effect can also be reduced productivity.

Given the problems created by all of the above "solutions" to an oversupply of human resources, it can only be expected that personnel directors and managers will find it difficult to develop appropriate answers. The best solution is to develop a human resource planning system that accurately forecasts the demand for and the supply of employees in various types of jobs, and to then adjust personnel policies and practices to keep demand consistent with supply. Since people are involved, and change is difficult, the system will have to be sold to the employees, managers, and regulatory agencies whose value preferences conflict in this area.

B. Job Analysis and Classification

Job analysis and classification are a paradox of human resource management. On the one hand, most personnel professionals consider them the building blocks of good human resource management. That is, before recruitment or selection can take place, it is necessary to write job descriptions that specify the duties of a position and the minimum qualifications required to perform those duties. In addition, it is essential to write job descriptions before setting pay rates for positions, because duties and qualifications are the primary factors used in determining job worth. These twin objectives of administrative efficiency and employee equity are fundamental to good human resource management, and it is for this reason that personnel professionals place so much importance on job analysis and job descriptions.

On the other hand, many employees and supervisors have less regard for job descriptions. They consider them to be inaccurate, incomplete, and of little use in meeting their primary needs in the organization. Employees wish job descriptions would include more specific information about what is expected of them and some concrete performance standards that would help them assess their own performance. Supervisors want job descriptions to offer more objective performance standards, in order to make performance appraisal easier and fairer, and disciplinary action or merit pay more certain (Klingner, 1979a).

To show how these problems with job descriptions occur, consider the position of social worker for a social service agency. Even among employees performing the same general duties (casework), performance expectations (number of cases) will differ depending on the type of clientele, the type of agency, and the geographic area covered. Before a job description can include a meaningful performance standard, it must include relevant information about the conditions that make task accomplishment easy or hard.

1. Job Descriptions

To do this, the traditional job description must be changed to include additional information relevant to the needs of employees and supervisors. Information on duties and qualifications must be expanded to include the following:

1. Tasks: What duties are important to the job?
2. Conditions: What factors make the job easy or hard to do?
3. Standards: What objective performance standards (quantity, quality, or timeliness of service) can be developed for each task?
4. Knowledge, skills, and abilities (KSAs): What KSAs are required to perform each task at the minimally acceptable standard?
5. Qualifications: What education, experience, or other qualifications are needed to ensure that employees will have the necessary KSAs for task performance?

These results-oriented job descriptions have several advantages over their traditional counterparts. First, they help employees understand what is expected of them. Second, they assist supervisors in establishing objective performance standards for use in merit pay or disciplinary action. Third, they establish a logical relationship between tasks, KSAs, and qualifications, which goes a long way to ensuring content validation of minimum qualifications. Their disadvantage, of course, is that major changes in conditions or performance standards will necessarily alter KSAs and, perhaps, minimum qualifications. Yet, some changes in jobs will always occur over time, and this gives employees and supervisors a natural interest in working with the personnel office to help keep them up to date.

2. Classification

Job classification is the process of categorizing positions according to the type of work performed or the level of skill required. The first of these categorizations is generally termed job classification; the second is usually considered job evaluation, in that the classification is based on job worth.

Job classification is generally based on broad occupational categories, such as administrative, professional, technical, laborer, or security-related positions. Other classifications may occur because of collective bargaining agreements or (in the public sector) laws establishing career service or civil service systems. For example, food service workers' positions may be classified separately by a hospital because their pay and benefits are set separately from other employees' under the terms of a union contract.

Or, social workers may be in a separate classification from their supervisors because the state civil service system has created separate categories for professional and administrative positions.

Classification is a contested issue in both public and private human service agencies because it affects pay and status. Normally, personnel departments resist attempts by supervisors to have jobs reclassified upwards because of the inflationary impact this has on the classification and pay structure. Supervisors, for their part, use reclassification as a means of winning more rewards for their employees and, perhaps, more status for themselves as well. In addition, most collective bargaining agreements prohibit supervisors from working employees "outside of classification," even though all job descriptions also require employees to perform ". . . all other duties as assigned."

In the public sector, the greater civil service protections afforded employees in "classified" positions makes these more desirable. In brief, classified positions are governed by civil service regulations regarding transfer, disciplinary action, dismissal, and layoffs. Managers have more control over employees in unclassified positions because these are exempt from civil service protections or collective bargaining agreements, thereby making layoffs or dismissals easier. These potential conflicts between employee rights and managerial efficiency make classification a continually contested issue in most agencies.

C. Job Evaluation and Compensation

Two terms common to personnel management are performance evaluation and job evaluation. Even though they may seem similar, they have different meanings. Job evaluation is the process of determining the worth of a position, usually by comparing the skill or responsibility required with that of other positions or some abstract scale of difficulty. Performance evaluation is the assessment of the quality of an individual's performance in a position. There is no necessary relation between the two factors. For example, a psychiatrist position is worth more money than a receptionist position, on the basis of qualifications, skill, responsibility, or other job worth factors. But an excellent receptionist may receive a higher performance evaluation than a mediocre psychiatrist. The two types of evaluation come together in the organization's pay system. General pay ranges for a position are established through job evaluation, and increments within these ranges are determined by performance evaluation.

1. Job Evaluation

Job evaluation, then, is a critical issue for employees because it determines within broad guidelines how much an employee is worth. It is critical for managers because it allows them to predict total personnel costs for budget preparation and control purposes. Finally, it helps the personnel department maintain pay equity throughout the organization and in comparison with other employers.

The easiest method of job evaluation is market comparisons. That is, the personnel department compares its salaries for selected positions with the salaries paid by other employers or with those advertised in newspapers for positions with the same title. The problem with this, of course, is that titles are not always an accurate indicator of job duties or qualifications required.

The alternative is to conduct a more formal type of job evaluation (Berg, 1976). While several methods are used, the most prominent today is the point-factor method. It compares jobs on an absolute scale of difficulty, using several predetermined job worth factors, which are quantified to make numerical comparisons easier. Here's how to do it:

1. Analyze all jobs in the agency to determine their tasks, conditions, standards, KSAs, and minimum qualifications.
2. Select factors that measure job worth across all positions (it may be necessary to break jobs into broad occupational classes first, and to develop job worth factors for each class).
3. Weight the job worth factors so that the maximum possible value is 100 points (for example, there could be four job worth factors, each with a worth of 25 points, or three job worth factors, two worth 40 points each and one worth 20).
4. Develop quality levels for each job worth factor, and apportion the points within that job worth factor to each quality level. For instance, if "working conditions" is used as a job worth factor worth 25 points, then the following quality levels might be established for it:
   a. 25 points: constant strenous activity (moving patients or materials)
   b. 10 points: some physical activity (moving patients or materials)
   c. 0 points: working in an office
5. Evaluate each job along each job worth factor, and compute the totals.
6. Establish realistic pay ranges for selected benchmark positions, based on market comparisons with similar jobs elsewhere.
7. Pay benchmark jobs the market rate, and pay other jobs in proportion to their comparative point totals.

Point-factor job evaluation methods are the best means of ensuring internal equity among employees doing similar work under similar conditions and external equity among organizations. Not surprisingly, their primary drawbacks are their complexity and the development costs associated with their use. It is also important to remember that the most critical aspects of point-factor evaluation are the choice and weighting of job worth factors and quality levels. These are basically judgmental decisions made by the job evaluator. But if they are done with concern and skill, they will result in the establishment of base pay rates for positions that are accepted by employees as equitable, and by managers as a realistic basis for budget planning.

The current controversy over comparable worth is a prime example of the controversy that can occur when administrators and employees disagree concerning the criteria to be used for determining job worth. Proponents of comparable worth believe that jobs entailing equivalent skill, effort, and responsibility should be compensated equally (Grune, 1980; Johansen, 1984, p. 14). Opponents believe that the labor market should set salaries, even if these are discriminatory on the basis of sex and at variance with job evaluation results (O'Neill, 1985). At the least, this debate raises questions about the validity of job evaluation (Emmert, 1985; Fogel, 1984; Neuse, 1982).

2. Other Compensable Factors

Job worth is only one of the factors that affects an employee's pay. Pay is based on a range of factors, including seniority, education, and performance (Sibson, 1974). Usually, the job evaluation system is used to establish the midpoint of the pay range for a position, and a range is established (usually five to ten percent on each side of the midpoint) within which employees' pay may vary on the basis of education, seniority, or performance. For instance, the position of police officer might be established with a midpoint salary of $20,000 and a range of plus or minus $2000. Under this system, new recruits might be brought in at $18,000, and officers could earn up to $22,000 on the basis of seniority, advanced education beyond the minimum needed to qualify for the position, or superior performance. The midpoint and range for the position would be adjusted periodically to compensate for inflation.

To be useful, a compensation system must combine elements of job worth (job evaluation) and employee characteristics (seniority and merit pay based on performance evaluation). It must be equitable in the rewards given for employee contributions, yet flexible enough to allow managers to exercise some discretion and employees to be rewarded for superior performance. These are frequently irreconcilable objectives; it is the job of the human resource manager to reconcile them (Ellig, 1983; Martel, 1982; McMillan and Williams, 1982).

3. Benefits

Employee benefits are a major part of the human service agency's personnel budget. Since 1960, they have increased in value from about twelve percent to almost forty percent of the typical employee's pay. The primary reasons for this are: (1) the need for increased employer contributions to pension systems because the federal Employee Retirement Income Security Act (ERISA) (1974) has increased concern for the actuarial soundness of pension systems, and (2) the increased cost of medical care funded by employer-financed group health insurance policies (Bracken, 1984).

Several groups have a legitimate interest in benefits. For employees, benefits constitute a large and increasing share of compensation, one that has the advantage of tax-exempt status. Managers can use benefits to increase the advantages of a compensation package, particularly such flexible benefits as training, merit increases, or desirable office locations (Gifford, 1984).

IV. DEVELOPMENT OF HUMAN RESOURCES

A. Productivity

Of the core personnel functions—procurement, allocation, development, and sanctioning of human resources—the development of human resources has historically received the least emphasis. The development function focuses on increasing the ability and motivation of employees to perform.

Recent economic and political conditions have forced companies and agencies to pay more attention to the development of their employees. With inflation, recession, and cutbacks in personnel expenditures, the value of administrative efficiency has emerged as a powerful influence on both public- and private-sector organizations. This call for increased productivity has forced employers to develop a more sophisticated understanding of employee motivation and satisfaction, the complex relationship between person and job through the design of work, and the impact of health and safety on employee performance; it also has resulted in the recognition that in labor-intensive work, turnover and absenteeism can significantly affect productivity (Bowman, 1984; Ukeles, 1982).

Despite the upsurge of interest in productivity improvement, a simplistic view of the way organizations operate often leads to high expectations and resultant disappointment because employees are not more efficient. The private sector is often assumed to have high productivity because of its constant emphasis on the bottom line—profit. Public agencies are often assumed to be less efficient because they lack a profit motive or because their employees are protected against discharge or discipline by civil service regulations.

While these beliefs are somewhat valid, reality is more complex. In reality, both public- and private-sector organizations strive to meet diverse or conflicting expectations in a changing environment. They must provide high-quality services, with efficiency, in accordance with complex and changing regulations of the federal government and state government or their private owners. Thus, the terms "employee efficiency," "productivity," and "organizational effectiveness" are not achievable goals, but are processes in which the organization and its employees are continually engaged (Gaertner and Ramnarayan, 1983).

1. Productivity Improvement Defined

Generally speaking, productivity concerns two specific assessments of performance. First, efficiency is measured as a ratio of outputs to inputs. In other words, measuring efficiency requires identification of a performance outcome, such as the number of miles of roads paved by a public works agency, and identification of the amount of resources used to produce the outcome, such as employee hours worked or funds allocated to client service or wages in the agency. The resultant ratio might measure clients per employee hours worked. Efficiency would be increased by increasing the number of clients while keeping the same number of employees, or by serving the same number of clients with fewer employees.

Yet, the obvious problem with efficiency measures is that either of the above solutions might lead to poorer quality mental health care being provided to the clients, or to acceptance of treatable clients and referral of clients with severe problems to other agencies. Thus, the need exists for an effectiveness measure, an assessment of the quality of the output measured against some standard. With effectiveness as a standard, the productivity measure for mental health care might look something like this: number of patients successfully treated (where success is defined in terms of such indicators as ability to hold a job, maintain family relationships, and live in a noninstitutional setting) per number of employee hours worked.

2. Personnel Management and Productivity Improvement

Productivity improvement programs seem to focus on three areas: (1) changes in structure or operating procedures (such as centralized purchasing or decentralized cost center control); (2) increased use of technology; and (3) improved human resource management (such as better orientation or training, improved job descriptions or performance standards, and alternative work schedules (Klingner and Nalbandian, 1985a). The personnel department is involved with all of these, though it is most directly responsible for the third.

The productive use of employees requires that four conditions be met. First, employees must have clear objectives, established through job descriptions or orientation sessions and reinforced through the agency's system of management by objectives. Second, employees must be able to perform the tasks assigned to them, by virtue of their either having necessary KSAs at time of hiring or receiving training. Third, employees

TABLE 3 Productivity Improvement and the Personnel Department

Condition	Role of the personnel department
Employees have clear objectives	Keep job descriptions current, coordinate orientation, train supervisors in management by objectives (MBO)
Employees able to do job	Validate selection procedures and criteria; provide training; train supervisors in performance appraisal
Employees allowed to do jobs	Reduce rigidities in personnel system; maintain safety standards; establish employee assistance programs
Employees motivated to do jobs	Train supervisors in dynamics of motivation and equity; design and maintain fair promotion, compensation, and disciplinary action systems

must have the opportunity to perform their duties; that is, their performance expectations must be reasonable, the working environment must be safe, and resources must be adequate to the task. Fourth, employees must be motivated to perform, through either rewards or discipline. The role of the personnel department in fostering these four conditions for improved human resource productivity is shown in Table 3.

To illustrate the role of the personnel department in productivity improvement, consider the impact of absenteeism and turnover on companies or public agencies. Abuse of sick leave results in decreased quality of goods or services produced when untrained workers must substitute for trained ones, and in increased costs to the agency when temporary employees must be hired or regular employees paid overtime. Employee turnover, which averaged twenty-two percent in the private sector from 1976 to 1979, represents other kinds of costs to the agency. First, there are acquisition costs, those required to recruit, select, hire, and place new employees. Second, there are development costs, those involved with orientation and training of new employees. Lastly, there are separation costs, separation pay, loss of efficiency prior to separation, and loss of productivity while the position is vacant.

However, turnover also has some potential benefits to the agency if the "leavers" are senior employees who are poor performers. In this case, they are likely to be replaced by more productive employees at a lower cost to the agency. However, in times of fiscal stress, turnover among productive but overworked junior employees will probably hurt more than it helps. In any event, turnover and absenteeism provide two examples of how the personnel manager's knowledge of the applied behavioral sciences and the development of systems for increasing employee productivity tie productivity measurement and improvement to the personnel function (Mobley, 1982).

B. Motivation

Much of the above discussion of productivity focused on structural or technological changes. A more concentrated analysis of employee performance related to agency productivity must directly address the two factors central to each employee's performance—motivation and ability.

Frequently the terms motivation and job satisfaction are used interchangeably. In fact, they are different. Satisfaction concerns the relationship between the benefits an employee derives from a job and the contributions expected. Motivation is the employee's desire to perform tasks expected by the organization (Campbell and Pritchard, 1976). Thus, it can be seen that motivated employees may or may not be satisfied, and satisfied employees may or may not be motivated. For example, an employee who receives a high salary and good working conditions in return for low productivity may be quite satisfied, but not motivated to high performance. Similarly, because of internal pressures for achievement or external threats, an employee may achieve high performance despite minimal rewards. The ideal is a work situation where employees are highly motivated and highly satisfied. The attainment of this condition requires deliberate action by management.

1. Causes of Job Satisfaction

Understanding job satisfaction and motivation requires some knowledge of two theoretical tools. Equity theory provides the best basis for understanding job satisfaction, and expectancy theory provides the best basis for understanding motivation.

Equity theory provides a basis for understanding why employees feel they are being treated fairly or unfairly (Adams, 1974). In brief, it offers a means of comparing each worker's inputs to a job with the outcomes derived from it. In general, employees feel they are treated equitably if their subjectively perceived inputs equal their subjectively perceived outputs. But even workers who see themselves as treated equitably (relative to their own outcomes) may still see themselves as treated inequitably compared with other employees. For example, a social worker with a large caseload of difficult clients may consider herself worth more than a caseworker with a smaller caseload. Yet, this other social worker may consider herself unfairly treated because all her client visits are out of the office and in the evenings. Thus, equity calculations require that employees compare their own inputs and outcomes, and compare their inputs and outcomes relative to those of other employees.

Equity issues are partly the concern of the personnel department, which uses job evaluation and merit pay systems to establish what constitutes a "fair day's work for a fair day's pay." But they are primarily the concern of the supervisor, who must listen to employees' perceptions of inequity and attempt to explain them if possible, or adjust them if necessary. Supervisors should also use the employee goal setting, counseling, and performance appraisal process to tell workers what types of behavior will and will not be rewarded; and they should consistently apply organizational rewards and discipline, and specify reasons behind these actions.

Expectancy theory attempts to logically reconstruct the mental processes that lead employees to expend energy in a certain direction (Lawler and Porter, 1975). It assumes that employees will work toward a certain goal if they see themselves as able to perform the task, if they see task accomplishment as being rewarded, and if they desire the rewards provided. In reality, these decisions are not reached separately; rather, they are all considered at the same time. For example, consider a social work supervisor who has been instructed to complete all pending cases within the next 48 hours. She may have serious doubts about the ability of her staff to do this, particularly if the lab is understaffed or if some social workers are trainees. In addition, the benefits of expending the effort to accomplish the task on time may not be that great. It may result in a commendation from the director of administration, but it is not likely to result in an increase in pay or benefits. It may even result in cancellation of her request for additional staff, since no additional staff would be needed if backlogs could be eliminated with existing personnel. Finally, the supervisor may not consider the benefits of a commendation to be that substantial, particularly when weighed against the greater chance of gaining additional personnel because of a continuing backlog.

Expectancy theory provides supervisors with a tool that they can use to assess motivational problems. By talking with the employee, the supervisor can find out whether the employee sees inadequate performance as due to a skill deficiency ("No matter how hard I try, I can't do this job right") or a motivational deficiency ("There are no rewards provided for successful performance, or successful performance is punishing because it disrupts my relations with other employees"). Supervisors can use expectancy theory to make sure that employees are able to do their jobs and to make sure that performance appraisal, merit pay, and disciplinary action systems actually reward desired performance and penalize undesired performance. For example, unless employers can identify why a particular employee received a merit raise and another did not, in terms of objective performance, then the merit pay system is unsuccessful, because other employees do not know what is expected of them to receive a similar raise.

2. Employee Needs

Both equity theory and expectancy theory refer to work outcomes and their perceived desirability to employees. What do employees want from their jobs? Two major theorists, Abraham Maslow and Frederick Herzberg, have developed multiple-factor explanations of human motivation focusing on the satisfaction of employee needs. For both theorists, the relevance of a particular motivator depends upon the worker's level of need. These models are shown in Table 4.

TABLE 4 Maslow's and Herzberg's Motivational Theories Compared

Hierarchy of unmet needs	Dissatisfiers (hygiene factors)	Motivators
Self-actualization		Achievement, recognition
Esteem		Work itself, responsibility, advancement
Belongingness	Company policy and administration	
Safety	Supervision, salary, interpersonal relations	
Physiological	Working conditions, job security	

Source: Klingner and Nalbandian, 1985a, p. 223).

According to Maslow, human needs can be arranged in a hierarchy of importance, with the higher needs becoming predominant motivators as lower ones are satisfied (Maslow, 1943). While each person's needs are different, organizations can create the conditions under which each person strives for self-actualization—the satisfaction of the highest level of unmet need. According to Herzberg, employees value two types of work outcomes (Wahba and Bridwell, 1983). *Hygiene factors* will prevent them from being dissatisfied with their jobs, but *motivators* are needed to elicit job satisfaction and performance. Although the validity and value of these theories is still disputed, there is no doubt that they have contributed to our understanding of job satisfaction. They both emphasize that motivation is a complex process, in which different factors serve as motivators under different conditions and for different employees. They both posit a hierarchical order among needs, supporting the conclusion that basic needs must be satisfied before higher ones can be fulfilled (Herzberg, 1984).

3. Job Design

The most critical application of motivation and job satisfaction theory is in job design (Hackman and Oldham, 1980; Locke and Latham, 1984). Historically, jobs have been designed with the emphasis on simplification, standardization of tasks, and specialization. These techniques increased the ability of employees to perform jobs satisfactorily, but they tended to ignore the fact that these jobs are boring. That is, the early applications of job design based on job simplification focused on workers' ability to perform work, not their motivation to perform it. The development of a more comprehensive approach to job design began with the Hawthorne Studies of the 1930s, in which researchers attempting to assess the effect of lighting levels on employee productivity were amazed to find that one group's productivity increased regardless of changes in lighting levels. The researchers concluded that workers' awareness of being singled out for attention, and group pressure and cohesiveness, caused productivity to increase without reference to lighting levels.

In its modern form, job design is exemplified by Hackman and Oldham, who have developed a model that ties core job characteristics to outcomes and critical psychological states. Briefly, this model holds that in jobs with certain characteristics (skill variety, task identity, autonomy, and feedback), where employees have certain critical psychological states (such as perceived meaningfulness of work, responsibility for outcomes, and knowledge of results), the result will be high motivation and job satisfaction—provided that the employee has the required knowledge and skill to do the job and receives external rewards for doing it (Naylor, 1984; Paul, 1985).

In summary, employee performance requires that four conditions be met:

1. The employee must know what is expected (adequate job descriptions, orientation, and training).
2. The employee must be able to do the job, and must believe he or she can do it (appropriate selection and training).
3. The organization must provide the employee with adequate opportunities to perform well (structure, resources).
4. The employee must be motivated to do well.
   - Does the employee connect high performance with the receipt of organizational rewards?

- Does the employee value these rewards?
- Does the employee think these rewards are distributed fairly?

In addition, some related methods of productivity improvement are quality circles, flextime, and compressed work schedules. Quality circles are an effort to increase employee involvement in solving job-related problems through scheduled but informal meetings aimed at identifying and resolving problems at the immediate level. Compressed work weeks involve reducing the number of days worked per week, but increasing the number of hours per day so that the total number of hours worked per pay period remains the same. Flextime establishes core working hours for all employees (such as 9:00 A.M. to 3:00 P.M.), and then allows employees to vary their remaining work hours (but according to a fixed schedule) on either end of this core. While employees generally report increased satisfaction with these last two innovations, the increased autonomy or leisure time these alternatives offer is unlikely to compensate for otherwise unacceptable working conditions, inadequate pay, or poor supervision.

In sum, the relationship among motivation, satisfaction, and performance is a complex one (Chung, 1977; Hanifin, 1986; Michaels, 1986; Naylor, 1984; Paul, 1985). With the help of equity theory, expectancy theory, and new methods of job design, we are becoming more aware that performance depends on ability, motivation, opportunity, and clarity regarding work expectations (Blumberg and Pringle, 1982).

C. Training and Development

Training is often considered the most visible and popular of all personnel activities. It promises managers that their employees will work better, and promises employees that they will do better on current or future positions. Yet training is not a cure-all—it will help only those performance problems caused by a skill deficiency rather than by some other problem, such as lack of clear expectations, feedback, or adequate rewards (Mager and Pipe, 1980). Table 5 illustrates the range of organizational responses to performance problems.

TABLE 5 Performance Problems and Responses

Situation	Organizational response	Personnel activity
Problem is insignificant	Ignore it	None
Selection criteria are inadequate	Change them	Job analysis
Employees unaware of expectations	Provide feedback	Orientation, training
Employees lack needed skills	Train them	Training
Good performance is unrewarded; bad performance is unpunished	Provide rewards and punishments, and connect them to performance	Performance evaluation, disciplinary action

From the above table, and remembering the discussion of performance and motivation from sect. IV.B, it can be seen that training is useful only in those situations where employees know what is expected of them, have enough basic skills or education to benefit from the training, are provided with feedback concerning their job performance, and are rewarded or disciplined on the basis of the adequacy of their performance. Too often, training is misused as a temporary or cosmetic solution when the real problem is faulty selection criteria, poor job design, or poor supervision. Not only is training inappropriate for these problems, but its indiscriminate use will cause training to be viewed with suspicion even in situations where its use is legitimate.

1. Orientation

Training begins with the new employee orientation process. Because orientation is usually the employee's first exposure to the employer, it is important that information be presented in a clear and accurate fashion.

The personnel department is usually responsible for presenting information about personnel policies, benefits, and services. Employees are usually asked to read, and to sign a statement attesting that they have read, an orientation handbook covering the following areas: AA and/or EEO, wages, hours of work, leave, benefits, performance evaluation, disciplinary action, grievances, promotion and reassignment, and unions. In addition, the personnel department may also coordinate brief presentations by agency officials clarifying the structure and purpose of the agency.

The employee's supervisor is responsible for orientation to the specific job. For this purpose, it is important that the job description be accurate and complete, and that the employee be assigned to a co-worker who understands the department's policies and procedures from a management perspective. In this way, the employee will receive at least some messages from the formal organization (management) in addition to messages received informally from other employees.

Also, the performance evaluation process appraises the employee's performance in light of the expectations previously established during orientation to the job through the initial MBO goal-setting process. Evaluation, done properly, provides the feedback and training that employees need to do their jobs well.

In this manner, orientation blends into on-the-job training, as employees learn about the structure of the organization, its personnel policies and benefits, their specific job duties and expectations, and evaluations of their performance.

2. Assessing Training Needs

Orientation assumes that new employees have relatively similar treatment needs, at least within similar job families. The assessment of training needs for existing employees is more difficult. Initially, management or training directors may require that all employees take some training if it is generally felt that this training will improve employee job performance in a current or projected job. For example, all new supervisory employees may be required to take a course in motivational techniques and disciplinary action. Or new technology or work methods may require that all employees in a certain job family take training to meet minimal job requirements, as was the case when data processing departments junked their keypunches in favor of video terminals. Lastly, training needs may be assessed on the basis of observable performance discrepancies, as part of performance evaluations or feedback from supervisors (Craig, 1976; Laird, 1978).

3. Designing the Training Program

Once the supervisor or training director has determined that a training need exists and that it is due to a performance problem for which training is an appropriate solution, he or she must design the training program in the following stages:

1. Define the training objective—what will each group with a performance deficiency need to know or to do by the end of the training?
2. Select the appropriate training method—for example, lectures or workbooks for general education, case studies and group discussion for management skills. Also, specify the type of trainer, training location, and format of the course.
3. Compute the cost of the training by considering the trainer's salary, trainee's salaries, training materials, and any other necessary expenses.
4. Determine if training is a cost-efficient solution to the problem. Training is *not* a cost-efficient solution unless the cost of the problem for a three- or six-month period is greater than the projected annual cost of the training program.

On the basis of the above information, it should be possible to recommend to top management or to the personnel department whether training is a good idea and, if it is, what kind of training program should be developed. It may well be that training will need to be combined with some other management improvement technique, such as job design, selection, rewards, or discipline (Gardner, 1976; Nadler, 1982; Wexley and Latham, 1981).

4. Training Program Evaluation

Even assuming that training is appropriate and cost-efficient, training can be evaluated at a number of levels (Zenger and Hargis, 1982; Measuring training effectiveness, 1983):

Reaction: How well did the trainees like the training?
Learning: How well did they learn the facts or concepts included in the training?
Behavior: To what extent did their job behavior change because of the program?
Results: What increases in productivity or decreases in cost were achieved?

The first two measures of effectiveness can be demonstrated by interviews or questionnaires distributed to trainees at the training site. Changes in behavior or productivity can be assessed by gathering data from supervisors. However, it is difficult to attribute any changes in behavior or productivity to training because of the usual absence of control—unless some employees do not undergo training, it cannot be determined whether the changes in behavior or productivity would have occurred anyway, without any training at all. Finally, the mere fact that employees are being observed may lead to productivity increases (a "Hawthorne effect") unrelated to the training itself.

5. Training and Career Development

Career development is the combination of future training needs and human resource planning (Nielsen, 1983). From the organization's viewpoint, it requires assessing future human resource needs and ensuring that employees receive the training they need to occupy future positions as well as current ones. From the employee's point of view, it requires the organization's giving information about future job possibilities within the agency, providing training related to employees, and thereby answering the question "What do I have to look forward to in this job?"

In cutback management situations, training is usually one of the first activities cut, because it is basically a supportive staff activity with a visible cost and less-visible short-term benefits (Bell, 1983). Ironically, imposing a hiring freeze or slowdown actually increases training needs, since the agency must meet the need for new skills by training existing employees rather than by hiring new employees who have the skills. The cutback of training, especially when combined with a hiring freeze or layoffs, has an uncertain impact on productivity (Rehder, 1983). Employees may work harder out of fear, or they may work less effectively because of increased stress or self-protective behavior. Whatever the outcome, there can be no doubt that cutback management reduces employees' and managements' career development interest in long-term employee development efforts.

6. Supervisory Training, Team Building, and Organizational Development

Supervisors are responsible not only for their own productivity, but for the performance of their subordinates. Consequently, one objective of training is to develop the supervisory skills of managers so that they can help their employees to "work smarter" (Galosy, 1983). This means educating managers about the building blocks for employee performance (clear standards, adequate skills, adequate feedback, and rewards or punishment).

Managers are also responsible for helping to improve productivity by improving the quality of work relationships within the agency. This process is called organization development (OD). One common OD technique is team building, which involves employees in identifying work problems that reduce organizational effectiveness, in proposing solutions, and in specifying who is responsible for seeing that the steps are carried out. OD resembles training in that both are intended to produce changes in productivity. But training is focused on tasks and the trainer, whereas OD focuses on relationships among the participants. OD resembles quality circles in that both are intended to involve participants in the change process. It differs in that OD focuses on relationships, while quality circles focus on work methods or procedures. All are efforts to increase productivity by unlocking employees' abilities and commitment (Burke, 1982; Levinson, 1982; Lippitt, 1982; Livingston, 1983; MacDonald, 1982; Robey and Altman, 1983; Watson, 1980).

D. Performance Evaluation

Performance evaluation (or appraisal) is central to employees' performance improvement because it is the process by which they are given feedback on their performance. But the effectiveness with which it is tied to rewards and punishments (through merit pay or disciplinary action systems), and the fairness with which supervisors evaluate employees' performance, will determine how much faith both parties place in the system. Frequently, performance evaluation systems that are poorly designed or haphazardly administered do a great deal of harm to agencies, their supervisors, and their employees.

1. Performance Evaluation Criteria

All performance evaluation systems measure one of two basic criteria, or some combination of both—personality and performance. Personality-based systems assess an employee's personality traits, characteristics, or aptitudes. Typically, a set of presumably desirable traits (such as enthusiasm, ability to follow orders, and appearance) is listed in a column down the left side of an evaluation form, and an evaluation scale runs horizontally for each trait or characteristic. The reviewer marks or checks the point on the scale corresponding to the extent to which the employee possesses each trait. Such systems are easy to design and administer, for ratings can be easily quantified and compared with those of previous time periods, other employees, or other organizational units.

The major problem with personality-based systems is their dubious validity and its effects on the relationship between employee performance and rewards (Cascio and Bernardin, 1981). The validity of personality-based evaluation depends upon the extent to which the selected traits are related to the duties of the position. But as we learned in our discussion of job analysis, different jobs require different knowledge, skills, and abilities. Innovativeness is a mandatory qualification for a hospital administrator, but it may land a financial manager in jail, or get a nursing director fired. Even if an organization went to the trouble of developing job-related traits for each position (through a construct validation process), the resultant trait evaluations would be of limited use because they would not identify areas of successful or unsuccessful performance, nor could they be readily changed by an employee who wished to improve his rating. Lastly, supervisory criticisms of an employee's personality usually lead to defensiveness and hostility.

For these reasons, most performance evaluation specialists advocate the use of performance-based systems, namely, those that evaluate job-related behaviors. In contrast to personality-based systems, these communicate managerial objectives clearly, are reliable, and provide a concrete basis for performance improvement and reward allocation. Because they are based on identifying the behaviors that measure satisfactory performance along the job elements (tasks) central to a position, performance-based evaluation systems are more logically related to content validity, to the organizational objective of productivity, and to objectivity of rewards and discipline. In addition, they make performance evaluation interviews more comfortable by focusing on specific examples of an employee's performance that are clearly related to job objectives previously established through an orientation and goal-setting interview as part of the MBO process (Cummings and Schwab, 1973; Latham and Wexley, 1981; Patten, 1982).

However, performance-based systems are considerably harder to develop than are personality-based systems. Because performance standards may vary even among positions with the same grade and title, performance standards must be developed or at least modified to suit the particular tasks or conditions of a particular position. This may require that supervisors spend more time working with employees to develop and clarify performance standards, and more time with subsequent evaluation interviews. This, in turn, may conflict with the supervisor's primary objective of getting the work done. Lastly, evaluating each employee on the basis of distinct job-related criteria causes problems in the equitable allocation of rewards and discipline. If two employees have both exceeded their performance standards, which is more deserving of a merit increase, and why (Edwards, 1983)?

2. Evaluation Methods

The choice between personality-based and performance-based evaluation systems largely dictates the choice of methods by which employees will be evaluated (Locher and Teel, 1977). Certain techniques are more frequently utilized in personality-based systems:

1. Graphic rating scales, which were described in the discussion of personality-based systems, are very easy to develop, administer, and score, but are of dubious validity.
2. Ranking techniques require the rater to rank order each employee along each trait.
3. Forced-choice techniques require the rater to select one statement that best describes an employee from among several choices; this technique can be valid if the evaluation form has been carefully designed to include traits related to job performance.
4. Essay evaluations, or narrative comments about an employee's personality or performance, are the oldest technique; they are adaptable to both performance- and personality-based evaluations, but they are time-consuming and require that supervisors be able to write well.

Other techniques are more suitable to performance-based systems:

1. Objective measures, the direct measurement of performance, measure the quantity, quality, or timeliness of an employee's work against previously established standards.
2. The critical incident technique records representative examples of an employee's work performance in relation to agreed-upon employee objectives.
3. Behaviorally anchored rating scales (BARS) are a refinement of the two above techniques that identify the primary tasks (elements) for a position and develops a range of possible levels of performance for each one; BARS fit logically with results-oriented job descriptions and management by objectives.

The choice among performance evaluation techniques is not an easy one. The techniques that have best withstood the test of validation challenges are those that have been developed on the basis of job analysis, which are performance-rather than personality-based (Giglioni, Giglioni, and Bryant, 1981; Kleiman and Durham, 1981). But these systems are also the most costly and difficult to develop.

3. The Human Dynamics of the Appraisal Process

The choice of which evaluation criterion and technique to use should not be used to obscure the fact that the human element of performance evaluation is the most important (Nalbandian, 1981). It is a truism that an organization in which relationships between supervisors and employees are characterized by openness and trust can use any type of performance evaluation system to provide objectives, feedback, and reward. Similarly, the most valid, most expensive, and best-publicized system can be subverted by employees, supervisors, or personnel specialists used to operating in a climate of misinformation and mistrust. It is therefore not surprising that performance evaluation systems are widely regarded either as a nuisance or as a necessary evil (Beer, 1981; Carroll and Schneier, 1983; Cederblom, 1982).

Why is this so? For some employees, no amount of feedback can increase productivity, because they are overworked already, or because they lack the training and technology to work more productively. In addition, performance evaluation may not be linked to an effective reward or discipline system. If civil service regulations protect unproductive employees from disciplinary action, or if budget constraints prevent meaningful merit pay systems, this is what will happen.

But the most important reasons for the failure of performance evaluation lie in the unwillingness of supervisors and employees to participate in the process (Graves, 1982a,b). Employees are likely to view any criticism with defensiveness and hostility, particularly if it is based on personality rather than performance. Supervisors, for their part, see little to look forward to in the performance evaluation interview. If employees react toward supervisors with indifference or hositility, and if supervisors are themselves dubious about the effectiveness of appraisal at improving performance, supervisors will develop ways of responding that minimize these reactions, such as rating everybody equally or avoiding disclosure of negative information during the evaluation interview. This is why in most organizations, most employees are rated "satisfactory." Ironically, because most employees consider themselves above average, they view "satisfactory" ratings as "unsatisfactory."

Even though performance-based rating systems are designed to make assessments more objective and, thus, more acceptable to employees, appraisal will inevitably produce anxiety, because it affects feedback and rewards. An effective performance evaluation system requires the following:

1. Supervisors who are willing to supervise and view appraisal as part of the supervisory process
2. A valid and reliable appraisal tool that has been developed with employee participation and that focuses on performance rather than personality traits
3. Training programs directed at the supervisory use of the appraisal instrument, and understanding of the human dynamics surrounding the appraisal process
4. Rewards for supervisors who competently and seriously approach the appraisal function
5. A superior-subordinate relationship at work characterized by understanding and trust

E. Employee Safety and Health

Under English common law, employees are entitled to a safe and healthy workplace. A number of factors have made this more difficult to achieve in recent years. First, our increased understanding of environmental health, employee psychology, and other fields has expanded our awareness of the kinds of issues we need to be concerned about. These include not only the traditional needs for fire prevention and health care, but also concerns for hazards caused by the workplace—lung disease from inhaling asbestos insulation fibers in older buildings, the uncertain effects of computer terminals on operators, and realization that job stress can cause or worsen employee health problems related to alcohol and drug abuse.

Companies' or agencies' concern for employees' safety and health is motivated by two factors. First, these conditions are required for employees to work productively, in that safety and health are basic physiological needs upon which employee performance depends. Second, recent increases in the cost of medical care, awareness of long-term health consequences of workplace conditions, longer life spans, and the litigiousness of society all place employers at greater risk when they ignore practices that are dangerous to employee safety or health (Chenoweth, 1984).

1. Occupational Safety and Health Act

Aside from general common-law protections, safety and health are legally required by the Occupational Safety and Health Act (OSHA) of 1970 (U.S. Department of Labor, 1976). While its provisions are generally assumed to apply to industrial facilities, it includes many standards that may apply to others as well, such as those for number and size of doorways, ventilation, fire protection, and first aid facilities. The act does not mandate federal standards in these areas. Rather, it requires states to either adopt the federal standards or develop standards of their own at least as effective as those promulgated under federal law and regulations, to designate and staff a responsible agency, and to submit required reports on employer compliance to the Department of Labor.

Under OSHA, employers and employees both have rights and responsibilities:

1. Employers are responsible for providing a hazard-free workplace, informing employees about OSHA, furnishing employees with safe equipment, recording and reporting injuries, and not conducting reprisals against employees who report OSHA violations.
2. Employees are responsible for following employer safety and health rules, wearing prescribed protective equipment, and reporting job-related injuries or illnesses promptly.
3. Employers have a right to help from the Occupational Health and Safety Administration (also called OSHA) in complying with standards, and to be advised of the reasons for an inspection.
4. Employees have the right to review copies of OSHA standards applicable to their type of agency, to request an OSHA inspection if they believe their workplace is unsafe, and to complain to OSHA if they believe they have been discriminated against as a result of filing an OSHA complaint.

2. The Personnel Department and OSHA

Private companies or public agencies may contain many conditions that violate health or safety standards. For example, the raised floor in one agency's centralized computer facility had a missing panel that had been temporarily replaced by an inverted milk crate. And one x-ray machine at a local hospital was powered by an unshielded electrical cable that passed within two feet of the operator's desk. To make matters worse, when employees complained about the unshielded cable and the heat produced by the cable's resistance, they were told that nothing could be done about the cable—the operator was given an electric fan to put under his desk to blow the heat away.

These are not isolated cases. The news is filled with stories of workers claiming lung damage due to exposure to asbestos; Vietnam veterans claiming a variety of ailments due to the herbicide Agent Orange; chemical exposure to painting or cleaning products; radiation in hospitals; and problems due to noise. The dangers of fetal damage for pregnant women or genetic damage for childbearing age employees (male and female) should also be considered (Ashford, 1983).

To prevent unsafe work conditions from becoming disasters, the personnel department should push for the establishment of an internal monitoring program or have this service contracted to a reliable firm. Either OSHA compliance inspectors or the outside consultants should inspect or survey the workplace. They should report directly to top management. Under no circumstances should they come under another department that might cover up any problems found, for financial or public relations purposes. While the personnel department will have some role in this process, by identifying jobs with a high rate of workers' compensation or disability retirement claims, inspections are best done by specialists in the field.

In addition, it is the responsibility of top management to stress the importance of safety and health to productivity and morale. In Japan and Europe, the number of accident-free workdays are carefully tabulated and publicized daily, so that employees and supervisors alike are aware of their significance. Here in the United States, it is more common for both managers and employees to avoid safety equipment—such as seat belts or earplugs—even when provided and required.

The personnel director has some specific responsibilities related to occupational safety and health. First, job descriptions should contain minimum medical qualifications where these can be defended as statistically or logically related to successful job performance. Persons with a history of back problems can be denied jobs requiring heavy lifting, or x-rayed to prevent them from filing workers' compensation or disability retirement claims based on preemployment conditions. If employees cannot be found who meet the minimum qualifications, then the job must be changed so that available employees can do it safely. Second, employees can be trained to perform their jobs safely, and supervisors to be more safety-conscious. Third, the savings derived from low workers' compensation claims or health insurance rates can be calculated, and employees and supervisors can be rewarded by having some of these savings passed on to them.

3. Employee Health and the Job

In addition to these direct links between occupational health and safety and employee well-being, there are other workplace conditions that may affect employee health. If employees are placed under conditions for which they lack clear objectives, adequate skills, feedback, or rewards, one likely result will be increased job stress. Employees may respond to this stress by alcohol or drug abuse, or by diminished productivity.

The personnel director can diminish the risk of these more subtle health problems by publicizing the well-documented relationship between these factors, and by working to maintain personnel and supervisory practices that ensure clear standards, adequate skills, timely feedback, and related rewards and discipline (Cirillo, 1983; Jordan and Simons, 1984; Matteson, 1982). The agency should have an employee assistance program (EAP) to which supervisors or the personnel department can refer employees who seek help with substance abuse or other personal problems that are affecting their job performance (Blair, 1984; Kindler, 1984). Lastly, employees should be encouraged to utilize preventive health care through exercise, diet, and greater reliance on health maintenance organizations rather than waiting until more costly and risky hospitalization and treatment for health problems becomes necessary (Chovil, 1985; Feuer, 1985).

V. SANCTIONS

The sanctions process represents the authoritative control, by interest groups inside and outside the organization, of the relationship between employees and management. The personnel activities most closely related to the sanctions process are collective bargaining, grievances, and disciplinary action.

The sanctions process is fundamentally different for public agencies and private companies. In private organizations, greater emphasis on the value of administrative efficiency means less concern for individual rights. In practice, this means that unless employees are covered by a collective bargaining agreement that includes provisions for protecting their rights in a layoff or disciplinary action situation, management may fire or discipline employees at will. By contrast, public agencies must temper their concern for administrative efficiency with maintenance of other values, such as individual rights. In practice, this means that public employees have constitutional protections that make it difficult for managers to fire or discipline them, in addition to any protections they may have as a result of collective bargaining agreements.

Thus, our discussion of the sanctions process will emphasize the important differences between private and public sectors with respect to labor-management relations, grievances, and disciplinary action.

A. Labor-Management Relations

Although many of the practices involved with private- and public-sector labor-management relations are identical, their underlying legal frameworks (and the agencies that ensure compliance with those frameworks) are completely different (Sloan and Whitney, 1981).

1. Laws and Administrative Agencies

In the private sector, the fundamental law regulating collective bargaining is the National Labor Relations Act (NLRA, or the Wagner Act), passed by Congress in 1935. The NLRA recognized the right of all private-sector employees to join unions for the purpose of collective bargaining, and it required that management recognize and bargain collectively with these unions in good faith. It established a federal agency (the National Labor Relations Board, or NLRB) responsible for certifying unions as appropriate bargaining representatives, supervising negotiations to ensure good-faith bargaining, adjudicating deadlocks (impasses) that might arise during contract negotiations, and establishing an arbitration process to resolve grievances between labor and management over contract administration issues. The NLRA was amended by the Taft-Hartley Act (1947), which allowed states to pass laws forbidding unions from requiring that employees be union members in order to apply for employment, and which prohibited unions as well as management from engaging in unfair labor practices (Getman, 1982; Kochan, 1980; Mills, 1982).

In the public sector, there is no single law or administrative agency that regulates the collective bargaining process (Chickering, 1976; Moskow, 1970). Rather, our federal system of government has dictated that the federal government is responsible for passing laws and creating administrative agencies to regulate collective bargaining for federal employees nationwide, and each state is responsible for passing laws and creating administrative agencies to regulate collective bargaining for state and local government employees within that state. Federal agencies and employees are regulated by the Federal Labor Relations Authority, under the terms of Title VII of the 1978 Civil Service Reform Act. Since most public human service agencies are run by state or local governments, this means that those wishing to familiarize themselves with the relevant laws, agencies, and practices must consult state statutes or published references particular to their state. These might include "looseleaf services" by major publishers in the area of labor relations, or *Labor-Management Relations in State and Local Government*, published annually by the Department of the Census.

2. Collective Bargaining Practices

Although the legal framework and regulatory agencies for collective bargaining differ between the public and private sectors (and among jurisdictions for public agencies), the collective bargaining process itself generally involves the same practices in all cases. The terms critical to an understanding of the process include the following: scope of bargaining, unit determination, recognition and certification, contract negotiation, impasse resolution, ratification, contract administration, and unfair labor practices.

a. Scope of Bargaining

Scope of bargaining simply concerns the range of issues about which management must negotiate. In most cases, the scope of bargaining is *open*; that is, management must negotiate about all items the union wishes to discuss. In some cases, such as public employees of federal agencies, salaries and benefits are set politically, through Congress, rather than bilaterally, between labor and management, so the scope of bargaining is *closed*.

b. Unit Determination

Before collective bargaining can occur, a primary responsibility of the agency regulating collective bargaining (the NLRB, or the appropriate public agency) is determining the suitability of a proposed bargaining unit. Bargaining units may be established among all employees of one agency or among employees of different organizations in similar occupations. The first option has the advantage of having a single set of managers involved in negotiations; the second offers greater commonality of interest among employees in the bargaining unit and greater equity for employees in the same "job family" of a state or local government classification system. Both agency-based and occupation-based methods of unit determination require some external coordination to ensure that negotiated contracts treat employees in different agencies or occupations equitably.

c. Recognition and Certification

Once bargaining units have been established by the NLRB or the appropriate federal or state collective bargaining agency, unions are free to organize employees for the purpose of bargaining collectively. While no uniform policies or procedures exist for these practices, generally an employer may voluntarily recognize a union as the exclusive bargaining agent for employees in that bargaining unit if the union can demonstrate that a majority of the employees in the bargaining unit want to be represented by that union. If the employer does not voluntarily recognize the union, recognition must occur through an election in which the union receives either a majority of the votes cast or a majority of the votes of employees in the bargaining unit.

Once a union has been voluntarily recognized or has won a representation election, it must be certified as the exclusive bargaining agent by the NLRB (for a private employer) or the appropriate regulatory agency (for a public employer).

d. Contract Negotiation

Contract negotiation begins immediately following certification. Management may be represented by a professional team of negotiators or by its own members. If the agency chooses to use its own managers as members of the negotiating team, this team should include an experienced chief negotiator who is the sole spokesperson for the team.

The most important aspect of negotiations is not the negotiations themselves, but the marshaling of information and arguments that takes place prior to negotiations (Neal, 1980). Management should develop its own preferred contract provisions and should anticipate those of labor. In particular, those proposed provisions with an economic impact must be costed to determine their short-term and long-term affect on the agency.

Once negotiations begin, each side should be represented by a single spokesperson. This person is responsible for working to support management's or labor's interests, bearing in mind that this will require proposing, accepting, or rejecting a variety of alternative positions on a range of issues. The way that skilled negotiators earn their money is by proposing or reacting to positions with a constant appearance of good-faith bargaining, while constantly striving to achieve agreement on positions that support their side's interests (Fisher and Ury, 1983).

e. Impasse Resolution During Contract Negotiations

An impasse is a breakdown in the contract negotiation process that occurs when labor and management disagree on proposed contract provisions and cannot resolve their disagreement by discussion, persuasion, or compromise. If this occurs, there are three impasse resolution procedures that may be used.

Mediation is the intervention of a neutral third party in an attempt to persuade the deadlocked negotiators to agree on contract provisions. The mediator functions in similar fashion to a marriage counselor. This person's suggestions are not legally binding, but the mediator may propose alternatives that neither party had thought of and that are voluntarily acceptable to both parties.

Fact-finding involves a formal hearing in which both sides present arguments in favor of a particular position. The fact finder then makes a formal decision supporting one side or the other or offering a compromise between them. While the fact finder's solutions are not binding, they are made public. This can affect the outcome of the negotiations, particularly for public agency collective bargaining situations where pressure from elected officials and the media is influential.

If these resolution techniques are unsuccessful, the last resort is *arbitration*, which is extensively used in private-sector collective bargaining but not in the public sector. Arbitration involves submitting the disputed provision to a third party, whose decision is binding (Chauhan, 1979; Elkouri and Elkouri, 1973).

Because labor and management will have to live with a negotiated contract once it is agreed upon, it is recommended that they make every effort to agree on contract provisions without resorting to impasse resolution techniques.

f. Ratification

Once the contract has been negotiated by labor and management, it must be ratified by the union's members before it goes into effect in the private sector. Management's negotiating team is presumed to speak for management, so no formal ratification by management is required other than the signature on the contract of management's chief negotiator. In the public sector, ratification requires approval by a majority of the voting members of the bargaining unit, and also approval of the legislature to which the public agency is responsible. This is because the legislature is the only body that can approve the appropriation of funds—the agency's managers or negotiators cannot agree to contract provisions that require spending additional funds for pay and benefits without first submitting these contract items to the appropriate legislature for approval.

g. Contract Administration

Once the contract has been negotiated, agreed to and ratified, each side is responsible for contract administration—that is, for conducting personnel policies and practices that carry out the contract's provisions. These usually involve items such as job classification, overtime or compensatory time provisions, disciplinary action, and working conditions.

Conflicts may arise because contract language is unclear or because one party finds that it cannot achieve its interests effectively unless the contract provisions are clarified. The collective bargaining agreement will include provisions for resolving disputes that arise under it. In the private sector, arbitrators appointed by the NLRB and paid by both parties are responsible for hearing both sides of the issues and making a binding decision. In the public sector, binding arbitration usually occurs, with arbitrators appointed by the state collective bargaining agency. Note that this form of binding arbitration applies only to the contract administration process in public agencies, and not to the contract negotiation process as well.

h. Unfair Labor Practices

In the private and the public sectors, employees have the undisputed right to join unions and bargain collectively. Management is prohibited from coercing or harassing employees as a consequence of their union membership, just as unions are prohibited from coercing employees in order to force them to join the union. But management does not have the same right to discourage employees from joining the union as the union does to encourage them to do so. That is because management's power to coerce employees is considered so great that reciprocity in this respect does not apply.

One method private-sector unions have of encouraging management to come to agreement during collective bargaining negotiations is the strike. Withholding services is one means by which unions can compel management to take their demands seriously. For its part, management can lock out striking employees and attempt to continue production using strikebreakers or management personnel. In the public sector, strikes are usually considered an illegal withholding of services, because public employees are considered to be employed by the public rather than just by agency managers. However, public unions and their employees have frequently subverted no-strike laws or contract provisions by engaging in sick-outs or other forms of resistance as a means of emphasizing or mobilizing political support.

B. Disciplinary Action and Grievances

The previous discussion of motivation introduced equity theory as a conceptual tool that could be used to explain why employees viewed their rewards as fair or unfair, relative to the performance required of them in return. Because the nature of the work relationship is dynamic, there are continual changes in employees' expectations of management and management's expectations of employees. The ongoing relationship between employees and supervisors is the informal means by which each party readjusts its expectations of and contributions to the other. At a formal level, two processes have been established for use by the organization and the employee when either feels its expectations of the other have been grossly violated. Disciplinary action is used to sanction employees for violations of work rules or expectations. Grievances are filed by employees who feel their rights have been violated by the organization. Thus, it is helpful to see these two processes as two sides of the same coin. For organizations covered by a collective bargaining agreement, grievances may be filed by either labor or management against the other party for alleged violations of the negotiated contract.

1. Performance Problems and Disciplinary Action

A disciplinary action is an employer-imposed reduction in organizational rewards for cause. Disciplinary actions may include written reprimands, suspensions, reductions in rank or pay, and firing. They do not include temporary layoffs or reductions in rank or pay that apply to a range of positions due to reductions in workload or budget. Rather, they are caused by specific behavioral incidents that result in low productivity or violations of agency work rules or procedures.

Disciplinary action is always the last step in dealing with an employee whose performance is substandard, never the first. It should be initiated only after the supervisor and the personnel department have made sure that the other conditions necessary for productivity are present:

1. Job design: Are the tasks, conditions, and performance standards of the job reasonable and equitable?
2. Selection: Does the employee meet the minimum qualifications established for the position?
3. Orientation: Were organizational rules, regulations, and position requirements clearly communicated to the employee?
4. Documentation and feedback: Has the employee's performance been clearly documented, and feedback provided?
5. Training: Does the employee have adequate skills to perform the expected tasks at the expected level of performance?
6. Rewards: Is good performance rewarded, or are there factors in the work environment that make good performance impossible or punishing?

2. Informal Counseling

If the supervisor has noticed a performance problem and thinks that all the conditions necessary to ensure productivity are present, the first step is to discuss the problem with the employee. This discussion is not a confrontation; rather, the supervisor uses it to determine whether the employee thinks there is a performance problem and what the employee considers the cause of it. The purpose of the discussion is to produce agreement on the need for improved performance and on the causes of poor performance.

The reason informal counseling is necessary is that supervisors frequently assume they know the cause of a performance problem, when in fact they may not. One employee was continually criticized for her tardy submission of a report due on the first of each month, until a conversation with her revealed that preparation of the report depended upon prior receipt of data from six other work units, who did not complete their work until the first of the month. Thus, informal counseling revealed that the solution to this problem was not discipline for the employee, but rescheduling the due date for the completed report (Davidson, 1985; Harrison, 1985).

The essence of information counseling is listening, to be sure that your initial understanding of the performance problem is in fact correct and that supervisory responsibilities for enhancing employee productivity have indeed been met.

The informal counseling session should end with agreement by the supervisor and the employee about the cause of the performance problem. If the cause is a supervisory responsibility, the supervisor should take the initiative to provide the conditions necessary for productivity—good job design, orientation, training, or feedback. If the cause is employee motivation, the supervisor should clearly tell the employee that performance will be monitored from now on, and should specifically describe the type of disciplinary action that will follow if performance is not improved to a certain level on those job elements that are unacceptable (Flynn and Stratton, 1981).

3. Progressive Discipline

If the employee's performance continues to be unsatisfactory, it will be necessary to provide discipline. If the key word for the informal counseling session is *listen*, the key word for the disciplinary counseling session is *tell*. During this session, the supervisor should summarize the previous informal counseling session, reminding the employee of the performance objectives that were mutually established and the disciplinary action that was promised if these were not met. The supervisor should close the session by telling the employee the discipline that will be applied and placing a formal notification of this in the employee's personnel file.

Before moving to disciplinary action, remember one thing—the only thing worse than not disciplining employees at all is attempting to discipline them and not being able to make it stick. To avoid having this happen to you, make sure that you have done everything possible:

1. Have you discussed the problem with the employee during informal counseling, resulting in the establishment of clear performance objectives and a time frame within which the employee's performance will be evaluated?
2. Have you documented poor performance relative to these previously established performance standards?
3. Are your performance expectations reasonable in terms of the agency's previously established personnel rules or policies, and are they applied equitably to other employees in the same circumstances?
4. On the basis of your previous experience or that of other supervisors, do you believe your boss and the personnel department will back you up, or will they side with the employee?

4. Positive Discipline

Recently, there has been renewed interest in tying discipline to management by objectives. Under this system, which is termed "positive discipline," the employee is notified about his performance problems. Clear standards are set, and the employee is given the opportunity to voluntarily meet those standards or resign from the organization. Proponents of this system feel it has the advantages of treating the employee as an adult and of avoiding adversarial disciplinary action (Bryant, 1984; Campbell, Fleming, and Grote, 1985; Heshizer, 1984).

5. Establishing Disciplinary Systems

The personnel department is responsible for establishing the preconditions necessary for supervisors to discipline unproductive employees effectively (Drost and O'Brien, 1983). First, it is responsible for developing and publicizing personnel rules for the agency. It is also responsible for clarifying rules in situations where different types of employees or different organizational units have legitimately different performance expectations. For example, an "established pattern of tardiness" might mean being 15 minutes late twice a year for a paramedic, because ambulances are required by law to have a full complement of paramedics, and the absence of one means that another will be forced to work overtime or comp time until the tardy employee arrives on the job. For employees who work on "job basis" (a required number of hours during the pay period, but a flexible work schedule depending on program requirements), the above standard would be unrealistic. To avoid having the least common denominator—the lowest standard—become the standard for the entire organization, the personnel department must define and justify different standards if they are necessary for certain units or types of employees (Pulich, 1983).

Second, the personnel department must train supervisors to view discipline as one means of ensuring employee performance, one that should be initiated only after they are sure the other conditions for employee productivity have been met.

6. Grievances

Grievances are the means by which employees seek redress for what they consider inequities in the organization's treatment of them. If the agency and its employees are covered by a collective bargaining agreement, grievances are filed with reference to specific provisions of the negotiated contract. In other circumstances, grievances represent a more general means of protesting what employees see as inequities in work assignments and promotions, poor supervision, and racial or sexual discrimination.

To begin with, supervisors remember that it is in management's best interest to treat employees consistently and fairly, and that the existence of a good grievance and appeal system is necessary to uncover management abuses of employee rights. The system should include the following steps:

1. Informal counseling: The employee and his or her supervisor should discuss the situation.
2. Grievance: If this is unsuccessful, the employee should be urged to file a formal grievance with the personnel department, both to protect the employee's rights and to provide a basis for response by the supervisor and the agency.
3. Consultation between the supervisor and the personnel director: The supervisor and the personnel director should meet to verify the facts in the situation and attempt to develop a solution that meets the employee's needs.
4. Adjudication: An agency supervisor or a panel of supervisors is appointed by the agency head to review the facts of the case and to hear testimony from witnesses. It is the responsibility of the personnel department to make sure that the agency's disciplinary action procedures have been followed.

Under a collective bargaining agreement, grievances are filed with the union steward rather than with the personnel department. The union steward then presents the grievance to the personnel director, and the consultation and adjudication processes follow. In either case, employees should have the right to a lawyer if they want one.

7. External Grievance Channels

Regardless of the resolution of a grievance by internal procedures, employees may also have the right to a review through one of many external channels. As we will learn in the next section, public employees enjoy much greater protection of their rights against arbitrary discipline or discharge than do private employees.

Private employees may appeal their disciplinary action to NLRB arbitration, if they are covered by a collective bargaining agreement and if the union agrees to support the appeal. They may appeal alleged violations of affirmative action laws to the appropriate federal or state compliance agency. As a last resort, they may file a private civil suit against the employer if the discipline or discharge involves a violation of a previous contractual agreement between them. But the time and cost involved in such suits make them rare.

By contrast, public employees have all of the channels available to private-sector employees, plus some additional ones. If they are covered by a collective bargaining agreement and if the union agrees to support the appeal, they may request grievance arbitration from the appropriate federal or state labor relations agency. And in addition to affirmative action compliance agencies and the courts, public agency civil service systems frequently have a civil service review board, which serves as an external appeal channel.

In addition, both public and private employees may request unemployment compensation following termination. If the employer rejects the claim on the grounds that the employee was fired for cause, the employment security office holds a review hearing to establish the nature of the termination. A determination that the employee was discharged without cause not only will result in chargebacks against the agency's unemployment compensation insurance account, but may also provide the basis for overturning the discharge on appeal to one of the many available external grievance channels.

To supervisors and personnel directors, it may sometimes seem as though it is harder to discipline employees than it should be. In one respect this is true, for the purpose of the sanctions process is to provide checks that limit management's ability to enforce unreasonable or inequitable performance expectations. However, private agency managers can reduce the number of external grievance channels available to employees by avoiding union recognition and documenting discharges for cause. Their public agency counterparts have a more difficult time, because public agencies are by necessity more responsive to employee rights. However, public agencies can also take steps to avoid union recognition and to ensure that civil service boards are composed of persons knowledgeable about personnel regulations and relatively immune to political pressure.

C. Employee Rights

The differences between public- and private-sector employment are nowhere as great as with respect to the issue of employee rights.

1. Private Sector Employee Rights

In the private sector, the primary objective is efficiency, and all other values, such as employee rights, are subordinate to this. While employers are encouraged to follow the steps in disciplinary action outlined in the last section to ensure that the relationships between employees and supervisors is fair and equitable, there is no legal requirement that they do this. For example, private-sector supervisors may discharge employees simply by telling them to go home and not come back. If the employee is not covered by a collective bargaining agreement, and if the discharge is not a violation of affirmative action laws, there will be no grounds for an employee appeal except the internal grievance process and the unemployment compensation review hearing, if the employer wishes to contest the payment of unemployment compensation on the grounds that termination was for cause. If the employee is disciplined rather than terminated, the internal review process is the only avenue of appeal, and one can assume that this process would be biased in favor of management.

In sum, private-sector employment is governed by a common-law doctrine called "employment at will." Under this doctrine, both employees and management are considered equal partners in the employment contract, and either party can dissolve an employment agreement by announcing its intention to do so. Unless a written employment contract exists that promises continued employment, employees have no recourse if they are discharged, even if their performance is exemplary and the discharge was arbitrary and capricious.

2. Public Sector Employee Rights

In the public sector, employees have much greater protection against arbitrary discipline or discharge. Although frustrated supervisors and personnel managers frequently blame this on civil service regulations, it is important to remember that the real reason is the Constitution (Rosenbloom, 1981). The Fourteenth Amendment guarantees persons the equal protection of the law and affirms that they may not be deprived of property (such as a job) without due process of law.

In recent years, federal courts have uniformly held that once an employee has held a job past a probationary period, he or she has a reasonable expectation of continued employment as long as performance is satisfactory and funds are available to support the position. Thus, because a job can become the employee's "property," employees are entitled to due process before they can be disciplined or discharged. In practice, due process means the right to be confronted with the reasons for the discipline or discharge, the right to respond to those reasons, and the right to have a decision made by an impartial hearing examiner.

This means that public agencies must follow the counseling and disciplinary action procedures specified previously, not only for the sake of maintaining employee productivity, but also to ensure that they can discipline or discharge unproductive employees. Particularly in public agencies, a continual conflict exists between management's right to discipline or fire unproductive employees, and employees' rights to due process in the deprivation of job-related property rights.

VI. CONTROL AND ADAPTATION OF THE PERSONNEL FUNCTION

Various sections of this chapter have described personnel management as the performance of systematic functions (allocation, procurement, development, and sanctions), the objectives of which differ according to the continual tension among values that influence outcomes for these activities (political responsiveness, individual employee rights, social equity, and administrative efficiency). The control and adaptation function enables personnel management, as an organizational activity, to remain responsive to the objectives of managers and to adapt to changes in environmental conditions.

A. Human Resource Management Evaluation

This involves an investigation of two activities: human resource management evaluation, and the role of management information systems in collecting and disseminating the information used to evaluate personnel management systems.

1. Program Evaluation

The section on productivity defined the differences among efficiency, effectiveness, and responsiveness. Private agencies are responsible to their owners or directors, primarily on the criterion of efficiency. For example, their prime concern is whether an agency delivers a needed service with a low unit cost, such that sales exceed expenses. In addition, larger concerns of effectiveness are also involved–is the service desired by customers or clients?

Public and not-for-profit agencies are concerned with efficiency and effectiveness, but the greater degree to which they are controlled by interest groups and legislatures dictates that they will be evaluated primarily on the basis of effectiveness and responsiveness. Do their programs meet the desired objective, and is that objective politically relevant? Within the agency, it is likely that program managers will use efficiency criteria to measure how well programs are doing once they have been established. But even an efficient program will not continue to be funded if it is not considered effective or politically responsive.

These considerations require that personnel managers understand the relationship between people and productivity (Cascio, 1982; Peters and Waterman, 1982).

2. Human Resource Management Information Systems

The collection and use of information for program planning, control, and evaluation purposes is essential to management of human service agencies. Yet, it can be seen from the previous discussion that different people have different needs for information of different types. A job development supervisor, for example, might want information on the total cost of job development and the total number of jobs developed in order to generate summary workload and unit cost figures. His boss, the director of a state department of occupational development, would also need information on total jobs developed compared with forecasted demand. The state legislature would have to assess the efficiency of the job development program, its effectiveness at meeting projected demand, and the overall level of priority for this agency compared with those of other programs competing for scarce resources.

While much of the information related to effectiveness and responsiveness is subjective and anecdotal, it is also possible to develop a management information system to collect data on various factors related to organizational effectiveness and, in particular, to the effectiveness of the personnel function (Smith, 1982a,b). For example, the agency could measure how well personnel practices met affirmative action guidelines by comparing its existing work force or current selections with the proportions of persons from affected groups in the relevant labor market. The impact of varying budget levels on agency staffing patterns could be projected by using microcomputerized spreadsheet programs to simulate the impact of alternative proposed budgets on the number of positions and their salaries. Employee development could be monitored by collecting information on employee skills and training. Lastly, the sanctions process could be affected by the use of information systems to monitor the impact of proposed economic contract items on the profitability of an agency.

Despite widespread recognition of the importance of personnel management information systems (PMIS) to personnel management, some confusion exists concerning the criteria that should be used to select such a system and the problems associated with its use (Ceriello, 1982). First, personnel managers need to specify the data elements they need to provide the information required to answer questions such as those raised above. For example, position data might include the salary range, occupation code, and organizational location of each position. Employee data might include each employee's classification, duty location, seniority, pay, benefits, and affirmative action status.

These data elements are summarized to form reports. For example, a payroll is simply the total personnel expenditures for a pay period. To produce it, one needs certain position data (the salary for a position) and employee data (name, and time and leave records). Thus, the PMIS is used to collect and store data, to produce reports used to control and evaluate current programs, and to develop simulations to support policy decisions. The personnel manager must decide what the system is to do before computer specialists decide how to do it; the PMIS must be designed to be compatible with the larger organizational management information system; and computerization should be recognized as a change in work technology that also involves such problems as employee insecurity, job redesign, and training needs.

In addition, the ease with which a PMIS can collect and disseminate information creates other problems, such as the conflict between employee rights and management efficiency.

B. Personnel Management in the Future

An understanding of the role of personnel management in the future requires both awareness of its role in the past and insight into the ways in which the interplay of conditions and values will affect its role in the future. Yet, several conclusions seem likely (Klingner, 1979b).

First personnel managers and supervisors will continue to be responsible for performing the functions of procurement, allocation, development, sanctions, and control and adaptation. In performing these functions, they will continue to be influenced by general societal values (social equity, political responsiveness, individual employee rights, and administrative efficiency) and by changing political, social, economic, and technological conditions within society.

Those personnel managers and supervisors who succeed will do so because they have recognized the importance of human resources to the survival or growth of their agencies and the key role of the personnel function in helping the human service agency to use its human resources efficiently and effectively (Klingner, 1984; Morse, 1984; Naisbitt, 1984; Newland, 1984; Nigro, 1984.

REFERENCES

Acuff, H. A. (1982). Improving the employment function, *Personnel Journal, 61*: 407.

Adams, J. S. (1974). Inequity in social exchange, *Organizational Behavior and Management: A Contingent Approach* (H. L. Tosi and W. C. Hamner, eds.), St. Clair Press, Chicago, p. 288.

Ashford, N. A. (1983). Legal mechanisms for controlling reproductive hazards in the workplace, *Occupational Health and Safety, 52*(2): 10.

Ayton, E., and Belohlav, J. A. (1982). Equal opportunity laws: Some problems, *Personnel Journal, 61*: 282.

Baker, D. D., and Terpstra, D. E. (1982). Employee selection: Must every job test be validated? *Personnel Journal, 61*: 602.

Beer, M. (1981). Performance appraisal: Dilemmas and possibilities, *Organizational Dynamics, 9*(3): 24.

Bell, C. R. (1983). How training departments win budget battles, *Training and Development Journal, 37*: 42.
Berg, J. G. (1976). *Managing Compensation*, AMACOM, New York.
Blair, B. R. (1984). Selecting an EAP contractor that will meet company needs, *Occupational Health and Safety, 53*(9): 40.
Blumberg, M., and Pringle, C. D. (1982). The missing opportunity in organizational research: Some implications for a theory of work performance, *Academy of Management Review, 7*: 560.
Bowman, J. S. (1984). Japanese management: Personnel policies in the public sector, *Public Personnel Management, 13*(3): 197.
Bracken, J. (1984). Getting through the maze: Knowing the fundamentals of employee health benefit planning, *Personnel Administrator, 29*(5): 64.
Bryant, A. W. (1984). Replacing punitive discipline with a positive approach, *Personnel Administrator, 29*: 79.
Burke, W. W. (1982). *Organization Development: Principles and Practices*, Little, Brown and Company, Boston.
Campbell, D. N., Fleming, R. L., and Grote, R. C. (1985). Discipline without punishment—at last, *Harvard Business Review, 63*(4): 168.
Campbell, J. P., and Pritchard, R. D. (1976). Motivation theory in industrial and organizational psychology, *Handbook of Industrial and Organizational Psychology* (M. D. Dunnette, ed.), Rand McNally College Publishing, Chicago.
Carissimi, D. C. (1982). Using management assessment centers in health care. *Training and Development Journal, 36*: 95.
Carroll, S. J., and Schneier, C. E. (1983). *Performance Appraisal and Review Systems*, Scott, Foresman and Company, Glenview, Illinois.
Cascio, W. F. (1982). *Costing Human Resources: The Financial Impact of Behavior in Organizations*, Kent-Wadsworth, Boston.
Cascio, W. F., and Bernardin, H. J. (1981). Implications of performance appraisal litigation for personnel decisions, *Personnel Psychology, 34*(2): 221.
Cederblom, D. (1982). The performance appraisal interview: A review, implications, and suggestions, *Academy of Management Review, 7*(2): 219.
Ceriello, V. R. (1982). The human resources management system: Part I, *Personnel Journal, 61*: 764.
Chauhan, D. S. (1979). The political and legal issues of binding arbitration in government, *Monthly Labor Review, 102*(9): 35.
Chenoweth, D. (1984). Health management consultants use diverse programs in achieving goals, *Occupational Health and Safety, 54*(2): 53.
Chickering, A. L. (1976). *Public Employee Unions*, Institute of Contemporary Studies, San Francisco.
Chovil, A. (1985). "Wellness" programs, *Business and Economic Review, 31*(2): 11.
Chung, K. H. (1977). *Motivational Theories and Practices*, Grid, Columbus, Ohio.
Cirillo, D. J. (1983). Coping with causes of stress in the automated workplace, *Management Review, 72*: 25.
Craig, R. L. (1976). *Training and Development Handbook*, 2nd Ed. McGraw-Hill, New York.
Cummings, L. L., and Schwab, D. P. (1973). *Performance in Organizations*, Scott, Foresman and Company, Glenview, Illinois.
Davidson, J. P. (1985). Giving and receiving criticism, *Supervisory Management, 30*: 11.
Dessler, G. (1978). *Personnel Management: Modern Concepts and Techniques*, Reston Publishing Company, Reston, Virginia.
Drandell, M. (1975). A composite forecasting methodology for manpower planning utilizing objective and subjective criteria, *Academy of Management Journal, 16*(3): 512.

Drost, D. A., and O'Brien, F. P. (1983). Are there grievances against your non-union grievance procedure? *Personnel Administrator, 28*: 36.
Dulewicz, V. (1982). Application of assessment centers, *Personnel Management, 14*: 32.
Edwards, M. R., Wolfe, M., and Sproull, J. R. (1983). Improving comparability in performance appraisal, *Business Horizons*, (September-October): 75.
Elkouri, F., and Elkouri, E. A. (1973). *How Arbitration Works*, 3rd Ed., Bureau of National Affairs, Washington, D.C.
Ellig, B. R. (1983). What's ahead in compensation and benefits, *Management Review, 72*: 56.
Elliott, R. (1985). *Public Personnel Administration: A Values Perspective.* Reston Publishing Company, Reston, Virginia.
Emmert, M. (1985). Pay equity and politics, *Review of Public Personnel Administration, 5* (Summer): 50.
Equal Employment Opportunity Compliance Manual (1982). Prentice-Hall, Englewood Cliffs, New Jersey.
Fallows, J. (1985). America's Changing Economic Landscape, *The Atlantic Monthly*, 255 (March): 47.
Feuer, D. (1985). Wellness programs: How do they shape up? *Training, 11*(4): 27.
Fisher, R., and Ury, W. (1983). *Getting to Yes: Negotiating Agreements Without Giving In*, Penguin, New York.
Flynn, W. R. and Stratton, W. E. (1981). Managing problem employees, *Human Resources Management, 20*: 28.
Fogel, W. (1984). *The Equal Pay Act: Implications for Comparable Worth*, Praeger, New York.
Gaertner, G. H., and Ramnarayan, S. (1983). Organizational effectiveness: An alternative perspective, *Academy of Management Review, 8*: 97.
Galosy, J. R. (1983). Curriculum design for management training. *Training and Development Journal, 37*: 48.
Gardner, J. E. (1976). *Helping Employees Develop Job Skill: A Casebook of Training Approaches*, Bureau of National Affairs, Washington, D.C.
Getman, J. C. (1982). *Labor Relations: Law, Practice and Policy*, 2nd Ed. The Foundation Press, Mineola, New York.
Gifford, D. (1984). The status of flexible compensation, *Personnel Administrator, 29*(5): 19.
Giglioni, G. B., Giglioni, J. B., and Bryant, J. A. (1981). Performance appraisal: Here comes the judge, *California Management Review, 24*(2): 14.
Graves, J. P. (1982a). Let's put appraisal back in performance appraisal: Theory and practice, *Personnel Journal, 61*: 844.
Graves, J. P. (1982b). Let's put appraisal back in performance appraisal: Part II, *Personnel Journal, 61*: 918.
Greenhalgh, L., and McKersie, R. (1980). Cost-effectiveness of alternative strategies for cutback management, *Public Administration Review, 41*(6): 575.
Grune, J. (1980). *Manual on Pay Equity*, Committee on Pay Equity, Conference on Alternative State and Local Policies, Washington, D.C.
Hackman, J. R., and Oldham, G. R. (1980). *Work Redesign*, Addison-Wesley, Reading, Massachusetts.
Hanifin, L. M. (1986). Communication barriers: Direct link to motivation, *American City and County, 101* (February): 38.
Harrison, E. L. (1985). Why supervisors fail to discipline, *Supervisory Management, 30*(4): 22.
Herzberg, F. (1984). Seeking answers that motivate, *Industry Week, 223*: 49.
Heshizer, B. (1984). An MBO approach to discipline, *Supervisory Management, 30*(3): 2.

Johansen, E. (1984) Managing the revolution: The case of comparable worth, *Review of Public Personnel Administration, 4* (Spring): 14.

Jordan, J. D., and Simons, R. D. (1984). It's no accident: What you think is what you do, *Personnel Journal, 63*: 16.

Kindler, H. S. (1984). Time out for stress management training, *Training and Development Journal, 38*: 64.

Kleiman, L. S., and Durham, R. L. (1981). Performance appraisal, promotion and the courts: A critical review, *Personnel Psychology, 34*(1): 103.

Klingner, D. E. (1979a). When the traditional job description is not enough, *Personnel Journal, 58*: 243.

Klingner, D. E. (1979b). The changing role of personnel management in the 1980's, *The Personnel Administrator, 24*(9): 41.

Klingner, D. E. (1982). Understanding affirmative action, *Administrative Comments and Letters, 2*(2): 1.

Klingner, D. E. (1984). Public personnel administration in the 1980s: Part of the solution, or part of the problem? *Public Personnel Management Journal, 13*(1): 59.

Klingner, D. E., and Nalbandian, J. (1978). Personnel management by whose objective? *Public Administration Review, 38*(4): 366.

Klingner, D. E., and Nalbandian, J. (1985a). *Public Personnel Management: Contexts and Strategies*, Prentice-Hall, Englewood Cliffs, New Jersey.

Klingner, D. E., and Nalbandian, J. (1985b). Public personnel management: A values perspective, unpublished.

Kochan, T. A. (1980). *Collective Bargaining and Industrial Relations*, Richard D. Irwin, Inc., Homewood, Illinois.

Kravetz, D. J. (1982). Selection systems for clerical positions, *Personnel Administrator, 26*(2): 39.

Laird, D. (1978). *Approaches to Training and Development*, Addison-Wesley, Reading, Massachusetts.

Latham, G. P., and Wexley, K. N. (1981). *Increasing Productivity Through Performance Appraisal*, Addison-Wesley, Reading, Massachusetts, pp. 28–30.

Lawler, E. E. III, and Porter, L. (1975). *Behavior in Organizations*, McGraw-Hill, New York.

Levine, C. H. (1978). Organizational decline and cutback management, *Public Administration Review, 38*(4): 316.

Levinson, H. (1981). Executive development: What you need to know, *Training and Development Journal, 35*(9): 84.

Levitan, S., Mangum, G., and Marshall, R. (1976). *Human Resources and Labor Markets*, 2nd Ed. Harper & Row, New York.

Lippitt, G. L. (1982). *Organizational Renewal*, 2nd Ed. Prentice-Hall, Englewood Cliffs, New Jersey.

Livingston, J. S. (1983). New trends in applied management development, *Training and Development Journal, 37*(1): 14.

Locher, A. H., and Teel, K. S. (1977). Performance appraisal: A survey of current practices, *Personnel Journal, 56*: 246.

Locke, E., and Latham, G. (1984). *Goal Setting*, Prentice-Hall, Englewood Cliffs, New Jersey.

Lubliner, M. J. (1981). Developing recruiting literature that pays off, *Personnel Administrator, 26*(2): 51.

MacDonald, C. R. (1982). *Performance-Based Supervisory Development*, Human Resource Development Press, Amherst, Massachusetts.

Mager, P., and Pipe, P. (1980). *Analyzing Performance Problems*, Wadsworth, Belmont, California.

Mangum, S. L. (1982). Recruitment and job search: The recruitment tactics of employers. *Personnel Administrator, 27*: 96.
Martel, P. (1982). A model of total compensation in a market comparability framework, *Public Personnel Management Journal, 11*: 148.
Maslow, A. (1943). A theory of human motivation, *Psychological Review, 50*: 370.
Matteson, M. T. (1982). The how, what and why of stress management, *Personnel Journal, 10*: 768.
McMillan, J. D., and Williams, V. C. (1982). The elements of effective salary administration programs, *Personnel Journal, 61*: 832.
Measuring training effectiveness (1983). A series of six articles in *Personnel Administrator, 28*(7).
Michaels, M. (1986). The new game of motivation. *American City and County, 101* (February): 36.
Mills, D. Q. (1982). *Labor-Management Relations*, 2nd Ed. McGraw-Hill, New York.
Mobley, W. (1982). *Employee Turnover: Causes, Consequences and Control*, Addison-Wesley, Reading, Massachuetts.
Moore, P. (1985). *Public Personnel Management: A Contingency Approach.* Heath, Lexington, Massachusetts.
Morse, M. (1984). Conflict and change in personnel management: An international challenge, *Public Personnel Management Journal 13*(1): 7.
Mosher, F. C. (1982). *Democracy and the Public Service*, 2nd Ed. Oxford University Press, New York.
Moskow, M. H. (1970). *Collective Bargaining in Public Employment*, Random House, New York.
Nadler, L. (1982). *Designing Training Programs: The Critical Events Model*, Addison-Wesley, Reading, Massachusetts.
Naisbitt, J. (1984), *Megatrends*, Warner Books, New York.
Nalbandian, J. (1981). Performance appraisal: If only people were not involved, *Public Administration Review, 41*: 392.
Naylor, P. (1984). Bringing home the lessons of Japanese management, *Personnel Management*, March: 34.
Neal, R. G. (1980). *Bargaining Tactics*, Richard Neal Associates, Falls Church, Virginia.
Neuse, S. (1982). A critical debate on the comparable worth perspective, *Review of Public Personnel Administration, 3*(1): 1.
Newland, C. A. (1984). Crucial issues for public personnel professionals, *Public Personnel Management Journal, 13*(1): 15.
Niehoff, M. S., and Romans, M. J. (1982). Needs assessment as step one toward enhancing productivity, *Personnel Administrator, 27*: 35.
Nielsen, R. P. (1983). Training programs: Putting them in sync with your company's strategic planning, *Personnel, 60*: 19.
Nigro, F. A. (1984). Public personnel administration: From Theodore Roosevelt to Ronald Reagan, *International Journal of Public Administration, 6*: 1–54.
O'Neill, J. (1985). An argument for the marketplace, *Society*, July–August: 55.
Patten, T. H. (1982). *A Manager's Guide to Performance Appraisal: Pride, Prejudice, and the Law of Equal Opportunity*, The Free Press, New York.
Paul, A. (1985). Motivating local government employees with incentives, *Public Management, 67* (November): 20.
Peters, T. J., and Waterman, R. (1982). *In Search of Excellence*, Harper & Row, New York.
Pulich, M. A. (1983). Train first-line supervisors to handle discipline. *Personnel Journal, 62*(12): 980.

Rehder, R. R. (1983). Education and training: Have the Japanese beaten us again? *Personnel Journal, 62*(1): 42.
Robey, D., and Altman, S. (1983). *Organization Development: Progress and Perspectives*, Macmillan, New York.
Rosenbloom, D. H. (1981). The sources of continuing conflict between the Constitution and public personnel management, *Review of Public Personnel Administration, 2*: 3.
Russ, C. F., Jr. (1982a). Manpower planning systems: Part I, *Personnel Journal, 61*: 40.
Russ, C. F., Jr. (1982b). Manpower planning systems: Part II, *Personnel Journal, 61*: 119.
Scarborough, N., and Zimmerer, T. W. (1982). Human resources forecasting: Why and where to begin, *Personnel Administrator, 27*: 55.
Schuster, F. (1985). *Human Resource Management*, Reston Publishing Company, Reston, Virginia.
Sibson, R. (1974). *Compensation*, AMACOM, New York.
Sloan, A. A., and Whitney, F. (1981). *Labor Relations*, 4th Ed. Prentice-Hall, Englewood Cliffs, New Jersey.
Smith, E. D. (1982a). Strategic planning and human resources: Part I, *Personnel Journal, 61*: 606.
Smith, E. D. (1982b). Strategic planning and human resources: Part II, *Personnel Journal, 61*: 680.
Spar, K. (1983). *Job Training Partnership Act: Background and Description*, Report No. 83-76 EPW, Congressional Research Service, U.S. Government Printing Office, Washington, D.C.
Stoops, R. (1981). Employer referral programs: Part I, *Personnel Journal, 60*(2): 98.
Thompson, J. D. (1967). *Organizations in Action*, McGraw-Hill, New York.
Ukeles, J. B. (1982). *Doing More with Less: Turning Public Management Around*, AMACOM, New York.
U.S. Department of Labor (1976). *All About OSHA*, U.S. Government Printing Office, Washington, D.C.
Wahba, M. A., and Bridwell, L. G. (1983). Maslow reconsidered: A review of research on the need hierarchy theory, *Motivation and Work Behavior*, 3rd Ed. (R. M. Steers and L. W. Porter, eds.), McGraw-Hill, New York.
Watson, C. E. (1980). *Management Development Through Training*, Addison-Wesley, Reading, Massachusetts.
Weiss, B. (1981). Hiring creative people: Three opportunities to make better decisions, *Personnel Administrator, 26*(4): 89.
Wexley, K. N., and Latham, G. P. (1981). *Developing and Training Human Resources in Organizations*, Scott, Foresman and Company, Glenview, Illinois.
Wilheim, S. J. (1980). Is on-campus recruiting on its way out? *Personnel Journal, 60*(4): 302.
Witkin, A. A. (1981). Commonly overlooked dimensions of employee selection, *Personnel Journal, 59*: 573.
Zenger, J. H., and Hargis, K. (1982). Assessing training results: It's time to take the plunge, *Training and Development Journal 36*: 15.

8

Supervisory Issues in Human Services Personnel Management

Norman Metzger Department of Health Care Management, The Mount Sinai Medical Center, New York, New York

The work environment is being dramatically changed, to a point where old supervisory styles are not only inappropriate but counterproductive. Franklin Roosevelt, in talking on the subject of introducing new ideas, said: "New ideas cannot be administered successfully by men with old ideas, for the first essential in doing a job well is to wish to see the job done at all." It is time to reject old ideas and old strictures about supervision, since they have, in the main, proved to be invalid. Workers are expressing different needs than those we perceived in earlier times. Old reward systems will not suffice for the remaining years in this century. More and more studies point out that workers are seeking jobs that provide personal satisfaction and growth.

There is a crisis of work in our country and in our industry. Agonizing over the purported loss of the "work ethic" cannot obscure the real nature of this crisis. It flows directly from our unfortunate adherence to old and tired ways of assigning work, and authoritarian leadership styles. The successful supervisor of the future will be a collaborative manager, rather than a control-centered one. Authoritarian leadership has failed and will continue to fail. Such leaders can manage to make gains temporarily, but in the long run, the will to work is eroded. The productive work force does not spring from personnel policies and rules, but is nurtured through a management style which has, as its hallmark, the respect of people and their contributions to the organizational success (Bassett and Metzger, 1986).

Supervisors are confronted with a new breed of employees, more assertive, more knowledgeable about their rights, more demanding. Such employees tend to accept less, trust less, and want more. To be a leader among this new breed, one must have a genuine interest in people as well as an interest in the work itself. The effective manager must gain the respect and admiration of subordinates and understand their motivations. The building of trust is the cornerstone of successful leadership. A relationship of trust springs from active commitment of employees. This can be done only when the leader listens to, respects, and rewards employees' contributions (Metzger, 1982).

I. PROFILE OF SUCCESSFUL SUPERVISORS

The critical difference between the successful manager and the failure is that the former is employee-centered. What do such leaders do, and why are they better than others?

1. They know the people who work for them. They are tuned in to employee needs, employee concerns, and employee moods.
2. They know how to speak to employees, and not down to them. They share much more information with their subordinates. They are open in their communication.
3. They are more often than not excellent listeners. They elicit and pay attention to and recognize suggestions. They patiently hear out complaints. They convert the results of their patient listening into action. They are willing to take their employees' cases forward (Munn and Metzger, 1981).
4. They are power sharers, not power hoarders. They realize that their power stems from the productivity of the group.
5. They consider their subordinates their equals; therefore, they treat them with dignity. Their primary concern is for the human aspect in management.
6. They are developers of subordinates, they are trainers, and they are mentors.

Leaders must have a sincere belief in basic values: human dignity, human fallibility, and human needs. They view workers not as instruments and factors of production, but as indispensable resources, capable of being motivated and subject to alienation; therefore, they have an understanding of the causes of alienation. Workers do not come to new jobs as alienated human beings. The work setting is the key dynamic in the alienation of workers. Ruch and Goodman (1983) tell us:

1. In the work setting, an alienated person believes his or her behavior cannot determine the outcome he or she seeks.
2. Alienated workers do not find fulfillment and meaning in their work.
3. Such alienation manifests itself in absenteeism, pilferage, sabotage, and a high degree of cynicism.

Need fulfillment or frustration results directly in either constructive or defensive behavior. Dissatisfied employees—those who become alienated—will not produce the excellence that is so desperately needed. When workers do not participate in decisions which directly affect the work that they do, they soon become resistant. An inordinate amount of time spent by modern-day managers is directed toward dealing with alienated and resistant workers. How do we change the supervisor's role?

II. THE MOTIVATION OF THE WORK FORCE

Some hospitals and health care institutions assert that people are their most important asset, while giving short shrift to the human factor when planning and preparing financial statements and long-range plans. The sad result of this sophistry in many cases is an impressive bottom line over the short run by managing employees as adversaries and neglecting the quality of delivery of service. Some three decades age, Rensis Likert and Daniel Katz (1953) embarked upon a research study to discover "the conditions making for a higher level of group functioning and a higher level of individual satisfaction of group members." These studies indicated that employee-centered supervisors, those that were cooperative and reasonable and exercised a democratic management style, were more successful than production-centered supervisors, who were more defensive and authoritarian in their styles. Leaders who are interested, supportive, and nonintrusive produced a higher level of motivation, a significantly more productive group, and a more satisfied work force. These researchers concluded that the key to a productivity-motivated work force is a management which enhances the workers' proprietorship in their jobs. The key to affecting employee attitudes or the success of the institution was the managerial behavior expressed in the work arena. They identified the specific supervisory practices that resulted in high productivity and the concomitant high level of job satisfaction. Such practices include:

1. An open approach; the understanding and appreciation or worker feelings; building leadership on the basis of motivational skills
2. A supervisory style which includes close personal interest in subordinates
3. An acute sensitivity to employee needs
4. A sharp awareness of the group process—specifically, pride and loyalty, and the role played by such pride and loyalty in productivity
5. A discriminating style of supervision, which is not overbearing—not too close, yet available
6. Encouraging participation and sharing in decision making by employees. Group consensus was the preferred mode of decision making.

The successful supervisors observed during the research conducted by Likert and Katz (1953) gave their subordinates a general outline of what was expected of them and how it should be accomplished. they did not closely supervise the work in progress. Employees solved problems as they encountered them. There was less insistence upon formal, rigid chains of command and lines of communication. These employee-centered supervisors viewed their subordinates as equals. Their employees turned out to be better motivated and, therefore, higher producers. This was a response to a specific style of leadership. The supervisor expressed interest in his or her employees, was supportive and nonintrusive. In effect, these studies indicated some three decades ago a style of leadership which has been slow to be accepted in our institutions, one that enhances the workers' proprietorship in their jobs.

Peters and Waterman (1982) point out the essential style of leadership which produces successful organizations. It is a style which has as its hallmark the concerns of people.

> The good news comes from treating people decently and asking them to shine. . . . A numbing focus on cost gives way to an enhancing focus on quality. . . . It is attention to employees, not work conditions per se, that has the dominant impact on productivity. . . . In short, we found the obvious, that the individual human being still counts. . . . Building up organizations that take note of his or her limits (e.g., information process ability) and strengths (e.g., the power flowing from commitment and enthusiasm) was their bread and butter.

Frederick Herzberg (1966) added to our knowledge of motivational factors, and, therefore, directed our attention to a style of management which produces long-term success. His research demonstrated that workers are more moved by the job itself than such maintenance factors as personnel policies, job security, and working conditions. He concluded that if you want to motivate workers, do not look to a newly painted office or work area, a water fountain, or a new employee benefit, but give the worker a larger shar of the job itself. The key, then, is to afford employees an opportunity for self-actualization and achievement. He stated that "the promise of money can move a man to work but cannot motivate him. Motivation means an innate desire to make an effort." Simply stated, he reiterated the old adage "Man cannot live by bread alone." He strongly believed that a motivated worker will do things on his or her own volition that far exceed what he or she could be made to do by offerings of food or money. It is self-motivation. This is nurtured by workers' participating in job decisions; by making suggestions which are appreciated; by playing a significant role in their own destinies in the work arena. Heeding Herzberg's findings, a supervisor will listen to and respect employees' suggestions. Such supervisors encourage participation. They solicit information, suggestions, and opinions. They keep their subordinates informed. Most importantly, they are sensitive to the need for appreciation. They dramatically and openly acknowledge positive contributions of their subordinates. They are interested in appropriate rewards. When one looks at the record of successful supervisors, it is clear that they are leaders in recommending promotions, merit increases, and transfers to more rewarding positions, and, more often than not, are spokespersons in the interest of their employees.

Blanchard and Johnson (1982) astutely observed that most managers seemed to be best at catching their employees doing something wrong, when they should be trying to catch them doing something right. They suggest that supervisors should help people reach their full potential by telling them up front what they are going to do and what they want the employees to do, and how well the employees are doing. Praising people immediately is a critical element in positive employee relations.

The Japanese model, and Japan's enormous success in the world markets, points to a management style which has much to offer us. The Japanese treat people as members o of their families, not as hired hands. Indeed, they see the institution in terms of the people who work for it. They emphasize management through shared values rather than through procedures and systems. They take a much longer term view of growth. Most important Japanese managers listen to the voice within their organization. Their management style is egalitarian; it engages fully the participation of employees in the running of the company. A key element is the development of trust. Ouchi (1984) defines trust as follows:

> Trust consists of an understanding that you and I share fundamentally compatible goals in the long run, that you and I desire a more effective working relationships together, and that neither desires to harm the other.

Ouchi states that a person of integrity treats secretaries and executives with equal respect, and approaches subordinates with the same understanding and values that characterizes his family relationships. A person with integrity can be counted upon to behave consistently, even as organizational conditions change. Such a style permits subordinates to regularly challenge, and occasionally even ridicule, superiors.

Daniel Yankelowicz (1981) pointed out a disturbing result of a survey that an overwhelming eighty-four percent of all Americans feel a certain resentment, and feel that those who work harder and live by the rules end up getting the short end of the stick. This is a direct result of work-induced alienation. Former Federal Reserve chairman

Arthur M. Burns commented on the decline in productivity in our country. He attributed this to a lessened sense of industriousness on the part of workers. What really has happened is a dramatic shift in the meaning and value of work. Our society is constantly changing.

In her book *Pathfinders*, Gail Sheehy (1981) made an astute comment:

> The inability of many Americans to find purpose in their work has helped to create the shift from the work ethic to a self-fulfillment ethic. Most people no longer want to work hard. They demand more leisure hours in which to seek some other purpose or pleasure under the catchall contemporary concept of "self-improvement."

It is true that as Hegel pointed out, we exist only when we are acknowledged, and our present age is characterized by the clamor for acknowledgment reflects an unfulfilled need. As Maslow (1970) has taught us, such unfulfilled needs rise to the top of the hierarchy of needs.

Bruno Bettelheim (1977), in his book *On the Uses of Enchantment*, stated it well:

> If we hope to live not just from moment to moment but in the true consciousness of our existence, then our greatest need and most difficult achievement is to find meaning in our lives.

It is difficult to find meaning in our lives when, indeed, much of our lives is spent in the work arena. If that arena is closed, severely controlled, and unresponsive, workers react counterproductively. Indifference and frustration resulting from such disconnection with control over their lives are basically the result of their being excluded from the planning function and being overlooked in the communication network. Most industrial behaviorists have found that there is a strong desire on the part of employees to be involved in their jobs. Such involvement includes the receipt of up-to-date information on deliberations and decisions flowing from the top. It also requires listening to employees.

Odiorne (1984) referred to the narcissistic character of Americans:

> People today are committed to finding a life-style and then a job to support it, rather than the reverse, which was characteristic of a Depression-raised generation before them. This will call for new participative styles of leadership, more listening, and considerable democracy in the workplace if these people are to be productive and creative.

III. LISTENING TO EMPLOYEES

The average supervisor, when asked to describe the process of communication, will paint a picture of a downward flow of formal communications: memos, orders, and meetings. The failure to include listening is a critical one. When one talkes about a failure to communicate, more often than not, it is a failure to listen. The better listeners supervisors are, the better listeners they will inspire. Half of the process of communication is listening. Communication, in effect, is a joint effort; there is a sender and there is a receiver; and the roles must be constantly reversed. Indeed, setting up an atmosphere where employees are encouraged to talk—to suggest, to criticize, to express feelings—is the key to more productive supervisor-subordinate relationships.

The establishment of a "feedback loop" is an essential part of communications. Feedback is a method of establishing understanding. It is a mirror, not a directive. In order to have reliable and valid feedback, subordinates must believe that they can "tell it like it is." You must make sure that you are on target. What you meant to say is not always what you actually said or what the other person heard. It is through the feedback loop that you establish whether you have hit the bull's-eye (Munn and Metzger, 1981).

Nichols (1960) directs our attention to analyzing our listening habits by offering a checklist:

1. Science says you think four times faster than the person usually talks to you. Do you use this excess time to turn your thoughts elsewhere while you are keeping general track of the conversation?
2. Do you listen primarily for facts, rather than ideas, when someone is speaking?
3. Do certain words, phrases, or ideas so prejudice you against the speaker that you cannot listen objectively to what is being said?
4. When you are puzzled or annoyed by what someone says, do you try to get the question straightened out immediately—either in your own mind or by interrupting the speaker?
5. If you feel that it would take too much time and effort to understand something, do you go out of your way to avoid hearing about it?
6. Do you deliberately turn your thoughts to other subjects when you believe the speaker will have nothing particularly interesting to say?
7. Can you tell by a person's appearance and delivery that he won't have anything worthwhile to say?
8. When someone is talking to you, do you try to make him think you are paying attention when you're not?
9. When you are listening to someone, are you easily distracted by outside sights and sounds?
10. If you want to remember what someone is saying, do you think it is a good idea to write it down as he goes along?

This is a soul-searching analysis of poor listening habits. The more "no" answers the better; every "yes" answer is an indication of a poor listening habit.

Some of the problems we face in the critical area of the communication process—listening—follow. Most of us talk too much. We are explaining out position without focusing on understanding, and without eliciting from the listener his or her position. We fail to frame questions properly, often taking the easy way out of structuring questions to get the answers we want to hear. We pay too little attention to the surroundings, the environment, the conditions for optimum communication. It is important to schedule discussions with subordinates in a timely manner, and in an appropriately private environment.

Cancelliere suggests that there are critical ways in which most people like to be listened to:

1. Without interruption
2. Without the listener's jumping to conclusions
3. Without evaluation
4. By a person who is attentive while the speaker is talking
5. With patience
6. By being looked at while speaking
7. By a person who asks questions to clarify meanings

8. Without being rushed, and without having sentences finished for them
9. By a person who, with the things that he says or by body movements, gives a strong indication that he is "tracking with" the speaker
10. By a person whose attitude conveys that what is being said is important

In our modern era of overspecialization, we no longer do the jobs ourselves; we as supervisors must deal through others. To the extent that we develop and refine the art of communicating, we will be effective supervisors. In order to do that, we need to develop our skills in listening, talking, and motivating. Before attempting to communicate with your employees, you should ask yourself six questions:

1. Do I assume that if an idea is clear to me, it will be clear to the receiver?
2. Am I endeavoring to make it comfortable for my subordinates and peers to tell me what is really on their minds? Or is the opposite true: Am I attempting to elicit only what I would like to hear?
3. Am I interested in understanding what the other person has told me? Or am I quick to frame my response?
4. Am I paying attention to my subordinates' and peers' feelings, fully cognizant that their feelings, which may well be different from mine, affect their communication?
5. Do I attempt to get into the castle of the other person's skin—do I try to listen from the sender's point of view before evaluating the message from my own point of view?
6. Do I fully appreciate the importance of feedback, since communication, even at its best, is an imperfect process?

IV. THE KEYS TO RETENTION

When a supervisor bemoans the high rate of turnover in his or her department, this person may well be looking at only one side of the coin, since retention is a critical part of the equation. What is needed is a bifocal lens, which gives the supervisor a view of why people leave the institution, and why others stay. The first impressionable days on a new job can make a critical difference between a productive, efficient employee and one who becomes alienated and leaves. First impressions are indelible. Early on, employees are impressed or depressed by whether the institution cares about them. This is clearly indicated in how they are treated, received, and respected in the initial interviewing stage, in the processing stage, and when they arrive as new employees into their departments. It should be clear that employees approach new jobs with some apprehension, with many predetermined attitudes, and with that difficult-to-deal-with aura of not belonging. To improve the retention rate—which must be recognized as the key to controlling turnover—your institution must subscribe to four general objectives of an induction and orientation program:

1. The reinforcement of employees' confidence in their ability to cope with new work assignments is primary. It is essential that you make the new employee feel worthy, appreciated, and needed.
2. An important phase of absorbing new employees into the mainstream is communication of complete and detailed conditions of employment. No surprises should be unfolded. The interview is not the only place to share such information. An employee who knows what is expected of him or her, and what part the employee plays in fulfilling to goals of the institution, is likely to be more efficient and, indeed, more comfortable and less likely to leave.

3. Rules and regulations often are negative motivators, but concealing such information is a greater risk. If you wish to obtain the cooperation of an employee, he or she must know at the onset of employment what the behavior expectations are in your institution.
4. Recognizing that pride in one's institution can nurture pride in one's self, it is essential to develop, as rapidly as possible in the mind of a new employee, a realization of the total objectives of the institution, its goals, and how that new employee relates to the ultimate success of the hospital's meeting its burden. It is not enough to say that employees are our most important asset. That has to be expressed in day-to-day treatment (Metzger, 1982).

Induction does not start the day the employee reports to work, but begins during the hiring process. One leading educator on child development responded to a mother who asked him "When should I begin teaching my six-month-old son the way to behave?" by saying "Madame, you are already six months too late." You start winning allegiance and building positive motivational conditions when the employee is an applicant. It is never too early to build trust and commitment. When you are asked to interview a new candidate, there are certain basic rules of behavior: Make the time; don't rush; don't give the impression that the process is a necessary evil; remember that the prospective employee is naturally nervous; find the right place to conduct the interview—not one where you are constantly interrupted; and, finally, remember that an interview is a two-way street—you talk, you listen, you obtain information, you give information.

There are four universal tenets of the induction process, none of which can be compromised or neglected:

1. A new member of a group must go through an extensive process of adjustment—which includes a learning process; he or she must adapt old habits to the new group.
2. To facilitate this absorption into the new group, facts relating directly to the job and expectations that you have must be communicated.
3. Although staff induction is critical to the process, in the final analysis, the first-line supervisor has the burden of responsibility.
4. Induction does not end in the first week or after the first month of employment. It is a long process, and is the link between good selection and good job performance.

Dubin (1958) identifies basic problems inherent in the orientation and induction process:

> Orientation and indoctrination of a new member are essentially processes of acculturation. He has to learn ways of behaving, a set of standards and expectations, and a point of view and outlook largely foreign to him in their specific details, although he may be generally familiar with them in their broad outline. . . . The adjustment process first involves becoming familiar with the language and its significant symbols that are used in the organization. . . . Accordingly, at the initial stage of orientation and indoctrination, a great deal of attention is paid both by the new member and by those who are teaching him to learn a vocabulary and a set of symbols that communicate significantly. In order to maximize understanding of what goes on, the new recruit has to become fairly familiar with the language of the organization.

It is the first-line supervisor's responsibility to familiarize the new employee with the language of the organization. The quicker the employee understands what the organization is all about, the sooner he or she will become accustomed to the way things are done in the new job and will become a productive member of the group. Turnover is a costly penalty. Much of it occurs with new employees. The basic challenge to supervisors is to make such employees feel at home in an alien land. This requires gaining acceptance of the work group for the new employee. It is the supervisor's primary duty to assist new employees and members of the department to become acquainted with each other and to develop an accommodation among each other.

The total objectives of the hospital or the health care facility, and the role that the new employee plays in relation to the successful attainment of these goals, must be shared at the onset; sharing of goals does not cease with the culmination of the probationary period. The cost of sound and formal induction and orientation is infinitesimal when compared to the cost of turnover and inefficiency. If there is one critical responsibility that the supervisor has in this process, it is to set up an atmosphere of receptivity. The new employee must know that he or she is wanted and needed. Unless the employee is integrated into the working force promptly and successfully, the full application of his or her productive ability can be delayed and, indeed, frustrated. The key, then, is to recognize that workers are individuals, with different personalities, with fear of new and unfamiliar situations, with a desire to succeed, and with fear of criticism. In addition, the great desire to belong makes this initial process of joining a new group even more emotionally trying. A new employee who knows what he or she is doing, why he or she is doing it, and why his or her task is an important part of the organization's total effort is much more likely to be efficient and loyal than an equally well-qualified worker who does not possess that knowledge. It is during the induction and orientation process that one addresses this task.

V. BURNOUT: HOW TO AVOID IT

Carl Rogers (1951) outlines certain patterns of behavior that he found consistently in people of exceptional emotional maturity. A discussion of burnout, a word often used to describe workers who no longer function properly and are alienated, should include a positive look at those who do more than survive, who grow. Rogers said that people of exceptional emotional maturity almost always manifest:

1. Willingness to accept experiences for what they are
2. Trust and confidence in their own ability and judgment
3. Greater reliance on self than on society or friends
4. Willingness to grow as a person

The real key to withstanding the pressures which produce burnout is not outside, but inside, oneself. Employees who succeed in maintaining high levels of dedication and productivity learn to have trust and confidence in their own ability and judgment. Most find strategies for coming to terms with adversity. The key is to translate their negative experiences into positive guidelines for their survival and their continuous growth. Coping with adversity really reveals an individual's true self. Maslow (1970) found the following characteristics of mentally healthy or self-actualized persons, those who never burn out:

1. They can accept the way things really are. Such people quit dwelling on what ought to be or what should be and start functioning in the arena of what is. They can

accept themselves no matter what they look like and what people think of them. They realize how futile it is to forever bemoan their weaknesses, and learn to accent their strong points. They are willing to take other people just as they come. They have developed strategies to deal with people the way they are, instead of refusing to have anything to do with them until they are the way they ought to be. They are action people and know they must start a project where the problem is.

2. They are not afraid to get close to others. Their inner feeling of security and happiness with themselves permits them to get closer to people. They are not threatened by others. These people are open and patient.

3. They are efficient judges of situations. They have an unusual ability to detect the spurious, the fake, and the dishonest in personality and, in general, to judge people correctly and efficiently (Moustikas, 1956). They get more done, because they spend less time spinning their wheels or relying on inappropriate easy answers. When a problem arises, they can solve it more efficiently, because they can make their decisions in terms of how things really are, rather than on how they wish they were.

4. They are creative and appreciative. For such people, even the casual workaday moment-to-moment business of living can be thrilling, exciting, and ecstatic (Peter and Hull, 1969).

5. They march to a different drummer. Having a good feeling about oneself generates confidence. Such people make their own judgments. They are more autonomous and independent in thought and action.

6. They are willing to learn from anyone. They are not threatened by the prospect of appearing dull or uninformed. They are more interested in understanding or getting the information than in maintaining any reputation of knowledgeableness.

These mentally healthy or self-actualized persons rarely burn out. The pattern of survival as contrasted to burnout deals with the possibility of change. This requires a greater reliance on self. No one can take away a person's pride unless that person gives it away. No one can take away a person's dignity unless that person grovels. Too much of the average supervisor's time is spent in seeking the approval of others. In seeking such acknowledgment, the supervisor seems unsure that he or she exists. Too often, such pursuits for acknowledgment isolate supervisors from the work force. Successful supervisors spend less time in seeking acknowledgment and more time in building trust. McMurray (1965) stated that self-relying, trusting, and decisive supervisors produce efficient subordinates. In the daily competition for employees' allegiance and loyalty, the strongest and most aggressive, decisive representatives will nearly always win out. Such supervisors rarely produce burned out employees. To succeed, the competent supervisor cares both about the goals and well-being of the institution, and about the needs and frustrations of his or her employees. Such leaders are ever sensitive to the signs of burnout and to its causes. They treat their subordinates as adults; they are the ultimate "sharers"; decision-making is a cooperative effort with them, which includes bringing their subordinates into the process; they not only are unafraid of diversity and "boat-rockers," but encourage such behavior; they reach out as often as possible to their employees; they are less rigid and authoritarian in their approach than those who fail (Metzger, 1986).

Any discussion of burnout must include a review of worker alienation. It is alienation, rather than burnout, that is a primary problem for supervisors today. Such alienation manifests itself in low productivity, dissatisfaction, inattention to quality, absenteeism, and many disciplinary problems. Ruch and Goodman (1983) describe the alienated employee as one who believes his or her behavior cannot determine the outcome he or she seeks. It is a corrosive state of mind that eats away at people over a long period of time, often several years. Such employees—often described as burned out—do not find fulfillment or meaning in their work. They identify four components of fulfilling and meaningful work experiences (McMurray, 1965):

1. *Knowledge.* The successful company is one that has a knowledgeable work force. Work alienation and lack of work knowledge go hand in hand. Knowledge, then, is the answer to the question "What's going on?"
2. *Care.* "Caring about what I do" was named as a key reason for feeling good about coming to work this morning.
3. *Respect.* These researchers state that in the context of work alienation, there is only one legitimate source of respect: one's humanity. They identify respect and care as the single most neglected aspect of leadership.
4. *Responsibility.* In the final analysis, it does not particularly matter what one is accountable for, so long as one has a feeling of being able to be accountable.

VI. DISCIPLINE: A POSITIVE APPROACH

The essence of a well-motivated, productive work force is self-discipline. The odious task delegated to supervisors is to mete out discipline to employees for breaches of policies, rules, and accepted behavioral patterns. Cause and effect are rarely considered. Too little attention is paid to the alienation which causes such problems. The workplace has been depicted as a management jungle. The new breed of employees is far more cynical than those we have dealt with in the past, far more educated, and, most importantly, far more concerned with the quality of life that work offers. To generalize about behavior in the work arena may lead us down a path of rigid rule making, inflexible punishments for deviators, and too little attention to the individuality now present among employees. Punishment may well be the least effective approach toward obtaining adherence to institutional standards of behavior. A growing cadre of managers is now directing its attention to correcting unacceptable employee behavior, rather than punishing it.

The goal of successful supervision is to build a trusting environment, which produces genuine agreement between supervisors and subordinates on the need to do the "right" thing. This requires obtaining cooperation of the subordinates. Cooperation is built upon consensus. Rules which make no sense to those who are ruled will be resisted. Rules unevenly applied will be scorned. The double standard is the bane of corrective disciplining. Let us, then, review the cornerstones of corrective disciplining:

1. Employees often act as individuals. They come to the workplace with diversity not amenable to generalized treatment. You must get to know your employees as individuals. This may well provide you with the answer to why a specific employee acted improperly.
2. Although it is impossible to universalize discipline, remember that when you discipline an individual, everyone else is looking at you. The primary criticism from employees regarding the disciplinary procedure is unevenness. When you discipline one employee, you are disciplining all. There may be nuances or special circumstances which you must consider, since not every case is the same. But beware the comparisons: A health care institution can ill defend the double and triple standards operative

between the medical staff, the administrative staff, and the "others." Preferential treatment can destroy the very essence of the disciplinary process.

3. Subjective disciplining is a destructive force. The first responsibility you have in deciding upon the necessity for discipline is to investigate, thoroughly and painstakingly, the facts. You can be engulfed and dragged under by your biases. Be alert to the necessity of ascertaining whether the behavior was temporary and transitory, rather than repetitious and permanent.

Redecker (1983) points to a critical area of the disciplinary process, realistic expectations of employees and responsibilities of management in the process:

1. Employees have a right to know what is expected of them and made aware of the consequences of not fulfilling those expectations. No surprises, please. No retroactive implementation of rules. Communicate fully and obtain understanding of the rules of behavior in your institution. Where arbitrators have been involved in the disciplinary process, a critical cornerstone to establishing "just cause" criteria to sustain management's action is whether the institution gave the employee forewarning or foreknowledge of the possible or probable disciplinary consequences of the employee's conduct. Notice is essential, understanding even more so.

2. The employee has a right to consistent and predictable employer responses to violations of rules. Here, we go back once again to single standards of acceptable behavior within the institution. Consistency is an essential ingredient of successful disciplinary procedures. One of the pervasive problems in meting out discipline is the uncertainty that many employees feel about management's application of such discipline. If there is a doubt that disciplinary action will actually take place, because of prior inaction on the part of management for similar offenses, there is clear encouragement for employees to continue unacceptable behavior. The deterrent value increases as the predictability increases.

3. The employee has a right to fair discipline based on facts. What may appear to be the facts often is not what actually happened. It is a cardinal principle in the application of fair and consistent discpline that supervisors painstakingly and unbiasedly search out the facts. Fact-finding methods must be established that are dependable and free from personal prejudices.

4. The employee has the right to question the facts and to present a defense. Due process is an inherent virtue of our society, and is no less essential in the workplace. The right to be heard is an inalienable one. The right to explain is a necessary one. If discipline is to be fairly applied, and perceived as such, employees must have the opportunity to defend themselves against charges which may lead to disciplinary action.

5. The employee has the right to appeal the disciplinary decision. Since most discipline is meted out by first-line supervisors—it is the first-line supervisor who sees the employee's behavior on a day-to-day basis—it is essential that an appeal from the decision of the first-line supervisor be available to the employee. We shall discuss this further when we deal with the grievance procedure.

6. The employee has a right to progressive discipline. It is an unquestionable management right to discipline up to and including discharge if there are sufficient and appropriate reasons. Management action is usually supported if progressive discipline includes first a verbal reprimand and a full explanation of what is necessary to remedy the situation, followed by a written reprimand for a second infraction and a clear warning of the future penalty that may be imposed. A final warning and suspension may follow and,

subsequently, the ultimate penalty of discharge. Of course, there are serious offenses which contract this procedure.

7. The employee has a right to be considered as an individual. It is essential that you know your employees. Many of the disciplinary problems which plague management spring from worker alienation. Many have individual causes, and rarely are two cases the same. If you wish to fairly apply discipline, then you must be interested in cause and effect, and in individual characteristics of employees. The essential ingredient is showing respect for people's humanness: showing appreciation for individual circumstnaces; carefully reviewing and evaluating the employee's prior records and performance.

The disciplinary process, to be successful, must be built upon employee understanding and acceptance of the need for rules and regulations. If such rules and regulations are ridiculous or perceived to be so by employees, there is little chance for adherence. Built upon this understanding for the need is a clear picture of uniform, consistent, and humane application of punishment. To discipline in the form of punishment may well be necessary, but to correct improper employee action is at the heart of a successful disciplinary process. If a disciplinary process is to work, then attention must be directed toward encouraging self-discipline (Metzger and Ferentino, 1983). This is not bought; this is not mandated. Rather, it is developed from an environment where employees trust their supervisors, and where supervisors believe in the importance of the contributions of their employees.

VII. THE GRIEVANCE PROCEDURE

The single most important interpersonal relationship in a health care institution is between the employee and the first-line supervisor. The organization reflects its value system in the general attitude of supervisors toward employee grievance. Whether handling employee grievances or gripes falls under the general rubric of a collective bargaining agreement or personnel policies, it presents to the supervisor and, in the final analysis, to the institution, a major opportunity to establish an atmosphere of firmness and fairness and to win employee respect and confidence. Grievances exist whether or not there is a formal mechanism for dealing with them. Consistency and fairness in the application of the grievance procedure are critical guideposts along the road to a productive and committed work force.

Earlier studies of the process, which continue to be valid, point out that a more harmonious union-management relationship can be expected when grievances are resolved in the early stages of the grievance procedure (Turner and Robinson, 1982). Still another study reached the following conclusions:

1. Top management depends significantly on first-line supervisors to resolve grievance-related issues.
2. First-line supervisors do not share this view, and, consequently, they probably do not exert adequate effort in the area of grievance administration.
3. By not perceiving their importance in the grievance procedure, supervisors do not realize that their role is fundamental in preventing minor grievances from becoming major disputes.
4. If the resolution of grievances in the early stages of the procedure is fundamental to harmonious labor/management relationships, the first-line supervisor may constitute the key to preserving or improving this relationship (Walker and Robinson, 1977).

These findings are critical to an appreciation of the role of the first-line supervisor in the adjudication of grievances. Contrary to the common belief, first-line supervisors are the most important people in the grievance procedure, as far as management is concerned. Handling grievances may well be one of their most important responsibilities. In any discussion of the supervisor's responsibility in the grievance procedure, we must start off with the appreciation of preventive action. Although there is no definitive mtho method for eliminating grievances, there are many basic guidelines which, if followed, minimize the number, frequency, and extent of grievances:

1. Be alert to the common causes of irritation in your department, and try to eliminate or alleviate minor irritations.
2. Be familiar with institutional policies, procedures, and practices, and do not knowingly violate them. In addition, explain all changes or deviations from the policy, procedures, or established practice.
3. If your employees are unionized, be familiar with the union contract.
4. If you make promises, keep them; but make no commitments that cannot be met.
5. Present all orders and instructions so that they can be understood by your employees. Do not talk down to them nor over their heads, keeping in mind that you are responsible for discussing why, when, how, and what of the matter.
6. Be impartial in making assignments and scheduling work. Favoritism breeds distress and frustration, which, in turn, breed grievances.
7. Let your employees know whether they are doing their jobs satisfactorily. If they are not measuring up to standards—which you have discussed with them in advance—not only let them know, but attempt to find out why and provide direction and instruction for their improvement (Metzger, 1986).

Supervisors who establish a healthy relationship with their employees can resolve many grievances before they reach the formal grievance stage; this, in turn, increases productivity. A little attention at the beginning goes further than a great deal of harried, stressful, and pressured attention at the end. Supervisors are learning that they can satisfactorily resolve most complaints before they become formal grievances. Yet, there are formal grievances which will be presented and must be adjudicated.

The supervisor usually is the first-step management representative in the grievance procedure. There are some rules which are universal in handling management's responsibilities in the grievance procedure:

1. Promptness is essential. A delayed consideration of a grievance often enlarges the problem and obfuscates the essential facts.
2. Employees should be encouraged to adjudicate disputes through the formal grievance procedure. Therefore, such procedures should be easy to utilize, and no stigma should be attached to their use.
3. Investigation of the material facts is at the heart of grievance adjudication. This requires discussing and analyzing all of the evidence presented.
4. To be effective, a grievance procedure must have avenues of appeal: The decision of the first-line supervisor can be appealed to a higher level. In the final analysis, in order to obtain employee commitment to the process, the last step should be voluntary arbitration by a disinterested party (Metzger and Ferentino, 1983).

The supervisor, in addition to the need to minimize grievances, has four major responsibilities in the process:

1. Hearing the complaint
2. Getting the facts
3. Making the decision
4. Communicating and decision

The following checklist includes the actions necessary to handle this responsibility properly:

1. Energetic pursuit of all the facts
2. Avoiding the temptation to form preconceived ideas about the validity of the grievance
3. The desire to protect the rights of both the institution and the employee in the disposition of the grievance
4. In such cases where management is wrong—the willingness to admit it

Beyond the technical application of the grievance procedure is a management ethos which cares about employees. In such an environment, grievances may not be completely eradicated, but employees will appreciate the inherent fairness of management practices, thereby reducing what is commonly present in the application of the grievance procedure—hostility and bitterness. The inherent adversarial nature of grievance adjudication can be softened by its fair and consistent application.

VIII. OVERCOMING RESISTANCE TO CHANGE

Nowhere is there a greater need to implement change than in the health care industry. There is constant activity in reviewing, planning, and implementing changes in the organizational structure, personnel policies and procedures, equipment, technologies, and, indeed, the very heart of delivering health care.

Change more often than not produces suspicions and resistance. To many it implies a move from familiar ways—mastered over long periods of time—to an unknown and threatening environment. In order to deal effectively with resistance to change, the supervisor must understand its causes.

There are many inappropriate explanations for resistance based upon the overt action of employees, but in the main, it is behavior intended to protect the employee from the effects of a real or imagined threat to the security of the individual or of the group. It is manifested when the following occur:

1. When a critical change is announced as a fait accompli
2. When the change and its effects are not clearly communicated and, more importantly, not understood by those affected
3. When employees have not been consulted in advance regarding the necessity for the change and have not been included in discussions of alternatives to nonproductive procedures or methods (probably the single most prevalent reason for resistance to change)
4. When the information which is disseminated about the change is distorted or unbelievable
5. When the change is based upon personal grounds, rather than requirements of the group or the institution
6. When excessive work pressures develop from the change, especially where employees perceive that there is an unfair distribution of the work load and a speed-up

7. When there is poor planning in advance of the change; when there is a failure to consider in detail exactly how the change will be brought about
8. When employees do not understand why the change is needed and what was wrong with the old ways of doing things
9. When the change to be instituted ignores established group norms or customs

Change requires a gradual weaning from the old habits and an alteration of attitudes. Facts alone will not suffice; experience is necessary and often frustrating. Almost every attempt to introduce change sets up a countervailing force, familiarly termed resistance to change, initiated by the employee whose job security seems to be threatened. Such employees will inundate the supervisor with anxious queries. The announcement of the change may be accompanied by wild rumors of impending disaster; grievances and slowdowns, refusal to meet new goals, and subtle group behavior to discredit the new system are other manifestations of this resistance.

Resistance to change may also be resentment of or anxiety over the way the change has been introduced, or the lack of consideration of employee feelings. Trying to convince someone of the advantages of the new method often sounds like criticism of the old—which the employee likes because it is familiar, or even because he or she sponsored it originally. More than one employee has flatly rejected a new procedure by saying, either in anger or in hurt, that there is nothing wrong with the performance of his or her department.

To effectively implement change, a supervisor should consider the use of feedback, permit the release of feelings and the blowing off of steam to bring out resistance, and get at its cause. The need to develop trust is never more essential than during the implementation of change. Supervisors can build a trusting work climate by helping those affected by the change to understand the need for it, and by allowing them to participate in decisions on how to implement the change and handle problems. This can best be done within the following framework:

1. Set up a nonadversarial environment by avoiding arguments. Understand that the other person is concerned about real or perceived problems and, therefore, look beyond the emotions being exhibited. Criticism should be minimized. The key to gaining agreement is to move from small points of consensus to overall and final agreement on the totality of the change.
2. Do not hesitate to admit when you are wrong. Admitting your mistakes when they are made will gain you immeasurable respect from your subordinates.
3. Establish a receptive frame of mind. This can be accomplished by explaining why the change has to be implemented and how it will benefit all. Receptivity seldom comes by fiat—you cannot legislate a receptive frame of mind. The supervisor needs to develop conditions that will encourage all subordinates to listen and be objective about the change.
4. Dispel the mystery surrounding the change by dramatizing ideas or suggestions. It is most helpful to use visual aids, including diagrams, charts, and films. You can never explain enough.
5. Set a fair challenge. Research has indicated that employees perform better and are more cooperative when they are presented with a challenging goal.
6. Appreciation and praise are essential ingredients in winning employees' trust. The need for appreciation stands at the top of the pyramid of employee wants. In the complicated and multitiered structure of most health care facilities, employees at the

bottom rung often feel like invisible people. Praise should not be bestowed grudgingly. The successful supervisor is able to find something to commend in even the least-able person.

When you convey to your subordinates that you value their ideas, that you will consider their suggestions objectively, and that they can be free to voice their concerns, you will be able to deal with employee resistance to change and maximize cooperation in implementing it.

IX. CONCLUSION

The role of the supervisor is one of the most stressful in health care management. Being in the middle—representing the employees to management and management to employees—requires much more than can be learned in classrooms and through books. Those who succeed develop positive relationships with their subordinates and their peers. Those who succeed have moved from an authority-obedience style of supervision to a participatory-commitment style. They are more willing to share power. They are not threatened by such sharing. Respect for employees' dignity is pervasive in interpersonal relationships. There is a high level of concern and attention to employee problems. In the final analysis, there is a belief in basic values: human dignity, human fallibility, and human needs.

REFERENCES

Bassett, L., and Metzger, N. (1986). *Achieving Excellence: A Prescription for Health Care Managers*, Aspen Systems Corporation, Rockville, Maryland.

Beatty, R. W., and Schneider, C. E. (1977). *Personnel Administration: An Experimental Skill-Building Approach*, Addison-Wesley, Boston.

Bettelheim, B. (1977). *On the Uses of Enchantment*, Random House, New York.

Blanchard, K., and Johnson, S. (1982). *The One Minute Manager*, William Morrow & Company, New York.

Cancelliere, Dr. (president of Listening Dynamics, New York). Personal communication.

Cherrington, D. J. (1980). *The Work Ethic*, American Management Association, New York.

Cribbin, J. J. (1972). *Effective Managerial Leadership*, AMACOM, New York.

Cribbin, J. J. (1981). *Strategies for Organizational Effectiveness*, AMACOM, New York.

Dubin, R. (1958). *The World of Work*, Prentice-Hall, Englewood, New Jersey.

Fulmer, R. M. (1983). *The New Management*, third edition, Macmillan, New York.

Herzberg, F. (1966). *Work and the Nature of Man*, World Publishing Company, New York.

Herzberg, F., Mausner, and Snydam.(1959). *The Motivation to Work,* second edition, John Wiley & Sons, New York.

Likert, R. (1953). Motivation: The core of management, *Personnel Series, 155*: 3 and 29.

Macoby, M. (1981). *The Leader: A New Face for American Management*, Ballantine Books, New York.

Maslow, A. H. (1970). *Motivation and Personality*, second edition, Harper and Brothers, New York, chaps. 3-7, passim.

McMurray, R. (1965). Clear communications for chief executives, *Harvard Business Review*, March/April: 58-62, 131.

Merrihue, W. (1960). *Managing by Communication*, McGraw-Hill, New York.

Metzger, N. (1979). *Personnel Administration in the Health Services Industry*, second edition, S. P. Medical and Scientific Books, New York.
Metzger, N. (1982). *The Health Care Supervisor's Handbook*, second edition, Aspen Systems Corporation, Rockville, Maryland.
Metzger, N. (1986). Beyond survival to excellence, *Health Care Supervisor, 4*: 4.
Metzger, N., and Ferentino, J. (1983). *The Arbitration and Grievance Process*, Aspen Systems Corporation, Rockville, Maryland.
Miner, J. B. (1969). *Personnel and Industrial Relations: A Managerial Approach*, Macmillan, New York.
Moustikas, C. E. (1956). Self-actualizing people: The study of psychological health, *The Self: Exclamations and Personal Growth*, Harper & Row, New York.
Munn, H. E., and Metzger, N. (1981). *Communications in Health Care: A Supervisor's Handbook*, Aspen Systems Corporation, Rockville, Maryland.
Nichols, R. (1960). Quoted in Merrihue, W. (1960). *Managing by Communication*, McGraw-Hill, New York, pp. 21–22.
Odiorne, G. S. (1984). Human resources strategies for the 90's, *Personnel*, November/December: 17.
Ouchi, W. (1984). Going from A to Z: Thirteen steps to a theory Z organization, *Management Review*, May: 9.
Peter, L., and Hull, R. (1969). *The Peter Principle: Why Things Go Wrong*, William Morrow & Company, New York.
Peters, T. J., and Waterman, R. H. Jr. (1982). *In Search of Excellence*, Harper & Row, New York.
Redeker, J. R. (1983). *Discipline: Policies and Procedures*, Bureau of National Affairs, Washington, D.C.
Rogers, C. R. (1951). *Client-Centered Therapy*, Houghton Mifflin Company, Boston.
Rowland, K. M., and Ferris, G. R. (1982). *Personnel Management*, Allyn and Bacon, Boston.
Ruch, R., and Goodman, R. (1983). *Image at the Top*, Free Press, New York.
Shaiken, H. (1984). *Work Transformed*, Holt, Rinehart and Winston, New York.
Sheehy, G. (1981). *Pathfinders*, William Morrow and Company, New York.
Shorris, E. (1981). *The Oppressed Middle*, Anchor Press, New York.
Simmons, J., and Mares, W. (1983). *Working Together*, Alfred Knopf, New York.
Turner, J. T., and Robinson, J. W. (1972). A pilot study of the validity of grievance settlement rates as a predictor of union/management relationship, *Journal of Industrial Relations*, September: 314.
Walker, R. L., and Robinson, J. W. (1977). The first-line supervisor's role in the grievance procedure, *Arbitration Journal*, December: 279.
White, W. F. (1983). *Worker Participation and Ownership*, ILR Press, Ithaca, New York.
Yankelowicz, D. (1981). *New Rules*, Random House, New York.

9

Employee Organizations in Human Services Administration

Paul E. Fitzgerald, Jr.* Health Sciences Administration, University of Arkansas at Little Rock, Little Rock, Arkansas

I. INTRODUCTION

The growth, development, and future of employee organizations (unions) in the health care industry and in human service organizations are discussed in this chapter. It is appropriate that these topics are discussed because of the volume of union activity in these industries and also because of the substantial growth of the service and health care sectors within our economy.

The U.S. economy has undergone a pronounced shift from being dependent on heavy industry to a "high-tech" and service orientation. Health care and human services comprise a substantial portion of the service sector. In fact, the health care industry is now responsible for over ten percent of the U.S. annual gross national product and continues to grow and diversify at a rate exceeding that of most other industries. Service industries are an important component of the economy and, thus, become important to unions and their existence.

Prior to 1975, fewer than five percent of the workers in the health care industry were unionized; now this figure approaches twenty percent. The rise in unionism for human service organizations began during the early 1960s and also grew at a rapid pace. Collective bargaining is a high-priority topic for managers in health care and other service industries because these industries are labor-intensive, with sixty to seventy-five percent of total costs being attributed to labor. There is a need for continuity of services, which is threatened through collective action by workers and the potential of strikes and work stoppages. Individual health and public health and welfare are threatened when services are halted or retarded, thus bringing great concern to managers and consumers alike.

Health care is a big business, and social welfare programs also constitute a substantial part of our economy. Health care institutions often have goals of monetary profit or intangible types of profit, while social welfare programs must operate within tight fiscal

**Present affiliation*: Director, Marketing and Strategic Planning, Arkansas Children's Hospital, Little Rock, Arkansas

constraints placed upon them by their sponsoring government unit. The delicate balance of delivering high-quality and marketable services with limited financial resources is a constant concern. The bottom line is that for any service industry to operate an efficient and cost-effective operation, administrators must be aware of unions, how they function, and their potential effect on human resource management and service delivery.

This chapter guides the reader through many of the pertinent areas related to the state of collective bargaining in health care and human services. Attempts are made to trace the unique development of collective bargaining and labor-management relations in health and human services, and to address the particular problems faced by administrators. The purpose of this chapter is to highlight what the author feels are the most vital topics for an introduction to the subject. Note that volumes of texts could be written about any of the topics covered in the chapter, and this material is presented in a limited scope.

First, the reader is introduced to the development of the union phenomenon in both the health care industry and human service organizations. The development in health care is traced through labor legislation, from the National Labor Relations Act of 1935 (Wagner Act) to the 1974 amendments to the Taft-Hartley Act, and the responses of administrators to these developments are emphasized. Growth in the human service industry is discussed in the context of legislation for unions of public employees in concert with social changes which fostered this development.

The next section presents current labor relations law for these industries, defining important terms, emphasizing specific health care sections and restrictions, and discussing the role of the National Labor Relations Board. The discussion of human service organizations presents federal policy and Executive Order 10988, as well as various state laws promoting or protecting union activities of public employees. These policies and laws provide the legal foundations for unionization of public employees, which generally typifies the employment status of employees in human service organizations. Some may find discussions of law a bit dry, but labor law lays the foundation for collective bargaining and must be introduced for a thorough understanding of labor relations.

The next section discusses the specific unions and associations that represent health care and human service organizations, presenting their similarities to and differences from unions in other industries. The trends of unionization are presented next, followed by an examination of the effects of collective bargaining, including the effect on the quality of care and services.

The next two sections look at the players involved, including workers, management, and the union. This examination will be placed in the perspective of current environmental conditions, focusing particularly on the changing marketplace for these industries.

Finally, the role of professional associations and professional employees as organized labor or unions is discussed, and projections are made for the future. This section is critical because unionization of professional employees has become more commonplace during the 1980s and will increase as our work force becomes more professionalized and service-oriented.

II. DEVELOPMENT OF UNIONS IN HEALTH CARE FACILITIES

This section guides the reader through a brief history of unions in the health care industry, with some emphasis on the social and legislative factors that have had the greatest influence on this development.

Union development in private enterprise preceded similar growth in the health care industry by several decades. The first union activities were initiated in hospitals as early as 1919 in San Francisco, stimulated by worker demands for shorter hours and adequate working conditions. There was other union activity in hospitals up through the 1960s, but this activity generally was isolated and of little general significance.

A. Legislative Developments

Labor legislation did not specifically address labor relations in health care facilities, and these early union activities presented many legal questions and a great deal of the confusion. The National Labor Relations Act (NLRA) of 1935, also known as the Wagner Act, addressed many inequities of the labor-management relationship in general, but did not specify situations in health care institutions. This law did not stimulate any noticeable growth of unions in the health care industry. The essence of the NLRA was to restore equality in the bargaining relationship and, in fact, establish this right for labor. A denial of this right had begun to build a great deal of resistance in labor during its dealings with management, but the NLRA did not deal specifically with health care workers and institutions.

The Taft-Hartley Act of 1947 amended the Wagner Act and had a specific exclusion for labor relations situations in voluntary, nonprofit hospitals. The Taft-Hartley Act was an influence in retarding the organizational activities of employees in voluntary, nonprofit hospitals. Unions had no legal power base in these institutions, and management was thrust into a favorable position.

The 1960s and the early 1970s brought considerable sentiment from labor to consolidate health care labor laws, but hospitals had an advantage in remaining nonunion because of labor's concentration of efforts in private enterprise, primarily heavy industry and manufacturing. The perceived professionalism and humanitarian nature of the industry, the limitations of the NLRA, and the nonprofit status of most health care institutions helped keep unions out. Significant social changes soon would become a focal point in the unionization of health care workers. These social changes accompanied the civil rights movement in the 1960s as the movement began to affect the social and economic structure of the country and contribute to the unification of minority workers proliferating in the health care industry.

Workers wanted to enhance their financial and social status, and one result was that they developed a positive perspective of the role unions could take in benefiting their position. Another factor that provided a firm foundation and stimulus for union expansion into hospitals was the firm power base of unions in the industrial sector (Metzger, 1978a). While hospitals underwent corporate and functional changes, moving away from the charitable image, new problems arose. One such problem was the potential for confrontations with organized labor. Health care was developing a big-business image, and unions historically have been a part of this phenomenon. Hospitals now had to face labor activities and the other consequences of change.

B. Response to the NLRA Amendments

Neither the AFL-CIO nor the American Hospital Association (AHA) was anxious to suggest any major changes in the Taft-Hartley Act. Labor interests feared that reopening the law might cause major changes that could weaken its position, whereas hospitals enjoyed their exemption and "looser" standards than other industries in dealing with employees and did not advocate change.

Despite the position of these groups, representative Frank Thompson (D.-N.J.) introduced an amendment that was meant to remove only the nonprofit hospital exemption. It is quite obvious that labor favored this proposal, but the AHA voiced its opposition and contended that the amendment was unreasonable, based on four beliefs. These beliefs were part of the AHA's testimony before the House Special Subcommittee on Labor on January 18, 1972:

1. Collective bargaining could not apply to hospitals.
2. Union strength was based on work stoppages and the threat of strikes, which cannot be tolerated in hospitals.
3. Loyalty divided between union and profession cannot be tolerated in the life-or-death situations existing in health care facilities.
4. The exemption was justified even more, based on labor situations of the day.

The federal government was not alone in its protection of health care management. Prior to 1974, workers in health care institutions had little support for collective action through state laws. Michigan and Wisconsin were the only two states that gave workers the right to strike, whereas Pennsylvania and Montana allowed work stoppages under very strict conditions. So the federal and state laws both discouraged collective action by health care employees. Table 1 gives a chronological listing of the development of federal labor relations laws relating to health care, and illustrates the point that management was protected.

With the passage of the 1974 amendments to the Taft Hartley Act, health care administrators became vulnerable to organizational activity, but did not have strong antiunion defenses. The health care administrator began to operate under a complex body of statutory, administrative, and case law that was foreign to him or her. The 1974 amendments were meant to protect workers and the rights of the public, but at the same time could be devastating to the unprepared manager.

The passage of amendments to the Taft-Hartley Act in 1974 brought drastic stimulation to union activity in heretofore nonunion health care facilities. Public Law 93-360 (1974), in conjunction with the NLRA, covered all nonpublic health care facilities

TABLE 1 Federal Labor Relations Laws Relating to Health Care Collective Bargaining

Law	Date	Implications
Wagner Act	1935	Applicable to all private hospitals
Taft-Hartley Act	1947	Gave specific exemption to nonprofit hospitals
Labor Management Reporting and Disclosure Act	1959	Allowed states to assume jurisdiction in labor relations situations not covered by the National Labor Relations Board, such as hospitals
Public Law 93-360	1974	Amended Taft-Hartley Act and removed exemption of nonprofit hospitals

and added provisions to "safeguard" their employees. Those amendments gave organized labor a new field to enter at a time when unions were searching for new industries to organize.

Union activity increased and was relatively successful after the passage of the 1974 amendments. Figures for National Labor Relations Board (NLRB) annual reports show that unions gained representation in sixty-one percent of the representation elections held in the final six months of 1974. The next two years saw union victories in fifty-two percent of elections in health care facilities, slightly above the success rate in all industries. Current figures show that the rate and success of union organizational attempts in health care are now comparable to those in other growth industries.

C. Health Care Environment

There have been two profound changes in the health care system which deserve mention because of their effect on, and relationship to, labor. These two changes are the transformation in image of the health care system from that of being charitable to that of being big business and the revision of Medicare (elderly and disabled) reimbursement from a cost-based system to a prospective payment system.

Until the 1970s, most health care institutions were generally perceived to be charitable in nature. Medical care was not considered competitive in nature, and the system was generally left to operate as it saw fit. As the consumerism movement grew and as health care costs began to skyrocket, individual and industrial consumers began to demand some control of costs. This demand spawned the development of alternative delivery settings to hospitals, and began a competitive era in hospital management which exists today and continues to intensify. The competitive nature of the industry has brought demands for greater cost-consciousness and increased productivity which directly impinge on labor and its role within the system. Labor also has less job security as a result of this changing environment and is viewed as more expendable by management. This change in image, with its greater demands on workers, has also stimulated greater demands by nonphysician health care workers who historically have encountered depressed wage levels and compensation packages. Thus, the change has generated more interaction between labor and management.

Another major change is the revision of Medicare reimbursement, which provides medical insurance for the elderly and disabled. Medicare provides a significant share of income for many health care providers and often exceeds fifty percent of revenues for many hospitals. Historically, Medicare reimbursed a health care institution for services rendered on a cost-based system. Costs were reimbursed if they were considered "usual, customary, and reasonable." Now, reimbursement is based not on cost, but on preestablished rates according to the diagnosis. Each illness is classified as one of 469 Diagnosis Related Groups (DRGs). A particular amount is reimbursed for each DRG regardless of actual cost, although some exceptions, called outliers, are made in extraordinary cases. The implication is that pressure exists to provide services and expend resources which will not exceed the reimbursement for the particular diagnosis. Of course, this pressure for productivity and efficiency will be felt by labor and management alike.

Competition, intensified by prospective payment has stimulated profound changes in hospitals, the major health care employers. The major impact is that hospital census levels are shrinking, thus bringing increased layoffs and job insecurity. A survey by the American Nurses Association revealed that eighteen percent of facilities had laid off registered nurses during the past two years. In addition, thirty-two percent said that other nursing staff (primarily licensed practical nurses and aides) had been laid off in that same time period. In Chicago alone, between 1982 and 1984, 15,000 jobs were lost in hospitals. Generally, these job losses were in the low-paying service classification, particularly affecting minority groups (Bureau of National Affairs, 1985).

As a result, these pressures are forcing more cost-consciousness among hospital managers. This pressure forces belt tightening and produces great strain and demands upon the work force. One final factor is that DRGs and cost containment have brought sicker patients to hospitals, requiring a higher level of care and more demands on staff.

III. DEVELOPMENT OF UNIONS IN HUMAN SERVICES ORGANIZATIONS

The unionization of human service and welfare employees is also a recent phenomenon. The vast majority of such workers are employed by governmental agencies at the federal, state, or local level; thus, the labor laws and directives of these various governmental tiers parallel union development and growth in each. At this writing, over twenty percent of all public employees are unionized, yet in 1960, unions for public employees were quite rare.

The early history of public unions is one of severe limitations. In the early 1900s, the president had power to prevent federal employees from bargaining collectively and being involved in union activities. Later, President Theodore Roosevelt issued executive orders to prevent lobbying by federal employees by prohibiting federal officials, employees, and their associations from soliciting pay increases in Congress under penalty of discharge. One positive move for employees was the 1912 Lloyd-La Follette Act, which allowed unaffiliated organizations to present their grievances to Congress without retaliation. But the NLRA in 1935 did not give relief to government employees, by specifically excluding them from coverage.

The question arises about how and why this phenomenal growth took place in the public sector, particularly since unions in traditional manufacturing industries were losing their foothold. Several factors could account for this growth, including:

1. An increasing number of service employees and career opportunities
2. Acceptance within white-collar occupations and professions that unions were not only acceptable, but a viable means to bargain collectively for work conditions
3. Acceptance by the public that public employees deserve reasonable wages and work conditions

This growth pattern is also accompanied by an attitudinal change both in the public and within professions that service work does not necessarily mean charity. Service workers and the public perceived a need for equitable wages and work conditions as in the private sector. Unions were one means to gain these needs in an accelerated fashion.

President Kennedy issued Executive Order 10988 in January 1962, which granted organizational and bargaining rights to employees of the executive branch of government. These rights were basically the same as those for private-sector workers, but the scope of bargaining issues and arbitration was limited. In addition, both the right to strike and the use of arbitration for negotiation impasses were prohibited. This executive order stimulated union membership, and by 1970, half of all eligible federal employees were represented by a union; at this writing, almost sixty percent of all federal employees are represented by a union. Executive Order 11491, promulgated by President Nixon in 1969, made several revisions in laws concerning federal employees. A parallel agency to the NLRB, the Federal Labor Relations Council, was created. In addition, the law was updated to bring consistency to election, bonding, and reporting procedures in both public- and private-sector unions.

The next step was in 1979, with the Federal Services Labor-Management Relations Act of 1978 (P.L. 95-454). The act was modeled after the NLRA, creating and setting the authority of a general counsel to investigate and prosecute unfair labor practice cases. In addition, the act provided for judicial review and enforcement of most cases.

States also began to pass various labor laws related to their employees. These laws vary greatly but do hold some common themes. These laws will be discussed later in this chapter.

The crucial point is that as public and professional sentiment changed in the 1960s and 1970s, a parallel change also occurred with labor legislation regarding public employees and their rights to bargain collectively. Increasingly, the law opened doors for public employees to unionize, and the law gave more strength and legitimacy to the movement.

IV. LABOR LEGISLATION IN SERVICE INDUSTRIES

A. Health Care

The 1974 amendments to the Taft-Hartley Act created opportunities for new and heightened union organizational activities, unparalleled since labor had penetrated the steel industry in the late 1930s. All nonpublic health care facilities now are covered by the amended NLRA, which provides safeguards to health care facilities in the conduct of their labor relations activities and protection of the workers.

This section highlights specific portions of the Taft-Hartley Act that are relevant to the health care industry, and clarifies some pertinent terms and the role of the NLRB.

1. Definitions

The text of the amended NLRA is too lengthy to be included in this chapter, but highlights of this act relating to health care must be mentioned. First, some terms are defined in Sec. 2 of the act that have importance in health care collective bargaining:

"Professional employee" means "any employee engaged in work predominantly intellectual and varied in character . . . involving the consistent exercise of discretion and judgement. . . . The output [of work] cannot be standardized in relation to a given period of time. . . . [Professional work requires] knowledge of an advanced type and study in an institution of higher learning or a hospital. . . ."

"Health care institution" includes any "hospital, convalescent hospital, health maintenance organization, health clinic, nursing home, extended care facility, or other institution devoted to the care of sick, infirm, or aged person."

It is also important to note that the American Nurses Association and other professional associations, which are numerous in health care institutions, fit the definition of "labor organization" in Sec. 2 of the act, leaving no legal question concerning their coverage by the NLRA.

2. Specific Health Care Sections

There are specific sections of the NLRA that address unique labor relations problems in the health care field. The most important provisions for health care include:

1. Unions must give a 10-day strike or picket notice to hospitals (Sec. 213).
2. Unions must give 90-day notice for terminating collective bargaining agreements (Sec. 213).
3. Mediation is mandatory (Sec. 213).
4. Management is protected from lockouts and interruptions of health service delivery (Sec. 213).
5. Health care employees having religious convictions against joining, or giving financial support to, a labor organization as a condition of employment, can pay sums equal to the specified dues to a nonreligious, tax-exempt, charitable fund (Sec. 19).

3. NLRB Influence

Another legal development occurred early in 1975, when the NLRB set guidelines for appropriate bargaining units in health care institutions. The board's interest was to prevent proliferation—that is, an excessive amount—of union contracts in an institution. Multiple contracts are a difficult situation with which to deal, particularly in a health care institution. The appropriate bargaining units established by the NLRB are as follows:

1. Registered nurses (RNs): If it is desired, RNs are entitled to be represented as a separate bargaining unit. RNs have a choice of representation separately or with other employees of the institution.
2. Professionals: A unit of all professionals with or without the RNs, as the RNs deem appropriate. This unit could include such individuals as physical therapists, pharmacists, and social workers.
3. Technicians: Technical employees are considered to be a separate unit. Employees such as X-ray technicians, certified operating room technicians, licensed practical nurses, and lab technicians could be included in this unit.
4. Business office clericals: These individuals comprise a separate unit that includes cashiers, patient accounts clerks, billing clerks, admitting clerks, and switchboard operators.

Although these bargaining units had been spelled out, problems began to develop with numerous bargaining units being formed within individual organizations. This trend continued for a decade after the 1974 amendments. The St. Francis decision of 1984 forced a revised look at the trend which had been developing in unit determination. The St. Francis decision requires there be "unusually sharp differences . . . of employees requesting separate bargaining units" (Furlane and Freeman, 1985). This decision did not invalidate any previous NLRB decisions or rulings concerning appropriateness of bargaining units or relieve an organization of its duty to bargain. The trend since this decision has been for much broader based bargaining units. Mutual interest is determined by common wage scales, labor grades, performance standards, shared facilities, centralized personnel policies, and other factors.

B. Human Service Organizations

As stated earlier, the typical human service employee is also a public employee. Thus, any discussion of pertinent legislation revolves around labor laws which govern federal, state, and local employment. This section will discuss, first, federal labor law and then relevant state statutes.

1. Federal Statutes

Executive Order 11492 is the law which covers all federal executive department agencies. This law created the Federal Labor Relations Authority (FLRA), which is the principal agency charged with administering the act. In many ways, the FLRA mimics the NLRB in its activities and scope of authority.

The FLRA has a general counsel appointed to a five-year term by the president. This counsel investigates and prosecutes unfair labor practices which violate the executive order. Decisions of the FLRA are appealable to a U.S. court of appeals, except in cases involving bargaining unit determination. In addition, the FLRA utilizes federal impasse panels to assist parties in resolving impasses. An impasse occurs when the two parties in a collective bargaining situation cannot agree on a particular issue and do not seem able to resolve their disagreement on the issue or set of issues.

Federal labor negotiations do have one very significant departure from private-sector activities, in that bargaining involves "work conditions" only, not including wages, which is the most significant issue, but also the most difficult upon which to agree. Wages for blue-collar employees are established by the Coodinated Federal Wage System, while white-collar wages are established in the General Schedule. All wages are formally set through executive order by the president. Because wages are intimately linked to our federal budget, this system ensures that an amount of money is budgeted which guarantees payment to federal workers and, at the same time, does not demand funds which are unattainable.

Federal labor law also stipulates that all labor agreements must have a grievance procedure. These grievance procedures must have a binding arbitration option as the final step.

Another significant section of federal labor law is sec. 7116(b)(7), which makes it illegal for a union representing federal employees to call or condone a strike or work slowdown. This section also stipulates that pickets may not interfere with the work of others, but does allow "informational picketing." This section is the most significant reason why there are so few strikes by federal employees. The FLRA has the right to revoke the recognition status of a union or take other very substantial measures when a strike is condoned for its membership. The most recent and significant such case was when the Professional Air Traffic Controllers (PATCO) walked off their jobs in late 1981. The FLRA did revoke the right of PATCO to be the sole agent for the controllers, and thousands of controllers were thus fired for noncompliance with the law.

Federal law included provisions familiar in the private sector including:

1. A clear definition of unfair labor practices by management (Sec. 7116[b]).
2. A clear definition of unfair labor practices by the union (7116[a]).
3. A mandate to negotiate in good faith (Sec. 7114[b]).

In summary, federal labor law is quite similar in many respects to labor law in the private sector, with two significant differences. First, wages are not an issue for negotiation; and second, strikes are illegal.

2. State Labor Laws

In many ways, labor laws of individual states are similar to both the laws that govern federal employees and those in the private sector. Federal statutes typically guide states in developing laws to regulate similar situations, and labor relations does not appear to be an exception. However, in numerous cases, state laws are even more rigorous than those that govern federal employees and the NLRA.

The first similarity is that many states have regulatory bodies similar to the NLRB. Most often they take the form of Public Employee Relations Boards (PERBs). All PERBs do not function the same or have the same responsibilities, but the typical duties of PERBs include the following:

- Handling designated unfair labor practices
- Certifying representation
- Determining bargaining unit composition
- Providing mediators
- Providing fact-finding

Several issues are of particular interest regarding laws governing state employees, including bargaining unit determination, the role of supervisors in bargaining units, and strikes. Each of these will now be examined.

The issue of bargaining units is extremely critical, as it is in all other industries, but particularly in governmental service agencies with a diverse range of employees and professions. The key is to develop units which are neither too small nor too large. A proliferation of small units develops a situation that is fragmented for workers and the organization. With many smaller units, more specific issues come to the forefront from special-interest groups, but the disadvantage is that the smaller groups often have less bargaining clout. Management also must face the prospect of an overbearing number of contract negotiation sessions. Larger units limit the number of bargaining sessions for management, but many significant issues for workers can get lost because they are not as wide in scope, yet they might still be appropriate for bargaining. It is in the best interest of both labor and management to develop appropriate bargaining units.

Supervisors, of course, are excluded from union activity by the NLRA, but states do have a different perspective in many cases. Most states allow some activity from supervisors in union activity. Some states allow supervisors in bargaining units with nonsupervisors, others have statutes allowing separate units only for supervisors, and, as in the NLRA, others exclude supervisors altogether. There is much debate over the appropriateness of having management (supervisors) bargain collectively, particularly in the same bargaining units as nonsupervisors. One justification is that the bureaucratic structure of many state systems creates supervisory positions in name only or with quite limited supervisory discretion and authority, thus creating no real conflict of interest for these individuals.

The final issue for discussion is the right to strike. Strikes are almost always illegal for public employees, although they have increased in number significantly over the past two decades. Most public employee strikes are by local government employees, and the one professional group of public employees most likely to strike is teachers. The quality of available data makes it difficult to speak with great certainty about human service professionals, but the data do indicate relatively few strikes for this classification of public employee.

Strikes by public employees are generally over the same issues as in the private sector, but strikes by public employees do not occur as frequently as those in the private sector. As in the laws governing federal employees, often there are very severe penalties in state laws for striking workers and labor organizations, but these penalties often are not imposed. The trend has been to resolve any labor disputes without the use of severe sanctions.

Strikes by public employees also are very complex because of the numerous interests that are involved. First of all, the general public and taxpayers are affected by loss of, or limitations on, services. Public sentiment has a great impact not only on the decision to strike, but also on the ultimate success or failure of a strike effort. There are also political ramifications from this activity which affect future funding or even continued existence of a particular agency or human service program.

V. UNIONS AND ASSOCIATIONS REPRESENTING SERVICE WORKERS

A. Health Care

The unions and organizations that represent health care workers are generally different from those representing workers in other industries. The differences, however, are generally only in the names of the organizations, rather than in their behavior, goals, and objectives.

No single union has recieved an exclusive charter from the AFL-CIO to represent hospital or health care workers. There are more than 40 unions and professional associations representing health care workers in collective bargaining. One reason that this number of unions is involved is not their inherent interest in health care workers, but simply that the workers sought out certain unions for convenience or because of reputation. It seems inconceivable that a meat packers union or stage workers union would represent health care workers, but these unions have been sought out in several areas because of their perceived strength or the convenience for the workers interested in organizing.

Although no single union has exclusive rights to organizing health care workers or institutions, more than seventy percent of all collective bargaining agreements in health care institutions are with three unions (Bureau of Labor Statistics, 1984). These three unions are the Service Employees International Union (SEIU); the American Nurses Association (ANA); and the National Union of Hospital and Health Care Employees, a division of the Retail, Wholesale, and Department Store Union (RWDSU, or 1199).

The SEIU represents employees working in private, nonprofit, and public institutions, including hospitals, nursing homes, schools, and public and private utilities. SEIU's most recent push has been to organize workers in nursing homes throughout the United States, particularly those working in large, for-profit chains. Most members of the SEIU are technicians, certain professionals, medical paraprofessionals, and maintenance workers. SEIU represents more than 150,000 health care workers and more than 600,000 workers in all industries (Bureau of Labor Statistics, 1984). In addition, the United Food and Commercial Workers Union, although not among the three largest health care unions, is quite active in organizing long-term care institutions, in efforts similar to that by the SEIU.

The ANA is a federation of 53 separate nursing associations, one each from the 50 states, the District of Columbia, Guam, and the Virgin Islands. Each state association operates autonomously, and members must be RNs in at least one state. The ANA has widespread membership, and more than 60,000 of its 185,000 active members work under collective bargaining agreements. Another section of this chapter deals with professional associations as organized labor in greater depth.

The National Union of Hospital and Health Care Employees is better known as Local 1199. Local 1199 may be the most publicized and well-known union in health care today.

Local 1199 began as an independent faction of the RWDSU representing pharmacists, drugstore workers, and eventually hospital employees. This faction evolved into the National Union of Hospital and Health Care Employees. Local 1199 is well known for its association with civil rights and similar causes. In fact, Martin Luther King, Jr., affectionately referred to Local 1199 as "my union."

The association with civil rights causes, plus the large number of minority workers in health care facilities, helped place Local 1199 into the public eye and strengthened its power, membership, and image. The National Union of Hospital and Health Care Employees defines its jurisdiction as all professional, technical, clerical, service and maintenance, and other employees in health care institutions. This union has its greatest base of power in the Northeast, and, specifically, New York City. Local 1199 represents approximately 100,000 health care workers (Bureau of Labor Statistics, 1984).

There certainly are peculiarities in the establishment of operations, goals, and demands of unions in health care facilities, but it appears they generally function in the same way as their non-health care counterparts. Unions in health care institutions demonstrate the same strengths and weaknesses as unions in other industries.

Continued unionization efforts appear likely for health care employees; thus, health care executives will be faced with unions and collective bargaining. The significant and rapid loss of union members in private enterprise ensures union movement into health care (Kobs, 1979). Unions have lost their base of strength from the typical "smokestack" industries of the 1950s and 1960s as workers have moved into more service-oriented and growing occupations. Workers in service industries, including health care, have now become inviting targets for union activity. Service industries have traditionally trailed other industries in their compensation packages, and unionization is the quickest route to receiving equitable pay and treatment.

The current prospective payment system for Medicare has added to increased job insecurity and increased layoffs (Bureau of National Affairs, 1985). One incident which lends evidence to this situation is that in the summer of 1984, 6,000 RN members of the Minnesota Nurses Association (MNA) struck 15 Minneapolis–St. Paul hospitals over a job security clause. Also, a review of major health care contracts and job actions in recent years reveals a consistent pattern of the following issues causing greatest concern: productivity issues and standards, job security, and staffing issues (Ibid., 1985).

Union organizers in health care are increasing, and large sums of money are being invested in union campaigns. Perhaps Jerry Wurf, an ex-president of the American Federation of State, County, and Municipal Employees (AFSCME), sums up the real reason that unions are here to stay. Wurf says: "Heavy hand and unreasonableness of management will always guarantee that there will be plenty of unions in this country." Health care managers certainly must recognize that many in their ranks demonstrate this behavior described by Mr. Wurf, and must be aware that organized labor has identified health care as one of its primary targets (Winpisinger, 1979).

B. Unions in Human Services

As in health care, no single union represents employees in human service occupations. However, there are fewer unions representing human service and public employees than health care workers. Consequently, there are a limited number of very strong unions in this sector.

The unions and associations which provide services to public employees generally operate exclusively in the public sector. This pattern is probably due to the differences in the laws regulating the public and private sectors, and the obvious difficulty of dealing with two complex bodies of law.

By far, the dominant public unions in both membership and media attention are the National Education Association and the American Federation of Teachers (AFT), which represent teachers, and the National Association of Letter Carriers (NALC) and the American Postal Workers Union, which represent Postal Service employees. It is unlikely, though, that these unions would represent a substantial number of human service employees. It is noteworthy that the AFT now has a health care subsidiary. The Federation of Nurses and Health Professional is the health care arm of the AFT.

The following unions represent the substantial majority of public human service employees: AFSCME, the American Federation of Government Employees (AFGE), and SEIU.

AFSCME is the largest public-sector union affiliated with the AFL-CIO, and generally represents state and local government employees. There are numerous smaller, specialized unions which will compete for other state and local employees, particularly for police, fire fighters, and health workers. AFSCME will represent virtually any type of public employee. The current membership of AFSCME, according to its international headquarters, is 1.1 million members, making it the largest affiliate of the AFL-CIO.

The AFGE is the employee association most likely to represent human service employees in the federal sector. The priorities of this federal union are no different than those of any other labor organization. The concerns of the AFGE addressed at their 1986 convention were the following:

1. Creating and protecting jobs
2. Security in old age with dignity
3. Fair compensation
4. Health and welfare both on and off the job
5. Equitable career development opportunity (AFGE Standard, 1986).

Thus are reflected the AFGE's more than 200,000 members' concerns about security on the job and professional career development. The words of Ken Blaylock, AFGE president, reflect the battle cry of unions today and particularly that of unions representing public employees when he said, "Our struggle to represent workers in collective bargaining and win better pay and working conditions from the powerful employer we're up against demands that we make the most of what we've got. In our unity is the power to win" (AFGE Standard, 1986).

The SEIU is the same union mentioned as a representative of health care workers. The SEIU represents not only health care employees in the public and private sectors, but rather a range of employees who work for governments.

It is important to stress that these three unions are not the only ones which represent public employees. Intense competition takes place in the public sector among various unions for representation rights of employees. As in health care and any other business, including the government, unions are a big business. They have a need to grow and develop with the work force and economy. As the economy changes to a service orientation, so must the unions change in order to survive.

VI. PRESENT TREND TOWARD UNIONIZATION IN SERVICE INDUSTRIES

Service workers are exhibiting a trend toward increased union representation in their labor-management relations, and labor unions are experiencing a relatively high success rate in their organizational activities. This section presents some information concerning these trends and the reasons for their development.

There are a variety of reasons why health care workers join unions and seek representation for collective bargaining. Joiner and Morris (1978) say that poor communication and a perception of inequitable treatment exhibited through policies in the areas of wages, benefits, and the organization itself are reasons that hospital employees contact and join unions. These reasons also hold true for workers in human services and other industries.

Flath (1980) cites more specific reasons why employees join unions:

1. Unions appeal to their fighting instinct.
2. Unions are "friendly" to minority groups.
3. Employees get a voice in job conditions.
4. Unions increase job security.
5. Employees participate in decision making.
6. Unions provide a chance to strike back at management.

Employees realize that government, taxation, and inflation are decreasing their real income, and feel that the union can better represent their needs in the financial bargaining position. This feeling has become an advantageous organizational point for unions. The power and impact of unions in service industries depends, to a large extent, on the worker's accepting this view of unions.

Historically, there was a delay in the penetration of these ideas into the health care system and the government. The climate was unfriendly toward unions, and various legislation were handicaps for union intervention. As unions gain respectability and legitimacy, they organize workers and perpetuate themselves in the organizations that have been most exploitative of labor. Worker unity and consistency in purpose negate the strength of the organization.

There are several factors that have affected union growth in service-oriented industries. One such factor is that the fundamental nature of these businesses has been an inhibiting force. The philosophy of helping and caring is widespread, particularly in the health care industry and to some extent in human services. Some labor philosophy and attitudes may contradict this humanistic outlook of health care and human service personnel.

Another inhibitor is that, generally, there is a great deal of inefficiency in generating interest to strike a health care institution or government agency. Besides these factors, there is public backlash accompanying strikes and work stoppages by health care or government employees. For instance, it could be destructive to the public image of a union to strike a children's hospital or cut off services to individuals dependent on public welfare. The unions also face other problems, including the dispersion and size of health care and human service organizations. On a broader scale, these unions have had an insignificant influence on social issues involving health care and human services. This situation must be seen as a paradox of the perceived purpose of these organizations, particularly professional associations, which contend to hold organizational goals and objectives beyond the basic demands for wages, benefits, and work conditions.

Labor movements throughout history have had different targets and varying degrees of influence. The current working relationships and employment situations in service industries have been shaped by prior labor movements, and are a product of a very dynamic process. Unions generally have a significant social, political, and economic effect on the field they are penetrating, but this has not been the rule in health service organizations. For example, the wide range of social and economic reforms considered for the U.S. health care system have not been priority items for unions. The unions have reacted to the reforms once they have been put in place, but have had virtually no impact on systematic reform or policy development. This mode of operation seems to be a real weakness of unions in health care, especially considering the general concern about the political relationships of the components of the health care system. Unions of public employees have had more political influence than those in health care, but more limited than those in nonservice industries.

There are many generally known conditions and situations that hinder unionization efforts in health care institutions and human service organizations. Most of these conditions are complicated by the union's demands and activities, but are inherent in health care and human service organizations. These conditions include:

1. Professionalism and professional values
2. Diverse work groups and bargaining units
3. Cost concerns by consumers or taxpayers
4. Noneconomic community pressures
5. Wage pressure
6. The charitable image of these organizations
7. Social accountability

VII. CURRENT SITUATION

This section presents the current situation of labor-management relations in the service industries from a managerial perspective. First, some of management's fears are discussed in detail; then, several of the reported liabilities associated with unionization of these workers are presented.

Administrators and managers who stimulate labor relation problems are thought to be major contributors to the general labor movement (Kobs, 1979). Health care and human service administrators, particularly ill-prepared or poor ones, assume an even more vulnerable position now that unions are protected in their industries. A bona fide labor movement has begun in these industries, with administrators facing pressures from unions attempting to gain support and new membership, placing management in a defensive position.

Despite the aggressive position of unions, these industries have not developed a counteracting policy or philosophy. For example, the American Hospital Association policy regarding unions is "for the hospital governing board to decide the hospital policy toward union recognition and collective bargaining." So, even though labor has targeted these industries for their own expansion, health care and human service organizations do not have a formal, unified strategy or philosophy to counter this union activity. In fact, since legislation has legitimized public employee unions, there cannot be a counteractive policy or legislation to fight these unions.

Health care and human service organizations began to experience unionization after the "golden age" of unions in the 1950s. This late start did present an ideal opportunity to the labor and management groups to select the best aspects of collective bargaining based on history and performance over time. This opportunity should have given the labor-management teams an opportunity to develop more practical forms of bargaining that could enhance the benefit to both parties. This practical and positive approach to the situation does not seem to be prominent. In fact, health care and human service management, with their bargaining units, are developing policies and agreements that bring the identical problems faced in union situations within other industries.

The health care or human service managers are faced with new problems, complicated by the presence of unions. The manager is faced with the possibility of strikes and other work actions. Remember that although strikes are often illegal for public employees, they are still a reality with the weak enforcement of the nonstrike statutes. The cost of a strike, in economic and social terms, is the first potential cost of unionization. Another complication of a strike is that management's power and autonomy are threatened. Conversely, the leadership of a union is never more out on a limb than in the strike situation (Metzger, 1978b). The question continues to be raised about the legitimacy of strikes in health care organizations or in public agencies. Labor answers with another question: Can there be genuine and equitable collective bargaining unless strikes are permitted?

Metzger (1975) identified another need of health care workers that was not satisfied without unionization. This need holds true for other predominantly white-collar, or professional, work groups, including human service employees. Managers now must be more productive and more sensitive toward preserving and enhancing the dignity of their employees. Unions were called upon to control some internal problems perceived by workers, and have forced managerial responses in revised policies and procedures. Those conditions that management would not provide willingly have now become union demands.

A. Management Fears

Management in health care and human services has been at a distinct disadvantage when interacting with sophisticated and mature labor unions, due to a lack of training and experience in dealing with them. Although this deficiency is diminishing, managers in service industries are often placed in subordinate positions, rather than being partners in decision making. Management slowly loses its autonomy in initiating changes without union sanction. Management is in a precarious position of losing rights but still holding responsibility. The rights of management affected by unionization include:

1. Hiring
2. Firing
3. Promoting
4. Expanding and creating positions
5. Setting work standards
6. Evaluating performance

7. Determining wages and fringe benefits
8. Revising policy and procedure
9. Scheduling
10. Disciplining
11. Conducting and formulating grievance procedures

Unionization can force numerous changes for managers, particularly unprepared or naive managers who have never faced this situation. Initially, unionization and collective bargaining are genuine handicaps for the manager of a health care or human service organization, but the long-term effect depends on the attitude adopted by management in its response to union activity. The initial adjustment may be difficult, but unions can become positive partners in the organization structure and organizational activities.

Health care managers expected turmoil and numerous unionization attempts, accompanied by intense and violent conflict following the 1974 amendments (Metzger, 1977). In retrospect, this was partially correct. Although unionization occurred with great frequency, statistics from the NLRB and the Federal Mediation and Conciliation Service show that unions in health care facilities are less likely to strike than those in other industries, and when striking, are less likely to take part in violence or aggressive behavior. This evidence does not dampen the reality that no matter how few, hospital strikes can have great social and economic costs.

Statistics also reveal that public employees are less likely to strike than their industrial counterparts. Of course, an overriding factor is that most strikes by public employees are illegal. Strikes by public employees are most likely on the local level, and least likely by federal employees, among whom strikes are quite rare.

Despite the evidence that unions have not been a problem to the degree expected, managers in these emerging industries maintain some basic fears concerning unionization, including the following:

1. The costs in increased salary and benefits will be devastating to the total cost of services delivered. The additional concern for the public sector is the need to increase taxes or deplete other program funding.
2. Unionization will interrupt service delivery and patient care.
3. Unions will impede administrative efficiency.
4. There will be a complication of administrative responsibilities.
5. Management will lose control of the organization.
6. Employees will reorder their professional priorities, which will lessen their concern for clients and patients. This issue is a particular concern in nursing.
7. One union will lead to another.
8. Worker productivity will decrease.

Research and common knowledge have shown that these fears have become reality in some situations, but evidence also reveals that these situations generally occur at a lesser rate and intensity than anticipated (Federal Mediation and Conciliation Service, 1979).

A review of the NLRB 1984 annual report found that the use of grievance and arbitration procedures in health care organizations is low relative to that in other industries. The data were not clear concerning the same information about human service organizations. This information reinforces the notion that labor-management relations in health care have shown little evidence of the conflict anticipated. Strikes are fewer and shorter in the health care industry, with the longest and most difficult strikes being in nursing homes and long-term care facilities, where wages are lowest and other work conditions often least desirable. Overall, there has been a lack of the expected violence and conflict.

The literature leads this author to believe that unions are not as critical a problem as expected by health care and human service managers. In fact, unions appear to be less of a problem than many other issues facing these managers in the next decade.

B. Proven Liabilities

There are potential liabilities associated with personnel problems in service organizations, particularly when the situation culminates in the establishment of a union. Potential liabilities of unions include the following:

A "fear factor" exists, as management must do its job in the shadows of the union (Miller, 1980).
A threat of conflict or physical conflict exists.
The threat of strike exists.
The community often exerts pressure to maintain a nonunion status (Kahn, 1978a).
The community exerts pressure to keep costs at a minimum.
The community exerts pressure for cost-effectiveness of services delivered.
Management fears loss of control.
Monetary costs are involved in fighting unionization attempts.
Communication is now forced into formal channels more often (Federal Mediation and Conciliation Service, 1979).
Personnel costs increase.
Higher wages accompany unionization (see Table 2).
Cost of services increases (see Table 3), reflecting cost of health care services.

TABLE 2 Wage Rate Differentials Attributed to Unions in Health Care Institutions

Author	Percentage differential in wage rates
Ashenfelter (Federal Mediation and Conciliation Service, 1979)	5
Becker (1980)	5
Block and Kuskin (1978)	5.3
Bristow (Federal Mediation and Conciliation Service, 1979)	16
Fottler (1977)	4.5–8.2
Hyclak (1979)	0–5
Kahn (1978a)	5
Lee (Federal Mediation and Conciliation Service, 1979)	28
Miller (1980)	0–5
Osterhaus (1979)	5
Schmidt and Strauss (Federal Mediation and Conciliation Service, 1979)	10
Sloan and Adamache (1984)	8.8
Wilson (1985)	8.8

TABLE 3 Increase in Total Cost of Health Care Attributed to Unionization

Author	Percentage differential
Fottler (1977)	5–8
Hyclak (1979)	0–5
Kahn (1978a)	5
Miller (1980)	0–5
Salkever (1984)	3–6
Sloan and Adamache (1984)	0–5

Although strikes and violence are less frequent in health care institutions, as well as in public employment, other actions are more prevalent, including:

Mass resignations
Sickout demonstrations
Refusal to bill patients
Refusal to document services
High absence rates (or Blue Flu)
Grievances
Slowdown of paperwork
Insubordination

A study for the Catholic Hospital Association (1979) analyzed the impact of unions and collective bargaining in hospitals and cites many specific liabilities associated with unions in health care institutions. These same factors are generally applicable in the human service industry and public employment. The Christopher study indicates that unions exert a negative impact on the management process, and the range of concerns is quite extensive.

First, costs increase for employers through wages and fringe benefits. The employee also feels increases in costs generated by the union through fees, fines, dues, and assessments, so neither side gains a financial advantage. There is a time loss dealing with union problems and more personnel relations matters, solidifying the polarity of the labor and management positions and eliminating teamwork. Unionization also has an impact on patients and clients, because direct and indirect costs are passed on to their bills. Another critical factor is that these costs are passed on to taxpayers, which has significant financial implications not just for clients, but for all parties contributing to the economy.

This effect is particularly problematic for unions at a time when technical procedures and professional services in health care are becoming more expensive, causing patient bills and third-party rates to rise. There is also great concern over taxes and public-sector expenditures. Some studies cited later in this chapter illustrate the effect that unions in health care institutions have on the wage rates of workers and on the total cost of health care.

Certainly, not all of these potential realities would be present in any single institution. The point is that these potential liabilities, accompanied by monetary, social, and human costs, are related to unionization of health care employees.

VIII. EFFECTS OF COLLECTIVE BARGAINING

Most discussions concerning unions and collective bargaining lead to the issue of wages and other monetary concerns. This issue is also of great concern in the health care system and in the funding of public programs. Therefore, this section will devote some discussion to wage rates plus other effects influenced by collective bargaining.

A. Wage Setting

It is obvious that there is pressure from unions that causes hospital managers and public service managers to meet prevailing wage rates for the community or industry. Miller (1980) calls this change "following the orbits of coercive comparison." There are wage leaders in every industry and community, so the union requests compensation that, in a social sense, has been deemed "fair and reasonable." This theory says that wages will rise regardless of a union's presence in a particular firm, because external influences already raise wages and affect the organizational structure. Therefore, a union does not have to be present in an institution to affect wages, so the presence of organized labor in a community or industry can influence wages even in a nonunion health care institution or public agency.

An interesting feature in health care institutions is that the demand for unionized, nonprofessional employees is relatively inelastic. Most unskilled labor is quite elastic, but hospital labor is essential and inelastic. Most human service organizations are not institutionally based, and thus they lack this demand for nonprofessional employees at the same level as a health care institution. This factor makes health care workers different in an economic sense, and makes their demands for wages more serious than those in many other collective bargaining situations.

Fottler (1977) tested the hypothesis that unionization has a significant impact on wage rates of nonprofessional hospital personnel. The study found that the bargains reached between a union and management generally set wage standards for the entire work force of an institution. This finding is rather obvious, but it shows that unions are reducing wage differentials between union and nonunion workers, and influencing wage rates and determination in the health care industry.

B. Evaluating Issues

In collective bargaining contracts, wages are the primary issue, as is the case in most other industries, but wages generally hold less overall value to health care workers than to those in other industries (Fitzgerald, 1984). The importance of wages varies for human service employees, because in some instances for public employees, wages are not a negotiable issue.

Issues that have the greatest overall importance in the health care and human service industries are job security and work conditions. The critical components appear to be grievance procedures, arbitration, and hours of work. A prime bargaining issue in public service is pensions, as well as the additional concerns related to paid time off (holidays, vacations, and sick leave).

Differences exist in contracts negotiated in health care and human services compared with those in other industries, but the differences are less striking than the similarities. As stated earlier, unions in the service industries generally behave as unions do in other industries, and this behavior also includes the approach to collective bargaining and the priority of bargaining issues.

C. Wage Rates

Wage rates in health care and human services have improved in the past 20 years relative to wages in other industries, yet overall these wage rates fall behind rates in other industries. An example of the differential is that in 1968 there was a thirty percent gap in average wages between nonsupervisory health care workers and their manufacturing counterpart. By 1979 the differential was reduced to nineteen percent, and in 1984 the difference was close to sixteen percent. Unions have made a difference in altering this wage rate, and this impact will be examined, but there are two other critical factors to consider in examining this difference: industry image and minority group representation.

The image of the health care and human service industries has been that of charitable and welfare-type organizations. Workers in these industries were expected to be special people, for whom concerns for patients and clients take priority over money. This image is changing as society has accepted the feeling that service workers deserve decent wages and work conditions, and has realized that health care and human service organizations are legitimate businesses. As this old image has eroded, wages have crept higher on a relative basis.

Another consideration is that many of the workers eligible for unionization in these service industries were women and from other minority groups. Historically, these groups have faced depressed wage levels. The civil rights and women's movements contributed to erasing some of the workplace bias which has kept wages depressed for women and other minorities. The bias has not been eliminated, but there has been some positive movement which has made a difference.

The gap is closing, but a union can close the gap faster than most management is willing to move. Statistics do show that unions in other industries have made up to fifteen percent greater changes in wage rates than has the health care industry. Even with the great rises in wages attributed to unions, as reflected in Table 2, the historically depressed wage rates minimize the effects of wage raises attributed to unionization (Miller, 1980).

Table 2 is a compilation of wage differential studies. The studies show that there is either no difference or a higher wage rate in union firms, ranging from nearly 5 to 28 percent. Table 3 examines the studies concerning the increase in the total cost of health care attributed to unionization. The figures show short-run effects, but give a better perspective to the wage studies. It may be significant that the most recent studies are among the lowest in differences measured.

These results may be evidence that the "quasi cartel" is quite effective in reducing differences in wage rates in the health care industry. The equalization of wage rates across industries makes wages a less flexible issue with less bargaining range; thus, wages become relatively stable.

One other factor worth mentioning is that Kahn (1978b), and others who use multiple equation models when examining unions and wages, reports a two-way causality. Unions affect wages, but wages also affect union membership. A very strong cycle of growth can develop. This factor also may be one reason why differentials have been dropping in the cited studies.

Another factor influencing total health care costs that cannot be ignored is increasing technology and equipment costs. The cost of labor has not risen as sharply as the cost of technology. Much of the increase in cost, and certainly the lack of benefit for costs in health care, is due to the dollars spent on technology (Fitzgerald, 1980). All of the blame for higher costs cannot be attributed to wage increases; rather, it is a complex set of internal and external factors that are responsible.

Unions do not create a differential between union and nonunion wages. This increase in wages is not welcomed by management, but the literature shows that differentials are diminishing and wage increases are less threatening. It appears that wage differentials are not as strong an argument for an antiunion stance as managers would expect.

There are nonmonetary costs attributed to unionization in health care and human services, as well as in all other industries. The greatest nonmonetary cost is that management has a new decision making partner, in the form of a union. Virtually all decisions which affect personnel in any way are now subject to union scrutiny. Management must fight hard to maintain its rights to manage the workplace, but even in situations where the technical rights have been maintained, management still has a handicap and the constant shadow of unionism.

All of the evidence leads this author to believe that unions in health care and human services present most of the same challenges to management that unions present in other industries. There are some complications and differences that do evolve, partly because of the laws guiding labor relations, the nature of these service industries, and the lack of preparation by health care managers for union organization attempts and activities.

IX. SERVICE WORKERS AND TRENDS IN UNION ACTIVITY

The movement to join unions is now an acceptable behavior for health care and human service workers, in both professional and nonprofessional job categories. This section discusses some of the factors which have stimulated this trend, including changes in the work force itself.

A combination of social pressures, workers' dissatisfaction with their jobs, and revised legislation is generating the movement to unions. In addition, so many more workers are now involved in the service industries than in the traditional "smokestack" industries, it seems only natural that unions should make the transition with the changing worker and employment opportunities. Modern management is complicated by employees who perceive their right in determining the future of their institution. The acceptance of unions by service employees has been generated in part by an evolutionary process among the workers. Part of this evolution involves a change in attitude, and a desire by employees to have some influence on decisions concerning organizational input and management.

A. The Worker's Profile

There are several differences between and among both health care workers and human service employees. This section will discuss, first, health workers, then human service workers.

Historically, the nonprofessional health care worker had been the person who could not work anywhere else, especially those workers in lower line, unskilled jobs. Hospitals particularly, were not the most desired place of employment for the nonprofessional. Pay was low, the work was unrewarding, and workers were viewed as transient and relatively easy to replace. This worker had very little education and relatively no career or job mobility. Today, most urban hospital workers are from minority groups, and up to

80 percent of all health care workers are female (Bureau of Labor Statistics, 1984; Wolfe, 1978). Some hospitals in the Southwest and limited urban areas also have had large numbers of illegal aliens working in their ranks.

The profile of the nonprofessional health care worker was that of a poor, unstable, and unprotected individual who was willing to work for low wages. This composite appears to be changing. Today's worker is more independent and better eduated, and will not accept the values, goals, and behavior patterns of the organization at face value. Workers realize that hospital wages are lower than those in other jobs, and this wage differential is the primary reason why more than 20 million employees in unions and professional associations in all industries bargain collectively.

Collective action becomes a reality for this new breed of health care employee. Unionization becomes a true social and economic movement, which creates powerful reactions, such as uniting health care workers into a single "fighting unit" (Metzger, 1978a). This unity generates a cycle that enables the health care industry to compete with other industries for the quality employee.

The health care field has several types of workers, including professional employees, with the potential to organize. In fact, the 1980s have even seen the development and growth of a union for physicians on house staff, the profession with the highest social status in health care, and among the highest in the general public. Health professionals often feel that unions would impede their personal progress and career growth, but rapid technological growth, social change, and a revised image of unions have diminished these sentiments. The present organization of professional workers is not meant to change the health system, but is an attempt by professionals to protect themselves and their professions. The professional and nonprofessional are frustrated because inflation is eroding their life-style, so collective action becomes a logical reaction to these social and economic pressures.

Some theorists, including this author, feel that the United States is on the brink of a major surge of professional and white-collar union organization. This movement may have particular strength in the allied health professions and in technical fields, which are already formed into well-defined, viable decision-making associations. The successful union, by providing greater status and prestige, reaches beyond the goals of survival and expansion. Unions in health care are confronting management and calling for the preservation of human values, which satisfies the needs of many professional associations.

Health care workers are aware of the middle-class status of other union employees and, of course, want this status, along with their other perceptions of union benefits. Most individuals, including health care workers, want more economic stability and greater social status. Therefore, workers can turn to unions as one alternative when they feel their needs are not being met by management.

Human service employees have the same priorities and concerns as employees in health care. The professional issues are the same, particularly those related to security. There seems to be a distinct pattern emerging which typifies union-related behavior from professionals. The key is that it is acceptable to be involved in such activities without professional alienation.

B. Union Movement and Growth

There is no doubt that unions have grown in the service industries. As stated earlier, it is a matter of simple mathematics and survival for the unions. Industry has changed from a manufacturing orientation to a service orientation. In turn, unions must make this same transformation. Unions are making this change, but it is lagging behind the change in industry.

With regard specifically to health care, there are interesting patterns of union activity. One instance is that larger hospitals receive more requests for recognition by unions, which parallels the same pattern related to size of manufacturing facilities (Metzger, 1978a). Furthermore, the extent of collective bargaining, organization attempts, and bed capacity of the hospital are positively associated. Not only are there more employees in larger facilities, but a greater proportion of them tend to organize (Metzger, 1978a). This relationship with facility size also holds true with work stoppages and strikes.

Public employees demonstrate similar patterns. First of all, the federal sector is the most heavily unionized and largest segment of public employees. As with larger health care facilities, a larger percentage of these employees than of other public employees are unionized. One deviation from the pattern exhibited by other unions is that unions of federal employees are the least likely of all employees to strike.

There is also a geographical relationship with unions. The Northeast and Midwest experience the greatest incidence of, and impact from, both union organizing and work stoppages in the industrial sector, and also experience the largest number and impact of similar activities in health care and human service organizations (Bureau of Labor Statistics, 1984). The Northeast and Midwest traditionally have been the strongest areas of union penetration for all types of union activity. This penetration and socialization to unions also produces more strikes and other work actions from the more aggressive unions in these areas.

Unions in all industries have been facing the prospect of losing membership and power since the early 1970s. Union membership in the United States was over 20 million in 1974, but by the start of 1977, membership had slipped about five percent, even with an increased labor force. Another illustration of this trend is that in 1945, 36 percent of all nonagricultural employees were unionized; this figure dropped to less than 25 percent in 1979 and by 1986 hovered at near twenty percent. Unions in health care facilities and in human service organizations did not follow this pattern because of the later penetration of unionism.

There are also indications that business lobbyists are gaining political influence and usurping the power base of organized labor. The point is that unions are experiencing difficulties in maintaining an income base and influencing political decisions. Health care facilities and government agencies, with their revised image and pro-organizational labor laws, are prime targets for organization. These organizations provide unions with an opportunity for income and a new base of political strength. The industrial sector seems less inviting for unions, so members in health care facilities are needed for unions to preserve their position of strength and, ultimately, for financial and organizational survival. It is evident from the information presented that unions are making this move to health care and human service organizations, and are experiencing enough success to generate continued activity.

X. PROFESSIONAL ASSOCIATIONS AS ORGANIZED LABOR

There is an organized labor movement in which professionals are seeking power and parity with management by acting collectively to attain desired goals. In health care, these professionals include physicians, nurses, pharmacists, and numerous allied health workers, while in human services they include social workers and a variety of white-collar employees.

Within health care, most of the activity involves nursing groups, particularly the ANA, while among public employees, the penetration is more widespread among particular groups of employees. Many theorists feel that the movement of professionals into organized labor activity is the "wave of the future." This hypothesis makes sense when one realizes how professionalized and white-collar the work force has become, and that this trend will only intensify in the future. Once again, it is a matter of numbers and survival.

For nurses, who represent a substantial portion of the hospital employees that have collective bargaining agreements, 1978 was the most active year on record for collective activity (Metzger, 1978a). Nurses follow the patterns established in non-health care unions and organize most frequently in health facilities located in large urban areas. Half of all ANA collective bargaining agreements are in California, Michigan, Minnesota, New York, Pennsylvania, and Washington.

The ANA not only has strong working state associations, but also gets assistance from labor groups, professional associations, and other unions in its organization efforts. This phenomenon reinforces the statement that organizing professional associations in health care is a practical growth decision for unions and demonstrates the unity of the labor effort in the organization of health care workers.

When the professional association becomes a collective bargaining unit, changes occur in interactions with management. The NLRA begins to influence the association's activities and decisions concerning its relationship with management. Relations that may have existed naturally will change, becoming more formal and adversarial (Bean and Laliberty, 1977). Management has a new set of rules governing this relationship and may perceive nurses in the new image of active union members. Nurses appear to feel a need to protect their own best interests and hold their allegiances tight, and having the right to engage in concerted activities appears to satisfy this need for active ANA affiliates.

Unionization of registered nurses also has monetary effects on the health care system. Studies by Block and Kuskin (1978) and Shapiro (1978) show that union/nonunion wage differentials are positive, but are smaller for nurses than for other health care workers. Two Federal Mediation and Conciliation Service (1979) studies determined that there is no difference between union and nonunion professional employees' wage rates or benefits. Additionally, one of these studies showed that unions have a greater impact on the wages of nonprofessional workers than on those of nurses.

Despite their common etiology, not all the activities of these professional associations mimic non-health care union activities. The association is a means to satisfy immediate needs, but the philosophical difference seems to be that individuals can then focus their attention on more distant, far-reaching issues. This focus may be a product of the goals of the professional employees and their association. Consequently, associations engage in fewer recognitional disputes than unions, but participate in far more work stoppages related to terms of employment demands.

Health care managers may need to adjust their operating procedures when dealing with the bright and mature collective bargaining units of the ANA and other bargaining units with professional employees. The same philosophy holds true with professional employees within the human services. Nurses have the membership and the influence to be a powerful force in the health care industry. Health care administrators need to be aware of the activities of such associations in their respective states and local areas. Administration is confronted with the alternatives of functioning with an active state association or an active unit in its institution, or practicing a management style that might make these unions unnecessary in the institution.

XI. THE FUTURE

Collective bargaining is a dynamic process, and the health care industry is a dynamic and changing entity. Much of collective bargaining in health care will change in the future, as economic, social, and legal revisions are implemented. The following are some changes this author feels may occur in the collective bargaining process relating to the health care and human service industries:

1. Health care managers in particular will be more likely to develop a preventive style of management. The goal of the preventive management style is to keep workers satisfied and unions out of their organizations.
2. Pressure will come on the federal government to regulate unions due to cost pressures. There will not be any immediate changes in the current labor relations law.
3. There will be significant movement to unionize allied health personnel and technologists. These workers are in natural bargaining units in their associations and are quite susceptible to unionization due to these units.
4. There will be more unions representing physicians, nurses, and other professionals.
5. The collective bargaining process may take on a more national flavor if national health insurance is implemented. There would be more centralized guidance in establishing wages and benefits. National health insurance could bring the recognition of one predominant health care union.
6. Health care and human service management will continue to become more professional and better equipped to manage institutions.
7. Cafeteria-style bargaining may become predominant in collective bargaining agreements. This style of bargaining allows workers to pick and choose from alternative benefits to suit individual tastes and needs.

Labor relations and collective bargaining are dynamic subjects, but certainly no more dynamic than the health care system or public employment. These factors in combination produce quite an exciting body of knowledge. Situations change almost daily with workers, regulations, and society. Managers who fail to keep abreast of these changes will not be able to place their organizations in a competitive position. In addition, the most critical factor is that managers in health care and human services will not be able to deliver the quality of services which their customers, clients, or patients deserve. This knowledge allows managers in these industries to meet the critical bottom line, which can often be, quite literally, a matter of life or death.

BIBLIOGRAPHY

American Federation of Government Employees (1986). *AFGE Government Standard*, Washington, D.C.

American Hospital Association (1985). *American Hospital Association Guide to the Health Care Field*, American Hospital Association, Chicago.

Bean and Laliberty (1977). *Understanding Hospital Labor Relations*, Addison-Wesley Reading, Massachusetts.
Becker, B. (1980). Hospital unionism and employment stability, *Industrial Relations*, Spring: 140.
Behling, S., and Schreischern, B. (1976). *Organizational Behavior: Theory, Research, and Application*, Allyn and Bacon, Boston.
Bentivegna, G. (1979). Labor relations: Union activity increase among professionals, *Hospitals, 13*: 63.
Block, F. E., and Kuskin, M. S. (1978). Wage determination in the union and nonunion sectors, *Industrial and Labor Relations Review, 1*: 183.
Bureau of Labor Statistics (1984). *Directory of National Unions and Employee Associations*, U.S. Department of Labor, Washington, D.C.
Bureau of National Affairs (1979a). *Labor Management Relations 1979–2020*, Washington, D.C.
Bureau of National Affairs (1979b). *Basic Patterns in Union Contracts*, Washington, D.C.
Bureau of National Affairs (1984). *Basic Patterns in Union Contracts*, Washington, D.C.
Bureau of National Affairs (1985). *DRGs: Impact on Employee Relations in the Health Care Industry*, Washington, D.C.
Byrd, S. F. (1979). *Front Line Supervisor's Labor Relations Handbook*, National Foreman's Institute, Waterford, Connecticut.
Catholic Hospital Association (1979). *A Guide to Employer Employee Relations*, Catholic Hospital Association, St. Louis.
Cawsey, T. F., and Wedley, W. C. (1979). Labor turnover costs, *Personnel Journal, 58*: 90.
Curtin, R. T. (1977). *Income Equity Among U.S. Workers*, Praeger, New York.
Dunlop, J. T. (1964). *The Theory of Wage Determination*, Macmillan, New York.
Eichner, A. S. (1979). *The Megacorp and the Oligopoly*, Cambridge University Press, New York.
Elkin, R. D. (1974). Recognition and negotiation under Taft-Hartley, *Hospital Progress, 12*: 50.
Federal Mediation and Conciliation Service (1979). *Impact of the 1974 Health Care Amendments to the NLRA on Collective Bargaining in the Health Care Industry*, U.S. Department of Labor, Washington, D.C.
Feldstein, P. J. (1979). *Health Care Economics*, John Wiley and Sons, New York.
Fitzgerald, P. E. (1980). *Flat of the Curve Medicine: A Discussion*, University of Alabama, Birmingham.
Fitzgerald, P. E. (1984). Worker perceptions: The key to motivation, *Health Care Supervisor, 3*(1): 13.
Flath, Carl I. (1980). Hospitals and the Labor Movement, *Southern Hospitals*, July: 24.
Fottler, M. D. (1977). The union impact on hospital wages, *Industrial and Labor Relations Review, 4*: 342.
Fuchs, V. R. (1976). The earnings of allied health personnel: Are health workers underpaid? *Explorations in Economics Research, 3*: 408.
Furlane, M. E., and Freeman, C. A. (1985). St. Francis decision signals broader-based bargaining units, *Health Progress, 4*: 66.
Hawk, D. C. (1976). Absenteeism and turnover, *Personnel Journal, 6*: 34.
Health Policy Advisory Center (1970). *Health/PAC Bulletin*, July–August.
Hyclack, T. (1979). The effects of unions on earnings inequality in local labor markets, *Industrial and Labor Relations Review, 10*: 77.
Jackson, D., Turner, H. A., and Wilkinson, F. (1972). *Do Trade Unions Cause Inflation?* Cambridge University Press, Oxford.
Joiner, C. L., and Morris, J. O. (1978). Management's response to the union phenomenon. *Hospital Progress, 5*: 59.

Kahn, L. M. (1978a). The effect of unions on the earnings of nonunion workers, *Industrial and Labor Relations Review, 1*: 205.
Kahn, L. M. (1978b). Unions and the employment status of nonunion workers, *Industrial Relations, 5*: 238.
Kahn, L. M. (1979a). Union strength and wage inflation, *Industrial Relations, 2*: 144.
Kahn, L. M. (1979b). *Industrial and Labor Relations Review, 7*: 520.
Kobs, D. R. (1979). *Unionization in Hospitals*, Catholic Hopsital Association, St. Louis.
Kovack, K. A. (1979). Do we still need unions? *Personnel Journal, 12*: 849.
Metzger, N. (1977). Preventive labor relations: Communication the key, *Hospital Progress, 4*: 79.
Metzger, N. (1978a). Labor relations: Recent statistics show reversed trend toward unionization, *Hospitals, 13*: 115.
Metzger, N. (1978b). *The Health Care Supervisor's Handbook*, Aspen Systems Corporation, Germantown, Maryland.
Metzger, N. (1979). Union impact on hospital management, *Journal of Health and Human Resources Administration, 8*: 28.
Metzger, N., and Pointer, D. D. (1975). *The National Labor Relations Act: A Guidebook for Health Care Facility Administrators*, Spectrum, New York.
Miller, R. U. (1980). *Hospital Labor Relations*. Graduate School of Business, University of Wisconsin, Madison.
National Labor Relations Board (1976). *A Guide to Basic Law and Procedures Under the National Labor Relations Act*, U.S. Government Printing Office, Washington, D.C.
National Labor Relations Board (1979). *44th Annual Report*, U.S. Government Printing Office, Washington, D.C.
Osterhaus, L. B. (1979). The effects of unions on hospital management, *A Guide to Employer Employee Relations*, Catholic Hospital Association, St. Louis.
Pfeffer, J., and Ross, J. (1980). Union-nonunion effects on wage status attainment, *Industrial Relations, 2*: 140.
Rakich, B., and O'Donovan, S. R. (1977). *Managing Health Care Organizations*, Sanders, Philadelphia.
Rees, A. (1962). *Economics of Trade Unions*, University of Chicago Press, Chicago.
Salkever, D. S. (1984). Cost implications of hospital unionization: A behavioral analysis, *Health Services Research, 5*: 639.
Shapiro, D. (1978). Relative wage effects of unions in the public and private sectors, *Industrial and Labor Relations Review, 1*: 193.
Sinicrope, A. V. (1979). *Current Issues in Labor Relations*, University of Iowa, Iowa City.
Sloan, F. A., and Adamache, K. W. (1984). The role of unions in hospital cost inflation, *Industrial and Labor Relations Review, 37*(2): 252.
Somers, G. S. (1980). *Collective Bargaining: Contemporary American Experience*, Industrial Relations Research Association, Madison, Wisconsin.
Stember, L., et al. (1978). Job satisfaction research: An aid in decision making, *Nursing Administration Quarterly, 4*: 75.
Szilagyi, A. D. (1979). Keeping employee turnover under control, *Personnel Journal, 6*: 42.
Teitelman, R. (1984). Labor pains, *Forbes, 134*(1): 68.
Walter, R. E., and McKersie, R. B. (1965). *A Behavioral Theory of Labor Negotiation*, McGraw-Hill, New York.
Ward, R. A. (1975). *Economics of Health Resources*, Addison-Wesley, Reading, Massachusetts.
Werther, W. B., and Lockhar, C. A. (1976). *Labor Relations in the Health Professions*, Little, Brown & Company, Boston.

Wilson, C. N. (1985). Unionization in the hospital industry: How are wages affected? *Healthcare Financial Management, 39*(8): 30.
Winpisinger, W. L. (1979). Labor's changing profile, *Nation's Business, 4*: 32.
Wolfe, S. (1978). *Organization of Health Workers and Labor Conflict*, Baywood, Farmingdale, New York.
Yoder, D. (1962). *Personnel Management and Industrial Relations*, Prentice-Hall, Englewood Cliffs, New Jersey.

Unit IV

Law and Regulation and Their Effect on Human Services Administration

10

An Overview of Law for Human Services Administrators

David H. Rosenbloom Department of Public Administration, The Maxwell School of Citizenship and Public Affairs, Syracuse University, Syracuse, New York

I. WHAT IS LAW?

Following *Black's Law Dictionary*, law can be given a concise definition as "in its generic sense, . . . a body of rules of action or conduct prescribed by controlling authority, and having binding legal force." More elaborately, and in the United States context, law can be considered a system for preventing and resolving disputes between individuals, groups, organizations, institutions, governments, and corporations. Law prevents disputes by defining and delimiting the conduct that will be considered acceptable in the society and by specifying punishments or penalties for breaches of such conduct. It establishes rights and obligations intended to control behavior. For example, law seeks to prevent disputes by individuals over private property by making stealing and trespassing punishable offenses. Law is used to resolve disputes by providing a method for determining whether rights have been violated or obligations met in any given context, or which party's rights or obligations should prevail over another's. This process is generally referred to as adjudication. It can be highly formal and complex, as in elaborate courtroom trials, or relatively informal and simple. In the fields of public health and human services, law is an important means of determining the rights of individuals to benefits, services, treatments, privacy, equal protection, and freedom. It also partly establishes the parameters of appropriate professional or administrative conduct, and determines the liabilities of administrators.

In the United States, law is a very comprehensive and powerful system for regulating conduct, but it is not the only one. Social control is exercised by families, various organizations, and peers. For instance, though it is legal, few people feel comfortable wearing formal dress to the beach or bathing suits to Internal Revenue audits. Economic control is evident in the forces of markets. There are many things we forego because they are unaffordable or unprofitable in an economic sense. Overlapping social and economic control is a category that could be called "professional or vocational control." Here, the values of a profession, such as law or medicine, or an occupation, such as public administration, may prescribe the character and content of legitimate conduct. For example, there are professional codes of ethics and administrative codes of conduct. Even though violations of these codes may not be illegal, they may provide for negative sanctions, such as the loss or suspension of an occupational license.

Control can also be based upon expertise. Individuals frequently comply with the directions or instructions of physicians because they defer to the expertise of the medical profession. They may suspend their personal judgment when accepting a doctor's directives. Administrative organizations often rely on expertise to obtain individuals' voluntary compliance. For instance, many individuals will be deferential to administrative decisions pertaining to eligibility for benefits or participation in human service programs. Deference to expertise is generally bolstered by the belief that the experts are impartial. Although perhaps personally interested in what happens to the individual client, experts are often expected to apply their expertise impersonally, in the sense of making decisions based on general principles, rather than in terms of individual persons or personalities. There are a number of other kinds of control as well, including physical and psychological control.

Each of these kinds of control will emphasize certain values and employ certain techniques for attaining them. Law can be highly developed in this respect, and in the United States, its values and techniques often conflict with those of other kinds of control. This fact emphasizes the need for American health and human service administrators to be familiar with law as a system for preventing and resolving conflict.

The United States polity makes law in four ways.

A. Constitutions

The federal and state constitutions define several legal relationships:

1. The relationship between the national and state governments. The U.S. Constitution provides for four kinds of powers in this regard: (a) powers that are vested exclusively in the federal (national) government (for example, the power to enter into treaties or coin money); (b) powers specifically denied to the states (those exclusively vested in the federal government, and the power of states to enter into compacts with one another without the consent of Congress); (c) powers that may be exercised, under some constraints, by both the federal and state governments (such as the power to tax); and (d) powers reserved exclusively for the states (these are largely unspecified, but the Tenth Amendment reads, "The powers not delegated to the United States by the Constitution, nor prohibited by it to the states, are reserved to the states respectively, or to the people").

2. The relationships between the state governments. For example, Article IV of the U.S. Constitution provides that "full faith and credit shall be given in each state to the public acts, records, and judicial proceedings of every other state."

3. The relationship among branches of the same government, such as the president and Congress at the federal level, or the legislature and executive in the state constitutions.

4. The relationships between governments and individuals. The federal Bill of Rights and the Fourteenth and Fifteenth Amendments are most familiar in this regard. For instance, the Fourth Amendment reads, in part, "the right of the people to be secure

in their persons, houses, papers, and effects, against unreasonable searches and seizures, shall not be violated." The Fourteenth Amendment prohibits each state from denying "to any person within its jurisdiction the equal protection of the laws." The Fifteenth Amendment specifies that "the right of citizens of the United States to vote shall not be denied or abridged by the United States or by any state on account of race, color, or previous condition of servitude."

5. The relationships between individuals. With one exception, the U.S. Constitution does not regulate the relationships among purely private individuals, that is, individuals who are not government officials, public employees, or engaged in state action[1] of some kind. The exception is the Thirteenth Amendment, which provides that "neither slavery nor involuntary servitude, except as a punishment for crime whereof the party shall have been duly convicted, shall exist within the United States, or any place subject to their jurisdiction." It is very important to note the distinction between the U.S. Constitution's direct regulation of relationships between the government and private individuals on the one hand, and its irrelevance in private relationships not involving slavery or involuntary servitude on the other. When one private individual is talking in a public place and another commands him or her to shut up, no constitutional issue of free speech is involved. On the other hand, if under the same circumstances, a police officer issued the order, a serious constitutional issue would be potentially present. Another illustration of the distinction is that while no government in the United States could constitutionally refuse to issue a marriage license to an individual based on his or her race, no individual would violate the Constitution by being unwilling to marry anyone of any race. Overwhelmingly, those purely private relationships that are regulated by law are controlled by kinds of law other than constitutions.

6. The relationships between governments and society. The Preamble to the U.S. Constitution states, in part, "We the people . . . do ordain and establish this Constitution for the United States of America." The government is accordingly conceptualized as the agent of the people or the society, and as having been created and authorized to accomplish certain purposes, such as promoting the general welfare. Thus, the government is separate from the society, and limits on its penetration of, intervention in, or interference with the society could be placed upon it. The U.S. Constitution prohibits the state and federal governments from doing a number of things, including granting titles of nobility, passing bills of attainder and ex post facto laws, and establishing religions (originally, this applied only to the federal government, but now is interpreted to apply to the states as well). Additionally, the Ninth Amendment reads, "The enumeration in the Constitution of certain rights shall not be construed to deny or disparage others retained by the people." This amendment has been interpreted as bolstering the rights of privacy and choices pertaining to family life which are not specifically mentioned in the Constitution.

B. Statutes

Whereas constitutions largely define what governments, rather than individuals, can do, statutes are generally aimed at regulating the behavior of private individuals and of public and private organizations. Statutes are usefully considered a legislative response to a problem that is present in the society or economy. For instance, the recognition of growing dangers from hazardous wastes may lead a legislature to enact a statute regulating their disposal or generation. The Civil Rights Act of 1964 was passed by Congress as a means of eliminating racial discrimination in private employment and in private facilities of public accommodation, such as motels and restaurants. Legislation is also addressed to what are considered harmful economic practices, such as monopolization, false advertising, fraudulent business practices, and the production of dangerous products. Today, a great deal of economic activity in the United States, including whole sectors of the economy—such as agriculture, labor relations, and the sale of stocks and bonds—are regulated by statutes.

Statutes not only regulate and specify appropriate conduct, they also place sanctions upon violators. Sanctions may be criminal or civil. A criminal case can be prosecuted only by the government, whereas either a private party or the government can bring a civil suit (that is, be the plaintiff) against another private party or government. Public administration in health and human services is regulated by both criminal and civil statutory law.

Although the goal of statutes is to regulate conduct, sometimes the letter of statutory law may be rather vague and indefinite. This is no secret. In *National Anti-Hunger Coalition v. Executive Committee of the President's Private Sector Survey on Cost Control* (1983, p. 530), a federal district court had occasion to inform Congress that one of its statutes was "another example of unimpressive legislative drafting. It is obscure, imprecise, and open to interpretations so broad" that it could threaten the constitutional separation of powers. But while the statutes may be obscure, the reasons for their obscurity is often clear. Legislatures respond to complex and dynamic social and economic problems. They can articulate the principles of conduct that should pertain in the areas they address, but it is difficult for them to specify precisely and in detail that which is to be prohibited in the future. As Leif Carter poses the problem, "Statutes speak for the future. Because legislators cannot tell precisely what shape the problem will take in the future and cannot predict what new methods of monopolizing trade or what new consumer fraud schemes people will dream up, statutes must address the future in general and flexible language" (Carter, 1983, p. 36). Less-benign reasons for imprecise statutory language are that members of the legislature are unable to agree on anything more than a general objective and that they prefer to avoid the conflict and controversy that may accompany specific statutory requirements. For example, it is easier to agree on the general objective of equal employment opportunity than on the specific requirement that affirmative action hiring and promotional goals be used (Rosenbloom, 1977). Not surprisingly, therefore, the Civil Rights Act of 1964 and the Equal Employment Opportunity Act of 1972 talk in terms of equal opportunity, and for the most part, it has been left to the courts and administrative agencies to fashion affirmative action strategies for achieving this general legislative aim.

C. Agency Rules and Adjudications

When the government's legislative and executive branches anticipate that a social or economic problem will require constant attention, they may establish an administrative agency to deal with it. For example, if the purity of food and drugs is considered to be an ongoing concern, or if fair economic practices are thought to be so, agencies such as the Food and Drug Administration and the Federal Trade Commission may be created. In more recent years, Congress created the Equal Employment Opportunity Commission (1965) to deal with prohibited discrimination in employment, and the Nuclear Regulatory Commission (1975) to deal with the development, use, and safety of nuclear energy. Such agencies are expected to make rules for the implementation of their general statutory mandates in order to adapt to new or unforeseen conditions. The issuance of these rules is itself regulated by the federal and state Administrative Procedure Acts (or similar legislation), but validly issued rules have the force of law. Violations of the rules can result in criminal or civil penalties. The volume of agency rules is tremendous. At the federal level, these are published in the *Federal Register*, which in bulk far surpasses legislation enacted by Congress. It is estimated that federal agencies issue 7,000 rules and policy statements pertaining to them each year, and that 2,000 of these apply directly to the citizenry (Carter, 1983, p. 15). Rules can and do range from the critical to the absurd. Matters of airline safety are regulated by the rules of the Federal Aviation Administration; the Food and Drug Administration has developed product standards that literally define the acceptable dimensions and appearance of food products, such as frozen fish sticks and potato chips.

Agency rules are binding on individuals and organizations. So are their adjudications, although appeals to the courts are possible. The volume of agency adjudication of the application of their rules is also extensive, although a precise figure of the number of cases resolved through adjudication of some kind is elusive. There are more federal administrative law judges to handle agency adjudication (about 1,100) than there are regular federal district court trial judges (about 710) (Carter, 1983, p. 15). Some agencies use adjudication more than rule making, whereas others prefer to rely mostly on comprehensive sets of rules. For instance, the National Labor Relations Board is heavily involved in adjudication of matters such as alleged unfair labor practices. The Internal Revenue Service, on the other hand, relies mostly on rule making to regulate conduct. In any event, agency adjudication is a way of making law, insofar as agency decisions become binding upon other parties in the future. In other words, if the NLRB declares a practice to be unfair, that practice is treated as unfair in future cases involving different parties (unless the adjudicatory decision is reversed). In this sense, adjudication builds a case law that specifies rights, obligations, and appropriate conduct. It is important to note that agency rules and adjudication are not administrative law. Administrative law consists of those portions of constitutional law, statutory law, and common law (discussed below) that establish the authority of public administrators, control their behavior, and determine their liabilities.

D. Common Law

American common law is derived from the long-standing English practice of judges deciding conflicts even in the absence of statutes. In other words, if two individuals had a dispute about a matter of property, contract, or other matter that was not covered by a specific statute, judges might resolve the conflict by relying on general principles of law as derived from prior cases, legal treatises, or legal philosophy. *Black's Law Dictionary* defines common law as follows: "As distinguished from law created by the enactment of legislatures, the common law comprises the body of those principles and rules of action, relating to the government and security of persons and property, which derive their authority solely from usages and customs of immemorial antiquity, or from the judgments and decrees of the courts recognizing, affirming, and enforcing such usages and customs; and, in this sense, particularly the ancient unwritten law of England." The extent to which the federal and state judiciaries make use of common law necessarily varies with the comprehensiveness of their statutory and constitutional law, as well as with the extent to which their legal systems favor allowing judges to make law, that is, to declare the common law.

Historically, the application of common law has often been viewed as a usurpation of power by the judiciary. In a famous critique of common law, Jeremy Bentham, an English political/social philosopher wrote:

> It is the judges . . . that make the common law. Do you know how they make it? Just as a man makes laws for his dog. When your dog does anything you want to break him of, you wait till he does it, and then beat him for it. . . . This is the way judges make laws for you and me. They won't tell a man beforehand what it is he should not do (Bentham, 1843, vol. 5, p. 235).

With regard to public administration, common law has been particularly important in establishing the extent to which public officials are immune to civil suits for damages arising out of the performance of their public duties. In recent years, as a good deal of public officials' historical common-law immunity has been eroded by judicial decisions, some public administrators may have come to view judge-made law as, in Bentham's terms, "dog law."

II. THE UNITED STATES LEGAL SYSTEM

A. Process

In seeking to resolve disputes, the legal system in the United States applies all of the types of law discussed above. It does this through adjudication based on adversary procedure. The fundamental principles of adversary procedure are simple to state, but their application can be exceedingly complicated and elaborate. Adversary procedure places two parties against each other in a contest presided over by a judge or hearing examiner. A jury may also be present to determine disputes over matters of fact, including intent. The adversaries present evidence and legal arguments or interpretations. Each side has the opportunity to challenge the material presented by the other. The judge applies established procedural rules to the contest, in order to assure that each adversary has a fair opportunity to present his or her side of the case. For instance, such rules specify that witnesses against an individual have to be identified (confrontation) and that an opportunity to cross-examine them will be available. Similarly, certain kinds of information, such as hearsay, cannot be presented or considered as evidence. The judge also applies relevant substantive law in deciding cases and in charging juries. For example, does a particular statute cover the conduct at issue? Does the liability of a party depend on his or her state of mind at the time the conduct occurred? Administrative hearings differ from judicial trials primarily in that juries are not used and the administrative law judge (or hearing examiner) plays a more active role in ferreting out information and in questioning the parties' legal contentions. Generally, administrative hearings are less formal and less rule-bound than trials.

A very central premise of adversary procedure is that factual information will be brought to the attention of the hearing examiner or judge and jury by the adversaries and will be screened by the rules of procedure. This is obviously a much different approach to ascertaining facts than that used by public administrators and natural and social scientists. Indeed, sometimes courts are compelled to treat information as fact simply because it is presented by one adversary and not controverted by the other. This can lead to all kinds of startling outcomes. In *Bishop v. Wood* (1976), the U.S. Supreme Court found itself in the odd position of having to decide the constitutionality of the dismissal of a police officer based on a record from the state trial court in which the policeman's claim that the charges against him were false was not contested. Therefore, the Supreme Court had to assume that his dismissal was erroneous, though, nevertheless, no constitutional relief was granted! A more important fact (or legal principle, to be precise) was established in *Wyatt v. Stickney* (1971), when both parties to a case agreed that involuntarily committed patients in state mental health facilities have a constitutional right to treatment. Although a constitutional right must depend on more than the adversaries' agreement that it exists, their failure to contest it in the *Wyatt* case influenced the federal district court's conclusion that there is such a right.

A more elaborate description of adversary procedure should make note of the following conditions delineated by Abram Chayes (1976, pp. 1282–1283):

1. "The lawsuit is *bipolar*. Litigation is organized as a contest between two individuals or at least two unitary interests, diametrically opposed, to be decided on a winner-takes-all basis."
2. "Litigation is *retrospective*. The controversy is about an identified set of completed events: whether they occurred and if so, with what consequences for the legal relations of the parties."
3. *"Right and remedy are interdependent."* In general, the plaintiff who prevails will be compensated for the harm or damages done to him or her at the level that will make him or her whole. In other words, the remedy is intended to restore the plaintiff to the position in which he or she would have been had not his or her rights been violated.
4. "The lawsuit is a *self-contained* episode. The impact of the judgment is confined to the parties. . . . Entry of judgment ends the court's involvement."
5. "The process is *party-initiated* and *party-controlled*. The case is organized and the issues defined by exchanges between the parties. Responsibility for fact development is theirs. The judge is a neutral arbiter of their interactions who decides questions of law only if they are put in issue by an appropriate move of a party."

Since the 1960s, the traditional adjudicatory model has been augmented by what is often called the "public law litigation" suit. This newer model of adjudication has been developed by the judiciary itself, largely in response to the difficulties posed by conflict resolution in the context of health and human service administration. Roger Cramton (1976, p. 552) describes the broad differences between the two models in terms of judicial review of public administration. One is "the traditional model . . . of a restrained and sober second look at what government has done that adversely affects a citizen. The controversy is bipolar in character, with two parties opposing each other; the issues are narrow and well defined; and the relief is limited and obvious." This model is useful as a corrective to the "tunnel vision in which particular values are advanced and others are ignored" by public administrative agencies. But the judiciary has not deemed the traditional model comprehensive enough to check contemporary public administration or allow for sufficient judicial participation in it. Consequently, there is

> a second model of judicial review that is growing in acceptance and authority. This model of the judicial role has characteristics more of general problem solving than of dispute resolution. . . . [There is] a modern tendency to view courts as modern handymen—as jacks of all trades available to furnish the answer to whatever may trouble us. "What is life? When does death begin? How should we operate prisons and hospitals? Shall we build nuclear power plants, and if so, where? Shall the Concorde fly to our shores?" (Cramton, p. 552).

Abram Chayes (1976, pp. 1282-1302) identified the following central aspects of the public law litigation model:

1. The structure of the public law litigation suit is not bipolar. Rather, the suit concerns whole communities, and the interests of the litigants may be overlapping. For instance, public school officials and parents suing for desegregation both have similar interests in the best public education possible at an acceptable cost. Prison officials have an interest in better correctional facilities, as do inmates. Public health officials and patients both favor better mental health care. The interests of the parties in a public law litigation suit are not identical, but it is possible for both sides to win. For instance, a court may order that a facility for the mentally retarded be upgraded in terms of physical plant and staff.

2. The public law litigation suit is prospective, rather than retrospective: "Instead of a dispute retrospectively oriented toward the consequences of a closed set of events, the court has a controversy about future probabilities." This change in focus poses difficulties in assimilating probabilistic, social scientific reasoning into the adjudicatory format.

3. Rights and remedies lose some of their independence. The remedies fashioned in public law litigation suits can be very extensive and essentially legislative in character. For example, in a public school desegregation suit, the court may find it necessary to consolidate and close schools, draw district lines, map out bus routes, and become involved in matters of finance. Such remedies generally fall within the equity powers of the judiciary. Equitable remedies go beyond what is authorized by statutory law in seeking to establish a fair resolution of a conflict that serves the broad public interest (McDowell, 1982). Chayes writes: ". . . if litigation discloses that the relevant purposes or [constitutional] values have been frustrated, the relief that seems to be called for is often an affirmative program to implement them. And courts, recognizing the undeniable presence of competing interests, many of them unrepresented by the litigants, are increasingly faced with the difficult problem of shaping relief to give due weight to the concerns of the unrepresented."

4. Fact-finding is no longer tied to "specific instances of past conduct," but like the remedies, is legislative in character. "The whole process begins to look like the traditional description of legislation: Attention is drawn to a 'mischief,' existing or threatened, and the activity of the parties and court is directed to the development of on-going measures designed to cure that mischief." However, establishing facts in a legislature is not quite the same as establishing them in a traditional lawsuit. Legislative facts tend to identify interests of various sectors or groups, such as automobile manufacturers, farmers, or minorities, and to treat the interest of the entire sector or group as identical to that of each of its members (Lowi, 1969). Traditional legal facts are much more oriented toward matters pertaining to specific individuals, such as the intent of a party to the suit—for instance, did he or she act in good faith? Interestingly, individual intent is treated as a matter of fact for determination by juries. In addition, legislative facts tend to be future-oriented and posed in the form of "if we do *x* (for example, subsidize farmers), then what effect will it have on *y* (say, the viability of family farms)?" Since courts do not have the same resources for establishing legislative facts as do legislatures, this aspect of the public law litigation model may be very problematic for the judiciary.

5. The public law litigation decree, which is the centerpiece of the emerging model, differs from the traditional judicial decree in that it ". . . seeks to adjust future behaviors, not to compensate for past wrong. It is deliberately fashioned rather than logically

deduced from the nature of the legal harm suffered. It provides for a complex, on-going regime of performance rather than a simple, one-shot, one-way transfer. . . . It prolongs and deepens, rather than terminates, the court's involvement with the dispute." The litigation to desegregate Boston's public schools in an excellent example. In *Morgan v. Kerrigan* (1975), a federal district court in Boston sought to integrate the public schools by creating eight school districts, closing 20 schools, and establishing a number of citywide magnet schools and examination schools. The court also mandated the use of parent councils to help facilitate the implementation of its plan. At one point, District Court Judge Arthur Garrity decided to eliminate a ninth planned school district, thereby requiring the busing of an additional 6,100 students. As late as 1981, Judge Garrity was still active in requiring Boston to fund aspects of the court's plan at an adequate level. Traditionally, as Chayes and Cramton observe, such ongoing involvement in administrative matters would be virtually unthinkable for the judiciary.

6. The public law litigation suit is not controlled by the parties initiating it. Since it involves broad issues of public policy and individuals and groups who are not formally parties to the suit (such as teachers or the parents of nonminority students in *Morgan*), the court places less dependence on the formal parties for the development of facts, assessment of injury, and explication of right. It also looks beyond the parties in developing a remedy.

7. The judge plays a more active role in the structure of the suit and assessing the desirability of various potential remedies. As Chayes notes, "The judge is not passive, his function limited to analysis and statement of governing legal rules; he is active, with responsibility not only for a credible fact evaluation but also for organizing and shaping the litigation to ensure a just and viable outcome."

The public law litigation suit provides a useful alternative forum to groups who are unable to convince legislatures to mandate far-reaching reforms of public administrative institutions. Members of minority groups, prisoners, and advocates for the mentally ill and retarded have been particularly successful in pressing such suits. Their votes often carry less weight in elections than do their rights in court. But public law litigation also has serious limitations. Some members of the judiciary, including Supreme Court justices, do not consider institutional reform a proper judicial function. For instance, in *Milliken v. Bradley* (1974, p. 744), Chief Justice Burger, speaking for the Court, admonished a district court that had sought to consolidate 54 independent school districts in the Detroit metropolitan area that "this is a task which few, if any, judges are qualified to perform and one which would deprive the people of control of the schools through their elected representatives." Moreover, by now the record is clear that many of the judicial decrees in public law litigation suits have met with only partial success in terms of implementation. They also have the effect of fragmenting public-sector budgeting to a greater extent. Nonetheless, it is important to bear in mind that the public law litigation suit is now common and does provide an important avenue for redress of rights to some of the least fortunate and most discriminated-against members of American society.

Whether in the form of the traditional lawsuit or public law litigation, adjudication has several advantages and disadvantages as a decision-making process (Shapiro, 1965). Among its advantages are the following:

1. It is incremental in its development of principles and decisions or rules. It builds on precedents, but makes continual adjustment to changing conditions possible. It avoids comprehensive mistakes and makes it possible to abandon unworkable or undesirable principles with relative ease. Thus, it is also flexible.

2. It is particularly useful where the issues are inherently judgmental. Many legal matters turn on the question of intent or good faith. These are not matters that can be decided categorically, but rather must be evaluated in light of the particular circumstances presented in a given case.

3. Adjudication is also desirable where the principles involved in a decision are highly complex. For example, it has long been held that the extent to which a public employee's speech is constitutionally protected depends on a number of factors, including the nature of his or her position and the content and context of the remarks.

4. Adjudication is highly desirable where it is possible to decide specific cases, but impossible to agree on general rules. This is sometimes evident in Supreme Court decisions in which there is a judgment of the Court, but no single opinion subscribed to by a majority of its members. This phenomenon occurred in such important cases as *Regents v. Bakke* (1978), dealing with affirmative action, and *Elrod v. Burns* (1976), declaring some patronage dismissals from the public service to be unconstitutional.

On the other hand, adjudication has some serious drawbacks:

1. In its classic form, it is retrospective and concentrates on harms already done.

2. It can lack uniformity if courts in separate jurisdictions decide similar cases differently. The federal circuit courts of appeals often do this, which makes the law in one circuit different from that in another—at least temporarily. Even judges of the same court may sometimes reach opposing decisions in similar cases.

3. The content of adjudicatory decisions is not always readily available to interested parties. The decisional principles and rules are not necessarily explicit, but instead must be derived from analyzing the case law. This can be a forbidding task and may take a great deal of legal training and skill.

4. Adjudication is time-consuming and repetitive.

5. Adjudication allows for minimal participation by those who are not formal parties to a case. Friend of the court briefs and expert testimony are allowed, but the adversary procedure is designed primarily to test individuals' rights, rather than to ascertain the broad public interest. The public law litigation model seeks to reduce this problem. But as Chief Justice Burger pointed out in *Milliken*, in terms of participation, it is no match for the electoral process.

However one evaluates the adjudicatory process, the main point is that it is the fundamental decision-making approach used in the United States legal system. Legislators may prefer lawmaking through the enactment of statutes. Administrators may favor rule making over adjudication. But the courts and the legal system are set up to adjudicate. That is their method and primary role in the separation of powers.

B. Structure

Structurally, the judiciary in the United States is essentially bureaucratic. The overall organization of the federal judiciary has been described in terms that would also apply to the states:

> The organization's basic subunits are its courts. Each has a unique geographical and/or functional jurisdiction. Lower courts are linked to higher courts through appellate review. Judges, in particular, but other court officials as well (including lawyers), must meet certain technical qualifications. Selection of permanent court officials is by appointment. Remuneration for the most important of these officials—the judges—is by set income that cannot be diminished. It is of such a scale that it is their primary or sole source of

> income. Judicial authority extends only to official acts. All official acts are set down as written transcripts, orders, rules, and opinions. The whole system is permeated by rigid rules relating to such matters as jurisdiction, procedure, admissibility of evidence, remedies, and appellate review (Goldman and Jahnige, 1971, p. 43).

As this description indicates, there are several types and levels of courts:

1. *Trial courts*. This is the level at which most cases are initially heard. Unlike other courts, trial courts may use juries. It is at this level that the record of the case is developed through sworn testimony and the admission of evidence.

2. *Appellate courts*. Appellate courts hear appeals from trial courts and from the adjudications of some administrative agencies. They can reverse the decisions of the lower courts when there has been a violation of proper judicial procedures or rules, or, more broadly, when the interests of justice seem to demand that they do so. Cases can be remanded to the trial courts or administrative agencies for rehearing or modification of the previous decision. Of course, appellate courts can uphold the trial court's decision, which is what occurs in the majority of cases.

3. *Supreme courts*. The U.S. Supreme Court sits at the apex of the American judiciary. It is the highest national court. The Supreme Court hears appeals from other federal courts and also from state courts. In some cases, appeals can go directly from U.S. district courts to the Supreme Court. It also hears appeals directly from the U.S. Court of Claims and the Court of Customs and Patent Appeals. Most other federal cases come by way of appeal from the U.S. courts of appeals. In some specific and relatively uncommon cases, the Supreme Court has "original jurisdiction" and sits in the capacity of a trial court. Perhaps the most important example is a suit between two states. The Court also hears appeals directly from the highest state courts having jurisdiction over a case that presents a question under the U.S. Constitution, such as abridgment of free speech or establishment of religion. Each state has the equivalent of a supreme court in its judicial system. An important function of supreme courts is to unify the law under their jurisdiction by resolving conflicting rulings of the appellate or trial courts.

4. *Special courts*. A number of courts have been established to deal with specific areas of the law. For example, at the federal level there is a Court of Claims to deal with cases in which a party is suing the U.S. government for monetary damages, often in connection with federal employment or federal contracting. There is also a U.S. Tax Court, a Customs Court, and, as mentioned earlier, a Court of Customs and Patent Appeals.

5. *Magistrates*. U.S. magistrates are empowered to try all but a few federal misdemeanors, administer oaths and affirmations, and set conditions, other than bail, for the release of persons accused of crime. Equivalent functionaries can be found at the state level as well.

Today, one of the major problems faced by the legal system in the United States is a very heavy workload. The dockets of courts at all levels are crowded, and several steps have been taken to ease the pressures on the judiciary. Some of these appear to be wholly functional in terms of maintaining the integrity of the legal system. For instance, more judgeships have been created and greater attention has been paid to court and docket management. However, at least two measures used to reduce the caseloads do pose serious problems for promoting justice. One is plea bargaining, which is now the predominant method of resolving criminal cases. In plea bargaining, the defense and prosecution bargain over the terms necessary to induce the defendant to plead guilty and thereby obviate the need for a lengthy or jury trial. The other measure is the growth of unpublished judicial opinions. These are written, but not published or circulated. Apparently, the practice serves to reduce the time required to write opinions. But the hallmark of the Anglo-American legal system has been the written judicial opinion explaining the judge's reasoning and explicating the legal principles involved, and unpublished opinions are less functional than published ones in this respect.

C. Judicial Roles and Values

In resolving conflicts presented to it in the form of litigation, the judiciary plays several important roles in American government and politics. Courts necessarily interpret the law when they decide cases. Generally, they pay great deference to the intent of the legislature that drafted a statute in question or to the expertise of the administrative agency that issued a rule. However, sometimes the legislative intent is uncertain or the administrative expertise questionable to the extent that the courts must essentially make law while trying to apply statutes or rules to particular cases. In other words, the courts must act as subordinate and supplementary lawmakers. A good example of both aspects of this role occurred in *Industrial Union Department, AFL-CIO v. American Petroleum Institute* (1980). The statute under interpretation was the Occupational Safety and Health Act of 1970, which authorized the secretary of labor to promulgate standards for dealing with toxic materials in the workplace that "most adequately assure, to the extent feasible, that no employee will suffer material impairment of health. . . ." Following this rule, and on the assumption that whenever a carcinogen is involved, there is no safe standard, the secretary issued a rule limiting exposure to benzene to the lowest feasible level (one part per million in its airborne state). In deciding whether the secretary's rule was legal, the Supreme Court had to try to decipher the legislative intent and to evaluate the rationality of the rule itself. The matter was so complicated that the Court could not reach a majority opinion, but rather issued a judgment that the rule was invalid. Justice Rehnquist, who subscribed to this judgment, had the following to say about the key issue of Congress's intent: "The legislative history demonstrates that the feasibility requirement . . . is a legislative mirage, appearing to some Members but not to others, and assuming any form desired by the beholder" (Industrial Union, 1980, p. 691). Necessarily, therefore, the Court had to supplement the statute with its own interpretation. The Court also found the secretary's rule lacking, in part because the risk involved from different levels of benzene in the workplace should have been quantified sufficiently to enable the secretary to characterize it as significant in an understandable way. The Court's approach consequently had the effect of requiring the agency to engage in risk analysis—that is, to apply a different kind of expertise—before seeking to promulgate rules for the regulation of toxic substances.

The courts must also interpret the Constitution in the process of determining its requirements in any particular case. This role lies at the heart of the courts' power of judicial review, which is the power to declare the acts of other government units to be unconstitutional. The U.S. Supreme Court can find the acts and actions of Congress, the federal executive branch, and any units of the state or local governments to be unconstitutional, and it can overturn the rulings of any of the federal or state courts that are properly appealed to it. The state supreme courts exercise a similar power with regard to their governments. The power of judicial review extends to laws, regulations, executive orders, policies and practices, and treaties. In declaring what the Constitution allows or requires, the courts generally analyze the intentions of the framers of the pertinent clause or amendment, prior judicial interpretations, and a variety of other materials, including scholarly treatises on the meaning of one clause or another. Nonetheless, in interpreting the Constitution, the courts must often augment it with their own views of what it requires. Sometimes members of the judiciary are quite candid about this role. For instance, Justice Powell once remarked, "Constitutional law is what the courts say it is" (*Owen v. City of Independence*, 1980, p. 669). Chief Justice Earl Warren was even more candid: "We have no constituency. We serve no majority. We serve no minority. We serve only the public interest as we see it, guided only by the Constitution and *our own consciences*" (emphasis added; Simon, 1973, p. 2).

More generally, the courts tend to view the Constitution as an expression of a set of fundamental legal and political values and principles that must be applied to changing circumstances. From this perspective, when the courts declare a "new" constitutional doctrine, it is new only in the sense that no previous case had required that it be articulated. In other words, the doctrines (values and principles) are always there, even if there has been no previous opportunity to announce them. On a few occasions, the courts may even overturn past cases on the basis that the proper legal reasons had not been applied. In any event, it is largely through interpretation, rather than amendment, that the U.S. Constitution can be continually adapted to changing political, economic, and social conditions. A good example of judicial augmentation of the Constitution occurred in two cases in which the Supreme Court declared some patronage dismissals from the public service to be unconstitutional (*Elrod v. Burns*, 1976; *Branti v. Finkle*, 1980). Apparently, there was no specific federal judicial precedent for these decisions.

In interpreting statutes and the Constitution, the courts unavoidably make public policy. Today, a good part of our political, social, and administrative universe has been the result of judicial policy-making. Some of the clearest examples are in the areas of public school desegregation, legislative apportionment, the application of the U.S. Constitution's Bill of Rights to the states, police conduct, abortion, public personnel administration, corrections, and public mental health care. Sometimes, policy-making of this type is best thought of as constitutionalizing some aspects of relationships that were previously considered not to be regulated by the Constitution. Public employment is one of the clearest examples. Today, in contrast to the past, many aspects of recruitment, selection, hiring, promotion, dismissal, discipline, and employee conduct are affected by the Constitution (Rosenbloom, 1971).

The courts also become directly involved in administering government institutions on occasion. This is largely an outgrowth of the public law litigation model. Prisons, public mental health facilities, and public schools are the leading examples. Judges have mandated rules for staffing, relieving overcrowding, regulating the physical and psychological environments of prisons and mental health facilities, and even for the stationing of prison guards. In many instances, the courts retain jurisdiction of a case while overseeing the implementation of such reforms.

The power of the judiciary is most obvious when the courts declare some government action to be unconstitutional or illegal. But even in the more frequent cases where the constitutionality or legality of government or private activity is upheld, the judiciary can play a very important role in legitimizing a public policy. For instance, in *Steelworkers v. Weber* (1979), the Supreme Court found nothing illegal in a private employer's voluntary agreement to use an affirmative action quota in allocating training to its employees. Such cases can help to resolve political disputes over important issues.

Once the law is clear, attention can be turned to how effective or desirable a practice or policy is. For instance, if affirmative action is legal, then the next step in evaluating it as a policy is to assess the conditions under which it works best.

A final judicial role that should be mentioned is that of agenda setting. The courts provide a forum for raising issues, provided the issues can be properly framed for litigation. A single individual can bring a case that has national ramifications. Interest groups—such as the National Association for the Advancement of Colored People, the American Civil Liberties Union, trade unions and trade associations, and many others—can assist individuals in bringing such cases when they believe their resolutions will create or maintain conditions that the groups favor. If such groups can show direct harm to their members or to themselves as corporate entities from some government or other practice, they may be able to bring cases directly. The important point is that the courts are a forum for raising issues in which, unlike the electoral system, it is not necessary to mobilize large numbers of people or even sums of money in order to be heard. This is one reason why members of society, such as prisoners and the mentally ill, who are relatively powerless in other government forums, may be especially inclined to seek policy changes and reforms through the courts. The same is true of individual citizens who are harmed by officially sanctioned activity.

In exercising their powers, the courts tend to express certain values in a relatively consistent way. At some points, these values converge with those embodied in prevailing public administration theory in the United States; but at other points, there is a marked divergence. It would be impossible to present a comprehensive exposition of judicial values here. However, the following are among the values informing judicial decision making that may be of greater interest to public administrators.

1. Judicial Restraint

In Federalist Paper Number 78, Alexander Hamilton perceptively observed, "The judiciary . . . has no influence over either the sword or the purse; no direction either of the strength or of the wealth of the society, and can take no active resolution whatever. It may truly be said to have neither FORCE nor WILL but merely judgment; and must ultimately depend upon the aid of the executive arm even for the efficacy of its judgments" (Rossiter, 1961, p. 465). Because the judiciary's chief power is judgment, it has to be especially careful to try to assure that other government actors and the general community will accept its rulings as legitimate. Consequently, courts often find it useful to be restrained in their decision making.

Restraint takes several forms:

1. The judiciary may rely on precedent, or at least show how precedents must be modified or why they must be abandoned if they are no longer deemed appropriate. Precedent is not the "imprisonment of reason," but it is relied upon as a guide. This helps legitimize judicial decisions because it militates against appearing to be highly politicized or whimsical. The Supreme Court occasionally makes dramatic turnabouts by overruling a decision handed down only a few years earlier. When it does so, it may simply admit that the first case was wrongly decided. However, the Court will generally try to avoid an indication that its abandonment of precedent is due to its changing membership or indecisiveness. More frequently, precedents are eroded slowly by the incremental appearance of new values and interpretations.

2. Another form of restraint is issuing narrow opinions as opposed to articulating comprehensive constitutional doctrines in any given case. As Alexander Bickel noted,

"A sound judicial instinct will generally favor deflecting the problem in one or more initial cases, for there is much to be gained from letting it simmer, so that a mounting number of incidents exemplifying it may have a cumulative effect on the judicial mind as well as on public and professional opinion" (Bickel, 1962, p. 176). He further observes that "the [Supreme] Court is a leader of opinion, not a mere register of it, but it must lead opinion, not merely impose its own; and—the short of it is—it labors under the obligation to succeed" (Ibid., p. 239). Narrow opinions are useful in this regard, because they can instruct the public as to what the Constitution requires and allow time for the society to make adjustments to fundamental changes. Perhaps the best historical example pertains to desegregation of public education. In *Missouri ex rel. Gaines v. Canada* (1938), the Supreme Court held that if a state provided law school education to whites, it had to provide it to blacks also (though not necessarily in the same university). In *Sweatt v. Painter* (1950), the Court held that the equal protection clause required that educational opportunities for blacks and whites be substantially equal in terms of tangible factors and, where this could not be accomplished on a segregated basis, that the educational facilities be racially integrated. In *McLaurin v. Oklahoma State Regents* (1950), the Court prohibited racial segregation within a single public university—that is, blacks and whites could not be segregated from one another in classes and other aspects of university life. In *Brown v. Board of Education* (1954), the Court held that segregation by law in public schools, regardless of tangible factors, was inherently unequal and in violation of the Fourteenth Amendment. Nevertheless, even then, the Court did not declare a specific remedy, but rather ordered that the schools be desegregated with all "deliberate speed." The opposition to public school desegregation has been substantial, but there seems to be every reason to believe that it would have been even greater if the Court had used the *Gaines* case in 1938 to reach the decision it finally handed down in *Brown* in 1954.

3. The judiciary also uses a form of statutory construction to enhance the legitimacy of its opinions. The general rule is that courts will interpret statutes in the way most favorable to their constitutionality. Judges work under the presumption that statutes are constitutional; they only infrequently seize upon ambiguous wording in an effort to find the statute unconstitutional.

4. Avoidance of "hot" political issues is another form of judicial restraint. American courts do not give advisory opinions. Within their jurisdiction, they decide actual cases or controversies, rather than hypothetical ones. In a broader sense, what comes before them for decision must be "justiciable," that is, suitable for resolution through lawsuit. Over the years, the judiciary has developed some general approaches that enable it to avoid cases that present highly controversial questions:

1. *Standing*. This requires that an individual have a legal right to bring the case to court. More generally, someone seeking to sue the government must show that government action has caused, or is imminently about to cause, some specific harm to that individual or to a group that he or she appropriately represents. This requirement prevents us from bringing suits to test the constitutionality or legality of policies to which we are opposed, but which do not affect us substantially differently from the way they affect the mass of other members of society.
2. *Political Questions*. The judiciary has refused to decide some cases on the grounds that they present political questions that are more appropriately addressed to the elected branches of government. In one such case, *Luther v. Borden* (1849), the Supreme Court found it inappropriate for the judiciary to decide, following a

rebellion of sorts in Rhode Island, which of two contending state governors was the rightful one. About a century later, in *Colegrove v. Green* (1946), the Supreme Court declined to enter the "political thicket" of legislative apportionment, though it has since overturned its holding in that case.

3. *Mootness*. A case can be considered moot when judicial decision can no longer have an impact on the resolution of the conflict. For example, the death of a party in a divorce case will make it moot. A recent highly political example of mootness occurred in *DeFunis v. Odegaard* (1974). The Supreme Court refused to decide the constitutionality of an affirmative action arrangement at a state law school on the grounds that regardless of its ruling, the student who brought the case was likely to graduate.
4. *Ripeness*. Mootness occurs when a case or controversy has already been resolved or is beyond judicial resolution. Ripeness presents a situation in which the dispute is not yet ready for resolution by the judiciary—for instance, when a genuine case or controversy might exist if a party is harmed, but the harm has not taken place and appears to be a remote prospect.[2] In one such case, *Poe v. Ullman* (1961), the Supreme Court refused to decide the constitutionality of a statute prohibiting the use of birth control devices, in part because it doubted whether the statute would ever be enforced, or could be in a way that did not violate well-established constitutional rights.

2. Adherence to the Rule of Law

The judiciary also highly values adherence to the rule of law. In a broad sense, the rule of law is a philosophy that encompasses judicial restraint (Carter, 1983, pp. 60-65). However, the concept can be used in a more limited sense to connote the use of law as a check on arbitrary government decision making or the exercise of unbridled official discretion. Here the issue is often posed less in terms of the substance of what government does than as a matter of how it decides to do it. Due process of law is the most important constitutional requirement in this context. Because it is so central to public administration, it will be discussed at some length later in this chapter. It is appropriate to note here, though, that due process is considered a very fundamental check on arbitrary government decision making. It requires that administrative or judicial decisions depriving individuals of life, liberty, or property must take a form that assures that the individual has an opportunity to contest, under reasonably fair conditions, the information or charges against him or her. This acts to safeguard against the possibility that the decision maker is simply misinformed. More elaborately, due process can require the rights to confrontation, cross-examination, open hearings or trials before impartial judges, legal assistance, and presentation of information and witnesses in support of one's position. Precisely how much process of this kind is "due," and what specific form it will take, depend partly upon the nature of what the individual stands to lose. For instance, loss of a government job or benefit will entail less due process than government efforts to incarcerate someone or confine him or her to a mental health institution.

The invocation of due process as a check on administrative discretion sometimes appears in another form as well. Due process can be violated by statutes or regulations that are so vague as to allow unchecked official discretion or to fail to specify the conduct required of private parties. Perhaps *Kolender v. Lawson* (1983) best illustrates the value the judiciary places on eliminating abuses of discretion. It concerned a

California statute that required individuals who wander or loiter to provide a "credible and reliable" identification and to account for their presence when asked to do so by a "peace officer." The Supreme Court found the statute to be unconstitutional under the due process clause of the Fourteenth Amendment. The crux of the statute's constitutional infirmity was that it was too vague and consequently allowed too great a range of discretion, did not restrain the exercise of police power, and actually encouraged arbitrary enforcement.

The judiciary's distaste for unchecked administrative discretion is also clearly illustrated in some Fourth Amendment cases. *U.S. v. Brignoni-Ponce* (1975) involved a practice by the U.S. Border Patrol. The patrol stopped motor vehicles within 100 miles of the Mexican border to check on the citizenship of their occupants. The basis for stopping any particular vehicle was that its occupants "looked Mexican." The stops took only about one minute, unless complications arose. However, the Supreme Court found the practice to be unconstitutional on the grounds that the Border Patrol needed a reasonable suspicion that the occupants of the vehicles were undocumented aliens in order to make the stops. Importantly, "looking Mexican" could not constitutionally constitute a reasonable suspicion. The larger point, of course, is that "looking Mexican" is an outrageously imprecise standard that places inadequate restraint on the exercise of police power and is insulting to U.S. citizens who are stopped because they do not fit the Border Patrol's stereotype of how they ought to look.

Delaware v. Prouse (1979) involved a practice by the police in Delaware of stopping cars on a random basis to check registrations and licenses. The Supreme Court again relied on the Fourth Amendment as a check on the unrestrained discretion involved: "We hold that except in those situations in which there is at least articulable and reasonable suspicion that a motorist is unlicensed or that an automobile is not registered, or that either the vehicle or an occupant is otherwise subject to seizure for violation of law, stopping an automobile and detaining the driver in order to check his driver's license and the registration of the automobile are unreasonable under the Fourth Amendment" (*Delaware v. Prouse*, 1979, p. 663).

3. Individuality

The judiciary also places a great deal of importance on treating each individual personally on his or her own merits. Adjudication is a decision-making process designed to assure that an individual can have his or her day in court. But the judiciary's emphasis on individuality goes farther, by promoting a great appreciation for diversity in terms of individuals' political and religious beliefs and social behavior. As Justice Jackson once succinctly expressed this value: "Compulsory unification of opinion achieves only the unanimity of the graveyard" (*West Virginia Board of Education v. Barnette*, 1943, p. 641). The number of cases emphasizing the value of individuality is so legion that it can be concluded that protection of individual choice in matters of politics, religion, association, and a variety of social contexts has become an important part of contemporary constitutional theory.

One of the most important ramifications of the judiciary's emphasis on individuality is that it can lead the courts to reject statistical generalizations as a basis for public policy formulation. *Craig v. Boren* (1976) presents an excellent example. The State of Oklahoma prohibited the sale of 3.2 percent beer to males under the age of 21 and to females under the age of 18. The state's rationale was that in the absence of such a regulation, males aged 18-20 were more likely than their female cohorts to be intoxicated while driving. There was some statistical support for this proposition. However, the Supreme Court found the regulation to be in violation of males' right to equal protection of the law under the Fourteenth Amendment. In the Court's words: "It is unrealistic to expect either members of the judiciary or state officials to be well versed in the rigors of experimental or statistical technique. But this merely illustrates that proving broad sociological propositions by statistics is a dubious business, and one that inevitably is in tension with the normative philosophy that underlies the Equal Protection Clause" (*Craig v. Boren*, 1976, p. 204). In his concurring opinion, Justice Stevens displayed even greater antipathy toward treating all males as identical for this purpose, without regard to their individual merits: "The empirical data submitted by the State accentuate the unfairness of treating all 18-20-year-old males as inferior to their female counterparts. The legislation imposes a restraint on 100% of the males in the class allegedly because about 2% of them have probably violated one or more laws relating to the consumption of alcoholic beverages. It is unlikely that this law will have a significant deterrent effect either on that 2% or on the law-abiding 98%. But even assuming some such slight benefit, it does not seem to me that an insult to all of the young men in the state can be justified by visiting the sins of the 2% on the 98%" (Ibid., pp. 213-214). An alternative, of course, is to prohibit driving while intoxicated and to punish those individuals, both male and female, who violate the prohibition.

Affirmative action is another area of public policy in which the difference between social scientific generalization and an emphasis on individuality is evident. Affirmative action tends to treat all members of a group as having been subject to identical discrimination. Although the judiciary has contributed much to the development of this approach, the Supreme Court and individual justices have displayed considerable uneasiness with its implications for individuality. For example, in the case of *Memphis v. Stotts* (1984), the Court had occasion to hold that "membership in the disadvantaged class is insufficient to warrant a seniority award [in public employment]; each individual must prove that the discriminatory practice had an impact on him . . . [citations omitted]" (p. 2588). In other words, the Court expressed its preference for individual adjudication (veritable case studies) over social scientific generalization.

4. Intent

In American law, the intent of a party may be equally important to, or even more important than, the result of that party's action. A good illustration is in the law of libel with regard to public figures. A libelous or slanderous statement may be actionable not because it is false, but because it was made with actual malice or wanton disregard for its truth or falsity. More dramatically, a death by shooting may be either a homicide or an accident, depending upon the intent of the individual who pulled the trigger. For health and human service administrators, a more important illustration of the place of intent in judicial values can be found in cases pertaining to equal protection. Under the Supreme Court's interpretation in *Washington v. Davis* (1976), the rule is that it will not be "held that a law, neutral on its face and serving ends otherwise within the power of government to pursue, is invalid under the Equal Protection Clause simply because it may affect a greater proportion of one race than of another" (*Washington v. Davis*, 1976, p. 242). Rather, it is necessary to show either (1) that a law or government practice establishes a racial or other social classification for which the state lacks either a compelling justification or a rational basis, or (2) that the law or practice has an invidious discriminatory intent or purpose. The Court expressed the importance of intent in this connection by indicating what might happen if it were treated as irrelevant: "A rule that a statute designed to serve neutral ends is nevertheless invalid, absent compelling justification, if in practice it benefits or burdens one race more than another would be far-reaching and would raise serious questions about, and perhaps invalidate, a whole range of tax, welfare, public service, regulatory, and licensing statutes that may be more burdensome to the poor and to the average black than to the more affluent white" (Ibid., 248).

5. A Robust Interpretation of Individual Rights

It is evident from much of the above discussion that the judiciary places great importance on the protection of the individual's civil rights and liberties. The U.S. Constitution and state constitutions are viewed as conveying rights and liberties that are a large part of the very reason for government in the United States and that cannot be abridged or infringed upon except under the most compelling of circumstances. This emphasis on individual rights has led the judiciary to develop some concepts for assuring that government regulations do not *needlessly* reduce the scope of constitutional protections. Public administrators should be especially aware of the following:

1. "Overbreadth." A regulation can be overbroad if it prohibits more than is necessary in order to achieve its intended purpose. For example, a statute intended to assure that public employees do not take part in partisan political activities would be overbroad if it also prohibited nonpartisan political speech or association.
2. "Chilling effect." A regulation can have the effect of chilling an individual's ardor for exercising his or her constitutional rights even though it does not directly prohibit individuals from doing so. For instance, borrowing from the example above, a regulation that did not penalize nonpartisan political association, but asked public employees to list all political organizations to which they belong, could have a chilling effect on the employees' exercise of freedom of association.
3. "Vagueness." A regulation can be so imprecise as to leave unspecified what it actually prohibits or allows. In this case, it will deprive individuals of the opportunity to know the limits of their constitutional rights and it may dissuade them from exercising their rights at all. Again using the example of public employees' political activities, a regulation that failed to distinguish partisan from nonpartisan activities could be considered unconstitutionally vague, since the line between the two types of activity is not always clear. In fact, the federal Hatch Acts, though constitutional, have a tendency toward vagueness. They allow political activity in "good government" organizations. Thus, presumably a federal employee could support the League of Women Voters in one of its registration drives, but could not do the same as part of an election or primary campaign for a partisan candidate, such as Jesse Jackson in 1984.
4. "Least restrictive alternative." Assuming that a regulation serves a compelling need and does not suffer from any of the above defects, it may still be unconstitutional if it is not the means of accomplishing the government's objective that is least restrictive of constitutional rights. For instance, if the only purpose of restrictions on public employees' political activities were to assure that individuals were not coerced by elected officials and political appointees to engage in campaigning, then the least restrictive alternative would be to outlaw the coercion itself, rather than the

opportunity to engage in electioneering. However, since the basis for the Hatch Acts is also to eliminate the appearance of partisanship in the public service, the acts are able to meet the least restrictive alternative test.

Another facet of the judiciary's value of robust constitutional rights is the downgrading of cost–benefit reasoning. The courts are not oblivious to the financial costs of implementing their interpretations of constitutional rights, including the reforms in administrative institutions and routines they may entail. However, the judiciary's predominant tendency is to assume that constitutional rights exist regardless of their financial cost, and the fact that they may be expensive is not a basis for abridging them. As one court said in an Eighth Amendment jail reform case, "Inadequate resources can never be an adequate justification for the state's depriving any person of his constitutional rights. If the state cannot obtain the resources to detain persons awaiting trial in accordance with minimum constitutional standards, then the state simply will not be permitted to detain such persons" (*Hamilton v. Love*, 1971, p. 1194). It is important to emphasize that while the judiciary tends to avoid cost-benefit approaches, sometimes it will take administrative costs and convenience into account, especially when determining precisely what due process requires in any given set of circumstances.

III. LAW AND HEALTH AND HUMAN SERVICES ADMINISTRATION

It should be evident that structure, processes, and values of the United States legal system may often be at odds with the predominant theories and practices of American public administration. As a self-conscious discipline and practice, American public administration often dates its origin to the publication of Woodrow Wilson's essay "The Study of Administration" in 1887. Wilson wasted no time in identifying what were to become the central values of orthodox public administration in the United States. In his opening paragraph, he wrote: "It is the object of administrative study to discover, first, what government can properly and successfully do, and, secondly, how it can do these proper things with the utmost possible efficiency and at the least possible cost either of money or of energy" ([1887] 1941, p. 481). In shorthand form, these values can be referred to as effectiveness, efficiency, and economy.

There are a number of reasons why public administration based on these values might tend to run counter to constitutional principles. Wilson and other scholar-practitioners in the orthodox tradition were uneasy with the constitutional scheme for the separation of powers. Since government had two functions, politics and administration, or expression of the popular will and its execution, traditional public administration found the Constitution's admixture of legislative, executive, and judicial powers something of a barrier to the notions of effectiveness, efficiency, and economy (Goodnow, 1900). Federalism also presented problems to these central values. After all, who today can find the fundamental orthodox administrative principle of unity of command in any complicated public administrative endeavor?

Even more problematic is the tendency for vigorous pursuit of orthodox values to lead to violations of individuals' constitutional rights. Effectiveness may suggest methods that are odious to the Constitution. This was true in *U.S. v. Brignoni-Ponce* and *Kolender v. Lawson*, discussed above. The Constitution does not favor unchecked official discretion, but effective public administration on the street requires a finely honed intuition (Lipsky, 1976). *Delaware v. Prouse* is even more to the point because there, the random stop by the police actually did uncover wrongdoing–a quantity of a controlled substance was in plain view in the car when the police approached it. Effectiveness in social welfare programs may require knowledge of the clients' behavior, but the Constitution rules out heavy-handed methods such as predawn raids on their dwellings (*Parrish v. Civil Service Commission*, 1967). Efficiency often requires standardization. In public mental health facilities, this can encourage handling patients in batches and failing to provide individual treatment. Yet in *Wyatt v. Stickney* (1971), it was held that anyone involuntarily confined to such an institution has a constitutional right to an individualized treatment plan. Economy has led to cost-cutting measures that violated individuals' due process and Eighth Amendment rights (*Holt v. Sarver*, 1970).

Perspectives are like lenses. How one sees an issue depends upon the apparatus with which one looks at it. In the health and human service areas of public administration, perspectives can make all the difference in determining what government can do and how it should do it. Jerry Mashaw (1983, p. 31) has identified three competing perspectives that are applicable in these administrative contexts:

1. Professional treatment. Here the legitimating value is service, the primary goal is client satisfaction, interaction between the public administrator and the client is personal, and the cognitive technique (intellectual process) is clinical application of knowledge. This is obviously a perspective for those health and human service administrators who consider themselves to be engaged in therapy.
2. Bureaucratic rationality. Here the legitimating values are accuracy and efficiency, the primary goal is program implementation, interaction is hierarchical, and the cognitive technique is information processing. Health and human service administrators who see their primary function as public management are apt to apply this perspective.
3. Moral judgment. The legitimating value is fairness, the primary goal is conflict resolution, decision-makers are organizationally independent, and the intellectual process is contextual interpretation. This perspective is closest to that of the legal system, and would be applied by officials in adjudicatory roles and by lawyers.

Considering these three perspectives, it is almost self-evident why professionals sometimes complain about bureaucrats who hinder their ability to render adequate service to eligible clients; why both may complain about being hampered by legal restrictions and lawyers' advice; and why judges and administrative hearing examiners may find the actions of the others defective.

It is important for the health and human service administrator to bear these competing perspectives in mind. It enables one to understand better the legal context of public administration in these fields. It also suggests that since all three perspectives are present and legitimate, the main challenge is to try to integrate them where possible and to make informed choices or rankings among them when integration is not feasible. If this challenge is met, the legal perspective will become as familiar to the health and human service administrator as are the professional and "bureaucratic" perspectives.

IV. CENTRAL CONSTITUTIONAL DOCTRINES

Public administrators in the fields of health and human services are not expected to be constitutional lawyers. But they are expected to understand those constitutional principles, values, and doctrines that are relevant to the performance of their jobs in the public interest. Additionally, many public administrators take an oath to support the

U.S. Constitution (and state constitutions). This section of the chapter provides a review of the constitutional doctrines or considerations that are most relevant to the general administration of health and human service functions in the public sector. The discussion emphasizes a broad understanding of the values and theories behind constitutional requirements, rather than a review of the latest cases.

A. Liberty and Property "Interests" in Health and Human Service Administration

The Constitution guarantees certain rights and liberties to individuals under the jurisdiction of governments of the United States. For example, one has a right to freedom of speech, association, and exercise of religion. These rights and liberties are not absolute; under some conditions and according to various judicial criteria, they can be limited. In the realm of public administration, a question often arises as to the constitutionality of conditions attached to the receipt of a government service or benefit. For example, a mother receiving financial assistance for her dependent child might be asked to allow a social worker to visit her home (*Wyman v. James*, 1971). This could be considered a violation of the Fourth Amendment's protection from government searches. An applicant for unemployment compensation might be required to express a willingness to work on the Sabbath, in violation of his or her religion (*Sherbert v. Verner*, 1963). An applicant for an occupational license might be questioned as to his or her morality or political ideology, and the application might be denied on the basis of the answers supplied (*Konigsberg v. State Bar of California*, 1957). A public school student might be prohibited from participating in extracurricular activities because he or she is married (*Starkey v. Board of Education*, 1963). The recipient of "old age assistance" might be told to live in conventional housing (*Wilkie v. O'Connor*, 1941). Public employees might be prohibited from engaging in partisan political activity or joining unions (*U.S. Civil Service Commission v. National Association of Letter Carriers*, 1973; *McLaughlin v. Tilendis*, 1968). These examples are all drawn from actual cases, and they all pose a serious constitutional question that has been difficult to resolve fully.

Historically, the judiciary was reluctant to hold that the allotment of government benefits could be regulated by the Constitution. Its reasoning, generally referred to as the doctrine of privilege, was as follows:

1. The government had no constitutional duty or obligation to supply the benefit, such as public housing, welfare, or even education.
2. The recipient accepted the benefit voluntarily, without government coercion.
3. Therefore, the government was largely free to establish the conditions upon which the benefit was provided to the recipient—if the recipient did not like the conditions, he or she could decline the benefit.
4. Benefits might even be withheld in a discriminatory fashion under some circumstances.

The key to understanding this approach was the distinction it drew between rights and privileges. Under the Constitution, a privilege can be obtained solely upon the terms set forth by the government; a right, on the other hand, is constitutionally protected and cannot be denied or abridged without due process of law.

A few cases conveniently convey the essence of the doctrine of privilege. In *Wilkie v. O'Connor*, New York State's highest court addressed the situation of a man who received old age assistance payments from the state commissioner of public welfare. The commissioner withheld the check on the basis that "despite all efforts to dissuade him, [Wilkie] insists upon his right to sleep under an old barn, in a nest of rags to which he has to crawl upon his hands and knees" (*Wilkie v. O'Connor*, 1941, p. 618). Wilkie challenged the commissioner's use of the welfare benefit to impose conditions upon his life-style. The court, relying upon the doctrine of privilege, gave short shrift to Wilkie's position: "He has no right to defy the standards and conventions of civilized society while being supported at public expense. This is true even though some of those conventions may be somewhat artificial" (Ibid., p. 619). For "in accepting charity, the appellant has consented to the provisions of the law under which charity is bestowed" (Ibid., p. 620).

The U.S. Supreme Court also embraced the doctrine of privilege in the past. *Hamilton v. Regents* (1934) is a good example. The issue was whether in establishing a state university, California could require students to enroll in a Reserve Officers' Training course. The students challenging the requirement claimed it infringed upon their religious freedom as conscientious objectors to war. The Court flatly rejected their argument:

> California has not drafted or called them to attend the university. They are seeking education offered by the State and at the same time insisting that they be excluded from the prescribed course solely upon grounds of their religious beliefs and conscientious objections to war, preparation for war and military education.
>
> Viewed in the light of our decisions that proposition must at once be put aside as untenable (*Hamilton v. Regents*, 1934, p. 262).

From a legal perspective, the doctrine of privilege incorporated a compelling logic. As one law professor explained: "If I have no ground for complaint at being denied a privilege absolutely, it is difficult to see how I acquire such a ground merely because the state, instead of denying me a privilege outright, offers me an alternative, however harsh" (quoted in O'Neil, 1966, p. 445). However, from a political perspective, the doctrine of privilege posed serious issues once public administration emerged as a major aspect of government. Charles Reich (1964, p. 733) framed the problem in a way that suggested why the doctrine of privilege had to be modified:

> One of the most important developments in the United States during the past decade [1950s] has been the emergence of government as a major source of wealth. Government is a gigantic syphon. It draws in revenue and power, and pours forth wealth: money, benefits, services, contracts, franchises, and licenses. Government has always had this function. But while in early times it was minor, today's distribution of largess is on a vast, imperial scale.
>
> The valuables dispensed by government take many forms, but they all share one characteristic. They are steadily taking the place of traditional forms of wealth–forms which are held as a private property. Social insurance substitutes for savings; a government contract replaces a businessman's customers and goodwill; the wealth of more and more Americans depends upon a relationship to government. Increasingly, Americans live on government largess. . . .
>
> The growth of government largess, accompanied by a distinctive system of law [the doctrine of privilege], is having profound consequences. It affects the underpinnings of individualism and independence. It influences the workings of the Bill of Rights. It has an impact on the power of private interests, in their relation to each other and to government. It is helping to create a new society.

If government benefits take the place of private property, as Reich argues, then some of the valuable functions previously performed by private property may be lost or altered. Reich contended that this possibility could be forestalled by creating a new legal approach to govern the rights of those receiving government largess. That approach would treat largess as a kind of property interest—a "new property"—that would be protected by due process and other constitutional rights. In Reich's words (Ibid., p. 787):

> If the individual is to survive in a collective society, he must have protection against its ruthless pressures. There must be sanctuaries or enclaves where no majority can reach. To shelter the solitary human spirit does not merely make possible the fulfillment of individuals; it also gives society the power to change, to grow, and to regenerate, and hence to endure. These were the objects which property sought to achieve, and can no longer achieve. The challenge of the future will be to construct, for the society that is coming, institutions and laws to carry on this work. Just as the Homestead Act was a deliberate effort to foster individual values at an earlier time, so we must try to build an economic basis for liberty today—a Homestead Act for rootless twentieth century man. We must create a new property.

Reich's discussion of the "new property" clarified the broad problems posed by the doctrine of privilege in the contemporary welfare or social service state. His analysis was part of a growing uneasiness with the implications and effects of the doctrine of privilege, and it eventually helped to crystallize the development of a new constitutional approach to regulating the conditions that could be attached to the distribution of largess. This approach is essentially to recognize that even though an individual may have no constitutional right to a government benefit, such as welfare payments or public education, the benefit must be considered more than a mere privilege because the individual may have a liberty or property interest in it that is sufficiently strong to require constitutional protection. The new constitutional approach has no agreed-upon label. However, it has replaced the doctrine of privilege, both legally and philosophically. It is no longer useful, from a legal perspective, for public administrators to conceive of their functions as dispensing privileges in which individuals have no constitutional rights.

The newer constitutional approach was solidified in the 1970s. It requires the courts (and public administrators) to consider two dimensions in assessing the extent of constitutional protection involved in the allocation of government benefits of various kinds. One is the strength of the individual's interest in the benefit: Does he or she need it to survive? Does it merely augment other income? Is it of substantial or minimal importance to the individual's ability to function in the society? The second dimension is the extent to which a constitutionally recognizable property or liberty interest is implicated by the conditions under which the benefit is granted or withheld. For instance, does the individual have a property interest in the form of a contractual right or legal entitlement to the benefit? Or is there merely a unilateral expectation on the part of the individual that he or she ought to receive it? Does acceptance of the benefit require the abridgment of a constitutional right or liberty? Is the abridgment severe? Is the right or liberty fundamental, or somewhat tangential? What is the administrative rationale for abridging the right or liberty?

The newer constitutional approach to the granting of government benefits is relatively complex and filled with distinctions in nuance. However, three Supreme Court decisions convey its essence in terms that should be familiar to public administrators in the fields of health and human services:

1. *Sherbert v. Verner* (1963) involved in Seventh-Day Adventist who lost her job when she refused to work on Saturday. She filed a claim for benefits under the South Carolina Unemployment Compensation Act. The claim was denied on the basis that the state Employment Security Commission "found that [Sherbert's] restriction upon her availability for Saturday work brought her within the provision disqualifying for benefits insured workers who fail, without good cause, to accept 'suitable work when offered' " (*Sherbert v. Verner*, 1963, p. 401). The administrative decision was upheld by the state's highest court on the basis of the doctrine of privilege. But on appeal, the U.S. Supreme Court flatly rejected this approach:

> Nor may the South Carolina court's construction of the statute be saved from constitutional infirmity on the ground that unemployment compensation benefits are not appellant's "right" but merely a "privilege." It is too late in the day to doubt that the liberties of religion and expression may be infringed by the denial of or placing of conditions upon a benefit or privilege. . . . To condition the availability of benefits upon [Sherbert's] willingness to violate a cardinal principle of her religious faith effectively penalizes the free exercise of her constitutional liberties . . . (Ibid., pp. 404–406).

In the Court's view, "governmental imposition of such a choice puts the same kind of burden upon the free exercise of religion as would a fine imposed against appellant for her Saturday worship" (404).

2. *Goldberg v. Kelly* (1970) concerned New York City's termination of welfare payments to an individual without first affording him a hearing. The Supreme Court found the procedure constitutionally defective in violation of the due process clause. In the Court's view, "The extent to which procedural due process must be afforded the recipient is influenced by the extent to which he may be 'condemned to suffer grievous loss,' . . . and depends upon whether the recipient's interest in avoiding that loss outweighs the governmental interest in summary adjudication" (*Goldberg v. Kelly*, pp. 262-263). Under the circumstances, in which Kelly might be deprived of "the very means by which to live while he waits" (Ibid., p. 264) for a full-fledged posttermination hearing, and in which no substantial administrative interest is served by the city's procedure, the recipient was entitled to a hearing prior to termination. Justice Black's dissent captured the shift from the doctrine of privilege to the "new property" approach:

> The Court . . . relies upon the Fourteenth Amendment and in effect says that failure of the government to pay a promised charitable installment to an individual deprives that individual of *his own property*, in violation of the Due Process Clause of the Fourteenth Amendment. It somewhat strains credulity to say that the government's promise of charity to an individual is property belonging to that individual when the government denies that the individual is honestly entitled to receive such a payment (Ibid., p. 275).

3. *Shapiro v. Thompson* (1969) concerned states' imposition of a requirement that an individual must have resided within their boundaries for at least a year in order to be eligible for welfare assistance. The Supreme Court found several constitutional defects with such residency requirements. They not only placed a chilling effect on the constitutional right to travel or migrate from state to state, but also violated the equal protection clause. In the Court's opinion, the states' reasoning "would logically permit the State to bar new residents from schools, parks, and libraries or deprive them of police and fire protection. Indeed it would permit the State to apportion all benefits and services

according to the past tax contributions of its citizens. The Equal Protection Clause prohibits such an apportionment of state services" (*Shapiro v. Thompson*, 1969, pp. 632-633).

The shift from the doctrine of privilege to the newer approach was succinctly summarized by Justice Powell in a dissenting opinion in *Goss v. Lopez* (1975, pp. 599-600):

> Not so long ago, state deprivations of the most significant forms of state largesse were not thought to require due process protection on the ground that the deprivations resulted only in the loss of a state-provided "benefit." . . . In recent years the Court, wisely in my view, has rejected the "wooden distinction between 'rights' and 'privileges,'" . . . and looked instead to the significance of the state-created or state-enforced right and to the substantiality of the alleged deprivation.

But by its very nature, the newer approach requires elaborate balancing of the individual's liberty or property interest and the extent of infringement upon his or her ordinary constitutional rights on the one hand, against the government's interest in viable public administration on the other. Consequently, the simplicity of the doctrine of privilege has been replaced by complexity, and the courts have been confronted with the need to assess each substantial case on its own merits in arriving at an appropriate balance. Therefore, it is not feasible in this chapter to explicate fully the body of constitutional law that has emerged since the demise of the doctrine of privilege. However, it is possible to review some of the main constitutional concepts presently governing the provision of benefits in the areas of health and human service administration.

B. Procedural Due Process

Today, under the Supreme Court's reasoning in *Mathews v. Eldridge* (1976), a threefold consideration is used to determine the requirement of procedural due process when public administrators act upon individuals:

1. The "private interest that will be affected by the official action"
2. The "risk of an erroneous deprivation of such interest through the procedures used, and the probable value, if any, of additional or substitute procedural safeguards"
3. The "Government's interest, including the function involved and the fiscal and administrative burdens that the additional or substitute procedural requirement would entail" (*Mathews v. Eldridge*, 1976, p. 335).

Balancing these considerations in any given case can require an elaborate analysis. Generally speaking, however, the following guidelines have evolved:

1. A hearing is needed except in certain cases. Hearings are not required if there is no dispute over the facts upon which the administrative decision is based. Hearings are not required where the individual has no legitimate expectation of receipt of the benefit or public-sector job.
2. Hearings prior to denial of the benefit must be held if, as in *Goldberg v. Kelly*, the individual needs the benefit in order to survive while awaiting a hearing *and* there is no overriding government interest in terminating the benefit earlier.
3. Individuals should be notified in advance of the administrative action and be given an opportunity to respond, in writing or otherwise.

4. The extent of due process in hearings, such as the right to an open hearing, confrontation, cross-examination, and the right to present witnesses on one's behalf, will depend on the facts involved, the nature of the deprivation, and the cost of an elaborate procedure to the government.

These guidelines may be useful to the health or human service administrator. However, it is important to emphasize that a highly legalistic approach may not be the best policy. Sometimes the law may require less than sound administration, and a broader adherence to the spirit of due process may be favorable.

C. Equal Protection

The Fourteenth Amendment, which was ratified in 1868, provides that no state shall "deny to any person within its jurisdiction the equal protection of the laws." It has been held that the Fifth Amendment imposes a similar restriction on the federal government (*Bolling v. Sharpe*, 1954). The original purpose of the equal protection clause was, at the least, to protect the freed slaves and blacks generally in the South. Over the years, a highly developed scheme evolved for interpreting equal protection in changing political and social circumstances.

1. Classifications. Public policies often intentionally classify individuals by social or economic attributes, such as sex, age, income, and, in earlier times, race. The judiciary uses a two-tiered approach to dealing with classifications of this kind. Some classifications are considered suspect because, on their face, they appear to be used to deny individuals equal protection of the laws. For example, a classification based on race is suspect. Classifications that do not appear to compromise equal protection are not considered suspect. A classification based on age is an example.

2. Scrutiny. Suspect classifications are subjected by the judiciary to "strict scrutiny." The courts will consider very carefully the origin, intent, and rationale for the classification. A nonsuspect classification is subject to weaker scrutiny.

3. Constitutionality. Classifications that are not "invidious"—that is, demeaning or harmful to a group—are less likely to be in violation of equal protection. Affirmative action has been accepted in some cases partly on this basis (*Fullilove v. Klutznick*, 1980; *Morton v. Mancari*, 1974). Invidious suspect classifications can be constitutional only if the government can demonstrate that they serve a compelling state interest that could not be equally well served in a fashion less invasive of constitutional rights. The burden of proof will be on the government where such classifications are involved, and justifying them will be extremely difficult. The constitutionality of nonsuspect classifications depends on whether there is a "rational basis" for them. Classifications based on sex are an example. Those that address conditions of biology, such as pregnancy, or of privacy, as when individuals are in custodial care, may be rational. Those that use gender as an "inaccurate proxy for other, more germane bases of classification" (*Craig v. Boren*, 1976, p. 198) are inherently irrational and consequently cannot meet the rational basis test.

The interplay of the nature of the classification, the degree of judicial scrutiny, and the test for constitutionality demonstrate the adaptive potential of equal protection. A classification may be nonsuspect at one time in history, but as the society changes, it may become suspect. This appears to be occurring with regard to gender-based classifications today. As the Supreme Court noted in *Craig v. Boren* (1976, p. 199), "increasingly outdated misconceptions concerning the role of females in the home rather than in the 'marketplace and world of ideas' were rejected as loose-fitting characterizations incapable of supporting state statutory schemes that were premised upon their accuracy."

D. The "Right to Treatment"

After a protracted debate among lawyers, medical practitioners, judges, and others, a federal district court unequivocally declared in *Wyatt v. Stickney* (1971, p. 784) that "when patients are so committed [involuntarily to public mental health facilities] for treatment purposes they unquestionably have a constitutional right to receive such individual treatment as will give each of them a realistic opportunity to be cured or to improve his or her mental condition." The court went on to hold that this right required: (1) a humane psychological and physical environment; (2) qualified staff in sufficient numbers, and (3) development of individualized treatment plans for all patients. In spelling out precisely what these requirements entailed, the court mandated a number of conditions to prevent overcrowding, to regulate the heating, cooling, and sanitation of the facilities, and to establish staffing ratios for professional and other employees per patient.

The right to treatment has been litigated in a number of contexts, but it has not been fully explained or endorsed by the U.S. Supreme Court. In *Youngberg v. Romeo* (1982, p. 324), involving a state facility for the mentally retarded, the Court held that an involuntarily committed individual had "constitutionally protected interests in conditions of reasonable care and safety, reasonably nonrestrictive confinement conditions, and such training as may be required by these interests." The Court indicated that the judiciary should be deferential to the judgment of appropriate professionals in ascertaining what is reasonable in these contexts.

However, professional values alone are not likely to be adequate in determining the acceptability of conditions and treatment or training. For as the lower court said in *Wyatt* (1971, p. 785), "To deprive any citizen of his or her liberty upon the altruistic theory that the confinement is for humane therapeutic reasons and then fail to provide adequate treatment violates the very fundamentals of due process." In particular, the right to treatment prompts public administrators in the field of mental health to balance their legitimate concerns with costs and efficiency against the constitutional right of the patients to more than being "warehoused." Importantly in this regard, those involuntarily confined to public mental health facilities may seek to develop a constitutional right to refuse antipsychotic drugs (*Mills v. Rogers*, 1982).

E. Privacy*

The constitutional right to privacy can be of great relevance to the administration of public health and human service programs. Under present Supreme Court interpretations, the right to privacy is both person-oriented and property-oriented. It is the right to be let alone, that is, the right to be free of undue government interference in matters of personal choice and to be free of unreasonable searches and seizures. However, like other constitutional rights, it is not absolute. The government's interest in intruding into personal privacy may sometimes outweigh the individual's right. Consequently, it is useful for public administrators in the fields of health and human services to be familiar with the Supreme Court's present construction of the right to privacy.

*The author is grateful to David Landsbergen for his assistance in researching this section.

The Court first declared the existence of the constitutional right to privacy in *Griswold v. Connecticut* (1965). The case followed *Poe v. Ullman* (1961), mentioned earlier in conjunction with the concept of ripeness. In *Griswold*, Connecticut's prohibition against the use of birth control devices and its attachment of criminal penalties to the provision of information or instruction about their function was at issue. The executive director of the Planned Parenthood League and a medical doctor were convicted of providing such information to married persons. They were fined $100. The Court's majority opinion observed.

> [Previous] cases suggest that specific guarantees in the Bill of Rights have penumbras, formed by emanations from those guarantees that help give them life and substance. . . . Various guarantees create zones of privacy. The right of association contained in the penumbra of the First Amendment is one. . . . The Third Amendment in its prohibition against the quartering of soldiers "in any house" in time of peace without the consent of the owner is another facet of that privacy. The Fourth Amendment explicitly affirms the "right of the people to be secure in their persons, houses, papers, and effects, against unreasonable searches and seizures." The Fifth Amendment in its Self-Incrimination Clause enables the citizen to create a zone of privacy which government may not force him to surrender to his detriment. The Ninth Amendment provides: "The enumeration in the Constitution, of certain rights, shall not be construed to deny or disparage others retained by the people." . . . The present case, then, concerns a relationship lying within the zone of privacy created by several fundamental constitutional guarantees. And it concerns a law which, in forbidding the *use* of contraceptives rather than regulating their manufacture or sale, seeks to achieve its goals by means having a maximum destructive impact upon that relationship. Such a law cannot stand in light of the familiar principle, so often applied by this Court, that a "governmental purpose to control or prevent activities constitutionally subject to state regulation may not be achieved by means which sweep unnecessarily broadly and thereby invade the area of protected freedoms" (*Griswold v. Connecticut*, 1965, pp. 484–485).

The Court's language in *Griswold* left open the possibility that the right to privacy in this context could be confined to marital relationships. In *Eisenstadt v. Baird* (1972, p. 453), it dispelled this notion as follows: "If the right of privacy means anything, it is the right of the *individual*, married or single, to be free from unwarranted governmental intrusion into matters so fundamentally affecting a person as the decision whether to bear or beget a child." This line of constitutional thought was further invoked in *Roe v. Wade* (1973), in which the Court held unconstitutional a Texas statute making it a felony for anyone to destroy a fetus in the absence of medical advice for the purpose of saving the life of the mother. In the course of its decision, which noted the sensitive and complex nature of abortion, the Court emphasized that its "decisions recognizing a right of privacy also acknowledge that some state regulation in areas protected by that right is appropriate" (*Roe v. Wade*, 1973, p. 154).

What are some examples, from the fields of health and human service administration, where government intrusion upon the right to privacy have been found appropriate? In *Wyman v. James* (1971), the Supreme Court found no constitutional impediment to a narrowly drawn New York administrative procedure requiring visits to the homes of recipients of Aid to Families with Dependent Children. The Court stressed that the procedure for visits included advance notice and prohibitions against forcible entry and snooping. In *Whalen v. Roe* (1977), the Court upheld New York's Controlled Substances Act, which was challenged on the basis that it required the names and addresses of individuals to whom such substances were prescribed to be collected in a central file. This aspect of privacy is sometimes called "informational privacy." Although the Court recognized that there is a "threat to privacy implicit in the accumulation of vast amounts of personal information in computerized data banks or other massive government files" (*Whalen v. Roe*, 1977, p. 605), it reasoned that the state had a sufficiently strong rational basis for collecting the information in this instance.

As in the case of other constitutional rights, the right to privacy presents public administrators in the health and human services fields with the need to strike an appropriate balance between the administrative demands of their programs and the rights of the individuals directly affected by them. Attention to such judicial concepts as compelling state interest, overbreadth, least restrictive alternative, vagueness, and chilling effect will facilitate this process.

V. LIABILITY

Public administrators in the fields of health and human services should be greatly concerned about legal doctrines pertaining to individual and agency liability. Under common law approaches in the past, most public administrators were *absolutely* immune to liability suits arising out of their official actions. Today, however, most enjoy only a *qualified* immunity in such suits. This change, which occurred in the 1970s and early 1980s, makes public administrators much more vulnerable to suits arising from the mistreatment or nontreatment of individuals under their care and from the wrongful denial of administrative services or benefits. The newer standard is connected to the emergence of the public law litigation model and to the demise of the doctrine of privilege. Consequently, it is best understood as part of a broad effort by the judiciary to exert greater influence or control over public administrators (Rosenbloom, 1983). Therefore, as in other areas of the law, it is important for public administrators to be cognizant of the theory behind the current approach to liability, as well as familiar with its specific standards.

A. From Absolute to Qualified Immunity

Historically, in Anglo-American law, there has been a doctrine of "sovereign immunity." It holds that the government cannot be sued for civil damages in the absence of its own consent. The doctrine developed in the English tradition of sovereignty in kings and queens who "could do no wrong." Why it was adapted through the common law to the United States is puzzling. Sovereignty is more diffuse in a federal system making use of the concept of the separation of powers and resting on popular consent. The original authorization of the constitutional regime was by the members of the citizenry who may have retained or ceded their sovereignty in the process. Nonetheless, the Supreme Court observed in *United States v. Lee* (1882, p. 207), "While the exemption of the United States and of the several states from being subjected as defendants to ordinary actions in the courts has . . . been repeatedly asserted here, the principle has never been discussed or the reasons for it given, but it has always been treated as an established doctrine." By implication, if the government could not be sued, neither could its agents who were acting within their official spheres of authority.

When applied to public administrators, the equivalent of sovereign immunity is best thought of as "official immunity," since the administrators themselves are not the sovereign. Moreover, the extent to which they enjoy immunity can be made to rest upon their behavior and intent as individuals. Traditionally however, the courts were reluctant to limit the scope of public administrators' official immunity on the basis that:

> In exercising the functions of his office, the head of an Executive Department, keeping within the limits of his authority, should not be under any apprehension that the motives that control his official conduct may, at any time, become the subject of inquiry in a civil suit for damages. It would seriously cripple the proper and effective administration of public affairs as entrusted to the executive branch of the government if he were subjected to any such restraint (*Spalding v. Vilas*, 1896, p. 498).

In other words, absolute immunity from civil suits for damages would protect the government and public administrators against frivolous suits or litigation brought chiefly for the purpose of harassment. On the other hand, absolute immunity would also foreclose suits against public administrators who, in the process of exercising their authority, violated individuals' constitutional or legal rights (*Stump v. Sparkman*, 1978).

Despite the one-sided nature of absolute immunity, it was the prevailing approach until the 1970s. As late as 1959, a plurality on the Supreme Court continued to adhere to the principle that:

> It has been thought important that officials of the government should be free to exercise their duties unembarrassed by the fear of damage suits in respect of acts done in the course of those duties—suits which would consume time and energies which would otherwise be devoted to governmental service and the threat of which might appreciably inhibit the . . . administration of policies of government (*Barr v. Matteo*, 1959, p. 571).

However, after the vast expansion of individual rights vis-à-vis public administrative actions that was associated with the breakdown of the doctrine of privilege and the strengthening of due process and equal protection, the doctrine of absolute official immunity was clearly out of place. Once the judiciary articulated new rights for individuals, it was obviously necessary to establish a new balance between the needs of the government for efficient and effective administration on the one hand, and those of the citizenry for protection of their rights on the other.

During the 1970s, the Supreme Court sought to establish a more appropriate balance in several cases.[3] In *Scheuer v. Rhodes* (1974, pp. 247-248), the Court abandoned the concept of absolute immunity for officials exercising executive functions:

> In varying scope, a qualified immunity is available to officers of the executive branch of government, the variation being dependent upon the scope of discretion and responsibilities of the office and all the circumstances as they reasonably appeared at the time of the action on which liability is sought to be based. It is the existence of reasonable grounds for the belief formed at the time and in light of all the circumstances, coupled with good-faith belief, that affords a basis for qualified immunity of executive officers for acts performed in the course of official conduct.

Thus, public officials—in this case, the governor of Ohio—enjoyed an immunity qualified by the reasonability of their actions and their intent in taking those actions.

Both of these elements subsequently underwent change as the present standard of official immunity developed.

In *Wood v. Strickland* (1975, pp. 321-322), reasonability was refined to mean whether the official "knew or reasonably should have known that the action he took within his sphere of official responsibility would violate the constitutional rights" of the private individual affected. In 1982, this standard was rephrased as: "Government officials performing discretionary functions generally are shielded from liability for civil damages insofar as their conduct does not violate clearly established statutory or constitutional rights of which a reasonable person would have known" (*Harlow v. Fitzgerald*, 1982, p. 4815).

The issue of intent proved more perplexing in terms of the balance the Supreme Court sought. Intent is subjective, but at law it is treated as a matter of fact. Consequently, when intent is an issue under dispute between two litigants, it must be determined through a trial, often incorporating elaborate adversary procedure and rules of evidence. In practical terms, allowing a public administrator's liability to turn on his or her intentions opens the door for frivolous or harassing suits. The plaintiff alleges a breach of good faith, and the public administrator has no choice but to settle out of court or to fight the charge in court. To the extent that in litigation, "the process is the punishment," even when the public administrator wins in court, he or she may pay a heavy price. Thus, under the good-faith approach, the public administrator was often in a no-win situation. In *Harlow v. Fitzgerald* (1982), after becoming cognizant of the problem of allowing insubstantial claims to go to trial, the Supreme Court eliminated the issue of intent as a determinant of qualified immunity. This has the practical effect of facilitating summary judgment by the courts in liability cases against public administrators. In a summary judgment, there are no issues of fact, but only those of law. Consequently, juries are unnecessary and extensive and expensive trials involving the presentation of witnesses and cross-examination, in an effort to establish the facts, are also obviated.

In sum, the central purpose of the current standard of public administrators' official immunity is twofold: (1) to deter insubstantial litigation that could impede effective administration, and (2) to deter public administrators from violating the statutory or constitutional rights of other individuals. The second objective emerged after the courts became more concerned with the rights of individuals vis-à-vis public administrative action. In the Supreme Court's words, the point has been to "create an incentive for officials who may harbor doubts about the lawfulness of their intended actions to err on the side of protecting citizens' constitutional rights" (*Owen v. City of Independence*, 1980, p. 652). The demise of the public administrator's absolute immunity from civil suits for damages has been part of a larger process of trying to square the administrative state with the judiciary's view of constitutional rights and values.

Three additional aspects of public administrative liability should be noted. First, the individual bringing a suit against a public administrator for violation of his or her constitutional or legal rights may sometimes seek punitive as well as compensatory damages. Punitive liability is intended to punish the wrongdoer and to serve as a deterrent. Such damages are awarded over and above those required by actual liability to compensate the injured party for the actual harm done to him or her. Historically, two general standards have evolved in determining whether punitive damages are appropriate. One is whether the individual found liable acted with malice when violating the other party's rights. Malice is essentially acting with "ill will, spite, or intent to injure"

(*Smith v. Wade*, 1983, p. 637). The second standard is recklessness, or a "callous disregard, or indifference to, the rights or safety of others" (Ibid., p. 637).

In terms of public administrators' liabilities, it is evident that the choice between the two standards makes a profound difference. If recklessness is the standard to be applied for punitive damages, then a showing that compensatory damages are appropriate can also support punitive damages. In other words, since the standard for compensatory liability is the violation of statutory or constitutional rights "of which a reasonable person would have known," recklessness, in the sense of a disregard for or indifference to such rights, may be construed to be a virtual redundancy. The public administrator who lacks knowledge of rights of which he or she should know has most likely been "reckless" in disregarding or being indifferent to acquiring knowledge of those rights. In *Smith v. Wade* (Ibid., p. 648), the Supreme Court embraced the recklessness standard, rather than malice, precisely for this reason. In the Court's view, "the conscientious officer who desires . . . [to] avoid lawsuits can and should look to the standard for actionability in the first instance," that is, the standard for compensatory damages. The Court's decision on this point underscores its concern that public administrators scrupulously avoid violating the legal or constitutional rights of those individuals upon whom they act.

In *Smith v. Wade*, the punitive damages were set at the amount that the jury thought would punish Smith, a prison guard, for violating Wade's Eighth Amendment rights and would deter other prison guards from acting in a similar fashion. The actual award was $25,000 compensatory damages and $5,000 punitive damages. However, punitive damages set in this fashion are relatively open-ended. Consequently, plaintiffs will often try to show not only recklessness, but also malice, in an effort to win greater punitive damages.

Another important aspect of public administrative liability pertains to the liability of cities (or their agencies) when their policies are the source of violation of individuals' legal or constitutional rights. In *Owen v. City of Independence* (1980, p. 651), the Supreme Court held that "a municipality will be liable for all of its injurious conduct, whether committed in good faith or not" if that conduct violates rights protected by federal law. In short, there is no issue of the city's "intent" or discussion of what it should have "known." On the other hand, cities are immune from punitive damages (*City of Newport v. Fact Concerts, Inc.*, 1981).

Third, some public administrators continue to enjoy a virtually absolute immunity. In *Butz v. Economou* (1978), the Supreme Court held that at least insofar as other remedies and avenues of redress are available:

1. Persons "performing adjudicatory functions within a federal agency are entitled to absolute immunity from damages liability for their judicial acts" (*Butz v. Economou*, 1978, p. 514).
2. "Those officials who are responsible for the decision to initiate or continue a proceeding subject to agency adjudication are entitled to absolute immunity from damages liability for their parts in that decision" (Ibid., p. 516).
3. "An agency attorney who arranges for the presentation of evidence on the record in the course of an adjudication is absolutely immune from suits based on the introduction of such evidence" (Ibid., p. 517).

For the most part, these limitations on the liability of such officials can be attributed to the Court's evident desire to maintain the absolute immunity of judges and public officials engaged in adjudication (*Stump v. Sparkman*, 1978). The Court also noted that federal officials engaged in administrative adjudication are strictly regulated by statute and that an individual injured by their actions has means for seeking relief other than suing them personally for damages.

B. Concomitant Rights

The substitution of qualified immunity for absolute immunity places new legal constraints upon many public administrators. It requires that they be cognizant of constitutional values and legal restrictions and that they pattern their official actions accordingly. However, since a public administrator's liability can be personal—that is, can be assessed directly against him or her—it is important to be aware of two concomitant rights that can serve as a defense for public administrators who might feel compelled by administrative hierarchies to engage in unconstitutional or illegal action. These are the right to disobey and the right to whistle-blow.

It may be something of an overstatement to refer to a right to disobey. Yet, there have been some cases on the matter that provide guidance. Moreover, such a right offers a reasonable prospect for the public administrator who is confronted with the choice of engaging in unconstitutional action, with its attendant risks for liability, or avoiding those risks and breach of public duty by resigning. *Parrish v. Civil Service Commission* (1967) offers the clearest example of the problem. Parrish was employed as a social worker in Alameda County, California. He was ordered to engage in a number of unscheduled, predawn visits to the homes of recipients of Aid to Needy Children. The purpose of the visits was to detect fraud in the form of the presence of male parents or unauthorized males in the homes. After discussing the matter with a supervisor, Parrish refused to participate on the grounds that the visits were "degrading, presumed the guilt of recipients, violated their rights of privacy, were not required under his job classification and were inconsistent with his training and the rehabilitation goals of the . . . program" (Vaughn, 1977, p. 264). He was thereafter fired for insubordination.

Parrish took the matter to the California state courts. He claimed that the unscheduled visits were in violation of the U.S. and California Constitutions and that if he had engaged in the action, he might have been subject to penalties under federal law. He was unsuccessful in the trial and appeals courts, but he won in the California State Supreme Court. In upholding his right to refuse to participate in the visits, the court addressed three elements. First, it found that the visits themselves were unconstitutional. Second, the information known to Parrish at the time did give him reasonable grounds to believe that the visits would be unconstitutional. Third, he actually did so believe—that is, his belief was sincere and in good faith, not an excuse to avoid an unpleasant aspect of work.

The *Parrish* decision places a heavy burden on the employee who would disobey unconstitutional orders, but insofar as it has value as a precedent, it does indicate how a right to disobey has been constructed in a major state. Most importantly, perhaps, it requires that the employee be correct in assessing the commanded activity as unconstitutional (Vaughn, 1977). Nevertheless, as Robert Vaughn points out, the right to disobey is a necessary concomitant to personal liability: "Congress and the courts have already adopted the concept of personal responsibility by providing penalties for the wrongful acts of public employees. The courts now have the opportunity to vindicate the concept of personal responsibility by accepting the right of public employees to disobey under appropriate circumstances" (Ibid., pp. 294-295).

The right to whistle-blow is more fully established. In some jurisdictions, including the federal government, it enjoys elaborate statutory protection (Vaughn, 1982). But it also rests on a sound constitutional footing. The Supreme Court provided whistle-blowers with broad protections under the First and Fourteenth Amendments in *Pickering v. Board of Education* (1968). The case involved a public school teacher who was dismissed for "sending a letter to a local newspaper in connection with a . . . proposed tax increase that was critical of the way in which the Board and the district superintendent of schools had handled past proposals to raise new revenue for the schools" (*Pickering v. Board of Education*, 1968, p. 564). The Court rejected the idea that Pickering's behavior was not constitutionally protected simply because he was a public employee. It stated that the general principle was "to arrive at a balance between the interests of the teacher, as a citizen, in commenting upon matters of public concern and the interest of the state, as an employer, in promoting the efficiency of the public services it performs through its employees" (Ibid., p. 568). In determining the appropriate balance, the Court relied heavily upon the important function that whistle-blowing can perform:

> The question whether a school system requires additional funds is a matter of legitimate public concern on which the judgment of the school administration, including the School Board, cannot, in a society that leaves such questions to popular vote, be taken as conclusive. On such a question free and open debate is vital to informed decision-making by the electorate. Teachers are, as a class, the members of a community most likely to have informed and definite opinions as to how funds allotted to the operation of the schools should be spent. Accordingly, it is essential that they be able to speak out freely on such questions without fear of retaliatory dismissal (Ibid., pp. 571-572).

The *Pickering* logic has been broad enough to sustain whistle-blowing by public employees other than teachers (*Bush v. Lucas*, 1983) and even "internal" whistle-blowing within an administrative hierarchy (*Givhan v. Western Line Consolidated School District*, 1979). However, in *Connick v. Myers* (1983), the Court indicated that when a public employee's speech focuses on office policies, additional weight should be given to the employer's concern about insubordination. It also noted that the employer has a legitimate interest in taking action against an employee whose speech threatens close working relationships and the government's ability to render service to the public in an efficient manner. Nevertheless, a public employee's public speech about public matters, delivered in a nondisruptive fashion, retains broad constitutional protection.

The right to whistle-blow is concomitant to public employees' liabilities because it offers them opportunities to challenge publicly (and privately) government policies that they believe are unconstitutional or illegal. This can accomplish at least two important objectives: (1) It can lead to a change of policy; and (2) it can promote a broad discussion that suggests the challenged policy is not unconstitutional. In the latter instance, the employee may be required to implement the policy, but after considerable debate, it is not likely that the courts will hold that he or she reasonably should have known the policy was unconstitutional, even if the judiciary eventually finds it so. Like a right to disobey, whistle-blowing gives the public employee some room to maneuver between vulnerability to liability and unchecked dismissal for insubordination.

VI. CONCLUSION

The purpose of this chapter has been to provide a broad general consideration of law that will prove useful to public administrators in the fields of health and human services. The character of law; the process, structure, and values of the legal system in the United States; the nature of some constitutional rights; and public administrators' liabilities were discussed. There is, of course, a great deal of technical law that is pertinent to the activities of health and human service administrators, some of which is discussed in the following chapters. Administrators, whose programmatic responsibilities often do not allow them sufficient time to become well versed in legal matters, may sometimes find legal concerns to be somewhat overwhelming. Consequently, it is helpful to arrange thoughts concerning law into a broad framework.

One such approach is for the administrator to consider himself or herself at an intersection of three major historical currents. One is the rise of the public service state—the polity in which the citizenry expects government to provide a wide range of protective services, including programs for health and human services. Another is the contemporary concern with public management—or the efficient, economic, and effective provision of these services, whether it be directly through government agencies or by contracting out to private service providers. In the past, the public service state was sometimes organized to dispense patronage, with relatively little concern for cost effectiveness or modern managerial methods. The third current is the growth of constitutional and human civil rights and liberties in the latter half of the present century. Each of these currents places particularistic demands upon the administrator: demands for more service, at less cost, and with proper attention to the fundamental rights of the recipients. The challenge becomes integrating the legitimate demands into successful programs. To do this effectively, the administrator must now view law, as well as concepts of management and cognizance of the political environment, as a fundamental aspect of professional competence. This is an onerous, but rewarding, task that requires continual attention to the broad values and principles embodied in the Constitution and the U.S. legal system. The principles and values provide a general framework that facilitates the understanding of many of the more technical aspects of law as it affects health and human service administration. The present chapter should provide a helpful beginning.

NOTES

1. Much of the discussion in this chapter is directed toward public administrators in health and human service programs. Many of the same constitutional concepts would apply to administrators of private health and human service programs and facilities if there were sufficient state action or government involvement in their financing or activities. For a brief discussion see: Pritchett, pp. 504–511.
2. Under the 1934 Federal Declaratory Judgment Act, parties seeking to test the meaning or constitutionality of a law can sometimes gain a judicial determination without first placing themselves in jeopardy by disobeying the law. See: *Abbott Laboratories v. Gardner*, 1967, for an example.
3. The federal statute of greatest importance to current interpretations of state and local public administrators' liability is 42 U.S. Code, section 1983 (originally the Civil Rights Act of 1871). The section reads, "Every person who, under color of any statute, ordinance, regulation, custom, usage, of any state or territory, subjects, or causes to be subjected, any citizen of the United States or any other person within

the jurisdiction thereof to the deprivation of any rights, privileges, or immunities secured by the Constitution and the laws, shall be liable to the party injured in an action at law, suit in equity, or other proper proceeding for redress." Although the statute does not apply to federal officials, the Supreme Court has held that liability is a direct derivative of certain constitutional rights. See: Rosenbloom, 1983, pp. 179-206, for a discussion.

REFERENCES

Abbott Laboratories v. Gardner (1967). 387 U.S. 136.
Barr v. Matteo (1959). 360 U.S. 564.
Bentham, J. (1843). *The Works of Jeremy Bentham* (J. Bowring, ed.), William Tait, Edinburgh.
Bickel, A. (1962). *The Least Dangerous Branch*, Bobbs-Merrill, Indianapolis.
Bishop v. Wood (1976). 426 U.S. 341.
Bolling v. Sharpe (1954). 347 U.S. 497.
Branti v. Finkel (1980). 445 U.S. 506.
Brown v. Board of Education (1954). 347 U.S. 483.
Bush v. Lucas (1983). 76 L.Ed. 2d 648.
Butz v. Economou (1978). 438 U.S. 478.
Carter, L. (1983). *Administrative Law and Politics*, Little, Brown & Company, Boston.
Chayes, A. (1976). The role of the judge in public law litigation, *Harvard Law Review, 89*: 1281.
City of Newport v. Fact Concerts, Inc. (1981). 453 U.S. 247.
Colegrove v. Green (1946). 328 U.S. 549.
Connick v. Myers (1983). 103 S.Ct. 1684.
Craig v. Boren (1976). 429 U.S. 190.
Cramton, Roger (1976). Judicial lawmaking and administration in the leviathan state, *Public Administration Review, 36* (September/October): 551.
DeFunis v. Odegaard (1974). 416 U.S. 312.
Delaware v. Prouse (1979). 440 U.S. 648.
Eisenstadt v. Baird (1972). 405 U.S. 438.
Elrod v. Burns (1976). 427 U.S. 347.
Fullilove v. Klutznick (1980). 448 U.S. 448.
Givhan v. Western Line Consolidated School District (1979). 439 U.S. 410.
Goldberg v. Kelly (1970). 397 U.S. 254.
Goldman, S., and Jahnige, T. (1971). *The Courts as a Political System*, Harper and Row, New York.
Goodnow, F. (1900). *Politics and Administration*, Macmillan, New York.
Goss v. Lopez (1975). 419 U.S. 565.
Griswold v. Connecticut (1965). 381 U.S. 479.
Hamilton v. Love (1971). 328 F. Supp. 1182.
Hamilton v. Regents (1934). 293 U.S. 245.
Harlow v. Fitzgerald (1982) 73 L.Ed. 2d 396.
Holt v. Sarver (1970). 309 F. Supp. 362.
Industrial Union Department, AFL-CIO v. American Petroleum Institute (1980). 448 U.S. 607.
Kolender v. Lawson (1983). 75 L.Ed. 2d 903.
Konigsberg v. State Bar of California (1957). 353 U.S. 252.
Lipsky, M. (1976). Toward a theory of street level bureaucracy, *Bureaucratic Power in National Politics* (F. Rourke, ed.), third edition, Little, Brown & Company, Boston.
Lowi, T. (1969). *The End of Liberalism*, W. W. Norton & Company, New York.

Luther v. Borden (1849). 7 Howard 1.
Mashaw, J. (1983). *Bureaucratic Justice*, Yale University Press, New Haven.
Mathews v. Eldridge (1976). 424 U.S. 319.
McDowell, G. (1982). *Equity and the Constitution*, University of Chicago Press, Chicago.
McLaughlin v. Tilendis (1968). 392 F2d 882.
McLaurin v. Oklahoma State Regents (1950). 339 U.S. 637.
Memphis v. Stotts (1984). 104 S.Ct. 2576.
Milliken v. Bradley (1974). 418 U.S. 717.
Mills v. Rogers (1982). 457 U.S. 291.
Missouri ex rel. Gaines v. Canada (1938). 305 U.S. 337.
Morgan v. Kerrigan (1975). 401 F. Supp. 216.
Morton v. Mancari (1974). 417 U.S. 535.
National Anti-Hunger Coalition v. Executive Committee of the President's Private Sector Survey on Cost Control (1983). 557 F. Supp. 524; 711 F2d 1071.
O'Neil, R. (1966). Unconstitutional conditions: Welfare benefits with strings attached, *California Law Review, 54*: 443.
Owen v. City of Independence (1980). 445 U.S. 622.
Parrish v. Civil Service Commission (1967). 425 P2d 223.
Pickering v. Board of Education (1968). 391 U.S. 563.
Poe v. Ullman (1961). 367 U.S. 497.
Pritchett, C. H. (1977). *The American Constitution*, third edition, McGraw-Hill, New York.
Reich, C. (1964). The new property, *Yale Law Journal, 73*: 733.
Regents v. Bakke (1978). 438 U.S. 265.
Roe v. Wade (1973). 410 U.S. 113.
Rosenbloom, D. (1971). *Federal Service and the Constitution*, Cornell University Press, Ithaca, New York.
Rosenbloom, D. (1977). *Federal Equal Employment Opportunity*, Praeger, New York.
Rosenbloom, D. (1983). *Public Administration and Law*, Marcel Dekker, New York.
Rossiter, C., ed. (1961). *The Federalist Papers*, Mentor, New York.
Scheuer v. Rhodes (1974). 416 U.S. 232.
Shapiro, D. (1965). The choice of rulemaking or adjudication in the development of administration policy, *Harvard Law Review, 78*: 921.
Shapiro v. Thompson (1969). 394 U.S. 618.
Sherbert v. Verner (1963). 374 U.S. 398.
Simon, J. (1973). *In His Own Image*, David McKay, New York.
Smith v. Wade (1983). 75 L.Ed. 2d 632.
Spalding v. Vilas (1896). 161 U.S. 483.
Starkey v. Board of Education (1963). 381 P2d 718.
Steelworkers v. Weber (1979). 443 U.S. 193.
Stump v. Sparkman (1978). 435 U.S. 349.
Sweatt v. Painter (1950). 339 U.S. 629.
United States v. Brignoni-Ponce (1975). 422 U.S. 873.
United States v. Lee (1882). 106 U.S. 196.
United States Civil Service Commission v. National Association of Letter Carriers (1973). 413 U.S. 584.
Vaughn, R. (1977). Public employees and the right to disobey, *Hastings Law Journal, 29*: 261.
Vaughn, R. (1982). Statutory protection of whistleblowers in the federal executive branch, *University of Illinois Law Review, 1982*: 615.
Washington v. Davis (1976). 426 U.S. 229.
West Virginia Board of Education v. Barnette (1943). 319 U.S. 624.

Whalen v. Roe (1977), 429 U.S. 589.
Wilkie v. O'Connor (1941). 25 NYS 2d 617.
Wilson, W. [1887] (1941). The study of administration, *Political Science Quarterly, 56* (December): 481.
Wood v. Strickland (1975). 420 U.S. 308.
Wyatt v. Stickney (1971). 325 F.Supp. 781; 334 F.Supp. 1341; 344 F.Supp. 387.
Wyman v. James (1971). 400 U.S. 309.
Youngberg v. Romeo (1982). 457 U.S. 307.

11

Health and Human Services Law and Regulation

Winsor C. Schmidt, Jr. Department of Political Science, Memphis State University, Memphis, Tennessee

The legal framework for health and human services governs every aspect of service administration, yet attention to health and human service law in public administration literature is minimal. One of the purposes of this chapter is to provide a bridge of understanding between the worlds of law and management.

I. INTRODUCTION: THE CONSTITUTIONAL FRAMEWORK

Law can be defined as "a body of rules of action or conduct prescribed by controlling authority, and having binding legal force" (Black, 1979). Less formally, and to paraphrase Oliver Wendell Holmes, law is a statement of the circumstances in which public force can be brought to bear upon people through courts.

A. The Ideal of Legality

The ideal of legality is significant for public administration, and for human service administration, because of the covenant that our government is a government of laws and not a government of men and women (Carter, 1983). No person is above the law. If humans were angels, there would be no need for law (Scallet, 1980). At the same time, humans have evolved to the point of capacity for self-government, self-rule, through law.

Health and human services are delivered within a framework of private and public law (Wing, 1985). The rules of conduct for health and human services in the free market economy are prescribed by such areas of the law as contracts and torts (civil wrongs). Government—specifically, the judiciary—provides a dispute resolution service for private conflicts, the results or cases constituting a body of private law. Private law defines and enforces the duties and rights of private individuals and organizations (Miller, 1986).

Government is active and regulatory in health and human services in response to qualitative or quantitative breakdowns in the free market economy and the family (Gates, 1980). The regulation and delivery of health and human services by government through law constitutes a body of public law defining the subfield of substantive health and human service law. Public law defines and regulates the relationship of individuals and government (Miller, 1986). Public human service law is generated not only by the judiciary in resolving disputes through cases involving public human service interests, but also by legislatures, and by administrative agencies through rule making and adjudication.

Public human service law is distinct from administrative law in that administrative law can be considered procedural (Carter, 1983; Gellhorn et al., 1987), generally governing the administrative process and the means by which administrators conduct public business. (An alternative definition of administrative law suggests "that the administrative process can be fully understood only in the context of the particular substantive program it accompanies" [Robinson, Gellhorn, and Bruff, 1980, p. xv]– such as environment, licensing, public employment, educational administration, or welfare administration.) Public human service law, at least for purposes of this discussion, delineates substantive service goals, or ends, and structure or legal organization–that is, what the service delivery system should look like and accomplish.

B. Constitutional Public Administration

Public administration began with the assertion that "the study of administration should start from the base of management rather than the foundation of law, and is, therefore, more absorbed in the affairs of the American Management Association than in the decisions of the courts" (White, 1926, pp. vii–viii). David Rosenbloom's (1983a, 1986) more coherent, sophisticated, and contemporary theory, summarized by Dwight Waldo, places the executive-managerial approach, with the legislative-political approach and the judicial-legal approach, in a public administration paradigm reflecting the constitutional separation of powers:

> David Rosenbloom has set forth the structure of the problem before us. For each of the three constitutional branches, he points out, there is a body of doctrine, set of values, collection of instruments, and repertoire of procedures. For the executive branch this "cluster" is administrative, managerial, bureaucratic, and the emphasis is upon effectiveness and efficiency. For the legislative branch the cluster is political and policy making and the emphasis is upon the values of representativeness and responsiveness. For the judicial branch the cluster is legal, and the emphasis is on constitutional integrity on one side and substantive and procedural protections for individuals on the other.
>
> Realistically our public administration does consist of varying mixtures of these three approaches or clusters. It is not just undesirable, it is impossible to narrow the concerns of public administration to any one of them. Our task is to find the proper way to put the three together (Brown and Stillman, 1985, pp. 463–464).

The three approaches, or perspectives, are merged in administrative agencies, like those regulating health and human services. The substantive law generated by legislatures, judiciaries, and executive and administrative agencies through the formal administrative process (rule making, adjudication, and other administrative law) constitutes health and human service law.

The balance of this chapter is divided into five major sections highlighting both significant and controversial areas of health and human service law. The sections will provide an overview of informed consent for services; voluntary and involuntary commitment; the right to treatment and the right to refuse treatment; institutionalization/deinstitutionalization; and record-keeping law and confidentiality.

The intention is to provide accurate and authoritative general information and a minimum, basic understanding of health and human service law. Emphasis is necessarily on the legal approach, or perspective, as reflected by judicial decisions. This chapter does not render legal advice or service; readers are encouraged to seek the services of local legal experts for such assistance.

II. INFORMED CONSENT FOR SERVICES

Health and human services are provided to recipients on the basis of some authority. One source of authority is the client's consent to services. In *Schloendorff v. Society of New York Hospital* [105 N.E. 92, 93 (N.Y. 1914)], Benjamin Cardozo stated:

> Every human being of adult years and sound mind has a right to determine what shall be done with his own body, and a surgeon who performs an operation without his patient's consent commits an assault, for which he is liable in damages, except in cases of emergency where the patient is unconscious and where it is necessary to operate before consent can be obtained.

The informed consent doctrine has been extended to require informed refusal in a case where a physician failed to inform a patient of the risks to not consenting to a recommended Pap smear, and the patient died from cancer susceptible to life-extending treatment [*Truman v. Thomas*, 27 Cal.3d 285, 611 P.2d 902 (1980)].

A. Elements of Informed Consent

There are several good secondary sources elaborating upon the law of consent (Kapp and Bigot, 1985; Miller, 1986; Pozgar, 1983; Reisner, 1985; Rozovsky, 1984). In brief, a valid consent is competent, informed, and voluntary. The physician or other practitioner must provide the necessary information and obtain consent, and a hospital is generally not liable for failure to obtain consent unless the practitioner is an employee or agent [*Fiorentino v. Wenger*, 19 N.Y.2d 407, 227 N.E.2d 286 (1967); Ohio Rev. Code Ann. section 2317.54 (Page 1981)].

1. Competence. A nice case illustrating consideration of the elements for a valid consent is *Kaimowitz v. Department of Mental Health* [No. 73-19434-AW (Cir.Ct. of Wayne County, Mich., July 10, 1973) reported in 1 *Mental Disability L.Rep.* 147 (1976)]. The Michigan court held that valid consent for experimental psychosurgery cannot be given by an involuntarily institutionalized mental patient. The court observed that competency is the ability to rationally understand the nature of a procedure, its risks, and other relevant information. There is a presumption of competence in law analogous to the presumption of innocence. In *Kaimowitz*, the patient's involuntary institutionalization diminished the legal capacity to consent.

2. Knowledge. The elements of disclosure that contribute to an informed or knowledgeable consent include the diagnosis of the problem; the nature and purpose of the proposed intervention; the risks and consequences of the services; the probability of

success; alternatives; the result anticipated without the service; limitations of the professional or facility; and advice (Kapp and Bigot, 1985). In *Kaimowitz*, the experimental nature of the proposed procedure rendered knowledgeable consent problematic.

3. Voluntariness. The final element for consent, voluntariness, involves freedom of choice without "any element of force, fraud, deceit, duress, overreaching, or other ulterior form of constraint or coercion" [1 *Mental Disability L.Rep.* at 150]. The *Kaimowitz* court cited these Nuremberg standards and concluded that the consent was not voluntary when every aspect of the patient's institutional life was decided without any opportunity by the patient to participate in the decision-making process.

B. Exceptions

There are exceptions to the general requirement of formal informed consent. These exceptions include legally required interventions (such as testing automobile drivers for intoxication); emergency; and waiver.

> The emergency exception applies when (1) immediate medical treatment is required to preserve life or to prevent a serious impairment to health; but (2) consent cannot be obtained from the patient (or from someone empowered to authorize treatment on the patient's behalf); and (3) there is no serious indication that the treatment would be refused were the patient then able to make his or her own wishes known (Kapp and Bigot, 1985, pp. 32–33).

Service recipients also retain the ability to waive the requirement of consent. Waiver should be explicit, competent, informed, and voluntary. When a client is legally incompetent, a guardian or other substitute decision maker should negotiate consent.

The requirement of consent is grounded in ethical responsibilities to respect individual autonomy, and to encourage rational decision making. While consent is perhaps seldom achieved to date (Lidz et al., 1984), it is a realistic possibility that can and should be legally enforced (Kapp and Bigot, 1985).

III. VOLUNTARY AND INVOLUNTARY COMMITMENT

Consent for services in a free market economy is essentially governed by considerations of contract. Public health and human services, in contrast, are so closely regulated that even voluntary services entail voluntary procedures or process. Commentators speculate that close regulation of such voluntary services reflects allegedly limited capacities by public service clients, abuses of or by "volunteer" clients, and securing the status of service recipients as "clients" (Lewis, 1977) through "voluntary" provisions authorizing institutions to temporarily retain "voluntary" patients pending involuntary proceedings (Brakel, Parry, and Weiner, 1985).

A. Voluntary Admission Procedures

Most states have voluntary admission procedures for the mentally ill, developmentally disabled, alcoholics, and drug addicts. Three types of voluntary procedures are informal admission procedures; traditional, formal, or conditional voluntary admission procedures; and third-party "voluntary" procedures. Some states explicitly prohibit using the threat of involuntary commitment to induce "voluntary" commitment [*Ex parte Lloyd*, 13 F.Supp. 1005 (E.D. Ky. 1936); Ill. Ann. Stat. ch. 91 1/2, section 3-402 (Smith-Hurd

Supp. 1982)]. At least one court has found unconstitutional a state's statutory scheme for converting involuntary patients to voluntary status, in which fewer rights and protections were accorded voluntary patients than involuntary patients [*In re Buttonow*, 23 N.Y.2d 385, 244 N.E.2d 677, 297 N.Y.S.2d 97 (1968)].

There are few exceptions to the voluntary contract model of free-market-economy health and human services. Chief Justice Burger points out that persons can be confined to protect society from communicable disease [*O'Connor v. Donaldson*, 422 U.S. 563, 583 (1975) (Burger, C.J., dissenting)]. Compulsory vaccination is uncontroversial [*Jackson v. Massachusetts*, 187 U.S. 11 (1905)]. So-called insane persons could be restrained without legal process at common law, but anyone exercising such prerogative assumed the burden of proving imminent dangerousness when civil damage suits were filed in response [Annot., 45 A.L.R. 1464 (1926)].

B. Involuntary Commitment

Public health and human services, on the other hand, seem to almost thrive on provisions for involuntary confinement (Lipsky, 1980). Indeed,

> the surrogate function is the heart and soul of a protective service program. It can be defined as the delegation by the client, or the substitution through legal means, of the client's decision-making power to another person, or persons, professionally responsible and legally accountable for the purposes of assuring that the client receives the necessary protection, whatever services this may require [Hall and Mathiasen, 1968, p. 11].

Rather than the traditional medical model of unconsented treatment constituting assault and being provided nonconsensually only for incompetents by legal guardians, "the therapeutic state" (Kittrie, 1971, p. 40) administers its services involuntarily.

Most states have statutory provisions for involuntary institutionalization of mentally ill persons, persons addicted to drugs or alcohol, and children and minors with mental disabilities (Brakel, Parry, and Weiner, 1985). At least 15 states have statutory provisions for involuntary adult (elderly) protective services (Schmidt, 1986).

1. Police Power

State power to commit individuals rests on two allegedly inherent derivations of sovereignty, the police power and the parens patriae power.

> While broad and extending to concern with the welfare of individuals (or their health, safety and morals—thus paralleling the parens patriae power), the essence of the police power is its authority to act in furtherance of the general welfare and the public safety. Rather than protect individuals from themselves or others, the police power tends to be invoked on behalf of society or societal interests *against* the individual (Brakel, Parry, and Weiner, 1985, p. 24).

The threshold requirement for invocation of the police power is diminished capacity to conform behavior to legal requirements or social tolerance, and inability to appreciate legal deterrence [*Minnesota ex rel. Pearson v. Probate Court*, 309 U.S. 270 (1940)]. Treatability is also a precondition [*Jackson v. Indiana*, 406 U.S. 715 (1972)]. Yet police power commitment is controversial to the extent that (1) it constitutes preventive detention of indiscretely defined populations [*Dash v. Mitchell*, 356 F.Supp. 1292

(D.D.C. 1972)]; (2) subject populations are no more dangerous than the general population; (3) dangerous behavior cannot be predicted (Monahan, 1981); (4) subject populations are too vaguely defined–for example, "disorderly persons" [*Papachristou v. City of Jacksonville*, 405 U.S. 156 (1972)], "psychopathic personality" [*Fleuti v. Rosenberg*, 302 F.2d 652 (9th Cir. 1964)]; (5) and individuals are unconstitutionally punished for a status, condition, or illness–for example, narcotics addiction [*Robinson v. California*, 370 U.S. 660 (1962)].

2. Parens Patriae Power

The parens patriae power is the alleged authority of the state to act as "the general guardian of all infants, idiots and lunatics" [*Hawaii v. Standard Oil Co.*, 405 U.S. 251, 257 (1972)]. The threshold requirement for exercise of this power is incompetency to make decisions (a competent person's refusal to seek services is "strictly a private concern and . . . beyond reach of all governmental power" [*In re President and Directors of Georgetown College, Inc.*, 331 F.2d 1010, 1016 (D.C.Cir. 1964)]). Legislatures and courts in at least 17 states explicitly require incompetency in order to involuntarily commit mentally ill persons (constitutionally) under the parens patriae authority (Schmidt, 1985a).

The difficulty with the parens patriae authority is not only that its legal precedent seems to be a 17th century printer's error in the English common law, but also that it justifies dangerously excessive and abusive discretionary power in the legislatures, courts, and agencies which use it (Gaylin et al., 1981; Schmidt, 1985a). "The Latin phrase [parens patriae] proved to be great help to those who sought to rationalize the exclusion of juveniles from the constitutional scheme; but its meaning is murky and its historic credentials are of dubious relevance" [*In re Gault*, 387 U.S. 1, 16 (1966)]. Another difficulty with parens patriae is that it is redundant to the legal system of guardianship and the state's more evident parens patriae obligation to provide public guardians for indigent incompetents [*Vecchione v. Wohlgemuth*, 426 F.Supp. 1297 (E.D. Pa. 1977); *In re Gamble*, 394 A.2d 308 (N.H. 1978); Schmidt et al., 1981, 1982].

3. Abolition of Involuntary Commitment

Difficulties underlying the alleged legal authorities for involuntary commitment are compatible with advocacy for abolition that is becoming too formidable to easily refute (Dybwad and Herr, 1979; Ennis, 1982; Ennis and Litwack, 1974; Goffman, 1961; Miller, 1976; Morse, 1978, 1982; Rosenhan, 1973; Szasz, 1968). Involuntary services are too expensive and ineffective to be a priority over voluntary services. What does it say about any profession that relies upon involuntary commitment for solicitation of its clients? The courts are slow but inexorable in remedying involuntary commitment deficiencies.

4. Right to Liberty

In its first civil commitment decision, the U.S. Supreme Court ruled that "a state cannot constitutionally confine without more [than enforced custodial care] a nondangerous individual who is capable of surviving safely in freedom by himself or with the help of willing and responsible family members or friends" [*O'Connor v. Donaldson*, 422 U.S. 563, 576 (1975)]. In upholding every person's constitutional right to liberty, the Court applied a survival standard rather than a paternalistic welfare standard; rejected mental illness alone as a justification for commitment; denied confinement to raise or ensure living standards; and prohibited deprivation of physical liberty for mere public animosity or intolerance. The Court also sustained the liability of public officials for such confinement where the official "knew or reasonably should have known that the action he took within his sphere of official responsibility would violate the constitutional rights of [Donaldson], or if he took the action with the malicious intention to cause a deprivation of constitutional rights or other injury to [Donaldson]" [*id.* at 577] (Rosenbloom, 1983b).

5. Standard of Proof

In its first decision concerning appropriate procedure for involuntary commitment, the Supreme Court held that under the due process clause of the Fourteenth Amendment, the standard of proof for the jury at a civil commitment trial must be at least "clear and convincing" evidence [*Addington v. Texas*, 441 U.S. 418 (1979)]. The function of a standard of proof is to instruct an adjudicatory fact finder about the degree of confidence society thinks there should be in the accuracy of factual conclusions. The Court reasoned that an individual's interest in liberty and the adverse social consequences and stigma of inappropriate commitment require the state to justify confinement by proof more substantial than the mere civil standard of "preponderance of the evidence" associated with monetary disputes between private parties.

On the other hand, the Court could not yet require proof beyond a reasonable doubt, as in criminal and juvenile proceedings [*In re Winship*, 397 U.S. 358 (1970)], or "clear, unequivocal and convincing" evidence, as in deportation and denaturalization, because of the doubt that a state could ever commit where psychiatric diagnosis and expertise are so uncertain and fallible. At least 15 states nevertheless used beyond a reasonable doubt, two states required "clear, unequivocal and convincing," and three states employed "clear, cogent and convincing." The Court specified that "clear and convincing" is a constitutional minimum, and that states are free to use higher standards. To satisfy due process requirements, the standard must inform the fact finder that the proof required is greater than the "preponderance of evidence" standard in other civil cases.

6. Other Procedural Requirements

In another procedural case, involving involuntary commitment of a convicted felon to a state mental hospital from prison, the Supreme Court ruled on other protections required by the due process clause of the Fourteenth Amendment [*Vitek v. Jones*, 445 U.S. 480 (1980)]. States are required to observe the following minimum procedures before such commitments:

1. Written notice that admission to a mental hospital is being considered
2. A hearing, after notice and preparation time, with disclosure to the prisoner of the evidence relied upon, and an opportunity to be heard in person and to present documentary evidence
3. Opportunity at the hearing to present testimony of defense witnesses and to confront and cross-examine state witnesses
4. An independent decision maker
5. The fact finder's written statement of the evidence relied upon and the reasons for commitment

6. Availability of qualified, competent, and independent assistance by a licensed psychiatrist, other mental health professional, or competent layman free to act solely in the inmate's best interest, furnished by the state if the inmate is indigent (the state is free to appoint a licensed attorney, but is not constitutionally mandated to do so)
7. Effective and timely notice of all the foregoing rights

The Court recognized the inmate's liberty interest, stigmatizing consequences, and grievous loss in any major change of confinement conditions.

7. Commitment of Children

The most difficult commitment case to date for the Supreme Court involved commitment of children to state-administered institutional mental health care by parents or guardians. In *Parham v. J. R.* [442 U.S. 584 (1979)], the Court held that the risk of error inherent in the parental decision is sufficiently great that some kind of prior, informal inquiry must be made by a neutral fact finder to determine whether statutory requirements for admission are met. Elements of the inquiry include:

1. Careful probe of the child's background using all available sources, including, but not limited to, parents, schools, and other social agencies
2. Interview with the child
3. Decision maker, with authority to refuse admission of any child not meeting medical admission standards, who can be a staff physician so long as conditions of independence are met
4. Periodic review of commitment by a similarly independent procedure

States are free to require a formal hearing, as a minority do.

Justices Brennan, Marshall, and Stevens disagreed vigorously with the majority's opinion, especially its trusting application to commitment of children by state social workers. The justices observed that the majority's criticism of "procedural minuets" could as easily justify elimination of criminal trials because prosecutors are not supposed to prosecute innocent people. The decision abused and ignored social science information on such matters as the efficacy of procedure and the competence of children to consent (Melton, Koocher, and Saks, 1983; Schmidt, 1985b).

Parham interrupted a trend toward recognition of children's rights and greater legal regulation of civil commitment. The controversy surrounding such issues as treatment of minors for drug and alcohol abuse is unabated. *Parham* was the iceberg tip of a whole dynamic, rapidly evolving body of law balancing the interests of children, parents, and the state (Melton, 1982; Murphy, 1974; Reppucci et al., 1984; Taylor, 1981; Wadlington, Whitebread, and Davis, 1983). But it did little to ameliorate the plight of this country's unclaimed children (Knitzer, 1982).

8. Acquired Immune Deficiency Syndrome (AIDS)

The judiciary is just beginning to address a new civil commitment issue, the compulsory detention, isolation, or hospitalization of Acquired Immune Deficiency Syndrome (AIDS) victims. Great Britain has reportedly authorized magistrates to quarantine AIDS carriers in limited situations, and officials in Connecticut, the District of Columbia, Maryland, New York, and Virginia have proposed quarantine as the appropriate response to AIDS in prisons (Parry, 1985a). Implementation of AIDS segregation in New York prisons has been preliminarily accepted as reasonable by a federal district court and a lower state court [*Cordero v. Coughlin*, 607 F.Supp. 9 (S.D.N.Y. 1984); *In re Application of Larocca v. Dalsheim*, 467 N.Y.S. 2d 302 (N.Y.Sup.Ct., Dutchess County, 1983)]. More recently, a federal court in Pennsylvania dismissed as frivolous a prisoner's request for restrictions on "possible AIDS carriers" in his prison wing [*Foy v. Owens*, No. 85-6909 (E.D.Pa. March 19, 1986)]. The commentary suggests that quarantine is illegal absent medical evidence of any need for isolating AIDS carriers. Statutorily compelled hospitalization of AIDS patients might pass constitutional muster if criteria included mental incompetence and accurate prediction of substantial dangerousness to self or others. The better approach, as with involuntary commitment generally, would be to allow commitment refusal by any competent person. Questions of dangerousness should be handled by the criminal justice or civil liability systems, and questions of health should be handled by the voluntary health care system (Miller, 1980), and guardianship in the event of incompetence.

IV. THE RIGHT TO TREATMENT AND THE RIGHT TO REFUSE TREATMENT

Dr. Morton Birnbaum is credited with the first formal discussion of a "right to treatment" in the delivery of mental health services, in a 1960 *American Bar Association Journal* article (Schmidt, 1976). Dr. Birnbaum defined the right as a legal right of a mentally ill inmate in a public mental institution to adequate medical treatment for his mental illness. In the context of health and human service regulation, however, the right to treatment has broader conceptual implications. A right to health care is increasingly viable in a variety of health and human service situations.

A. Statutory Right to Treatment

The first mental health judicial decision to recognize a right to treatment was *Rouse v. Cameron* [373 F.2d 451 (D.C.Cir. 1966)]. Chief Judge Bazelon, writing for the majority, upheld the application of a statutory right to treatment provision to an insanity acquittee involuntarily committed to St. Elizabeth's Hospital. The court also noted three potential constitutional bases for a right to treatment: (1) the lack of due process protections for criminal defendants automatically committed without treatment upon acquittal by reason of insanity; (2) due process and equal protection questions concerning four years of confinement without treatment, for the purpose of treatment, on a one-year misdemeanor acquittal; and (3) cruel and unusual punishment considerations for persons indefinitely confined without treatment who are not criminally responsible. The court did not require cure or improvement, but only a bona fide effort to cure or improve.

B. Constitutional Right to Treatment

The first litigation to directly recognize a constitutional right to treatment for civilly committed patients was *Wyatt v. Stickney* [325 F.Supp. 781 (M.D.Ala. 1971), *hearing on standards ordered*, 334 F.Supp. 1341 (M.D.Ala. 1971), *enforced*, 344 F.Supp. 373 (M.D.Ala. 1972), 344 F.Supp. 387 (M.D.Ala. 1972), *affirmed sub nom. Wyatt v. Aderholt*, 503 F.2d 1305 (5th Cir. 1974)]. The case was precipitated when a cut in cigarette tax revenue resulted in the firing of 99 Bryce Hospital staff. The staff and patients sued, claiming that the patients would not receive adequate treatment as a result of the staff reductions.

1. Institution Conditions

Conditions in the state system were execrable. Because of understaffing, lack of supervision, and brutality, four Partlow State School and Hospital residents had died.

> One of the four died after a garden hose had been inserted into his rectum for five minutes by a working patient who was cleaning him; one died when a fellow patient hosed him with scalding water; another died when soapy water was forced into his mouth, and a fourth died from a self-administered overdose of drugs which had been inadequately secured [503 F.2d at 1311 n.6].

Severe health and safety problems were described:

> Patients with open wounds and inadequately treated skin diseases were in imminent danger of infection because of the unsanitary conditions existing in the wards, such as permitting urine and feces to remain on the floor; there was evidence of insect infestation in the kitchen and dining areas. Malnutrition was a problem: The United States described the food as a coming closer to punishment by starvation than nutrition. At Bryce, the food preparation and distribution systems were unsanitary, and less than 50 cents per day per patient was spent on food [less than for Alabama's zoo animals] [503 F.2d at 1310].

The court found that treatment programs were medically inadequate, conforming to no known minimum standards. The U.S. Department of Justice and the Department of Health, Education, and Welfare were invited to appear as amicus curiae, joined by the American Psychological Association, the American Ortho-Psychiatric Association, and the American Civil Liberties Union. Citing *Rouse v. Cameron*, the court concluded: "When patients are . . . committed for treatment purposes they unquestionably have a constitutional right to receive such individual treatment as will give each of them a realistic opportunity to be cured or to improve his or her mental condition" [325 F.Supp. at 784].

2. Constitutional Minimum Standards

Rather than inappropriately prescribing treatment, the court, after weeks of expert testimony, defined the constitutional minimum standards without which adequate treatment could not occur; "(1) a humane psychological and physical environment, (2) qualified staff in numbers sufficient to administer adequate treatment, and (3) individualized treatment plans" [344 F.Supp. at 373]. These minimum standards for adequate treatment of the mentally ill, and for adequate habilitation of the mentally retarded, were elaborated in specific detail [344 F.Supp. at 379-386, 395-407].

3. Impact

As of 1978, at least 11 states had overhauled their institutional mental health facilities at the prompting of federal courts. While such judicial intervention causes some consternation in medical and public administration circles (Straussman, 1986; Yarbrough, 1985), "it should always be borne in mind that the current judicial approach was brought on largely by legislative and administrative neglect of the plight of mental patients and prisoners. In this sense, the judiciary is simply filling a vacuum left by these other branches of government" (Rosenbloom, 1983b, p. 176).

4. The U.S. Supreme Court's Response

While the U.S. Supreme Court has not recognized a right to treatment or habilitation, it has held that involuntarily committed mentally retarded persons have substantive rights under the due process clause of the Fourteenth Amendment to (1) safe conditions of confinement, (2) freedom from bodily restraint, and (3) minimally adequate or reasonable training to assure safety and freedom from undue restraint [*Youngberg v. Romeo*, 457 U.S. 307 (1982)]. Nicholas Romeo was a 33-year-old profoundly retarded man committed by his mother, after his father's death, to Pennhurst State School in Pennsylvania. Between July 1974 and November 4, 1976, Nicholas suffered injuries on at least 63 occasions.

5. Professional Judgment

The Court emphasized, in defining reasonable training, that the courts must defer to judgment exercised by qualified professionals. Subsequent cases have interpreted the professional judgment standard to include accreditation by the Joint Commission on Accreditation of Hospitals and certification by the U.S. Department of Health and Human Services [*Concerned Citizens for Creedmore, Inc. v. Cuomo*, 570 F.Supp. 575 (E.D.N.Y. 1983); *Woe v. Cuomo*, 729 F.2d 96 (2d Cir. 1984); Cook, 1983]. The right to treatment cases for mentally disabled persons provide that if the state intervenes in their lives, it can do so only in a constitutionally permissible manner [*Welsch v. Likins*, 373 F.Supp. 487, 498-499 (D.Minn. 1974), *aff'd* 550 F.2d 1122 (8th Cir. 1977)].

C. Right to Health Care

Beyond the constitutional rights to treatment and habitation in mental health law, courts are crafting a right to health care. The general common-law rule is that no person is legally compelled to give aid or take action to save or rescue another person. However, exceptions are accumulating. For example, concerning abandonment, a physician who is ill should attempt to arrange for a substitute [*Kenny v. Piedmont Hospital*, 136 Ga.App. 660, 222 S.E.2d 162 (1975)]. Noncooperative and disruptive patients should not be arbitrarily denied services from such "public service enterprises" as hospitals and physicians without notice and exploration of such alternatives as conservatorship (guardianship) [*Payton v. Weaver*, 131 Cal. App.2d 38, 182 Cal.Rptr. 225 (1982)]. Concerning emergencies, patients in unmistakable emergencies have a right to care in a hospital that maintains an emergency room [*Wilmington General Hospital v. Manlove*, 174 A.2d 135 (Del. 1962); *Stanturf v. Snipes*, 447 S.W.2d 558 (Mo. 1969)]. This right to emergency care includes nonresident aliens at private hospitals [*Guerrero v. Cooper Queen Hospital*, 537 P.2d 1329 (Ariz. 1975)]. Constitutionally, a right to health care is identified for prisoners [*Newman v. Alabama*, 349 F.Supp. 278 (M.D.Ala. 1972); *Estelle v. Gamble*, 97 S.Ct. 285 (1976)] and interstate travelers [*Memorial Hospital v. Maricopa County*, 415 U.S. 250 (1974)].

A question related to the rights to treatment, habilitation, and health care involves the power of the state to interfere with access to treatment that would otherwise be available. California statutory provisions requiring mandatory notification of a relative, and approval by a panel of physicians, prior to electroconvulsive therapy violated patients' constitutional right to privacy and due process in giving competent, informed, and voluntary consent [*Aden v. Younger*, 57 Cal.App.3d 662, 129 Cal.Rptr. 535 (1976)].

Regulation of the use of a nontoxic substance (laetrile) in connection with one's personal health care was also found to violate the constitutional right to privacy [*Rutherford v. U.S.*, 430 F.Supp. 1287 (W.D. Okla. 1977)]. Another federal court found that patients have a constitutional right of privacy to obtain acupuncture treatment from practitioners other than licensed physicians [*Andrews v. Ballard*, 498 F.Supp. 1038 (W.D. Tex. 1980)].

D. Right to Refuse Treatment

The right to consent to treatment implies a right to refuse treatment, the necessary analogue of the right to treatment. Legal bases for the right to refuse treatment include (1) the common-law right to freedom from nonconsensual invasion of bodily integrity (informed consent doctrine and the law of battery); (2) the constitutional right of privacy; and (3) the constitutional right to freedom of religion. The common-law right to refuse is illustrated by Brother Fox's right to decline respiratory support through his guardian [*In re Storar,* 52 N.Y.2d 363, 420 N.E.2d 64 (1981)]. The Massachusetts Supreme Court recognized that a noninstitutionalized incompetent with a guardian has a right to refuse antipsychotic drugs; the guardian must seek judicial determination of substituted judgment concerning the patient's choice if he were competent [*Guardianship of Roe*, 421 N.E.2d 40 (Mass. 1981)].

1. Right to Privacy

The right to refuse treatment on the basis of the right to privacy is illustrated by the Karen Ann Quinlan decision, involving a woman in a permanent vegetative state [*In re Quinlan*, 70 N.J. 10, 355 A.2d 647 (1976)]; a 77-year-old woman's refusal to have her gangrenous leg amputated [*Lane v. Candura*, 6 Mass.App. 377, 376 N.E.2d 1232 (1978)]; and a 73-year-old competent man's constitutional right to discontinue the use of a respirator in treating his amyotrophic lateral sclerosis (Lou Gehrig's disease) [*Satz v. Perlmutter*, 379 So.2d 359 (Fla. 1980)]. The privacy right to refuse treatment extends both to involuntarily institutionalized mental patients who are competent [*Rennie v. Klein*, 462 F.Supp. 1131 (D.N.J. 1978), *suppl.*, 476 F.Supp. 1294 (D.N.J. 1979), *vacated and remanded*, 653 F.2d 836 (3d Cir. 1981), *vacated and remanded*, 458 U.S. 1119 (1982), *modified on remand*, 720 F.2d 266 (3d Cir. 1983), *dismissed by consent*, Aug. 20, 1984 (D.N.J.); *Rogers v. Okin*, 478 F.Supp. 1342 (D.Mass. 1979), *aff'd in part, rev'd in part and remanded*, 634 F.2d 650 (1st Cir. 1980), *vacated and remanded sub.nom. Mills v. Rogers*, 457 U.S. 291 (1982), *on remand*, 738 F.2d 1 (1st Cir. 1984); *In re K.K.B.*, 609 P.2d 747 (Okla. 1980)] and to those who are incompetent [*Rogers v. Commissioner of Dep't of Mental Health*, 458 N.E.2d 308 (Mass. 1983)]. The freedom of religion refusal cases involve Jehovah's Witnesses refusing blood transfusions [*In re Osborne*, 294 A.2d 372 (D.C. 1972)] and Christian Scientists refusing all treatment, including psychotropic drugs [*Winters v. Miller*, 446 F.2d (2d Cir. 1971), *cert. denied* 404 U.S. 485 (1971); *In re Boyd*, 403 A.2d 744 (D.C. 1979)].

2. Refusing Treatment for Mental Illness

The right to refuse treatment in mental disability law has been particularly controversial, but should be seen in appropriate context. The mental health system is conceptually more rational as a health system than as a preventive detention criminal justice system.

As a health system, mental health clients are legally presumed competent. As legally competent persons, they can either consent to or refuse treatment, whether institutionalized or not. Whether or not society chooses to institutionalize them, mental health clients should not have their judgment substituted unless they are legally adjudicated incompetent and a substitute decision maker (guardian) is appointed. Otherwise, they retain the same legal capacity to consent to or refuse treatment as any other service recipients.

The feared epidemics of clinically significant treatment refusal have not materialized; virtually all refusers end up accepting medication without harm from the refusal (Applebaum and Hoge, 1986). Recipients of mental health services are fundamentally and unalterably opposed to involuntary hospitalization and forced medication (Lecklitner and Greenberg, 1983). The real problems with mental health services are inequitable funding, inadequate training, resource misallocation, and deficiences in knowledge about mental illness.

V. INSTITUTIONALIZATION/DEINSTITUTIONALIZATION

Institutionalization involves commitment of "captives" to such "total institutions" as prisons, public mental hospitals, public facilities for the mentally retarded, nursing homes, boarding homes, and the like (Goffman, 1961; Miller, 1980; Rosenbloom, 1983b; Talbott, 1978). From an administrative perspective, institutionalization accomplishes control, economies of scale, centralization of services, and segregation of captive client groups

Deinstitutionalization is the policy of placing such health and human service clients as the mentally ill and retarded, juvenile delinquents, alcoholics, addicts, the elderly, and criminals outside of large, isolated public facilities and into community situations (Bachrach, 1976). Administratively, deinstitutionalization makes control and economies of scale more difficult, decentralizes services, and integrates segregated service recipients.

A. Institutionalization as Discriminatory Segregation

The segregation-integration discrimination model is appropriate insofar as such discriminatory practices as racism against blacks reverberate in ageism against the elderly (and children) and "sanism" or "mentalism" against the mentally ill and retarded (Perlin, 1979). Common manifestations include physical isolation and segregation, social stigma and myths, and delimited opportunities in education, employment, and housing (homelessness) (Hayes, 1987). Deinstitutionalization ultimately fails only to the extent exclusionary zoning is successful (Lippincott, 1979; Mental Health Law Project, 1985; Perlin, 1979). Promulgation of deinstitutionalization policy in law proceeds by legislative, administrative, and judicial means, with the judiciary leading in the face of legislative and administrative neglect and impasse (Schmidt, 1983).

B. The Least Restrictive Alternative Principle

A legal basis for deinstitutionalization is the least restrictive alternative principle. The principle originated in a U.S. Supreme Court decision invalidating an Arkansas statute that required schoolteachers to annually reveal all of their organizational associations and contributions for the past five years [*Shelton v. Tucker*, 364 U.S. 479 (1960)]. The Court said:

> [E]ven though the governmental purpose be legitimate and substantial, that purpose cannot be pursued by means that broadly stifle fundamental personal liberties when the end can be more narrowly achieved. The breadth of legislative abridgment must be viewed in the light of less drastic means for achieving the same basic purpose [364 U.S. at 488].

The principle has been applied in a variety of constitutional contexts, including the right to vote, freedom of association, right of privacy, right to travel, freedom of religion, freedom of speech, and interstate commerce (Schmidt, 1985a). Application of the principle to health and human services has most actively occurred in mental disability law.

1. Application to "Homelessness"

In *Lake v. Cameron* [364 F.2d 657 (D.C.Cir. 1966)], the District of Columbia Court of Appeals held that a 60-year-old wandering woman, who suffered from chronic brain syndrome associated with aging, could not be committed to St. Elizabeth's Hospital until the state made an inquiry into all alternative courses of treatment. The court reasoned that deprivation of freedom because of dangerousness to self should not go beyond what is necessary for protection. (Warren Burger, then a judge on that court, argued in dissent that courts are not set up to inquire about or study social welfare facilities and problems, curiously ignoring court experience in criminal sentencing, probation, and disposition, as well as traditional judicial review in administrative law.)

2. Application Within Institutions

In 1969, the same court expanded the least restrictive alternative principle to application within a mental institution: "The range of possible dispositions of a mentally ill person within a hospital, from maximum security to outpatient status, is almost as wide as that of dispositions without" [*Covington v. Harris*, 419 F.2d 617, 623-24 (D.C.Cir 1969)].

3. Application to Mentally Retarded Persons

The federal district court in *Wyatt v. Stickney* applied the least restrictive alternative concept to mentally retarded persons, as well as mentally ill persons: "Patients have a right to the least restrictive conditions necessary to achieve the purposes of commitment," and "no person shall be admitted to the institution unless a prior determination shall have been made that residence in the institution is the least restrictive habilitation setting feasible for that person" [344 F.Supp. at 379, 386]. Implementation of the least restrictive habilitation was ordered as follows:

> Residents shall have a right to the least restrictive conditions necessary to achieve the purposes of habilitation. To this end, the institution shall make every attempt to move residents from (1) more to less structured living; (2) larger to smaller facilities; (3) larger to smaller living units; (4) group to individual residence; (5) segregated from the community to integrated into . . . community living; (6) dependent to independent living [344 F.Supp. at 396].

4. Impact

The right to treatment, or habilitation, in the least restrictive setting was used to mandate the development of community-based treatment programs, chronologically: for the retarded in Minnesota [*Welsch v. Likins*, 373 F.Supp. 487 (D.Minn. 1974), *aff'd in part and remanded in part*, 550 F.2d 1122 (8th Cir. 1977)], Maine [*Wuori v. Zitnay*, No. 75-80-SD, 2 *Mental Disability L.Rep.* 693, 729 (D.Me. July 14, 1978)] and Massachusetts [*Brewster v. Dukakis*, C.A.No. 76-4423-F, 3 *Mental Disability L.Rep.* 44 (E.D.Mass. Dec. 6, 1978)]; for the mentally ill in the District of Columbia [*Dixon v. Weinberger*, 405 F.Supp. 974 (D.D.C. 1975); and for delinquent and antisocial juveniles in Texas [*Morales v. Turman*, 383 F.Supp. 53 (E.D.Tex. 1974), *vacated*, 535 F.2d 864 (5th Cir. 1976), *reinstated*, 430 U.S. 322 (1977)]. By 1977, at least 35 states explicitly or implicitly recognized the least restrictive alternative principle.

5. Dissent

Some courts have resisted application of the least restrictive alternative principle in mental disability law. An early New Mexico decision held that due process did not require the state to consider less restrictive alternatives to total institutionalization [*State v. Sanchez*, 80 N.M. 438, 457 P.2d 370 (1969), *appeal dismissed for want of a substantial federal question*, 396 U.S. 276 (1970)]. *Sanchez* was initially ignored by federal courts [e.g., *Lynch v. Baxley*, 386 F.Supp. 378, 392 n.10 (M.D.Ala. 1974)], including the U.S. Supreme Court. In *O'Connor v. Donaldson*, the Supreme Court affirmatively cited *Shelton v. Tucker* for the proposition that "while the state may arguably confine a person to save him from harm, incarceration is rarely if ever a necessary condition for raising the living standards of those capable of surviving safely in freedom, on their own or with the help of family or friends" [422 U.S. at 575]. The only other case in accord with *Sanchez* was a Georgia case that was reversed on the authority of *Wyatt v. Aderholt* [*Burnham v. Department of Pub. Health*, 349 F.Supp. 1335, 1340–41 (N.D.Ga. 1972), *reversed*, 503 F.2d 1319 (5th Cir. 1974), *cert. denied*, 422 U.S. 1057 (1974)].

However, in *Pennhurst State School v. Halderman*, the Supreme Court revived *Sanchez*, citing it for the proposition that the Court had never found a right to treatment, and going on to hold that the federal Developmentally Disabled Assistance Program and Bill of Rights Act of 1975 does not create substantive rights to appropriate treatment in the least restrictive environment [451 U.S. 1, 16 n.12 (1981)]. (The Development Disabilities Act, the Education of All Handicapped Children Act, Section 504 of the Rehabilitation Act, the Civil Rights of Institutionalized Persons Act, the Protection and Advocacy for Mentally Ill Individuals Act, Section 1983 of the Civil Rights Act, and the Community Mental Health Centers Construction Act, all provide federal statutory avenues for deinstitutionalization.) But *Halderman* was a narrowly decided statutory interpretation case that did not inhibit the Court from later sustaining the principle, as predicted (Schmidt, 1983), that "the nature and duration of commitment [must] bear some reasonable relation to the purpose for which the individual is committed" [*Jackson v. Indiana*, 406 U.S. 715, 738 (1972)]. In *Youngberg v. Romeo* [457 U.S. 307 (1982)], the Court held that involuntarily committed mentally retarded persons have constitutional interests in reasonably safe conditions of confinement, freedom from unreasonable bodily restraints, and such training as is required by these interests, so as to comport fully with the purpose of commitment.

C. Constitutional Right to Community Services

In conjunction with *O'Connor v. Donaldson*, nondangerous mentally disabled persons may not be institutionalized if they can survive in the community alone or with available help; and if they cannot survive alone or with available help, they must receive more than enforced custodial care in an institution: safe confinement, freedom from restraints, and enough habilitation to assure these interests. *Youngberg* is generating a constitutional right to community services for the mentally retarded [*Clark v. Cohen*, 613 F.Supp. 684 (E.D.Pa. 1985); *Thomas S. v. Morrow*, 781 F.2d 367 (4th Cir. 1986); *Lelsz v. Kavanagh*, 629 F.Supp. 1487 (D.Tex. 1986)].

D. Implementation

Legal provisions like the right to treatment in the least restrictive setting generate implementation problems and opportunities (Bradley and Clarke, 1976; Harvard Law Review, 1977; Horowitz, 1983; Lottman, 1976; McCormack and Mandel, 1985; Note, 1975; Yarbrough, 1985). Some mental health professionals suggest that the least restrictive alternative principle poses a dilemma between restrictiveness and treatment effectiveness: Is 30 days of effective programming in a state hospital more, or less, constraining than one year in a less effective community program (Stromberg and Stone, 1983)? What does not seem universally appreciated are not only the benefits and effectiveness of conscientious deinstitutionalization (Kiesler, 1982; Stein and Test, 1978), but also the right of legally competent persons to prefer home to the comforts of an institution [*O'Connor v. Donaldson*, 422 U.S. at 575], and to decide for themselves the most appropriate level of care [*In re Borgogna*, 121 Cal.App.3d 937, 175 Ca.Rptr. 588 (1981); Parry, 1985b]. This is consistent with legal opportunities to choose between medication and surgery, between walk-in surgery and inpatient care and convalescence, between dying and extraordinary treatment measures. Implementation for legal incompetents necessitates a viable guardianship system (Schmidt et al., 1981).

E. Outlawing Exclusionary Zoning

One of the most recent Supreme Court decisions continues the momentum against discriminatory segregation and restriction. In *City of Cleburne v. Cleburne Living Center* [105 S.Ct 3249 (1985)], the Court held that the exclusionary zoning practice of requiring a special use permit for a proposed group home for mentally retarded persons violates equal protection of the laws where other facilities (boardinghouses, hospitals) are permitted without such permits. The special use permit requirement rested on an irrational prejudice against the mentally retarded that would not pass judicial scrutiny and application of a revitalized rational relationship equal protection test.

The "new partnership" between public administrators and the judiciary continues in the face of administrative muddling and coping (Rosenbloom, 1987). Whether public administration can forge a new administrative culture more consistent with judicial and "new public administration" values remains to be seen.

VI. RECORD-KEEPING LAW AND CONFIDENTIALITY

With the recent attention to public management information systems (Bozeman and Bretschneider, 1986; Kraemer and King, 1987), it is appropriate to consider record-keeping law in the context of health and human services. Since timely and more comprehensive summaries are available in other sources (Kapp and Bigot, 1985; Miller, 1986), this section will cover highlights and new developments.

A. Confidentiality

An important beginning point for record-keeping law is confidentiality. Confidentiality protects the client and the therapeutic relationship with the individual provider. Confidentiality is not a veil to hide professional or organizational wrongdoing.

1. Professionalism

Health and human service personnel secure professional status with adherence to the ethical obligations of their profession. The Hippocratic oath for physicians provides: "And whatsoever I shall see or hear in the course of my profession, as well as outside my profession in my intercourse with man, if it be what should not be published abroad, I will never divulge, holding such things to be holy secrets" (Miller, 1986, p. 294). Principle 6 of the code of ethics for the American Psychological Association states that "safeguarding information about an individual that has been obtained by the psychologist in the course of his teaching, practice or investigation is a primary obligation of the psychologist" (Preisner, 1985, p. 204). The *Code of Ethics of the National Association of Social Workers* (1979) says, regarding confidentiality and privacy: "The social worker should respect the privacy of clients and hold in confidence all information obtained in the course of professional service." The American Society for Public Administration's *Code of Ethics and Implementation Guidelines* (1985) commits its members to "respect and protect the privileged information to which we have access in the course of official duties."

Health and human service professionals thus have a general duty to maintain the confidentiality of personal client information, and the client has a right to expect fulfillment of the duty. The law assures confidentiality through privileges that protect the disclosure of particular information, and through a right of privacy protection against invasion of confidentiality.

2. Privileges

Privileges against disclosure of private communications did not exist in the common law (Brakel, Parry, and Weiner, 1985). The legal system depends upon the whole truth's emerging through the adversarial process, and privilege laws inhibit this quest. Evidence law experts argue that illnesses at one time were publicly known and, except for "loathsome disease," disclosable without embarrassment or stigma. There is a sense in which secrecy in a relatively open, democratic society fosters social myths and stigma.

Using the attorney-client privilege as a precedent, legislatures balanced judicial access against privacy, and began to authorize privileges of confidentiality for other relationships: priest-penitent; physician-patient; psychiatrist-patient; psychologist-patient; psychotherapist-patient; and social worker-client. Privilege statutes address the kind of professional conduct, prescribe the degree of confidentiality, describe the nature of uniquely professional information, and limit coverage to designated types of professionals. Brakel and colleagues (1985, p. 462) describe the following minimal criteria that justify limiting court access to information:

> (1) The communications are made in a situation in which both parties have an expectation of confidentiality, (2) confidentiality is essential if the relationship between [professional] and patient is to be complete and satisfactory, (3) the therapeutic relationship is one that should be fostered by society, and (4) in many instances, the injury caused by disclosure of therapeutic information would outweigh the benefit gained by improving the judicial result.

3. The Client's Privilege

The right of privilege is held by the client, who decides whether to exercise or waive it. Efforts by professionals to exercise the privilege on the client's behalf have not been successful [*Caesar v. Mountanos*, 542 F.2d 1064 (9th Cir. 1976), *cert. denied*, 430 U.S. 954 (1976); *In re Lifschutz*, 467 P.2d 557, 85 Cal. Rptr. 829 (1970)]. Exceptions to the privilege include child abuse, civil commitment, court-ordered examinations, and patient-litigant situations (child custody disputes, malpractice cases, personal injury suits, worker's compensation cases, will contests).

4. Right of Privacy

The other way in which the law protects confidentiality is through the right of privacy. The broadest, but most unsettled, legal theory supporting confidentiality began with *Griswold v. Connecticut* [391 U.S. 429 (1965)]. In *Griswold*, the U.S. Supreme Court held that married couples had a right to be free from a Connecticut state law banning the sale and use of contraceptives. The Court identified a right of privacy grounded in the First, Third, Fourth, Fifth, Ninth, and Fourteenth Amendments of the Constitution. The Court subsequently extended the constitutional right of privacy to the use of contraceptives by unmarried people [*Eisenstadt v. Baird*, 405 U.S. 438 (1972)], a woman's right to seek an abortion [*Roe v. Wade*, 410 U.S. 113 (1973)], and parental notification requirements for minors seeking abortions [*H.L. v. Matheson*, 450 U.S. 998 (1981)]. Justice Douglas wrote, "[t]he right of privacy has no more conspicuous place than in the physician-patient relationship, unless it be in the priest-penitent relationship" [*Doe v. Balton*, 410 U.S. 179, 219 (1973) (concurring)]. Justice Stevens concluded that these cases "involved at least two different kinds of interests. One is the individual interest in avoiding disclosure of personal matters, and another is the individual interest in independence in making certain kinds of important decisions" [*Whalen v. Roe*, 429 U.S. 599, 599-800 (1977)].

In *Whalen v. Roe*, a New York law required doctors to report all prescriptions for dangerous drugs to a centralized computer file. The Supreme Court upheld the statute only because it was limited by such security provisions as a bar on disclosing patient identity. The Court said:

> We are not unaware of the threat to privacy implicit in the accumulation of vast amounts of personal information in computerized data banks or other massive government files. The collection of taxes, the distribution of welfare and social security benefits, the supervision of public health, the direction of our Armed Forces, and the enforcement of the criminal laws all require the orderly preservation of great quantities of information, much of which is personal in character and potentially embarrassing or harmful if disclosed. . . . Recognizing that in some circumstances . . . [the concomitant statutory or regulatory] duty [to avoid unwarranted disclosures] arguably has its roots in the Constitution, nevertheless New York's statutory scheme and its implementing administrative procedures evidence a proper concern with, and protection of, the individual's interest in privacy. We therefore need not, and do not, decide any question which might be presented by the unwarranted disclosure of accumulated private data—whether intentional or unintentional—or by a system that did not contain comparable security provisions [429 U.S. at 605-606].

5. Sensitive Information

Several courts have identified fundamental privacy rights when such especially sensitive information as mental health records are revealed [*Merriken v. Cressman*, 364 F.Supp. 913 (E.D.Pa. 1973); *Roe v. Ingraham*, 403 F.Supp. 931 (S.D.N.Y. 1975)]. In *In re B* [394 A.2d 419 (Pa. 1978)], the Pennsylvania Supreme Court held that a mother's constitutional right of privacy prevented disclosure of her psychiatric hospitalization history in the dispositional phase of her son's delinquency proceeding. A federal district court struck down a state Medicaid statute permitting fraud investigation seizure and examination of psychotherapists' clinical notes because it violated individuals' constitutional right of privacy [*Hawaii Psychiatric Society v. Ariyash*, 481 F.Supp. 1028 (D.Hawaii, 1979)]. In making the injunction permanent, the court stated:

> The disclosure of a patient's innermost thoughts, feelings, conduct, and beliefs is, quite simply, not justified by the State's interest in verifying the necessity or performance of psychotherapeutic treatments, in preventing fraud, or in catching those who commit fraud. In short, the court concludes, the State could implement a statutory scheme that would strike a more appropriate balance between preserving the integrity of the Medicaid program and minimizing any intrusion on an individual's right to confidentiality (Brakel, Parry, and Weiner, 1985, p. 572).

6. Privacy and Computers

One of the most interesting recent cases involved the state of Washington's Department of Social and Health Services regulations requiring disclosure of name and diagnosis of patients utilizing state and federal subsidized mental health facilities for inclusion in a centralized computer information system [*Peninsula Counseling Center v. Rahm*, 719 P.2d 926 (Wash. 1986)]. Two University of Washington professors testified that the mental health centers could generate a unique patient code using computer "hashing" or encryption. A 10-character hash code would make the chance of a duplicated client count smaller than two-tenths of one percent, or one in 1.78 million on a population of 60,000. The Washington Supreme Court nevertheless overruled the trial court's preliminary and permanent injunction against the system's violation of privacy and of the less intrusive alternative principle. The court held that the system was permissible when carefully tailored to meet the government's interest in accountability. Specifically, the system was acceptable because only four people had access to the raw data; a person's information would remain in the system for only five years after treatment; only priority patients (acutely ill, chronically mentally ill, seriously disturbed) were targeted by the system; no more than the patient's name and diagnostic code were kept in the system; and the centralized records were strictly confidential.

B. Affirmative Record-Keeping Requirements

The general duty of health and human service professionals to maintain confidentiality is juxtaposed against limitations on the duty and affirmative record-keeping requirements. Record-keeping is essential for quality services; it is an administrative activity without which quality service can neither be said to occur nor, as suggested by *Wyatt*, be reviewed or evaluated. There is a general legal duty to properly document provision of services to clients. Failure to properly document and resulting injury may constitute actionable negligence against the responsible professional.

1. Responsibility for Documentation

The professional who makes the observation, performs the test, or provides the service is responsible for documentation (Kapp and Bigot, 1985). Team approaches to provision of services should induce professionals to read the record entries of all team members. Documentation responsibilities cannot be delegated. Guidelines for documentation are as follows:

1. Written client records should be accurate and truthful.
2. Documentation must be thorough and complete.
3. Records should be legible.
4. Documentation should be timely.
5. Mistakes must be corrected so that the change is evident, and not overcorrected, obliterated, or destroyed.
6. Notations should be objective, value-neutral, and nonjudgmental (Kapp and Bigot, 1985).

2. Access to Records

The law provides for access to records pursuant to subpoenas and other judicial discovery orders (Miller, 1986). Reporting laws relating to vital statistics, public health (venereal and other communicable diseases) (Kapp and Fortess, 1986), child and adult abuse, wounds, and other situations (including industrial accidents, blood transfusions, and investigational medical devices) define a statutory duty to disclose. Access laws relating to worker's compensation, the federal Freedom of Information Act, state public records laws, and various governmental review functions (such as peer review organizations, Medicare surveyors, hospital licensing) also define statutory duties to disclose. Patients have a right of access to their own records by statute, or case law over the past 25 years (Miller, 1986), although almost half the states do not yet allow mental patients to have access (Brakel, Parry, and Weiner, 1985).

3. Duty to Warn

One of the most controversial disclosure requirements comes from *Tarasoff v. Regents of University of California* [131 Cal.Rptr. 14, 551 P.2d 334 (1976)]. The California Supreme Court held:

> When a therapist determines, or pursuant to the standards of his profession should determine, that his patient presents a serious danger of violence to another, he incurs an obligation to use reasonable care to protect the intended victim against such danger. The discharge of this duty may require the therapist to take one or more of various steps, depending upon the nature of the case. Thus, it may call for him to warn the intended victim or others likely to apprise the victim of the danger, to notify the police, or to take whatever other steps are reasonably necessary under the circumstances [131 Cal.Rptr. at 32, 551 P.2d at 340].

This duty to warn (disclose) not only jeopardizes confidentiality and the therapeutic relationship, it also disregards the inability to accurately predict dangerousness (Ennis and Litwack, 1974; Monahan, 1981), and risks increasing inappropriate commitments.

4. Model Statutes

Unlike other areas of health and human service regulation, the law is struggling to keep pace with rapid technological changes in the recording and use of information. Several model laws have been enacted or suggested to better balance confidentiality and record-keeping requirements. The Illinois Mental Health and Developmental Disabilities Confidentiality Act [Ill. Ann. Stat. ch. 91 1/2, section 801 (Smith-Hurd Supp. 1984] was enacted after much work by a panel of mental health professionals, judges, attorneys, and lay people. Two other model law suggestions are the Model Law on Confidentiality of Health and Social Service Records (American Psychiatric Association, 1979) and the Suggested Statute on Therapeutic Confidentiality (Mental Health Law Project, 1977).

REFERENCES

American Psychiatric Association (1979). Model law on confidentiality of health and human service records, *American Journal of Psychiatry, 136*: 137.

American Society for Public Administration (1985). *Code of Ethics and Implementation Guidelines*, American Society for Public Administration, Washington, D.C.

Applebaum, P., and Hoge, S. (1986). Empirical research on the effects of legal policy on the right to refuse treatment, *The Right to Refuse Antipsychotic Medication*, American Bar Association Commission on the Mentally Disabled, Washington, D.C., pp. 87–97.

Bachrach, L. (1976). *Deinstitutionalization: An Analytic Review and Sociological Perspective*, U.S. Government Printing Office, Washington, D.C.

Black, H. (1979). *Black's Law Dictionary*, West Publishing Company, St. Paul, p. 795.

Bozeman, B., and Bretschneider, S., eds. (1986). Public management information systems, *Public Administration Review, 46*: 473.

Bradley, V., and Clarke, G. (1976). *Paper Victories and Hard Realities: The Implementation of the Legal and Constitutional Rights of the Mentally Disabled*, Georgetown University Health Policy Center, Washington, D.C.

Brakel, S., Parry, J., and Weiner, B. (1985). *The Mentally Disabled and the Law*, American Bar Foundation, Chicago.

Brown, B., and Stillman, R. (1985). A conversation with Dwight Waldo: An agenda for future reflections, *Public Administration Review, 45*: 459.

Carter, L. (1983). *Administrative Law and Politics: Cases and Comments*, Little, Brown and Company, Boston.

Cook, T. (1983). The substantive due process rights of mentally disabled clients, *Mental Disability Law Reporter, 7*: 346.

Dybwad, G., and Herr, S. (1979). Unnecessary coercion: An end to involuntary civil commitment of retarded persons, *Stanford Law Review, 31*: 753.

Ennis, B. (1972). *Prisoners of Psychiatry: Mental Patients, Psychiatrists, and the Law*, Harcourt Brace Jovanovich, New York.

Ennis, B., and Litwack, T. (1974). Psychiatry and the presumption of expertise: Flipping coins in the courtroom, *California Law Review, 62*: 693.

Gates, B. (1980). Guess who's coming to dinner? Developments in human services administration, *Public Administration Review, 40*: 286.

Gaylin, W., Glasser, I., Marcus, S., and Rothman, D. (1981). *Doing Good: The Limits of Benevolence*, Pantheon Books, New York.

Gellhorn, W., Byse, C., Strauss, P., and Rakoff, T. (1987). *Administrative Law: Cases and Comments*, Foundation Press, Mineola, New York.

Goffman, E. (1961). *Asylums: Essays on the Social Situation of Mental Patients and Other Inmates*, Doubleday, Garden City, New York.

Hall, G., and Mathiasen, G. (1968). *Overcoming Barriers to Protective Services for the Aged*, National Council on Aging, New York.

Harvard Law Review (1977). Mental health litigation: Implementing institutional reform, *Mental Disability Law Reporter, 2*: 221.

Hayes, R. (1986). The editors interview Robert M. Hayes, *New England Journal of Human Services, 6*: 10.

Horowitz, D. (1983). Decreeing organizational change: Judicial supervision of public institutions, *Duke Law Journal, 1983*: 1265.

Kapp, M., and Bigot, A. (1985). *Geriatrics and the Law: Patient Rights and Professional Responsibilities*, Springer Publishing Company, New York.

Kapp, M., and Fortress, E. (1986). Screening for AIDS: Legal and ethical issues, *New England Journal of Human Services, 6*: 19.

Kiesler, C. (1982). Mental hospitals and alternative care: Non-institutionalization as a potential public policy for mental patients, *American Psychologist, 37*: 349.

Kittrie, N. (1971). *The Right to be Different: Deviance and Enforced Therapy*, Johns Hopkins Press, Baltimore.

Knitzer, J. (1982). *Unclaimed Children: The Failure of Public Responsibility to Children Services*, Children's Defense Fund, Washington, D.C.

Kraemer, K., and King, J. (1987). Computers and the Constitution: A helpful, harmful, or harmless relationship? *Public Administration Review, 47*: 93.

Lecklitner, M., and Greenberg, P. (1983). Promoting the rights of chronically mentally ill in the community: A report on the patient rights policy research project, *Mental Disability Law Reporter, 7*: 422.

Lewis, E. (1977). *American Politics in a Bureaucratic Age: Citizens, Constituents, Clients, and Victims*, Winthrop, Cambridge, Massachusetts.

Lidz, C., et al. (1984). *Informed Consent: A Study of Decisionmaking in Psychiatry*, Guilford Press, New York.

Lippincott, M. (1979). "A sanctuary for people": Strategies for overcoming zoning restrictions on community homes for retarded persons, *Stanford Law Review, 31*: 767.

Lipsky, M. (1980). *Street-level Bureaucracy: Dilemmas of the Individual in Public Services*, Russell Sage Foundation, New York.

Lottman, M. (1976). Enforcement of judicial decrees: Now comes the hard part, *Mental Disability Law Reporter, 1*: 69.

McCormack, F., and Mandel, D. (1985). How to manage an institution during litigation, *Mental and Physical Disability Law Reporter, 9*: 73.

Melton, G. (1982). Legal reforms affecting child and youth services, *Child and Youth Services, 5*: 1.

Melton, G., Koocher, G., and Saks, M. (1983). *Children's Competence to Consent*, Plenum Press, New York.

Mental Health Law Project (1977). Suggested statute on therapeutic confidentiality, *Mental Disability Law Reporter, 2*: 343.

Mental Health Law Project (1985). The effects of group homes on property values, *Mental and Physical Disability Law Reporter, 9*: 309.

Miller, K. (1976). *Managing Madness: The Case Against Civil Commitment*, Free Press, New York.

Miller, K. (1980). *The Criminal Justice and Mental Health Systems: Conflict and Collusion,* Oelgeschlager, Gunn and Hain, Cambridge, Massachusetts.

Miller, R. (1986). *Problems in Hospital Law*, Aspen Publishers, Rockville, Maryland.

Monahan, J. (1981). *The Clinical Prediction of Violent Behavior*, U.S. Government Printing Office, Washington, D.C.

Morse, S. (1978). Crazy behavior, morals, and science: An analysis of mental health law, *Southern California Law Review, 51*: 527.

Morse, S. (1982). A preference for liberty: The case against involuntary commitment of the mentally disordered, *California Law Review, 70*: 54.
Murphy, P. (1974). *Our Kindly Parent–The State: The Juvenile Justice System and How It Works*, Penguin Books, New York.
National Association of Social Workers (1979). *Code of Ethics of the National Association of Social Workers*, National Association of Social Workers, Inc., Washington, D.C.
Note (1975). The *Wyatt* case: Implementation of a judicial decree ordering institutional change, *Yale Law Journal, 84*: 1338.
Parry, J. (1985a). AIDS as a handicapping condition, *Mental and Physical Disability Law Reporter, 9*: 402.
Parry, J. (1985b). Least restrictive alternative: An overview of the concept, *Mental and Physical Disability Law Reporter, 9*: 314.
Perlin, M. (1979). Protecting civil and legal rights of the de-institutionalized elderly, *Returning the Institutionalized Elderly to the Community: Proceedings of a Training Institute*, Florida State University Center of Gerontology, Tallahassee, pp. 20–52.
Pozgar, G. (1983). *Legal Aspects of Health Care Administration*, Aspen Publishers, Rockville, Maryland.
Reisner, R. (1985). *Law and the Mental Health System: Civil and Criminal Aspects*, West Publishing Company, St. Paul.
Reppucci, N., Westhorn, L., Mulvey, E., and Monahan, J. (1984). *Children, Mental Health, and the Law*, Sage Publications, Beverly Hills.
Robinson, G., Gellhorn, E., and Bruff, H. (1980). *The Administrative Process*, West Publishing Company, St. Paul.
Rosenbloom, D. (1983a). Public administration theory and the separation of powers, *Public Administration Review, 43*: 219.
Rosenbloom, D. (1983b). *Public Administration and Law: Bench v. Bureau in the United States*, Marcel Dekker, New York.
Rosenbloom, D. (1986). *Public Administration: Understanding Management, Politics, and Law in the Public Sector*, Random House, New York.
Rosenbloom, D. (1987). Public administrators and the judiciary: The "new partnership," *Public Administration Review, 47*: 75.
Rosenhan, D. (1973). On being sane in insane places, *Science, 179*: 250.
Rozovsky, F. (1984). *Consent to Treatment: A Practical Guide*, Little, Brown and Company, Boston.
Scallet, L. (1980). Mental health law and administration: Who is "on the side of the angels?" *Journal of Health and Human Resources Administration, 2*: 320.
Schmidt, W. (1976). *The Right to Treatment in Mental Health Law*, National Association of Attorneys General, Raleigh, North Carolina.
Schmidt, W. (1983). Deinstitutionalization following *Pennhurst State School v. Halderman*, *Journal of Health and Human Resources Administration, 5*: 481.
Schmidt, W. (1985a). Critique of the American Psychiatric Association's guidelines for state legislation on civil commitment of the mentally ill, *New England Journal on Criminal and Civil Confinement, 11*: 11.
Schmidt, W. (1985b). Considerations of social science in a reconsideration of *Parham v. J.R.* and the commitment of children to public mental institutions, *Journal of Psychiatry and Law, 13*: 334.
Schmidt, W. (1986). Adult protective services and the therapeutic state, *Law and Psychology Review, 10*: 101.
Schmidt, W., Miller, K., Bell, W., and New, E. (1981). *Public Guardianship and the Elderly*, Ballinger Publishing Company, Cambridge, Massachusetts.
Schmidt, W., Miller, K. Bell, W., and New, E. (1982). Alternatives to public guardianship, *State and Local Government Review, 14*: 128.

Shadish, W. (1984). Lessons from the implementation of deinstitutionalization, *American Psychologist, 39*: 725.

Stein, L., and Test, M., eds. (1978). *Alternatives to Mental Hospital Treatment*, Plenum Press, New York.

Straussman, J. (1986). Courts and public purse strings: Have portraits of budgeting missed something? *Public Administration Review, 46*: 345.

Stromberg, C., and Stone, A. (1983). A model state law on civil commitment of the mentally ill, *Harvard Journal on Legislation, 20*: 291.

Szasz, T. (1968). *Law, Liberty, and Psychiatry: An Inquiry into the Social Uses of Mental Health Practices*, Macmillan, New York.

Talbott, J. (1978). *The Death of the Asylum: A Critical Study of State Hospital Management, Services, and Care*, Grune and Stratton, New York.

Taylor, R. (1981). *The Kid Business: How It Exploits the Children It Should Help*, Houghton Mifflin Company, Boston.

Wadlington, W., Whitebread, C., and Davis, S. (1983). *Cases and Materials on Children in the Legal System*, Foundation Press, Mineola, New York.

White, L. (1926). *Introduction to the Study of Public Administration*, Macmillan, New York.

Wing, K. (1985). *The Law and the Public's Health*, Health Administration Press, Ann Arbor, Michigan.

Yarbrough, T. (1985). The political world of federal judges as managers, *Public Administration Review, 45*: 660.

12

Legal and Ethical Dilemmas in Modern Medical Technology

John F. Hough Division of Community Health and Patient Advocacy, California Medical Association, San Francisco, California

Marc D. Hiller Department of Health Management and Policy, University of New Hampshire, Durham, New Hampshire

I. INTRODUCTION

Health administrators, health planners, and clinicians are today more frequently prompted to deal with the problems of the new medical ethics. These problems are of a social, governmental, political, economic, medical, and legal nature. To be effective, administrators must stay abreast of both the advances in medical care and the precedent-setting responses to them in law that will doubtless follow.

This chapter is designed to address the needs of administrators, planners, practitioners, and "good bureaucrats" in this endeavor, toward a more earnest reception of the role medical ethics must play in today's health care environments. This chapter represents an attempt to synthesize the variety of challenges and problems prompted by rapid technological change in medicine, some responses of the legal system to them, and the nature of the decisions that law and medicine have created for administrators in the last decades of this century.

II. HEALTH ADMINISTRATION TODAY

A. Medical Technology

Essentially, administrators and planners will continue to be charged with the responsibilities of both implementing new technologies and responding to moral and legal considerations about their use. Their decisions about implementation will affect the quality of their administration within their particular health care environment, and in turn, will affect the quality of health care provided to the public.

The daily work of health care administrators is affected by the massive transformations wrought by the development, allocation, and standardization of new technologies. Conclusions arrived at in the courts and the nation's legal system about the use of these new technologies will affect the concomitant decisions of these persons in their work.

Precedent is equally important in health administration and in law: today's court decisions influence tomorrow's hospital decisions and have an impact on next year's technology allocation and resource purchase decisions. Given these manifestations of the proliferation of high-technology medical devices and procedures, administrators and planners must remain vigilant, forwardthinking, and always anticipating the future needs and demands of their constituencies which will at some point be the needs and demands of both their patients and institutions.

B. Medical Ethics

Just as the administrator must remain abreast of the new technologies that exit the laboratory and soon head for the examining rooms or operating theaters, he or she must also remain abreast of ethical responses to these technologies and their sometimes antagonistic partnership with court decisions. The effective administrator must presume that ethical theories often overlap with and occasionally provide theoretical foundations for public policy, law, and in turn for medical practice and administration. Therefore, medical ethics or bioethics, either in theory or practice, can no longer be only a "parlor activity" or area of sublime or passing interest for administrators. A working knowledge of medical ethical dilemmas and precedents in moral decision-making should be considered a job function and, at least tacitly, an occupational responsibility for today's administrators (Friedman, 1986; Gregory, 1984). A subset of the body of ethical knowledge we consider important for administrators to pursue is that which applies specifically to dilemmas posed by modern medical technology.

The range of ethically relevant topics pertaining to medical technology is quite broad. We have elected to focus on the economics of medical technology and how cost constraints can affect resource allocation; on organ transplantation, the once-"exotic" technology that is becoming commonplace but still must be examined under the microscope of ethical scrutiny; on issues of death and dying, because these are the most pressing patient cases in which ethical decision-making and law will determine the extent to which technology intervenes; and on the development of the "bioethics committee" model, in which ethics and law merge with medicine and administration in the effort to categorize and provide direction for optimal health care among patients usually near death. We hope that focusing on these areas will sharpen the reader's awareness to the fact that effective health administration today requires a firm grounding in ethical analysis.

III. ON LAW AND ETHICS

Increasingly, administrators face ethical dilemmas for which they seek legal solutions. Within our highly litigious society, legal considerations have moved to the forefront of successful health management. Many administrators or their health systems have hired staff attorneys; most at least have placed legal counsel on retainer. The law may constitute one, and some may even argue "the best" approach to dealing with issues that bear seemingly intractable value conflicts. However, it ought never be viewed as the only, or even the most satisfactory, means to attempt to resolve moral dilemmas in a rational manner.

While legal resolutions may alleviate fears of potential liabilities, administrators should still recognize that meaningful solutions to moral problems require both a careful analysis of the ethical principles involved in a particular case, and a clarification of their own professional and personal values that influence decision-making.

Laws can be seen as a codification of ethics, but not all laws are necessarily ethical or even bound by ethical norms. To the extent that law is considered to be a codification of ethics, such an assertion reflects the view that laws attempt to establish socially agreed-upon norms to govern society and to prompt necessary decisions in difficult situations. However, deriving ethical resolutions to problems may be more meaningful and far-reaching. As Pellegrino and Thomasma (1981, p. 247) point out, legal intervention marks a "forceful commentary on the tardiness" of institutions in meeting their ethical obligations.

Whereas law usually mandates minimum standards and is enforced through sanctions and penalties, ethics tends to reach for the ideal. Ethics, which differ from morals per se, is a discipline that is unbounded, voluntary, and cannot be mandated (Hiller, 1986, pp. 7-8; also see Beauchamp and Childress, 1983, for succinct operational definitions of the philosophical terms used hereafter). Law is standardized, filled with procedure and protocol, and is often impersonal. It fosters an adversarial process with a singular goal: winning. In contrast, ethics tends to be more humanistic, personal, and largely dependent on conscience. In most cases, it is sensitive to the kinds of situations that arise in health care. Winning is not at issue, and therefore choices are not as clear-cut. Rather, ethical analysis seeks to determine the best possible outcome from all possible alternatives. In wrestling under conditions of uncertainty, as is so often the case in modern technological medicine, the absolute nature of law is not always applicable or helpful to the administrator.

Though outcomes based on law and ethics may be similar, such outcomes may result from their being based on common theoretical principles such as utility or justice; after all, it is often possible to reach similar decisions based on very different (or even opposing) arguments. However, there is often a large gap between what is deemed legal and what is ethical. Consider, for example, the debates that arise over high-risk human experimentation when there is little or no potential gain for the subject, or, given the advances in neonatal technologies, the inability of law to resolve the dilemmas associated with abortion and/or foregoing life support on defective newborns. In both cases, laws have contradicted values held by large segments of society, including many health administrators. The ethical approach to understanding and deciding issues in modern technological medicine is therefore requisite in today's health administration, while the legal approach may or may not provide substantive solutions or even satisfactory guidelines in resolving the hardest problems.

IV. A SYSTEMS VIEW OF ETHICAL APPROACHES TO HEALTH ADMINISTRATION

Our chapter has in theme a "systems view" of the close relationship between decisions in the legal or medical arenas and the practice of administration. Decisions of a medical, legal, or ethical nature involving the net effects of modern medical technology in one state, in one medical specialty, or in one patient's serious case will influence the decisions of administrators, planners, or practitioners in other states, specialties, or serious cases.

In a sense, the process and products of health administration now more than ever constitute a kind of institution or "system," like a corporation or a human body, in which the whole is more than the sum of its parts. In his landmark work on health planning, Blum describes this systems view in great detail, stating at the outset that one of the paradoxes facing administration or planning is that "planning is shaped by the same forces that created the problems that planning is supposed to correct" (Blum, 1981, p. 6). This is especially true in the context of the "rapid deployment" of medical technology: the reason that administrators need to consider the ethical ramifications of allocating modern medical technology is that technology itself has proliferated, creating problems of fair allocation, extending lives perhaps against the desires of the patient or family members, and all the while costing an incredible amount of money (Anderson and Russe, 1987; Jennett, 1985). Technology is driving the American health care system; clinical options are very often technological options. When clinicians and administrators make decisions about the implementation of technology, they make decisions about technology's effects throughout the health care system: costs increase, persons live or die with or without technological intervention, or health care product manufacturers produce more or fewer machines almost in direct response to trends throughout the system.

Making that system effective will require that administrators have knowledge of more than the operation of the particular hospital or clinic or government program at hand. Effective administrators will need to know what others in the field are saying when they are "doing ethics," especially as it pertains to new technology. As an institution or system, health care administration and its practitioners will be called upon more than ever to articulate their moral decisions or to make more explicit the rules by which they and their institutions make moral decisions affecting patient care in a technology-dependent medical model.

V. ADMINISTRATORS AS MORAL AGENTS

Also in theme, we attempt to address the role of health administrators as "moral agents" for patients and institutions in the health care system. Several authors have expressed their view that physicians, administrators, and policymakers must step outside their own particular professional codes of ethics or their personal moral opinions to act as expositors for a new kind of institutional ethics, a set of normative principles defining the way institutions "ought" to act on behalf of patients (Pellegrino, 1979).

This is especially relevant in today's health care environment. The stakes have become decidedly higher because of the influence of proliferating medical technology. Physicians have been removed from acting as the traditional moral agents for individual patients whose sick role has deprived them of the ability to act for themselves or decide the course of their treatment. Now, physicians and hospitals are no longer quite as much in control of the course of treatment, in that treatment decisions are more often driven by the available technological options in the hospital environment. Their proclivity to act as "moral agents" appears to have been minimized, because the ability to prolong life through the available technological interventions virtually demands that physicians exercise that ability. Given that new technologies expand the way human life can be medically altered, shortened, or extended, the obligation of hospitals and physicians to act as agent for the infirmed person takes on an "exquisite significance" when treatment decisions involve a moral question. That is, physicians more than ever can and often will attempt to "play God." If it may be in the best interest of the patient, for example, to allow him or her to die with dignity, the availability of the technological option of keeping the patient alive may be too "tempting" to physicians, and they may be more likely to exercise that option.

What do we mean by "moral agent"? Essentially the term is derived from the premise that a patient, as an autonomous individual, has the obligation to act morally but also in his or her own best interest in all decisions, and specifically within health care to take responsibility for his or her own actions that may jeopardize or improve their health. When ill, however, the patient's ability to act morally or even in his or her own best interest may be compromised. Then, another person or institution must act on behalf of that patient, making decisions about treatment on the basis of what he or she might have decided had they been able to express and justify the decision. Our focus here is not to suggest exactly what physicians and hospitals should decide in specific cases, but rather to suggest that advances in medical technology have placed these agents in the position of having to articulate their moral premises and then act on them (DeGeorge, 1982). Pellegrino (1979, p. 149) states "We can foresee a time, not too far distant, when hospitals will have to declare their positions on the major medico-moral questions for the patient's guidance." He cites the example of Catholic hospitals having customarily articulated their positions on certain specific procedures, such as abortion. As we shall see, today's hospital bioethics committees can also fulfill this need by deliberating over hospital guidelines in the most controversial ethical problems.

Interestingly, this idea is based on the notion that patients will ordinarily delegate the agency for their moral decision-making to physicians. There may be a trend, however, for patients to reserve the right not to delegate that agency, instead taking advantage of innovations such as Durable Power of Attorney for Health Care statutes to state from the outset that they do not want some technological interventions administered during a medical crisis. Administrator and physicians must remember that the patient's wishes about humane treatment demand full respect, and that moral agency is not automatically delegated to clinicians, but rather is essentially transferred only through the patient's autonomous choice.

Pellegrino's interesting article on this subject continues: "Most decisions in a hospital are decisions in which technological and value choices are intermingled. Our society has developed a deep concern, not without foundation, that in deferring to the expert in technical matters it has lost control of the values and purposes of that technology" (1979, p. 149). He cites an article by Kantrowitz (1975), calling for the separation of the technical and value components of the use of technology. It is becoming more crucial to assess the social and philosophical attributes of technology, certainly on an individual level in that each person should decide to what degree they might want to have life-sustaining treatment administered. On an aggregate level, hospitals and health systems will need to "distinguish between the professional medical advocacy for introduction and use of high technology and the social values of its employment" because "Institutions are not immune to irrationality, the abuse of power, or the usurpation of morals" (Pellegrino, 1979, p. 150), and medical technology provides fertile ground for either potential "irrationality" or moral usurpation, or both.

Therefore, as the members of our medical establishment go about their business in assessing medical technology for its marvelous capabilities, the point for administrators is that their assessment must also take into account the net effects of technology on personhood, autonomy, and values for patients (Hiller, 1984). Acting as moral agent for patients, and by extension, for the hospitals and health systems they oversee, administrators must ask whether their own administrative decisions enable an ethical context to be infused in particular treatment decisions (Oglesby, 1985). Pellegrino continues, "The main tasks of American medicine's third century are not managerial, fiscal, or technological, though such things pressure us daily. They are unequivocally moral and spiritual." Hospitals and health systems must pursue "a simple, sincere, voluntary and expeditious show of concern for moral issues untainted with self-interest" if they are to respond adequately to the moral challenges presented in this technological age (Pellegrino, 1979, p. 152).

VI. A WORD ABOUT TECHNOLOGY ASSESSMENT

The concept of evaluating the social and ethical features of a new technology along with its clinical or practical efficacy is important, but only in the context of recognizing the vital role of technology assessment itself. Many authors have addressed topics pertaining to technology assessment, including who or what profits from determining whether a technology is efficacious and safe (Banta and Behney, 1981; Banta et al., 1981; Greenberg and Derzon, 1981; Institute of Medicine, 1985; Jonsen, 1986; Office of Technology Assessment, 1978; Preston, 1985; Schwartz and Joskow, 1978). However, technology assessment should go beyond determinations of risks and benefits, perhaps to include a focus on the social and ethical features of introducing and implementing the new technology under scrutiny. Evans cites the example of an announcement by former Secretary of Health and Human Services Patricia Roberts Harris, who in 1980 declared that new health technologies must be evaluated not only on the basis of their medical efficacy but also on their "social consequences" before any consideration could be given to federal reimbursement for the new device or procedure (Knox, 1980, cited in Evans, 1983). The Secretary's edict at the time dictated that new medical technologies were to be evaluated on the basis of their cost-effectiveness and their cost-benefit ratios, and additionally on their ethical implications and their potential long-term effects on society.

Banta and Behney suggested that "Technology assessment is seen as a comprehensive form of policy research that examines short- and long-term social consequences (e.g., societal, economic, ethical, legal) of the application of technology. Technology assessment is an analysis of primarily social rather than technical issues, and it is especially concerned with unintended, indirect or delayed social impacts. . . . The goal of technology assessment, as of all policy research, is to provide decision makers with information on policy alternatives, such as allocation of research and development funds, formulation of regulations, or development of legislation" (Banta and Behney, 1981, p. 448). The "social impacts" to which they refer are probably related to the ethical issues concerning selection of recipients of the technology, the allocation of resources to health care programs, and individual patient rights to health care regardless of cost and availability.

VII. HEALTH ECONOMICS AND RESOURCE ALLOCATION

The moral effects of medical technology on health care delivery have been spawned by the exorbitant costs of lifesaving technology. It can be said in simple terms that if saving the lives of terminally ill patients were not so very expensive compared to other activities in health care, concern about resource allocation would not be so vivid (Menzel, 1983; McCullough, 1985).

Additionally, in the United States the economic and moral costs of high-technology medical care have approached a zenith only recently, because the development of such technology has been closely associated with the emerging role of the federal government as a leading payor for the regulator of health care expenditures. The expanding role of government in health care spending and the resulting reality that we all are paying the costs of high-technology medical care have reshaped the questions from purely medical or even ethical ones to social ones. Now, legislators and other policymakers are forced to deal with and perhaps provide partial answers to these social questions. However, these persons and the institutions they represent are probably more inclined simply to make fiscal or resource allocation decisions within their purview than to grapple with the net long-range ethical quandaries at hand.

Occasionally in the recent history of economic policy decision-making in health care, "half-baked" approaches to cost containment have placed the onus of responsibility for appropriate medical care and resource allocation squarely on the shoulders of health planners, hospital administrators, trustees, and clinicians. The best example is Medicare prospective payment, instituted in 1983. Of course, Medicare provides the most expensive, life-saving or life-prolonging care for probably the most severely ill patient population; this care generally requires the most advanced technologies. Casting aside for the moment all the arguments for and against prospective payment as a satisfactory tool for successful cost containment, it can be said that the individual hospital administrator, in conjunction with the hospital medical staff, has been forced to act as the chief agent for implementing prospective payment (Veatch, 1986). This example illustrates how health economics, and in particular the federal government's role in managing the affairs of health economics, can place the administrator more on the cutting edge of ethical decision-making than even legislators or regulators who actually formulate health policy.

Finally, administrators need to have a working knowledge of the recent infusion of "competition" into the modern health care vocabulary. More than anything before it, the privatization of medical care has prompted analysts to observe how and why the profit motive can be injurious to patient care, and to raise the screen of ethical analysis across the resource allocation decisions that are intimately related to a "bottom line." It is not safe to say that an administrator or planner operating under conditions presented by a corporation or for-profit entity will decide high-technology resource allocation questions differently than a counterpart in the not-for-profit sector. However, it is safe to say that they are looking at different pages of the same book of rules. For the administrator more often coaxed to watch a bottom line, making a decision about the cost of care either across the board or in an individual case is effectively also a decision about allocation of care. Therefore, the increasingly competitive nature of economic decisions by administrators also places them on another kind of ethical cutting edge (Veatch, 1983).

VIII. COSTS OF TECHNOLOGY, RESOURCE ALLOCATION, AND RATIONING DECISIONS

Roger Evans of the Battelle Human Affairs Research Centers in Seattle has provided the seminal article in recent years on the nexus of high-technology medical care and ethical decision-making or resource allocation. Doctor Evans bolstered his observations made earlier in this decade on the topic with the landmark research performed under his direction at Battelle, the federally financed National Heart Transplantation Study (Evans et al., 1984), in which issues of cost and ethically based resource allocation were discussed thoroughly for the benefit of federal policymakers.

Evans' premises (1983) include the prediction that all questions pertaining to constrained resources will inevitably yield questions on rationing medical care. He cites the increasingly important role of technology assessment through clinical trials as a strategy that can eventually streamline and improve the efficiency of the health care resource allocation. However, some observers point to extensive clinical trials as only a panacea for improving the cost/benefit equation in high-technology medical care. Regardless of which side of the debate an administrator takes, though, Evans implies that persons within the medical community must simply begin to devote more energy to improving their own individual and collective decision-making processes about rationing and resource allocation.

Naturally this new analysis on such a comparatively personal scale will not be easy nor even readily embraced by clinicians or administrators, but that like rationing, it will become necessary and inevitable. In an arena more traditionally reserved for biomedical ethicists, suddenly clinicians and planners find that their thinking about resource allocation may be more appropriately pursued at a higher or "macro" level, rather than continuing the grueling strategy of deciding about allocation essentially on a piecemeal basis: case-by-case, hospital-by-hospital, payor-by-payor. This dispassionate recommendation is presented by Evans in stark recognition of the fact that administrators and clinicians are increasingly making such decisions in a policy environment essentially devoid of adequate ethical thinking, and that if appropriate ethical decision-making is going to be done, it will most likely by done by persons in the field.

Biomedical research already has been detrimentally affected by reductions in the budget of the National Institutes of Health. Moreover, it appears that a kind of unanticipated "trickle-down" effect has occurred during the years of the Reagan presidency bringing decisions about medical technology out of the laboratory to rest squarely in the administrator's office (Iglehart, 1982). Essentially, over time the lack of funds for pursuing expensive clinical trials to demonstrate the efficacy of new procedures or products will yield less reliable analyses of the new technologies. Instead, decisions about the utility of new procedures will be within the purview of clinicians and planners, and, to an increasing degree, of patients asked to provide informed consent for the use of the new procedure or product within their own case. A new spectrum of risks and benefits is created. As an example, the informed consent forms presented to recipients of the Jarvik-7 artificial heart have drawn attention because of their detail and length and the fact that they vividly refer to the unprecedented degree of risk assumed by on the patient himself (Annas, 1983a; Rachels, 1983). For each patient or planner so affected, this new responsibility represents new ground to be broken, and given the choice, each would probably defer the enormous responsibility back to the purveyors of laboratory knowledge.

Unfortunately, few technology assessors exist who could take back that responsibility. In fact, beyond the political exigencies of budget cutting lies the fact that no satisfactory, relatively objective technology assessment institution has ever been established or allowed to flourish. The National Center for Health Care Technology was allowed to die a slow fiscal death in 1981, brought on by entreaties from the Health Industry Manufacturers Association and other groups that posited that only practitioners are best able to assess the clinical usefulness of medical innovations. Other federal entities, including the congressional Office of Technology Assessment and the Prospective Payment Assessment Commission have contributed to the body of knowledge about the costs and benefits of new technologies, but their efforts have also been underfunded, and their mandates are always broader than pursuing the nuts-and-bolts analysis of test data on new products.

Besides Evans, several other authors emphasize this important point. In the absence of mutually acceptable policies and methods by which the efficacy of medical technologies can be determined, Bunker (1982) and his colleagues suggest that a kind of half-baked technology assessment in the context of insurance reimbursement will be performed. A clinical vacuum exists that can only be filled by accurate, objective, long-term performance data, but no agency appears on the horizon capable of providing that kind of support to clinicians or planners, according to Frederickson (1981).

Furthermore, Callahan (1980) places these facts into the unsettling realm of ethical decision-making, suggesting that treatment decisions become intimately related to allocation decisions: in making a treatment decision, the physician must at least consider whether utilizing a questionable new procedure or device will be reimbursed by the patient's insurance carrier, which for better or worse constitutes an allocation decision. Stein (1978) suggests that none of these decisions should be within the immediate purview of practitioners, although he does not doubt their ability to handle them satisfactorily; rather, physicians' skills are simply more appropriately invested in patient care, not determining whether some new untested device or procedure would make a difference in more than his own patient's individual case. Again, Evans notes that clinicians increasingly "find themselves being forced to confront problems that traditionally have been reserved for biomedical ethicists" (1983, p. 2048).

Because clinicians are sometimes legally precluded from and morally reluctant to engage in allocation decisions, the responsibility befalls health planners, or worse, legislators. The track record of lawmakers does not favorably predispose the observer to presume that future allocation decisions will be viable or even remotely correct. The prime example is the unsettling performance of Congress in making the allocation decision to extend Medicare coverage to patients with end-stage renal disease (ESRD) in 1972. The legislative response to the problem of limited resources was to increase the available supply of resources, essentially by throwing money at the problem and allowing all ESRD patients to be fully covered (Moskop, 1987). This solution is unlikely to be engaged ever again, not because it did not save lives or enhance the quality of life for thousands of patients, but simply because the pool of available monetary resources is (finally) perceived to be quite limited; if there is a next time, Congress will have to expand its license to print money (Evans et al., 1981). Evans says this decision has only "staved off the inevitable–deciding which patients should be treated under public and private insurance programs" (1983, p. 2048).

IX. TECHNOLOGY AS THE PRECURSOR TO TODAY'S PREVALENT DISEASES

In keeping with Blum's quote that today's planning is a response to problems created yesterday, it is interesting to examine those disease conditions in which technology has played its largest role and around which the most vexing ethical problems have developed.

The positive forces of technology have certainly reduced the risks Westerners face from infectious diseases–smallpox, polio, and diphtheria to name only a few–as one "miracle cure" after another has helped to improve life expectancy throughout this century. The technology that led to treatment and virtual elimination of these diseases was yielded by a clearer understanding of the disease themselves.

Now, however, the chronic diseases have increased in incidence as an indirect result of people living longer. Diseases like cancer, stroke, chronic obstructive pulmonary disease, and other regressive conditions are much more complex and are often related to lifestyle, requiring treatment demanding even more technologically advanced procedures and therapies, yielding higher costs for care than ever before. In a sense, medical technology has rescued us from the death toll of certain diseases, but in so doing has begotten an epidemiological pattern of other diseases for which cures are either nonexistent or extremely complex (and expensive) to achieve.

Given the vast expense to treat and potentially cure the chronic diseases, medical technology would not have such economic importance without this present epidemiology of chronic disease. A relatively conservative estimate indicates that 80 percent of the health resources expended in this country are committed to the treatment of or research about chronic diseases (Cluff, 1981). But the chronic diseases are essentially incurable, and learning more about a disease will not necessarily lead to its elimination. A leading cancer combatant and observer of medical sociology, Lewis Thomas, notes that treating the infectious diseases was comparatively easy in contrast to today's fight, because curing them "comes from a genuine understanding of disease mechanisms" (1977, p. 1367), preceding some new immunization or nutritional augmentation, in his words, to "cheat or defeat" the disease.

But for all its advanced character, today's technology cannot perform the same marvelous feats. Thomas calls today's therapies "halfway technologies," enabling a patient to enjoy some functionality or favorable quality of life but not appreciably minimizing the role of the disease in the rest of his or her life.

Crane (1975) suggests that, in this epidemiological and economic new day, the nature of the diseases we are vigorously combatting has also raised the ethical stakes. Physicians "suddenly" have much greater prescience about and control over the moment of the patient's journey into death. Influence over the dying process may now be seen even in patients who are not elderly or seemingly decrepit: technology has also allowed clinicians the chance to enable persons with genetic disorders such as Down's syndrome or even juvenile diabetes to live at least peaceful lives whereas once they surely would have died.

Therefore physicians and, in turn, administrators, now face a variety of ethical situations that would not have been presented in the absence of proliferating medical technology. One of the series of consequences that must be addressed in any technology assessment effort are the ethical consequences, including the selection of recipients of any new technology, allocation of new resources according to fiscal constraints, and the rights of all patients to refuse technological interventions of any kind. Failing to give more than just a sidelong glance at these consequences makes it fruitless to evaluate the long-term capacity of any new technology as a tool to reduce health care costs or to improve upon the "new" epidemiological patterns (National Academy of Sciences, 1979).

X. TECHNOLOGY AND HEALTH CARE COSTS

Health care spending in the United States reached $425 billion in 1985, an increase of 8.9 percent over spending in 1984, representing 10.7 percent of the nation's Gross National

Product. Nationally, 59 percent of the funding for health care resources in 1985 came directly from the private sector, mostly through private health insurance (34 percent) and the cost sharing through direct payments among consumers and their families (25 percent). The remaining 41 percent was funded through government health programs, especially Medicare and Medicaid (Waldo et al., 1986).

Not surprisingly given these figures, the rapid rise in the cost of health care over the last two decades and the associated role of medical technology have combined to make technology itself the perceived "culprit" in the health cost spiral (Altman and Blendon, 1979). Yet how much does technological advancement contribute to the actual cost of hospital care today? There are a variety of answers focusing on the effect of technology on the per diem costs of hospitalization, but the range generally yields about fifty percent as the average cost cited (Waldman, 1972).

While it may seem straightforward that medical technology now requires the devotion of half a hospital's per patient resources during an episode of illness, this fact may be misleading. Several authors (Fineberg and Hiatt, 1979; Moloney and Rogers, 1979; Scitovsky and McCall, 1976) have cited a notable increase in the use of diagnostic tests and therapeutic procedures for each diagnosis. These are not the futuristic devices or machines that are commonly perceived to manifest medical technology. Rather, they are the more mundane laboratory and "nuts-and-bolts" devices and procedures that support the influence of big-ticket technology. Especially since the advent of Medicare prospective pricing, hospital stays have grown progressively shorter, but the cost of ancillary services has increased rapidly in conjunction with two factors: the increased consumption of resources during the shorter inpatient stay, and also the concomitant increase in nursing home or skilled nursing facility utilization that is an expected product of prospective payment. Total ancillary costs per case increased 17.5 percent between 1981 and the first full year of prospective payment among Medicare hospitals, compared with only an increase of 4.5 percent for "routine care" associated with daily nursing care, which would be expected to increase at a slower rate due to the effect of shorter inpatient stays (Prospective Payment Assessment Commission, 1987). Together these facts suggest that while more advanced equipment may improve efficiency and conceptually can save or prolong lives, from a cost viewpoint their increased use may yield more "induced costs," deferring any potential savings that might have been anticipated from the more efficient technology.

Furthermore, new technologies do not necessarily perform old services more efficiently, but instead provide new and ever-more expensive services. A prime example is described in impressive detail by Knaus and Thibault in their account of the utility of the intensive care unit, in which not only critical activities are performed more efficiently but also newer, much more expensive activities are performed (Knaus and Thibault, 1982).

In essence, brand new "showcase" technological procedures like computerized tomographic scanning "actually account for far less of the annual growth in medical expenditures than do the collective expense of thousands of small tests and procedures . . . that individually cost little" (Moloney and Rogers, 1979, p. 1417). Indeed, Stoughton flatly says that "control over large technology distribution, whether clinical or diagnostic, is only part of the answer to the issue of health care costs. Another part of the equation is control over small technology utilization" (1982, p. 47).

XI. DISTINGUISHING BETWEEN "EXPERIMENTAL" AND "THERAPEUTIC" TECHNOLOGIES

What kind of clutch, then, could ever be placed on the gears of spending for either high or low technologies? The clutch relates to the strategies of reimbursement common in the United States today, but it is a crude one that often skips gears. Returning to technology assessment for a moment, the point should be made that these expenditures on technological devices or procedures would be less likely if the direct relationship between costs and third-party reimbursement were not such a motivator. Hospitals and physicians are inclined to prescribe interventions or perform procedures if it is demonstrated to them that nearly total reimbursement is likely to follow.

Commercial health insurers or service plans are sometimes beholden to the edict or example of the federal government, because as the payor for Medicare, the government often decides whether a new device or therapy is worthy of coverage. Many other payors follow suit. But the federal government is hardly the purveyor of "straight information" the private payors may expect. In fact, frequently Medicare relies on the coverage decisions manifested by the fiscal intermediaries with which it has contracted to process claims to determine whether Medicare coverage for a relatively untested device or therapy will be justified. But these fiscal intermediaries can rarely pronounce the new intervention anything but "experimental" or "therapeutic." These intermediaries fulfill a vital role, but it can be argued that their influence may be disproportionate to even their own ability to determine which technologies are effective enough to warrant reimbursement.

A kind of policy vacuum exists for determining whether a new device or therapy should be reimbursable. Some intermediaries, notably Blue Shield of California, have instituted their own medical policy committees for assessing new therapies and making coverage decisions solely for their own insureds; Medicare is welcome to accept the "advice" of Blue Shield on whether a particular therapy should be covered under Medicare, but essentially the activities of the carrier's technology assessment committees apply only to the expenses of their own policyholders and not specifically to the carrier's role as a Medicare fiscal intermediary. In sum, there is really no satisfactory uniformly applied method of limiting the proliferation of medical technology through alternative reimbursement policies (Greenberg and Derzon, 1981; Schaeffer, 1982).

Distinguishing between an experimental and a standard treatment—and who decides such—also raises ethical questions. With a novel or untested procedure, the reimbursement incentive for physicians and manufacturers is to prompt its widespread acceptance. An obvious example would be the economic incentives behind the development of the totally implantable artificial heart. A second ethical issue in the current system of reimbursement for innovations involves distributive justice: the just distribution of benefits *and* risks among all patients. Whether insurance coverage is available to a patient for a medical innovation often depends on what policy he or she has purchased, because in the absence of an independent medical technology center providing reliable recommendations, there is wide variability among carriers about which innovations are experimental and which have been standardized. Paying patients can be said to have been thrown into yet another "lottery": not the natural lottery, but an insurance policy lottery (Hough, 1986). For them, the question must be "Can I take advantage of this technology given the constraints of my particular health insurance policy?"

XII. ETHICS AND ECONOMICS DURING THE LAST YEAR OF LIFE

There is no doubt that the cost of treating the terminally ill is very high. However, Bayer and his colleagues have presented an analysis suggesting that it is not prudent to label that high cost as disproportionate, saying "it is not appropriate to conclude that such expenditures represent a morally troubling misallocation of resources" (Bayer et al., 1983, p. 1490). Insofar as the cost of treating terminally ill patients involves the utilization of innovative technological devices or therapies, their moral analysis on this point is worth reviewing in some depth.

Morally speaking, medical care for the terminally ill cannot be denied on the grounds that it would not offer sufficient return on the very sizable investment required; dying persons are not "second-class" persons. But it is just as improper to presume that the terminally ill "deserve" a greater proportion of resources than other patients; resources are not infinitely available, and some allocation might always be necessary or likely. "The real problem is to determine when and in what way a consideration of costs is reasonable either in clinical or administrative decision-making, and then to devise acceptable criteria for making cost-conscious decisions," according to Bayer (1983, p. 1492).

Devising such criteria leads first to a focus on those treatments that are labelled "marginally useful." It is easier to verbalize this term than to apply it in decision-making, for there is a range of interpretations as to which features of a treatment—and which treatments—provide only marginal benefits. Some therapies for terminally ill patients are only beneficial for a few patients, and often there is no satisfactory means to predict which patients will experience the benefit or at what stage of their illness it might occur. Other therapies portend only psychological benefits; their cost must be vigorously justified, especially when their expenditure might jeopardize the physical benefits some other therapy would bring to another patient or group of patients. Responding to this dilemma can bring administrators and physicians to loggerheads, at least in principle if not in practice: "What the administrator may view as a pattern of unjust or wasteful expenses for statistically miniscule benefits the clinician . . . may consider a pattern of justified expenses for a series of individual treatments, each undertaken in the best interests of the particular patient" (Bayer et al., 1983, p. 1492).

Bayer and his colleagues conclude that efforts at controlling costs must have an ethical bias: more vigorous promotion of patient and family autonomy in decision-making (now bolstered more by the spreading acceptance of the Durable Power of Attorney for Health Care); broader governmental and insurance support for alternative forms of institutional care, such as hospices; and an assessment of which diagnostic therapies will actually provide the clinician with more information about the terminally ill patient. This last strategy will help to mitigate the cost and questionable benefits derived from those "marginally useful" therapies, which of course need to undergo a more effective definitional scrutiny. The reader is referred to Bayer's article for a concise discussion of issues of morality in allocating resources to the least well-off patients, and of the tools necessary for beneficent decision-making in their very expensive care.

XIII. ORGAN TRANSPLANTATION: EQUITY AND POLICY

Certainly, it is within the area of organ transplantation that health administrators face their most vexing and highly publicized quandaries in the ethical maelstrom surrounding medical technology. Fortunately, there is a large body of literature on the topic of equitable distribution of organs for transplantation. Additionally, no administrator or clinician enters this arena without some precedent, for even though medical advances occur seemingly weekly in transplanting organs or in improving the survivability after surgery, many of the pertinent ethical questions in the topic have already received at least some scrutiny by professionals.

Kutner (1987) provides the administrator with a brief but thorough review of the recent course of solid organ transplantation in the United States since the first kidney transplant performed in 1954, with special attention given to the political and legislative influence in the proliferation of transplant surgeries. She refers to the so-called "modern era" of organ transplantation beginning with the introduction of powerful drugs administered to transplant patients to diminish the degree of rejection of transplanted organs, including azathioprine and cyclosporine. With cyclosporine, cardiac transplant patients' two-year survival rates improved from less than half to more than 75 percent of patients (Austen and Cosimi, 1984). Casscells (1986) reported that five-year heart transplant survival rates have climbed to between 50 and 60 percent in recent years. Similar improvements were gained in liver transplantation through the widespread use of cyclosporine. In 1987 the first "piggyback" transplantation occurred, in which a cardiac patient received a heart from a living donor, who himself immediately received transplanted cadaver lungs and heart, signalling a new period in which formerly "exotic" therapies would suddenly become commonplace.

Kutner also provides the administrator with an overview of the legislative support for organ transplantation in the United States, a chapter in the story with defined peaks and valleys. Like other authors, she points to the passage of P.L. 92-603, an amendment to the Social Security Act that established the ESRD program providing Medicare funding for dialysis and transplant technologies and therapies for kidney disease patients, as the watershed event. Not surprisingly, as dialysis treatment facilities began to increase, the number of transplant candidates maintained by dialysis therapy also increased at a rather dramatic pace, placing an ever-greater demand on the number of cadaver kidneys required. This trend indicates again that while the Medicare ESRD benefit has maintained a reasonable quality of life for many persons, more funding for expensive, life-saving therapies is not necessarily the solution to the problem of an insufficient supply of donor organs (Kutner, 1987, pp. 25-26).

Combined with the introduction of the immunosuppressant drugs in the 1970s and 1980s, the equitable distribution of scarce organs became increasingly problematic. Congress, having learned from the rapidly escalating cost overruns unanticipated when the ESRD program was established in 1972, seemed at first unwilling to tackle the growing problems of improving the supply of solid organs for transplantation. Cited in another section of this chapter is the perception that Congress and the Health Care Financing Administration (HCFA) were virtually content to allow policies on the financing for these and other expensive therapies—and thereby the diffusion of these therapies to sick patients—to be decided by states or even by health insurers acting as Medicare fiscal intermediaries.

This "laissez-faire" approach to organ transplantation led to the pragmatic but nevertheless unsettling trend in the early 1980s for "media campaigning" for transplantable organs, most prominently by the parents of young Jamie Fiske who tearfully (and, eventually, successfully) pleaded before a group of pediatricians and television cameras for a liver for their daughter. Even the President became involved in the effect to procure a donated liver for this little girl, a fact that underscored in bittersweet terms the policy vacuum in which life and death questions were being answered. Throughout this decade, only a loose network of organ procurement and matching agencies, often supported only by the medical centers at which the surgeries will be performed, have provided patients on organ transplant waiting lists with the tantalizingly slim hope of receiving cadaver organs before their terminal diseases take their final toll.

With the signing into law of the Organ Procurement and Transplantation Act (P.L. 98-507) in October 1984, a new era of proactive federal involvement in the transplantation effort began. The net effect of the Act's passage is not yet clearly perceived, but it marks at least an initial step to meet more adequately the needs of persons on organ donation waiting lists. The Act established the National Organ Transplantation Task Force to examine the medical, legal, ethical, economic, and social issues presented by human organ procurement and transplantation, provided grants to organ procurement agencies, mandated establishment of an organ procurement and transplantation network and a scientific registry of persons awaiting transplants and the clinical success of transplant patients, and strengthened federal statutes prohibiting the sale or purchase of organs (Kutner, 1987). The Act provided $31 million in funding for these important activities, although political machinations and the lukewarm reception for the Act by the Reagan Administration have served to diminish the available funding at least during the initial fiscal years of implementing the Act (Casscells, 1986). Continually, the result seems to have been that the distribution of organs is still influenced by highly publicized individual cases, in which the news media fan the hot flames of questions about which patients will receive desperately needed organs in time (Annas, 1985a; Reiner et al., 1986).

In sum, Kutner decries the Organ Procurement and Transplantation Act as only a partially successful first step. Administrators need to recognize the lessons learned from its passage and that of the ESRD Program: federal responses in this arena represent only compromises, usually political compromises, not real solutions. She notes that while the Act suggests a federal endorsement of organ transplantation as a commonplace "fact of life" in the American health care system, it did not go far enough to present transplantation as something ordinary or necessary enough to continue appropriate planning for future needs. For example, despite all its other benefits, the Act did not include strategies such as establishing an optimal number and regional distribution of medical centers performing transplants, or address the very serious economic problems associated with affordable immunosuppressant medications for transplant patients (Kutner, 1987).

Furthermore, the federal response to Medicare coverage for heart transplants indicates that it would be unwise to presume adequate solutions will be forthcoming from Washington. After release of the National Heart Transplantation Study, led by Doctor Evans and his colleagues, in 1986 the Health Care Financing Administration elected to extend coverage for heart transplants to beneficiaries meeting selection criteria that essentially nominated only the "healthiest ill" persons for the new benefit. Generally, only those Medicare beneficiaries under 55 years of age would enjoy coverage and only at specified medical "centers of excellence." Naturally the pool of patients is substantially diminished just by this age restriction, given that most beneficiaries are elderly. And at least initially HCFA was unwilling to address the difficulties of paying for immunosuppressant drug therapies for Medicare transplant patients. In sum, federal solutions are only compromise solutions, and administrators still must often roll up their sleeves to handle these problems on their own.

XIV. HEALTH CARE COSTS AND ORGAN TRANSPLANTATION: ISSUES FOR ADMINISTRATORS

It is no surprise that advances in medical technology contribute a large part of the overall increase in the nation's share of the Gross National Product devoted to health care, now over eleven percent of the GNP. The cost effectiveness of a new technology can be compromised when clinicians and administrators expand the application of the technology beyond a "prudent" degree. The context in which "prudence" is exercised, however, is influenced by politics and economics, and administrators and planners must wade through a forest of interpretations of data sets that may yield entirely different conclusions about the cost effectiveness of the same new technology. An excellent give-and-take "dialogue" exists on this aspect of the problem in the medical ethical literature between ethicist George Annas and two of the foremost analysts of costs of organ transplantation, Thomas Overcast and Doctor Evans, in which they wrangle over interpreting and implementing the conclusions of the Massachusetts Task Force on Organ Transplantation (Annas, 1985b, 1985c; Overcast and Evans, 1985).

In this interchange, even comparing the costs of transplantation recovery, prevention of organ rejection, and the possibility of subsequent diseases, versus more conventional drug therapies as the treatment of choice for persons with pertinent terminal diseases represents an "apples versus oranges" comparison that spawns vitriolic disagreement among these health policy analysts. Overcast and Evans suggest that it is unreasonable to assess the net "opportunity cost" of transplanting an organ without also assessing the "cost of dying," or in other words, while transplant patients can incur heavy cost burdens beyond the actual surgical costs, the same can be said for treatment of end-stage diseases in which transplant surgery is not involved.

Kutner raises an interesting point that is valuable for administrators and planners to note. She states that, according to insurance company surveys, there is strong public support for transplantation regardless of its cost, and that it represents a medical technology that many persons deem justifiable and no longer particularly exotic. Additionally, while there is some public awareness of the potential for bankrupting the Medicare trust funds, publicly funded coverage for transplant coverage is not viewed as a "major culprit" creating the strain on economic resources (Kutner, 1987).

XV. THE SUPPLY OF ORGANS: ETHICAL AND LEGAL CONSIDERATIONS

Beyond economics, distributing the scarce resource of donor organs represents the crux of the transplantation problem for administrators and planners. Merrikin and Overcast (1985) noted that as many as 75,000 Americans (not to mention foreign nationals also on American waiting lists) may require transplanted hearts, but probably no more than 2,000 donor hearts are made available each year for them in this country. And even though there is broad public support for expanding transplantation efforts and for organ donation efforts, perhaps fewer than one in two supporters indicate a willingness to donate their own organs; even fewer comply with the solicitation for organ donations through Uniform Anatomical Gift Act (UAGA) mechanisms such as drivers' license affidavits (Blendon and Altman, 1984).

The pervasive influence of clinicians is present here too, with many physicians or hospital staff members remaining unwilling to harvest organs of persons who had executed a UAGA declaration before their deaths without first obtaining approval from the next of kin. Usually notions of liability exposure affect such decisions by physicians, although this fact defeats a central purpose of establishing the UAGA in 1968: to expedite the removal of organs from willing donors unable to declare their wishes, while offering a measure of liability protection for clinicians with the ultimate goal of enabling another life to be saved. Some states such as California are implementing legislation to bolster the net effect of the UAGA, such as requiring hospital staffs to establish and follow protocols for "required requests" of kin promptly to approve the harvesting of organs from their deceased or brain-dead relatives regardless of the decedent's status under the UAGA; generally such protocols are mandated as part of a hospital's licensure or accreditation criteria. Nevertheless, after nearly twenty years of utilization it appears that donor cards under the UAGA are more useful as a tool for educating about the need for transplantable organs, rather than an effective means of augmenting the supply of available organs.

Caplan (1983) provides an excellent summary of the status in this decade of "presumed consent" efforts. Beyond the more conventional "encouraged voluntarism" now in effect that, through public education, prompts persons to become organ donors through provisions such as the UAGA, advocates of presumed consent suggest that the only viable method of substantially increasing the supply of donor organs is to presume that all persons would donate, and that only those who have demonstrated their desire to refrain from donation should not have their organs harvested upon death. Physicians would simply extract needed organs and tissues from cadavers unless the individual carried a card prohibiting such removal or unless the next of kin objected. This system has had its share of both critics and supporters, but its legal justification is based on the treatment of bodily organs as property and on the constitutional authority of the state to dictate the manners in which bodies must be treated upon death.

When the debate over presumed consent flared up for the first time in the 1960s, another political compromise prevailed in that round, with the public policy see-saw tipping toward encouraged voluntarism and the establishment of the UAGA. Stating that encouraged voluntarism has failed to close the gap between supply and demand of donor organs, however, Caplan presents a variety of convincing ethical arguments in support of presumed consent and its less impactful cousin in this policy arena, "required request" or "routine inquiry." He states that "A centralized system for the mandatory salvaging of organs, with protections for those who wish to dissent, could help to increase the supply, reduce the cost, and alleviate the emotional problems that encouraged voluntarism has produced" (Caplan, 1984, p. 25).

Kutner (1987, p. 27) reports that the United States lags behind other western nations, thirteen of which have presumed consent laws without nearly the demand for cadaver organs experienced in the United States. And while there may be ethical justification for presumed consent reported by Caplan and others, and with more than fifty percent of Americans polled supporting "required request" policies (Caplan, 1984), Manninen and Evans (1985) report that fewer than ten percent of Americans polled support the concept of presumed consent even while supporting expansion of transplantation services in the main. Even in the best circumstances or in an ethically justifiable "required request" hospital environment, physicians and hospital staffs are still remarkably unwilling to approach grieving kin, despite the observations of social scientists that surviving family members derive substantial psychological benefits from participating willingly in the organ donation process upon request (Corlett, 1985; Batten and Prottas, 1987). Yet again, for administrators and planners, this debate should indicate that legislative remedies to ethical dilemmas in modern medical technology are only half-baked solutions; without a well-developed system of institutional supports, efforts to expand the organ donation pool even bolstered by the best *pro bono* legislation can be avoided by key personnel and therefore can fail.

XVI. ISSUES OF SOCIAL EQUITY IN TRANSPLANTATION: WHO SHALL LIVE?

An area that will only expand in legal importance in the next decade is that of selection criteria for transplant candidates that are not directly related to a person's specific medical condition warranting the transplant. To this point in the history of transplantation, purely medical considerations have been utilized to determine which persons "deserve" one of the organs from the limited supply available. Generally only those patients for whom transplants represent the best chance for survival and with reasonable expectations to survive the procedure and subsequent therapies for "enough" years to justify the expense have been the best candidates for transplants.

However, predicting which patients will "do best" with their new organ remains a tough nut to crack. Discounting the prominent problems of affordability of these transplants and equitable insurance coverage, it may be fair to say that patients having a history of prior emotional or family problems might be less likely to be selected to receive a scarce organ than, say, a person within a higher socioeconomic class with strong family support whose only discernible defect would be the clinical condition warranting the extraordinary surgery. Merrikin and Overcast have written that "As the cost and complexity of medical care advance, both physicians and society will increasingly be faced with the necessity of allocating scarce medical resources. Whether through assessment of treatment suitability, by lottery, or by chance, these allocations must stay within the confines of the applicable antidiscrimination laws" (Merriken and Overcast, 1985, p. 26). It seems fair to say that in the near future legal challenges to the authority of persons or institutions deciding on the allocation of organ resources may become more commonplace, providing administrators and planners with some of their most vexing dilemmas.

Regarding the problem of transplant queues for foreign nationals, the debate continues without much abatement. Many argue that scarce organs should be reserved for U.S. citizens because more often than not the donors are American and because American tax dollars may be invested in organ procurement efforts or even the surgeries themselves. On the other hand, some argue that relatively wealthy foreign nationals willing to spend large sums on such procedures might benefit the U.S. economy, or at least that providing a specialized medical service to persons able to pay can be seen as a humanitarian effort on the part of Americans. (This may be a somewhat specious argument given the fact that just as many foreign nationals spend all their resources just getting to the United States and surviving without employment due to their serious medical condition, frequently without the means to pay for their postsurgical medical care.) The National Task Force on Organ Transplantation finally concluded that ten percent of the kidneys harvested in the United States could be reserved for nonresident immigrant recipients, but that hearts and livers should be provided for foreigners only as a last resort. The Task Force employed the rationale that Americans denied access to hearts or livers probably would die in the queue and that complete follow-up care would need to be anticipated if maximum chances for long-term survival could be attained (Kutner, 1987, p. 30).

Finally in this topic of organ transplantation, it should be clear to administrators and planners that the volume of transplantation will only expand, not contract. The vagaries of implementing this new technology on such a much larger, unprecedented scale, however, may prompt some health administrators almost to wish the technology were not so pervasive. Indeed, today's quandaries reviewed in this section will become somewhat moot if the pool of available organs expands. That would present yet another set of problems, however. For example, in a study reported by Doctor Evans and colleagues, a quality of life outcome assessment was performed on kidney dialysis patients. Dialysis patients in the post-Medicare funding era seemed to have received much less agressive encouragement to achieve maximum rehabilitation when compared to their counterparts undergoing dialysis before the Medicare funding option was available; the former population seems to demonstrate a significantly different diminished capacity to return to productive, gainful activity than the latter group (Evans et al., 1981). Their conclusions underscore the notion that implementing a new technology (whether nonsurgical like dialysis or surgical like a kidney transplant) without full regard to the entire range of quality of life issues involved beyond "simple" survival and nonrejection of the organs essentially limits the true value of the new technology, or ignores the fact that the new technology brings with it new challenges practically unrelated to the surgery or new device.

Kutner comments that "When a technology becomes so available that it is no longer necessary to offer it only to those patients most likely to return to active lives (the 'best-risk' patients), the patient population becomes a more challenging one to treat and rehabilitate, and the system must include more patient service and dedicated medical personnel in order to further patients' total rehabilitation" (Kutner, 1987, p. 33). This is important for administrators struggling with methods for ethically determining the future course of transplantation or any technology in their health systems. The question becomes "to use or not to use?" given that the utilization of the new technology yields unanticipated ethical and legal questions when evaluating and implementing a new technology that holds promise. Plough answers the question by stating that "The ability of a treatment to significantly extend a patient's life where no treatment would surely result in immediate death is almost in itself an operational standard for clinical effectiveness. . . . If a technology extends life, use it!" (Plough, 1986, p. 39). The conclusion to be drawn is that organ transplantation presents our health care system with the bellwether questions for ethically determining "who shall live," and while proceeding apace with implementing transplantation on a large scale might seem to be the best answer for administrators and planners faced with these questions, it is only fair to assume that another unfair share of very difficult questions will await them once such a policy is in full operation.

XVII. DEATH AND DYING: PARAMOUNT DILEMMAS FOR ADMINISTRATORS

In no other context than the new issues surrounding death and dying are the legal and ethical problems in medical technology more profound for administrators and planners.

The progress made during the last two decades in the effort to define death satisfactorily actually represents a monumental triumph in the cooperation between clinicians and health care policymakers, and gives context to the bulk of issues in death and dying today. It may be difficult to remember a time not very long ago when cessation of breathing and cardiac function were the best indicators of death. However, the ability to resuscitate patients through technological means who might otherwise have died has changed all that (Ramsey, 1978). In the enabling legislation that established the functions of the President's Commission for the Study of Ethical Problems in Medicine and Biomedical and Behavioral Research, that group was directed to study "the ethical and legal implications of the matter of defining death, including the advisability of developing a uniform definition of death" (P.L. 95-622, 1978).

Responding to that mandate, the President's Commission did conclude that a restatement of the standards traditionally recognized for determining death was necessary, and to that end developed a model statutory definition of death that seems workable and has been adopted by several states. In conjunction with health care provider groups and the National Conference of Commissioners on Uniform State Laws, the Commission recommended adoption of a "Uniform Determination of Death Act." It read, in part: "An individual who has sustained either (1) irreversible cessation of circulatory and respiratory functions, or (2) irreversible cessation of all functions of the entire brain stem, is dead. A determination of death must be made in accordance with accepted medical standards" (President's Commission, 1981, p. 2). Presciently, the Commission recommended that this or any other model uniform determination of death act should address general physiological standards rather than medical criteria and tests, which are more likely to undergo change as medical science advances and the influence of technology increases. The reader is commended to this volume from the President's Commission for a broad overview of the very important legal and ethical status of the pronouncement of death.

XVIII. DECIDING TO FOREGO LIFE-SUSTAINING TREATMENT

While hers was not the first case in which decisions about the eventual course of life-sustaining treatment were made in a very tentative fashion, most observers point to the case of Karen Ann Quinlan as the milestone in prompting broad public awareness of the problems now upon our health care system as products of technological intervention. Many readers will be familiar with the Quinlan case decided in New Jersey, and the details of it are richly accounted in a number of seminal articles and short books (Annas, 1976, 1979; Beresford, 1977; Doudera and Peters, 1982; Wong and Swazey, 1981). The reader who is interested in the role of bioethics committees, described in more detail below, is well advised to invest time in scanning these articles, because the genesis of today's bioethics committees can be justifiably attributed to the furor surrounding the Quinlan case and other similar cases.

The media attention deservedly given to the Quinlan case certainly prompted many legislators and health administrators to ask "What if that happened in my state or my hospital?" The ethical questions were as clear as the anguished look on the faces of Karen's parents as they were shown appealing before the New Jersey Supreme Court for the fully protected right to decide the course of their daughter's treatment, which was one of minimal intervention during the last years of her life. Additionally, the legal questions were becoming clearer, and certainly appeared even more challenging.

A more recent case also deserves the attention of interested administrators or students of health administration, particularly in the legal context so omnipresent in these situations. The case of Clarence Herbert, a security guard at a Southern California race track, is more interesting for its precedent-setting effect on the activities of physicians and hospitals than necessarily for the clinical features of decisions about brain-dead patients. Recovering from routine surgery, Mr. Herbert's pulse and respiration stopped and he was put on life-support treatment, including a respirator. During the lapse before the respirator could be put in place, Mr. Herbert suffered brain damage and remained in a vegetative state which was likely to be permanent.

His surgeon, Doctor Robert Nejdl and the attending internist, Doctor Neil Barber, communicated to his family that the chance of his recovery was extremely poor (although in later court proceedings the actual language employed by Doctors Nejdl and Barber underwent contentious scrutiny and criticism). The family members wrote a statement to the effect that they wanted all machines employed to sustain his life removed. Much like Karen Ann Quinlan, to the surprise of the physicians and the family, Mr. Herbert continued to breathe on his own even after the respirator was detached upon the orders of the physicians. After two more days, the doctors, having consulted with the family, then ordered the removal of the intravenous tubes that provided hydration and nourishment. Six days later Mr. Herbert died.

This case is set apart from others like it in that Doctors Nejdl and Barber were then charged with murder and conspiracy to commit murder. A protracted legal battle ensued, with a magistrate ordering the charges dismissed only to have a superior court judge order the reinstatement of the charges. Without a full trial, however, an appeals court dismissed the charges for the final time.

The attention of the courts was focused not so much on the quality of care provided to Mr. Herbert or on the removal of the respirator, but rather on the particular features of withdrawing food and water. Judges on the appeals court decided that withdrawing food and water was no different from withdrawing any other medical treatment, such as the respirator in this and the Quinlan cases. That court distinguished between a person's normal eating and drinking and the administration of nutrition and hydration through medical means. The appeals court judge's opinion stated that "the use of an intravenous administration of nourishment and fluid, under the circumstances [is] the same as the use of the respirator or other form of life support equipment" (*Barber v. Superior Court*, 1983, p. 490). Perhaps more importantly for physicians and hospital administrators, the judge also wrote that "Although there may be a duty to provide life-sustaining machinery in the *immediate* aftermath of a cardio-respiratory arrest, there is no duty to continue its use once it has become futile in the opinion of qualified medical personnel" (*Barber v. Superior Court*, 1983, p. 491, emphasis in original). Thus, in a precedent at least for California physicians and hospitals, the prevailing notion is that there is no duty to continue useless treatment, and that that "brand" of treatment can be foregone at nearly the same time that what might be considered as "still useful" treatment such as a respirator can be discontinued. Other accounts of the Herbert case can provide a thorough overview of the serious issues involved for physicians and hospital administrators (Breo et al., 1983; Kirsch, 1982; Paris, 1985; Steinbock, 1983).

In a series of 24 recommendations, the President's Commission entered the fray with a broad interpretation of "life-sustaining treatment" that encompassed "all health care interventions that have the effect of increasing the life span of the patient," including of course respirators and kidney machines but also the "paraphernalia of modern medicine" such as home physical therapy, special feeding procedures, and nursing support, "provided that one of the effects of the treatment is to prolong a patient's life" (President's Commission, 1983, p. 3). The Commission essentially encouraged respect for the wishes of competent patients in the extent to which extraordinary treatments should be administered during the final days or weeks of life, and for persons unable to express their wishes, the Commission heartily encouraged the development of legally viable instruments with which designated proxies could make health care decisions for those persons, such as Durable Powers of Attorney for Health Care.

On the other hand, the Commission also emphasized that many constraints on patients' decisions exist and some are justified in almost all circumstances, including the premise that "Health care institutions may justifiably restrict the availability of certain options in order to use limited resources more effectively or to enhance equity in allocating them" (1983, p. 3). Members of the Commission were astute in separating the particular areas of concern by classes of patients, from incompetent patients in general, to patients with permanent losses of consciousness, seriously ill newborns, and patients for whom cardiopulmonary resuscitation constituted an "extraordinary" treatment at the end of life. Perhaps the main advantage of these recommendations in the ongoing dialogue was their emphasis on clarity and explicitness within each institution, uniformity in state laws, and a delicate balancing of actions in the best interests of each patient with the constraints of equitable allocation and availability of resources for treatment. These were expressed in conjunction with descriptions of "shared decision-making," adequate informed consent with full disclosure of treatment options and presumed consequences, and the influence of civil and criminal laws on decision-making.

Once again the reader is encouraged to invest the time in scanning the Commission's report on the topic as an entree into the legal precedents and summaries of the crucial questions at hand. The Commission's report has not been received without controversy (see, for example, Capron, 1983), but it remains a seminal document and a good starting point for further investigations on the role of administrators and planners in decisions about the extent of treatment at the end of life.

XIX. ARTIFICIAL FEEDING: A SPECIAL CASE OF "LIFE-SUSTAINING TREATMENT"

The brief account of the Clarence Herbert case given above was provided in the context of decisions concerning the removal of life-sustaining therapies. It actually constitutes a special case in foregoing these treatments, however, in that it manifests a much broader definition of "life-sustaining treatment." Given the President's Commission's far-reaching definition of such treatment, it seems that any attempt to narrow that definition might be counterproductive to a "death with dignity" movement, which administrators and planners will need to acknowledge or even contend with. Physicians have already been confronted with the feeding and hydrating issue, with a group of physicians counseling that the issue can be decided on the basis of perceiving the (albeit unconscious) patient's sense of comfort or relief: "Naturally or artificially administered hydration and nutrition may be given or withheld, depending on the patient's comfort" (Wanzer et al., 1984, p. 958).

Arguing essentially that the rough equation between a respirator and a feeding tube is inappropriate, however, Meilaender writes that "For the permanently unconscious person feeding is neither useless nor excessively burdensome. It is ordinary human care and is not given as treatment for any life-threatening disease" (Meilaender, 1984, p. 13).

In a very brief but moving piece on the subject of the cultural disinterest in truly implementing a policy of removing feeding tubes, Callahan writes "Feeling and sentiment are rarely absent from a well-ordered moral life" (Callahan, 1983, p. 22). Even though detaching intravenous feeding and hydrating tubes is not really a new subject, through cases like Herbert's and a similar one, that of Claire Conroy in New Jersey, a variety of commentators have heralded it as something akin to the "last frontier" in foregoing life-sustaining treatment (see, for example, Annas, 1983b, and Lynn, 1986). In fact, Callahan suggests that "a denial of nutrition may in the long run become the only effective way to make certain that a large number of biologically tenacious patients actually die" (Callahan, 1983, p. 22). He points out, however, that clinicians, administrators and judges would be remiss if they overlooked the cultural and emotional repugnance of, essentially, starving patients, even though there exists at least a modicum or "moral licitness" in discontinuing feeding. In fact, given that the courts have passed at least partial judgment on the allowability of the discontinuation of feeding, perhaps the only thing that prevents our medical care system from implementing a rational, regular policy of removing nasogastric tubes is that emotional quality, the sentiment in the well-ordered moral life that discourages legitimate but perhaps distasteful activities at the end of life. Callahan declares that "this struggle between head and heart" can be resolved, and in fact that the struggle itself helps to preserve elements of conscience in what otherwise might become dry, clinical decisions made for ostensibly right reasons.

The bioethical literature on the topic of discontinuing feeding is growing richer, and the reader is referred to a few seminal articles for an adequate description of the proscribed limitations to a policy of inducing a justifiable death through removal of the most basic "life-sustaining treatment" (Green, 1984; Lynn and Childress, 1983; Micetich et al., 1983).

XX. SELECTIVE REFUSAL OF TREATMENT: THE CASE OF ELIZABETH BOUVIA

Another powerfully important case in the body of information about death and dying is that of Elizabeth Bouvia, a victim of cerebral palsy who has asserted her right to refuse life-sustaining treatments–including feeding–and therefore prompted moral and legal dilemmas for hospital administrators and physicians distinctly different from those they face in other cases of withholding treatments. The Bouvia case still remains one of only a few like it, and although "the last chapter" has not yet been written in her life and therefore the full impact of the case has not been realized, administrators would be wise to expect other cases like it because an understandable "backlash" against technological interventions has arisen for which there are few ethical landmarks upon which to negotiate this unfamiliar terrain. The reader is referred to a pithy account in the commentary by Annas of the Bouvia case's many ethical and legal twists (Annas, 1984).

In brief, Bouvia's palsy has left her without motor function in any of her limbs except limited movement in her right hand that enables her to operate a motorized wheelchair; her ability to speak is impeded, but she has enough control over her facial muscles to articulate reasonably well and to eat with the feeding help of another person. A college graduate, when Ms. Bouvia's family support network deteriorated and the level of state support for her range of disabilities was diminished, she arranged for a voluntary psychiatric admission to Riverside County General Hospital with the intent to be left alone and, eventually, to starve herself.

In response, her physician threatened to have her declared mentally ill and therefore dangerous to herself so that force-feeding could be implemented. Obviously concerned about the liability of the medical staff and the hospital itself, administrators and county supervisors were very reluctant to allow Ms. Bouvia's ultimate wishes to be carried out or assisted in any way. (For an excellent discussion on improvements in the liability situation affecting physicians and hospitals in this context, the reader is referred to a recent article by an attorney and physician team, Gilfix and Raffin, 1984.)

The intervention of the American Civil Liberties Union in the case on behalf of Ms. Bouvia marked the importance of this being an important patients' rights case. The legal literature on patients' rights to refuse treatment is sizable, particularly in cases of voluntary psychiatric commitment in which, through informed consent and the preeminence of the patient's best interests, such rights have been upheld. Ms. Bouvia's attorney convinced her to accept nourishment while the case could be heard.

At her hearing, she indicated that she no longer was interested in being dependent on other people for her care, calling it "humiliating." In equally stern tones, the hospital chief of psychiatry testified that he would continue to feed her with the nasogastric tube even if the court ordered him not to do so. Allied with the medical staff, the county pled that the issue was whether any person had a right to commit suicide in the county's hospital, and specifically with the tacit cooperation or even assistance of the medical staff. The judge eventually decided more in favor of the county and the hospital staff, indicating that in the best interests of the staff, other patients and unnamed other physically handicapped persons in the United States, Ms. Bouvia's right to privacy and therefore her right to refuse treatment did not outweigh the responsibility of the hospital to prevent her from committing suicide.

In the context of medical technology, the Bouvia case may not be entirely germane, but it represents the extent to which the perceptions of patients about their medical care are vitally important in deciding whether to forego that care or portions of it. Annas (1984) saw the Bouvia case as one in which the attempt at suicide was the crucial issue. More importantly, regardless of their level of technological advancement, medical interventions–in this case force-feeding–that must be administered in a "brutal" manner perhaps against the wishes of a competent patient or the family of an incompetent patient may in fact diminish the quality of "care" and "therapy." That had been at issue in *Bouvia*: at least four attendants were required to hold her down while the nasogastric tube was forcibly inserted into her nose and stomach, virtually negating the true context of "care." As Annas notes, "Medical care must be consensual or it loses it legitimacy" (Annas, 1984, p. 46).

Therefore, for administrators and planners, the issues involved with death and dying have taken a few twists and turns in recent years. No longer will concurrence with the Quinlan decision be enough for persons operating or managing hospitals and health systems. Now issues of whether too little or minimal levels of treatment–for example, the removal of feeding and hydration–and too much treatment–for example, the hospital's refusal to remove feeding tubes while rejecting a patient's wishes–must be confronted. Only the administrator who attempts to operate his or her hospital or health system in a manner akin to what Pellegrino called "moral agency" will satisfactorily respond to these vexing quandaries.

XXI. THE CARE OF IMPERILED NEWBORNS: ADMINISTRATORS AND THE "BABIES DOE"

As we have seen, the intervention of high technology in medical care can dramatically affect the course of treatment for adults at the end of their lives. Not to be overlooked by any administrators are the cases in which medical technology has affected the course of treatment for newborns, particularly for infants formerly considered not viable either due to low birthweight or the vagaries of genetic or teratogenic diseases. Now, however, the lives of these babies can be moderated, even saved, through technology. The blessing that such advances present, however, also constitutes a double-edged sword, because survival of some severely deformed or diseased infants can often mean a torturous and perhaps short life-time for them and prohibitive expense and anguish for their parents and families. Because dealing with these cases on an individual basis is so draining for hospital personnel and physicians, some ethicists believe that standard courses of treatment or nontreatment should be developed and implemented. The influence of bioethics committees is perhaps most profound in these cases. And finally, because the difficulties associated with these cases are so emotionally charged and fraught with the influence of religious and political agendas, administrators need to wade through all the options open to them and their institutions so that informed and ethically moderated medical decisions in the best interests of these children will be the end result of their activities.

The moral problems in caring for imperiled newborns are numerous, as are the medical conditions and diagnoses that are at hand in these cases. For this chapter, we will focus only on those considerations we feel are important for administrators in withholding life-sustaining treatment for infants, with an emphasis on the recent governmental interventions in this area. Most notably, these include the Baby Doe regulations.

Again, the President's Commission report on foregoing life-sustaining treatment provides a good starting point for the discussion. The Commission's recommendations included one specifically aimed at the role of administrators in these cases: "The medical staff, administrators and trustees of each institution that provides care to seriously ill newborns should take the responsibility for ensuring good decision-making practices. Accrediting bodies may want to require that institutions have appropriate policies in this area. An institution should have clear and explicit policies that require prospective or retrospective review of decisions when life-sustaining treatment for an infant might be foregone or when parents and providers disagree about the correct decision for an infant. . . . The best interests of an infant should be pursued when those interests are clear; the policies should allow for the exercise of parental discretion when a child's interests are ambiguous" (President's Commission, 1983, p. 7). An engaging and thorough analysis of this "best interests" standard is provided by John Arras in a recent article, to which readers are referred for context on this crucial criterion employed so often in these cases (Arras, 1984).

In 1982 and 1983, the U.S. Department of Health and Human Services (DHHS) instituted its strategy of offering a "Baby Doe Hotline" telephone number for confidential reporting of suspected violations of provisions of the Rehabilitation Act of 1973 affecting treatment and feeding for infants. A few publicized cases early in the decade of parents and physicians deciding to withhold palliative medical care or even nutrition and hydration prompted this strategy; these included the case of Baby Doe in Bloomington, Indiana, a Downs syndrome baby who survived six days without aggressive medical intervention. It seemed clear to many observers at the time that the Reagan Administration's overall goals of thwarting abortions and emphasizing conservative values in health care had led to this hotline effort.

Annas has called it a "strategy of fear" (Annas, 1983c, p. 14), designed to intimidate physicians and hospital administrators into treatment decisions more akin to those conservative values than necessarily the clinically relevant best interests of the child in each individual case. Furthermore, the strategy harshly minimized the role of parents who normally act as surrogates for their infants; parents' anguish even seemed to be minimized, with the unspoken presumption in the strategy being that parents, like physicians and hospitals, were somehow biased and unable to speak effectively for the infant. Annas summarized by writing "Treatment should be denied to a handicapped infant for only one reason: that the treatment is not in the infant's best interests. Withholding treatment in the interests of others would be a monumental and unjustified change in the law, and runs contrary to child abuse and neglect statutes" (Annas, 1983c, pp. 15-16).

The Baby Doe Hotline was eventually thrown out in court as "arbitrary and capricious" enforcement of the Rehabilitation Act's Section 504 statutes against discriminating against handicapped newborns. The DHHS has implemented nearly the same strategy through the regulatory process, but at least in not the same inflammatory manner as initially done, what with large posters and the toll-free number; it has been observed that the net result of the controversy is not substantially different or better than the preexisting restrictions manifested already in Section 504. However, later the government did amend its Baby Doe rules by encouraging hospitals to establish "Infant Care Review Committees" to monitor and advise all parties on ethically relevant features of withholding care; DHHS considers the committees only a "buffer" between itself and the hospital, with DHHS reserving the right to ignore the recommendations of any such committee. The crux of the issue still remains obfuscated by the government's activities: "It should be clear by now that what is needed in neonatal decision-making is precise articulation of agreed-upon principles and improved procedures for applying them to individual cases. . . . Indeed, a more constructive federal strategy would entail legislation to ensure that no one, handicapped or not, is denied needed medical services because of inability to pay . . . [or] on the basis of handicap" (Annas, 1983c, p. 16).

A similar case (if in name only) without as much overt governmental intervention but with many of the same political and religious motivations can be assessed similarly. The Baby Jane Doe case involved a baby born in 1983 in New York with serious disorders, including meningomyelocele (a form of spina bifida), hydrocephaly, and microcephaly. Her parents were informed by the attending physicians that without surgery she could be expected to live between two weeks to two years; with surgery, she might survive twenty years but would be severely retarded, paralyzed, epileptic, bedridden, and subject to constant bladder infections. After lengthy discussions with neurologists, religious counselors, and social workers, the parents decided against the surgery, which in this case constitutes a rather high-level technological intervention into the infant's care. Instead, they chose to have antibiotics injected into the infant to ward off spinal infection and to let nature take its course (Steinbock, 1984).

However, an attorney with a long history of pressing "right-to-life" lawsuits in several states on behalf of unborn fetuses, handicapped infants, or severely ill patients, encouraged a judge to initiate a proceeding to halt the withholding of treatment and to prompt the surgery to be performed. A protracted legal battle ensued, with a not insignificant fact being that the attorney pressing for the courts to intervene against the parents' wishes was not in any fashion related to the child and therefore had insufficient standing to sue. The New York Court of Appeals threw out a lower court's finding against the parents, now holding that the parents' decision was in the best interests of the infant and that, accordingly, there was no basis for judicial intervention as had been requested by the "right-to-life" attorney.

In her article, Steinbock provides a pithy account of many of the twists and turns in this legal squabbling, noting that while the judicial actions ended in favor of the parents' right to privacy, the issue was decided on mere procedural grounds and not on philosophical lines that could have been helpful for determining courses of treatment by parents in future cases. The issue eventually did undergo scrutiny in the federal courts, with the Justice Department filing suit against the hospital, claiming that it had obstructed the Department from seeing Baby Jane Doe's medical records so that it became unable to determine if Section 504 had been violated. The government's request was dismissed when the U.S. District Court for the Southern District of New York agreed with the hospital and the parents that it would be a dangerous precedent to allow the government access to confidential medical records as well as an intolerable invasion of the parents' right to privacy (Steinbock, 1984, pp. 15, 19).

Steinbock concludes that "there should always be a presumption in favor of treatment, when there is doubt about whether to treat" (1984, p. 19). Nevertheless, she distinguishes between the criteria that doctors and hospitals should follow, and the criteria for government intervention against the wishes of the child's parents and doctors. "Since competent doctors can disagree about an infant's prognosis, it would be improper for the state to intervene against the wishes and best judgment of an infant's doctors and parents whenever it can find another doctor ready to testify that the child would benefit from some other treatment" (Steinbock, 1984, p. 18).

In terms of technology, performing or not performing the surgery qualifies in this case as the specific intervention creating the moral burden. Baby Jane Doe did not survive much longer after the court battles were concluded, but what if she had? Assuming that the baby would have died quickly without surgery was crucial to the parents' decision to forego the surgery, although she did survive the many months during the court proceedings. If the "best interests of the child" criterion is employed, indeed relied upon, would an imperiled newborn who did not receive the technological intervention of surgery then benefit from a longer life? There are substantial disagreements in answering that question, but there seems to be broad consensus that "prolonged life is not in every case a benefit" (Steinbock, 1984, p. 18).

However, in cases in which a spina bifida baby survives to such an extent that the parents begin to have second thoughts and perhaps would support the idea of surgery later in life, it should be noted that, according to the *amicus curiae* brief filed by the Spina Bifida Association in the Baby Jane Doe case, surgery should take place within twenty-four hours of birth if any of the maximal benefits can be accrued. Given that relatively short "window of opportunity," it is worth noting Steinbock's reference to James Rachels' advocacy for active euthanasia in cases such as this (Rachels, 1975, cited in Steinbock, 1984, p. 18). That is, once it is decided that continued existence is not in the child's best interests, passive euthanasia—in this case, the administration of only antibiotics to ward off a painful and eventual death—becomes a much less desirable option. Active euthanasia, in this case infanticide, ought to be allowed, according to Rachels, as an option as permissible as withholding the life-prolonging technological intervention of surgery. However, obviously infanticide is not legal, and is generally morally unacceptable. The question for parents, and in turn for physicians and administrators, is whether the quality of life of the infant having undergone the life-prolonging technological intervention would be sufficiently good to warrant the risk that, upon the surgically-assisted child's eventual death several years later, the parents would not themselves suffer an even greater tragedy.

XXII. DURABLE POWERS OF ATTORNEY FOR HEALTH CARE

An important development that enables patients to state their wishes about medical intervention and to designate a surrogate who may articulate their health care decisions if they are incompetent is the formulation of the Durable Power of Attorney for Health Care (DPAHC). Because the acceptance of these documents is expanding among physicians, attorneys and the courts, and most important among the general public, administrators and planners need to stay abreast of activities concerning the DPAHC.

The DPAHC represents a "second generation" of the so-called "living wills" established by many states in the 1970s to enable persons to describe their wishes about life-sustaining treatment before the need arose for such treatment. The early living wills were based on the model established by the initial passage of the California Natural Death Act in 1977 (codified at Sections 7185 et seq., California Health and Safety Code, 1987). More than two-thirds of the states had passed some form of similar natural death acts by 1985, each having in common the opportunity for the patient's forbiddance of extraordinary treatment that would artificially prolong the dying process.

However, despite their precedent-setting character and the overall victory for patients' rights to designate the nature of their treatment, living wills were quite flawed (Bok, 1976; Eisendrath and Jonsen, 1983). In general such documents could be ignored by physicians without much legal liability for the disregard, and more than a few controversial cases emerged in which incompetent persons executed a living will near to the time of their deaths or during severe illnesses (Hilfiker, 1983). In addition, many families blocked adherence to the wills when they disagreed with their infirmed family member's wishes to forego extraordinary treatment, usually successfully dictating that a full battery of medical technological interventions were administered to the patient perhaps against his or her wishes (Lo and Steinbrook, 1983). Finally, the legal viability of the documents was suspect; not many courts would uphold the tenets of the living wills because they lacked uniformity and often placed hospitals and attending physicians in difficult positions that compromised their protection against civil and criminal liability.

The emergence of the DPAHC, first in Pennsylvania, then in California and in many states since then encouraged by the President's Commission's recommendation for Durable Power statutes, represents a positive force to correct the shortcomings of living wills (President's Commission, 1983, pp. 145 et seq.).

The DPAHC has many advantages, including statutorily defined uniformity within each state, the capacity to make the executed form a permanent part of the medical record, and the provision for nominating a surrogate. The latter can exercise the responsibility for making legally binding health care treatment decisions for the executor in the event of his or her incompetence. Further, the context of living wills almost always dictated that less treatment should be administered in a clinical crisis; DPAHC forms enable the executor to be comparatively specific about the nature of treatment he or she does and/or does not want administered, including statements about increasing the level of treatment administered or pursuing extraordinary care in some situations. In contrast, Steinbrook and Lo (1984) noted that the language used in many living wills had often been vague or ambiguous or too general for adequate interpretation, and that they would only apply in irreversible, terminal illness.

Finally, the legal viability of the DPAHC is not substantially questioned. Although to date there have been few significant test cases, the presumption is that most courts would uphold the DPAHC, protecting from liability not only the surrogate but also the hospital and any participating physicians. In the sense that administrators and planners are probably very often concerned about the liability of their institutions in cases of significant medical technological intervention, their support for the widespread acceptance of DPAHC documents should be encouraged.

A variety of innovative safeguards have been included in the California DPAHC, such as the restriction against any person with "conflicting interests" in the health care of the patient—such as the treating physician—from acting as the "proxy" or as witnesses to the execution of the document. Additionally, the proxy cannot participate in any decisions about health care for the incompetent patient in a circumscribed milieu of medical environments or certain treatments, such as placement in a mental health facility, psychosurgery, electroconvulsive therapy, abortion, and sterilization. There are some other procedural safeguards for patients in nursing homes as well (Steinbrook and Lo, 1984). The DPAHC also encompasses a "statute of limitations": once executed the authorization of the proxy becomes void in seven years. It can be revoked either orally or in writing at any time during that seven year period, but only by the principal, not the physician or proxy. Perhaps the most important safeguard built into the DPAHC statutes is the legal immunity from criminal prosecution, civil liability, and professional disciplinary action for physicians acting in "good faith" with the designated proxy. It is only with that authority that meaningful compliance with the wishes of the patient can be achieved, and that the fullest possible participation by the physician community can be anticipated.

In general, the evolution of the DPAHC constitutes a welcome development for physicians, patients, and health care administrators alike. In a sense, for the first time patients are enabled to have an element of meaningful control over the modern technological armamentarium that can place all parties in the kind of critical ethical dilemmas that have been the focus of this chapter.

XXIII. BIOETHICS COMMITTEES: INSTITUTIONAL STRATEGIES FOR MORAL DECISION-MAKING

For the administrator and planner, the rise of "institutional ethics committees," "hospital ethics advisory panels," "infant care committees," or, generically, "bioethics committees" crystallizes many of the most interesting and challenging issues facing nonclinical health care personnel today.

The rise of bioethics committees in health care systems and hospitals is a striking recent development and response to moral and legal problems spawned by new technologies. Endorsements of the concept of the institutional ethics committee have come from the American Medical Association (1985), the National Hospice Organization, and seminally, the American Hospital Association (see, for example, American Hospital Association, 1985). Congress has encouraged their prudent use in cases involving the treatment of babies born with severe disabilities. And the President's Commission went so far as to propose model state statutes to formalize bioethics committees and to outline the nature of legal protection for committee members and the responsibilities of health care institutions as the sponsors for the committees (President's Commission, 1983, pp. 439 et seq.; Lynn, 1984).

Although it would be very difficult to ascertain the exact number and nature of all the bioethics committees in this country, about one-fourth of U.S. hospitals have established them. Many hospices and nursing homes are beginning to establish such committees as well (Fost and Cranford, 1985; Hosford, 1986).

Members of these committees educate themselves on bioethical aspects of medical decision-making, counsel other health care providers, patients and their families, and establish working guidelines for the handling of categorized cases that could again confront the institution in the future. Their services are both tangible and intangible. Committees help facilitate decision-making by clarifying and distilling important issues for physicians and administrators, providing a measure of legal protection for the institution's officers and medical staff, and offering the opportunity for professionals and clinicians to express disagreements over treatment or to share assumptions about the handling of particular cases or categories of cases.

The membership of these committees can include administrators, health planners, physicians, philosophers, attorneys, chaplains, social workers, hospital trustees, nurses, patients' rights advocates, and members of the community at large. Their activities are best pursued in comparatively low levels of media attention, although the general public may be justifiably interested in the degree to which the committees' advice might reflect the community's conscience. While they are not without controversy, bioethics committees can help formalize the brand of ethical decision-making required in today's technological medical environment in ways that are not exploitative or adversarial (Veatch, 1977).

Hosford provides an interesting and thorough account of the rise of bioethics, and hence the rise of bioethics committees in the past twenty-five years. Importantly for administrators or students of health administration, he cites the fact that more than ever patients and their families are participating in their own health care decisions, acting on the movement toward greater autonomy and a prevailing rejection of the authority of many professionals, including physicians. Also, medicine's inability to cope with the new dilemmas that are a product of medicine's own expansion and seemingly superhuman capacities to preserve or prolong life have spawned the growth of bioethics committees: "When medical people were almost powerless, they were confronted with relatively few ethical dilemmas" (Hosford, 1986, p. 21).

In addition to these forces, he points to other factors yielding the new bioethics: the postwar concern for human rights; the civil rights movement; a relatively tarnished image for physicians; the "right to die" movement; the promulgation of living wills and Durable Powers of Attorney for Health Care; the consumer movement and better consumer education; influential lawsuits over violations of informed consent laws; and most pertinently, the advances in new medical technology.

The particular aspects of medical technology that are germane to this discussion are not the "exotic" expensive ones we might expect, but rather the now-mundane procedures or devices that only a few years ago were unknown, including antibiotics, cardiopulmonary resuscitation (CPR), and the widespread dissemination among physicians and nonphysicians alike of the skills necessary to perform CPR. Additionally, in an echo of Ivan Illich, the expanding volume of cases of clinical iatrogenesis resulting from inappropriate or overused capacities to resuscitate patients who may not desire resuscitation have yielded the occasional outrage against some medical capabilities. Father Paris has given color to this development by writing "For the individual whose journey has indeed come to its conclusion, . . . we do not say, 'At last he is at peace.' Instead, we shout, 'Code Blue.' That is the problem" (Paris, 1982, p. 122).

Hosford also cites the Karen Ann Quinlan case as a watershed event in which the courts gave the first element of legal credibility to the emerging role of bioethics committees. The New Jersey Supreme Court observed that the persons making decisions on

Karen's behalf and pertaining to the quality of her life should it continue would have been well served by a consensus-building advisory committee familiar with medicine and ethics. Chief Justice Richard J. Hughes wrote:

> The most appealing factor . . . seems to us to be the diffusion of professional responsibility for decisions, comparable in a way to the value of multi-judge courts in finally resolving on appeal difficult questions of law. Moreover, such a system would be protective to the hospital as well as the doctor in screening out, so to speak, a case which might be contaminated by less than worthy motivations of family or physicians. In the real world and in relationship to the momentous decision contemplated, the value of additional views and diverse knowledge is apparent (*In re Quinlan*, 1976, cited in Hosford, 1986, p. 70).

It should be noted, however, that while the opinions of bioethics committee members in a particular case constitute a tremendous advantage to physicians and administrators in carrying out the contentious and difficult decisions about incompetent patients, the ultimate decision-making authority lies with the family in consultation with the physician and, by extension, the courts when it may appear that the best interests of the patient may not be served by the intervention of physicians and the family (Siegler, 1986).

Next, bioethics committees are frequently the primary resource for establishing guidelines for hospital Do-Not-Resuscitate (DNR) policies and procedures. An important feature of DNR guideline writing is to emphasize that they are indeed guidelines, not edicts or commands. Not only will this emphasis serve to minimize the potential legal liability of the committee, but it may also elicit greater respect for the guidelines and eventually greater compliance. Hosford writes "They are [merely] maps of the moral terrain" (1986, p. 172).

This activity prompts the medical staff and the hospital administration to grant greater weight to the directives within living wills or DPAHC forms executed by a critically ill patient. Indeed, this activity also engages the fullest possible participation of patients in determining their own care in a medical crisis, because having guidelines promulgated by the bioethics committee may enable more physicians to converse openly with terminally ill but competent patients about the general implementation of DNR orders. That is, as Lo and Steinbrook noted, physicians are not often willing to discuss the meaning of DNR orders with their patients, but might be more willing when the influence of a learned committee is cited: "It is essential for the patient's complete understanding that the DNR order be recognized for what it is—a statement that futile gestures will be avoided while constructive actions will be continued" (Lo and Steinbrook, 1983, p. 1562).

Having thorough guidelines also enables families to understand and possibly agree with the treatment decisions recommended by physicians or decided upon by the physician and the patient, when possible; this prospect for understanding is essential in these cases because of the potential for legal liability if the family members are not consulted or if their wishes are not followed. In fact, Hosford relates that at least one bioethics committee, that at the University of Minnesota Hospitals and Clinics, has incorporated features of dealing with families into the committee's DNR guidelines.

Continuing, bioethics committees can also invest their energies in developing guidelines and advisory policy statements in the area of "limited therapy" protocols, which may highlight the institution's activities regarding feeding and hydration for terminally ill patients. These protocols may be a corollary to the hospital's DNR guidelines. Similarly, some institutions have established "brain death criteria," for although the medical indicators of brain death are rather straightforward and not necessarily within the realm of questions up for philosophical discussion, criteria developed by a bioethics committee can help physicians and others distinguish between brain death and "persistent vegetative states." More to the point, the timely declaration of brain death is obviously very important for the sake of procuring organs for transplantation. It is conceivable that some hospitals might want to append a policy of "Americans first" for organ transplantation within these brain death criteria. Other hospitals might want to emphasize the equitable allocation of medical resources. They could stipulate that an element of decision-making when very little hope for recovery exists for a patient might be the scarcity and expense of some resources, but also that scarcity in itself would not be a sufficient reason to decide to withhold those resources.

Still other areas within the purview of bioethics committees include policies on abortion, fetal surgery, genetic counseling, extraordinary life support for severely disabled newborns, transfers to hospice care, truthtelling in diagnosis and prognosis, and therapeutic abortion. It should not be overlooked that, given the prevalence of religiously affiliated hospitals and health systems in the United States, religious themes or tenets of the operators of these hospitals can certainly be documented and emphasized in the products of bioethics committees. Within such guidelines, these themes do not have the full impact of law, but make the institution's own philosophies apparent to the medical staff, administrators, patients, and their families without untoward legal implications or jeopardizing the hospital's accreditation.

The rising influence of bioethics committees is a trend that administrators and planners would be wise to monitor (Gibson and Kushner, 1986). In a sense these committees make the jobs of health administrators easier by sharing the full burden of infusing a moral direction in the care that is provided. Even patients can participate in the decisions about their own care. In cases in which the impact of modern medical technology is profound, the potential legal liability and ethical indecision that are always present during the last days of a patient's life may be reduced.

XXIV. CONCLUSIONS

In this chapter we have attempted to address the legal and ethical dilemmas presented to clinicians and administrators alike due to the growing influence of modern medical technology. Our analysis has focused on the richness of the literature in medicine, sociology, philosophy, and law that pertain to this topic. The reader should have at least a working knowledge of the most pressing difficulties in these areas, and be equipped to investigate the learned examinations of these topics already engaged by authors in these disciplines, toward a more appropriate role for ethics in administration and day-to-day medical decision-making.

Rarely is there total consensus among physicians, administrators, and other health care personnel regarding the proper role of technology or assessing technology for the most appropriate implementation in medicine. However, examining topics such as organ transplantation, death and dying and the assistance made available within the bioethics committee model can enable these personnel to make informed decisions about the role of technology in the context of saving lives, not merely extending them, and about cost effectiveness, not merely cost saving. Given the possibility that health administrators, in cooperation with their colleagues, can act as moral agents toward a more morally conscious health care system, the enlightened administrator and planner should be attuned to these questions and potential answers.

REFERENCES

Altman, S. H., and Blendon, R. J. (1979). *Medical Technology: The Culprit Behind Health Care Costs*? Department of Health, Education and Welfare, U.S. Public Health Service, Government Printing Office, Washington, D.C.

American Hospital Association (1985). *Values in Conflict: Resolving Ethical Issues in Hospital Care—Report of the Special Committee on Biomedical Ethics*, American Hospital Publishing Company, Chicago.

American Medical Association (1985). Guidelines for ethics committees in health care institutions, *Journal of the American Medical Association, 253*: 2698–2699.

Anderson, G. F., and Russe, C. M. (1987). Biomedical research and technology development, *Health Affairs, 6*(2): 85–92.

Annas, G. J. (1976). In re Quinlan: Legal comfort for doctors, *The Hastings Center Report, 6*: 30–32.

Annas, G. J. (1979). The Quinlan case: Death decisions by committee, *The New Physician, 28*: 53–56.

Annas, G. J. (1983a). Consent to the artificial heart: The lion and the crocodiles, *The Hastings Center Report, 13*(2): 20–22.

Annas, G. J. (1983b). Nonfeeding: Lawful killing CA, homicide in NJ, *The Hastings Center Report, 13*(6): 19–20.

Annas, G. J. (1983c). Disconnecting the Baby Doe hotline, *The Hastings Center Report, 13*(3): 14–16.

Annas, G. J. (1984). When suicide prevention becomes brutality: The case of Elizabeth Bouvia, *The Hastings Center Report, 14*(2): 20–21, 46.

Annas, G. J. (1985a). Regulating the introduction of heart and liver transplantation, *American Journal of Public Health, 75*(1): 93–95.

Annas, G. J. (1985b). Regulating heart and liver transplants in Massachusetts: An overview of the Report of the Task Force on Organ Transplantation, *Law, Medicine and Health Care, 13*: 4–7.

Annas, G. J. (1985c). The dog and his shadow: A response to Overcast and Evans, *Law, Medicine and Health Care, 13*: 112–129.

Arras, J. D. (1984). Toward an ethic of ambiguity, *The Hastings Center Report, 14*(2): 25–33.

Austen, W. G., and Cosimi, A. B. (1984). Heart transplantation after 16 years, *New England Journal of Medicine, 311*: 1436–1438.

Banta, H. D., and Behney, C. J. (1981). Policy formulation and technology assessment, *Milbank Memorial Fund Quarterly, 59*: 445–479.

Banta, H. D., Behney, C. J., and Willems, J. S. (1981). *Toward Rational Technology in Medicine*, Springer Publishing Company, New York.

Barber v. *Superior Court, Nejdl* v. *Superior Court*, (1983). *195 Cal. Rptr.* 484 (Cal. App. 1983).

Batten, H. L. and Prottas, J. M. (1987). Kind strangers: The families of organ donors. *Health Affairs, 6*(2): 35–47.

Bayer, R., Callahan, D., Fletcher, J., Hodgson, T., Jennings, B., Monsees, D., Sieverts, S., and Veatch, R. (1983). The care of the terminally ill: Morality and economics, *New England Journal of Medicine, 309*: 1490–1494.

Beauchamp, T. L., and Childress, J. F. (1983). *Principles of Biomedical Ethics*, (2nd ed.), Oxford University Press, New York.

Beresford, H. R. (1977). The Quinlan decision: Problems and legislative alternatives, *Annals of Neurology, 2*: 74, 77.

Blendon, R. J., and Altman, D. E. (1984). Public attitudes about health care costs: A lesson in national schizophrenia, *New England Journal of Medicine, 311*: 613-616.

Blum, H. L. (1981). *Planning for Health: Generics for the Eighties* (2nd ed.), Human Sciences Press, New York.

Bok, S. (1976). Personal decisions for care at the end of life, *New England Journal of Medicine, 295*: 367-369.

Breo, D. L., Lefton, D., and Rust, M. E. (1983). MDs face unprecedented murder charge, *American Medical News*, September 16, 1983, *26*(34): 1, 13-22.

Bunker, J. P., Fowles, J., and Schaffarzick, R. W. (1982). Evaluation of medical technology strategies: I. Effects of coverage and reimbursement, *New England Journal of Medicine, 306*: 620-624.

California Health and Safety Code (1987). Sections 7185-7191, Bancroft-Whitney, San Francisco.

Callahan, D. (1980). Shattuck lecture: Contemporary biomedical ethics, *New England Journal of Medicine, 302*: 1228-1233.

Callahan, D. (1983). On feeding the dying, *The Hastings Center Report, 13*(5): 22.

Caplan, A. L. (1983). Organ transplants: The costs of success, *The Hastings Center Report, 13*(6): 23-32.

Caplan, A. L. (1984). Ethical and policy issues in the procurement of cadaver organs for transplantation, *New England Journal of Medicine, 311*: 981-983.

Capron, A. M. (1983). Looking back at the President's Commission, *The Hastings Center Report, 13*(5): 7-12.

Casscells, W. (1986). Heart transplantation: Recent policy developments, *New England Journal of Medicine, 315*: 1365-1368.

Cluff, L. F. (1981). Chronic disease, function and quality of care, *Journal of Chronic Disease, 34*: 299-304.

Corlett, S. (1985). Professional and system barriers to organ donation, *Transplantation Proceedings, 17*: 111-119.

Crane, D. (1975). Decisions to treat critically ill patients, *Milbank Memorial Fund Quarterly, 53*: 1-33.

DeGeorge, R. T. (1982). The moral responsibility of the hospital, *Journal of Medicine and Philosophy, 7*(1): 87-100.

Doudera, A. E., and Peters, J. D. (eds.) (1982). *Legal and Ethical Aspects of Treating Critically and Terminally Ill Patients*, Association of University Programs in Health Administration Press, Ann Arbor, Michigan.

Eisendrath, S. J., and Jonsen, A. R. (1983). The living will: Help or hindrance? *Journal of the American Medical Association, 249*: 2054-2058.

Evans, R. W., Blagg, C. R., and Bryan, F. A. (1981). Implications for health care policy: A social and demographic profile of hemodialysis patients in the United States, *Journal of the American Medical Association, 245*: 487-491.

Evans, R. W. (1983). Health care technology and the inevitability of resource allocation and rationing decisions, (In two parts), *Journal of the American Medical Association, 249*: 2047-2053 and *249*: 2208-2219.

Evans, R. W. Manninen, D. L., Overcast, T. D., Garrison, L. P. Jr., Yagi, J., Merriken, K. J., Jonsen, A. R., et al. (1984). *The National Heart Transplantation Study: Final Report*, Battelle Human Affairs Research Centers, Seattle.

Fineberg, H. V., and Hiatt, H. H. (1979). Evaluation of medical practices: The case of technology assessment, *New England Journal of Medicine, 301*: 1086-1091.

Fost, N., and Cranford, R. E. (1985). Hospital ethics committees: Administrative aspects, *Journal of the American Medical Association, 253*: 2687–2692.

Frederickson, D. S. (1981). Biomedical research in the 1980s, *New England Journal of Medicine, 304*: 509–517.

Friedman, E. (1986). *Making Choices: Ethics Issues for Health Care Professionals*, American Hospital Publishing Company, Chicago.

Gibson, J. Mc., and Kushner, T. K. (1986). Will the "conscience of an institution" become society's servant? *The Hastings Center Report, 16*(3): 9–11.

Gilfix, M., and Raffin, T. A. (1984). Withholding or withdrawing extraordinary life support: Optimizing rights and limiting liability, *Western Journal of Medicine, 141*: 387-394.

Green, W. (1984). Setting boundaries for artificial feeding, *The Hastings Center Report, 14*(6): 8-10.

Greenberg, B., and Derzon, R. A. (1981). Determining health insurance coverage of technology: Problems and options, *Medical Care, 19*: 967–978.

Gregory, C. L. (1984). Ethics: A management tool? A profile of the values of hospital administrators, *Hospitals and Health Services Administration, 29*(2): 102–119.

Hilfiker, D. (1983). Allowing the debilitated to die: Facing our ethical choices, *New England Journal of Medicine, 308*: 716–719.

Hiller, M. D. (1984). Ethics and health care administration: Issues in education and practice, *Journal of Health Administration Education, 2*(4): 147–192.

Hiller, M. D. (1986). *Ethics and Health Administration: Ethical Decision Making in Health Management*, Association of University Programs in Health Administration Press, Arlington, Virginia.

Hosford, B. (1986). *Bioethics Committees: The Health Care Provider's Guide*, Aspen Systems Corporation, Rockville, Maryland.

Hough, J. F. (1986). Transplant financing: Ethical and economic decision-making, Paper presented before the 114th Annual Meeting of the American Public Health Association, Las Vegas, Nevada.

Iglehart, J. K. (1982). Health policy report: Prospects for the National Institutes of Health, *New England Journal of Medicine, 306*: 879–884.

Institute of Medicine (1985). *Assessing Medical Technologies*, National Academy Press, Institute of Medicine, Washington, D.C.

Jennett, B. (1985). High technology medicine: How defined and how regarded, *Milbank Memorial Fund Quarterly, 63*(1): 141-173.

Jonsen, A. R. (1986). Bentham in a box: Technology assessment and health care allocation, *Law Medicine and Health Care, 14*(3-4): 172–174.

Kantrowitz, A. (1975). Controlling technology democratically, *American Scientist, 63*: 505-509.

Kirsch, J. (1982). A death at Kaiser Hospital, *California 7*: 79–81, 164–175.

Knaus, W. A., and Thibault, G. E. (1982). Intensive care units today, *Critical Issues in Medical Technology* (B. J. McNeil and E. G. Cravalho, eds.), Auburn House, Boston, pp. 193-215.

Knox, R. A. (1980). Heart transplants: To pay or not to pay, *Science 209*: 570–575.

Kutner, N. G. (1987). Issues in the application of high cost medical technology: The case of organ transplantation, *Journal of Health and Social Behavior, 28*: 23–36.

Lo, B., and Steinbrook, R. L. (1983). Deciding whether to resuscitate, *Archives of Internal Medicine, 143*: 1561-1563.

Lynn, J. (1984). Roles and functions of institutional ethics committees: The President's Commission's view, *Institutional Ethics Committees and Health Care Decision Making* (R. E. Cranford and A. E. Doudera, eds.), Health Administration Press, Ann Arbor, Michigan, pp. 22–30.

Lynn, J. (Ed.) (1986). *By No Extraordinary Means: The Choice to Forego Life Sustaining Food and Water*, Indiana University Press, Bloomington, Indiana.

Lynn, J., and Childress, J. F. (1983). Must patients always be given food and water? *The Hastings Center Report, 13*(5): 17-21.

Manninen, D. L., and Evans, R. W. (1985). Public attitudes and behavior regarding organ donation, *Journal of the American Medical Association, 253*: 3111-3115.

McCullough, L. B. (1985). Moral dilemmas and economic realities, *Hospital and Health Services Administration, 30*(5): 63-75.

Meilaender, G. (1984). On removing food and water: Against the stream, *The Hastings Center Report, 14*(6): 11-13.

Menzel, P. T. (1983). *Medical Costs, Moral Choices*, Yale University Press, New Haven.

Merriken, K. J., and Overcast, T. D. (1985). Patient selection for heart transplantation: When is a discriminating choice discrimination? *Journal of Health Politics, Policy and Law, 10*: 7-32.

Micetich, K. C., Steinnecker, P. H., and Thomasma, D. C. (1983). Are intravenous fluids morally required for a dying patient? *Archives of Internal Medicine, 143*: 975-978.

Moloney, T. W., and Rogers, D. E. (1979). Medical technology: A different view of the contentious debate over costs, *New England Journal of Medicine, 301*: 1413-1419.

Moskop, J. C. (1987). The moral limits to federal funding for kidney disease, *The Hastings Center Report, 17*(2): 11-15.

National Academy of Sciences (1979). *Medical Technology and the Health Care System*, Committee on Technology and Health Care, National Academy of Sciences Press, Washington, D.C.

Office of Technology Assessment (1978). *Assessing the Efficacy and Safety of Medical Technologies*, U.S. Government Printing Office, Washington, D.C.

Oglesby, D. K. (1985). Ethics and hospital administration, *Hospital and Health Services Administration, 30*(5): 29-43.

Overcast, T. D., and Evans, R. W. (1985). Technology assessment, public policy and transplantation: A restrained appraisal of the Massachusetts Task Force approach. *Law, Medicine and Health Care, 13*(3): 106-111.

Paris, J. J. (1982). Terminating treatment for newborns: A theological perspective, *Law, Medicine and Health Care, 10*: 120-124.

Paris, J. J. (1985). Court responses to withholding or withdrawing artificial nutrition and fluids, *Journal of the American Medical Association, 253*: 2243-2245.

Pellegrino, E. D. (1979). Hospitals as moral agents, *Humanism and the Physician* (E. D. Pellegrino, ed.), University of Tennessee Press, Knoxville, pp. 141-152.

Pellegrino, E. D., and Thomasma, D. C. (1981). *A Philosophical Basis of Medical Practice: Toward a Philosophy and Ethic of the Health Professions*, Oxford University Press, New York.

Plough, A. L. (1986). *Borrowed Time: Artificial Organs and the Politics of Extending Lives*, Temple University Press, Philadelphia.

President's Commission for the Study of Ethical Problems in Medicine and Biomedical and Behavioral Research (1981). *Defining Death: Medical, Legal and Ethical Issues in the Determination of Death*, United States Government Printing Office, Washington, D.C.

President's Commission for the Study of Ethical Problems in Medicine and Biomedical and Behavioral Research (1983). *Deciding to Forego Life-Sustaining Treatment: Ethical, Medical and Legal Issues in Treatment Decisions*, United States Government Printing Office, Washington, D.C.

Preston, T. A. (1985). Who benefits from the artificial heart? *The Hastings Center Report, 15*(1): 5-7.

Prospective Payment Assessment Commission (1987). *Medicare Prospective Payment and the American Health Care System: Report to the Congress, February 1987*, United States Government Printing Office, Washington, D.C.

Rachels, J. (1975). Active and passive euthanasia, *New England Journal of Medicine, 292*: 78–80, cited in Steinbock, B. (1984), Baby Jane Doe in the courts, *The Hastings Center Report, 14*(1): 13-19.

Rachels, J. (1983). Barney Clark's key, *The Hastings Center Report, 14*(2): 17-19.

Ramsey, P. (1978). *Ethics at the Edge of Life: Medical and Legal Intersections*, Yale University Press, New Haven.

Reiner, M., Eagles, W., and Watson, K. (1986). Organ bingo: Choice or chance? *Dialysis and Transplantation, 15*: 441-442.

Schaeffer, L. D. (1982). Role of the HCFA in the regulation of new technologies, *Critical Issues in Medical Technology* (B. J. McNeil and E. G. Cravalho, eds.), Auburn House Publishing Company, Boston, pp. 151-161.

Schwartz, W. B., and Joskow, P. L. (1978). Medical efficacy versus economic efficiency: A conflict in values, *New England Journal of Medicine, 299*: 1462-1464.

Scitovsky, A. A., and McCall, N. (1976). *Changes in the Costs of Treatment of Selected Illnesses, 1951-1964-1971*, Department of Health, Education and Welfare, Health Resources Administration, United States Government Printing Office, Washington, D.C.

Siegler, M. (1986). Ethics committees: Decisions by bureaucracy, *The Hastings Center Report, 16*(3): 22-24.

Stein, J. (1978). *Making Medical Choices: Who is Responsible?* Houghton, Mifflin Company, Boston.

Steinbock, B. (1983). The removal of Mr. Herbert's feeding tube, *The Hastings Center Report, 13*(5): 13-16.

Steinbock, B. (1984). Baby Jane Doe in the courts, *The Hastings Center Report, 14*(1): 13-19.

Steinbock, R., and Lo, B. (1984). Decision making for incompetent patients by designated proxy: California's new law, *New England Journal of Medicine, 310*: 1598-1601.

Stoughton, W. V. (1982). Medical costs and technology regulation: The pivotal role of hospitals, *Critical Issues in Medical Technology* (B. J. McNeil and E. G. Cravalho, eds.), Auburn House Publishing Company, Boston, pp. 37-50.

Thomas, L. (1977). Notes of a biology-watcher: The technology of medicine, *New England Journal of Medicine, 285*: 1366-1368.

Veatch, R. M. (1977). Hospital ethics committees: Is there a role? *The Hastings Center Report, 7*(2): 22-25.

Veatch, R. M. (1983). Ethical dilemmas of for-profit enterprise in health care, *The New Health Care For Profit: Doctors and Hospitals in a Competitive Environment* (B. H. Gray, ed.), National Academy Press, Institute of Medicine, Washington, D.C., pp. 125-152.

Veatch, R. M. (1986). DRGs and the ethical reallocation of resources, *The Hastings Center Report, 16*(3): 32-40.

Waldman, S. (1972). Effect of changing technology of hospital costs, *Social Security Bulletin, 35*: 28-30.

Waldo, D. R., Levit, K. R., and Lazenby, H. (1986). National health expenditures, 1985, *Health Care Financing Review, 8*: 1-21.

Wanzer, S. H., Adelstein, S. J., Cranford, R. E., Federman, D. D., Hook, E. D., Moertel, C. G., Safar, P., Stone, A., Taussig, H. B., and van Eys, J. (1984). The physician's responsibility toward hopelessly ill patients, *New England Journal of Medicine, 310*: 955-959.

Wong, C. B., and Swazey, J. P. (1981). *Dilemmas of Dying: Policies and Procedures for Decisions Not to Treat*, G. K. Hall and Company, Boston.

Unit V

Innovation and Change in Human Services Administration

13

Innovation and Change in Organizations: The Absorbing and Sustaining of New Attributes

Marcia B. Steinhauer Graduate Program in Human Services Administration, School of Education, Rider College, Lawrence, New Jersey

I. INTRODUCTION

The topic of formal organizations engaging in innovation activities has generated increasing interest among both students of organizational phenomena and practitioners. The result of this interest has been the development of a wide body of literature related to the topic, but the development has been diverse and fragmented and often unrelated to previous endeavors. Mohr noted that the literature consists of "scattered projects representing different disciplines, motivated by different considerations, and employing a strikingly heterogeneous selection of independent variables" (Mohr, 1969, p. 112).

The purpose of this chapter is to gain an understanding of the wide range of approaches, the major areas of investigation, and the various units of analysis, and to explore the conceptual bits and pieces that have emerged. The diversity of sources and perceptions in the literature on innovation in organizations is presented in a manner which gives the broadest possible overview of the field.

There are many overlapping areas in the literature, and no one article or book can be said to fit best in only one conceptual category. The materials presented in this chapter are organized by a conceptual scheme that can both highlight their contribution and show points of congruence and variance within the literature. Section II notes the different definitions of the term "innovation." The connotations of the term directly influence the research intent, scope, and findings. Section III deals with the major orientations behind the examination of innovation. The intents behind the studies can be demonstrated by the various purposes and paths the research has taken, especially in disciplines outside of political science. The literature is conceptualized for purposes of this review into diffusion research; factors conducive to creativity; research utilization; and aggregate multiorganizational analysis.

The last section contains the contributions from organization theory. The section is divided into the following major conceptual categories: kinds and properties of innovation; organization characteristics of the individuals involved affecting innovation; and the dynamics of organizational adoption.

II. PROBLEMS OF DEFINING INNOVATION

There has not been conceptual agreement on the term "innovation." It has been used within three different contexts (Zaltman, Duncan, and Holbek, 1973). The first context is that of invention, whereby a creative process occurs to produce new phenomena. The literature on creativity and technological development use the term in this manner. Utterback's definition of innovation is that of "an invention which has reached market introduction in the case of a new product" (Utterback, 1971, p. 77). In Milo's study of the resource getting of a health organization, the term means to create a means to respond to the demand of building a new organization (Milo, 1971).

Marquis and Myers emphasize technological development, but view innovation as a process beginning with awareness of a demand and the feasibility of its development, and proceeding to an item and its utilization:

> A technical innovation is a complex activity which proceeds from the conceptualization of a new idea to a solution of the problem and to the actual utilization of a new item of economic or social value (Marquis and Myers, 1969, p. 1).

The second context in which innovation is found is in the process of adoption and institutionalization—that is, there are changes in the organization. Knight's definition of innovation is "the adoption of a change which is new to an organization and to the relevant environment" (Knight, 1967, p. 478). His view implies that the organization has gone beyond conception of a new idea and has begun to apply it, thus stressing adoption. The definitional focus of Evan and Black is similar in that they take the adoption context of the term and carry it a step further, to "the implementation of a new procedure or idea, whether a product of invention or discovery" (Evan and Black, 1967, p. 519). Clark, on the other hand, puts emphasis on the institutionalization aspect by noting that it "is a process whereby specific cultural elements or cultural objects are adopted by actors in a social system" (Clark, 1968, p. 1). Given this emphasis, he notes that innovation can be depicted as "new forms of knowledge that result in structural change" (Ibid, p. 2).

The creation of ideas is not included in the definition by Becker and Whisler, but they posit the idea of organizational risk. Their view of innovation is "the first or early use of an idea by one of a set of organizations with similar goals" (Becker and Whisler, 1967, p. 463). To them, an organization is credited with being innovative if it assumes the risks inherent in being among the first to use an idea, regardless of the source. They also note that innovation can be separated in time and space from an invention, because an invention is a creative act of an individual, but an innovation requires a cooperative group action.

Mohr omits from his definition the aspects of creation, but does point to the notion of success (and early use). This perspective of organizational innovation involves "the successful introduction into an applied situation of means or ends that are new to that situation" (Mohr, 1969, p. 112). Success implies acceptance of the innovation by those in the situation. Mohr's definition also allows for use of the term even though adoption is based on information previously developed outside the organization where the innovation is adopted.

The first contextual usage implies a more widespread process, beginning with the creation of an item; the second usage, adoption and internalization, does not include an act of creativity. Both contexts do imply a dynamic situation, or that a process is occurring.

The third use of the term does not involve a process; rather, it is used in a descriptive mode. The emphasis is on why something is new or different, regardless of its implementation. This use focuses on the delineation of the characteristics of the innovation. The various attributes an innovation can possess will be considered in a later part of this chapter. However, within this context there is agreement by several authors—including Knight, Becker and Whisler, and Zaltman and colleagues—that what is considered "new" or "novel" results from the perceptions of the social units which adopt it.

To summarize, the first two contexts of innovation, that of invention and adoption, imply processes occurring. The first context includes the notion of the generation of an idea or artifact and may or may not include the process of adoption. The adoption connotation may be used with the notions of risk or success being added. In the last context, simple description, innovation is determined by the perceptive capacities of the adopting social unit.

The diversity of the definitions has promoted a range of orientations to both the empirical and the theoretical research applications of innovation. The orientation presented will demonstrate the research development and the several emergent paths within the literature. The two major deficiencies that will emerge from the review of these groups of literature is an absence of rigor in both the conceptual and the operational definitions of the term. The lack of a clear conceptual reference has already been demonstrated. But the lack of a clear operational definition has led researchers to imply they are examining a process when they are actually focusing on nondynamic phenomena. The next section considers four of the major alternative approaches and the nature of the resultant studies.

III. ALTERNATIVE APPROACHES TO THE STUDY OF INNOVATION

A. Diffusion Research

Sociology, using the adoption context of the term innovation, has produced much on the subject. The major area of consideration has been with "diffusion" research. The focus of this research is "the earliness of knowing about something new . . . and the rate of adoption of something new" (Rogers and Shoemaker, 1971, p. 100). The orientation of diffusion research has been extensively applied in the fields of marketing, anthropology, rural sociology, and communications on a diverse range of subject matter, from hybrid corn to marijuana use (Feller and Menzel, 1977; Pontius, 1983; Ray, 1983; Rogers, 1983; Rogers and Shoemaker, 1971). In diffusion studies, the unit of analysis has usually been the community. Gross, Giacquinta, and Bernstein give a cogent description of these studies:

> (1) They generally deal with the spread or adoption of rather simple technical innovations such as hybrid seed, tranquilizers, or audiovisual aids; (2) the agricultural studies have focused on the spread or adoption of

> innovations among farmers residing in a particular county, state, or region; (3) the studies of medical innovations have primarily dealt with their diffusion and adoption by doctors in a single community; (4) the anthropological studies have focused on the spread of such practices as the use of new tools, wells, and modern farming techniques within nonindustrial societies; and (5) the education studies have primarily dealt with the adoption rates of innovations in school systems (Gross, Giacquinta, and Bernstein, 1971, p. 20).

To illustrate the multiformity of subject matter, several examples of diffusion studies are presented. Bennett (1969) focused on groups of individuals in different socioeconomic categories and their acceptance of contraception. Katz (1961) did a comparative analysis of two studies: how hybrid seed corn gained acceptance among farmers in two Iowa communities; and how physicians in four communities responded to the availability of a new miracle drug called gammanym. Public response within two different socioeconomic neighborhoods to new medical technology was the focus in a study by Yeracaris (1961). Becker (1970) studied the adoption of a new program, diabetes screening, in local health departments. He was especially interested in the peer influence in the two-step flow of information.

The narrow nature of this view of innovation as early knowledge or first adoption has a limiting effect on studying the dynamics of political phenomena. Walker, a political scientist, utilized the diffusion literature to study spatial patterns in order "to measure the speed with which states adopt new programs" (Walker, 1969, p. 880). The study was at a macro level, with all 50 states included, and defined an innovation to be a policy or program new to the state, but there was no follow through on what happened after the legislature adopted the program. The states has been the focus of other policy studies as well (Foster, 1978; Henry, 1975; Savage, 1978).

There have been theoretical attempts to explain entire systems in terms of diffusion. Clark (1969) looked at the variations in development of the university as an institution in several countries. He used Rogers's scheme of knowledge, information collection, evaluation, and trial and error to describe the development of the German university system.

Schon (1969) developed theoretical variations of the diffusion model in looking at social movements. The "center-periphery" system depends on a high level of resources and energy at the center because it is limited in its capacity for handling feedback. The "proliferation of centers" system adds secondary centers or outposts, an example being missionary installations. His "Johnny Appleseed" design has a primary center which roams a given territory to disseminate information. His last construct is the "magnet model," where the adopters flock to a central point and then return to their own locale.

Criticism of this approach to the study of innovation has come from several authors. The study of diffusion has promise as an approach, notes Thompson (1969), on new products and procedures that seem to be in the interests of prospective users. He goes on to mention that they are actually studies of technological change, but have not yet been sufficiently integrated theoretically to be of general application.

Gross and his associates posit that this approach has little application in explaining the implementation of innovations in organizations.

> One of its basic assumptions is that . . . the individual is free to decide himself whether the innovation shall be tried and if tried whether it should be

> continued. If the innovation does not interest him, he is free to reject it. If he is not pleased with his evaluation of it, he can discontinue his use of the innovation (Gross, Giacquinta, and Bernstein, 1971, p. 21).

Moreover, to emphasize the point that adoption does not always mean change, a study by Carlson (1965) revealed that mere adoption of programs by top-level education administrators does not necessarily lead to the desired changes at school levels.

The remarks of Gross and colleagues are concise statements on the inapplicability of the diffusion approach to complex organizations:

> It is concerned with the adoption of simple technological innovations of individuals, and it assumes that they can try out innovations on a small scale without the help or support of other persons. It also assumes the persons can undertake trials in an either/or fashion and that short trials are sufficient to render an effective evaluation. Many organizational innovations cannot be tried on a small scale and cannot be implemented unless there is cooperation and support among colleagues. . . . And some require several years of full implementation before an adequate evaluation of their effectiveness can be made. . . . In short, although this may be useful in understanding the adoption of simple innovations among aggregates of individuals, it appears to be of little value for explaining the implementation of organizational innovations (Gross, Giacquinta, and Bernstein, 1971, p. 22).

B. Factors Conducive to Creativity

Within the literature presented in this section, the conceptual connotation of innovation is linked to the context of invention. There is a statement of the creative process and the bureaucratic conditions needed to foster it (Udell and O'Neill, 1977). The importance of the literature in this section is its limited approach. While there is a notion of a dynamic situation, only the creative part of an innovation process is considered, not the adoption and implementation parts. However, several of the concepts dealt with here also hold significance in a wide connotation of innovation, and will be reviewed again in sections which consider organizational and individual characteristics affecting innovation.

The description of the creative process by Steiner which is used by Hlavacek and Thompson appears to be the most concise statement on the subject:

> First, the creative process is an irregular one, and it often seems aimless and unpredictable. It is characterized by sudden leaps. From the point of view of production norms, it seems inefficient. . . . Second, the creative process is characterized by slowness of commitment, by suspended judgment. . . . It is inclined to make a painfully full exploration at the analytical stage and to continue search long after satisfactory solutions have been found (Steiner, 1973, p. 363).

Several conditions within organizations have been identified as relevant to creativity. Thompson names the following: "(1) psychological security and freedom, (2) a great diversity of inputs, (3) an internal or personal commitment to search for a solution, (4) a certain amount of structure of limits to the search situation, and (5) a moderate amount of benign competition" (Thompson, 1969, p. 10). There are other internal conditions, such as freedom from unusual external pressures, group interaction, a sense of professionalism, and uncommitted resources, which enhance the likelihood for innovative or creative behavior to occur (Ibid.).

There is empirical support for the conditions posited by Thompson in the work of Pelz and Andrews (1966) on creativity in research and development laboratories. They found that creative abilities of scientists and engineers were enhanced where coordination was loose, where individuals worked on particular specialties as main projects for relatively short periods of time, where there were methods for communicating ideas, and where there was an opportunity to influence decision makers. In general, the factors identified by Thompson empirically support the notion that innovation is fostered in a loosely structured, professional organization with some minimal excess resources.

C. Research Utilization

The approach taken in the literature discussed in this portion is most closely linked to the discipline of economics. The definitional context of innovation is closest to that of adoption; but it is an external, rather than internal, incidence. It is an adoptive nexus between an organization and knowledge development by its environment.

The emphasis of this approach is on the sources of new ideas and products, and the time lag between research output (Cohen, Keller, and Streeter, 1979; Frosch, 1984; Millman, 1983; and Ribes et al., 1981). Knight (1967) notes that economists have been concerned with the spillovers into civilian endeavors from research and development (R&D) defense efforts, and the number of innovations from small firms.

Doctors's (1969) study of the National Aeronautics and Space Administration (NASA) is one of the best single sources for a detailed presentation of R&D expenditures by the U.S. government. He highlights the fact that much of the promotional activity of NASA for securing government funds was based on the promise of future beneficial nonspace developments. He uses a quote of two NASA officials to emphasie this point: "A considerable portion of the technology resulting from military/space/nuclear work is relevant to needs outside those mission areas" (Doctors, 1969, p. 27). His analysis shows that the field which utilized the most innovation from both space and defense was computer manufacturing. In looking at the rate of technological development, or the diffusion of innovation from conception to end item usage, he notes, "Our studies suggest that major technological discoveries may wait as long as 14 years before they reach commercial application even on a small scale, and perhaps another five years before their impact on the economy becomes large" (Ibid.).

Mansfield (1968) also examined the time lag of utilization of an invention. He found that in industry, there is a lag of about 10 to 15 years between invention and usage. He found that mechanical innovation requires the shortest interval, and electronic innovations require the longest. He also found that the lag seems shorter for consumer products than for industrial products, and shorter for new products and processes developed with government funds than for those developed with private funds. Moreover, he mentions a bandwagon effect, in that as the number of firms in an industry using a new product or technique increases, the probability of its adoption by a nonuser increases. In another study, examining the speed of adoption of new techniques within a given industry, such as the railroads, brewing, and steel, he found that investment is directly related to a perceived profitable situation (Mansfield, 1963).

Utterback (1971) confirms Manfield's findings in that firms innovate in cases where there is clear short-term potential for profit. He has pointed out that innovations that represent breakthroughs of industry-changing magnitude are from sources other than firms within a particular industry. As an example, he gives the case of DuPont, where 12 out of 18 major product innovations originated outside the firm. Lastly, because of the lag of 10 to 20 years, he posits that the stimulus for innovation is not new technological information.

Marquis and Myers (1969), in their study of innovation in American firms, support some of the earlier points. Their analysis of 157 case studies of innovation has shown that in 96 cases, or 61 percent of the cases examined, the ideas for new products and processes came from outside the firm. They also hold that the major sources of ideas for innovation come from marketing factors, as opposed to technological factors.

The foregoing studies indicate that organizations try to reduce risks. They do this either by promoting the possible spillovers from their work or by assessing the potential market demand and the developed technical sources.

The Third World, or developing nations, has been the most recent focus for research utilization studies (Brown et al., 1979; Fischer, 1981; Goldman, 1981; Jundt, Ostrom, and Schlaeter, 1976; Kinsey and Ahmed, 1983; Lall, 1977; McCulloch and Yellen, 1982; McDonald and Leahey, 1985; Mench, 1977; Shelp et al., 1984).

D. Aggregate Multiorganizational Analysis

The common thread of the studies represented in this group is that they relate community socioeconomic variables with aggregate organizational variables in attempts to measure successful innovation. These organizational studies of innovation have been operationalized at a macro level and have centered mostly on private enterprise. The focus is not on innovation as a process within a given organization, but rather on the quantitative adoptions within given sets of similar organizational entities.

While most of this kind of study has been on private, profit-motivated organizations, examples have been taken from the literature to demonstrate the range of applicability in the public sector also (Kraemer, 1977; Lambright et al., 1979; Perry and Danziger, 1980; Polsby, 1984; Roessner, 1977; Weimer, 1980). Becker and Stafford (1967) had as their unit of analysis 140 savings and loan associations with assets of at least \$5 million in Cook County, Illinois. They used organizational efficiency as the dependent variable and operationalized it with two monetary measures: future growth (assets) and current profit (surplus). In examining whether organizational efficiency, or success, was related to innovativeness, they examined organizational size, administrative size, number of innovative adoptions, community growth, and the management team's leadership style. The range of innovations they counted included bonus plans, advertising, premiums for new accounts, and the purchase of municipal bonds. They found that the initial growth of the organization was highly related to the growth of the surrounding community. After this easy growth period (growth in terms of adding surplus to their funds), there was usually an increase in administrative size. With this increase in the number of administrative staff came an increase in the number of innovations adopted. Lastly, they found that group atmosphere is important for adoption of new ideas, in that it generates communication within the managerial staff about how to improve business.

Carroll selected 85 American and Canadian medical schools as her units of analysis in an attempt to determine which of a number of variables were associated with innovation. The variables related to size and composition of the student body and of faculty and administrative personnel, to volume and sources of support of research, and to number and location of clinical facilities. A medical school was classified as either innovative or conservative on having initiated major revisions of its curriculum, in either content or organization (Carroll, 1967, p. 531).

The author used the construct of a "federal-type" organization structure to analyze her findings. In the federal type of organization, there were a number of unitary departments, each with a field of study in the curriculum. Research funds were secured by department chairmen and certain of their faculty, and thus power centered in the departments. With the entrance of the government into allocation of research funds, a change began. The funds were allocated directly to the schools, rather than to individuals or departments. The power balance shifted, and departmental autonomy began to erode in the more innovative schools. Lastly, Carroll found the innovative schools to have the following characteristics: larger faculties; more part-time faculty members; and a large number of departments in the basic sciences and clinical areas.

Mohr used as his unit of analysis 94 local health departments in Michigan, Illinois, Ohio, New York, and Ontario, each one "serving a jurisdiction of not greater than 600,000 in population, whose chief executive—the local health officer—had occupied his current position during the entire period of 1960-1964" (Mohr, 1969, p. 111). He was looking for program response to advancing technology and to the changing needs of the public. Earlier, programs were designed to control communicable disease. More recent service demands have been in the areas of mental health, dental needs, and prevention services. He proposed that the extent of innovation in nontraditional programs is a negative function of obstacles and a positive function of the motivation to innovate and the availability of relevant resources. He operationalized the study by examination of the health-officer activism-ideology, the extent of public health training of key employees, health department expenditure, and aggregate community variables, such as population of the health jurisdiction and percentage of the population in white-collar occupations. His findings supported his proposition, but the relationships were weak. He found size of the organization important, but only insofar as it implied the presence of motivation, obstacles, and resources.

While the approach this literature represents has yielded many significant findings on the comparative aggregate level, the notion of innovation as a process is conspicuously absent. The emphasis has been on adoptive output, or major changes in substantive programs (McKinnan, 1980; Millman, 1983; Musmann, 1982). However, the studies did yield some important concepts, such as management team style, professionalism, and motivation, which lend themselves to operationalization within a single complex organization.

IV. ORGANIZATION THEORY AND THE ANALYSIS OF INNOVATION

A. Classification Schemes and Dimensions of Innovations

Part of the literature on innovation has been concerned with the description of the various types and properties of innovations. The typologies are broad classes of phenomena grouped by the changes they imply. The properties, or characteristics, of innovations are more unidimensional and detailed. Typology categories are not mutually exclusive in attribute descriptions. Indeed, typologies can be combinations of characteristics.

1. Typologies of Innovations

The typologies are examined by initial focus, degree of anticipation, and outcome. Evan, in trying to understand the differential response to innovation, designed a twofold classification aimed at identifying the initial focus of the innovation. He makes a distinction between technical and administrative innovation with the following definition:

> A technical innovation is the implementation of an idea for a new product, process, or service; by an administrative innovation [is meant] the implementation of an idea for a new policy pertaining to the recruitment of personnel, the allocation of resources, the structuring of tasks, of authority, of rewards (Evan, 1966, p. 51).

Evan hypothesizes that administrative innovations in organizations tend to lag behind technical ones. His rationale is that new technical ideas are more likely to be viewed by management as related to the profit goal of an industrial organization. Also, administrative innovations are likely to require more time for a discernible effect.

The degree of anticipation of the appearance of an innovation into the system, or the recognition of a need for change, is the basis of the typology put forth by Knight (1967). The recognition of a need for change is also linked to whether an organization is successful or not. Knight posits that many innovations are routine—that is, they are scheduled in advance. He gives the example of style and color changes in products as being programmed in advance. This kind of innovation usually occurs in a successful atmosphere.

A nonprogrammed or nonroutine innovation can occur under either successful or unsuccessful organizational conditions. If a nonroutine innovation takes place when an organization perceives itself as successful, it is called a slack innovation, because it is promoted and adopted when there is an excess of resources and an opportunity to exchange the status and prestige of subunits and individuals (Knight, 1967, p. 486).

Another form of nonprogrammed innovation is a distress innovation. This occurs when the organization perceives itself as unsuccessful. "Internal changes will occur rather than changes in products or processes. The company does not have the excess resources to look outside. It cannot afford the risk and high cost of introducing a new product or processes and, instead, the company will emphasize cost-reduction projects" (Knight, 1967, p. 486). Knight hypothesizes that stress conditions can be either mild or great. Under mild stress, one can expect moderate measures, internal in nature, and focused on reducing costs, changing organizational structure, or reshuffling personnel. Under great stress, the search for distress innovations is wider and more random, and more radical steps are made for an improvement in organizational conditions.

Bradshaw and Mapp (1972), building on Knight's typology, have devised a variation on a nonprogrammed innovation. They posit that this type of innovation can result from a power strategy applied to the innovating organization by another agency. They give as an example the adoption of consumer participation panels in a family planning program, in compliance with pressure from the federal government in the form of a threat to withhold funding. Thus, a government agency can specify the implementation of a specific innovation as a prerequisite for the funding of the usual services of the agency.

Normann's typology focuses on the outcome or effect of innovation patterns. Outcome is considered in terms of minor and major changes, called variations and reorientations, respectfully: "A new product may be a variation, that is, a product with a set of dimensions basically similar to those [of] earlier products of the organization, through refinements and modifications" (Normann, 1971, p. 206).

The annual model changes of American cars would be a typical example of a variation. Reorientations, on the other hand, imply more fundamental changes, in which some product dimensions may be eliminated and entirely new ones added. Variations can be accommodated within the framework of the existing political system of an organization, while reorientations tend to be associated with changes in the system.

Normann posits that reorientation falls into three typical patterns: systematic, idiosyncratic, and marginal. Systematic orientations are related to the development of the organization and phases in a longer orientation process. Their legitimation comes with their relation to the longer series of events in the organization. Expansion into new markets is a ready example.

Idiosyncratic reorientations lack consistency with other events in the development of the organization. "They are typically initiated because the center of power–most often the managing director–is exceptionally strongly influenced by some event and then legitimizes and promotes a project" (Ibid, p. 208). Normann points out that these projects are not easily integrated in the value system and tend to suffer from low-concept consensus. He gives an example of a medical products firm which traditionally had a policy to manufacture only highly developed products. A consultant outside the firm urged the director to make a skin cream. A subsidiary was formed around the new product, and new marketing channels had to be developed. Thus, the nature of the product itself differed from those produced by the company, from medical to cosmetic. Development, as opposed to just manufacturing, became an operation. Lastly, distribution patterns were not consistent with previously established ones.

Marginal reorientations are relatively small projects which do not substantially affect the structure and goals of the organization and are easy to legitimize. This kind of reorientation usually fits into existing production or distribution systems and "may initiate learning processes that lead to greater reorientations by changing the focus of attention and the perception of some new part of the environment" (Ibid., p. 210). An example of this pattern is a drug firm which used only chemists to conduct research. Within several years after the employment of two pharmacologists, the research efforts and the structure of the company were changed in a pharmacological direction.

2. Properties of Innovations

Several writers have been concerned with the probable effects of the properties of attributes of innovations on the likelihood of their adoption. Many innovations are items of modern technology and can be complex entities, having various properties. Each property can have a positive or negative effect on the rate at which an innovation is adopted in a given population. Fliegel and colleagues have noted that to study the adoption of innovations

> via their attributes is a compromise between treating each new ideas as essentially unique and, on the other hand, treating various new ideas as equivalents. Different innovations cannot be compared. By denying the existence of differences among innovations, the research has simply substituted one type of unexplained variability for another (Fliegel, Kivlin, and Seklon, 1968, p. 438).

a. Compatibility

The literature posits that innovations are more acceptable if they are compatible or consistent with the adopter's previously established norms, values, and experiences. In his exploration of past research findings, Katz (1973) notes that the adopter must perceive an innovation as compatible with his values on such factors as risk and profitability before an innovation is accepted. Miles (1964) found that innovations must be congruent with the potential adopting system. Innovations which are perceived as threats to existing practices are less likely to be adopted, he found, while those innovations which can be added to an existing system without disturbing it are more likely to be accepted. Thio's (1971) thorough review of the property of compatibility offers a succinct analysis. He adds two organizationally related dimensions to the concept: symbolic compatibility, which refers to the perception of the innovation by members of the organization; and functional compatibility, which concerns what is required by the adopter to utilize the innovation.

b. Divisibility

The literature posits that an innovation which can be introduced in segments or parts, with each segment having an opportunity to be assimilated into an existing situation, will arouse less resistance than would comprehensive change. Fliegel and Kivlin (1966), in their study of Pennsylvania dairy farmers, found that divisibility of trial, the extent to which an innovation lends itself to a small-scale tryout before full adoption, was an important factor in encouraging rapid adoption. Zaltman, Duncan, and Holbek (1973) state that divisibility may facilitate adoption for either or both of the following reasons: by minimizing threatening situations; by maintaining current practices during implementation; or by providing a set of components that can be implemented gradually with the use of feedback. The last idea is reinforced by Bright (1964), in his distillation of principles from case studies. He suggests that innovations be introduced in stages, since resistance is lessened if only slight changes are required.

c. Complexity

The degree to which an innovation is perceived as difficult to understand and use will have an effect on its adoption. According to some of the literature, the more complex the innovation, the less likely it is to be put into operation. In the cross-national study by Fliegel and colleagues, it was found that in a range of innovations related to dairy farming, the more complex ones were less rapidly adopted (Fliegel, Kivlin, and Seklon, 1968). In examining the attribute of complexity as both an idea and an operation, Zaltman and colleagues posit that "an innovation which is easy to use but whose essential idea is complex is more likely to be adopted than an innovation which is difficult to use but whose essential idea or concept is readily understood" (Zaltman, Duncan, and Holbek, 1973, p. 39). However, in the analysis of innovations in higher education by Clark (1968), the attribute of complexity serves a different purpose. In examining the criteria for institutional acceptability, Clark found that the degree of development of an innovation assumes importance because in universities, the more intellectually sophisticated and conceptual a scheme is, the better it conforms with university values. Hence, in this setting, the attributes of complexity and compatibility are linked.

d. Efficacy

There are various observations in the literature that the uncertainty associated with an innovation will be reduced if the innovation has been proven before in another system. Becker and Whisler have noted that the cost to late adopters is smaller because of "reduced risk to late adopters where the innovators have demonstrated the possibility of a new idea" (Becker and Whisler, 1967, p. 462). The literature refers to efficacy under several headings. Mansfield (1963) uses the term "observability" to denote that when there is tangible proof of utilization, the probability of adoption is greater. Lin and Zaltman (1973) advance the notion of "result demonstration," which shows the benefits of adopting a particular innovation. They hold that the more visible the innovation's advantages, the more likely it is to be adopted. Fliegel and Kivlin (1966) use the term "clarity of results" to signify the communication of the results of a new practice, and suggest that this should contribute to a more rapid adoption.

e. Physical Manifestation

The physical properties of innovations have been given rather superficial treatment in the literature. The reason is probably that most innovations studied are mechanical devices or items of a tangible nature; and the properties discussed above naturally lend themselves to descriptions of material artifacts. Doctors points out:

> We tend to view technology primarily in terms of machines and physical tools, that is, hardware. Increasingly, however, such software as systems concepts, management control techniques, and computer programs may all be viewed as being as much a part of the common store of technology as a rocket vehicle or a linear accelerator (Doctors, 1969, pp. 3-4).

Evan and Black (1967) found in their study of acceptance of staff proposals that software innovations, which they classify with administrative rather than technological innovations, may be more difficult to sell to management because in dealing with ideas and concepts, potential payoff is more uncertain. Lin and Zaltman (1973), commenting on the perceptions of potential adopters toward the attributes of an innovation, query if the visibility of a physical object is more readily acceptable than ideas and practices which are abstract.

B. Organizational Characteristics Affecting Innovation

1. Environment

Organizations operate and interact within a contextual setting. The relationship between the organization and its environment is an important determinant of the innovative process. The literature dealing with this characteristic is mostly theoretical, but empirical findings are noted to the extent they have appeared. Zaltman and colleagues note that environment of a multimember adoption unit is important in two different ways:

> First, changes in the environment create a *situation* of stress and pressure to which an adoption unit must respond if it is to remain in a relationship of dynamic equilibrium with the environment. Thus an adoption unit is more likely to innovate when its relevant environment is rapidly changing than when it is steady. . . . Second, if the response to the situation is an innovative *solution*, environmental norms may or may not favor the changes this solution implies (Zaltman, Duncan, and Holbek, 1973, p. 110).

Burns and Stalker (1961) were interested in whether management systems could alter in conformity with the changes in "extrinsic factors." For them, these extrinsic factors were different rates of technical or market change brought on by the appearance of new scientific discoveries, inventions, and consumer demands. Utterback (1971) reinforces this point in his theoretical analysis of the firm's social and economic relationship to its environment. He says that the process of innovation is embedded in the environment because it is the use of existing products and processes which leads to recognition of needs and wants for new products and processes. As noted earlier, Utterback demonstrated that the technological environment was often the stimulus for innovation because most product innovations originated outside the firm. Thus, he concluded, it was neither cost nor technical knowledge which acted as crucial restraints on the firm. "The primary limitation on a firm affecting its innovative ability is in recognizing the needs and demands in its external environment" (Utterback, 1971, p. 81).

The environment is also important to innovation in that the solution must be acceptable to the larger social environment to which the adopter unit belongs. Thompson (1967) suggested that many organizations are subject to authoritative specification for permissible action and must adjust to the constraints and contingencies imposed by the larger system. An example would be government units having to exist on the financial inputs of legislative bodies, and having no option regarding their clientele. An empirical example to substantiate the correspondence between environmental factors and organizational change is described by Becker and Stafford (1967), who found that the most important variable to explain adoption of innovations by savings and loan associations was community growth rate.

Duncan (1972) contributes to our understanding by dividing the environment into components and factors. First, he makes a distinction between internal and external environments by using the notion of relevant physical or social factors falling either inside or outside the boundaries of an organization. The components of the internal environment are organizational personnel, organizational function and staff units; and organizational levels. The external components are customers, suppliers, competitors, and sociopolitical and technical factors. He found in this study of 22 decision units that the more dynamic the environment, the more likely it is that the organization will experience innovation in order to reduce disequilibrium.

2. Structure

The literature on organizational structure as it applies to the innovative process stresses its multidimensionality. The consensus seems to be that different configurations of the dimensions comprising organizational structure can either facilitate or hinder the innovative process. A discussion of the salient structural dimensions of centralization, formalization, and specialization, as well as of other research findings can serve as illustrations.

a. Centralization

The dimension of centralization focuses on the location of authority and decision making in an organization. Thompson posits that the modern bureaucratic organization is dominated by the monocratic stereotype which dictates centralized control over all resources. The monocratic organization is resistant to innovation because the conditions which generate creativity call for free communication, flexible structure, and intrinsic rewards. Moreover, the hierarchy of authority is a procedure whereby legitimacy is dispensed. "It is a procedure that works in such a way as to give the advantage to the veto. . . . [It] does not provide for appeals. . . . Thus, even if the monocratic organization allows new ideas to be generated, it will probably veto them (Thompson, 1969, pp. 19-20). The Burns and Stalker study amplifies the discussion of highly centralized organization with a partial description of their "mechanistic" model. "Management, often visualized as the complex hierarchy in organization charts, operates a simple control system, with information flowing up through a succession of filters, and decisions and instructions flowing downward through a succession of amplifiers" (Burns and Stalker, 1961, p. 5). In his descriptive model of intrafirm innovation, Knight (1967) argues that one needs power to innovate. This, he says, comes in great part from the formal hierarchy, in that the higher a person's position, the more likely one is to be a successful innovator and the more radical the development that one can introduce.

The Hage and Aiken (1967) study of program change in 16 social welfare agencies operationalized centralization as the degree of participation in organization decision making, and contrasted this with hierarchy of authority. The investigators found a positive relationship with the first; when there was greater participation in agency-wide decisions, there was a greater rate of program change. They found a negative relationship between hierarchy of authority and program change.

A case against expecting much innovation within a decentralized organization is made in Sapolsky's study of department stores. He described department stores "as federations of quasi-independent merchants" (Sapolsky, 1967, p. 498). He found that because of the decentralization, tactics used to innovate in one subunit can be known and resisted in another.

b. Formalization

The dimension of formalization emphasizes the rules and regulations that ensure predictability of performance. The theorized relationship between formalization and innovation is that strict emphasis on rigid rule observation, job codification, and specification of roles inhibits diffusion and communication of ideas, suppresses creativity, and consequently is negatively associated with innovation. Lawrence and Lorsch (1967), examining differentiation and integration within the subsystem of six industrial organizations, found that those aspects of behavior in organizations subject to preexisting programs and controls were more defined or rigid when there was a certainty of performance from their relevant environment. Burns and Stalker's field studies confirm this point, in that they found that organizations that were profitably coping with uncertain and changing situations had a low degree of formalized rules and job specification, instead of the higher degree of formalized structure associated with financial success in the more certain situations of the mechanistic model. They note that in the mechanistic model "there is a precise definition of rights and obligations and technical methods attached to each functional role [and] a tendency for operations and working behavior to be governed by the instructions and decisions issued by a superior" (Burns and Stalker, 1961, p. 94).

Hage and Aiken (1967), in their study of welfare organizations, found that many rules and procedures cause restraints for an organization. They found that job codification is inversely related to the rate of organizational change. However, the relationship between the degree of rule observation and the rate of change was much weaker than expected. Shepard (1967) postulates an unstable relationship between formalization and innovation by distinguishing stages of innovation. In essence, he advocates an oscillating organizational model. He calls attention to periodicity, or alterations associated with innovating groups, and holds that at the idea generation stage, there should be a loose and open organization. At the implementation stage, there should be a functional division of labor, discipline, and control of internal communications.

c. *Specialization*

The structural dimension of specialization, or complexity, focuses on the number of occupational specialties in an organization and the training and degree of professional activity associated with them. Hage and Aiken (1967) determined that in welfare agencies, there was a high positive correlation between the rate of acceptance and implementation of new programs and the number of occupational specialties within the organization. They also found that the number of occupational specialities was one of the best predictors of future program innovation. They indicated that this was because the most innovative organizations were more likely to have many cooperative relationships with other agencies, which might suggest that the focus of the staff was on professional organizational goals, rather than on departmental self-interests.

Along a similar line, Carroll (1967) found that innovative medical schools had a larger number of departments in the basic sciences and clinical areas. She presumed that the diversity in subcultures stimulates proposals, but it is centralized authority which leads to their acceptance. Thus, in this study, the innovative schools reflected a lessening of departmental autonomy along with a larger number of departments.

The degree of autonomy or interdependence of the differentiated organizational subunits is a factor in determining the effects of specialization. Sapolsky (1967) held that the department store's structural arrangement of a larger number of autonomous subunits deterred the implementation of any proposed centralized innovations.

The various findings pertaining to the several dimensions of organizational structure and its relationship to innovation indicate that different configurations of structure facilitate the innovation process in its varying stages. Zaltman and colleagues have made the most succinct statement on this point:

> Specifically, it is emphasized that in stimulating the initiation of innovations, a higher degree of complexity, lower formalization, and lower centralization facilitate the gathering and processing of information, which is crucial to the initiation stage. It is also emphasized that in the implementation stage, a higher level of formalization and centralization and a lower level of complexity are likely to reduce role conflict and ambiguity which could impair implementation. This conclusion thus implies that the organization must shift its structure as it moves through various stages of innovation; at the earlier initiation stage, a more organic or less bureaucratic structure seems more appropriate. Then, as the organization moves to the implementation, more bureaucratic structure becomes appropriate (Zaltman, Duncan, and Holbek, 1973, p. 155).

3. Climate

A part of the literature examining organizational climate has been reviewed earlier under the various research approaches—namely, the factors conducive to creativity. The bureaucratic conditions identified previously include psychological security and freedom;

a great diversity of inputs; an internal or personal commitment to search for a solution; a limited structure to the search situation; and a small amount of benign competition (Cohen, Keller, and Streeter, 1979). It was noted that while this approach is important, it is limited to only the earliest stages of an innovation process, that of the creation of innovative ideas. There are some other relevant dimensions that can be identified from the literature which are applicable to organizational climate and that have possible significance for the large view of an innovation process.

a. Communication

In the journal articles aimed at practitioners of public administration, one of the principles deemed essential for an innovative organization climate is open communication. Patrick advocates both formal and informal free communication. "Creativity is encouraged by free and open channels of communication. Employees must feel free to use the existing channels of communication and should be encouraged to communicate with colleagues and associations outside the organization" (Patrick, 1970, p. 33). Siepert and Likert advocate open communication for an innovative climate because of the informational interdependence on which decision making is based (Siepert and Likert, 1973).

The communication problem between technologists and managers within the same organization is an important consideration of informational exchange for decision making. Under any organizational situation, the problem exists; but within the framework of an innovation process, informational interdependence is highly relevant. A theoretical scheme developed by Churchman and Schainblatt analyzes effective relationships based on communication between managers and scientists. The investigators focused on the distinct forms which emerge with the problem of implementation of innovation, or the manner in which results of scientific efforts may come to be used by managers. The fourfold scheme takes into account the actor's perception of how information should be communicated. The "separate functionalist" thinks of management and science as separate functions. "For him, implementation consists of designing the operation solution, which is a specification of the physical changes that must take place in the organization in order for it to be able to accommodate the optimal mathematical solution" (Churchman and Schainblatt, 1965, p. B71).

The "communicator" emphasizes the need for creating more understanding on the part of the manager—that is, creating better lines of communication. It is vital for the scientist to appreciate this need, but a detailed understanding of the manager is not required in order to have the manager understand the scientist. Communication is a fairly direct process which is independent of the personality of the manager.

The "persauder" views the implementation problem in terms of the manager's personality.

> Hence the problem is not to provide for the manager's complete understanding of the scientist, but to ensure that the scientist understands enough about the manager so that the scientist can overcome managerial resistance to change per se, alter specific managerial attitudes, or persuade managers to accept recommendations (Ibid., p. B79).

The "mutual understander" takes a synthetic position in order to bring about a successful union of the other communication patterns. This type of actor would argue against the separation of technology and management because "if science is to become a method of managing, then management must become a method of science" (Ibid., p. B82).

b. Staff Cohesiveness

Another dimension of organizational climate which can influence innovation is the level of staff cohesiveness, or reciprocal collegial support. Thompson, commenting on the reward system relevant to an innovative environment, notes the importance of this extrinsic source of satisfaction: "It appears that they take the form of improved esteem in the eyes of similarly committed peers rather than an increase in interpersonal power relative to peers or a more improvement in income as such" (Thompson, 1969, p. 11). This point was reinforced by the government-sponsored Arthur D. Little study aimed at formulating the optimum conditions of successful innovations. It was found that an atmosphere of collaboration, where relationships are governed by mutual confidence and trust and long personal associations exist between parties, was most conducive to implementation of innovation (Arthur D. Little, Inc., 1965).

Becker and Stafford (1967), in studying savings and loans associations, included a factor similar to staff cohesiveness. They examined the management team's leadership style, using a sociometric approach to discovering both the most and the least preferred co-worker. They found that group atmosphere is important for innovation because if it is congenial and mutually supportive, communication will be frequent and easy, thus allowing for creation and adoption of viable innovations.

c. Morale

A dimension of organizational climate closely related to staff cohesiveness is that of the level of staff morale, or job satisfaction. Hage's theoretical explanation of organizational adaptiveness to change posits that high job satisfaction, measured by attitude batteries and rate of turnover, can provide a climate for innovation. There are empirical studies which substantiate this relationship. Marcum (1973) studied innovation adoption in schools, and found that in an open climate, there is high morale with regard to work; furthermore, she found, there is a relationship between high morale toward one's work and innovation adoption.

Hage and Aiken's research on social welfare agencies found the performance variable of job satisfaction was correlated to the rate of program change. However, the investigators also found that "job satisfaction may be a necessary precondition for the introduction of changes, but after this change has been introduced. It may have disruptive and negative effects on social relationships among members of an organization" (Hage and Aiken, 1967, p. 513). This brings up again a point considered earlier–namely, that the climate required for introduction of an innovation does not guarantee its implementation.

d. Tenure of Leadership

A final dimension of organizational climate which is relevant to innovation is that of the length of time a particular high-level position is filled by the same individual. The literature on tenure of leadership does not have an empirical base, and the theoretical propositions do not attempt to explain similar phenomena. Tenure is significant to organizational climate and innovation because of the very importance of managerial roles per se in adoption and implementation, and because it is a measurable phenomenon which can be studied. Thus, although the contributions from the literature are sparse, recognition of this variable is noted for later methodological utilization.

Siepert and Likert, speculating on high managerial mobility patterns in public service organizations, hold that:

> There is some job mobility because a manager tries to innovate and fails, but we suspect there is more job switching because the manager does not risk the necessary innovation and sits tight until organizational pressures overwhelm him (Siepert and Likert, 1973, p. 2).

The organizational climate can be determined by the organizational leadership. It is for this reason, Griffiths states, that the number of innovations is inversely proportional to the tenure of the chief administrator.

> The longer an administrator stays in a position, the less likely he is to introduce change. . . . All of the processes which bring about a steady state have had time to operate. Feedback channels have become structured and have gained independence. Change is thus more difficult, because the frequency of interaction between subsystems is decreased (Griffiths, 1964, p. 434).

It was noted above that the organizational climate has a similarity to organizational structure as a variable, in that it may be necessary for differing configurations to emerge at various stages of an innovation process. Wilson (1966) hypothesized that different climates are required for generation, approval, and implementation of innovation proposals. According to him, the climate required to induce innovative behavior in organizations may be the same climate which will prohibit the implementation of innovative proposals.

The Evan and Black (1967) study on the factors associated with the success and failure of innovative staff proposals provides support for this hypothesis. It is of interest at this point, additionally, because it is an empirical application of clusters of both structural and climate variables. They investigators found that staff proposals were more likely to be successful in an organization where formalization of rules, specialization, communications between management and staff, quality of proposals, competitive position of the organization, and perceived need were high, and where the professionalization of management was low.

Rowe and Boise have synthesized the theories and findings on this point and suggest the following about the total climate required for organizational innovation:

1. During the knowledge accumulation and diffusion stages, both rational and open-ended operational climates may be required.
2. During the formulation stage, a loosely structured, diverse, professionalized, mildly competitive, psychologically secure climate operating under the presumption of available resources and some freedom from external pressures may be appropriate.
3. During the decisional stage, the climate must be sufficiently rational to assure the quality of proposals, their orderly transmission to decision makers, and the adequacy of communication between proposers and decision makers.
4. During the implementation stage, a generally rational and efficiency-inducing climate seems required.
5. Externally, the innovative process within the organization seems likely to be fostered by the availability of fiscal resources, organizational diversity, and extensive patterns of communications, information, and knowledge (Rowe and Boise, 1974, p. 289).

4. Size

One of the variables which has been highly correlated with innovation is organizational size. This variable has been used in aggregate multiorganizational studies where large numbers of similar firms and agencies have been studied. The findings indicate more change takes place in larger organizations. For example, Hage and Aiken (1967) found that a rate of program change in social welfare agencies was highly related to larger organizations. Mansfield's (1968) study of technological innovation in industry found that the largest organizations will do a disproportionately large share of innovation in situations where the investment required to innovate is large relative to the size of the organizations that could use the innovation; the minimum size of the organizations required to use the innovation is large relative to the average size of similar organizations; the average size of the largest organizations is much greater than the average size of all potential users of the innovation.

5. Resources

The organizational characteristic of availability of uncommitted financial resources has been favorably linked in both the theoretical and the empirical literature to the innovation process. Clark (1968), in his analysis of innovation models descriptive of higher education, holds that among the characteristics which influence the universities to be open to innovation is financial support—that the more extensive the financial support, the greater the propensity of institutional innovativeness. Mohr (1969), studying health departments, emphasizes the significance of excess resources. He found empirical support for the hypothesis that innovation was a function of the interaction among motivation, obstacles, and resources.

The concept of resources is expanded by Thompson to mean more than financial affluence and excess. His concept of "slack" denotes the existence of a comprehensive affluent situation in the organization.

> By "slack," I mean uncommitted and unspecified resources of appropriate personnel, finance, material, and motivation. . . . A situation in which there is such slack apparently makes it possible for various psychological variables that are supportive of innovation to operate. . . . Slack at the organizational level is the counterpart of psychological security in the creative process. It makes it easier for management to back innovations. The presence of slack encourages the decentralization of control over resources (Thompson, 1969, pp. 42–43).

The Arthur D. Little study on successful research and exploratory development in new weapons empirically substantiated Thompson's points. One of the findings was that in nearly all cases of successful research and development, a vital element present for the triggering of the event was "resources, usually facilities, materials, money, and trained and experienced men, which could be committed to do a job" (Arthur D. Little, 1965, p. II-5). Also present were an explicitly understood need, goal, or mission, and a source of ideas, or pool of information. Another finding dealing with patterns of funding revealed that a common pattern for initial funding of successful research and development was on the basis of local decisions. It was recommended that further allocations also be made at local, or decentralized, points because centralized controls involve justification of work and introduce delay.

6. Professionalism

The organizational characteristic of professionalism is closely related to the structural dimension of complexity or occupational specialization. However, professionalism covers more than the number of occupational specialties; it conveys the notion of very extensive preentry training and extraorganizational involvements. Thompson holds that professionalism involves specialization of people, not of task, and that it "is based on the concept of investment of human 'capital' rather than of labor as a commodity" (Thompson, 1969, pp. 42-43).

The findings in the literature relate professionalism positively to innovativeness in organizations. Hage and Aiken (1967) found that the main effect of staff professionalism is the input of new knowledge into the organization because of a heightened awareness of programmatic and technological developments within a profession. This was related to involvement in extraorganizational activities. (However, the amount of professional training did not appear significantly associated with the rate of innovation in social welfare agencies.)

An interesting finding about professionalism was made by Evan and Black (1967) in their study of organizational factors affecting the success of staff proposals submitted to management in business firms. Among the characteristics of organizations in which proposals were more likely to be successful was the combination of a higher degree of professionalization of management. The authors offer the possible explanation that under such conditions, management is more disposed to rely on the judgment of its professional staff.

C. Characteristics of the Individual Affecting Innovation

The literature pertaining to the relationships between individual characteristics and organizational innovation is sparse. However, there are some items of a demographic and perceptional nature that lend themselves to research on the innovation process. The very scarcity of such materials indicates the need for more empirical research in this area.

1. Age

It is a rather common assumption that younger people are more favorably disposed to organizational innovation. Marcum (1973) found in her study of educational innovation that the professional staff was younger in the more innovative schools.

2. Professionalism

This characteristic was treated before as an organizational characteristic. It has been previously stated that extraorganizational professional activity of social welfare workers was found to be related to a higher innovation rate, while the amount of training they received was not. Sapolsky (1967) also found in his department store research that it was the increased involvement of professional comptrollers in outside activities that lead them to propose innovative management techniques.

The type of training received by individuals can also be significant in furthering innovation. Radner, Rubenstein, and Bean (1968) did a field study of 66 firms which were attempting to integrate operations research and management science skills into their organizations. The researchers found personnel fell into five general categories: former military; professional scientists from engineering; operations research/management science specialists with training in systems analysis; mangement specialists with training in business administration; and organization men with special training serving in an interim capacity. They also found that as management science activities became integrated in the firms, the management specialists succeeded to leadership of the units, and that these units were moved to the top management levels.

The dearth of materials reviewed in this section pointed out possible areas of research. The individual as a member of a social system has both demographic and cognitive characteristics that are relevant to institutional research. Age, amount and type of educational background, career patterns, and organizational rank are but a few of several important aspects of the members of an organization. The relationship of these aspects to an innovation process clearly needs to be explored.

D. Dynamics of Organizational Adoption

The innovation literature on the dynamics of organizational adoption concentrates on integrative interfaces which reduce resistance and assist implementation. The output of previous research efforts can best be grouped under the following headings: linkage mechanisms; boundary personnel; participation of workers; and power relations.

1. Linkage Mechanisms

There are several contributions in the literature which treat the organizational devices for facilitating and integrating change. Lynton (1969) presents a comprehensive model which lends itself to a variety of settings and conditions. He distinguished four different assessments of the environment regarding the need for change and the linkage mechanisms these assessments lead to. The needs for change can be assessed as negligible; frequent, but temporary; frequent, but specific; or continuous. Linkage mechanisms to integrate change range from project orientations and ad hoc committees to permanent differentiated subsystems. He found that where the environmental assessments are inaccurate, the linkage mechanisms are inadequate to support the required integration. Inaccurate assessments, therefore, will tend to provoke a multiplication of innovative subsystems.

Lawrence and Lorsch found in their study of integration devices in six organizations that supplementing the hierarchical and administrative systems, there is a great development of "voluntary" integrating activities. They discuss the tendency for such voluntary activities to become increasingly formalized:

> One has only to note the proliferation of coordinating departments (whether called new product, marketing, or planning departments), task forces, and cross-functional coordinating teams to find evidence that new formal devices are emerging to achieve coordination (Lawrence and Lorsch, 1967, p. 12).

Two authors offer suggestions for linkage mechamisms within extremely hostile organizational situations. Knight (1967) describes the use of formal powers for the creation of a new organization. This new creation contains a subsystem of the formal power system which may be able to introduce innovations. This type of situation occurs because the parent firm ignores new developments. Evan (1966) holds that members of an organization who find resistance to their attempts to incorporate an innovation can adapt to the situation and develop sub-rosa strategies to circumvent organizational policies. They can incorporate the developed innovation by "bootlegging"—that is, by attaching it to other projects which have already gained acceptance.

2. Boundary Personnel

Specific and formalized organizational positions charged with reducing attitudinal and communication barriers to innovation are sometimes established. The idea of establishing such positions is found in the literature under a variety of labels: boundary personnel; boundary spanner; change agent; or linking agent. The purpose of these organizational positions is to establish the function of transferring innovations between units within the same organization or from one organization to another (Egan, 1985).

The research in this area is quite supportive of the boundary personnel concept. In Corwin's (1972) experiment in training Teachers Corps personnel for low-income schools, he found that one of the most important factors for technological innovation was competent and receptive boundary personnel in the host organizations. In his study of technology utilization from the space program, Doctors (1969) found that moving the technical personnel along with the innovation was a key element in a successful transfer.

3. Participation of Workers

One method of reducing resistance to an organizational change is to allow workers to participate in its development—the notion being that they will accept the change if they have a part in its occurrence. As Stewart said:

> If a change is arbitrarily imposed, there will be great resistance. However, participation in the discussions on how the change is to come about will lower resistance (Stewart, 1957, p. 36).

Research studies such as those by Coch and French (1948) in a textile factory, and Watson and Glaser (1965) in mental health agencies and group therapy, support the "participation hypothesis."

4. Power Relations

A line of thought contrasting to the participation hypothesis is found in the literature on power relations. The underlying premise is that an organization's subunits (including individuals), common claimants to the same resources, will have varying amounts of conflict during the process of an organizational change.

Power relations in organizations are defined by Harvey and Mills "as relations between individuals or subunits in which each is attempting to impose its own inner structure on the organization's internal environment aims which to some extent are incompatible" (Harvey and Mills, 1970). They do attempt to operationalize these terms.

With power defined as an individual's capacity to obtain performance from other individuals, Bachman (1968) found in his study of college administrators that an individual may exercise power over other individuals because of his control of sanctions, the respect accorded his knowledge, the existence of norms which legitimate his exercise of power, or his personal attractiveness. In a comparative study of five organizational settings, which included business and industry, Bachman, Bowers, and Marcus (1968) duplicated these findings. It is interesting that they found the powers of coercion and regard to be the least influential ones for motivating organizational behavior.

One final insight into the nature of organizational power is suggested by Mann and Neff. They propose that an executive understand the use of expert and referent power in such a manner that as he acts to bring complex change, "he would be respected for his command of technical knowledge, . . . his ability to see administrative problems, . . .

and his skills in helping others grow as they face large, unfamiliar organizational problems (Mann and Neff, 1963, p. 56).

BIBLIOGRAPHY

Argyris, C. (1970). *Intervention Theory and Method*, Addison-Wesley, Reading, Massachusetts.

Argyris, C. (1965). *Organization and Innovation*, Dorsey Press, Homewood, Illinois.

Arthur D. Little, Inc. (1976). *Management Factors Affecting Research and Exploratory Development*. For Director of Defense, Research Engineering under Contract No. SD 235.

Bachman, J. G. (1968). Faculty satisfaction and the dean's influence: An organizational study of twelve liberal arts colleges, *Journal of Applied Psychology, 52*: 55.

Bachman, J. G., Bowers, D. G., and Marcus, P. (1968). Bases of supervisory power: A comparative study in five organizations, *Control in Organizations*, (A. S. Tannenbaum, ed.), McGraw-Hill, New York, p. 229.

Barnard, C. A. (1938). *The Functions of the Executive*, Harvard University Press, Cambridge, Massachusetts.

Becker, M. H. (1970a). Factors affecting diffusion of innovations among health professionals, *American Journal of Public Health, 60*: 294.

Becker, M. H. (1970b). Sociometric location and innovativeness: Reformation and extension of the diffusion model, *American Sociological Review, 35*: 267.

Becker, S. W., and Stafford, F. (1967). Some determinants of organizational success, *Journal of Business, 40*: 511.

Becker, S. W., and Whisler, T. H. (1967). The innovative organization: A selective view of current theory and research, *Journal of Business, 40*: 462.

Bennett, C. (1969). Diffusion within dynamic populations, *Human Organizations, 28*: 243.

Blau, P. M. (1956). *The Dynamics of Bureaucracy*, Random House, New York.

Blau, P. M., and Scott, W. R. (1962). *Formal Organizations: A Comparative Approach*, Chandler Publishing, San Francisco.

Bradley, H. B. (1969). Designing for change: Problems of planned innovation in corrections, *Annals of the American Academy, 381*: 89.

Bradshaw, B. and Mapp, C. B. (1972). Consumer participation in a family planning program, *American Journal of Public Health, 62*: 972.

Bright, J. R. (1964). *Research, Development, and Technological Innovations: An Introduction*, Richard D. Irwin, Homewood, Illinois.

Brown, L. A., Schneider, R., Harvey, M. E., and Riddell, J. B. (1979). Innovation diffusion and development in a Third World setting: The cooperative movement in Sierra Leone, *Social Science Quarterly, 60*: 249.

Burns, T. and Stalker, C. M. (1961). *The Management of Innovation*, Tavistock Publications, London.

Carlson, R. O. (1965a). Barriers to change in public schools, *Change Processes in the Public Schools* (R. O. Carlson, ed.), Center for the Advanced Study of Educational Administration, University of Oregon, Eugene, p. 3.

Carlson, R. O. (1965b). *Adoption of Educational Innovations*, Center for the Advanced Study of Educational Administration, University of Oregon, Eugene.

Carroll, J. (1967). A note on departmental autonomy and innovation in medical schools, *Journal of Business, 40*: 531.

Churchman, C. W., and Schainblatt, A. H. (1965). The researcher and the manager: A dialectic of implementation, *Management Science, II*: B69.

Clark, T. N. (1968). Institutionalization of innovations in higher education: Four models, *Administrative Science Quarterly, 13*: 1.
Coch, L. and French, J., Jr. (1948). Overcoming resistance to change, *Human Relations, 1*: 512.
Cohen, H., Keller, S., and Streeter, D. (1979). The transfer of technology from research to development, *Research Management, 22*: 11.
Corwin, R. G. (1972). Strategies for organizational innovation: An empirical comparison, *American Sociological Review, 37*: 441.
Crosby, A. C. (1968). *Creativity and Performance in Industrial Organizations*, Tavistock Publications, London.
Derthick, M. (1975). *Uncontrollable Spending for Social Service Grants*, The Brookings Institution, Washington, D.C.
Doctors, S. I. (1969). *The Role of Federal Agencies in Technology Transfer*, MIT Press, Cambridge, Massachusetts.
Doctors, S. I. (1971). *The NASA Technology Transfer Program: An Evaluation of the Dissemination System*, Praeger, New York.
Downs, A. (1966). *Inside Bureaucracy*, Little, Brown and Company, Boston.
Dubley, D. H. (1971). Impact of organizational climate, *Personnel Journal, 50*: 196.
Duncan, R. B. (1972). Characteristics of organizational environments and perceived environmental uncertainty, *Administrative Science Quarterly, 17*: 313.
Dymsza, W. (1972). *Multinational Business Strategy*, McGraw-Hill, New York.
Egan, G. (1985). *Change Agent Skills in Help and Human Service Settings*, Brook/Cole Publishing Company, Monterey, California.
Elbing, A. C. (1970). *Behavioral Decisions in Organizations*, Scott, Foresman, Glenview, Illinois.
Estafen, B. D. (1970). System transfer characteristics: An experimental model for comparative research. *Management International Review, 10*: 2.
Etzioni, A. (1961). *A Comparative Analysis of Complex Organiations*, Free Press, Glencoe, New York.
Etzioni, A. (1964). *Modern Organizations*, Prentice-Hall, Englewood Cliffs, New Jersey.
Evan, W. M. (1966). Organizational lag, *Human Organization, 25*: 51.
Evan, W. M., and Black, G. (1967). Innovation in business organizations: Some factors associated with sources or failure of staff proposals, *Journal of Business, 40*: 519.
Feller, I., and Mensel, D. C. (1977). Diffusion milieus as a focus of research on innovation in the public sector, *Policy Science, 8*: 49.
Fischer, B. (1981). Interest rate ceilings, inflation and economic growth in developing countries, *Economics, 23*: 52.
Fliegel, F. C., and Kivlin, J. E. (1966). Attributes of innovations as factors in diffusion, *American Journal of Sociology, 72*: 235.
Fliegel, F. C., Kivlin, J. E., and Seklon, G. (1968). A cross-cultural comparison of farmers' perceptions as related to adoption behavior, *Rural Sociology, 33*: 437.
Foster, J. L. (1978). Regionalism and innovation in the American states, *Journal of Politics, 40*: 179.
French, J. R. P., Jr., and Raven, B. (1959). The bases of social power, *Studies in Social Power* (D. Cartwright, ed.), Institute for Social Research, University of Michigan, Ann Arbor, Michigan, p. 150.
Frosch, R. A. (1984). R&D choices and technology transfer, *Research Management, 27*: 111.
Globe, S. Levy, G. W., and Schwartz, C. M. (1973). Key factors and events in the innovation process, *Research Management, 16*: 8.
Goldman, A. (1981). Transfer of a retailing technology into the less developed countries: The supermarket case, *Journal of Retailing, 57*: 5.

Golembiewski, R. T. (1964). Innovation and organization structure, *Personnel Administration, 27*: 3.

Goodenough, W. H. (1963). *Cooperation in Change*, Russell Sage Foundation, New York.

Griffiths, D. E. (1964). Administrative theory and change in organizations, *Innovation in Education* (M. B. Miles, ed.) Teachers College, New York, p. 425.

Gross, N., Giacquinta, J. B., and Bernstein, M. (1971). *Implementing Organizational Innovations: A Sociological Analysis of Planned Education Change*, Basic Books, New York.

Gruber, W. H., and Niles, J. S. (1972). Put innovation in the organization structure, *California Management Review, 14*: 29.

Hage, J. (1965). An axiomatic theory of organization, *Administrative Science Quarterly, 10*: 289.

Hage, J., and Aiken, M. (1967). Program change and organizational properties: A comparative analysis, *American Journal of Sociology, 72*: 503.

Hage, J., and Aiken, M. (1970). *Social Change in Complex Organizations*, Random House, New York.

Hage, J. and Dewar, R. (1973). Elite values versus organizational structure in predicting innovation, *Administrative Science Quarterly, 18*: 279.

Hall, R. H. (1962). The concept of bureaucracy: An empirical assessment, *American Journal of Sociology, 69*: 32.

Hall, R. H. (1972). *Organizations: Structure and Processes*, Prentice-Hall, Englewood Cliffs, New Jersey.

Harvey, E., and Mills, R. (1970). Patterns of organizational adaptation: A political perspective, *Power in Organizations* (M. M. Zald, ed.), Vanderbilt University Press, Nashville, p. 181.

Havelock, R. G. (1969). *Planning for Innovation Through Dissemination and Utilization of Knowledge*, Center for Research on Utilization of Scientific Knowledge, Institute for Social Research, University of Michigan, Ann Arbor, Michigan.

Henry, N. (1975). Bureaucracy, technology, and knowledge management, *Public Administration Review, 35*: 572.

Hlavacek, J. D., and Thompson, V. A. (1973). Bureaucracy and new product innovation, *Academy of Management Journal, 16*: 361.

Hlavacek, J. D., and Thompson, V. A. (1974). Bureaucracy and venture failures. Research Report. (mimeographed.)

Holt, K. (1970). Management of technological innovation, *Management International Review, 10*: 21.

Homer, P. W. (1973). Technology for local and state governments, *Public Management, 55*: 2.

Hughes, H. (1983). Capital utilization in manufacturing, *Finance and Development*, p. 6.

Jundt, J. E., Ostrom, L. L., and Schlaeter, J. L. (1976). Closing the technology transfer gap, *Akron Business and Economic Review, 7*: 21.

Kahn, R. L., and Cannell, C. F. (1957). *The Dynamics of Interviewing*, John Wiley and Sons, New York.

Kar, S. B. (1974). Implications of diffusion research for a planned change, *International Journal of Health Education, 17*: 192.

Katz, E. (1961). The social itinerary of technical change: Two studies on the diffusion of innovation, *Human Organization, 20*: 70.

Katz, E. (1973). The characteristics of innovations and the concept of compatibility, pp. 157–158, *Planning for Creative Change in Mental Health Services*, National Institute of Mental Health, DHEW Publication No. (HSM) 73-9148. United States Government Printing Office, Washington, D.C.

Katz, E., Levin, M. L., and Hamilton, H. (1963). Traditions of research on diffusion and innovation, *American Sociological Review, 28*: 237.

Kinsey, B. H., and Ahmed, I. (1983). Mechanical innovations on small African farms: Problems of development and diffusion, *International Labour Review, 122*: 227.

Knight, K. E. (1967). A description model of the intra-firm innovation process, *Journal of Business, 40*: 478.

Kraemer, K. L. (1977). Local government, information systems, and technology transfer: Evaluating some common assertions about computer application transfer, *Public Administration Review, 37*: 368.

Kuhn, T. S. (1962). *The Structure of Scientific Revolutions*, University of Chicago Press, Chicago.

Lall, S. (1977). Medicines and multinationals: Problems in the transfer of pharmaceutical technology to the Third World, *Monthly Review, 28*: 19.

Lambright, W. H. (1972). Government and technological innovation: Weather modification as a case in point, *Public Administration Review, 32*: 1.

Lambright, W. H., Flynn, P. J., Teich, A. H., and Lakins, A. B. (1979). *Technology Transfer to Cities: Processes of Choice at the Local Level*, Westview Press, Boulder, Colorado.

Lawrence, P. R. and Lorsch, Jay (1967). Differentiation and integration in complex organizations, *Administrative Science Quarterly, 12*: 1.

Leavitt, H. J. (1965). Applied organizational change in industry: Structural, technological and humanistic approaches, *Handbook of Organizations*, (J. G. March, ed.), Rand McNally, Chicago, p. 1144.

Levine, R. A. (1968) Rethinking our social strategies, *The Public Interest, 10*: 27.

Likert, R. (1967). *The Human Organization*, McGraw-Hill, New York.

Lin, N., and Zaltman, G. (1973). Dimensions of innovation, *Processes and Phenomena of Social Change*, (G. Zaltman, ed.), Wiley Interscience, New York, p. 93.

Lynton, R. (1969). Linking an innovative sub-system into the system, *Administrative Quarterly Review, 14*: 398.

Mann, F. C., and Neff, F. W. (1963). *Managing Change in Organizations*, Foundation for Research on Human Behavior, Ann Arbor, Michigan.

Mansfield, E. (1968). *Industrial Research and Technological Innovation: An Econometric Analysis*, W. W. Norton, New York.

Mansfield, E. (1963a). Size of firm, market structure, and innovation, *Journal of Political Econony, 41*: 556.

Mansfield, E. (1963b). The speed of response of firms to new techniques, *Quarterly Journal of Economics, LXXVIL*: 290.

Marcum, L. R. (1973). *Organizational Climate and the Adoption of Educational Innovation*, pp. 191-192. *Planning for Creative Change in Mental Health Services*. National Institute of Mental Health, DHEW Publication No. (HSM) 73-9148. U.S. Government Printing Office, Washington, D.C.

Marquis, D. G. (1969). The anatomy of successful innovations, *Innovation, 1*: 28.

Marquis, D. G., and Myers, S. (1969). *Successful Industrial Innovations*, National Science Foundation, Washington, D.C.

McCulloch, R., and Yellen, J. L. (1982). Technology transfer and the national interest, *International Economic Review, 23*: 421.

McDonald, D. W., and Leahey, H. S. (1985). Licensing has a role in technology strategic planning, *Research Management, 28*: 35.

McKinnon, L. M. B. (1980). The corporate library as a source of new technology, *Long Range Planning, 13*: 102.

Menck, K. W. (1977). Fundamental concepts of the transfer of technology to the developing countries, *Economics, 15*: 30.

Merton, R. K. (1965). The environment and the innovating organization, *The Creative Organization* (G. A. Steiner, ed.), University of Chicago Press, Chicago, p. 50.

Miles, M. B. (1964). Innovation in education: Some generalizations, *Innovation in Education* (M. B. Miles, ed.), Teachers College, New York, p. 631.

Millman, A. F. (1983). Licensing technology, *Management Decision, 21*: 3.

Milo, N. (1971). Health care organization, *Journal of Health and Social Behavior, 12*: 163.

Mohr, L. (1969). Determinants of innovation in organizations, *American Political Science Review, 63*: 111.

Musmann, K. (1982). The diffusion of innovations in libraries, *Libri, 32*: 257.

Normann, R. (1971). Organizational innovativeness: Product variation and reorientation, *Administrative Science Quarterly, 16*: 203.

Patrick, J. F. (1970). Organizational climate and the creative individual, *Public Personnel Review, 31*: 31.

Pelz, D. C., and Andrews, F. M. (1966). *Scientists in Organizations: Productive Climates for Research and Development*, John Wiley and Sons, New York.

Perry, J. L., and Danziger, J. N. (1980). The adoptability of innovations: An empirical assessment of computer applications in local governments, *Administration and Society, 11*: 461.

Polsby, N. W. (1984). *Political Innovation in America: The Politics of Policy Initiation*, Yale University Press, New Haven.

Pontius, S. K. (1983). The communication process of adoption: Agriculture in Thailand, *Journal of Developing Areas, 18*: 93.

Price, J. L. (1972). *Handbook of Organizational Measurement*, D. C. Heath, Lexington, Massachusetts.

Randor, M., Rubenstein, A., and Bean, A. (1968). Integration and utilization of management science activities in organizations, *Operations Research Quarterly, 19*: 117.

Ray, G. F. (1983). The diffusion of mature technologies, *National Institute Economic Review, 56*: 62.

Ribes, B., et al. (1981). *Domination or Sharing? Endogenous Development and the Transfer of Knowledge*, Unesco, Paris.

Robertson, T. S. (1967). The process of innovation and the diffusion of innovation, *Journal of Marketing, 31*: 14.

Robertson, T. (1971). *Innovative Behavior and Communication*, Holt, Rinehart and Winston, New York.

Roessner, J. D. (1977). Incentives to innovate in public and private organizations, *Administration and Society, 9*: 341.

Rogers, E. M. (1983). *Diffusion of Innovations*, 3rd ed., Free Press, New York.

Rogers, E. M., and Shoemaker, F. F. (1971). *Communication of Innovations: A Cross-Cultural Approach*, Free Press, New York.

Rosner, M. M. (1968). Administrative controls and innovation, *Behavioral Science, 13*: 36.

Ross, P. F. (1974). Innovation adoption by organizations, *Personnel Psychology, 27*: 21.

Rowe, L. A., and Boise, W. B. (eds.) (1973). *Organizational and Managerial Innovation: A Reader*, Good Year Publishing Company, Pacific Palisades, California.

Rowe, L. A., and Boise, W. B. (1974). Organizational innovation: Current research and evolving concepts, *Public Administration Review, 35*: 284.

Sapolsky, H. M. (1967). Organizational structure and innovation, *Journal of Business, 4*: 497.

Savage, R. L. (1978). Policy innovativeness as a trait of American states, *Journal of Politics, 40*: 212.

Schoen, D. R. (1969a). Managing technological innovation, *Harvard Business Review, 47*: 156.

Schoen, D. R. (1969b). The diffusion of innovation, *Innovation, 6*: 42.

Selltiz, C., Jahoda, M., Deutsch, M., and Cook, St. W. (1960). *Research Methods in Social Relations*, 2nd ed, Henry Holt, New York.

Shannon, G. W., Bashshur, R. L., and Metzner, C. A. (1971). The spatial diffusion of an innovative health care plan, *Journal of Health and Social Behavior, 12*: 216.

Shelp, R. K., Stephenson, J. C., Truitt, N. S., and Wasow, B. (1984). *Service Industries and Economic Development: Case Studies in Technology Transfer*, Praeger Scientific, New York.

Shepard, H. A. (1967). Innovation resisting and innovation producing organizations, *Journal of Business, 40*: 470.

Siepert, A. F., and Likert, R. (1973). The organizational climate for successful innovation, *Public Management, 55*: 2.

Slevin, D. (1971). The innovative boundary: A specific model and some empirical results, *Administrative Science Quarterly, 16*: 515.

Steiner, G. (1973). *The Creative Organization*. Selected papers Number 10 Graduate School of Business, University of Chicago, 1962. Quoted in James D. Hlavacek and Victor A. Thompson, Bureaucracy and new product innovation. *Academy of Management Journal, 16*: 361.

Stewart, M. (1957). Resistance to technological change in industry, *Human Organization, 16*: 36.

Taylor, J. (1970). Introducing social innovation, *Journal of Applied Behavioral Science, 6*: 69.

Terreberry, S. (1968). The evolution of organizational environments, *Administrative Science Quarterly, 12*: 590.

Thio, A. O. (1971). A reconsideration of the concept of adopter innovation compatibility in diffusion research, *Sociological Quarterly, 12*: 56.

Thompson, J. D. (ed.) (1966). *Approaches to Organizational Design*, University of Pittsburgh Press, Pittsburgh.

Thompson, J. D. (1967). *Organizations in Action*, McGraw-Hill, New York.

Thompson, J. D., Hammond, P. B., Hawkes, R. W., Junker, B. H., and Tuden, A. (1959). *Comparative Studies in Administration*, University of Pittsburgh Press, Pittsburgh.

Thompson, V. A. (1961). *Modern Organization*, Alfred A. Knopf, New York.

Thompson, V. A. (1965). Bureaucracy and innovation, *Administrative Science Quarterly, 10*: 1.

Thompson, V. A. (1969). *Bureaucracy and Innovation*, University of Alabama Press, University, Alabama.

Tilton, J. E. (1971). *International Diffusion of Technology: The Case of Semiconductors*, The Brookings Institution, Washington, D.C.

Udell, G. G., and O'Neill, M. F. (1977). Technology transfer: Encouraging the noncorporate inventor, *Business Horizons, 20*: 40.

Utterback, J. M. (1971). The process of technical change within the firm, *Academy of Management Journal, 14*: 75.

Walker, B. (1970). On the contrasts between private firms and governmental bureaus, *Power in Organizations* (M. M. Zald, ed.), Vanderbilt University, Nashville, p. 322.

Walker, J. L. (1969). The diffusion of innovations among the American states, *American Political Science Review, 63*: 880.

Watson, G., and Glaser, E. M. (1965). What we have learned about planning for changes, *Management Review, 54*: 34.

Weimer, D. L. (1980). Federal intervention in the process of innovation in local public agencies;A focus on organizational incentives, *Public Policy, 28*: 93.

Wildausky, A. (1972). The self-evaluating organization, *Public Administration Review*, p. 509.

Wilson, J. Q. (1966). Innovation in organization: Notes toward a theory, *Approaches to Organization Design* (J. D. Thompson, ed.), University of Pittsburgh Press, Pittsburgh, p. 193.

Yerocaris, C. A. (1961). Social factors associated with the acceptance of medical innovations: A pilot study, *Journal of Health and Social Behavior, 3*: 193.

Zald, M. M., ed. (1970). *Power in Organizations*, Vanderbilt University Press, Nashville.

Zaltman, G., ed. (1973). *Processes and Phenomena of Social Change*, Wiley Interscience, New York.

Zaltman, G., Duncan, R., and Holbek, J. (1973). *Innovations and Organizations*, John Wiley and Sons, New York.

14

Innovation and Change in the Delivery of Drug Services

Dale B. Christensen and William H. Campbell Department of Pharmacy Practice, University of Washington School of Pharmacy, Seattle, Washington

"Even if you're on the right track, you'll get run over if you just sit there."

Will Rogers

It has been said that nothing is so constant as change. Yet, there is a strong and often unsettling undercurrent in our lives that leads to the perception that the rate of change is accelerating and may soon overwhelm our abilities to cope. Several authors have played on this theme (in such works as *Future Shock, The Third Wave,* and *Megatrends*) and, apparently, struck a responsive chord among a large number of people. An examination of the medical care system dramatically illustrates that it has not been immune to either the process or the rapidity of change. Several megatrends can be highlighted within medical care. These include:

1. Transition from medical care controlled by physicians to an activity coordinated by interprofessional colleagues
2. Evolution of the patient from passive subject to active participant in medical care decision making
3. Illness and death as adversaries to be combated at all costs, versus natural states to be accommodated with comfort and compassion
4. Life as a sacred gift versus life as a technological process attainable through manipulation of genetic materials
5. Medical care as a market commodity to medical care as a rationed public resource

Significantly, each of the above changes has a ripple effect throughout the various sectors of the medical profession.

Change seems to be endemic, yet it would seem at first glance that very little has changed within the drug industry. The typical patient still receives tablets and capsules in vials that appear unchanged from the early 1900s, except for the replacement of a safety cap for the time-honored cork. While the drugs themselves may have changed, there are still pharmacists behind the counter preparing prescriptions for patients. Closer examination reveals this to be a thin veneer, however, masking powerful forces of change that affect not only the profession, but the products and services it delivers. In this chapter, we will identify some of the major shifts that are affecting the delivery and use of drug products and drug-related services. To better understand them, it is helpful to first have a historical perspective of technological developments affecting the drug industry and pharmacy practice over the past 150 or so years.

Historically, pharmacy and medicine were closely tied and indistinguishable. However, as more drugs were discovered and as techniques for their extraction became increasingly complex, task specialization occurred. The pharmacist's professional role evolved to include three basic functions: (1) extracting and preparing drugs from botanical sources, (2) guaranteeing the freshness and genuineness of drugs (particularly when adulterated products proliferated the U.S. market), and (3) safeguarding the acquisition and use of drugs. The historical importance of extemporaneous compounding is reflected in the symbol that the profession informally adopted: the mortar and pestle.

By the nineteenth century, the pharmacist had secured a firm position as a supplier of drugs to the physician or patient. However, emergence of the drug manufacturing industry in the mid-1800s as part of the Industrial Revolution gradually supplanted pharmacists' extraction and compounding responsibilities. Pharmacies became storehouses for manufactured medicinals and emerged as entrepreneurial establishments. During the 1900s, pharmacy legislatively established a near exclusive domain as distributor of drug products to patients via prescriptions. As drugs themselves became increasingly potent and important as a therapeutic tool, the importance of this function was enhanced, as was the status of the profession itself. Beginning in the 1970s, pharmacy education and training began a shift from being exclusively drug-centered to a patient-centered, "clinical pharmacy" orientation. This transition, however, is incomplete and represents a service ideal, rather than a reality, in many settings.

As can be seen, change is nothing new to pharmacy. But we may well ask what forces are changing the profession and drug distribution system today. To answer this question, we direct our examination to the following contemporary forces of change:

Technological impact
Drug product formulations
Drug development
Computerization and automation
Drug information
Financing of drug services: The emergence of the third party
Market factors affecting community pharmacy
Market factors affecting hospital pharmacy
Changes affecting the work activities of pharmacists

I. TECHNOLOGICAL IMPACT

It is appropriate to first address the broader technological explosion in medical care and examine how it affects drug service delivery. Table 1 presents a view of technology based upon patient impact (prevention, diagnosis, therapy, or rehabilitation) and clinical function (medical, surgical, ancillary).

TABLE 1 Classifying Medical Technology: Selected Examples

Clinical function	Patient impact			
	Prevention	Diagnosis	Therapy	Rehabilitation
Medical	Multiphasic screening	Ambulatory cardiac monitoring	Neonatal intensive care	Continuous passive motion devices
	Pap smears	Fiberoptic endoscopes	Lithotripsy	
	Home glucose monitoring			
	Home cancer tests	Ultrasound diagnosis in obstetrics and cardiology		
Surgical	Telemonitoring of cardiac patients	Cardiac catheterization and angiography	Coronary angioplasty	Cochlear implants
		Arthroscope joint examination	Implantable drug pumps	Prosthetics for cosmetic and reconstructive applications
Ancillary	Electrocardiogram, stress test	Radioisotope diagnosis	Antipsychotic drugs	Ambulatory aids
	Vaccines	Automated chemistry analyzers	Antiulcer drugs	Durable medical equipment
	Prophylactic antibiotics			
	Beta blockers for heart attacks			

It is apparent that a large number of technologies are sweeping the medical care landscape, covering a broad spectrum of patients and conditions. Interestingly, drugs are represented in virtually all levels of the technology matrix. The key will be to select for mass adoption those technologies having a high cost-effectiveness ratio as well as a high impact on quality of care. In that sense, the various technologies are in competition with one another, and drugs must compete with arthroscopic surgery or a lithotripsy procedure, for example, for limited health care dollars. Future allocations of medical care resources will pit one medical care modality against another (for example, drugs versus surgery) to optimize the medical care system. This will increase an already acute need for rigorous cost-effectiveness research on drugs and program evaluation studies on pharmacy services.

Technology manifests itself in virtually every aspect of change we choose to address, from the development of product formulations to computer applications. This is more clearly illustrated below.

II. DRUG PRODUCT FORMULATIONS

For centuries, the human body has been anointed externally with drug concoctions of various sorts, and drugs have been inserted into one end or the other of the gastrointestinal system to induce therapeutic effect. Neither of these routes of drug administration is likely to be replaced, but we are seeing the development of major new approaches to drug administration. These include transdermal patches, intravenous (IV) pumps, subdermal implants, and ion-differential exchange systems. Many of the new systems share the characteristic of controlled release of medicinals into the bloodstream. Insulin pumps, for example, provide a steady infusion of insulin to better meet the body's physiological needs for glycogen. Nitroglycerin transfermal patches provide more consistent control of peripheral vasodilation of coronary arteries in angina. Implants render obsolete many concerns about patient compliance, and decrease the need for physician or pharmacy visits.

Some have speculated that the trend to develop miniature devices, such as insulin pumps, that combine physiological measurement with drug metering will lead to constant monitoring of a variety of other physiological parameters (for example, glucose, electrolytes, creatinine, prothrombin time, heart rate, blood pressure, and biogenic amines). If unobtrusive physiological-measuring and drug-dosing devices can be developed, it would seem that the next logical step is to develop a telecommunications system allowing the patient to "download" these physiological parameters into a computer for monitoring and dosage adjustment.

III. DRUG DEVELOPMENT

The drug development process has also undergone major change. Traditional methods called for a mass screening of compounds extracted from soils or plants to identify those with biological activity. This trial-and-error method was costly and time-consuming, requiring as many as 10,000 compounds to find one potentially useful drug, and eight to 10 years of research (and many millions of dollars) before a drug product could be approved for marketing (Brodie and Smith, 1985).

This "shotgun" approach has been considerably improved. There is now a much better understanding of the relationships between biological activity and chemical structure of organic compounds. This knowledge about structure-activity relationships is important in helping scientists predict the probability of a certain type of biological activity for a new agent. Time-consuming and expensive screening procedures can be minimized, and synthesis of new compounds can be guided by probability estimates of biological activity. Computer graphics, mass spectrometry, and nuclear magnetic resonance imaging techniques have helped pharmaceutical scientists unravel the mysteries of structure-activity relationships.

Our discussion of technological developments would not be complete without discussing the "second pharmacological revolution." According to Teeling-Smith (1983), the first pharmacological revolution bloomed in the early 1900s, with the discovery of aspirin, sulfonamides, antibiotics, psychotropics, and other drug families. In each case, the pharmacological intervention involved an exogenous substance that, upon being ingested, modified physiological function. Anti-inflammatories, beta blockers, calcium channel blockers, and angiotensin converting enzyme inhibitors are results of this line of research. As the first pharmacological revolution reaches maturity, scientists are on the brink of discovering new neurotransmitters for treating neurological conditions (such as Parkinson's disease and Alzheimer's disease), and new mood-altering drugs with specific affinity for binding sites in the brain which can serve as definitive treatment for severe mental illnesses.

The second pharmacological revolution arose from Crick and Watson's pioneering work in the 1950s to elucidate the structure of the DNA molecule. Their work helped explain intracellular processes and led to the current explosion in research on the body's immune system. Through manipulation of the autoimmune system, the actual cause of the disease is attacked, and cure can be the goal, rather than merely palliative treatment. Moreover, these techniques will contribute new diagnostic methods for early detection and treatment of previously untreatable or undetectable pathologies. If the second pharmacologic revolution fulfills its promise, we may eliminate such scourges as acquired immune deficiency syndrome, various cancers, and immune system pathologies before the twenty-first century.

IV. COMPUTERIZATION AND AUTOMATION

The impact of the computer has been pervasive through health care delivery, as in many other sectors of our society. There is a vast literature describing physicians' use of computers in research, education, and patient care. Some familiar as well as not-so-familiar examples are computerized tomography, patient risk assessment based on population demographics, and computer-assisted diagnosis. Yet, most of the mainstream of medical practice occurs the way it has occurred for centuries. A physician office visit consists of a verbal exchange with the patient; the physician reviews handwritten notes on the patient chart; some procedures are performed; and some drugs are prescribed in handwritten fashion on a small piece of paper that is given to the patient. Delivery and presentation of this small piece of paper to the pharmacist stimulates his work and contribution to the health care process.

While all professions are advancing at a rapid pace toward routine computer usage, pharmacy is especially poised for such an advance and, in fact, has incorporated computers extensively into its practice (Campbell, 1986). An examination of selected characteristics of the prescription dispensing process reveals some clues as to why this has occurred. For example, the traditional practice of pharmacy includes:

1. Frequent patient-pharmacist encounters of relatively short duration;
2. Definable units of service (e.g., a prescription) centered around an identifiable product or products;
3. Responsibility to record and analyze information within a relatively limited dataset (e.g., patient, drug, program); and
4. Unscheduled and unpredictable nature of encounters with attendant need for immediate response.

Pharmacy has now reached a point of interdependence between the practitioner and the computer. The American Pharmaceutical Association/American Association of Colleges of Pharmacy Report on Standards of Practice states that a pharmacist in any setting is responsible for: (1) maintaining a current medication record, (2) checking the record before dispensing a medication, and (3) advising the patient or prescriber on any significant problems or special directions for use (Kalman and Schlegel, 1979). This process requires accurate, complete, and accessible data, a task that computers perform quite readily.

To date, computer systems have been used more extensively in community, as opposed to hospital pharmacies. Two basic needs have compelled retail pharmacists to adopt computers. One is to assist in prescription record retrieval. Prescription records must be rapidly retrieved for refills and for review of drug usage. While this is a relatively easy, if time consuming manual task, changes in pharmacy regulations and practice standards in the 1970s made it more complex. Pharmacists in many states are now required to also maintain records chronologically by patient as a patient drug profile. Patient drug profiles permit pharmacists to perform certain clinical functions as part of the dispensing process, such as: checking for drug interactions, reviewing the pattern of drug usage of a patient for purposes of determining appropriateness of a new or refill prescription request, monitoring patient drug-taking compliance with chronic drug therapy over time, and checking for potentially interacting combinations of drugs. Computerized maintenance of prescription records in a data base greatly facilitates these tasks.

A second need fulfilled by the computer is third-party billing. The diversity of third-party programs and the volume of drugs dispensed and billed through them have generated substantial paperwork demands on practicing pharmacists. Most of these demands can be reduced or eliminated through computer automation.

A typical computer system also performs other valued tasks. For example, it can query the prescription data base to tabulate drug usage reports of particular interest to a pharmacy manager. The computer's ability to maintain actual acquisition cost prices and current replacement cost prices on the thousands of drug products in a typical pharmacy inventory greatly facilitates pricing and billing activities. This is especially important during periods of frequent price changes, as it allows automated pricing of prescriptions in a manner that reflects changes in drug replacement costs.

The computer's impact on pharmacists in the institutional environment is somewhat different. In this setting, pharmacists have used the computer to enhance the efficiency of existing drug distribution tasks. Further, the computer's data base management capabilities have allowed more efficient access to drug use data in a manner that has facilitated implementation of new clinical services. Some typical computer-generated reports in use in the computerized institutional environment are listed below (Fassett and Christensen, 1986):

Patient record data base management
Medication order entry
Production of drug labels and fill lists
Preparation lists for intravenous solutions and admixtures
Drug utilization review
Drug information literature retrieval
Drug therapy problem detection
Drug therapy monitoring
Drug formulary search and update
Purchasing and inventory control
Billing for pharmacy services

Drug utilization reports and management information
Integration of drug data base with other hospital departments

V. DRUG INFORMATION

Two notable observers of the pharmacy scene have stated that just as robots have displaced workers from the assembly line, the computer will reduce the need for the dispensing pharmacist and increase the need for supervisory personnel (Brodie and Smith, 1985). They assert that clinical and managerial skills, particularly those involving the transfer of drug knowledge and information, will be in demand, and that the shift in emphasis from dispensing medicines to dispensing information could be the single most transforming effect of technology on the profession. Let us further reflect on this notion by considering information management needs within the integrated health care system.

One focus has been the development of drug information services. The increasingly complex nature of medical practice and the breadth, as well as diversity, of drug information have made it difficult for the average health professional to stay current with the state-of-the-art of drug therapy. Specialization has helped, but health care systems such as hospitals and health maintenance organizations have sought more organized approaches to resolving this problem.

An early approach was to designate a pharmacist as a drug information specialist, who would be responsible for providing drug information services to the medical staff. This service consisted of a passive role in responding to drug information questions as they were raised, as well as a more active role in disseminating pertinent new information in a timely manner through newsletters or other media. The institution's pharmacy and therapeutics committee typically uses this resource in fulfilling its charge of assuring appropriate drug distribution and use within the institution. Drug formulary systems are common to the institutional environment, and their maintenance requires a constant review of new information about drug products.

The computer has been particularly helpful in meeting drug information retrieval needs. First, and most obvious, is the time saved in conducting literature searches. Formerly, a pharmacist would expend several hours searching *Index Medicus* to thoroughly research a particular therapeutic question. Second, a computerized search is more accurate and more pleasant. Several data base services exist for conducting searches, and these can be easily and quickly conducted over telephone lines using a logical set of data base query commands (Malone, 1986).

There is also a need for organized drug information to facilitate drug distribution and patient care. A particularly evident change in the institutional environment is the growing interdependency of information systems between pharmacy and other operating units. To understand this transition, an understanding of hospital practice as it existed 30 years ago is helpful. Hospital departments and service units functioned autonomously and more or less independently. Up to the early 1960s, a hospital pharmacy performed what was essentially a wholesaling function. Stock bottles of drugs were maintained on hospital floors by nurses, who prepared individual doses for patients in soufflé cups prior to each administration period. The pharmacy's primary role was to periodically replenish this supply, and to prepare extemporaneous compounds when needed.

In contrast, today's hospital drug distribution system illustrates multiple departmental interdependencies. Drug orders are directed to the pharmacy from the hospital floor as before, but are generated by the physician via chart drug order notations. The hospital pharmacy's data base consists of patient information gathered from the hospital's admission, discharge, and transfer (ADT) system and typically includes data on patient location, age, sex, admitting diagnosis, drug allergies, past medication history, blood chemistry, and organ (for example, kidney) function (Fassett and Christensen, 1986). This information is used by pharmacists for drug monitoring and dosage calculation. A close interdependency exists with the laboratory system as well, since laboratory values can affect drug-dosing decisions, and the presence of drugs in patients can affect laboratory values. Computer systems have become invaluable tools to gather, store, and process these diverse information needs.

Finally, the information needs for the management of the integrated drug systems must be recognized. Within pharmacy, information needs can be differentiated into that needed to assist drug distribution, drug information flow to facilitate patient care, and that needed for purposes of administration and management. In the last area, an organized system is especially needed for purchasing and inventory control, third-party billing, drug use review, cost accounting, and budgeting. Once again, these information needs are most effectively met by an integrated computer system.

VI. FINANCING OF DRUG SERVICES: THE EMERGENCE OF THE THIRD PARTY

Public policy and private enterprise arrived at the same conclusion during the 1980s: Health care could no longer be funded on a cost-reimbursed basis. As providers of care incurred and passed along higher and higher costs of operation, payers (insurance companies, state and federal government) encountered greater difficulty in raising the necessary revenue through premiums, taxes, or out-of-pocket patient expenses. Eventually, when the medical care equivalent of a $500 defense contract screwdriver became commonplace, cost-based reimbursement systems were scrapped in favor of negotiated payment systems. In such programs, the provider of care was offered a "take it or leave it" price for services offered, with the price often representing less than the total costs of delivering services. While unpopular with providers, negotiated payment systems have rendered obsolete the cost-reimbursed systems that forced some insurance programs to (and sometimes past) the brink of insolvency.

The situation with regard to prescriptions is somewhat unique. While medical care in general has been moving toward becoming a fully insured commodity, prescriptions have remained largely uninsured. Currently, about twenty percent of per capita payments for prescriptions are covered by insurance, while nearly ninety percent of per capita payments for hospital days are covered by insurance. The reasons for this are not hard to discern; insurance is intended to pay for high-cost, unpredictable expenses which have low incidence in a population. Prescriptions are (at least relative to hospital days) low-cost and widely distributed in the population. Thus, coverage for outpatient prescription drugs has developed slowly in the private insurance industry, and outpatient prescriptions drugs were notably omitted from coverage when Medicare legislation was enacted in 1966.

Insurance coverage for prescription drugs is, however, likely to be much more extensive by the end of the decade. In some metropolitan areas, coverage for prescription drugs already approaches fifty percent of per capita expenditures, and political pressure is mounting to add outpatient prescription drugs to Medicare. As coverage expands, there will be greater pressure to control costs through administrative means, and to develop alternatives to fee-for-service reimbursement for providers. Newer methods of case-based reimbursement (for example, capitation) will impose further incentives to pharmacies to reduce utilization and reduce costs of drug services.

Population-based risk sharing is new to the community pharmacy and is only slowly being accepted. Individual patients' use of services will continue to require careful scrutiny at the point of medical care contact. It will also be necessary to monitor population use rates and detect early deviations from projections. Providers will be compelled to select lowest-cost products (for example, generic and therapeutic equivalent drug products) for dispensing, and to prevent costly overutilization or misutilization. This is proving to be a difficult, and some would say unfair, assignment to pharmacists. While the pharmacist does have some control over refill patterns and the use of generic drugs, present practice standards and regulations provide the pharmacist with little discretionary power in influencing the selection of the drug product for dispensing. Pharmacists can exert some influence over drug utilization by monitoring compliance rates and checking for drug interactions and therapeutic duplications. However, the optimum application of capitation-generated incentives for control of drug costs clearly involves collaborative risk sharing and cooperative working arrangements between the prescriber and the pharmacist.

VII. MARKET FACTORS AFFECTING COMMUNITY PHARMACY

Several effects are obvious in this shift of financing. One is the hastening of new forms of competition for prescription services. At one time, chain and independent pharmacists battled in the marketplace for the loyalty of individual consumers, who paid cash for prescriptions. This battleground was well understood and time-honored. More recently, new entrants have entered the marketplace competing for segments of the merchandise mix traditionally offered by community pharmacies. For example, nearly half the market for over-the-counter cosmetics, toiletries, and nonprescription drugs today is accounted for by supermarkets and mass merchandisers. The market for home health and durable medical equipment is burgeoning and is increasingly dominated by specialty retailers.

In the 1980s, new forms of competition for prescription services have emerged. Mail-order firms are proliferating. So, too, is office-based physician dispensing of prescription drugs. Economic incentives have fostered a rapid growth in prescriber dispensing, despite concerns raised by professional associations that this practice represents a flagrant conflict of interest and is, therefore, unethical. Other forms of competition for retail pharmacy are small to moderate-size medical clinics, such as emergency care centers, that dispense directly to their patients.

Networks of retail pharmacies have been formed to negotiate and deliver prepaid prescription services to third-party programs. In some cases, a chain pharmacy organization can demonstrate sufficient geographic distribution to deliver prepaid prescription benefits. In other cases, a group of independent pharmacies may form voluntary networks (called pharmacy service administrative organizations, or PSAOs) to negotiate and deliver prescription services. The competitive model to medical care organization has created a system where organizations are willing to accept discounted reimbursement rates in return for exclusive access to a group of eligible recipients.

As the third-party prescription market increases, it will be increasingly difficult for the independent pharmacist to survive without affiliating with other pharmacies through provider networks. It may be expected that these networks not only will proliferate, but will begin to take on the characteristics of a voluntary chain, with common name identity, standardization of prescription product/service offerings, and group purchasing to capitalize on economy of scale efficiencies.

VIII. MARKET FACTORS AFFECTING HOSPITAL PHARMACY

Perhaps the most dramatic change affecting the environment of the hospital has been the method of reimbursement. For years, retrospective, "cost-plus" reimbursement was the order of the day. For the pharmacy, as well as other hospital departments, this amounted to an open policy to develop and expand services with little financial worries. The Tax Equity and Fiscal Responsibility Act was passed in 1982, and final regulations affecting Medicare program funding were published by the Health Care Financing Administration in 1984. These regulations set forth a new basis for payment of hospital care for Medicare beneficiaries based on groupings of diseases with similar treatments costs.

This change is having a dramatic ripple effect on all service departments within the hospital. Reimbursement based on Diagnosis Related Groups of diseases (DRGs) places hospitals at a financial risk to provide care in an efficient manner, and provides incentives for earlier discharges, shorter lengths of stay, and, if possible, less costly in-hospital care.

Early discharge results in a greater need for home-based care, an area as yet unaffected by the prospective reimbursement. Hospitals have expanded to meet these needs by developing home care programs. Pharmacy services in the home care environment are also needed, and hospital pharmacies have geared up to offer services such as home total patient nutrition, home IV antibiotic therapy, and home-based pain control systems involving drugs (for example, so-called pain cocktails) as well as nondrug devices (such as TENS machines).

Drug usage in the hospital is directly affected by these incentives. Cost control is, for the moment, the factor driving changes in the nature of pharmacy services. Systems for monitoring drug usage and drug costs per day and per DRG episode are being developed. Drug costs are being examined and compared to peer group hospitals linked through management/utilization information sharing networks.

Most large hospital pharmacies now have in place several programs to control drug costs. Examples are pharmacokinetics consultation and similar services aimed at influencing drug prescribing and use, greater use of drug formulary systems, drug use review, and target drug programs. Other programs to control drug acquisition and distribution costs include bid purchasing, automated inventory control programs, and the use of technicians.

There is also a new emphasis on use of cost-benefit and cost-effectiveness criteria to evaluate pharmacy service programs. While the primary emphasis is on reducing drug costs, a more farsighted approach recognizes increases in drug costs as acceptable where it can be shown that they contribute to shorter lengths of stay or are a trade-off for more expensive modalities of care (for example, that they avoided surgery). New service programs are increasingly being assessed using these criteria. For example, pharmacokinetics consultation services performed by pharmacists have been shown to be cost-effective in reducing the number of laboratory tests (serum drug assays) conducted, and have been shown to contribute to shorter lengths of stay or greater patient survival for particular drugs and disease states (Bootman et al., 1979; Horn, Christensen, and deBlaquiere, 1985).

IX. CHANGES AFFECTING THE WORK ACTIVITIES OF PHARMACISTS

The trends discussed above clearly point to major changes in the manner in which drugs are used and how pharmacy is practiced today and will be practiced in the future. These changes have been the subject of considerable discussion by pharmacy leaders and educators. In fact, future crystal ball-gazing has been the popular parlor activity for pharmacy over the past few years (Bezold et al., 1985; Gourley et al., 1985; Study Commission on Pharmacy, 1975; Zellmer, 1986). Several other major trends destined to have an impact on the nature of the future pharmacist's work are briefly discussed below.

Third-party coverage of prescription services and a shift to capitation-based reimbursement is producing two countervailing forces in community pharmacy. One is a tendency to reduce contracted pharmacy services to a minimum common denominator: a prescription-only dispensing service. Related clinical and counseling services are not specifically reimbursed at present. On the other hand, capitation-based reimbursement provides pharmacists additional incentives to provide ancillary services aimed at achieving more appropriate drug use or reduced costs. Unfortunately, the profession to date has not convincingly documented its contribution in this area, particularly in the community practice environment.

A strong cost control orientation toward health service delivery will continue to affect the practice activities of pharmacists. At least in the near term, there is every reason to believe that the rigorous application of cost-benefit and cost-effectiveness criteria will continue. The institutional pharmacy administrator will need to justify existing services such as unit dose and satellite distribution systems, as well as nondistributive services. This is in contrast to a decade earlier, when assessments of the effectiveness of clinical services (if performed at all) consisted of reports of helpfulness and perceived improvements in patient care by physicians, nurses, and patients. Today, documentation and outcome-focused justifications are essential to the continued existence of clinical programs, and it is imperative that these programs describe a reduction in overall costs. It will be increasingly necessary to document how service-specific clinical programs reduce drug toxicity, drug incompatibilities, inappropriate use, costs, and lengths of stay.

Within the ambulatory environment, increased market competitiveness among third-party programs will drive efforts to control costs. There will be greater use of current cost-cutting techniques such as patient copays, generic drug incentives, and drug formularies, as well as lower reimbursement levels for pharmacies. For pharmacists, this means exploring ways to acquire and dispense drugs at lower cost.

The "graying of America" deserves mention as another major trend affecting the delivery of health care. Increasing attention will be directed to this population segment, not only because people are living longer, but because of the graying of the baby-boomers. Because of their sheer numbers, this segment will demand more attention of the health care delivery sector. Their health needs reflect both the physiology of aging and longevity. The problems of health maintenance when multiple chronic disease states are involved contribute to increased use of medical services and drugs. The complexities of the drug regimen (more drugs, more doses) increase the potential for drug interactions as well as the potential for inappropriate drug-taking behaviors. By way of training and accessibility, pharmacists are ideally situated to perform drug-use monitoring and patient instruction services to address these problems, but whether or not they do so will depend on numerous factors, notably reimbursement arrangements.

Consumer-based marketing and consumer behavior are further factors likely to affect health care delivery for some time to come. The competitive model has spawned high levels of competition for patients. Just a few years ago, it was unheard of for hospitals or health care insurers to advertise for patients. The winners in the new health care entrepreneurship race will be those who are best able to keep patients satisfied, quite aside from the types of services provided or not provided. Naisbitt's observations (*Megatrends*) of the high-tech–high-touch phenomenon would seem to apply to health care. Consumers' enrollment and patronage decisions will be affected by mass media advertising and by the interpersonal skills that health care providers, including pharmacists, demonstrate.

It has been predicted that many traditional medicines as we know them will be readily available without a prescription, their safety and efficacy having been proven by decades of use (Bezold et al., 1985). Consumers will increasingly self-diagnose, self-prescribe, and favor the use of generic drugs. But they will need some source of education and counsel in the process. Consumer segments continuing to pay for drugs out of pocket (such as the elderly) will favor outlets offering low prices (for instance, mail-order houses), while others with some third-party coverage will patronize those pharmacies offering high-touch services.

X. SUMMARY

It seems clear that the identified forces of technological change will have some dramatic effects. The very shape of drugs will differ, as will the manner in which we administer them to our bodies. The practice activities of pharmacists will be much different in institutional, as opposed to ambulatory, settings. At the same time, a trend toward earlier hospital discharge and extended home-based services is blurring the traditional distinction between the hospital and community pharmacy. It is easy to envision the next step: a focus on continuity of patient care from hospital bed to home bed to full recovery, and coordination of this care by a single health professional team.

The question of who will provide drug dosage adjustment and drug monitoring is much less certain. Physicians' assistants now perform routine diagnoses of uncomplicated cases and monitoring of chronic disease under the general supervision of the physician. Nurses are increasing their drug knowledge base, and are performing many more patient monitoring functions. Pharmacists are now trained in pathophysiology, patient therapy monitoring, and patient interaction skills, and are involved in patient dosage adjustment and monitoring activities.

The pharmacist's clinical roles will ultimately be determined by some combination of the nature of evolving drugs and drug delivery systems available, continued training in drug monitoring techniques, and the success of efforts to document via cost-effectiveness criteria contributions to patient care. In the final analysis, however, roles will probably be most directly shaped by the outcome of internecine turf battles with other health professionals attempting to provide the same services. The ancient Chinese curse "May you live in interesting times" would seem to apply.

REFERENCES

Bezold, C., Haperin, J. A., Binkley, H. L., and Ashbaugh, R. A. eds., 1985. *Pharmacy in the 21st Century–Planning for an Uncertain Future*, Institute for Alternative Futures, Project Hope, Bethesda, Maryland.

Bootman, J. L., et al. (1979). Individualizing gentamicin dosage regimens in burn patients with Gram negative septicemia–A cost benefit analysis, *J. Pharm. Sci., 68*: 267.
Brodie, D. C., and Smith, W. E. (1985). Implications of new technology for pharmacy education and practice, *Am. J. Hosp. Pharm., 42*: 81.
Campbell, W. H. (1986). Future directions, *Computer Applications in Pharmacy* (W. E. Fassett and D. B. Christensen, eds.), Lea & Febiger, Philadelphia, p. 244.
Fassett, W. E., and Christensen, D. B., eds. (1986). Hospital pharmacy computer systems, *Computer Applications in Pharmacy*, Lea & Febiger, Philadelphia, p. 202.
Gourley, D. R., Hadsall, R. S., Gourley, G., Fine, D. J., and Wiener, M. (1985). ASHP members' concepts of institutional pharmacy in the year 2000, *Am. J. Hosp. Pharm., 42*: 96.
Horn, J., Christensen, D. B., and deBlaquiere, P. A. (1985). Evaluation of a digoxin pharmacokinetic monitoring service in a community hospital, *Drug Intell. Clin. Pharm., 19*: 45.
Kalman, S. H., and Schlegel, J. F. (1979). Standards of practice for the profession of pharmacy, *Am. Pharm. NS19*: 133.
Malone, P. M. (1986). Drug information retrieval and storage, *Computer Applications in Pharmacy* (W. E. Fassett and D. B. Christensen, eds.), American Pharmaceutical Association, Washington, D.C.
Study Commission on Pharmacy (1975). *Pharmacists for the Future*, Health Administration Press, Ann Arbor, Michigan.
Teeling-Smith, G. (1983). An historical perspective, *The Second Pharmacological Revolution* (N. Wells, ed.), Office of Health Economics, London, p. 7.
Zellmer, W. A. (1986). Perspectives on Hilton Head, *Am. J. Hosp. Pharm., 43*: 1439.

Unit VI

Data Administration and Information Systems in Human Services Administration

15

Integrated Information Systems Concepts: An Information Resource Management Approach

Edward M. Jackowski Graduate Program in Human Services Administration, School of Education, Rider College, Lawrence, New Jersey

Barbara Stevens New Jersey Department of Corrections, Trenton, New Jersey

I. INTRODUCTION

Data are, and continue to be, the most valuable and least accountable resource that managers have under their supervision and control. This chapter discusses several methods and techniques that can be used to integrate information systems in organizations which vary in size (small to large), longevity (under development to fully operational), and complexity (single-celled to multidimensional). As a highly productive undertaking, the integration of information systems is a complicated process and requires the complete involvement and dedication of senior management and their staff. Imperative to a successful data management program is that senior management initiate and mandate the processes required to manage, control, and share the data resource. An umbrella approach that recently came into existence for the purpose of maximizing the use of the data resource is information resource management (IRM).

IRM suggests that the joint efforts of both the human being (abstract and heuristic thinking) and the computer (high-technology configurations and structured thinking), working in unison, are essential if we intend to harness data as a valued resource. In order to achieve relatively successful data integration, the chapter's theme focuses on the use of highly flexible data integration design standards to obtain the desired results. Data integration causes organizations to behave in manners which are contrary to the norms found in the management literature of the Industrial Revolution and, therefore, requires a retooling of the organization's human and computer resources. Organizations will have to adapt to new work situations and management requirements unavoidably created as a result of the IRM approach.

The effective management of the corporate data resource necessitates the use of standardized approaches to integrate information systems. Systems designed according to first-generation design principles have their underlying foundation in early schools of management. Not understanding the effects of high technology, and the changes it would bring, managers had no way of recognizing the need to merge the data requirements of the different functions of the organization. To move from first- to second-generation design principles associated with data integration and IRM is a gradual process, building upon principles developed by early management schools, not a traumatic changeover.

The chapter reviews basic data integration principles, concepts, and foundations that will assist organizations in making the transition from stand-alone, first-generation environments to second-generation integrated information systems using the IRM approach. Section II reviews the management and organizational functions of an organization and describes an integrated information systems framework. Section III discusses the merging of the three information systems technologies (data processing, office automation, and data communications) and reviews the responsibilities of information systems design teams (executive steering committees and project management design teams).

Section IV defines basic information systems terms and proposes the use of a five-phase, IRM-SDLC (systems development life cycle) method. Section V discusses several integration design tools, such as a three-stage data integration model, data dictionaries, and the characteristics and features of data base management versus file management systems. It also reviews several codification structures associated with the successful employment of data integration principles. Lastly, sec. VI provides closing comments and a propositional inventory concerning the future directions an organization should follow when contemplating the management, control, and sharing of the data resource.

II. INTEGRATED INFORMATION SYSTEMS FRAMEWORKS

As the lifeblood of contemporary organizations, information systems cut across, and are typically designed, according to each of their management and organization functions. In an effort to operate productively and with the fewest problems, management has as a prime responsibility the division of the organization according to diverse labor specializations. These artificially contrived specializations (also known as boundaries or functions) are one part of an organizational mosaic that scientific management has labeled information systems (Mescon, Albert, and Khedouri, 1981, pp. 35-60). From a parochial standpoint, each information system in an organization represents the sum total of data elements required by a particular functional area, such as finance, personnel, facility planning and design, research and development, and program management.

During the 1960s and 1970s, information systems were developed and viewed as isolated, disposable systems constructed for one particular purpose: the fulfillment of the myopic needs of one functional area. They were designed with a shortsightedness or lack of relationship to other functions. In reference to automated information systems, this myopia was quite understandable, since software associated with the period was developed to solve specific problems within an organization. Known as file management system (FMS) software, its use in the realm of integrated environments was limited by the training and knowledge of the information system department's staff and by the lack of knowledge or ignorance on the part of senior and middle management. Informed information systems designers and programmers were not encouraged to develop applications that sought maximum use of the data resource.

Only recently (in the late 1970s and 1980s), through integrated data design strategies, have information systems been viewed from a total data resource management perspective. Administrators and technicians armed with relational data base management system (DBMS) software of this recent era are now beginning to understanding the benefits gleaned from systems planned in an integrated fashion. DBMS software fosters the sharing of the data resource by identifying solutions to a problem through an integrated IRM approach (Fosdick, 1985).

FMS software of earlier periods did not provide for the integration of smooth and uncomplicated applications and the user-friendliness associated with DBMS software. Furthermore, an FMS method traditionally was used to develop information systems as isolated files and entities (records) instead of using advanced DBMS methods when designing systems. (A discussion of the characteristics of DBMS software methods is provided throughout the body of this chapter.)

A. Information Systems Framework

Integrated information systems frameworks are now possible because of advanced (flexible) information systems design methods coupled with relational DBMS software (Konsynski, 1984-1985). Flexible systems are those designed to be user-friendly and provide maximum data utilization. The integrated information systems framework proposed in this section capitalizes on flexible and modular information system designs that take into consideration the unique data requirements of the major functions within an organization. To be effective, an integrated information system must first consider the data needs of each organizational function and then provide information for use by each of the firm's or agency's management functions.

Basically, an organization has two functions that must be satisfied by an information system: Both organizational and management functions are required to meet an organization's goals and objectives as dictated by the governing board or chief executive officer. Each function is necessary to provide the input required to meet the organization's purpose. Organizational functions pertain to the specialized work breakdowns of an organization—personnel, finance, research and development. Management functions relate to the responsibilities of senior, middle, and supervisory management—the decision-making processes of planning, organizing, directing, controlling, and evaluating the organization.

Before continuing with a discourse on integrated information systems, a knowledge and understanding of an organization is essential. To best illustrate the complexities and the cross-impacts that occur within an organization, a management and organization function matrix is discussed. Then, an integrated information systems framework is described from the viewpoints of an organization's operating information system, management information system, and decision support system.

1. Management and Organizational Function Matrix

The management and organizational function matrix shown in Fig. 1 recognizes the relationships between the management and organizational functions within an organization.

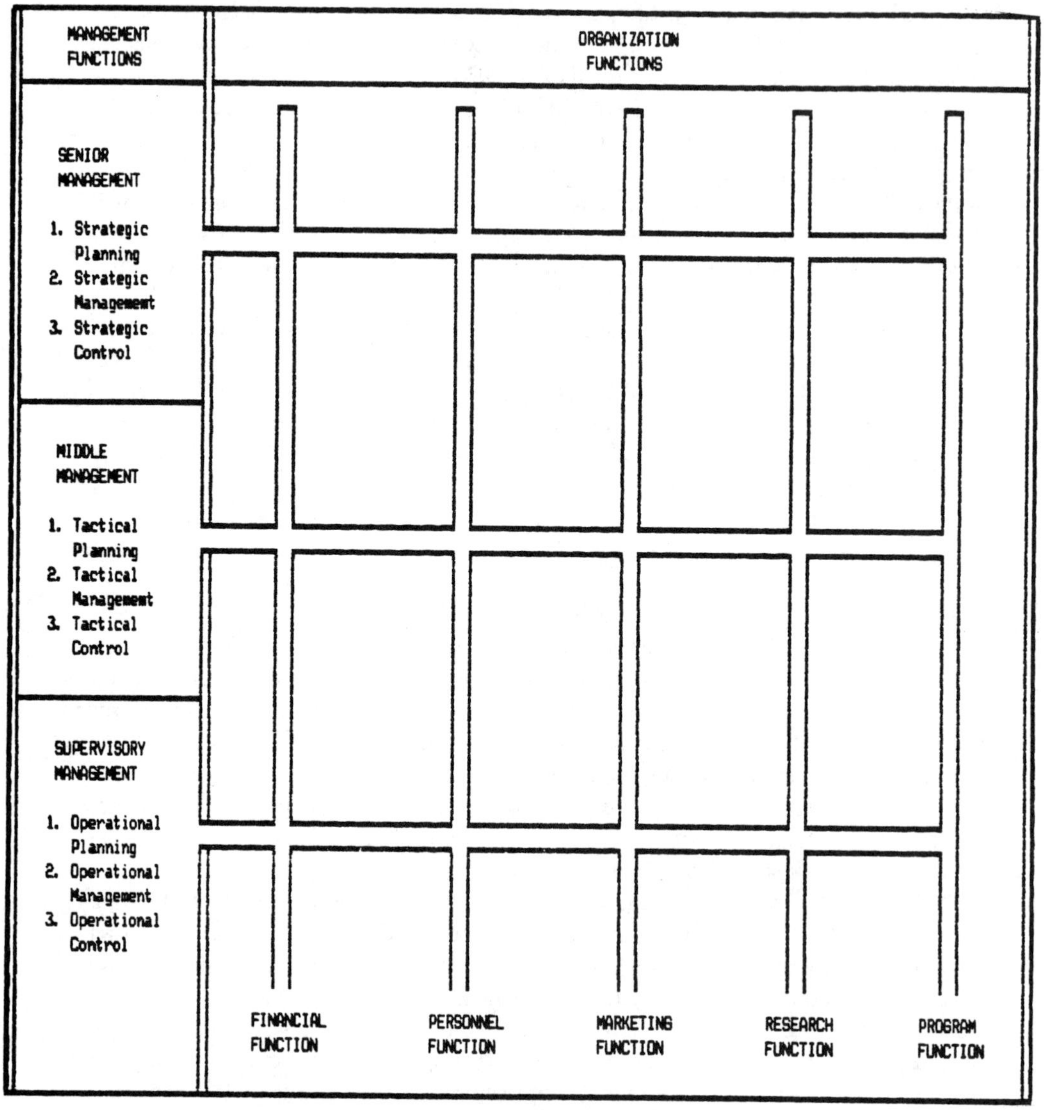

FIGURE 1 Management and organization function matrix.

A description of the management functions (horizontal cells) and organization functions (vertical cells) in the matrix is as follows:

a. Management Functions

The horizontal cells differentiate the management levels of the organization by senior, middle, and supervisory distinctions. Each management function is described below.

1. The senior management function relates to the role the chief executive officer performs in planning the strategies and policies concerning where the organization as a

whole and individual organizational functions are proceeding in the short- and long-range future (1 to 10 years). Paramount to this management function are the major policy-setting and coordinating issues that relate to how the organization intends to function in the future. What makes this level so complex are the numerous political, societal, and economic issues that influence the organization and at times throw off its equilibrium.

2. The middle management function is responsible for assisting and providing senior management with data needed to plan for the short- and long-range future, and to monitor or control present development or operating conditions within the organization. Middle management develops the tactical planning, management, and control activities necessary to accomplish the goals of senior management and direct the workload of supervisory management. In their unique, catch 22 role, middle managers function as organizational buffers to satisfy the needs and wants of both management extremes (i.e., #1 and #3).

3. The supervisory, or operational, management function is responsible for the efficient day-to-day use of the resources allocated by senior management to their respective areas of operation (Kallman and Reinharth, 1984). Supervisory managers are concerned with providing the services or products needed by their clients and with supervising personnel under their jurisdiction. Operational decisions emanating from this management function concern the execution of specific, production-oriented tasks that must be carried out in an efficient and effective manner (Hicks, 1984).

Kallman and Reinharth (1984) studied the supervisory management function in depth and state that it has experienced significant change within the last 20 years. Prior to the development of automated systems, a supervisory manager and his or her staff were often under enormous stress to generate data summaries upon which management could make a decision. As a normal part of their responsibilities, they processed and manipulated thousands of transactions of data internal to the organization. Because of the enormous volumes of data associated with this management function, supervisory managers were limited to the use of internal data when they developed alternative choice, or what-if, statements concerning their sphere of decision making; external data were not considered an important and useful resource for this level of management.

Each management function shown in Fig. 1 is responsible for planning, organizing, directing, and controlling the goals and objectives of the individual organizational functions falling under its jurisdiction.

b. Organization Functions

The vertical cells in the function matrix pertain to each of the distinct organizational functions necessary to administer the organization: finance, personnel, marketing, facility planning and design, research, and program management. The decomposition of the function of an organization into these separate specializations is a result of the need to cope with the various responsibilities associated with operating a complex configuration containing numerous regulations and procedures. Each function operates in conjunction with, and under the direction of, any one of the three management functions previously described.

It must be understood that an organization's functions are not limited to those contained on the function matrix or mentioned above. These are used for illustrative purposes only.

2. An Integrated Information Systems Framework

Organizations intending to remain competitive in the marketplace require data to be integrated across each management function—senior, middle, and supervisory. All arenas require decision- and conclusion-oriented information—information that collectively aids a particular management and organization function in performing its daily operations.

Figure 2 delineates the different types of information systems required by each function in an organization. As shown, the classic management pyramid, as constructed by Anthony (1965), has been superimposed over the management and organizational function matrix (Fig. 1) to form an integrated information systems framework. The open grid lines in the matrix denote a data channel that enables data to flow freely from one organizational function to another, as well as between the management functions in the information systems hierarchy.

Detailed, transaction-oriented reports are needed by supervisory management. As the data moves up the pyramid and are provided to middle or senior management, they are summarized to provide an overall view of the organization. In some cases, reports only are generated when an exception to the norm occurs (commonly referred to as variance reports). Through this process, management is provided with exception reports based upon hard data generated from transaction level information in the operational information system (OIS).

As a strong foundation, the data contained in the OIS are summarized, and management information system (MIS) "management by exception" and short-range planning reports are generated for use by middle management. From the other extreme, OIS and MIS data are summarized and manipulated through various forecasting techniques to provide senior management with a decision support system (DSS) that calculates both short- and long-range projections for advanced decision making. Without a well-structured and though-out OIS, it would be impossible to provide management with its long sought-after MIS and DSS capabilities.

Descriptions of the three information systems follows.

a. Operational Information System

The OIS is the foundation for both the MIS and the DSS, and is a response-oriented system, processing data at a detailed, operational level (Inmon, 1984). An OIS performs significant, transaction-oriented data processing, such as payroll, accounts payable, accounts receivable, student scheduling, and order processing. Transactions generated through the OIS are identified and recorded through specific organizational determinants and codification structures.

Sprague (1980) succinctly traced the electronic data processing (EDP) OIS, MIS, DDS evolution, and isolated five commonalities of operational information systems. Although Sprague does not strictly define the five commonalities as OIS characteristics, they certainly demonstrate the components and goals of an OIS functioning to the satisfaction of management. These commonalities are as follows:

1. Focused data inputs, storage, processing, and system flows
2. Efficient transaction processing
3. Scheduled and optimized computer runs
4. Integrated files for related jobs
5. Management by exception (variance) reports

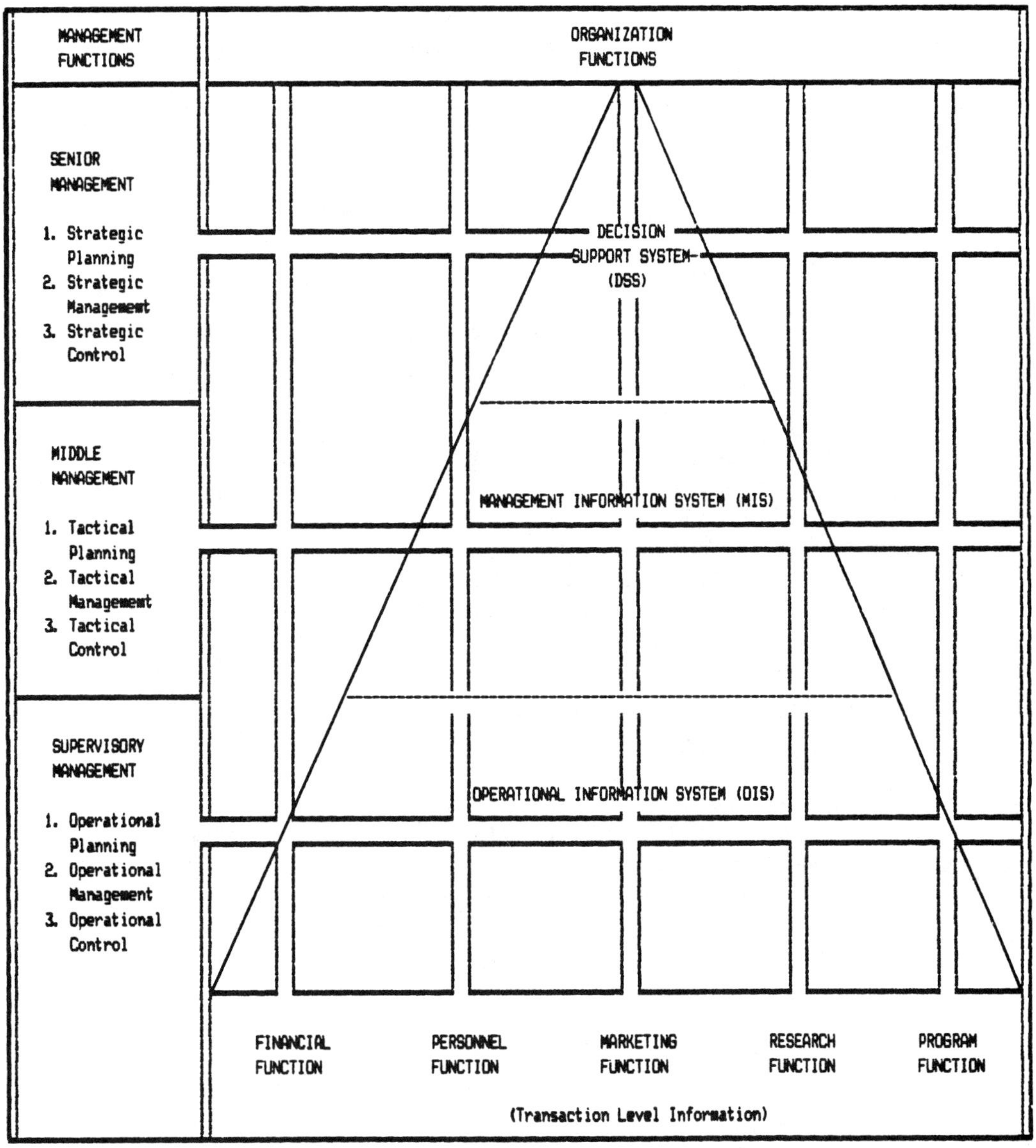

FIGURE 2 Integrated information systems framework.

From an integration standpoint, the data in each discrete OIS of an organization must be capable of sharing and exchanging data through open channels of communications. Open channels must be architecturally designed to enable an organization to operate effectively and efficiently by reducing the need for redundant data. Data integrity is a principal concern of the OIS; therefore, the type of data on which operational systems run remains fairly static (Inmon, 1984).

When using an integrated systems design, it is of the utmost importance to have a moderately or, if possible, a fully functional OIS before advanced decision-making capabilities are realized. It is through the OIS that detailed data enter the information systems framework and become validated, processed, and then used by supervisory, middle, and senior management for the sundry responsibilities required of these respective positions.

b. Management Information System (MIS)

The MIS concept, as shown in Fig. 2, is linked to the tactical functions performed by middle management. The purpose of an MIS is to provide middle managers with an integrated set of data files and entities which produce reports that assist middle managers in making sound and practical management decisions.

An MIS is not built over night. It requires a sound OIS foundation consiting of numerous building blocks. The foundation cannot be realized without long-range systems planning being understood, designed, and strategically and tactically monitored by senior and middle management.

Once an OIS is operating for a particular organizational function, the MIS can then draw upon the data in a summarized fashion, using information already captured and stored by the data processing system (Hicks, 1984). The summarized data (historical and current) are available to middle management to understand the organization's present and short-range situation and also to monitor and control its operation. What-if questions about the organization's current operations are capable of being generated for the purpose of enabling decision-oriented answers.

c. Decision Support System (DSS)

DSS is a relatively new term in the information systems (IS) field, and was coined by Morton and Keen (1971). Unlike both OIS and MIS, DSS-generated questions pertain to sophisticated, what-if statements about the short- and long-range future. They are built on the knowledge gained from the MIS area. DSS information is used in the realm of senior management's highly unstructured decision making. As shown in Fig. 2, DSS is at the apex of the management pyramid, draws upon the universe of data contained in other information systems to aid in the senior management decision-making and planning process by making assumptions about the future, and is a distinct activity, differing from both the MIS and the OIS areas.

Computers are support mechanisms for DSSs and, when linked with appropriate IS architectural designs, assist managers in the decision-making processes (semistructured tasks), support rather than replace managerial judgment, and improve the effectiveness of decision making (Keen and Morton, 1978). Critics contend that DSS is simply another buzzword, while others argue that DSS is a subset of MIS, since MIS includes all systems which support any management decision (Carlson, 1977). As used in this chapter (Fig. 2), a DSS is an entity seprate and distinct from an MIS.

Regardless of one's perspective concerning DSS, it has identifiable characteristics much as OIS and MIS have. DSSs are built upon the unstructured, implied needs of a user, while OISs and MISs are built upon the structured, explicit needs of a user. DSSs are high-risk, decision-oriented systems used by senior management strategists and other high-level decision-makers who require flexibility, adaptability, and quick data responses. Moreover, DSS is a user-initiated and controlled system which supports the personal decision-making styles of individual managers (Sprague, 1984). Ultimately, higher level decisions established from the data in the DSS must be coupled with the judgment and intuition of management.

The state of the art regarding implementation of an integrated information systems framework, as presented in this section, is still in its early stage of development. Such frameworks draw heavily upon the knowledge of other disciplines and can exist only if senior and middle managers want to increase effectively the use of the data resource.

The integration of an organization's information systems (management and organization functions) is a strategic and tactical management issue. Organizations must understand that integrated frameworks require discipline, flexibility, standard operating procedures, and long-range planning. Integrated frameworks are not givens, and must be installed in an organization which possesses the climate needed for a successful information systems operation. The next section focuses on integrated design assumptions and prerequisites related to merging of information systems technologies and project management design teams.

III. INTEGRATED INFORMATION SYSTEMS TECHNOLOGIES AND DESIGN TEAMS

Advances in information technology (data processing, office automation, and data communication) occurring over the past three decades have caused integrated information systems design efforts to be continually refined and redesigned. Design concepts employed by the information systems community have changed not only because of information technological improvements, but also because of the overwhelming need to manage the unprecedented amount of paperwork occurring throughout all organizational environments as we entered further into the Age of Information.

Another factor affecting information systems designs is the shift in the corporate placement of the information systems function. Prior to the 1970s, information systems were housed mainly under the direction of the finance department. Their position was one of a second-class citizen catering to the needs of a specific area of responsibility. Only recently, due to the competitive advantage offered by integrated information systems designs and the clamoring for responsiveness by the user community, is the reverse true, with the status of the information systems department and its responsibility being elevated to a noteworthy member of the senior management team.

Assumptions and prerequisites concerning the design of information systems and their infrastructures have been ever changing. An important assumption associated with the construction of today's information systems is the existence of a need to design organization-wide data structures (architectures) which reflect intradata and interdata relationships between and among the different information systems and data elements in the organization. This design should be identified as a high prerequisite before the selection, if possible, of computer hardware and software. State departments, municipalities, school districts, hospitals, and other institutions or agencies, when preparing their information systems plan, should be attentive to the design of an organization-wide data architecture before attempting to identify the resources needed for integrated information systems. The development of an integrated architectural (data structure) design should be addressed by the information systems department through a rigorous analysis and synthesis of the data requirements of the organization.

Under current conditions, it is inevitable that many advances will occur in information systems designs now and in the future. As an information-prevalent society, we are only beginning to enjoy the fruits of such endeavors. To provide orderliness in the design of information systems, senior, middle, and supervisory management design teams should be formed and provided with the tools and knowledge for designing and using integrated information systems data structures—data structures that will provide them with a means of easily communicating in today's competitive environment.

In keeping with the topic of integrated information systems (the linkage of like data elements), this section defines and describes the technologies and terms associated with contemporary information systems and the responsibilities of an executive steering committee and project management design teams. Their understanding is necessary for systems designers (users and information systems staff) and their management counterparts to harness the full capability and integration of the data resource. As information technology and its terms change, the information designer's mind must be open to conceptual and physical design situations that have an impact on information systems under development (Edwards, 1985).

A. Information Systems: Three Related Technologies

Information systems may be defined as the "merging of the technologies of data processing, office automation, and telecommunications" (McFarlan and McKenney, 1983). For the purpose of this chapter, "data communications" is a more descriptive term than telecommunications and will be substituted for that third field of technology. Each technology, their combined use, and an example are discussed.

1. Data Processing

Contemporary electronic data processing has existed since the 1960s; the term refers to the automated recording, processing, and dissemination of numeric data (rows and columns), rather than data associated with words and letters (word processing). EDP became popular in the 1950s, with the development of unit record equipment and the standard 80-column Hollerith card (Orilia, 1986). Today, punched cards are almost a phenomenon of the past, with data being entered on-line and stored directly on magnetic tape or disk instead of indirectly with punched cards. Data processing accounts for approximately 10 percent of an organization's information processing requirements (Taggart and Silbey, 1986).

2. Office Automation

Office automation is an all-inclusive term referring not only to word processing, but also to such functions as electronic mailing, calendar management, electronic filing, and facsimile copying (Martin, 1984). Word processing is the basic building block for office automation. It is the manipulation of an organization's words into various types of office correspondence (memos, letters, and reports). In reference to EDP, office automation accounts for approximately ninety percent of an organization's workload (Taggart and Silbey, 1986). Yet, only recently, with the advent of the microcomputer in the late 1970s and early 1980s, has word processing become the dominant contender for the use of the computer resource.

3. Data Communications

Data communications is the transfer of data from one destination to another. It includes not only distributive data processing (DDP) and other means of transmitting data through telecommunications, but also hard-wired local area networks (LANs). DDP, or the linking of computers in different geographic locations, would not be possible without telecommunications. LANs communicate data over hard-wired (coaxial or optical cables) lines from one terminal or computer to another in one geographic area.

Telecommunications is the subset of data communications responsible for the transmission of data and words over non-hard-wired communication lines (such as satellites, microwaves, and multichannel radios). This technology is responsible for new dimensions in the field of information systems, and enables information transfers from one computer to another in different parts of the country. Telecommunications is used, for example, by state governments to communicate between their data centers and the diverse counties within their geographic boundaries; by school districts wanting to time-share the computer as a common resource and thereby maximize cost savings; and, extensively, by the Department of Defense (Haverty and Tauss, 1986, pp. 54–58). Simply stated, telecommunications enables data to be communicated from one point to another, whether it be across a street or to the other side of the world.

As a result of telecommunications, on-line transaction processing (OLTP) systems are possible at remote sites; OLTP makes possible, through common data bases, the interactive use of terminals by users for adding, inquiring, and updating data bases (Serlin, 1985). Future telecommunication systems in the 1990s and beyond must be designed to incorporate the emerging technology of integrated services digital networks (ISDN) with other technologies of information systems. ISDN is the transmitting of voice, data, text, and video over telecommunication lines (Horwitt, 1986).

4. Integrating Information Systems Technologies

Information systems traditionally have been designed to process quantitative data as opposed to words; however, office automation, at its current rate of growth, will surpass data processing. Therefore, information systems designers can no longer limit their designs to data processing alone. The design of integrated information systems data structures must incorporate the full range and power of both word and data processing capabilities. Future-oriented systems must be designed to capture data (alpha and numeric) that can be extracted from data files (sets) and incorporated directly into the body of a letter, memo, or other type of reporting medium.

5. An Example of Integrating the Three Information Systems Technologies

The San Diego city school system's definition of office automation (as presented at the 1986 Association of Educational Data Systems conference in New Orleans) is all-inclusive and merges the three technologies of information systems (data processing, office automation, and data communications) into an integrated whole. Specifically, office automation is defined as "a system that provides a full set of office functions to every office worker through workstations that are connected through a network which supports communications and information sharing."

Based on this definition, the San Diego city schools divided office workers into three categories: support staff (secretaries, clerks, typists, and word processing operators), professionals (accountants, specialists, analysts, and technicians), and managers (principals, directors, assistant superintendents, and vice principals). Office functions addressed consisted of typing, filing, word processing (documentation revision and origination), document retrieval, mail, duplicating, calendar management, personal computing, data processing, and records management. Data processing involved using data base management system software to establish data structure schemas, data elements, data entry and query screens, and output reports and searches.

By identifying, categorizing, and synthesizing the data structures of several offices, the integration of data processing, office automation, and data communications technologies is enabling office workers to interface their data needs between and among themselves in highly productive communicative environments. As illustrated by the San Diego city schools, the "office of the future" is a reality that is being achieved through the use of advanced data integration and architectural data structure design concepts.

B. Information Systems Design Teams

Highly productive information systems are those which utilize integrated information management data structure design concepts. Ideally, these systems communicate across organizational boundaries and attain maximum cost savings for each dollar spent to process information. Although achieving this goal is not an easy task, farsighted managers must begin to think in ways that cut across the functions (management and organizational) of the organization; they must understand, from a design and architectural standpoint, that efficiencies never can be realized if information systems engineers are not consulted, and managers continue to model their systems designs (data structures) according to the discrete stand-alone functions of the organization.

Information systems engineers (data architects) must provide systems designers and managers with directions which open their minds and enable them not to be burdened by the political pressures related to separate, unconnected ownerships of data.

Every organization has a wealth of data which serve as an essential resource (Popek and Jacobsohn, 1983). The recognition of data as a vital strategic resource has only emerged in recent times. As Martin (1982, p. 265) states, "Overall management is needed for most data." He is alluding to the need to identify and treat data as an organization-wide integrated resource, instead of fostering the design of independent data structures for the explicit purpose of solving a given problem.

Managing data as an organization-wide resource requires an IRM project management system (PMS) and corresponding information systems design teams. The IRM-PMS identifies, monitors, and controls past, current, and future data requirements.

After an IRM-PMS is in operation, interactive information systesm design teams can be formulated to share and inhibit the redundant use of the data resource. The design teams' purpose is to function as the fulcrum for the design of integrated data structures. Design teams work in conjunction with the staff of each production or support service program area in the organization. They assess their individual data and reporting requirements before interfacing their requirements with other information systems data structures in the organization.

To ensure adequate data structure designs, criteria must be developed against which information systems design teams (executive steering and project management) can measure their results. The evaluation criteria selected must be based upon the strategic goals and objectives of the corporate organization and the intrinsic needs of user management. If information systems and their data structures are designed in isolation, and managers do not consider the integration and sharing of the data resource between and among organizational segments, these criteria never will be used successfully. Now, more than ever, as systems designers begin to use advanced information systems technologies and second-generation design techniques, systems integration is a requirement that cannot be ignored; neither can its evaluation.

1. Executive Steering Committee

When designing integrated systems, project management design teams should receive their overall direction from an executive steering committee composed of senior management from the various divisions of the organization as well as from the chief information systems officer. An executive steering committee's purpose is to oversee the entire mix of new and enhanced information systems being proposed through the IRM-PMS (the information systems department and user-management are jointly responsible for identifying new developments and enhancements to existing systems). Information systems projects receiving approval are used as inputs into the organization's IS plan. If necessary, when beginning the data integration process, the committee need do nothing more than review existing information systems to gain an understanding of their effective utilization.

As a top-level management committee, the information systems executive steering committee is crucial to the data integration process. It has many responsibilities, such as setting policy, planning, monitoring, and settling organizational disputes arising over the sharing of a program's data. As an information system nears completion, special attention must be paid by the steering committee to monitoring and controlling each project. Nolan (1982) reported that in a 1982 survey of 127 companies, eighty-five percent had corporate-wide executive steering, whereas in the mid-1970s, fewer than fifty percent of the organizations had such committees. The purpose of the steering committee is to translate the organizational strategy set into an information resources strategy set (King, 1985)—that is, to define the strategies of an IRM system based upon both the intrinsic and the extrinsic goals and objectives of the organization.

2. Project Management Design Team

Once an information systems project is identified for inclusion in the IRM-PMS and approved by the steering committee for development or enhancement, the next step is the organization of a project management (PM) design team. The PM design team should consist of users (managers and professionals) and information systems specialists (systems analysts and programmers). To ensure project integrity, a user-manager and data administrator (a person or organizational unit responsible for controlling and reducing the fragmented use of data) should function in an advisory capacity to the PM design team.

The PM design team, during its initial phase of operation, must identify the needs of the data user in a systematic mode. This is crucial if desired outcomes—user satisfaction and nonfragmentation of data across organizational lines—are to be achieved.

It is very important that users be totally involved in the design of information management systems. In organizations with advanced understanding of the processes that must transpire, a user is the manager of an IS project. Grindly (1984) notes 10 critical measures for evaluating an MIS department. His sixth critical measure states that a project manager for application systems approved by a steering committee (the creation of a committee is the fifth critical measure) should be a user.

An industry-wide lack of information systems personnel, coupled with advanced views on how information systems should be constructed, requires that organizations become responsible and initiate user training programs. These programs must educate end-user personnel regarding the general methods and techniques associated with an IRM-PMS and the functions of a PM design team.

When integrating information systems, the PM design team must understand that data elements (attributes of a record) in reports generated from proposed information systems should be concatenated, if possible, with data contained in other information systems in the organization. Each management function in the organization then will be provided with those reports necessary to perform its particular decision-making functions; this is especially important for senior management, which cuts across the functions of the organization.

The data administrator is an important member of the PM design team, and acts in an advisory and change agent role. In the broadest organizational responsibility, the data administrator (incorrectly identified as the data base administrator by some authors) establishes and enforces standards for the use, control, and security of all files and entities comprising the data base (Burch, Grudnitski, and Strater, 1983).

The data administrator, along with user-management, plays an ancillary, but important, role in the functioning of the PM design team. Both the data administrator and user-management are concerned with maximizing the limited resources of the organization. User-management wants reports generated that can provide the best possible answers to questions needing resolution; the data administrator wants to ensure the integrity of the data elements contained in the overall data structure.

This discussion assumes that the PM design team is functioning within a future-oriented organization, where managers approach data as a corporate resource and take full advantage of the three IS technologies described: data processing, office automation, and data communications. It is important to understand that concepts of integrated information systems can be utilized only in highly organized systems which use sophisticated hardware and data base management methods in their design. Without a proper design method, integrated information systems data structures are doomed to failure.

In the future, PM design teams should incorporate data base management, word processing, graphics, spreadsheets, and communications in the formulation of information systems that are geared toward the full decision-making needs of the entire organization. As improved software is made readily available, information systems PM design teams will be challenged. The entire organization inevitably will change along with the character of its evolving information systems.

IV. INTEGRATED INFORMATION SYSTEMS DESIGN TERMS AND METHODS

Armed with an understanding of the frameworks, technologies, and design teams (personnel) associated with information systems, it is equally important to understand widely used terms and methods. The terms and methods must be viewed from the standpoint of the corporate organization and each of the organization's segments. Consistency in terms and methods is essential for the design of integrated information systems. In this highly complex field, there are many different terms and methods. This section discusses the definition of integrated information systems and integrated design methods.

A. Integrated Information Systems Defined

Integrated information systems have many meanings. Before proceeding with a definition, it is most appropriate to understand the basic components necessary for any system to exist. Information systems, no matter how simple or complex, require four basic components: inputs, processes, outputs, and dissemination.

1. Inputs

Inputs are data elements, source data derived from source documents (data collection instruments). Once the source documents are gathered, or collected, the distinct data elements are entered into the computer.

2. Processes

Processes are performed in the computer, and are ways of manipulating data elements. Processing can be as simple as sorting or merging a list of clients being served by an organization; it also can be as complex as performing a statistical analysis—for instance, a factor analysis to derive an equitable funding rate for school districts receiving Aid to Families with Dependent Children or hospitals developing Diagnosis Related Group information.

Data elements involved in processing can be source data or derived (calculated) data. Source data elements are those inputted into the computer from a data collection instrument (source document), sight inspection (visual), or audio (telephone) conversation. A derived or calculated data element is one generated by adding two or more source data elements together or performing any Boolean operation to create its existence.

3. Outputs

Outputs are the products or reports generated by the computer after both source and derived data elements are arranged in a manner which can be used by the decision maker. Outputs can be simple listings of data elements or single calculated data elements generated in response to complex queries. They can be generated in the format of a select query language, a customized payroll (OIS report), a performance analysis statement (MIS report), or an alternative repositioning statement (DSS report). Outputs can be in the form of pure data, information (data with meaning), or knowledge (information with intuitive value).

4. Dissemination

Dissemination is the last component; data outputs are distributed in the form of storage media, paper reports, or responses produced on a visual display unit (computer terminal). Data outputs can be carried by hand from one location to another or transmitted electronically. If dissemination does not occur, there is no reason for collecting the data in the first place.

Keeping within this four-component discussion, integrated information systems must be designed in view of the total environmental communication system within which they exist. As organizations move into the realm of advanced systems design methods, managers must be cognizant that an information systems schema consists of both internal and external environmental subschemas. In designing an overall conceptual design for integrated information systems, systems architects must take into consideration all data elements having an impact upon an information system's productivity. Data schemas and subschemas, whether they be internal or external, all have input, process, output, and dissemination characteristics associated with their design.

Figure 3 identifies terms associated with the parts of a hypothetical financial information system. The diagram is designed in the format of an interlocking mosaic that, for illustrative purposes, shows the overall schema for a financial system. The data schema is broken down into both internal and external subschema (data modules). Internal and external subschema must be designed modularly and provide a capability that allows them to be joined together, if necessary, through highly complex data relationships which foster an integrated, yet flexible, design. A mosaic IS design enables internal and

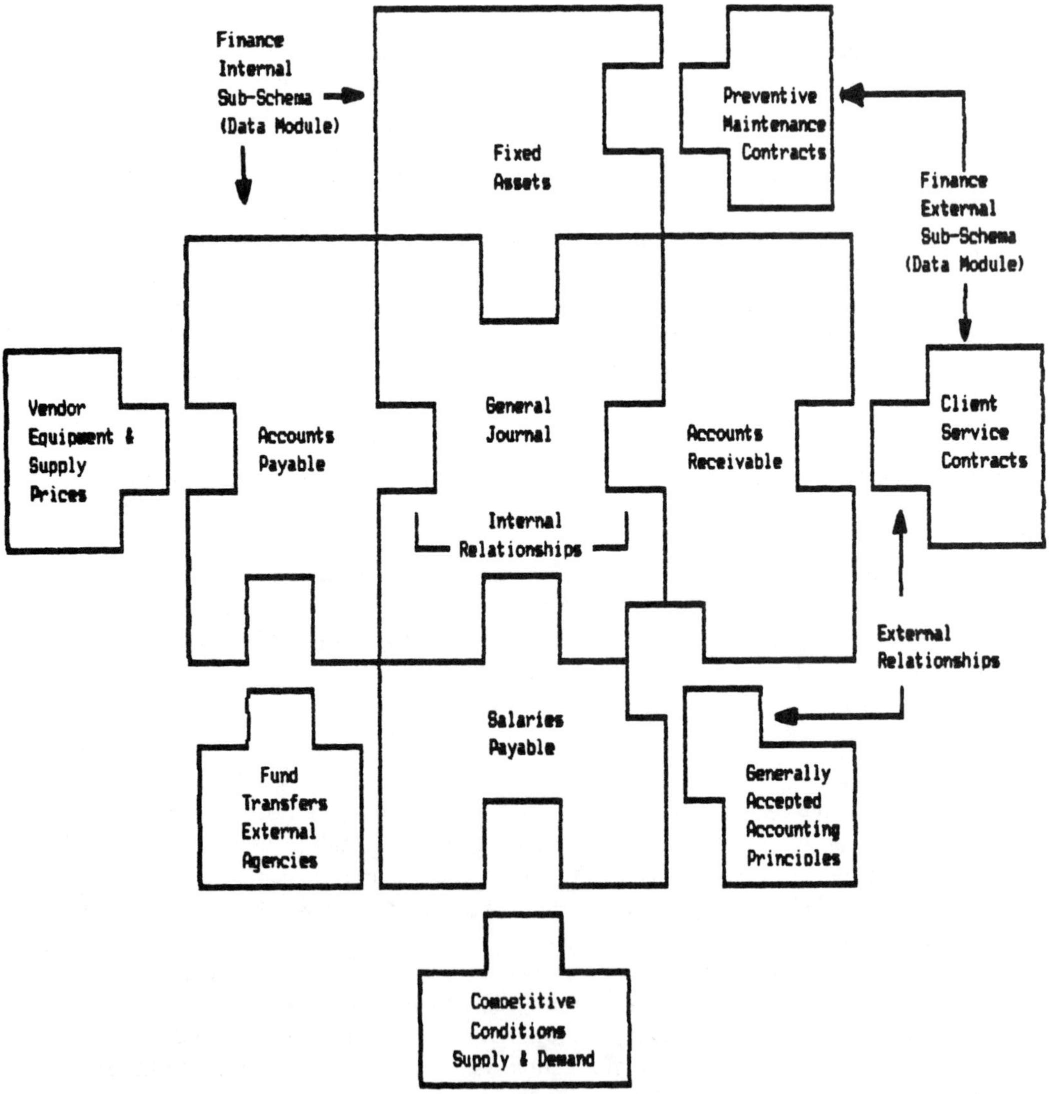

FIGURE 3 Financial information system: Schema (information system) and sub-schema (data modules).

external subschema data modules to be integrated and linked together through data relationships fashioned in a style similar to the interlocking pieces of a jigsaw puzzle.

As shown in Fig. 3, the internal data modules consist of fixed assets, accounts payable, salaries payable, accounts receivable, and general journal. The external data modules consist of vendor equipment and supply prices, fund transfers to external agencies, generally accepted accounting principles, client service contracts, and preventive maintenance contracts. Each of these data modules contains data elements unique to its existence. It is through these data elements and their internal or external data relationships that systems architects are provided with a capability to integrate and link the data modules in an information system. A linked set of data elements and their corresponding data modules form either an internal or an external subschema.

By designing information systems in a mosaic configuration, systems architects are able to visualize how to integrate and link data elements in any part of the schema (overall environment) with various subschemas; for example, the external subschema pertaining to vendor equipment prices is joined to the internal fixed assets subschema, and through this relationship, data elements have a capability of flowing not only to the fixed asset module, but also through internal subschema data flow channels to the general ledger subschema.

Just as in a jigsaw puzzle, all of the pieces in the internal and external subschema relate to form the whole. A missing piece in the puzzle can lend a distorted view to the overall picture; therefore, in an information system, a missing link will produce a distorttion in one's logical view and may affect relationships that could be formed. Logical views of IS designs are the perceived views of users versus physical views that pertain to how a schema's or subschema's data elements are structured, stored, and accessed by a computer's hardware or software (Martin, 1977).

The terms "schema" and "subschema," which became popular with the use of data base management system software packages in the 1970s, are interchangeable with the terms "systems" and "subsystems." The term "subsystem" also has been used interchangeably with "application."

At different points in the evolution of an information system, a system can be called a subsystem, and a subsystem can be called a system. For example, an organization's information system consists of several subsystems. They are finance, personnel, research, marketing, and production. Each of these in its own realm is known as an information system and has subsystems or subschemas (data modules) associated with it. The finance information system shown in Fig. 3 has a general journal, accounts payable, accounts receivable, fixed assets, salaries payable, and inventory subsystems. Each of these subsystems, in turn, has its own particular applications represented by various types of inputs or outputs.

The meaning of an organization's information system can cause confusion to both user and IS managers alike. An information system can be defined as the organization's entire communications system or a specific type of information system in the organization; that is, it can refer to an OIS, MIS, or DSS. When used with an adjective, such as finance, personnel, student, or client, it refers to an information system performing a specific function. The use of an adjective plus operational, management, or decision support provides us with a further breakdown of an information system; for example, a finance OIS, finance MIS, or finance DSS. An integrated information system is one that contains minimum data element redundancies, whether it is by type or function. It refers to a system that has data independency and shareability.

B. Integrated Design Methods

The majority of IS departments in existence today follow a standard design method when constructing an information system. The methods are known as systems development life cycles (SDLC); (King and Srinivasan, 1988; Taggart and Silbey, 1986). These SDLCs normally follow a common theme, have several phases associated with their accomplishment, and are used to define, design, implement, and evaluate new information systems, or to modify or enhance existing systems. Traditionally, SDLCs have been used to design stand-alone (nonintegrated) systems constructed along the dimensions of programming languages such as COBOL, BASIC, PL/1, and Pascal, and were utilized to design information systems that have one purpose to accomplish. The use of complex integrated data structures formulated by IS engineers and the organization's design teams have only recently become capable of being accomplished due to technological breakthroughs in the area of high-level, user-friendly software.

Before reviewing the phases of an integrated SDLC, it is important to understand that data integration will require existing stand-alone information systems to be retrofitted. The time commitment and funding put forth to accomplish this conversion endeavor will more than justify the resources and effort involved. The rationale for the retrofit should not be compared to an upgrade of computer hardware and the corresponding conversion of existing applications programs. That would be like comparing apples and oranges. The retrofitting of existing information systems to an integrated environment will have a much greater impact on the organization than witnessed in past hardware or software conversion efforts.

SDLCs coupled with the principles of IRM assume that an organization intends to manage its information systems in a unified, nonfragmented, and integrated manner. When integrated IS data structures are designed through the use of an IRM-SDLC, they will be able to identify intricate data interrelationships, and make possible the most complex user-initiated revisions, which designers cannot begin to realize. An IRM-SDLC should be used by organizations seriously contemplating the integration of their data resource within the confines of a single, multidimensional data base. The purpose of an IRM-SDLC is to design an organization's information systems under a unified umbrella approach versus the traditional stand-alone approach. Figure 4 is a paradigm which explains a five-phase IRM-SDLC designed by Jackowski. The upper portion of the figure identifies the five phases (IRM conceptual data flow model; integrated information systems cross-impact matrix; definition; system development and implementation; and evaluation, training, and maintenance) and feedback channels of the IRM-SDLC. The lower portion provides generalized descriptions of each of these phases. Phases III and IV are traditional SDLC phases; phases I, II, and V ensure that information systems are not being designed in isolation and that data are being shared and treated as a corporate resource. Following is an in-depth discussion of each of the phases of the IRM-SDLC.

1. Phase I (IRM Conceptual Data Flow Model)

The IRM conceptual data flow model is the first, and most important, phase, and considers the entire organization as one function with many facets and logical views. Facets are the different functions and information systems currently existing in contemporary organizations; logical views represent the combined views (information systems) of all users of the IRM system (Martin, 1977).

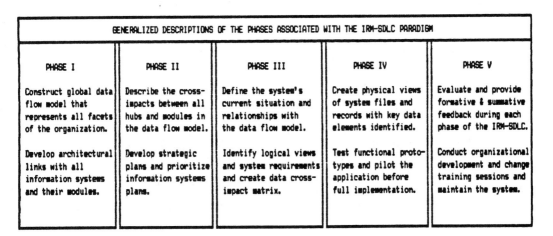

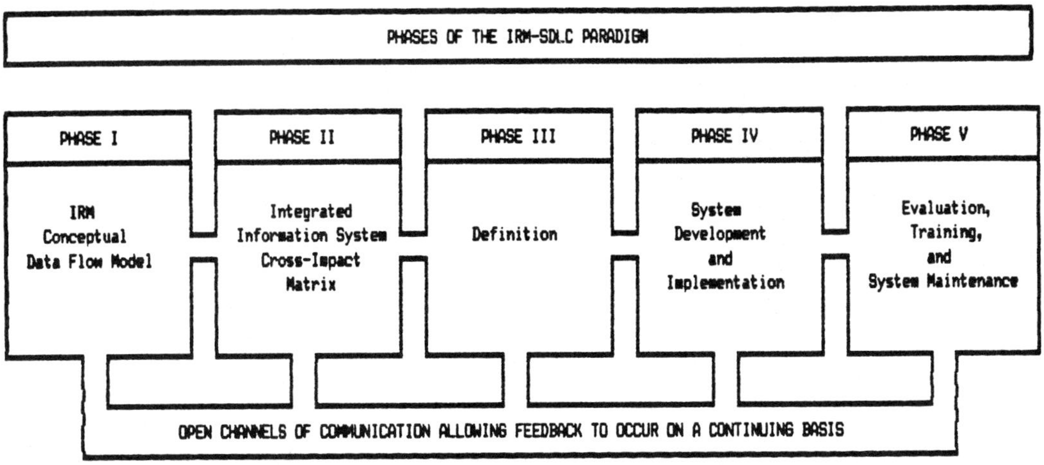

GENERALIZED DESCRIPTIONS OF THE PHASES ASSOCIATED WITH THE IRM-SDLC PARADIGM				
PHASE I	PHASE II	PHASE III	PHASE IV	PHASE V
Construct global data flow model that represents all facets of the organization. Develop architectural links with all information systems and their modules.	Describe the cross-impacts between all hubs and modules in the data flow model. Develop strategic plans and prioritize information systems plans.	Define the system's current situation and relationships with the data flow model. Identify logical views and system requirements and create data cross-impact matrix.	Create physical views of system files and records with key data elements identified. Test functional prototypes and pilot the application before full implementation.	Evaluate and provide formative & summative feedback during each phase of the IRM-SDLC. Conduct organizational development and change training sessions and maintain the system.

FIGURE 4 Information resource management system development life cycle (IRM-SDLC) paradigm.

The IRM model should be engineered by systems architects, who develop relational information hubs about every facet of the organization. A relational information hub represents those data elements that pertain to a common function. A hub can be subdivided into data modules that categorize a given function's purpose. For example, a finance information system can be classified as an information hub, with its subsystems being the data modules. An acronym used to describe the model development process a systems architect must follow is LORIE (for logical organization of relationships in an integrated environment).

Systems architects responsible for the design of the IRM model must consider the logical views of all current and future users of the system in the organization. They must understand the different relationships (indigenous and exogenous) that currently exist and those which may evolve and become integrated in the future. Environmental modifications may be required due to external and internal forces; for instance, government regulatory changes might necessitate system modifications. If it is to be effective, the IRM model must respond to questions arising from all facets of an organization's environment. Due to the complex design processes associated with IRM systems, systems architects must be able to conceive multiple relationships; the architects also must understand the effects their deliberations will have on the organization and the behavior of personnel whose job descriptions eventually will change.

Ultimately, the IRM-SDLC conceptual data flow model is a global representation of the organization. It has consistency, but remains fairly liquid over time, in order to allow flexibility and periodic modifications to occur as dictated by the organization's rules and regulations.

2. Phase II (Integrated Information Systems Cross-Impact Matrix)

The construction of an integrated information systems cross-impact matrix is the second phase of the IRM-SDLC. The matrix has several dimensions associated with its construction, and describes the cross-impacts which exist between each data module in an information hub. A data module, as noted above, relates to an information system's subfunctions. Each of the IRM model's different IS data modules must be prioritized by an executive steering committee, whose purpose is to identify the impact each data module has upon the strategic plans of the organization. This process also should determine information system planning strategies and identify when a data module should be slated for programming and implementation. It is important to understand that relationships exist between data modules, and the prioritization of one data module may have a major impact on whether or not another can be programmed.

The executive steering committee is responsible for developing both the strategic and the system implementation plans for each IS in the organization. The committee's main responsibility is to review, evaluate, and prioritize the inclusion of new developments or major enhancements to existing systems. During phase II, the committee reviews the impact each module has upon the short- and long-range goals of the organization. As a focal point, members can relate their decisions to external regulations and requirements, and to the internal needs of middle and operational management. In addition, as long-range planners, members should, through the help and guidance of their staff, identify those data elements they need in the decision support system.

Because the steering committee is composed of members of senior management, its attention should not focus heavily on operational systems. Committee members should approve data modules and data elements which receive the highest conversion priority from middle and supervisory management. Conversion priorities are associated with existing stand-alone information systems or data modules slated to be integrated into the IRM system. (Phase II receives its input from the IRM conceptual data flow model constructed in phase I, and is similar to the first two phases in the SDLC proposed by King and Srinivasan [1988], strategic planning and system planning.) Once approved for development, a data module or application can be scheduled for movement into the definition phase (phase III).

An information systems planning method developed by IBM to aid management in the process of identifying priorities is business systems planning (BSP). As stated by Murray (1988), BSP "concentrates on the applications systems portfolio of an organization, identifying areas lacking effective systems . . . and setting priorities for their development."

McFarlan (1981) has provided extensive research regarding the portfolio approach to systems planning and development. The approach entails an assessment of the individual risks associated with a project and a mix of projects in the organization's overall IS portfolio in advance of implementation. McFarlan traced the failures of major organizational information systems projects, attributing failure to the following: the failure to assess individual project risk, the failure to consider the aggregate risk of a portfolio of projects, and the lack of recognition that different projects require different managerial approaches.

3. Phase III (Definition)

The definition phase of the IRM-SDLC consists of three steps: (1) defining the current situation relevant to the information system or data module under development, (2) identifying the required outputs based upon user and management interviews, and (3) reviewing existing IRM information hubs and their corresponding data structures to ensure the data requirements defined in step 1 and identified in step 2 are nonduplicative.

Step 1 requires existing data relationships and logical views of users and management to be defined and considered by the PM design team and the data administrator before the required outputs of step 2 are identified. As part of defining the current situation, step 3 requires a review of all information hubs' data structures influencing the desired results of the IS data module as it currently exists. Data relationships identified in other information hubs also must be incorporated into the design of the outputs identified in step 2. The cross-impact matrix, discussed in phase II, is a vital part of this process. From a data administrator's viewpoint, step 3 requires the matrix of phase III to be defined further and constructed for each of the data elements in the different data modules of an information system. This step involves an intense scrutiny of the data relationships which exist between and among the organization's information systems.

The process suggested here is similar to Shah and Davis's (1988) "service analysis," which calls for the functional decomposition and development of workflow charts used in the process of analyzing an entity's data requirements. As input to the information system planning process noted in phase II, service analysis, coupled with a data element cross-impact matrix, is a data management tool that provides excellent assistance in deliberating which IS data modules should be prioritized for development. In addition, this tool provides systems architects, integraters, designers, analysts, programmers, and users with a total view of the organization when conducting an analysis of the proposed impacts of the new or enhanced development.

As part of step 3, each information system data module selected for development or enhancement by the executive steering committee must be defined in regard to its relationship with the IRM system. System flow diagrams of existing information hubs and data structures must be constructed and then reviewed with the data administrator and user-management. As part of step 2, prototypes of each required output report should be constructed and reviewed with each user in order that feedback on its design can be secured (Adamski, 1986). If the prototypes meet the requirements of the users, system flow diagrams then should be developed showing the relationships that the proposed system has with the rest of the organization.

4. Phase IV (Systems Development and Implementation)

The fourth phase in the IRM-SDLC, systems development and implementation involves the designing of the processes necessary to write and test computer programs, and prepare and implement the system by either a direct or a parallel cutover. Whereas the logical views of the users were defined in the previous phases, this phase relates to the physical view of the system. It is important that the application be integrated into the design of existing systems; thus, physical views of the file (data sets) layouts must be prepared to show the data relationships that exist between tables or files (relations) in the data base. This is accomplished by identifying key data elements in the relationships and specifying the codification structure required for each data element to perform its function.

When constructing either tables (files), reports, or listings, it is important to show the data entry screens or documents that are used for each particular data element and the outputs to be generated. The outputs should identify lookups that are required. Lookups refer to the identification of other relationships (tables) that are necessary to prepare a report in addition to the primary relation (tables). Complete documentation is mandatory, since it would be almost impossible for a PM design team to retrace the steps followed by an analyst or programmer without a proper paper trail. The interrelationships involved are rather complex and must be taken into consideration when systems outputs are scheduled for production.

Testing of the prototype system should be intensive, to ensure proper implementation without loss of data integrity. The system must incorporate the knowledge of all PM design team members, as procedures are prepared for both systems and user personnel. If the testing of the application is successful, the next step is the application's implementation. Before doing either a direct or a parallel cutover, a pilot test should be performed by the project team. The pilot organization should be selected with utmost care, in order that it not destroy the credibility of the system under development. Implementation strategies, especially those in an integrated environment, must consider all relationships newly formed or currently in existence. The choice of implementation strategies is the key to the success of any type of information system under development, especially, an IRM system.

5. Phase V (Evaluation, Training, and System Maintenance)

Evaluation, training and system maintenance are conducted concurrently with the other phases in the IRM-SDLC. Evaluation concerns whether or not the PM design team has implemented successfully the new or enhanced system according to the objectives defined in phases III and IV. Evaluative criteria should be delineated, obtained, and provided concerning both the logical and the physical views of the system under development. Evaluations must take into consideration productivity gains made in regard to the organization's goals and objectives and the individual objectives of the users. Feedback must be provided, not only during the different phases of the IRM-SDLC, but also after the system is in operation for a given time period and, afterward, during the system's life span, to ensure the proper management of changes that may be required periodically.

Evaluative interviews (formal and informal) are essential and must be prepared and conducted with PM design team members, users, and the data administrator alike while the integrated system is under development. The dynamic changes and business impacts associated with integration must be understood by each member of an organization, especially in an IRM environment, where major climatic and behavioral changes are inevitable. These changes, if not understood, planned for, and evaluated by management, could possibly have a precarious effect and jeopardize the entire IRM project.

Management must recognize the impact of an IRM system and foster the employment of organizational change and development techniques (Beckhard and Harris, 1977). It is suggested that a change agent, acting on behalf of the executive steering committee, be consulted during and after the evaluative interviews for the purpose of resolving conflicts and assisting in the settlement of disputes. Astute managers understanding the effects of integration must initiate corporate-wide training programs which enable a smooth transition. The traditional functions of the organization will undoubtedly change as a result of the installation and operation of IRM concepts. Therefore, personnel must be reeducated through specialized training courses provided by senior management on a periodic and continuing basis throughout the IRM-SDLC. Training is an imperative and crucial element to the success of an IRM.

Because of the nature of an IRM-SDLC, periodic maintenance should be conducted to ensure the system is functioning in an integrated manner. Maintenance is particularly important because the data modules in the data base system must operate in unison. If one data module or data element in the system is out of synchronization, it could cause problems that affect the entire integrated environment. Change management is important and was recognized several years ago by IBM, when it introduced a method similar to SDLC called information systems management architecture (ADPers Recognize . . ., 1986).

6. The IRM-SDLC Method: Summary

The phases of the IRM-SDLC are important to the successful integration of information systems. As mentioned, a standardized development process is required if systems are to be built which satisfy the needs and wants of the entire organization. If systems are not designed in an open environment, confusion can reign and impede progress towards an integrated data management system that follows the principles of IRM. It is crucial to understand that systems designed in closed surroundings can cause integration efforts to be convoluted.

Integrated design methods require the members of an organization to function in ways not normally associated with today's philosophies of how an organization should function, and demand a rethinking of philosophies and internal management styles. Team management and long-range planning must be practiced above all else if data integration is to remain a high priority. The harnessing of scarce resources is an issue that all management levels must understand.

V. INTEGRATED DESIGN TOOLS AND CODIFICATION STRUCTURES

Organizations intending to integrate, manage, and control their data resource must incorporate fundamental data mangement design tools and codification structures into the design of their information systems. These tools and structures are mandatory for the survival of organizations intending to enter into advanced stages of data processing growth (integration, data administration, and IRM). All information systems (functions) in an organization require analytical tools; without tools and standardized processes, an organization's IS department would continually be in a state of confusion.

Data management, which cuts across all organization and management functions, is no different and, in turn, requires its own set of tools and structural standards to assist in the process of delineating, obtaining, and providing useful information to management.

The integration of an organization's data resource is an extremely complicated process. To assist in the development of sound tools and structures, data management borrows ideas, knowledge, and understanding from contemporary management disciplines (operations research, evaluation, organizational behavior and change). Standardized tools and structures are needed to aid systems architects in recording their inputs and the relationships between different data elements, and to achieve answers to management questions.

The practitioner must be cautioned against a sole reliance on design tools to produce a system accessible and efficient to management and end-users. A critical factor in successful IS development is the structuring and codification of the data so that software designs can be integrated adequately in the design process. For the data to be available to all potential end-users, it must be stored and accounted for according to a structured design which reflects the entire organization's use of the data, rather than just one application's logical view (Wilson, 1985).

No matter how useful data management's tools and structures are, it must be recognized that managers, professionals, and clerical staff are resistant to change—especially when they are not absolutely sure of the consequences of the actions to be initiated. As a matter of fact, even informed managers resist change and inadvertently try to maintain the status quo. To effectively integrate information systems, PM design teams are receiving training provided by consultants and training groups to cope with change and be able to direct project outcomes by learning "to think in terms of change sponsors, change agents, and change targets" (Sullivan-Trainor, 1987).

Under adverse conditions, long-range strategic planners must be made cognizant that the longer fragmentation and nonintegration of systems continues, the harder and more costly it becomes to use data management tools and structures in the process of reducing data redundancy and developing common cores of data. This impediment is due partly to the software conversion process, and mainly to the modification of older applications designed using FMS methods. The purpose of integrated data systems is to curtail the fragmentation of data throughout an organization and enable the various levels of management to function in an environment which generates accurate and expedient information.

Tools and codification structures employed in the design of integrated information systems include data models, data dictionaries, and data base management system software. The effective use of these tools, however, will depend directly upon the organization's readiness and propensity to adhere to highly flexible, yet standardized, codification structures. These structures should enable systems integraters to develop architectural blueprints of all infrastructures within an organization. Blueprints are needed to identify and code linkages and types of interfaces that occur throughout the organization.

This section describes (1) general characteristics associated with data models, data dictionaries, and data base management systems, and (2) basic codification structures essential to the development of flexible, integrated environments.

A. Data Integration Design Tools

Three tools mentioned—data models, data dictionaries, and data base management systems—are necessary for the successful design and implementation of a sound IRM plan. These tools should be used in as much a sequential manner as possible to ensure proper standardization and normal progression during the integration process; thus, a step-by-step process should be followed with backward looping (feedback) occurring in a uniform fashion.

1. Data Models

Data models and prototypes of existing and proposed systems should be prepared for each information system and its data modules to provide management with an understanding of the multidimensional relationships that flow from one system to another. For strategic planning purposes, the models should be sophisticated enough to identify all possible relationships that can exist in both the short and the long term. This ensures that proper IS planning evolves in regard to the prioritization and logical implementation of the different data modules in the overall IRM system. Besides understanding data relationships, a data model should be supplemented with reports that identify who in the organization utilizes the data. The IRM data model proposed in Fig. 5 follows a minimum, three-stage (nine-step) process, which corresponds to the IRM-SDLC discussed earlier in the chapter. A description of each of the stages and steps in the IRM data model follows.

a. Stage One (Information Systems Model)

Step 1 is the design of a conceptual view of each information system found in the organization, along with a description of each system's data modules. Step 2, the decomposition of the IS model designed in step 1, shows the relationships that exist between the data elements and the users of the information. Step 3 describes how all of the subschemas (data modules) are integrated to form the schema (information systems model).

b. Stage Two (IRM Data Model)

This stage uses the IS data models designed in the previous stage to develop an overall IRM data model which can be used by managers to identify and prioritize the information systems or data modules that should be slated for full or partial implementation. Based upon the IS data models constructed in step 3 above, step 4 allows systems architects to use advanced data modeling (relationship matrix) techniques to develop, in step 5, an IRM data model that shows how each IS data model fits together. Instead of waiting for each IS data model to be completed, systems architects can (as soon as two or more information systems models are completed) begin to develop the IRM data model concurrently with stage 1. Once the IRM data model is constructed, step 6 involves the prioritization of information systems and data modules for inclusion in the information systems plan.

Stage Two is used to provide designers with the capability to construct a flexible and integrated coding structure which can be used by the organization as a means of integrating its data resource. This aspect of the model will be discussed later. Overall, the IRM data model can eliminate many of the bottlenecks and misinterpretations concerning data ownership and the fragmentation of data throughout the organization.

c. Stage Three (System Prototypes)

Once all relationships are defined and known, the third stage is to identify the reports and corresponding data elements and files (data sets) associated with each of the IS modules. Step 7 is an extension of the models developed in Stages One and Two, and requires the

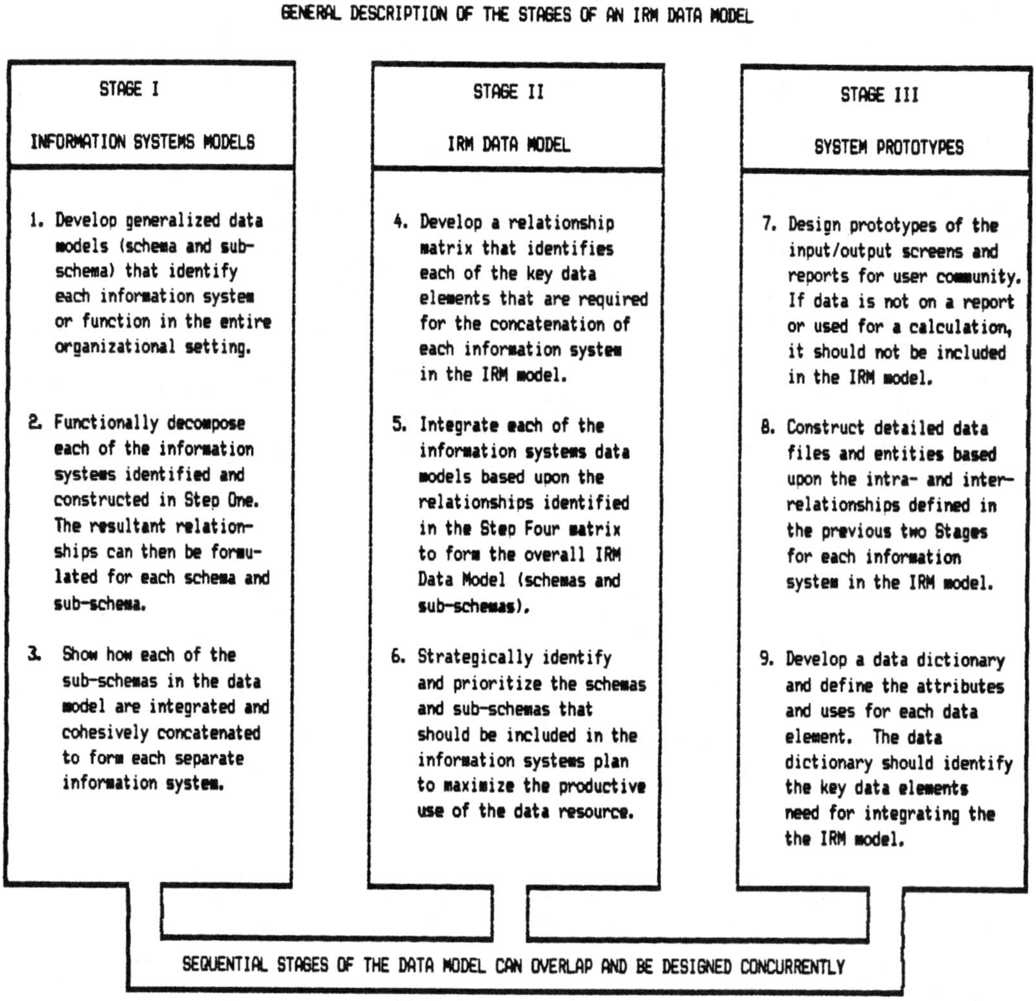

FIGURE 5 Information resource management data model (IRM-DM).

prototyping of the input and output screens and reports used by the user community; it is needed to construct the data sets and entities (records) that are used in the data base management and data dictionary systems.

Based upon the relationships identified in the previously constructed data models and the prototypes of step 7, step 8 is the construction of detailed data sets and entities for each IS data module under development. The number of data sets required for a particular data module may range anywhere from one to 20 files, depending upon the complexity of the data being captured or derived. What is of the utmost importance is that key data elements be established, and relationships identified between each of the data sets and entities in the data submodules, data modules, and information systems of the IRM model. Step 9 involves the development of a data dictionary, as discussed in the next section, which identifies several characteristics and uses for each data element.

Before the establishment of files and key data elements, prototypes (sketches) of the reports and other types of documents to be generated by the proposed system must be designed. When constructing the prototypes, systems architects should take into consideration the various requirements and views of the different management functions, each manager's personalized style, and logical views of the system under development. Prototypes developed in an IRM environment should not be limited by the parameters of an FMS. They must cut across all functional boundaries and suggest the generation of reports that utilize the maximum potential of the entire data base of data elements available to management operating at either the OIS, the MIS, or the DSS management level.

Current prototyping practices are still somewhat controversial, and their use is not an agreed upon axiom in the overall MIS environment. Specifically, the prototype model should include the following: major program modules, the data base, screens, reports, and other inputs and outputs that the system will use for communicating with other interfacing systems (Lantz, 1986). Lantz stresses that prototyping is a method that is teachable, measurable, and comparable, and that lends itself to modification; it is therefore a logical design tool, which is, however, underutilized by organizations. Data elements from each of the organization's functional areas should be combined where appropriate to generate reports and documents that were not possible to create in the past.

2. Data Dictionaries

Data dictionaries or directories are a natural outgrowth of data models. If an organization is small and just entering the automated data processing field, it is imperative that data modeling and dictionaries be immediate goals. As data repositories containing metadata (data about data), data dictionaries or directories are not only used to control data redundancies and provide data security, but are used also by the data administrator (change agent) as a means of eliminating conflicts over the collection and use of the data in the IRM system. Data models and dictionaries are the most important tools that a data administrator, responsible for the effective and efficient use of data resource, can use.

Regarding the prerequisites for the development of a data dictionary, Jackowski (1979) notes that:

> The development of a data dictionary should not occur until system designers have a precise knowledge of existing data flows and an understanding of data control concepts. This may be accomplished through:
>
> 1. An analysis of an agency's paperwork volume, which will document whether there is a need for better data management.
> 2. A definition of the purpose, scope, advantages, and disadvantages of a data control and forms management system.
> 3. The assignment of responsibility and authority by the chief administrative officer to a centralized office which will handle forms control, analysis, monitoring, and design procedures.
> 4. The establishment of written policies and procedures for the operation of the data control and forms management system, to include such activities as: forms or data review committees; in-service training to familiarize staff with the system; an annual data acquisition plan that lists all authorized data collection for a given year; and the monitoring of approved data collection activities to assure timeliness, accuracy, validity, and availability of the data.

In a cross-impact matrix, Jackowski (1979) lists 18 uses and 14 characteristics for the data dictionary. An example of the uses are the identification of available data (general reference), input instruments, output documents, and the development of data base structures and content.

Data dictionaries normally are associated with data base management systems; however, they can stand alone in the form of either a manual or an automated system designed for identifying and maintaining the data base management system's data elements in the organization (Jackowski, 1985). Ross (1981, pp. 82-86) notes that a data dictionary can be used for data modeling, and states "that it allows the data administrator to precisely model the specific definition, control, and procedure requirements of his particular environment." He describes some of its uses as modeling of specific system design methods, design of automation of forms, modeling of project control systems, establishment of a report distribution schedule, building models for distinct data base management systems, file management schemes and output subsystems, and data flow and structure diagrams.

An important point to remember is that data dictionaries are crucial tools in the development of an integrated data system, since they identify how each specific data element is used in an IRM system. The term "data directory" refers to a collapsed version of a data dictionary.

3. Data Base Systems

A data base system or method allows users to develop absolute linkages between its parts for the purpose of achieving maximum effectiveness in the design and use of the data resource. In addition, it enables an organization to manage its data resources through the elimination of possible fragmented and redundant data by developing relations for the purpose of sharing data in all segments of the organization. Finally, a base system works under the premise that an organization is a single entity composed of many functions which operate in numerous one-to-one and one-to-many relationships.

The term "data base" has different meanings and can be, for example, conceived as a single, massive file that contains medical, legal, educational, or other types of data. This view does not necessarily reflect an integrated environment; often, when one encounters the term "on-line data base" it usually refers to a nonintegrated data base type.

The term "on-line data base" and "data base," as used in this chapter, refer to the use of integrated computer files and associated applications in a growing and mature data processing organization. The two data organization and design methods that exist today are the FMS and DBMS. This section reviews the basic features and characteristics associated with both of these approaches to managing and integrating the data resource.

Integrated information systems designs use generalized file management systems and data base software. The FMS methods use COBOL, FORTRAN, PL/1, BASIC, and Pascal. According to Cardenas (1985, pp. 7-9) they are "self-contained systems integrating: all the facilities of report writers, report program generators, and sort packages; various facilities of program languages; and a number of other useful file handling (not data base) facilities. Functionally, they can perform a great portion of what a programming language can do plus a lot more in areas where a programming language is weakest, namely, storage/retrieval and report writing." He notes that the main objectives of data base technology are data independence, data shareability, nonredundancy of stored data, relatability, integrity, access flexibility, security, performance and efficiency, and administration and control.

Higher level, fourth-generation DBMS methods operating in multidimensional organizational climates use a relational DBMS data structure. Relational data structures are flat files with key data elements which allow relationships between several files to be formed. Seveal relational DBMS software packages available on the market are, for example, IBM's SQL/DS and Query-by-Example; Relational Software's ORACLE SQL*CALC; Relational Technology's INGRES.SQL PLUS; Mathematica's RAMIS II; Microrim's RBase System V; Cosmos's Revelation; Ashton-Tate's DBase III Plus; and Cullinet's GoldenGate.

Both ORACLE and INGRES run identically on mainframes, minicomputers, and microcomputers. ORACLE is the first to combine a mainframe class relational DBMS with a Lotus 1-2-3-compatible spreadsheet user interface. RBase System V, initially developed for a microcomputer, is being developed to run on a minicomputer.

In an unpublished document, Jackowski (1980) noted the characteristics of FMS and DBMS methods:

File Management System (FMS) Characteristics

1. Increases speed and accuracy of clerical and professional functions.
2. Cost and effort of modifications considerable.
3. Suboptimal with respect to the entire information system.
4. Special reports often costly, untimely, or even impossible to prepare.
5. Difficult to update existing procedures.
6. File-oriented systems impose restrictions on data relationships and data formats.
7. Requires that data be duplicated or stored repeatedly, if used for multiple purposes.
8. Lack of easy, well-defined ways to measure productivity.

Data Base Management System (DBMS) Characteristics

1. Increases speed and accuracy of clerical and professional functions.
2. All data regardless of organization and file structure is stored in one place.
3. All data is available for routine and special variance reports.
4. Cross-office applications are possible without file duplication and reprogramming.
5. Access to data of other office subunits is possible without the intervention of data processing personnel (multiuser environments).
6. Maintains logical relationships among data elements.
7. Individual data formatted to user specifications through customized report writers.
8. Security provisions built into the system.
9. Data updated once instead of in several different files scattered throughout the organziation.

The development of a forms management and data control unit for the recording, monitoring, and control of all source documents (manual and automated) is a first step in using DBMS software. In general, a DBMS increases the ability to develop and change program applications, preserves the integrity of data, expands and simplifies the use of data processing facilities, and provides greater capacity for ease in system-wide use.

Regardless of the method chosen, the system design must consider the requirements of the system's users. Systems designed now and in the future must be user-friendly and menu-driven. Menus should be constructed that enable a user to move freely from one option to another and contain, at a minimum, three types of screens (help, input, and output). All menus should be linked together in a logical and orderly fashion.

Help screens are essential and should describe the simplest to the most complex explanations required for user understanding. Input screens must enable a user to add, delete, and edit records. If possible, a browse feature also should be available on the input screen that enables users to search through a file and edit any of the data elements requiring a change. Output screens should list various types of query and customized reports which are needed by the user.

Documentation must be underscored and stressed throughout the entire IRM-SDLC process, especially during the design phase. It is vital at the onset of the design process to establish the role documentation will play. Documentation is the most vital mechanism that administrators have at their disposal to manage the design and programming of the different data modules. Since information systems do not exist in a stable or stationary form, documentation is the only means the PM design team has for capturing and reflecting the dynamics, requirements, and parameters of the system under design (Kirk, 1973).

B. Integrated Coding Structure

For successful integration to take place, an organization must develop a set of coding structures for the explicit purpose of standardizing the coding of data elements in the IRM system. Coding structure designs should follow the same basic guidelines noted in the design of an IRM data model (Figure 5); they should be prototyped prior to actual use.

An integrated coding structure is a set of interrelated coding structures working in unison for the purpose of developing an organization's overall data structure. Without it, a data structure could not exist. It is a plan that enables data element integration to occur between and among the various pockets of information in an organization.

If an organization is contemplating the integration of existing systems, it is important that the PM design team develop common coding structures which accommodate the integration of existing and planned applications. Three major coding structures which form the base for an organization's data structure are (1) a program structure, (2) an IRM structure, and (3) a data element structure.

1. Program Structure

Foremost is the need for a comprehensive program structure which reflects the structure of the organization. Information or data must be capable of being assigned to each of the discrete segments (department, division, program, and project) in an organization for the purpose of recording inputs and providing outputs relevant to each segment. A program coding structure is the vehicle used to record employee, finance, facility, client or student, equipment, supplies, and other data to each segment of the organization. It is a road map which enables data to be reported singularly for each segment or aggregately for different organizational groupings. A program structure is a reflection of an institution's or agency's organization chart.

Flexibility and maneuverability in adding, changing, and deleting program segments must be designed into the program coding structure. It is an important building block in the design of the organization's data structure (data sets and entities). Data must belong to some organizational unit in order for it to have value to the organization. "No matter how large or multifaceted an organization is, it should only have one comprehensive structure" (Jackowski, 1985).

2. IRM Structure

In an integrated environment, each data element must be given not only a program structure code, but also an IRM code relevant to the information system and data module it is assigned. As part of the organization's data structure, the IRM code must be specific enough to enable a data dictionary to be constructed that has depth and meaning associated with its use. To achieve this, data elements must be structured according to a generalized data schema.

The IRM coding structure's purpose is to categorize an organization's data elements according to the type of data they represent. For example, data elements can be categorized according to the IS (finance) and data module (accounts receivable, accounts payable, fixed assets, general journal, and so on) in which they belong. In addition, in a user-friendly menu-driven application, the IRM coding structure can be used to assist the PM design team when coding application menus, data entry and help screens, and reports.

Strict adherence to a standard IRM coding structure by the PM design team is important to the success of an integrated environment. As noted above, it has been stressed that flexibility and adaptability be built-in to the design of an integrated coding structure. Flexibility is the ability of the system to manage a wide variety of circumstances as it is developed; adaptability is the ability to meet major changes in environments with a minimum of modifications (Mathews, 1971).

3. Data Element Structure

The data element coding structure works in conjunction with both the program and the IRM coding structures. Its purpose is to identify the program and IRM code, and the data set and entity to which a data element belongs. The data element coding structure encompasses the codes from the other coding structures, plus codes for the data set, entity, and data element itself. The coding structure must be specific enough to enable a data element dictionary to be constructed which has depth and meaning associated with its use.

VI. CONCLUSION

Information is the most valuable and expensive resource that an organization has at its disposal. Its use presupposes that all members of the IS community acknowledge the impact it plays on their respective organizational units.

When information systems are maintained as distinct entities, and are not integrated, the use of information is diminished, and synergism within the organization is difficult to achieve. Fragmented and nonintegrated information systems detract from an organization's ability to gain the full competitive potential of the data resource.

If an integrated information system, functioning under the principles of an IRM, is used by any organization, the following propositions should be followed:

1. Information systems managers must be retrained continually and made aware of future products (hardware, software, and data communications, design methods) on the market.
2. Senior management must ensure that a joint responsibility exists between all team members (IS specialists and end-users).
3. Information systems engineers (architects) must provide systems designers and end-user managers with directions to enable them not to be burdened by the political pressures related to separate, unconnected ownership of data.
4. A lack of IS personnel, coupled with advanced views of how systems should be constructed, requires that organizations take their own initiative to develop user-training programs.
5. Users of automated information systems must understand that if systems are to be effectively integrated, they must be designed not only to take into consideration the needs of their sphere of responsibility, but also to provide information to other segments of the organization.
6. Consistency in terminologies, methods, and codification structures is essential for the design of integrated information systems.
7. The design of centralized or decentralized integrated systems now or in the future must follow a given set of rules or procedural standards if they are to result in a successful product.
8. The main criterion for a successful design is that architects of the system under contemplation follow a data base versus file management method.
9. Integrated design methods require the members of an organization to function in ways not normally associated with today's philosophies of how an organization should function.
10. Team management must not exist merely as a design principle; it must be practiced above all else if data integration is to remain a high priority.
11. The effective use of data integration tools will depend directly upon the organization's readiness and propensity to adhere to highly flexible, yet standardized, codification structures.
12. Without a data model of the organization and the internal and external relationships that form the *gestalt*, it would be almost impossible to determine the most productive means of concatenating the various independent data systems existing in an organization.

Having the capability to achieve high results in the form of high technology is not sufficient in itself; a retraining of all levels of management, information specialists, and end-users is required. Research into the methods of achieving high data structure design results through organizational development, change, and design principles demands more than the breakthroughs witnessed in hardware and software; it goes beyond, to the need for a basic research program in our colleges and universities.

REFERENCES

Adams, M. M. (1984). Data administration function at core of system success, *Computerworld 18*(39): SR40.

Adamski, L. (1986). The prototyping methodology: Designing right the first time, *Computerworld, 29*(13): 69.

ADPers recognize need to manage system changes, *Government Computer News, 5*(7): 49.

Alter, S. L. (1980). *Decision Support Systems–Current Practice and Continuing Challenges*, Addison-Wesley, Reading, Massachusetts.

Anthony, R. N. (1965). *Planning and Control Systems: A Framework for Analysis.* Graduate School of Business Administration, Harvard University, Boston.

Appleton, D. S. (1985). The technology of data integration, *Datamation, 31*: 106.

Beckhard, R., and Harris, R. T. (1977). *Organizational Transitions: Managing Organizational Change*, Addison-Wesley, Reading, Massachusetts.

Burch, J. G., Jr., Grudnitski, G., and Strater, F. R. (1983). *Information Systems: Theory and Practice*, John Wiley and Sons, New York.

Business Systems Planning, Executive Overview (1981). Technical Publications Department Document GE20-0630-1, IBM, White Plains, New York.

Callahan, J. (1985). Need for the systems generalist, *Journal of Systems Management, 36*: 32.

Canning, R. G., ed. (1984). *Fourth Generation Languages and Prototyping.* EDP Analyzer Special Report, Canning Publications, Vista, California.

Cardenas, A. F. (1985). *Data Base Management Systems*, 2nd ed., Allyn and Bacon, Boston.

Carlson, W. (1977). A paradigm for management information systems, *A Paradigm for Management Information Systems* (Philip Ein-Dor and Eli Segev, eds.), Praeger, New York.

Casey, W., and Curtice, R. M. (1985). Database: What's in store?" *Datamation, 31*: 83.

Chester, J. A. (1985). Demystifying relational data base management systems, *Infosystems, 32*(10): 60.

Crane, J. (1986). "Office Automation–The Future is Now. The San Diego Schools Office Automation Strategy and Implementation." Association of Education Data Systems (AEDS) Annual Conference (April 24), New Orleans.

Crescenzi, A. D., and Reck, R. H. (1985). Critical success factors: Helping IS managers pinpoint information needs, *Infosystems, 32*(7): 52.

Danziger, J. N., Dutton, W. H., Kling, R., and Kraemer, K. L. (1982). *Computers and Politics: High Technology in American Local Governments*, Columbia University Press, New York.

Durell, W. R. (1985). *Data Administration, A Practical Guide to Successful Data Management*, McGraw-Hill, New York.

Edwards, P. (1985). The designing mind, *Datamation, 31*(18): 105.

Filley, A. C., House, R. J., and Turner, J. H. eds. (1972). *Studies in Managerial Process and Organizational Behavior*, Scott, Foresman, and Company, Chicago, Illinois.

Fosdick, H. (1985). IRM putting theory to work, *Infosystems, 32*(8): 33.

Garrison, R. H. (1985). *Managerial Accounting*, 4th ed., Business Publications, Plano, Texas.

Grindly, A. (1984). Sizing up your MIS department: Ten critical measures, *Business Quarterly, 49*: 87.

Haverty, J., and Tauss, G. (1986). How good is TCP/IP? *Government Data Systems, 15*(3): 23.

Hicks, J. O., Jr. (1984). *Management Information Systems–A User Perspective*, West Publishing Company, Minneapolis, Minnesota.

Horton, F. W., Jr., and Marchand, D. A. (1982). *Information Management in Public Administration*, Information Resources Press, Arlington, Virginia.

Horwitt, E. (1986). Net values: Users watch ISDN, opt for current solutions, *Computerworld, 20*(7): 1.

Hovey, H. A. (1976). Some perspectives on data processing in state government, *Computer Systems and Public Administrators* (R. A. Bassler and N. L. Enger, eds.), College Readings, Alexandria, Virginia.

Hughes, J. W. (1984). MIS for State and Local Governments, *Journal of Systems Management, 35*(11): 25.

Inmon, W. H. (1983). *Management Control of Data Processing–Preventing Management-By-Crisis*, Prentice-Hall, Englewood Cliffs, New Jersey.

Inmon, W. H. (1984). *Integrating Data Processing Systems in Theory and in Practice*, Prentice-Hall, Englewood Cliffs, New Jersey.

Jackowski, E. M. (1977). An educational data element dictionary, *Journal of Systems Management, 28*(8): 38.

Jackowski, E. M. (1979). Uses and attributes of an educational data element dictionary, *AEDS Monitor, 17*(7-9): 24.

Jackowski, E. M. (1980). Characteristics and features of file management and data base management system, unpublished document.

Jackowski, E. M. (1985). Information systems in state and local governments, *State and Local Government Administration* (J. Rabin and D. Dodd, eds.), Marcel Dekker, New York.

Kallman, E. A., and Reinharth, L. (1984). *Information Systems for Planning and Decision Making*, Van Nostrand Reinhold, New York.

Kami, J. M., and Ross, J. E. (1973). *Corporate Management in Crisis: Why the Mighty Fall*, Prentice-Hall, Englewood Cliffs, New Jersey.

Keen, P. G. W., and Morton, M. S. S. (1978). *Decision Support Systems–An Organizational Perspective*, Addison-Wesley, Reading, Massachusetts.

King, W. R. (1985). Information, technology, and corporate growth, *Columbia Journal of World Business, 22*(2): 29.

King, W. R., and Srinivasan, A. (1988). The systems development life cycle and the modern information systems environment, *Handbook of Information Resource Management* (J. Rabin and E. M. Jackowski, eds.), Marcel Dekker, New York.

Kirk, F. G. (1973). *Total Systems Development for Information Systems*, John Wiley and Sons, New York.

Konsynski, B. R. (1984–1985). Advances in information system design, *Journal of Management Information Systems, 1*(3): 3.

Kroenke, D. (1978). *Database: A Professional's Primer*, Science Research Associates, Chicago.

Lantz, K. E. (1986). The prototyping methodology: Designing right the first time, *Computerworld, 20*(11).

Lay, P. M. W. (1985). Beware of the cost/benefit model for IS project evaluation, *Journal of Systems Management, 36*(6): 30.

Marchand, D. A. (1985). The 4 roles of an IRM manager, *Government Data Systems, 14*(8): 24.

Martin, J. (1977). *Computer Data-Base Organization*, 2nd ed., Prentice-Hall, Englewood Cliffs, New Jersey.

Martin, J. (1982). *Application Development Without Programmers*, Prentice-Hall, Englewood Cliffs, New Jersey.

Martin, J. (1984). *An Information Systems Manifesto*, Prentice-Hall, Englewood Cliffs, New Jersey.

Mathews, D. Q. (1971). *The Design of the Management Information System*, Auerbach, New York.

McFarlan, W. F. (1981). Portfolio approach to information systems, *Harvard Business Review, 59*(5): 142.

McFarlan, W. F., and McKenney, J. L. (1983). *Corporate Information Systems Management: The Issues Facing Senior Executives*, Richard D. Irwin, Homewood, Illinois.

Mescon, M., Albert, M., and Khedouri, F. (1981). *Management: Individual and Organizational Effectiveness*, Harper and Row, New York.

Mills, J. A. (1985). A pragmatic view of the systems architect, *Communication of the ACM, 28*: 708.

Mills, J. A. (1985). A pragmatic view of the systems architect, *Communication of the ACM, 28*: 708.
Mimno, P. (1985). 4GL: Power to the users (part one), *Computerworld, Indepth* (April 8): Indepth 19.
Mimno, P. (1985). 4GL: Power to the users (part two), *Computerworld, Indepth* (April 15): Indepth 1.
Morgan, H. (1985). The microcomputer and decision support, *Computerworld, 19*(33): 39.
Morton, S., and Keen, M. S. (1971). *Management Decision Systems; Computer-Based Support for Decision Making*, Harvard University Press, Boston.
Murray, J. M. (1988). Information systems and data processing organizations, *Handbook of Information Resource Management*, (J. Rabin and E. M. Jackowski, eds.), Marcel Dekker, New York.
Nolan, R. L. (1982). Managing information systems by committee, *Harvard Business Review, 60*(4): 72.
Orilia, L. S. (1986). *Computers and Information: An Introduction*, 3rd edition, McGraw-Hill, New York.
Popek, B. and Jacobsohn, H. (1983). Managing information as a resource, *Data Management, 21*(9): 32.
Roche, E. (1983). Information architecture, *Computerworld, 17*(40): 9.
Rockart, J. F. (1982). The changing role of the information systems executive: A critical success factors perspective, *Sloan Management Review, 24*: 3.
Rosenthal, L. (1986). A guide to integrated software, *Government Data Systems*, 15(3): 23.
Ross, R. G. (1981). *Data Dictionaries and Data Administration*, AMACOM, New York.
Serlin, O. (1985). Exploring the OLTP realm, *Datamation, 31*(15): 60.
Shah, A. D., and Davis, R. K. (1988). Defining end user requirements through service analysis, *Handbook of Information Resource Management* (J. Rabin and E. M. Jackowski, eds.), Marcel Dekker, New York.
Sprague, R. H., Jr. (1980). A framework for research on decision support systems, *Decision Support Systems: Issues and Challenges* (G. Fick and R. H. Sprague, Jr., eds.), Pergamon Press, New York.
Sprague, R. H., Jr. (1984). A framework for the development of decision support systems, *Information Systems for Planning and Decision-Making* (E. Kallman and L. Reinharth, eds.), Von Nostrand Reinhold, New York.
Communications News Staff Report (1983). Integration opens world to better information sharing, *Communications News, 20*: 52.
Sullivan, C. H. (1985). Systems planning in the information age, *Sloan Management Review, 26*(2): 3–12.
Sullivan-Trainor, M. (1987). Three team leaders master a framework for management change, *Computerworld, 22*(9): 5.
Taggart, W., and Silbey, V. (1986). *Information Systems: People and Computers in Organizations*, Allyn and Bacon, Boston.
Thompson, Stewart (1975). *The Age of the Manager Is Over*, Dow Jones-Irwin, Homewood, Illinois.
Wilson, A. H. (1985). Pitfalls, in data design, *Datamation, 31*: 114.
Wood, M. (1985). Converting systems requires a "common ground" approach, *Data Management, 23*: 16.
Zand, D. E. (1981). *Information, Organization, and Power–Effective Management in the Knowledge Society*, McGraw-Hill, New York.

16

New Technological Advances in Hardware and Software and Their Impact in Human Services

John Abbott Worthley Center for Public Service, Seton Hall University, South Orange, New Jersey

Andrea Camerlingo-Aluisi Department of Epidemiology, United Hospitals Medical Center, Newark, New Jersey

Computerized information systems in health care and human service organizations have advanced in recent years at a rapid rate. This chapter describes the current state of the art in health and human services with regard to the use of modern computer technology. It also analyzes the impact of the technology on these organizations and suggests some significant managerial implications. Our emphasis is decidedly on the actual rather than the possible, although we do give some attention to probable future developments.

I. STATE OF THE ART

After briefly reviewing the history of the use of computer technology in health and human service organizations, this section describes the various types of computer systems currently used and presents, in some detail, illustrations of the application of the technology in health and human service organizations.

A. Historical Background

While computers have been used in organizations since the 1950s, it was not until the 1960s and 1970s that computerization had an impact on the health and human service field. Hodge (1977) relates that during this time, a few hospitals, relatively unknown except to the regions they served, committed themselves to one common goal—to serve as a site for the development of computerized patient information systems. This effort was often assisted by companies that shared the vision of applying the technology to hospitals. Soon these organizations were the topic of discussion at national meetings, and their activities were recounted in the hospital literature. They also served as on-site observation centers for visitors from as far away as Asia. Despite these early hopes, efforts failed. Enthusiasm was replaced with skepticism and, eventually, cynicism. Many hospitals returned to conventional methods for handling patient information, and technology companies found other commodities to promote.

Despite these early disappointments, progress was made, and in the mid-1970s, success stories began to emerge. Skilled administrators and health professionals began to consider the timing and approach for the installation of automated patient information systems within their organizations.

Over the past 20 years, the use of computers in health and human services has evolved from an accounting focus in the 1960s to an emphasis on expediting patient care in the 1970s. The current effort focuses on integrating clinical, financial, and operations management data, and is designed to facilitate the transformation of raw data into decision-assisting information (Winfree, 1986). Though the optimal use of computerized information systems in health and human services is yet to be realized, major advances have been made.

B. Current System Types

Today there are six major types of computer systems in use in health and human service organizations. They can be classified as follows:

1. Financial/Administrative Systems. These systems automate many activities, such as patient billing, accounts receivable, accounts payable, general ledger, personnel/payroll, and property management. Typically, this type of system operates on large mainframe equipment or minicomputers.

2. Departmental Information Systems. These systems are designed to assist an individual department with its information management. They function independently, although they may share data with other systems. Examples include laboratory and pharmacy systems.

3. Decision Support Systems. These systems assist management in the analysis of data produced by other computerized systems. Examples of this type of system include case-mix analysis, planning, and financial modeling.

4. Office Automation Systems. These systems combine the existing proven areas of word processing and data processing with new advancements such as electronic data transfer. Examples are scheduling, memo writing, and record-keeping systems.

5. Microcomputer Systems. These systems are used in health and human service organizations in three different ways: (1) as data downloading devices from a mainframe or minicomputer, which allows the user to examine or manipulate the information without affecting the operations of the central computer; (2) as query devices for order entry or results reporting; and (3) as a processing device that independently performs a specific application, such as word processing or financial analysis.

6. Patient Care Systems. These systems are frequently referred to as patient information systems, medical information systems, or order entry and communications systems. A patient care system tracks patient information from the time of admission to the time of discharge. It also provides automated functions for enabling outpatient clinics and physician offices to communicate with inpatient areas and ancillary services (Ginsberg and Browning, 1985).

Specific applications for which computers have been used with success in the health and human service industry are the following:

1. Patient data
    a. Demographic data
    b. Financial data
    c. Health care data—the comprehensive medical record
2. Ancillary services
    a. Clinical laboratory
        pathology
        chemistry
        hematology
        histology/cytology
        blood bank
        virology
    b. Pharmacy
    c. Noninvasive cardiac laboratory
    d. Electrocardiology
    e. Electroencephalography
    f. Radiology
        special procedures (for example, angiography)
        ultrasound
        CT scanning
        magnetic resonance imaging labs
    g. Respiratory therapy
    h. Physical therapy
    i. Nutritional support (dietary services)
    j. Social services
    k. Central services
    l. Environmental services (housekeeping)
3. Clinical services
    a. Operating room
    b. Emergency room
    c. Nursing care units
    d. Critical and special care units
    e. Outpatient clinics
    f. Patient transportation
    g. Patient education
4. Administrative services
    a. Medical records
    b. Utilization review
    c. Quality assurance
    d. Infection control/epidemiology
    e. Materials management
    f. Personnel and human resources
    g. Education and staff development
    h. Staffing and scheduling
    i. Data processing
    j. Payroll
5. Accounting services
6. Medical research

7. Marketing and fund-raising services
8. Public health application
   a. Epidemiologic studies
   b. Population health profiles
   c. Immunization histories
   d. Program evaluations
   e. Census statistics
   f. Special studies and research
   g. Educational processes
   h. Social services
   i. Mental health services
   j. Contagious disease services
9. Home health care services
10. Extended care/nursing home facility services

These last two application services are in the beginning stages of development as of this writing. They are included in this summary of application areas because of their impending impact on health care delivery.

In order to gauge the progression of information systems, Ball and Boyle (1980) have classified hospital information systems according to the degree of integration and communication present in the systems. This classification is as follows (Fedorowicz, 1983):

Class A: These are individual systems which address the specific requirements of single departments or specialties (such as laboratory system, pharmacy system, accounting system).

Class B: This is a type of information system which crosses departmental and specialty boundaries. Its base is institutionally and administratively oriented and has a communications network superimposed on it. The network may extend to the transmission of orders between patient floors and departments. It may also include integrated ancillary applications.

Class B, Level 1: This system includes an admission discharge transfer (ADT) subsystem and a data collection message switching subsystem. On-line terminals are in place throughout the hospital for order entry, communications of orders, and charge capture. Periodically, once or twice a day, the system must be cleared of captured charges. The only permanent data base for the duration of the patient stay is the demographic data maintained by the ADT system.

Class B, Level 2: This type of a system includes all the capabilities of a level 1, but in addition maintains some archival for retaining the patient medical record of orders, results, progress notes, and so forth. It also maintains data bases for ancillaries. As such, it can generate medication schedules, nursing care plans, cumulative lab results, and so on. It can also provide a wealth of information upon inquiry, such as all active orders, medication profiles, and uncompleted lab tests.

Class C: This is another type of hospital information system which is oriented to the patient medical record. Historical patient information is the foundation. When communications networks are superimposed on class C systems, they have many similarities to class B systems. The major difference lies in structure. Class B systems use administrative or fiscal systems for a base, while class C systems use the patient medical record as a base. Class C systems by design include fully integrated ancillary subsystems.

Anthony and Young (1984) further define three levels of information systems: (1) systems to support ongoing production; (2) systems to support control and measuring; and (3) systems to support analysis and planning. Shapin (1986) argues that the traditional view of information systems in health care, and in other industries, has been that of a pyramid with operational systems at the bottom, tactical systems in the middle, and strategic management systems at the top. Further, he believes that from the start, the primary purpose of computers in health care and human services has been to facilitate transaction processing. Transaction systems are characterized by a bottom-up design. They are designed by asking end-users what information and functions are needed to perform one's job. Transaction systems are also characterized from a performance point of view; they are designed for rapid processing of data in present ways. Ad hoc requests for information in ways not anticipated by the original designers may be virtually impossible or require the aid of a programmer. Management information systems, on the other hand, are designed from the top down. Their primary consideration is the information needs of managers. They provide decision-assisting information and are designed for flexibility more than performance.

C. Specific Applications of Computer Technology

In order to achieve a clearer understanding of the scope of computerization in health and human service organizations, specific uses in some key areas will be discussed. These areas are

1. Clinical laboratory
2. Pharmacy
3. Nursing
4. Administrative services
5. Discharge planning
6. Home health care
7. Community mental health centers

These areas were chosen because of one or more of the following considerations. First, areas such as the laboratory and pharmacy have had considerable experience with computerization. As such, past and present successes and problems are readily identifiable, as are future trends. Areas such as nursing and administrative services have utilized computerization for a shorter period of time than have the laboratory and pharmacy; however, computerization is increasing at a rapid rate in these areas. Further, the application processes in these areas have met with unique concerns which managers must be able to address if the technology is to be utilized to its potential. The final clinical areas—application, discharge planning, home health care, and community mental health centers—are relatively new to computerization. As such, the evolutionary process can be highlighted, and future advances predicted.

1. Clinical Laboratory

The clinical laboratories were among the first medical applications of computer technology within the health field. One need only walk through the laboratory of any hospital to appreciate the impact that computerization has had on laboratory testing. In addition to the vast array of clinical analyzers available to laboratories today, information systems include the following functions which are basic to laboratory automation:

On-line order entry interface
Results reporting interface
On-line admission, discharge, transfer interface
On-line instrument data acquisition
Batch work lists
Batch reports

The laboratory relies on increasingly sophisticated diagnostic equipment and is one of the most technologically advanced departments within the hospital. Test results provided by laboratory departments are critical to diagnosis, treatment, and monitoring of patient care. Statistics provided by labs aid health care research. Pressures from reimbursement methods are demanding that laboratories be aware of service utilization statistics. An automated laboratory system can provide increased departmental productivity, as is reflected in test performance and results reporting increases, which, in turn, can improve the practitioner's ability to render effective patient care (Packer, 1985f).

The benefits of an automated laboratory system are described by Evans and colleagues (1986). For example, they report that through the development of a computer program that translates the patient's microbiology test results from the laboratory computer into a hierarchical data base that is stored in a computerized medical record, medical personnel are able to identify patients with hospital-associated infections, patients who were not receiving antibiotics to which their pathogens were susceptible, patients who could have been receiving a less expensive antibiotic, and patients who were receiving prophylactic antibiotics for too long a time period. Thus, through the use of computerized screening, the potentially life-saving information that may have been overlooked is brought to the attention of staff.

Future developments in laboratory computerization are being prompted by issues facing health care in general. For example, prospective reimbursement methods are causing laboratory work to be viewed in a different light. Prospective payment demands that hospitals save money in order to make money, thus turning the laboratory from a potential profit source into a cost center. In order to stay in the black while maintaining quality care, hospitals must seek ways to increase the speed and cost-effectiveness of diagnosis, leaving maximum time and resources for therapy. One result of this is pressure for faster turnaround time. A 200-bed East Coast hospital, for example, is planning to computerize most clerical functions and test reporting in answer to this reimbursement demand (Becker, 1984). Laboratories must address the institution of procedures and systems that will cut costs, improve productivity, and assure accuracy. Thus, instruments that can "talk to," or interface with, other laboratory computers will become a valuable asset to the modern lab. Further issues to be considered are the increasing emergence of intelligent instrumentation. More and more of the old in-lab functions previously handled by the laboratory computer are being conducted at the laboratory instrument panel. Some futurists believe that control of instruments from a single console will represent greater control with enhanced productivity (Walker, 1985).

2. Pharmacy

The use of computer technology in drug dispensing dates back to the early 1960s, when the National Institutes of Health were involved in drug control studies. With the advent of unit dose drug administration came the necessity for a data processing system. During the course of their duties, pharmacists must maintain a sufficient, but not excessive, inventory for future use; must be aware of possible adverse drug interactions; and must keep appropriate historical data for administrative, billing, and research purposes.

Operating under pressure, pharmacists have little time to complete required paperwork. Automated pharmacy systems assist with paperwork and enhance departmental productivity. System functions can be integrated with other components of a hospital information system to provide management with better and more timely data for decision making.

Some of the functions basic to a pharmacy information system are as follows:

On-line order entry
Medication administration records
Automatic refill dispensing reports
Order crediting and debiting
Label generation
Drug compatibility checks
Drug duplicate order checking
Drug reference lookup

In addition, certain pharmacy software programs have the availability of other functions, such as:

Allergy screening
Automatic intravenous scheduling
Historical data bases for medical research
Automatic dosage calculation based on the physical attributes of individual patients

Future developments in pharmacy computerization are promising. New systems can interface with the laboratory computer to access blood and microbiological profiles in order to enhance accuracy in drug ordering by the physician. In addition, disease/drug monographs can be developed by the individual institution to meet population specifics when treating certain diseases and can be instantaneously available to the practitioner at the time of treatment. Increased utilization in the pharmacy of intravenous admixture programs allows an automated pharmacy system to access work-flow and quality assurance needs with daily departmental activities, thus increasing productivity and efficiency by the pharmacy. This benefit of automation was reported by a 200-bed Midwest hospital. Through integrated computerization, this hospital pharmacy realized an annual growth rate of 20 percent in unit dose dispensing, sixty percent in the hyperalimentation admixture program, and fifteen percent in dispensing of medications to outpatients (Ford, 1985).

3. Nursing

Of all hospital personnel, nurses are the ones who are most directly affected by hospital-wide medical information systems. Half or more of the system's users are nursing personnel, and they account for an even higher proportion of its daily transactions. Some functions basic to a nursing information system are as follows:

Patient demographic data
Admission, discharge, transfer data
Order communication
Result reporting

Medication administration and reporting
Patient scheduling
Requisitioning of tests and supplies, including medicines
Reporting of nursing data
Care planning instructions (Hodge, 1977)

Illustrative of the state of the art is a 476-bed Milwaukee teaching hospital's nursing department which has developed and employed a patient-centered, automated system of patient information. All of the system's aspects were formulated from the patient's perspective, rather than from those of particular departments. The aspects of patient care were defined as assembling patient information, nurse care planning, order processing, patient scheduling, results reporting, and patient billing. The approach was integrated in design. The automation of 150 previously existing standardized care plans was a substantial part of the initial development of the system. Through the availability of on-line care planning, the nursing staff was able to utilize the care plans in a flexible and creative way, while collecting hours of nursing care data. Further, utilization of the on-line care plans facilitated the selection of desired nursing diagnosis, desired outcomes, and desired approaches to care. This system also allowed for evaluation and update of the patient's care plan at any time during the hospital stay. Patient care backup worksheets were printed every 24 hours. A complete patient care plan was generated after discharge by the medical records department. In addition, a Patient Care Discharge Summary, which contained all outstanding nursing diagnosis and discharge planning information, was included as a permanent part of the patient's record and was utilized as referral information for other care agencies (Albrecht and Lieske, 1985).

Institution of this integrated nursing care information system also brought with it additional benefits for nurse managers. Through the data generated from the patient care system, patients could be classified according to care needs. In turn, hours of care could be automatically calculated from nursing and physician orders, thus constituting the basis for determining the level of nursing skill and degree of nursing care each patient required. This allowed nurse-managers to efficiently allocate resources, effectively trace the impact of new developments in clinical practice, and accurately monitor adherence to standards of care, thus increasing patient-specific decision-making activities and providing an efficacious quality assurance program.

Prospective payment reimbursement methods are placing pressures upon nursing to support its claim that nurses make a difference in the patient's recovery process. Computerization is one method which is assisting nurses to provide exact indicators for patient care requirements, care delivered, and resulting changes in patient status. Viers (1983) reports that in an Omaha hospital, charting time for nursing staff decreased by 7.7 minutes per patient per shift. Further, since the inception of computerization at this hospital, overtime decreased from an average of 50 to 70 hours per unit per week to only 10 to 15 hours per unit per week. Some vendors touting the benefits of bedside computer terminals claim that clerical work time is decreased by as much as fifty percent, which means more time for care at the bedside.

4. Administrative Services

Administrative services involve those departments which deal with the activities of planning, organizing, staffing, and controlling in order to achieve the organization's goals. As such, these areas may deal explicitly with administrative matters, or they may have a dual focus which includes not only administrative activities but clinical inputs as well. This section will include responsibilities ranging from personnel administration to medical records administration; from inventory control (materials management) to data processing; from peer review activities and quality assurance programs to infection control and epidemiologic requisites.

Packer (1984d) reports that hospitals are spending an estimated $8 billion a year on administrative information systems. About 350 vendors sell systems products and services to hospitals. Management information systems are expected to grow faster than any other segment of the hospital information systems market, at a rate of thirty-five percent per year.

The modern chief executive officer (CEO) in today's health care organization is continually faced with changing fiscal constraints. As such, he or she must be aware of the organization's performance over time. Matters pertaining to admissions, bed utilization, occupancy rates, length of stay rates, and service utilization rates are of critical importance in the ever-changing environment which surrounds health care today. Strategic decision-making processes must be utilized effectively if the organization is to remain healthy.

Computerization is assisting the CEO in many of the above problems. First, computers are measuring projected versus actual performance, thus revealing problems or opportunities. Second, computers provide possible responses to potential problems. Third, computers suggest consequences that each response might generate. This can be done through simple expression in English or through complex mathematical simulations.

Packer (1984d) also reports that hospital-based information systems have come a long way in a short time to deliver to administrators the capacity for strategic management assistance. The earliest systems were designed for transactional processing and some operational activities, such as patient billing, accounts receivable, and payroll. In the late 1960s, a management information system that would provide transactional processing and operational activities and, in addition, managerial control and strategic management activities was conceived. The early 1970s saw implementation of these systems fall short of their goals with respect to the managerial control and strategic management programs, because these systems were unable to respond to the needs of upper-level managers who were faced with problems that were nonrecurring and were difficult to quantify or even estimate. Today, as an alternative to a management information system, a two-level structure appears to be emerging. Routine, structured activities comprise the lower level, while decision support systems which assist in the less routine, less structured decision-making activities of managerial control and strategic management, are the upper level. Strategic management systems are becoming a fact of life in today's competitive hospital.

One component of successful strategic management is the proper creation, completion, storage, and access of the patient medical record. Historically, medical records activities have been labor-intensive in nature and have been prone to delays caused by the tremendous volume of medical records. Today, automation of the modern medical records department allows for improvement in management of information, patient care, financial viability, and competitive position in the marketplace.

The automation of the medical records department may be broken into four fundamental activities (Packer, 1985b):

Master patient index
Chart location
Diagnosis Related Group (DRG) classification
Abstracting

Today, the medical record is in essence the patient's bill. Third-party payer requirements for completion of the medical record prior to submission of a bill can have a significant effect on a hospital's cash-flow status. Automation offers a way to increase the efficiency of this process. Automated DRG analysis application allows hospitals to provide and maintain a high quality of care and provides a method for review and evaluation of treatment modalities to be accomplished by clinicians and managers alike.

Future trends in medical records automation deal with the availability of charts to two people in two different locations at the same time. Through the use of optical disks and local area network (LAN) technology, this problem may be solved. Optical disks have the capacity to store enormous amounts of textual data and video images. For most hospitals, one optical disk could permanently store a year's worth of admission data (in unaltered form). LAN technology allows hospitals to have the capability to transmit textual, video, and audio data simultaneously along one path to geographically remote sites, a consideration of growing importance as hospitals diversify their delivery of services. Through such technology, clinicians in different parts of the hospital could access the record simultaneously. New data, once entered, would be immediately available without any inconsistencies to all who might have need of it. Further, the medical record could be identified in a specific fashion whenever data had not been added in a timely fashion. With proper and effective safeguards and security and privacy protocols, physicians and other health care providers could access a patient's medical records from other geographic locations, thus allowing them to follow the patient's progress more intensely (Packer, 1985b).

Personnel departments are using computers for maintaining current employee records. These records can contain the most basic information or may contain special needs related to staff positions, such as certification requirements, performance appraisals, job-related benefits and claims, and employees' health-related information. Personnel departments are also charged with responsibility for maintaining accurate job descriptions on all employee positions. Those organizations with formal union representation must be familiar with contract specifics at all times. The automated personnel department finds that paperwork is decreased and productivity enhanced through computerization. Further, computerization can assist in strategic planning as it relates to attrition rates and changes in staffing needs (Christensen and Rupp, 1986).

The benefits of computerization for inventory control are also impressive. Through a systematic automated system, materials managers can keep abreast of current inventory so that supplies are not depleted or underutilized. This enables the organization to efficiently use supplies and resources, thereby increasing the economic benefits associated with accurate inventory control.

Computerization of peer review and quality assurance programs allows for immediate analysis of large amounts of data concerning actual processes and outcomes of patient care. These programs are most effective if they function concurrently with criteria immediately available for the most common diagnoses and with a method for determining which patient's care meets these criteria and which represents exceptions. An information system which provides both criteria for care and data on actual care on-line and in real-time, permits implementation of standards of care as patients are being cared for, not after-the-fact (Hodge, 1977).

In addition to the problem of patient morbidity, nosocomial (hospital-associated) infections are now an economic issue for hospitals. Today, approximately four to five percent of patients in hospitals develop a nosocomial infection. The severity of infection is reflected in extended length of stay and escalating health care costs. Recently published research has estimated the cost of nosocomial infections to be over $1 billion annually. In this era of prospective reimbursement, nosocomial infections constitute lost revenue to the hospital; and infection control programs are now challenged to meet the demand of cost containment, as well as the prevention of hospital-associated infections. Since data are the key to an active infection control program, computer assistance has been used. A computer can offer a mechanism to store, organize, and retrieve data in a highly efficient manner. In addition, computerization can result in staff hours saved, improved analysis of data, increased sensitivity for identifying at-risk patients, improved efficiency and productivity of the department, and the ability to expand services without increasing staff (Troxler and Escott, 1985).

To continue to provide quality care at a competitive price, hospitals need to get maximum mileage out of their data. A large percentage of hospitals are merging their financial and clinical information. In the future, information on consumer and payer needs may be integrated with hospital financial and clinical data. Such integration would help the hospital to better realize its strengths, weaknesses, areas of service dominance, and new areas to investigate which have future market value (Packer, 1985d).

5. Discharge Planning

Discharge planning is directed toward ensuring continuing health care for a person moving between home and the health care system. To be effective, discharge planning must use a systematic approach that integrates activities surrounding the goal of coordinating patient needs with available resources. The preparation for discharge is emphasized from the time of admission and should identify the linkages among the care providers, the providers as participants in the plan of care, and the achievement of mutually agreed upon goals (Romano, 1984).

The components of discharge planning utilizing an automated system consist of:

Admission assessment
Screening
Access/referral
Multidisciplinary assessment
Integrated care plan
Documented progress
Discharge summary
Multidisciplinary outcome summary

In an environment that fosters cost containment through efficient resource consumption, and with current reimbursement methods, early discharge planning allows for quality care to be rendered without sacrificing the economic needs of the organization. At a Maryland hospital, computerized discharge planning activities allow for the communication of patient care needs as the individual moves between home and inpatient or outpatient settings. The computer allows for communication to occur between the community and referring physician by providing an organized nursing summary document that highlights nursing diagnosis and contains information about the multidisciplinary involvement that occurred at the hospital (Romano, 1984). As the emphasis on ambulatory and home care grows, successful organizations are likely to be those that can integrate acute care needs with ambulatory and home care requirements. The potential for linking physician's offices to hospital-maintained acute care and ambulatory care records accentuates the need for integration in all hospital computerization activities.

6. Home Health Care

Although home health care is not new, rising hospital costs have helped to redefine its importance in our health care delivery system. Today, home health care is emerging as a cost-effective alternative to prolonged hospital stays. Prospective payment methods have forced hospitals to develop strategies for reducing length of stay. As stated previously, early discharge planning is one method being utilized for reducing hospital stay. Because of increasing demands for services, home health care agencies are experiencing a need for automated financial and management information systems. The freestanding agency is faced with the need to provide Medicare services, private duty nursing, Medicare billing, private client billing and receivables management, payroll, accounts payable, and general ledger (McIlvane, 1986b).

Because of these needs, coupled with the pressure to stay competitive in a rapidly changing marketplace, strategic planning and marketing are essential for home health care agencies. While home health care experts have identified the information needs for the present, future trends are focusing on networking and data exchange of patient information among different components of the health care delivery system. Costs, control, confidentiality, security, responsibility, and usefulness are all factors to be considered. The exchange of basic patient demographic information upon hospital discharge, and later if the patient situation changes and hospital reentry results, is essential. It is further believed that the trend toward accessing patient demographic information will be forced by economics, as it can reduce data entry time when patients are referred from hospitals to home health agencies or back to hospitals again (McIlvane, 1986a).

7. Community Mental Health Centers

The need for cost-effective information processing in this era of cost containment has touched all areas of service, including community mental health. Hennage (1983) reports on the efforts of an Indiana mental health agency's efforts to computerize. This agency employed 200 people, had a client roster of 3,000, provided 50,000 activities annually, and had an annual budget of $6 million. This agency's fundamental concern was to purchase a data base which could answer the questions "Where and why does who do what, with what result, and at what cost?" Because of various vested interests, this center received little to no encouragement in its search for an adequate system. However, through commitment and involvement of managers and staff, the agency was able to successfully implement an integrated computer system which could produce monthly productivity reports; prepare the state budget; keep personnel files; produce personnel reports; increase the timeliness and accuracy of the billing process, thereby improving revenue-generating procedures; and provide general ledger and accounts payable statistics. Future trends in community agency automation also deal with the issues of networking and linkage to other agencies on a statewide basis. Once again, it is anticipated that matters of citizen's rights and privacy will be a major part of the challenge.

II. ANALYSIS OF COMPUTER UTILIZATION

The focus of our discussion to this point has centered on the various computer systems available to the health and human service manager today and key clinical areas in which these systems are in use, as well as on some future developments that may be expected in these areas. This section presents a statistical analysis of computer use in the nation's health care organizations in order to help clarify the magnitude and scope of the computerized environment of health and human services.

While there are numerous studies on computerization in health care available today, statistics cited here are taken from three major studies: (1) C. L. Packer and the research staff of Shared Data Research, Hudson, Ohio, examined the use of computers in hospitals from 1981 through 1984 for the American Hospital Association. The data base consisted of 4,367 hospitals, of which more than 1,300 hospitals participated through either telephone or mail survey. (2) Joyce Jensen, of the National Research Corporation, Lincoln, Nebraska, has charted overall data processing and microcomputer usage in hospitals from 1983 through 1985 by telephone survey of 450 administrators selected randomly and stratified by bed size and geographic area. (3) Sheldon I. Dorenfest, of Dorenfest and Associates, Highland Park, Illinois, has monitored trends in microcomputer usage in the nation's hospitals from 1979 through the present by utilizing a statistically representative sample of 250 community hospitals in the United States. These three studies were chosen because of the inclusiveness of the data provided. Taken together, these studies provide some significant insights for health and human service managers.

A. Changes in Data Processing Budgets

Packer (1985a) found that between 1981 and 1984, the average hospital increased its data processing budget by sixty-five percent. While the percentage of hospitals with computer budgets under $200,000 decreased from approximately thirty percent in 1981 to 13 percent in 1984, the percentage of hospitals having data processing budgets greater than $1 million grew from 14 percent in 1981 to almost 31 percent in 1984. More than fifty-seven percent of the sample hospitals had budgets in excess of $500,000 in 1984. These increases in data processing expenditures are symptomatic of the importance of accurate and timely information. Not only does information support the hospital's day-to-day operations, but it also provides the basis for the organization's strategic management system. This statistic is further supported by data supplied by Dorenfest (1985), who found that in 1980, none of the 250 community hospitals surveyed used microcomputers, whereas 218 (eighty-seven percent) were using computers by the end of 1984, and by Jensen and Miklovic (1985), who found that four out of every 10 hospitals surveyed planned a major purchase, replacement, or enhancement of their information systems hardware.

B. Trends in Approaches to Data Processing

The four principal approaches to using computer technology within hospitals have been in-house, turnkey, facilities management, and shared services. Packer (1984a) defines each as follows:

In-house: A hospital employing this approach purchases and controls its own hardware, has a professional staff to manage the computer system, and assumes responsibility for obtaining the requisite software to implement desired functions.

Turnkey: Under this approach, a hospital contracts with a third party for its computer services. For a set fee, the third party provides both the hardware and the software. Once the system is set up, its operation is under the hospital's control; however, the third party remains available to answer questions and provide assistance, maintenance, and improvements.

Facilities management: This approach gives a hospital computer services that are under its control but are staffed by professionals working for a facilities management company. Typically, the company contracts with the hospital to perform all data processing activities at the hospital using the company's staff.

Shared services: This approach utilizes a third party to perform all data processing activities. Usually, the site is in a different geographic location from the hospital and data processing activities occur with the hospital sending and receiving data over existing communication lines.

Jensen and Miklovic (1985) found that more hospitals have developed in-house data processing capabilities, while hospitals' arrangements with outside data processing companies have declined. Thus, each year since 1983, five percent more hospitals have developed in-house data processing systems to meet the need for information. Growth of total in-house systems occurred in hospitals of every bed-size group with only one exception. Hospitals with 100 to 199 beds showed substantial increases in the amount of data processing performed outside the hospital, while still maintaining some kind of in-house data processing. Fifty-six percent of hospitals with more than 500 beds used only in-house data processing, making it the bed-size group with the highest percentage of hospitals using only in-house processing. Further, sixty percent of the hospitals in the Southwest used in-house systems, the highest concentration, while the Northeast showed the lowest current in-house capabilities, at thirty-nine percent. However, eleven percent more of the region's hospitals had internal data processing systems in 1985 than in 1984, and twenty-six percent more hospitals in the Northeast purchased hardware and software during 1985 to help the hospital cope with prospective pricing. Jensen has further revealed through her survey that through 1985–1986, six out of 10 hospitals that currently use outside data processing facilities plan to bring data processing in-house, at least partially, and fifty percent of those who currently rely primarily on outside systems want to rely more on in-house systems.

In addition, Packer (1985a) found that of the hospitals that utilized the in-house approach to data processing in 1981, approximately seventy-seven percent retained the in-house system in 1984, while nineteen percent had switched to shared service vendors, and three percent to the facility management approach. Likewise, eighty percent of the facility management hospitals had shifted to in-house (forty percent), turnkey (twenty percent), or shared services (twenty percent) by 1984. Over fifty percent of the turnkey approach hospitals had shifted to either shared services or in-house by 1984. These results suggest that shared service is the preferred approach for those hospitals leaving the turnkey approach, while hospitals terminating facility management contracts have a fifty percent likelihood of going in-house.

Much of the growth in data processing budgets and applications, as well as shifts in data processing approach used, can be explained by hospitals' attempts to meet the challenges of the current turbulent health care environment. The manager in today's health care organization must be sensitive to these changes and able to adapt to those methods which will allow the institution to continue to provide quality care at a competitive price.

C. Trends in Computer Hardware

A computer is usually classified as either a mainframe computer, a minicomputer, or a microcomputer. The exact definition of each is not clear; however, Packer (1984a) comments that most people would agree that a million dollar computer is a mainframe, whereas a thousand dollar computer is a microcomputer. Somewhere between $20,000 and $40,000, an ill-defined line is crossed, and one moves from the microcomputer world to the minicomputer world.

Differences other than costs can distinguish the three types of computers. The original computers, large mainframes, required specialized staffs and controlled environments. They were usually located in a data processing department, away from the users. As technology advanced, it became possible to access mainframes from distant locations using terminals or printers. Like mainframes, the development of minicomputers often required a specialized staff for their use and programming, and tended to be housed in remote locations. However, with the development of microcomputers, the way people view and use computers is changing. These self-contained units can sit on the corner of a desk completely under the control of the user. Software for micros is now designed to be user-friendly and so eliminates the need for a specialized computer staff.

Packer (1984c) has found that approximately thirty percent of all hospitals sampled utilized a mainframe computer, while sixty-five percent utilized minicomputers, and sixty percent used microcomputers. Fifty-five percent of hospitals use more than one type of computer. Dorenfest's (1985) survey revealed that among the 250 hospitals sampled, the number of microcomputers in use has almost tripled each year from 1981 through 1984. He further revealed that microcomputer hardware is used in many hospital departments. The fastest-growing and largest users of microcomputers include finance and accounting, medical records, and laboratory departments. By the end of 1984, more than three-quarters of the sample hospitals with microcomputers used them in the finance and account departments, and almost half used them in the medical records and laboratory areas. Other areas with substantial microcomputerization are nursing, pharmacy, respiratory therapy, and radiology departments. Administrative areas using micros include general administration, data processing, public relations, personnel, materials management, engineering, and education. Jensen and Miklovic (1985) reported that one-third of the hospital administrators surveyed had microcomputers for their own use, and that of those who did not have a microcomputer at the time of the survey, thirty-six percent planned to be using one within 12 months. They further reported that seven out of 10 administrators utilize their microcomputer for spread sheet analysis or data base management. Fifty-nine percent use them for general word processing, and 24 percent utilize them for accessing the mainframe computer. While microcomputer use is widespread in all bed-size facilities, significantly more metropolitan hospitals than rural facilities utilize the micro. Thus, ninety-one percent of metropolitan hospitals surveyed utilize a micro, versus seventy-four percent of rural hospitals. Nevertheless, administrators and managers alike are using micros as immediate information access becomes necessary for decision making in a rapidly changing environment.

D. Satisfaction Levels Associated with Computerization

As has been previously stated, most hospitals employ three basic data processing activities: financial management, patient care, and strategic management. Likewise, a hospital can utilize one of four major systems to implement those activities: in-house, turnkey, facilities management, and shared services. Further, hospitals may have mainframe computers, minicomputers, microcomputers, or a combination of the three as the basis of their computer hardware. Of primary concern to health care managers today is the level of satisfaction associated with computer use in health care settings. Packer (1984b) reports that hospitals surveyed from 1981 through 1984 cited nine factors affecting their level of satisfaction. They are:

1. Technology—the ability of the system's hardware/software combination to meet the hospital's needs
2. People—the extent to which the people necessary to implement and operate the system are available
3. Cost—the cost of the system
4. Flexibility—the extent to which the system can be adapted to environmental changes
5. Integration—the system's ability to interface two functions, such as patient billing and accounts receivable
6. Performance—the efficiency and speed with which the system performs the functions it is designed for
7. Growth—the extent to which the system can accommodate increasing demands placed upon it
8. Support—the availability of technical and personnel resources when needed to correct system problems and provide assistant to the users
9. Size—the system's ability to satisfy the hospital's needs in a cost-effective manner, providing neither too much nor too little power or cost.

Packer (1984a) found that among the hospitals that are satisfied with their systems, twenty-one percent cited performance as the reason, nineteen percent cited flexibility, sixteen percent cited cost, and four percent cited growth. Dissatisfied hospitals cited those same factors in the following proportions, respectively: seventeen percent, twenty-nine percent, ten percent, and seven percent. These statistics indicate, according to Packer, that reasonable cost and high performance are more likely to be associated with systems that satisfy hospitals, and inflexibility and low growth capability are more likely to be associated with systems that do not satisfy. Packer also found that there was no statistical significance between satisfied and dissatisfied ratings for the factors of support and technology. These statistics can be helpful to the health and human service manager who is faced with a choice between two affordable systems. The flexibility and growth capability of each system should be thoroughly investigated, since these factors appear to be more likely associated with dissatisfaction.

Packer (1984b) also reports that when hospitals were examined for the level of satisfaction associated with the data processing approach utilized (such as in-house versus turnkey), the overwhelming majority of hospitals sampled were either very satisfied or satisfied with their existing systems, whatever the approach utilized. Thus, this statistic appears to indicate that existing systems are meeting hospital needs currently.

Today, well over 300 different companies offer software to the hospital industry. Their products range from single application software to entire systems. Software is a major and often misunderstood expense. It may be a onetime purchase of a package or a recurring lease arrangement with a third party. If software is developed by the hospital, actual costs are more difficult to identify than when it is obtained from an outside source (Packer, 1985a). Since the modern health and human service manager may be involved with the purchase of a software program, it is helpful to examine how satisfied hospitals are with current software applications.

Distinctions between computer hardware and types of computer software often are confusing. Hardware describes the physical components of the computer—that is, pieces that can be seen or touched. However, these items are useless until given instructions, via computer programs, that specifically define the steps to be taken to perform an activity. Programs are stored in electronic states and are called software. There are two important types of software to distinguish. The first, known as system software or the operating system, is obtained from the company which manufactures the hospital's computer hardware. For mainframe computers, the operating system is usually leased on a cost per month basis, while microcomputer users can purchase system software for a onetime fee.

While system software controls the use of hardware components, the second class of software, application software, directs the computer to perform activities to support specific operational and managerial functions, such as payroll, pharmacy, laboratory, and DRG. There are six widely used applications which represent the three major data processing systems within the hospitals: financial management, patient care, and strategic management. These applications are patient billing and general ledger for financial management systems; admission/discharge and transfer, and nurses' station order entry for patient care systems; and financial planning and DRG software for strategic management systems (Packer, 1985c).

When assessing hospitals for their level of satisfaction with application software, Packer (1985c) asked participating hospitals to compare the actual cost of each application software with the amount budgeted. It was reported that hospitals with a system developed in-house were most likely to be at or under budget (eighty-nine percent), while twenty percent of hospitals using the other three approaches–turnkey, facility management, and shared service–tended to be over budget.

When hospitals were asked if they would recommend their applications to other hospitals, patient billing rated a twenty-seven percent response for "would not recommend." Hospitals listed inflexibility, inadequate technology, and cost as factors in their rating. Further, in-house and facility management hospitals were least satisfied with their patient billing applications, with thirty-five percent and thirty-seven percent, respectively, saying they would not recommend it to other hospitals. General ledger applications revealed that twenty-six percent of in-house hospitals and thirty-nine percent of facility management institutions would not recommend their applications. Primary reasons for dissatisfaction for all approaches were inflexibility, inadequate technology, and poor performance. Admissions applications revealed that facility management institutions were by far the least likely to recommend their admissions software to another hospital. Thirty-eight percent reported dissatisfaction with the software. Primary reasons cited for dissatisfaction for all approaches were inflexibility, cost, and inadequate technology. Order entry software appeared to be an application process with which most hospitals were satisfied: Ninety-eight percent of all hospitals with shared services would recommend their software to another hospital.

Where users were dissatisfied, the most frequently cited reasons were inadequate technology and insufficient ability to integrate the software with other components of the hospital information system. Financial planning software analysis revealed that thirty-six percent of hospitals utilizing facility management would not recommend their software to another hospital, and twenty-nine percent of hospitals using the turnkey reported that they would not recommend their software. Cost was the leading reason for dissatisfaction with financial planning software. Other reasons were inflexibility and lack of growth capability. DRG software was the application with which most hospitals were satisfied: Ninety-eight percent of shared service hospitals would recommend their application to another hospital, while ninety-three percent of in-house hospitals showed satisfaction. Facility management hospitals fared the worst, with twenty-seven percent stating that they would not recommend their software. Hospital satisfaction and dissatisfaction hinged on the same three factors. Satisfied hospitals cited good performance, flexibility, and cost as reasons for their satisfaction, while dissatisfied institutions cited cost, inflexibility, and poor performance as the major reasons for dissatisfaction.

Overall, these studies suggest that today's health care manager is faced with the responsibility for making technology management decisions in an environment in which this technology is rapidly changing. Macaleer (1985) argues that managing technology is both a demanding and an ongoing process. However, he further states that managerial decisions can be considerably easier if managers carefully analyze the market, stay skeptical of trends, and focus on issues that clearly articulate their particular institution's needs. The issues Macaleer believes are most central to modern managerial input are cost, growth, and flexibility.

Costs must be considered relative to the issues of growth and flexibility. An early misconception was one that hinged on the issues surrounding computer purchase. Once the computer was bought and programmed, the organization considered itself as having an information system. However, with rapidly changing technology, hospital managers quickly realized that the issue is not one just of purchase cost of the system, but rather of cost-effectiveness over the long run. A system can be considered cost-effective when it can support both the change and the growth needs of the organization.

Finally, systems which are flexible and able to grow with changing organizational needs will have a positive impact on the organization's ability to increase its control over information.

III. MANAGERIAL IMPLICATIONS

It is reasonable to conclude that the use of advanced computer technology in health and human service organizations has been impressive, and that its impact on both quality of care and productivity has been significant. But this state of the art report, as thus far presented, should not give the impression that the experience to date has been a milk-and-honey phenomenon. Quite to the contrary, use of the technology (as suggested in the previous section), has been problem-laden, and there have been as many horror stories as success stories. Moreover, the successful applications of computer technology in health and human services have not come easily—they all required rigorous managerial action. This final section addresses that other side of the story.

A. Problems Encountered

The use of computer technology in health and human service organizations is a story of wonders, but it is also a tale of woes. Hardly an organization has gone untouched by downtime, computer error, cost overruns, personnel upsets, or some other "horror story" associated with use of the technology. Major areas of difficulty have been design and planning processes, operational matters, organizational impacts, psychological reactions, and political or legal realities.

1. *Design and Planning Processes.* The coalition of vendors, technicians, and information users needed to make a computer application effective has proven to be elusive. Computer vendors have often been difficult to control, technicians have more than occasionally been incomprehensible, and users have tended to be easily intimidated

and uninvolved. The result has been computer systems that don't work—that is, systems that do not produce what the user was promised or thought, and that don't meet the users' need. Thus, we hear tales, lots of them, about reams of printouts beautifully generated by sophisticated hardware, as directed by advanced software, that are unreadable or inaccurate, out of date, or otherwise unusable by the intended user. We hear stories of expensive hardware remaining in unopened crates in organizations' offices. We hear of users spending hours at terminals or microcomputers trying to access one piece of information that formerly was available quickly in manual form. In short, planning and designing systems that actually meet the needs of users has been a serious challenge.

2. *Operational Matters*. Two of the more notorious examples of operational problems with computer applications have become so common that the terms "computer downtime" and "computer error" need little explanation in the lexicons of health and human service professionals. Patients have been billed incorrectly, or not at all, because of computer error; clients have become hypertensive while waiting to be issued a medical record number because a computer was down. More subtle, but no less common, operational problems have been data pollution and security. Many health and human service organizations have experienced a debilitating overabundance of data as a result of computerization. Health care professionals, for example, have reported an inability to find needed information among mountains of data generated from computer systems. But perhaps the most serious operational problems have involved security breakdowns. Loss of computerized data, unauthorized access to data, even manipulation of data are problems that have occurred again and again after installation of advanced computerized systems.

3. *Organizational Impacts*. Probably the greatest problems encountered in using advanced hardware and software have involved organizational dynamics. Unintended and often subtle impacts have proven to be the nemesis of many computerization projects in health care and human service organizations. Chief among these have been user resistance and shifts in organizational power. Caseworkers, clerks, doctors, and nurses, fearful of the technology or angry at the way it was introduced, have found subtle ways to resist such that technically sound computer systems do not work. In addition, use of the technology has tended to relegate previously important employees to less significant roles, and to raise computer technicians to lofty heights. Antagonism between aloof technicians and intimidated users has been common.

4. *Psychological Reactions*. The history of the use of computers in health and human services is replete with behavioral patterns caused by fear, anxiety, and distrust. Increased absenteeism, declines in morale, and staff disruption have been typical adjuncts of advanced hardware and software. Based on a study of 40 hospitals, Dowling (1980) concluded that computers are ego-threatening. He found professionals who feared the loss of prestige, and clerks who seemed paranoid that the computer was usurping their power. Increased isolation also seems to have produced feelings of anomie in many organizations. These psychological reactions have been behind the resistance to new hardware and software that has plagued many health and human service organizations.

5. *Political/Legal Realities*. Two pieces of federal legislation, and hundreds of similar statutes in state and local jurisdictions, have complicated the effort to employ advanced computer technology. Freedom of information laws have placed legal responsibilities on health and human service organizations to make available information that they hold. On the other hand, privacy laws place legal restrictions on information

processing. Health and human service professionals have frequently been caught in the middle. When computers are used, more data tend to be collected and stored, which means, under freedom of information laws, that more data must be made available. Under privacy laws, this means that more data must be protected, with computer error being an unacceptable excuse for breaking the law. These legal requirements are becoming both more stringent and more applicable.

B. Lessons Learned

Our analysis suggests that nearly all the difficulties and problems that organizations have experienced with advanced hardware and software are nontechnical in nature; rather, they are managerial. Austin and Greene (1978) have observed concerning problems with computers in health care: "While there appear to be several factors that cause [problems] . . . the main one seems to be hospital managers themselves." This conclusion is also reached by Herzlinger (1977) in her analysis of computer use in nonprofit organizations generally. For practical purposes, advanced technology is high in quality, reliability, and sophistication; management of this technology, on the other hand, has generally been underdeveloped in comparison.

Significant managerial advances have, however, been made. The experience with advanced technology, related above, has produced insights and lessons, the application of which is making the use of advanced computer systems both more productive and less traumatic. Some of the more important of these insights are the following.

1. *Become computer literate.* Most of us effectively use and manage two advanced technologies today—the telephone and the automobile. To use them well, we become, in a sense, technologically literate. To use a telephone, we all learn what a dial tone is, which end of the phone to speak into, area codes, and so forth—things that we take for granted, but which are actually technical aspects that a user must know. Similarly, to effectively use a car, we do not need to understand principles of internal combustion, hydraulics, and electricity, but we do need to know how to read a fuel gauge, where the brake pedal is located, what a red light or green light means, and so forth. The same kind of literacy is needed to effectively use and manage computers. Health and human service professionals do not need to know and understand principles of electronics or programming. But we do need to understand basic computer jargon and concepts—the equivalents of dial tone, brake pedal, area code, and miles per hour.

2. *Be involved in system planning, design, and implementation.* A common tendency has been to turn the management of advanced computer technology over to the technicians. Case after case has taught us that user-managers must be involved if the systems are to work well in the organization. While we do use automobile mechanics to ensure that our cars run well, we do not let the mechanic tell us where we should drive the car. Similarly, information needs can be determined only by the users; and organizational realities that computer systems enter into are best understood and managed by user-managers.

3. *Think systematically.* Systematic analysis needs to take place before, during, and after the introduction of advanced computer technology. This involves identifying user objectives, gathering information on how to meet them, formulating alternatives, and monitoring what happens. Good systematic analysis is asking the right questions and getting the best answers possible. Good management is ensuring that all the right questions are asked and that the best answers are sought. Experience shows that most

challenges and problems of computerization can be anticipated if the relevant questions are posed; most obstacles can be recognized if the development process is systematically monitored; most difficulties can be handled if users and managers systematically observe and learn.

4. *Anticipate and manage organizational impacts.* In addition to identifying areas of organizational impact, health and human service managers need to understand how these arise and develop. They should plan and implement precise actions to mitigate, enhance, or otherwise control anticipated impacts.

5. *Anticipate and understand resistance.* The fundamental lesson for managing resistance is to focus on the user. Involving the user in the computerization project, selling the user on the system, keeping the user fully informed—these are the kinds of managerial actions that produce success.

6. *Attend to security.* Managing the security of computer systems is an administrative task requiring creative user-manager action. Organizing information, assessing vulnerabilities, installing procedural and technical measures—these and other efforts need attention.

7. *Establish privacy policies.* Dealing with the privacy issue in computerization is a serious responsibility that requires the perception and sensitivity of the manager. Knowing the laws and regulations and establishing policies and procedures are first steps.

In sum, as a result of efforts to use advanced computer technology in health and human service organizations, the state of the art in managing the use of these systems has advanced considerably. We now realize that the key to successful use of sophisticated hardware and software is advanced managerial perspective and skill.

BIBLIOGRAPHY

Adams, G. A. (1986). Computer technology: Its impact on nursing practice, *Nursing Administration Quarterly, 10*(2): 21.
An excellent work dealing with the social and ethnical implications of computerization and nursing practices.

Albrecht, C. A., and Lieske, A. M. (1985). Automating patient care planning, *Nursing Management, 16*(7): 21.
Valuable case study highlighting the needs for a well-integrated system in a nursing practice.

Anthony, R. N., and Young, D. W. (1984). *Management Control in Non-Profit Organizations,* 3rd ed., Richard D. Irwin, Homewood, Illinois.
Provides valuable insights into managerial control issues in non-profit organizations.

Austin, C. J., and Greene, B. R. (1978). Hospital information systems, *Inquiry, 14,* June: 95. A comprehensive summary of hospital uses in the 1970s.

Bagby, P. R. (1985). Orienting nurses to computers, *Nursing Management, 16*(7): 30.
Good case study pointing out the need to assess adult learning needs prior to instituting computers.

Ball, M. J., and Boyle, T. M. (1980). Hospital information systems: Past, present and future, *Hospital Financial Management, 10,* February: 12.
Traces the progression of hospital information systems and provides a classification scheme for information system.

Becker, G. L. (1984). The impact of DRGs on New Jersey labs, *Medical Laboratory Observer, 15,* January: 30.
Fascinating report on how New Jersey labs are coping with prospective pricing and how computerization can help.

Bellinger, K., and Laden, J. (1985). Nurse use of general purpose microcomputer software, *Nursing Outlook, 33*: 22.
Good explanation of basic software programs that have use for nursing application.

Bergmann, C., and Johnson, J. (1986). Managing nursing care with a personal computer, *Nursing Management, 17*(7): 29.
Case study of personal computer use in a medical/surgical unit. Sample charts available.

Blomberg, R., and Beebe, C. (1986). Needs-based micro training—A case study, *Health Care Computing and Communications, 3*: 92.
Needs-based computer training emphasized in this study on micro training.

Buisson, C. J. (1985). Computer applications in nursing continuing education, *Nursing Clinics of North America, 20*: 505.
Excellent case study on a continuing education department's transition to computerization.

Carpenter, C. R. (1983). Computer use in nursing management, *Journal of Nursing Administration, 13*(11): 17.
Outlines a role for the nurse administrator in preparing and implementing automatic data processing plans.

Childs, B. W. (1985). Nursing home information systems, *Health Care Computing and Communication, 2*: 64.
Outlines the need for information systems in nursing home facilities.

Christensen, W. W., and Rupp, P. R. (1986). *The Nurse Manager's Guide to Computers*, Aspen Publishers, Germantown, Maryland.
Excellent text on computer basics, implementation processes, and computer potentials for the nurse-manager.

Counte, M. A., Kjerulff, K. H., Salloway, J. C., and Campbell, B. S. (1983). Implementation of a medical information system: Evaluation of adaptation, *Health Care Management Review*, *8*, Summer: 25.
Study which reveals that employee attitudes affect computer implementation processes.

Cucciarre, D. (1985). Choosing a computer system: Guidelines for the small hospital, *Health Care Computing and Communication, 2*(5): 40.
Key questions a manager should consider when choosing a computer in a small hospital are presented.

Curtain, L. L. (1984). Nursing: High-touch in a high-tech world, *Nursing Management, 15*(7): 7.
Thought-provoking editorial on the impact of technology in health care settings.

diMonda, R. (1984). Keeping abreast of technology, *Hospitals, 58*: 85.
Provides sources of information about new and developing technology in the hospital industry.

Donovan, W. (1986). Federal regulation of software: Widespread, impact, *Computers in Healthcare, 7*(6): 48.
Interesting article dealing with the impact of potential regulation on software development.

Drazen, E. L. (1983). Planning for purchase and implementation of an automated hospital information system: A nursing perspective, *Journal of Nursing Administration, 13*(9): 9.
Discusses the planning process as it relates to the purchase of a computer in the nursing department.

Dorenfest, S. I. (1985). Hospital computer use soars, *Modern Healthcare, 15*(13): 79.
Fascinating study addressing the use of computers in hospitals from 1979 through 1984.

Dowling, A. F. (1980). Do hospitals interfere with computer implementation? *Health Care Management Review*, *5*, Fall: 23.
A survey of a community hospital staff's resistance to the use of computers.

Durel, T. J. (1985). Obstacles to direct use of information systems, *Healthcare Computing and Communications*, *2*(11): 56.
Excellent work which reveals some obstacles to a manager's direct use of information systems.

Evans, R. S., et al. (1986). Computer surveillance of hospital-acquired infections and antibiotic use, *Journal of the American Medical Association*, *256*: 1007.
Describes how computer screening can help focus the activities and improve the efficiency of hospital personnel.

Fedorowicz, J. (1983). Hospital information systems: Are we ready for case mix applications? *Health Care Management Review*, *8*(4): 33.
Interesting work which discusses the need for case-mix applications which are automated.

Ford, P. (1985). Choosing and fitting a pharmacy system, *Healthcare Computing and Communications*, *2*(12): 38.
Experiences of one hospital pharmacy in evaluating and implementing a computerized system.

Ginsberg, D. A., and Browning, S. J. (1985). Selecting automated patient care systems, *Journal of Nursing Administration*, *15*(12): 16.
Provides an overview of the key issues that must be examined in the selection process for a patient care system.

Gustafson, D. H., and Thesen, A. (1981). Are traditional information systems adequate for policy makers? *Health Care Management Review*, *6*(1): 51.
Interesting article exploring the information needs that decision makers rely upon and traditional methods for meeting these needs.

Halverson, C., and Huesing, S. (1984). Hospital information systems: The next three generations, *Healthcare Computing and Communication*, *1*(11): 33.
An examination of the direction that automated hospital systems will take in the future.

Hanson, R. L. (1982). Applying management information systems to staffing, *Journal of Nursing Administration*, *12*(10): 5.
This article defines a seven-step process for establishing a management information system, from defining the management objective to implementing the system.

Happ, B. (1986). Computers: Integrating information-world into nursing, *Nursing Management*, *17*(7): 17.
Excellent work which examines present and future information systems and their ethical impact on nursing.

Henchbarger, T. L. (1986). HMO health education enters the computer age, *Healthcare Computing and Communications*, *3*(7): 86.
Article which examines the issue of computerization in a health maintenance organization.

Hennage, D. W. (1983). Microcomputers: The effective low-cost alternative, *Health Care Management Review*, *8*(3): 35.
One mental health center's experiences with computer selection, purchase and utilization.

Herzlinger, R. (1977). Why data systems in non-profit organizations fail, *Harvard Business Review*, *44*, January–February: 81.
An insightful analysis of problems in non-profit organizations when computers are introduced.

Higgins, L. (1984). Are you glad you have a computer? *Healthcare Computing and Communications, 1*(8): 49.
Discusses issues of increased productivity, decreased costs, and improved efficiency.

Hinson, I., Silva, N., and Clapp, P. (1984). An automated kardex and care plan, *Nursing Management, 15*(7): 35.
One nursing staff's experiences with an automated patient care profile. Sample records provided.

Hodge, M. H. (1977). *Medical Information Systems–A Resource for Hospitals*, Aspen Publishers, Germantown, Maryland.
Helpful text whose purpose is to assist health care managers in understanding the rationale behind medical information systems and the major management issues in selection, implementation, and benefit realization associated with computerization.

Hoffman, F. M. (1985). Evaluating and selecting a computer software package, *Journal of Nursing Administration, 15*(11): 33.
Outlines topics to be considered during software evaluation.

Hulm, C., and Burik, D. (1984). Evaluating the new case-mix systems, *Hospitals, 58*: 92.
Examines the strengths and weaknesses of various data processing systems and their relationship to DRG applications.

Javitt, J. (1986). *Computers in Medicine–Applications and Possibilities*, W. B. Saunders, Philadelphia.
Addresses the use and benefits of computerization for physicians in various health care settings.

Jensen, J., and Miklovic, N. (1985). Half of hospitals plan to purchase software: 40% will buy hardware, *Modern Healthcare, 15*(19): 86.
A study of trends in hospital computer purchases from 1980 to 1984.

Lant, T. W. (1986). Computerized nurse staffing systems: You'd better shop around! *Nursing Management, 17*(7): 37.
Discussion of how to evaluate a system's performance.

Lenkman, S. (1985). Management information systems and the role of the nurse vendor, *Nursing Clinics of North America, 20*: 557.
Discusses the role of the vendor in assisting in the acquisition of computerization.

Lenkman, S. (1985). The case for shared data between hospitals and alternative care settings, *Healthcare Computing and Communications, 2*(4): 45.
Examines the issue of computerization alternatives in multiorganizational settings.

Levine, J., and Tobias, T. (1985). What is your hospital information fitness score? *Healthcare Computing and Communications, 2*(10): 38.
Allows readers to evaluate and recognize the strengths and weaknesses of their information system.

Macaleer, S. C. (1985). Managing technology to manage change, *Healthcare Computing and Communications, 2*(12): 46.
Valuable discussion of pitfalls associated with computerization.

MacArthur, A. M., and Sampson, M. R. (1985). Screen design of a hospital information system, *Nursing Clinics of North America, 20*: 471.
Explores the influence of screen design on the effects of implementation of an information system.

McCarthy, L. J. (1985). Taking charge of computerization, *Nursing Management, 16*(7): 35.
Presents a practical strategy for getting nursing management's interests into the hospital's data base and retrieval programs.

McConnell, C. R. (1985). Video display terminals: A new source of employee problems, *Health Care Supervisor, 3*: 81.
The comparatively new video display terminal and creative problem-solving techniques managers need to know for its use.

McHugh, M. L. (1986). Information access: A basis for strategic planning and control of operations, *Nursing Administration Quarterly, 10*(2): 10.
Presents the role of information in strategic planning.

McIlvane, M. E. (1986a). A roundtable discussion on home health and information systems, *Computers in Healthcare, 5*(1): 34.
Discusses the need for computerized information management in the fast-growing and changing home health marketplace.

McIlvane, M. E. (1986b). Value of computerization–Home health executive viewpoints, part 1, *Computers in Healthcare, 5*(2): 38.
Focuses on the managerial awareness of the importance of computerized information systems in home health care.

McIlvane, M. E. (1986c). Value of computerization–Executive viewpoints, part 2, *Computers in Healthcare, 5*(3): 50.
Continuation of the article on managerial awareness.

Maimis, R. A. (1986). A "mainframe" on every desktop, *Inc.*, November: 17.
Brief explanation of tomorrow's "wunderchip."

Mayo, G. E. (1986). Total community healthcare network, *Healthcare Computing and Communications, 3*(8): 60.
Explores the benefits of a community computerized network for healthcare.

Meason, R. (1986). A case for system security, *Computers in Healthcare, 5*(6): 60.
Security management considerations for a successful computerized system.

Newbern, V. B. (1985). Computer literacy in nursing education, *Nursing Clinics of North America, 20*: 549.
Discusses new language today's nurse must learn to speak and understand.

O'Desky, R. I. (1986). An infocentric view of the hospital information system, *Healthcare Computing and Communications, 3*(1): 44.
Examines the development of an integrated system from an infocentric viewpoint.

Packer, C. L. (1984a). The four principal approaches to data processing and the satisfaction they provide, *Hospitals, 58*(11): 88.

Packer, C. L. (1984b). Why hospitals like–or dislike–their approaches to data processing, *Hospitals, 58*(13): 81.

Packer, C. L. (1984c). Computer hardware in the hospital industry, *Hospitals, 58*(21): 111.

Packer, C. L. (1984d). Management information systems: Key tools for CEOs, *Hospitals, 58*(22): 107.

Packer, C. L. (1985a). Historical changes in hospital computer use, *Hospitals, 59*(2): 115.

Packer, C. L. (1985b). Automation in the medical records department, *Hospitals, 59*(5): 100.

Packer, C. L. (1985c). What hospitals think of application software, *Hospitals, 59*(8): 101.

Packer, C. L. (1985d). Integration, performance key to ambulatory care information systems, *Hospitals, 59*(10): 120.

Packer, C. L. (1985e). Automation in the hospital pharmacy, *Hospitals, 59*(18): 106.

Packer, C. L. (1985f). Turnkey systems dominate hospital lab market, *Hospitals, 59*(20): 96.
Series presents the results of a major, ongoing study on computerization in hospitals.

Poggio, F. L. (1986). Information system flexibility, *Computers in Healthcare, 7*(4): 36.
Focuses on the importance of flexibility in an information system.

Powell, M. N. (1982). Designing and developing a computerized hospital information system, *Nursing Management, 13*(8): 40.
Focuses on the importance of defining variables when considering computerization.

Randall, A. M. (1985). The computer did it, *Healthcare Computing and Communications, 2*(4): 72.
A lighthearted look at computer errors.

Reeves, D. M., and Underly, N. K. (1982). Computerization of nursing, *Nursing Management, 13*(8): 50.
Examines nursing department's success with automation.

Repogle, K. J. (1986). A computer at every bedside, *Critical Care Nurse, 6*(1): 14.
Examines how nurses have utilized computers in critical care for many years.

Romano, C. A. (1984). A computerized approach to discharge care planning, *Nursing Outlook, 32*(1): 23.
Documents how computers can coordinate and record care needs of the patient as he or she moves between the hospital and home.

Romano, C. A. (1986). Development, implementation, and utilization of a computerized information system for nursing, *Nursing Administration Quarterly, 10*(2): 1.
Analyzes the components to be considered when planning a computerized system for nursing.

Sanders, D. H., and Birkin, S. J. (1980). *Computers and Management in a Changing Society*, McGraw-Hill, New York.
Provides a broad managerial orientation to data processing in society today.

Shapin, P. G. (1986). The expanding role of information systems, *Healthcare Computing and Communications, 3*(6): 50.
Discusses the necessity of two systems, one designed for flexibility, the other for transactions.

Silverman, M. R. (1986). Departmental computer systems—Reevaluating the issues of control, *Computers in Healthcare, 7*(9): 49.
Computing is undergoing a fundamental change away from the traditional centralized facility, toward various distributive processing methods which will require control measures to assure accuracy.

Stern, S. K. (1986). Microcomputers—Becoming hospital-wide productivity tools, *Healthcare Computing and Communications, 3*(2): 18.
Explores the effects of computerization.

Suding, M. J. (1984). Controlling the computer input, *Nursing Management, 15*(7): 44.
Presents computer-related challenges to personal accountability and decision-making activities.

Tamarisk, N. K. (1982). The computer as a clinical tool, *Nursing Management, 13*(8): 46.
Discusses the need for nursing leadership to move beyond emotion-laden myths about computers, to solid understanding of the clinical applications and potential future impacts.

Tarrent, C. A. (1986). Computer conversion: The neglected phase, *Healthcare Computing and Communications, 3*(5): 26.
Emphasizes the need for careful planning and user support when computer implementation begins.

Thomas, A. M. (1986). Management information systems: Determining nurse manager requirements, *Nursing Management, 17*(7): 23.
Presents a model to assist management in determining nursing management information requirements.

Tindal, C. L., and Bursley, H. M. (1985). Using nursing expertise for non-nursing computer systems, *Nursing Clinics of North America, 20*: 595.
Contends that nursing's experience with key cognitive and intuitive skills has provided the individual nurse with a deeper understanding and appreciation of computer applications.

Troxler, S. H., and Escott, S. P. (1985). Computer utilization in infection control, *Healthcare Computing and Communications, 2*(9): 47.
Presents the benefits of a computerized infection control surveillance program.

U.S. Department of Commerce. (1976). *Computers, Health Records and Citizen Rights*, U.S. Government Printing Office, Washington, D.C.
Examines the sensitive area of privacy issues in medical record keeping, with particular emphasis on computerized systems.

U.S. Department of Health, Education, and Welfare. (1977). *Demonstration and Evaluation of a Total Hospital Information System*, National Center for Health Services Research, National Technical Information Service, Springfield, Virginia.
Contains the findings from the demonstration and evaluation of a comprehensive hospital information system at a general community hospital over a four-year period.

Viers, V. M. (1983). Introducing nurses to computers, *Nursing Management, 14*(7): 24.
Explores how to convince nurses that computers are the best "staff assistants."

Wagner, J. B. (1986). Measuring user satisfaction, *Healthcare Computing and Communications, 3*(6): 40.
Considers how to successfully critique your hospital's information system in a way that is not only productive, but a good communication vehicle for users to talk to upper management.

Walker, L. (1985). The laboratory system—A new generation, *Healthcare Computing and Communications, 2*(7): 76.
Explores factors affecting laboratory computer system changes and future trends.

Walker, L. (1986). Healthcare personal computer usage explodes, *Healthcare Computing and Communications, 3*(2): 26.
Suggests that the use of personal computers in hospitals needs to have strong managerial input to assure integrity and accuracy for output produced.

Winfree, R. G. (1986). Teamwork: The key to information systems success, *Hospitals, 60*(8): 104.
Discusses the importance of teamwork to the successful application of computer technology in health care.

Worthley, J. A. (1982). *Managing Computers in Health Care—A Guide for Professionals.* AUPHA Press, Ann Arbor, Michigan.
Focuses on assisting health care professionals in reaping the potential benefits and in solving the problems associated with computer usage.

Zielstorff, R. D. (1985). Cost effectiveness of computerization in nursing practice and administration, *Journal of Nursing Administration, 15*(2): 22.
Provides definitions of terms used and documents each type of evaluation process for one who is studying the cost-effectiveness of computers in nursing.

17

Implementing Medical Information Systems

Michael A. Counte Center for Health Management Studies and Department of Health Systems Management, Rush-Presbyterian-St. Luke's Medical Center, Chicago, Illinois

Kristen H. Kjerulff Center for Nursing and Health Services Research, School of Nursing, University of Maryland at Baltimore, Baltimore, Maryland

Jeffrey Colman Salloway Department of Psychology and Social Sciences, Rush Medical College of Rush University, Chicago, Illinois

I. INTRODUCTION

A. Chapter Focus: Implementation Impacts vs. Implementation Processes

It has long been accepted by organizational researchers that organizations must be able to acquire or develop and successfully implement new technologies in order to ensure their basic survival (Pasmore et al., 1982; Rousseau, 1983). As Allen (1982) has observed: "The 1980s will see businesses in many industries outperforming their competitors largely because of an ability to manage the new technology and develop information systems of strategic importance to the company."

The simple adoption or acquisition of new technologies, such as contemporary information systems, is not sufficient, however. An organization must also ensure that the implementation of the new technology is successful. In other words, the change must be an effectively planned or managed change. As Robbins (1983) has stated, without the capability to successfully implement new technologies, "organizations that persist in keeping 'their heads in the sand' eventually find themselves running going-out-of-business sales, in bankruptcy courts, or just phasing out of the scene."

The purpose of this chapter is to review what behavioral scientists and other researchers have learned about the dynamics of one problem area in the planning of technological change in health care organizations: the implementation of computerized medical information systems (MIS). Our primary intent is to address issues that often arise during implementation which concern employee responses to the MIS. In other words, under what conditions when attempting to introduce an MIS do health care organizations (especially hospitals) confront problems such as employee resistance, decreased job satisfaction or morale, and increased attrition and turnover?

During this introductory section of the chapter, we will present a brief historical overview to highlight the definition, scope, and diffusion of MIS, and a description of each of the specific topics that are covered in the chapter. Our goal by the end of the chapter is to show the reader how the findings of research on MIS implementation may help future change agents increase their effectiveness in introducing such new technologies.

B. Historical Overview

1. Definition of a Medical Information System

Although there have been a multitude of definitions offered of medical information systems, most focus upon either general attributes or specific functions. An example of the former type is offered by Austin and Greene (1978): "A clinical (or medical) information system involves the organized processing, storage, and retrieval of information to support patient care activities in the hospital." The second type of conceptual approach is exemplified by the position of the U.S. Office of Technology Assessment (1977): "A medical information system is a computer-based system that receives data normally recorded about patients, creates and maintains from these data a computerized medical record for each patient, and makes the data available for the following uses: patient care, administrative, and business management; monitoring and evaluating medical care services; epidemiological and clinical research; and planning of medical care resources." In both approaches, the major emphases are using computer hardware and software to record and store data that describes patients who use a health care facility and to subsequently allow the information to be used by health care professionals (clinical, ancillary, and managerial) in their decision-making. Individuals who utilize such information systems are referred to as users or end-users.

2. Shift from Manual to Automated Procedures in Health Care Organizations

The definitions offered by Austin and Greene (1978) and the Office of Technology Assessment (1977) provide insight into the technical functions of the MIS. What is even more interesting to consider, however, is the remarkable impact that this technology has had upon both the organization of activity in the hospital and patient care itself. In general terms, we can see that the MIS has the potential to redefine the entire business of providing care. However, to understand how this occurs, we have to consider the history of the shift from manual recording and sharing of information to automated data systems.

The computer officially arrived as a tool for information processing with the installation of the first Univac computer in the Office of the Census in 1951. This was followed in 1953 by IBM's marketing of its 701 mainframe. These were very large, expensive, and complex machines built for batch processing of information. Thus, for example, an enormous stack of punch cards could be fed into the machine, and the machine could count, sort, array, and calculate on that batch. Each time a new count, sort, array, or calculation was required, the batch was reentered into the machine. The replacement of punch cards with tape drives did not alter the fact that these were batch processing machines (*The Economist*, 1986).

The next developmental stage came in 1963, with Digital Equipment's PDP machines. These computers changed the face of computing in two significant ways. First, they were not nearly as expensive as the IBM and Univac machines, thus making them widely available for a variety of applications. Second, unlike batch processing machines, the PDPs enabled data input directly into the machine in a continuous stream. This change made possible a host of on-line and interactive functions, such as word processing, manufacturing process control, and interactive queries in which the user can ask questions of an on-line data base.

Initially, the batch processing computer did away with tedious, repetitive tasks better done by machines than by people. With on-line capabilities, however, the computer could now transform real-world events far more rapidly than people could. This did not occur without problems, however. Making the machine into an on-line participant in real-world behavior meant making the machine accessible to people who did not commonly use computers: clerks, secretaries, managers who would input data and ask questions of data bases. Data processing people could be made to think in machine-compatible paradigms, but could clerks, secretaries, and managers? Errors might be tolerable in processed payrolls or inventories. But what would be the impact when errors occurred in medical records, pharmacy orders, or surgery schedules? Thus, the implementation of computer systems in hospitals has occurred more slowly than in other industries.

Hospitals have traditionally floated on a sea of paper. In addition to the normal paper transactions found in any industry—payrolls, purchasing, personnel, and the like—crucial records must be maintained on prescriptions, procedures, and processes which affect life and death. Though it was not difficult to entrust accounting and personnel functions in hospitals to machines, the transfer of patient care functions to a computer was (perhaps justifiably) fraught with concern.

Austin (1983) provides us with a chronology of the steps by which hospitals made the transition into the automated age. He points out that prior to 1960, there were no genuine computer systems in hospitals. Hospitals, like hotels, were using bookkeeping machines developed principally by firms such as Burroughs to do patient billing. The link between the patient and the machine was the embossed metal plate which was kept at the nursing station with the patient's name and account number on it. Key records, billing slips, lab report forms, and so forth were run under the pressure of the embosser to keep track of charges and information.

The concept of the computer in the hospital began to gain credence in the late 1960s and really took hold in the early 1970s. The era of the 1970s was what Austin calls a developmental period, in which batch processing was applied to the same tasks in hospitals as in other industries, such as payroll, accounts receivable, and inventory control. Note that processes central to the care of patients are conspicuously absent. These inroads occurred on an application-by-application basis. What is important here is that each of these applications developed separately, often with its own hardware and business forms. In fact, it was the advanced hospital which at that time had a single mainframe handling all these tasks. Nevertheless, this established the primacy of the business computer in the hospital industry.

Through the late 1970s, there was a shift from an application-by-application approach in computerization to the development of systems. Hospitals hired data management consultants who understood the potential of computers in hospitals long before hardware and software were available. As a result, even though the conceptual foundations of modern systems were present, early attempts at integrated systems failed.

At the same time that these early systems were being attempted, the shift to on-line computers was occurring in the computer industry. Minicomputers dedicated to single functions began to show up in specific departments. This occurred for several reasons. This was the period of the Regional Medical Programs and of rapid expansion of research funding by the National Institutes of Health. As a result, basic and clinical scientists in research-oriented institutions were able to procure funds for their own computer systems. The PDP 1100 became a standard fixture in the well-equipped lab. The lesson was not lost on hospital administrators, who saw the potential applications of these devices to operations.

The net result was the movement of the health care industry toward the form of on-line computing pioneered by Digital Equipment. This implied local access to the minicomputer (called "distributed data processing") and the growth of "packaged" systems. It was through these local minicomputers that the notion of integrated systems as workable entities really emerged. The early attempts at integrated systems had failed for a variety of reasons. There had been no integrated software to build such systems. Though integrated systems were possible in theory, the programming tasks to make them operational were a nightmare of conflicting languages and incompatible commands. Attempts to integrate already existing subsystems required that programmers build interface programs that enabled one computer to talk to another. This language skill simply did not exist. Again, it was all theoretically possible—but not practically possible.

Instead, the industry took a rather different turn. After 1980, the availability of the microprocessor and its offspring, the desktop computer, entered the scene. With the desktop computer, it was possible to do local processing of data for scientific purposes or word processing. Systems of distributed data processing grew in hospitals. Keep in mind, however, that all this time, hospitals had available large mainframes on which business functions were still being handled routinely. It now became possible to begin integrating the mainframe and these desktop computers by using the desktops for remote entry of data. All that was required was wiring or telephone modems and a system of software that permitted data to be entered or retrieved.

All of this evolution has gone on in the context of the business, administrative, and research sides of hospital operation. At the same time, there has been movement toward the development of software for patient services and on-line patient information systems. The end-point in this evolution is the so-called integrated system, which will be described in a later section of this chapter. The current era is marked by the development and marketing of patient information systems. To date, such patient management systems have been implemented in a relatively small number of hospitals, but offer enormous potential for expansion. This raises for us the question of applications and functions of medical information systems. This is our next concern. We will discuss at greater length the possibilities of the patient information system when we discuss typologies of systems below.

3. Applications and Functions of Medical Information Systems

Given the complexity of the modern hospital and the wide range of diverse needs of clinical and administrative personnel, many types of separate, or stand-alone, information systems have been developed and implemented (Randall, 1985). Typical systems applications focus upon automation of a specific area within a diverse range of functions, such as general ledger; payroll; accounts payable; accounts receivable (billing); supply and distribution; laboratory analysis; pharmacy; admissions, discharge, and transfer of patients; radiology; dietary; and patient scheduling (MacFarlane, 1982). In most, if not all, of these functional areas, systems developers have over the years gradually improved the systems through the introduction of new generations. The current movement in the health care industry toward integrated, or total, hospital information systems will be discussed later in this chapter.

4. Environmental Forces Influencing Hospital Adoption of Medical Information Systems

During the last decade, hospital managers have encountered an increasingly turbulent environment (Morris, 1986; Whitehead, 1985), and there is currently no indication that such pressures will decrease in intensity. As Brady and Bergstein (1978) have noted: "Hospital management's task will grow more complex as the trends toward more diverse patient care, more severe regulatory and governmental requirements, more acutely ill patients, diminishing budgetary growth, and more sophisticated hospital organizations continue."

In the face of such challenges, information systems have continued to be an attractive technology for hospital managers who are faced simultaneously with pressures both to reduce costs, or obtain more for less, and to improve the quality of patient care services that they offer to the public (Jay and Anderson, 1982). As public concern with cost control and quality continue into the future, there is a strong likelihood that reliance upon such information systems will only increase in scope and magnitude.

C. Focal Issues and Problem Areas of this Chapter

As we will persistently repeat throughout this chapter, it is nearly a universal contention among observers of the health care industry that hospitals will either increase their capability to successfully acquire and implement MIS in future years or they will substantially decrease their chances for survival. Thus, the specific topics that we will address are concentrated upon three areas: increasing the reader's understanding of the types of information systems that have been created and their range of uses; explaining what types of systems have been adopted by different types of hospitals, as well as current trends; and discussing how information systems ultimately affect hospitals and individual end-users. An underlying contention of the authors is that it is imperative that future managers in the health care system be fully aware of not only the potential benefits of such systems, but also the unintended problems that arise during system implementation that may lessen such positive impacts.

Subsequent topics of this chapter are organized in the following manner. Our initial attention will be directed toward an examination of what types of MIS have been purchased by hospitals, what the future looks like in terms of technological advances, and how changes in technology will influence future MIS diffusion patterns among hospitals. Next, we will review the results of research that has examined the empirical impacts of information systems on both organizational and personal/social levels. Finally, we will introduce the concept of adaptation to automation and attempt to show how research findings concerning adaptation to automation and the impacts of computerization can be used to improve current methods of planning and monitoring the implementation of medical information systems.

II. MEDICAL INFORMATION SYSTEMS: DIFFERENTIATION AND ADVANCES

A. Toward a Typology of Medical Information Systems

Medical information systems are not a unitary phenomenon in hospitals. As discussed above, they have evolved substantially over time. Moreover, they differ on a number of dimensions—some obvious, some not. Understanding the implementation of these systems requires that we have some notion of the different types of systems which exist. Austin and Greene (1978) suggest a typology based on two dimensions: the type of information base used and the realm of activity addressed by the MIS. These two dimensions tend to fall along the same lines, with the result that Austin and Greene find three basic types of information systems:

1. Clinical or medical information systems
2. Information systems to support administrative operations
3. Management planning and control systems

The first of these, clinical or medical information systems, supports direct patient care activities. Operational administrative systems, the second type, are responsible for finance, personnel, payroll, purchasing, inventory control, and similar activities. The final category is based on policy-relevant data and supports strategic planning. The authors suggest that putting these three together leads to a total hospital information system.

In fact, what Austin and Greene describe is, in some ways, a categorical system for only a single stage in the development of an integrated hospital information system—a stage at which hospitals have tended to create three separate subsystems which manage three seemingly disparate subfunctions of the hospital. An alternative perception is that this is a single point in an evolutionary transition in which the totally integrated information system will be the final result.

If the most important dimension of hospital information systems is in fact evolving, and if the integrated system will be the result, then we may construct an alternative typology of medical information systems based on evolutionary types. Such an evolutionary typology would then be linked to our earlier discussion of the chronology of implementation of medical information systems. That typology would include seven types of systems, as follows:

1. The hand accounting system
2. The machine accounting system
3. The electronic accounting system
4. The electronic information management system
5. The remote entry information system
6. The integrated system
7. Artificial intelligence: the computer-generated diagnosis

As we discussed earlier, hospitals began with hand accounting systems. These included not only manual accounting for patient costs and administration, but the entire paper system of tracking patient care. This was part and parcel of the entire institution of the medical records department of the hospital and the occupation of the medical records librarian.

The machine accounting system was also a historical epoch, just as the period of hand accounting was. Here, however, we find the application of the machine only to accounting functions. The only analog to the machine in medical records was the installation of the pneumatic tube, a system of tubes or pipes which ran throughout the hospital. Medical records, lab reports, or specimens were placed in special containers which could be sent to most locations in the hospital by air pressure. This was a primitive but effective system of mechanical mail.

With the introduction of batch processing computers, the era of electronic accounting began, and with it came a whole type of automated processing which is still prevalent in hospitals. The electronic accounting system is, in reality, little more than the machine accounting system with gears replaced by capacitors. For the hospital with limited resources today, this may be the extent of the development of computerized systems.

More commonly, however, hospitals are in transition from electronic accounting systems to electronic information management systems. This transition occurs as hospitals acquire limited-function computer subsystems. Thus, for example, there are commercial packages available which computerize pharmacy functions; lab functions; admitting, discharge, and transfer systems; and purchasing functions. Most often, at least at the present, these are autonomous subsystems available for a particular department. However, they rarely talk to one another.

More toward the end point of this transitional type lies the electronic information management system. The early electronic information management system is typified by the Spectra system, which appeared in a number of hospitals in the late 1970s. Spectra was a patient information system. This is in some contrast to the electronic accounting systems mentioned above. Rather than replacing the accounting machine, or integrating with it, it was intended to manage patient care functions. As such, it was a kind of electronic medical records system. Spectra was generally typical of the category. It offered enormous promise. Much of that promise was never realized.

The brains of the early electronic information management system is the centralized computer. Remote terminals are scattered in various departments of the hospital for data entry and retrieval. In theory, such an information management system has the potential to handle all information functions related to patient care. Thus, one could enter new patients; bring up admitting data; and order and schedule diets, diagnostic tests, medications, and procedures. It is, in some ways, an electronic pneumatic tube, shifting information from one place to another wherever it is needed. Further, because all the data are available and integrated in a single source, it is theoretically possible to add on functions which were previously handled by separate subsystems, often with separate, dedicated computers. One could abstract drug prescriptions from such systems to determine rates of usage and to schedule reordering for the hospital pharmacy. One could evaluate the seriousness of illnesses, to schedule nursing staff. With all kinds of patient care data available in one place, the possibilities for management are theoretically endless.

One difficulty with the early systems was that they were effective data management systems, but not sophisticated data analysis systems. For maximum impact on administration, analysis was crucial; but it was not present. To perform analysis, data had to be dumped off such machines onto other computers which are capable of analysis. This required interfaces with those other machines, language protocols which enable one computer to talk to another. The problems of disparate languages and operating systems doomed these attempts to failure.

Just as these systems were failing to deliver on their promise, the remote entry information systems were making their debut. These were a real conceptual breakthrough. Instead of a dedicated system, such as the electronic information system, these did not rely exclusively on a central computer to operate. They could run software locally without regard to a central computer, or they could enter and retrieve data from a central core when necessary. This sheer level of flexibility made them very attractive as a hardware base on which to build systems. This was the state of the art in 1986. Data are entered into the patient care data base from any number of points around the hospital.

However, pharmacy can run its own programs locally, as can nursing, dietary, admissions, and so on. The next key problem is whether anyone can access the entire data system to make administrative decisions that affect the system and the hospital as a whole. The solution to this problem is the integrated system.

The integrated system is the goal of every manufacturer who designs computer systems for hospitals. Such a system would combine the best features of the electronic information system and the remote entry information system. It would integrate the electronic mail functions and patient data base functions of the former and permit the remote data processing functions of the latter. In this way, it could be used not only to transfer information around the hospital, but also for accounting, policy, and administrative analysis. It would further add logical extensions, such as inventory control, staff scheduling, prompts for routine consultations, routine purchasing, and alerts for contra-indicated orders. Such a system has the power to redefine the whole business of delivering patient care. An example will illustrate.

Dr. Perry Neeham returns from his evaluation of a recently admitted patient, Mr. King, and approaches the Electronic Patient Protocol Information System (EPPIS). He logs on to EPPIS and calls up the patient record. Asking for drug prescription options, he orders the new drug Regenticide for his patient. EPPIS asks for dose and administration schedule. Already entered into EPPIS is Mr. King's admitting information and the name of his primary care nurse. At the entry of the drug, Regenticide, EPPIS has already alerted the pharmacy that a dose of Regenticide has been ordered on the floor for administration, that the supply of doses in the pharmacy is now at 10 and will be at nine after administration of the drug, that this supply is normally enough for a three-day period under average circumstances, and that it is now scheduled to reorder 10 doses of Regenticide from the manufacturer in 24 hours for resupply three days hence. When that order is received at shipping and receiving, and entered into EPPIS, the system will place that information in its inventory for the pharmacy and will notify accounts payable that it will issue a check to the drug manufacturer on the tenth of the month.

Meanwhile, Mr. King's primary care nurse, Ann T. Vyrol, has logged on to EPPIS. The system has notified Ms. Vyrol that Dr. Neeham has prescribed a drug for her new patient and that it has been ordered from the pharmacy. She draws up her meds, and as she brings the Regenticide to Mr. King, she passes a laser light pen across the bar code on the unit dose drug. EPPIS records the administration of the drug on Mr. King's chart, subtracts one dose of Regenticide from the hospital pharmacy inventory, and bills Mr. King for the drug. The next time Dr. Neeham logs on to the system, EPPIS notifies him that Mr. King has received his medication and asks, by the way, if Dr. Neeham would like to order a medical consult for the patient or perhaps a social service consult, inasmuch as Mr. King does not show any insurance coverage and his bills are adding up.

This is just the beginning. EPPIS can aggregate this information for administration, can print overall statistical reports for the Joint Commission on the Accreditation of Hospitals, and can provide a data base for the annual meeting of the board. This is a fanciful system, of course. Such a comprehensive system is probably not yet in operation—not yet. But it is only a short time away. The important consideration for us at this time is that the integrated information system has the power to redefine the business of delivering care. In our example above, the system has redefined the purpose of medical records. It is no longer merely a vehicle for transferring patient information. It serves in inventory control, purchasing, and accounts receivable. Moreover, with such a system in place, the pharmacy can operate with minimum inventory, just-in-time delivery (similar to the auto industry), and one-hundred percent cost capture on medications–a substantial improvement over current methods. The same potentials exist for scheduling, staffing, and other administrative functions.

A final category of medical information systems is artificial intelligence–the computer-generated diagnosis. This rather separate development is not a matter of hardware at all, but a matter of software. It is exemplified by the PROMIS system. PROMIS, developed at the University of Vermont, is a series of queries to an examining physician which takes the user along a logic-branching pathway toward a diagnosis. Thus, it might have asked Dr. Neeham if Mr. King had a fever. If the answer had been yes, PROMIS would pursue alternative bits of data to formulate a diagnosis. Does Mr. King have any localized tenderness? If yes, PROMIS would pursue the matter of a local infection. If no, PROMIS might ask for a white cell count. It would then proceed along such logically branching chains until it arrived at a number of potential diagnoses which it would lay out for Dr. Neeham.

Systems such as PROMIS have not been accepted easily by medical staffs and may not be widely available in the immediate future for hospitals. Nevertheless, it has been demonstrated to be feasible and will eventually arrive in tandem with the integrated medical information system.

A number of questions follow: How quickly will such systems emerge as technical possibilities? How rapidly will they be adopted by hospitals? What will be the constraints on their adoption? And what will be the effect on employees and on the organization itself?

B. Advances in Medical Information Systems

Pressures upon health care organizations to simultaneously control their costs and improve the quality of their patient care services, coupled with rapid improvements of information systems technology, are likely to lead to major changes in the next 10 to 15 years. New forms of hardware architecture foster the development of distributed networks; computer software is becoming increasingly user-friendly; and the increased availability of health care professionals who are sophisticated in information systems design and utilization (the field of medical informatics) are all changes that will accelerate the computerization of health care organizations (Jenkin, 1982). In light of projections that such developments "are going to revolutionize the practice of health care in the United States" (Whitehead, 1985), it is useful at this juncture to examine the specifics of how information systems will change in the foreseeable future and discuss the likely impacts of these innovations.

The development of integrated information systems that are characterized by clinical and financial information stored in a single repository which can be accessed by any authorized user is already an important goal and will continue to be a priority area into the future (Klinger, 1985; Morris, 1986; Whitehead, 1985). As mentioned earlier, up to this point, most MIS applications have been constructed as stand-alone systems with few, if any, communications links that would allow users to consolidate patient information. Presently, hospitals are trying to eliminate such past difficulties by attempting to purchase or develop integrated systems that overcome such fragmentation. According to Randall (1985), "most hospitals during the next 10 years–even those in bed ranges now considered too small–will be installing (single-system) totally integrated financial, clinical, and data communications systems to replace (out of sheer information processing necessity) their fragmented, interfaced information processing systems that seem to be the rule rather than the exception in the markeplace today."

In addition to the integration of in-house data, multihealth care systems—which have a single owner but are comprised of various types of facilities, from hospitals to nursing homes—are seeking to develop comprehensive information systems. These would eventually allow them to track patients as they flow through different components of their systems. They would monitor the continuity of care and resource consumption of their clients. Among other important tasks, such multihealth care information systems will allow the owners to "aggregate data by patient, track patients throughout the multilevel system, follow competitors' movements in the marketplace, develop new measures of performance and quality health care, and strike a balance between central control of data management and local control of data processing" (Sandrick, 1985). The key elements in such integrated systems will be (1) that the patient will be the focal point of all information versus organizational units or functions and (2) that health care professionals and managers for the first time will be able to draw upon a vast repository of information.

Another major area of activity is the rapid development of information systems that can be employed in medical diagnosis and treatment. Primarily spurred on by the rapid development of the field of artificial intelligence, clinicians are becoming more frequently involved in the development and utilization of information systems in their clinical activities. As Jenkin (1982) observed several years ago: "In the past, the application of computers to patient care has been limited to extending administrative applications into the more formalized tasks characteristic of the operation of various ancillary services. The increasing presence and accessibility of these systems and their increasing relevance to clinical issues is now stimulating many medical professionals to seriously consider their potential extension into the areas of clinical decision-making and problem-solving." Advances in computer technology such as digital-based radiography, full-voice recognition, networking, and decision trees, plus ready access to an MIS at the patient's bedside, are all developments that make it easier for the physician to use information systems as an adjunct to their decision-making. Perhaps the most important development of all is that of bedside terminals, or "point-of-service workstations" (Klinger, 1985), because they should enhance the productivity of clinical personnel and their ability to provide high-quality patient care.

Solely from a technological perspective, there is widespread agreement that current and future improvements of MIS will continue at a rapid rate. In addition, there is a wide consensus that these new information systems hold great promise for both the improvement of patient care services and an increased capability to identify, monitor, and eventually control the costs of health care delivery.

III. DIFFUSION PATTERNS OF MEDICAL INFORMATION SYSTEMS

A. Information Systems as Technological Innovation

The study of the spread of new ideas and technologies among organization types, such as hospitals and individual users (physicians, nurses), has long been of interest to health service researchers (Gordon and Fisher, 1978). Three concepts are typically differentiated (Christman and Counte, 1981): "invention (the creation of a new product), adoption (the decision to purchase), and implementation (the actual use of an innovative technology.)"

In regard to information systems adoption and implementation, it has been suggested that "the speed of technical change in this field has been far greater than the speed of social adaptation" (Lindberg, 1979). In other words, over the years, the technical advances in information systems have consistently outpaced hospital decisions to purchase them and the ability of health care workers to use them. At this point, we will briefly review advances in information systems and prevailing adoption patterns over the last three decades. Implementation issues will be covered in depth during subsequent sections of this chapter.

B. Trends in Hospital Adoption of MIS

1. Pre-1960

Although by the end of the 1950s the first generation of computers had been developed and there was a recommendation by the American Hospital Association that they be utilized by hospitals (Shaffert and McDowell, 1978), very little interest was expressed by hospitals in incorporating computers in their operations. Most hospital functions were accomplished using manual systems and mechanical devices such as bookkeeping machines, and activities were highly self-contained and segregated, in that there was no central storage or processing of patient data (Austin, 1983).

2. The 1960s

The situation began to change during the next decade. This period marked the first time that hospitals began to extensively purchase and utilize computer-based information systems. Although the early 1960s saw only a sluggish rate of adoption (according to Shaffert and McDowell [1978], only 39 out of 6,000 hospitals were using computers in 1962), by the end of this period, automated systems were much more widely available and used for routine hospital operations, such as payroll preparation and patient billing. Although there were obstacles that confronted hospital adoption of MIS, such as misunderstanding by vendors of the complexity of medical care processes, high purchase costs, and a shortage of computer specialists in hospitals (Shaffert and McDowell, 1978), there were even a small number of attempts by the late 1960s to develop integrated or total information systems.

3. The 1970s

A much more rapid diffusion of information systems in hospitals became apparent in the early 1970s. One study (Herner and Company, 1970) found that forty percent of hospitals surveyed used computerized accounting or billing systems, while another report stated that by the end of this period, the spread of such systems had expanded both in number and in scope (that is, to nonbilling functions) (Jay and Anderson, 1982). Major factors that facilitated the diffusion of computerized information systems during this period included the development of minicomputers, which assisted small hospitals in addressing their data processing needs; the availability of outside (shared) data processing services for hospitals without in-house systems; and continued improvements in computer hardware and software packages accompanied by decreased costs (Shaffert and McDowell, 1978).

4. The 1980s

A recent analysis of hospital data processing activity during the period of 1982 to 1984 (Grams et al., 1985) isolated major trends apparent during the first half of the current decade. This national survey discovered that:

1. Many, if not most, hospitals use financial and admissions/registration systems, while a lesser number employ nursing station/order entry, laboratory, pharmacy, radiology budgeting systems.
2. All hospitals surveyed are increasing their data processing budgets, and the biggest increase is among hospitals that have from 101 to 200 beds (perhaps because larger hospitals have already made substantial investments in information systems).

C. Adoption versus Use of Hospital-Based Information Systems

In one of the few extensive studies of MIS diffusion ever reported, Lindberg (1979) suggested that despite technical advances and the great promise of medical information systems, their rate of diffusion has been quite slow (compared to the diffusion of information systems in other industries). Although in a small number of areas, such as financial functions, hospitals have been very receptive to purchasing computerized systems, automation in other functional areas (especially those involving patient care activities) has proceeded very slowly.

Lindberg suggests that three types of barriers have led to the hospital industry's lagging behind others in the rate of automation. First, hospital information systems have been plagued by distinct operational problems. Technical problems such as slow response time and frequent system breakdowns, as well as management errors, typify major operational issues. Second, there are certain diffusion barriers that are unique to the field of health care, such as the limitations of current medical knowledge that hinder the development of expert systems, irregular terminology, and the sheer complexity of the health care industry and its constituent organizations. Finally, there have been major social obstacles to the diffusion of MIS, especially the fact that few health care professionals have had any formal education or training in the field of computer science.

In spite of these widespread obstacles, the fact remains that health care information systems have become a quite common fixture in hospitals, and often the associated costs represent a major component of their budgets. The simple act of adopting an information system, however, does not ensure that the system will be appropriately utilized by its users or that it will have its intended impacts upon the adopting organization. As Greer (1981) has observed: "Most studies of organization innovation, including those in medicine, focus on the adoption stage, i.e., on the acquisition of new equipment. Few look at successes in implementation, level of utilization, or abandonment. Failure to examine implementation or utilization is unwarranted both because it leads to confusion in thought about adoption and also because an increasingly substantial literature suggests that adoption and utilization may be at best tenuously related."

The remainder of this chapter will be directed toward an examination of impacts of information systems on the organizational and individual levels. Our major assertion throughout our discussion of impacts and personal adaptation to automation will be that the effectiveness of any system's implementation is heavily influenced by organizational factors and personal and social attributes of individual users.

IV. ORGANIZATIONAL IMPACTS OF MEDICAL INFORMATION SYSTEMS

A. Issues in Technology Assessment

Organizational scientists from many disciplines have had a long-standing interest in the study of technology in organizations (Pasmore et al., 1982; Rousseau, 1983). Several factors have prompted this interest. First, from a practical perspective, the acquisition and implementation of new technologies is often a very costly and significant purchase. Thus, many organizations are interested in monitoring the impacts of technology primarily because the purchase decision is often expensive. A second factor that underlies technology assessment is the interest of various groups, from organizational researchers to government agencies and managers, in the actual impacts of technology on organizations (or the impacts upon social systems). Most technologies are introduced because they are intended to alter work arrangements in order to improve the quantity or quality of outputs (goods or sevices). The question that ultimately arises is whether the benefits achieved are worth the costs that are involved.

A number of perplexing issues have confronted technology researchers who study organizations. First, it is often difficult to determine whether any one type of technology is the predominant one in an organization (Rousseau, 1983). Thus, for example, in the case of computer information systems, it is difficult to ascertain which specific type of system located within an organization is the most important one to study. As one might suspect, some types of technology directly support the production of a good or service (core-conversion technologies), while others exist to support these core activities (support technologies) (Hancock, Macy, and Peterson, 1983). In view of the conceptual problems that arise in attempting to measure aspects of technology in organizations, most organizational researchers have compared only gross differences in technical resources across organizations. Second, technology assessment is frequently done from different perspectives. On some occasions, the researcher's interest is in technological factors as independent variables (that lead to changes), while at other times technological conditions are viewed as dependent variables that result from organizational attributes or conditions (such as studies of the diffusion of new technologies). Third, researchers studying the effects of new technologies have often failed to distinguish whether they are interested primarily in understanding the impacts of technological change upon organizational effectiveness, which represents the fulfillment of organizational objectives, or upon organizational efficiency, which indicates simply how well designated resources are being utilized. Both elements are clearly important, but as Krobock (1984) has stated, "being ineffective for a period of time can result in only one outcome for an organization in a competitive environment—its demise." Finally, it has gradually become apparent to technology researchers that technological changes may well have impacts that vary in the directness of their effects. First-order impacts are those that directly influence productivity (such as work motivation), but there may also be effects upon role relationships (second-order), employee selection procedures (third-order), and even interorganizational relations (fourth-order) (Pasmore et al., 1982). Clearly, the assessment of technology in organizations is not a simple matter.

B. Information Systems and Organizational Change

In spite of the thorny issues that have hampered efforts to monitor the effects of new technologies in general, new studies of the impact of information systems and computerization in health care and other industries have proliferated. There is a widespread recognition that advances in computer technology (for instance, improvement in ease of use) have the clear potential to alter significantly the structure of organizations and the work life of organizational workers, from clerks and secretaries to professionals and managers (Fleischer and Morell, 1985). In addition, there is growing recognition that many of the effects of computer technology are not intended or planned; organizational impacts may substantially determine the success or failure of computer applications; and organizational impacts often have been simply unanticipated and poorly managed (Worthley, 1982).

At this point, we will proceed to examine what is known about the organizational effects of information systems. We will purposefully present both speculation and research findings, because at this early stage, both types of information are equally plausible. Also, our explicit emphasis will be upon structural impacts versus individual-level changes, which will be discussed in a subsequent section of this chapter. Finally, material will be presented from studies of information systems both in and outside the health care industry in order to better ascertain the generalizability of ideas and evidence.

C. Organizational Impacts of Office Automation in Industry

A multitude of different types of computer-based office information systems have appeared since the mid-1970s, and they have been acquired by a rapidly increasing number of corporations from many sectors of American industry (Fleischer and Morell, 1985). There are many differences in such systems, but they all have several distinguishing attributes. First, they are multifunction systems. Such functions often run the gamut "from electronic mail and spread sheets to complex management information systems and decision support systems" (Gutek, Bikson, and Mankin, 1984). A second major characteristic is that the functions of a system are typically independent, and a variety of users can use the system for different purposes in parallel.

Overall, there is very little evidence concerning the empirical impacts of office-based information technology upon organizational structure. Allen (1982) argued that computer-based technology offers great promise to corporations, but in many cases the systems are unmanaged. He cites decentralization of authority (a structural phenomenon) as an area of particular concern. On the one hand, modern management information systems offer companies the opportunity to decentralize decision-making to lower levels than ever before by users who have ready access to timely information. This, in turn, conflicts with management's traditional bias toward centralized decision-making structures to control the power to make decisions (Robbins, 1983) and makes it harder to integrate the results of decisions being made by a larger number of decision makers (Allen, 1982).

Because researchers have focused relatively little attention on the effects of office automation, Olson and Lucas (1982) offered a series of 18 research hypotheses concerning the possible effects of information systems on the nature of work, individual employees, organizational communications, interpersonal relations, interdepartmental relations, and organizational structure and processes. Space limitations prohibit our listing all of their ideas except those that primarily concern organizational impacts. First, with regard to organizational communications, they propose that automated office systems will improve the efficiency (speed and accuracy) of communications functions; decrease the frequency of face-to-face contacts; and increase the sheer volume of communications between individuals and organizational units. Second, they suggest that information systems will likely have the following impacts upon management behavior: more rational decisions will be made because of less withholding of information; managers will need to develop methods to control the activities of subordinates who work off-site; and it will be possible to increase the span of control of managers (that is, the number of people who report to a manager) and to reduce the total number of managers that are needed by an organization. Third, they suggest that because information itself will be more readily available to separate departments, there will be less withholding of information and, thus, decreased interdepartmental conflict. Finally, they propose that in the future, the widespread use of office information systems will eliminate the necessity for organizations to have a central physical location and, because of significant improvements in organizational communications, organizations will be much more capable of adapting to changes in their environments.

In addition to the speculation of authors such as Olson and Lucas, there has been a slow emergence in recent years of empirical studies of the organizational impacts of computer-based office information technology. One study reported by Fleischer and Morell (1985) examined the impacts of office automation systems on 22 user-managers from eight large companies in Philadelphia and Pittsburgh. The investigators identified three major impacts. First, managers reported that they spent their time differently after the introduction of the systems, in that they began to delegate more routine tasks to their staffs and to spend more of their efforts on decision-making and planning. Second, the managers reported that the information systems changed their beliefs about the amount of information they needed to make decisions. In particular, "once they saw what a computer made possible, they became unwilling to settle for less." Finally, the researchers found that the implementation of the information systems led to increased decentralization of decision-making because adequate information was available to make decisions at lower levels; yet, higher-level managers could continue to monitor decisions that were being made. Since many of the companies had already planned to decentralize decision-making prior to the introduction of the information systems, however, it was difficult to determine how much of an impact could be specifically attributed to the introduction of the information systems.

Another study, by Frederiksen, Riley, and Myers (1984) was a case study of a life and health insurance company after its implementation of an on-line information system. They found that decentralization of the company's units into self-managed work teams that had considerable autonomy and a "flattening" of the company's hierarchical authority structure were facilitated by the implementation of the information system.

Finally, the results of a study reported by Gutek, Bikson, and Mankin (1984) are worthy of examination, since it is one of the few studies reported in the literature that have multiple organizations in the study sample. Their project was a two-year study of the individual and managerial effects of computer-based information technology in 55 offices in 26 different private-sector companies. They found that initially, the companies purchased the systems in order to aid the individual productivity of office workers. At the least, there were subjective reports that productivity had increased, and there was a minor decrease in labor costs. Also, the authors found that both managers and their subordinates generally favored the information systems.

It is very difficult to make many preliminary conclusions based upon the above speculation about the organizational impacts of office automation systems and empirical studies of their utilization. This is partially because the systems themselves are so different in their designs and applications, and partially because the organizations are rarely studied over time in order to identify trends or changes that emerge over time. Perhaps the most interesting speculation and tentative finding that has emerged is the observation that these information systems make it feasible for decentralization of decision-making to occur, while at the same time they leave higher levels of management with the opportunity to effectively monitor such decisions. Fleischer and Morell (1985) suggest: "in a sense, total power in the organization is increased, with more decision-making information available at lower levels, but with no accompanying decrease above."

D. Effects of Medical Information Systems on Health Care Organizations

Despite the fact that hospitals are heavily information-dependent and also highly complex institutions (with diverse labor forces, fragmented and often disparate subunits, and so forth), there has been a paucity of research done on the impacts of MIS on organizational structure. However, since this issue is our primary concern at this point, and a number of authors have speculated about the subject, their views are worthy of examination.

Perhaps the first authors to discuss potential organizational impacts of MIS were Goldstein and Farlee (1973), and Farlee (1978). Based on the model originally developed by Hage and Aiken (1965), they argued that our attention should focus upon four organizational variables that are important to organizations because they are means that enable social systems to achieve their stated objectives (goals, outputs): (1) formalization, or the number of rules and procedures that dictate how tasks will be accomplished; (2) centralization; (3) specialization/complexity; and (4) stratification. They predicted that the introduction of information systems in hospitals will likely be to increase formalization, centralization, occupational specialization, and status differences among occupations.

Another approach to projecting the organizational impacts of MIS was that developed by Worthley (1982). He suggests that MIS can affect organizations on two different levels: formal and informal (or latent). On the formal organizational level, he postulates that MIS will lead to structural reorganization of a hospital's units in order to more efficiently utilize the MIS; substantial decentralization of organizational units and a greater diffusion of decision-making capability due to the increased availability of information at lower levels; greater formalization or standardization of work procedures and tasks; and new responsibilities for support units (such as the need for greater attention of legal offices to privacy legislation concerning patient data). On the informal level, he postulates that a number of developments are likely, such as a shift of power from line managers to those who are more sophisticated users of the MIS and, possibly, increased cooperation among departments because of the increased standardization of procedures.

Although it is evident from the above discussion that the impacts of information systems in hospitals and other types of organizations are often widespread and occasionally quite subtle, it is imperative that managers be sensitive to their possible occurrence and ramifications. As Worthley (1982) has indicated, "Experience in health care organizations strongly indicates that, left unmanaged, these impacts do derail computerization efforts that are otherwise viable. Successful use of computer technology depends on the ability of managers to understand, anticipate, and manage these organizational impacts."

Thus far, we have restricted our analysis of MIS impacts to the organizational level of analysis. At this point, we will shift the discussion toward an analysis of impacts of MIS at the individual and interpersonal, or social network, levels.

V. INDIVIDUAL AND SOCIAL IMPACTS OF MEDICAL INFORMATION SYSTEMS

A. Importance of Individual-Level and Social-Level Impact Assessment

The vast majority of presentations and published papers in the area of medical computing focus on descriptions of new computer systems or software developments (Symposium on Computer Applications in Medical Care, 1977–1986). Any type of innovation in medical computing creates great interest among the medical community and intense competition among the medical computing vendors. When these computer systems are developed, advertised, and eventually sold, there is considerable discussion concerning their technical qualities, but very little discussion concerning the "people impacts."

The people impacts are the effects the computer system has on the individuals who use it or are affected by it. When a medical information system is implemented, its initial effects are usually felt by clerical employees, particularly those working in the business and financial offices.

For many hospital employees, the switch from manual to computerized procedures represents a major change in the way that their work is performed. For example, in a noncomputerized admitting department, incoming patients wait to be interviewed by admitting clerks. Admitting clerks ask each incoming patient a series of questions about insurance coverage, sleeping and smoking habits, and so on. Answers to these questions are recorded manually and sent by messenger or pneumatic tube to the business office and the patient's eventual patient care unit. The admitting clerk may then call the patient's unit and ask if a bed is available. The ward clerk or nurse checks to see what is available and calls the admitting clerk back when a bed is ready for occupancy. These types of procedures work fine in a small hospital with a small number of patients admitted each day; however, in a large hospital, there may be several hundred patients admitted every day. In that case, reliance on manual procedures frequently means a backup during peak admitting hours and a wait of several hours for patients to go through the admission process. When an admission, discharge, and transfer (ADT) system is implemented, the admission clerk changes from manual forms of data collection to computerized data collection procedures. As incoming patients are interviewed, their answers are keyed directly into the computer. Pertinent information is then sent instantaneously to each of the appropriate departments in the hospital. The admitting clerk can query the computer as to bed availability and match the patient with an appropriate roommate if necessary. For the admitting clerk, a switch from manual to computerized procedures represents a switch from paper-and-pencil forms and communication with other employees in the hospital by phone or pneumatic tube to continuous interaction with a computer terminal. The substance of the job has not changed, but how the job is conducted has changed dramatically.

Assuming that all has gone well with implementation of the ADT system, several questions arise: Has the computer system made the admitting clerk's job easier or harder? Does the clerk feel more or less stressed? Does the clerk feel more or less isolated? Does the clerk feel more or less happy about the job? An administrator might argue that answers to these questions are irrelevant as long as the job is accomplished. However, if computerization leads to increased absenteeism, turnover, and more subtle forms of resistance, the cost to the hospital can be quite high.

It is important, therefore, to measure and understand the impacts of a medical information system on the individuals who are expected to use it. An MIS requires that individuals across many hospital departments input and transmit information in a timely and appropriate manner. If even one individual fails to input information at the appropriate time, the consequences can be unpleasant for many others using the system.

B. Measuring Individual and Social Impacts

Although there are many aspects of an individual's work life that one could expect to be affected by computerization, there are several areas that provide particularly valuable information about the people impacts of a specific computer system. These are as follows:

1. Job Satisfaction

Some authors have suggested that a medical information system will increase job satisfaction because it decreases the extent to which a person must perform mundane clerical tasks (Hodge, 1977). Others have suggested that job satisfaction will decrease after computerization because the system standardizes the way that people do their work (Farlee and Goldstein, 1972). Hodge (1977) reported an increase in job satisfaction after the introduction of an MIS, but this was measured only among the professional staff.

2. Job Stress

During training and implementation, it is to be expected that a period of increased stress and tension will be experienced by the hospital staff. However, after the system has been implemented and is performing smoothly, one would expect levels of job stress to be less than they were prior to implementation.

If there are some individuals for whom computerization has created higher levels of job stress, tension and ambiguity, then further investigation is warranted. It could be that for some individuals, the system creates double work. It is also possible that the system is poorly designed or poorly implemented, such that for some or all of the employees working with the system, it is not providing them with the information that they need. Another possibility is that some individuals simply do not work well with computers, for reasons of basic personality or cognitive style, and are continuously stressed while working with the system.

3. The Balance of Power

Dowling (1980) has suggested that the implementation of an information system can change the balance of power among employees. Dowling described a case study of an administrator who resisted the new computer system because he would no longer have exclusive control over the information in his department. Since the information would be entered directly into the computer system, he would no longer be able to act as gatekeeper for that information.

On the other hand, clerical employees, who work extensively with the system, suddenly have a great deal of information at their fingertips that the administrators and clinical staff must request. When an MIS is fully implemented, much of a patient's clinical information is stored on the system, rather than on a chart. If a physician or another member of the clinical staff wants the most up-to-date clinical information about a particular patient, he or she must ask someone to get it or must query the computer. Frequently, physicians choose to have the information acquired for them, rather than to deal with the computer themselves (Anderson and Jay, 1984; Kwon, Vogler, and Kim, 1983).

4. Social Networks

Introduction of an MIS is a structural change which has the capacity to affect not only the individual and his or her relationship to the job, but also relationships between people. Every person in the hospital can be said to have a social network of contacts, a pattern of persons to whom they normally talk, whom they often see, and with whom they exchange information vital to the job. This specialized social network can be labelled a "job network" to distinguish it from the more general concept of social networks, as it has been used in the network literature.

One of the primary functions of an MIS is to transmit information from one hospital department to the next. In a hospital which does not have an MIS, communication between departments is a continuous process of phone calls and paper-based information delivered by messenger and pneumatic tube. Many patient services, such as a late meal or transport (someone to transport a patient from one part of the hospital to another), are requested by telephone. Medications are ordered via a messenger who visits each ward several times a day. Thus, in a busy hospital, there exists a complex communication network based primarily on person-to-person contact. A ward clerk may communicate with a hundred or more people throughout the hospital every day. Most of these people are acquaintances known by name.

Such networks clearly have a job-related function. In addition, they often develop social functions. They tie an individual to a work setting, providing gossip, respite from work concerns, and reinforcement for the normative system. This informal social network is a supplement to the formal job network which maintains vital functions for the organization. What happens when an MIS is implemented and the formal job network is altered?

After a system is implemented, much of the communications which previously passed from hand to hand and from mouth to ear is conducted on the computer. In contrast to receivers of personal communications, the receiver of information often doesn't know who the sender is. Transmission is faster, more accurate, and decidedly more impersonal. The implication here is that personal social networks may be weakened and the balance shifted to specifically task-oriented interaction, a form of job depersonalization. Were this the case, the tie between the worker and the organization might be weakened.

Three studies have addressed this issue in one way or another. In a discussion of the implementation of a computer system at Rochester Methodist Hospital, Remsberg and Anderson (1984) point out that the hospital encouraged the formation of a user's group to help staff learn to use the computer to best advantage. Though the authors do not document the outcomes, this represents a de facto change in the structure of communications.

Of more immediate interest is the work of Salloway, Counte, and Kjerulff (1985a,b). In a longitudinal, cross-lagged study of the implementation of an MIS among clerks in a major hospital, the authors noted with curiosity that job satisfaction increased over time, while attitudes toward the computer system became more negative. In their studies, they draw some initial inferences from the data which suggest that the increase in job satisfaction may be a function of changes in the job network. This phenomenon requires some explanation.

The authors report that the staff who were introduced to the MIS were bound by a dense network of communications which traversed department lines and bound together this lower stratum of the organization. With the implementation of the MIS, communications links within this stratum began to be eroded.

However, as we have discussed above, the clerical staff in this study found that even though these lower-stratum links were compromised, they had a great deal of information at their fingertips that the administrators and clinical staff needed. Because these higher-stratum personnel had to ask for this information, the clerks became gatekeepers to the computer system. The decreased communications with other workers at the same level in the organization was attended simultaneously by an increase in communications with nurses, physicians, medical students, and other professionals. This shift in the job network of ward clerks led to a redefinition of their role within the organization. They approached the personnel department of the hospital with a request for change of job title from ward clerk to computer operator. In short, the definitions which they made of themselves and their work changed as their job networks changed. Thus, one of the categories of impact which must be observed in the process of implementing an MIS is the pattern of job networks.

An additional research effort in this area is the work of Anderson and Jay (1985). The authors have been interested primarily in the impact of computerized information systems on physicians. The approach here is a traditional social network methodology using block-model analysis. With this technique, the authors demonstrate that physician location in a network of referral and consultation is a key variable in determining whether they will use the computer system or not. Thought the sample is small (24) and the study population is comprised of different specialities, the research is nonetheless important in demonstrating the importance of the network concept to understanding the process of implementing an MIS.

What we find then is that the MIS imposes changes on the communications patterns and job networks of hospital personnel. These, in turn, may alter perceptions of the job. In the research reported by Salloway and colleagues (1985a,b), the locus of solidarity for the ward clerks shifted from the class group (lower stratum) to the ward as a unit, across professional lines. In the long run, this may be a rather positive outcome, though data are not yet available to substantiate this assertion.

5. The Way the Job is Performed

There has been very little research on the effects of an MIS on how people perform their jobs. There are several reasons for this. The first reason is that for those implementing the computer system, it is quite obvious how people's jobs change. An individual no longer writes specific information on paper, but enters it into the computer, by typing or using a light pen. So people have not thought it necessary to measure this change. However, every computer system is different in a multitude of ways, and every position in the hospital uses the MIS differently. So, in order to understand fully the people impacts, we must first understand the job impacts. The second reason that there is little research in this area is that it is very difficult to measure. An instrument designed to measure the job impacts of computerization does not exist at this point.

There have been several studies which have attempted to measure the impacts of an MIS by examining how it changes the amount of time people spend on various tasks. Generally, these studies have reported that people spend less time doing clerical tasks and paperwork (Barrett, 1975; Schmitz, Ellerbrake, and Williams, 1976). However, the primary purpose of an MIS is not to decrease clerical work, but to increase the speed and efficiency with which information is stored and transmitted throughout the hospital. So the primary impact of the MIS on individuals' jobs should be in terms of the quality, quantity, and accessibility of the information they work with.

C. Research Design in Impact Assessment

The vast majority of research on impacts of medical information systems or other types of computer systems has been retrospective in nature. Data are collected from individuals only after the system is implemented. This is a very weak research design and does not allow one to measure change with sufficient confidence. A much stronger research design involves the measurement of study variables prior to implementation of the computer system and then at several points after implementation. This type of design allows one to assess both short- and long-term impacts.

It is also important that one measure the same individuals at each stage of data collection, in order to be able to examine changes occurring at the individual level. This involves the collection of a large enough sample of individuals prior to implementation so that attrition over the course of time does not render one's study sample too small to allow valid conclusions. The researcher must also be able to identify each individual in order to be able to match baseline, or preimplementation, data with postimplementation data. This type of design is known as a panel study (Campbell and Stanley, 1963). It is clear from even a rudimentary understanding of research design that unless one can study the same individuals over time and measure dependent variables before and after the intervention of interest, one cannot assess impacts with any confidence (Campbell and Stanley, 1963; Suchman, 1967). Nonetheless, there has been very little research conducted on the impacts of an MIS using this type of design.

In early 1980, the authors were asked to design a study to assess the people impacts of a medical information system which had not yet been implemented. This provided the authors with the unique opportunity to conduct a study of the impacts of an MIS utilizing a panel study design. Following is a brief summary of the results of this study.

D. A Study of Short-Term and Long-Term Impacts of an MIS

1. Individual Impacts

This study was conducted in a large tertiary care hospital in the Midwest. The first module of the MIS scheduled to be implemented was the ADT system. This system was designed to allow communications between 13 hospital departments and 40 hospital units. The departments were admitting, the business office, medical records, surgical reservations, nonsurgical reservations, emergency room, and a variety of smaller departments. All clerical and supervisory employees in each of these departments, as well as all ward clerks, were scheduled to be trained on the system. Prior to the beginning of training, a random sample of 68 employees was drawn from a list of 305 individuals scheduled to be trained on the ADT system. These 68 employees were asked to participate in a study measuring the impacts of the new computer system. Each employee chosen to participate was given a packet of questionnaires which were to be filled out during work hours. The following individual-level measures were taken:

1. *Job Satisfaction.* A modified version of the work scale of the Job Description Index (Smith, Kendall, and Hulin, 1969) was used to measure job satisfaction. Employees indicated the extent to which their job could be characterized by 20 adjectives, including challenging, lonely, boring, and pleasant.
2. *Role Ambiguity and Conflict.* Two subscales from the Job Perceptions Inventory (Rizzo, House, and Litzman, 1970) were used. One subscale measured role ambiguity using 11 items (such as "I feel uncertain as to how much authority I have"), while the other measured role conflict with 12 items (for example, "I work under incompatible policies and guidelines").
3. *Attitudes Toward the MIS.* A 20-item questionnaire was developed by the authors (Kjerulff and Counte, 1984, 1986) to measure attitudes toward the specific computer system being implemented at the hospital. This scale consisted of 20 attitude statements, such as "I am looking forward to having the MIS in operation" and "I plan to avoid using the MIS as much as possible." Individuals indicated the extent to which they agreed with each item using a five-point Likert scale, ranging from "strongly agree" to "strongly disagree."
4. *Work Role Activities.* Each employee was given a list of 10 work activities, such as talking on the telephone, talking with patients and their families, and data processing. The employees were asked to indicate the amount of time they had spent in each of these activities on the previous workday, and then to indicate the extent to which that day had been a typical day.

Data were collected from each of the employees in the study at three points in time: shortly prior to implementation, six months after implementation, and a year after implementation. By the second data collection stage, the panel sample had been reduced to 53 people; by the third stage, it stood at 45. Statistical comparison of those who left the institution during the study period versus those who stayed indicated that those who left were slightly younger and better educated than those who stayed, but did not differ on any of the impact measures.

Summated scores were derived for four of the inventories, and Cronbach's alpha coefficients were obtained. Cronbach's alpha is a measure of the reliability or internal consistency of a summated rating scale. The Cronbach's alphas were as follows: attitude toward the MIS, 0.88; job satisfaction, 0.78; role ambiguity, 0.71; and role conflict, 0.79.

Each of the impact variables was then entered into a two-factor (3×3) repeated measures analysis of variance software program that tested for the significance of changes in each variable over time by occupational group (Counte et al., 1985). The cell sizes of the three occupational groups were as follows: 23 ward clerks, 14 general clerks, and eight departmental supervisors. There were 45 subjects for whom complete data were available across all three data collection stages.

The results of the analysis indicated that job satisfaction decreased slightly at six months postimplementation, but was significantly higher at the end of one year. On the other hand, attitudes toward the computer system decreased significantly by the six month postimplementation data collection stage and remained significantly lower at the one year postimplementation data collection stage. There were no significant differences across time for role ambiguity or role conflict. In terms of the 10 work role activities, the most significant difference over time was an increase in time spent in data processing activities. There was also a significant decrease in amount of time spent helping other departments acquire information. The amount of time spent talking on the telephone increased at six months postimplementation and then decreased significantly at one year postimplementation. The amount of time spent filling out forms decreased at six months postimplementation and then increased to baseline levels at the one year data collection stage. There was also a decrease in amount of time spent traveling around the hospital. There were no significant time changes by occupational group interactions.

In summary, the results indicated that job satisfaction increased for this sample of employees learning to work with a medical information system. The three indicators of job stress, role ambiguity and role conflict, remained the same after implementation of the MIS. In terms of job impacts, the two strongest changes were an increase in amount of time spent in data processing activities and a decrease in amount of time spent helping other departments acquire information. The results concerning changes in amount of time spent talking on the telephone were curious. It is surprising that there was an initial increase in time spent talking on the telephone, since the computer system should lessen the necessity of many of the clerical employees' having phone conversations. Anecdotal evidence indicates that employees were, at that point in time, spending an increased amount of time on the phone discussing the computer system itself. By the one year postimplementation data collection stage, the amount of time spent talking on the telephone had decreased significantly.

As discussed previously, reported amount of time spent in work activities is only a crude measure of the job impacts of computerization. There are undoubtedly many more subtle changes in the way that people do their jobs, and these should be studied.

VI. ADAPTATION TO AUTOMATION: DEFINITIONAL ISSUES AND EXPLANATORY VARIABLES

Innovation theory suggests that no matter what the innovation is, or how potentially valuable the innovation is, some people will not like it, at least initially (Brewer, 1980). Some people simply do not adapt well to change. Implementation of a medical information system typically requires individuals to make major changes in the way that they do their work. No matter how clearly useful and valuable the MIS will be, not everyone will like it or be happy with it. Besides requiring major changes in work patterns, implementation of an MIS is also a trial-and-error process. The hardware and software must always be fine-tuned for each hospital, since many flaws and bugs in the system emerge only during the first few months of use. For those individuals who are negative toward the system to begin with, the problems and flaws which crop up during implementation will serve only to reinforce their attitudes toward the system. Therefore, when an MIS is implemented, there exists a strong potential for organized resistance to the system and, perhaps, even for attempts to sabotage the system (Dowling, 1980; Hodgdon, 1979; Zaltman, Duncan, and Holbek, 1973). Thus, it is important that individual adaptation to medical technology be measured and studied in order to help us better understand the process involved with learning to work with this type of technology, and begin to understand how to foster improved acceptance of new technologies.

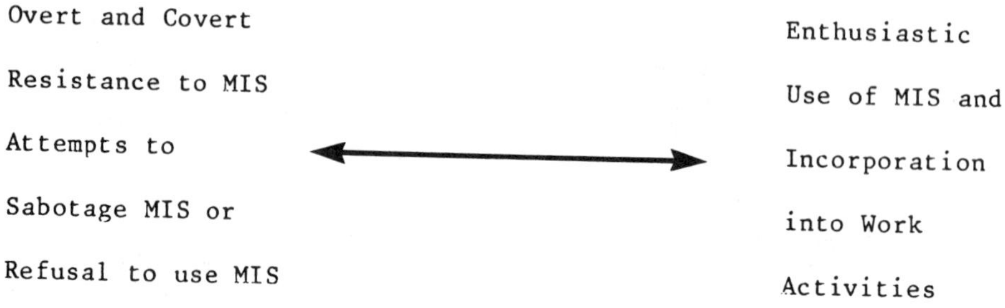

FIGURE 1 Continuum of personal adaptation.

A. Conceptualizing Adaptation

Several papers have been written on the topic of resistance to automation (Dowling, 1980; Hodgdon, 1979; Zaltman, Duncan, and Holbek, 1973). It is our contention that resistance is the negative pole of a continuum of adaptation, with willing and enthusiastic use of the system representing the positive pole of the continuum. A thorough understanding of the adaptation process must involve the study of individuals who fall along this continuum. Figure 1 illustrates this continuum.

The negative pole of the adaptation continuum represents resistance to the MIS, which would include refusal to use the MIS, complaining about the MIS, circumventing the MIS if possible, or even attempts to sabotage the system. The positive pole is characterized by enthusiastic and willing use of the system, helping others to learn to use the system, and readily incorporating it into work activities.

The average user probably falls somewhere in the middle of the continuum. This person is willing to cooperate, but is not very enthusiastic about the system and will reserve judgment until implementation is completed.

How a person adapts to a new technology is a function of many different factors. Interaction theories of human behavior provide a framework for understanding the interplay of these factors. Interaction theory states that behavior is a function of the individual in interaction with his or her environment (Moos and Insel, 1974). In other words, what a person does is determined in part by forces originating within himself or herself (internal) and in part by forces originating from the environment (external). The internal forces are basic personality characteristics, past experiences, and attitudes about and perceptions of the world. The external forces are social forces, information presented, and characteristics of one's environment. These forces interact to determine the way that a person will respond to computerization. This interplay is described in Figure 2.

There are several individual or personal characteristics which have been suggested as being relevant to adaptation to automation. Theses are as follows:

1. Individual Characteristics

a. Attitude Toward Computers

People tend to have opinions about many things, so it is to be expected that each of us may hold some type of opinion about computers. Even those who have had little or no

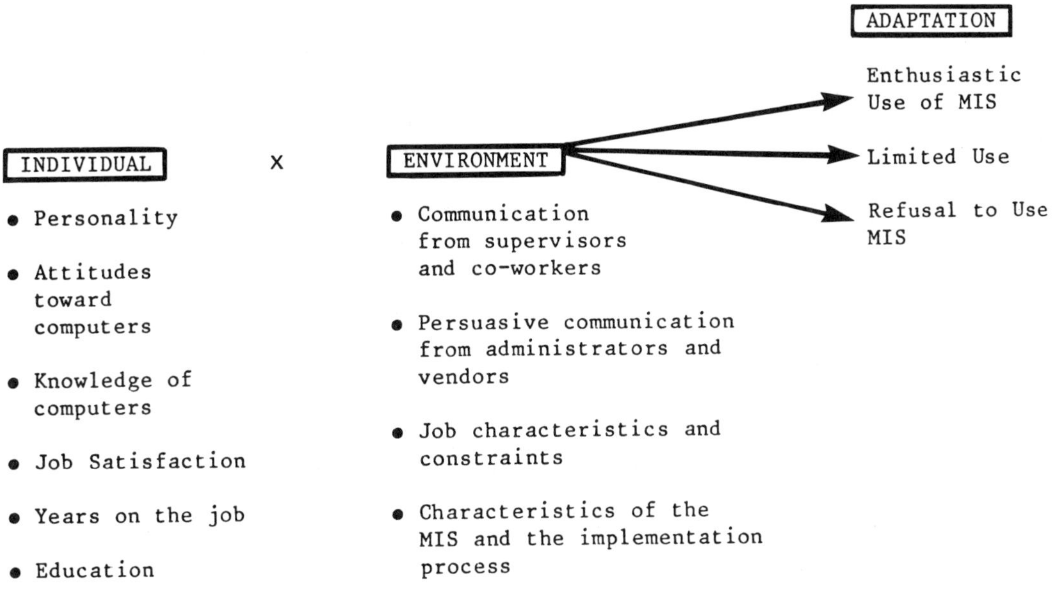

FIGURE 2 Interaction perspective.

exposure to computers usually feel quite willing to express an opinion about them. Prior to exposure to computers, individuals may possess general or stereotypic attitudes toward computers. Once they have begun to work with a specific computer system, they then develop attitudes and opinions about that specific system. An individual can have different attitudes toward computers in general than toward a specific computer system (Kjerulff and Counte, 1984).

There have been quite a few studies involving the measurement of attitudes toward computers. The underlying assumption of this body of research is that attitude is a reflection of adaptation. That is, individuals who are positive toward computers will adapt well to a particular computer system, and those who are negative toward computers will adapt poorly. Although this is not an unreasonable assumption, there are so many factors of potential relevance to adaptation to computerization, that relying solely on a measure of attitude to gauge employee acceptance can be very limiting. One must first begin to ascertain the extent to which attitude is, in fact, a relevant force in the adaptation process (Kjerulff and Counte, 1984, 1986).

b. Personality

Champion (1975) has suggested that personality may play a role in the way that an individual responds to automation. We would like to refine this hypothesis, by suggesting that different personality traits may be relevant to adaptation to automation among different groups of individuals. For example, among scientists, who have the option of developing expertise in a wide variety of computer technologies, perhaps achievement motivation would be a pertinent personality trait. Scientists, who are high on achievement motivation, would be particularly active in learning new computer technologies in order to increase their level of productivity. Among groups characterized by an hierarchical status structure, individuals high on the need for social recognition and approval from others might be particularly motivated to become proficient with a new computer system. Across all groups, a basic willingness to accept change in one's life and an enthusiastic willingness to learn new skills would help one adapt to computerization.

Nearly every type of computer requires a fairly high degree of structure in the way that people must interact with it. It is suggested, therefore, that individuals who are perfectionists, meticulous, and willing to accept structured constraints on the job (for example, rules) will adapt well to the demands of automation.

c. *Knowledge of Computers*

It is not unreasonable to assume that individuals who know something about computers or have some previous computer experience will feel less trepidation when they are expected to learn to use a new computer system than individuals with no previous computer experience or knowledge of computers. It is also possible, though, that if they are knowledgeable about one MIS and are switching to a new MIS, they will be more critical, because they are more sophisticated in their expectations.

d. *Personal Characteristics*

Certain characteristics, such as age and educational level, have been found to be related to attitudes toward computers (Melhorn, Legler, and Clark, 1979; Startsman and Robinson, 1972). Years on the job and previous work experience could also contribute to the way that a person adapts to a new computer system.

e. *Job Satisfaction*

It is suggested that individuals who are happy with their jobs will be more willing to stick with their jobs through the change and upheaval expected to occur when an MIS is implemented. It is also possible, however, that if they are happy with their current jobs, they won't want anything to change.

2. Environmental Characteristics

There are many forces in the environment of potential relevance to the way individuals respond to a new computer system. These are described as follows.

a. *How the System Is Introduced*

The manner in which the system is implemented, the way that the system is introduced to employees, the extent to which the employees are part of the decision-making process, and the training procedures used should be highly relevant to the extent to which the employees are willing to adapt to the new system (Fisher, 1984; Kjerulff et al., 1984; Ochs, 1984). It has been frequently contended that employees at all levels like to feel that they have been part of the decision-making process concerning the choice of an MIS and the various options to be put on the system (Rayman, 1984; Weaver and Johnson, 1983).

b. *One's Social Network*

The prevailing attitude and level of adaptation that one's peers adopt, or that is adopted by individuals or groups of people one respects, should be an influential factor in determining how an individual will respond to the new MIS. Anderson and Jay (1984) examined patterns of referral and consultation between physicians and identified specific groups of physicians who tended to perform similar roles in the social network. Some of these groups were heavy users of the MIS, while other groups were not. Use of the MIS seemed to be closely related to membership in a group. The researchers suggest that computer use may be partially a matter of consensual validation among physicians, with physicians on the periphery of the social network or in isolated groups being slower to adopt the new technology.

For clerical employees, it is not unlikely that the attitude expressed by each supervisor toward the new MIS would have an impact on the degree of commitment and enthusiasm felt by the employees in each work unit.

c. *Job Characteristics*

There are several job characteristics which would be expected to be relevant to the adaptation process. In the research reported by Counte, Kjefulff, Salloway, and Campbell (1982, 1986), there were differences in level of adaptation between shifts, with people on the day shift experiencing lower levels of adaptation. These differences persisted over the course of a year after implementation of the MIS under investigation. These results will be described in more detail in the next section. Other factors, such as the stress level, role conflict, and role ambiguity, which normally characterize a specific position or department, could also influence the extent to which individuals are capable of coping with the added demands of learning to use and incorporate a new computer system. If an individual's position is highly demanding, he or she simply may not have the time to learn to use the MIS and become comfortable with it.

An individual's position itself may be a determining factor in the extent to which he or she learns to use the new MIS. For the vast majority of currently implemented medical information systems, there is little or no use by physicians or nurses (Grams, 1984). The majority of work done on the typical MIS is done by clerical employees. Usage of the MIS by administrators and clinical staff varies greatly from one setting to the next.

d. *Characteristics of the Innovation Itself*

Attributes of the MIS will clearly have a major impact on the way individuals adapt to it. If the MIS is, in fact, functioning poorly, then adaptation to it is inappropriate and counterproductive. The appropriate response to a poorly functioning MIS is organized resistance. Organized resistance would include documenting the system's problems and complaining about these problems to the appropriate administrators.

Assuming that the MIS is functioning more or less adequately, there are still many characteristics of the way that it functions that may have an impact on the ease with which people are able to adapt to it. It may be that within certain programs on an MIS, specific screens are difficult to work with, or certain procedures are difficult to accomplish. One MIS may be less user-friendly than another or require more memorization or training in order to be able to use it proficiently.

B. Studying Adaptation to Computerization

Earlier, we described a study of the long-term impacts of a medical information system. As part of this study, the process of employee adaptation to the new MIS was also examined. As described previously, 68 employees were chosen randomly from a list of 305 employees who had been scheduled to be trained to use the ADT system. Data were collected from these employees at four points in time: prior to training, after training but prior to implementation, six months after implementation, and a year after implementation. At the two data collection stages prior to implementation, measures were taken of attitude toward computers, personality, job satisfaction, and other personal characteristics (such as age and educational background) which the authors hypothesized would be relevant to adaptation to the MIS. Adaptation to the MIS was then measured at six months and one year postimplementation. In the following sections, the questionnaires used to measure adaptation will be described, and the predictors of adaptation will be explained in more detail, as will the results of statistical analyses used to predict adaptation at six months and one year after implementation of the MIS.

1. Measurement of Adaptation

Adaptation to the new MIS was measured by means of two separate instruments. One instrument was completed by the employees, while the other instrument was completed by each employee's supervisor.

The questionnaire given to the employees consisted of two subscales, which we called the "use scale" and the "change scale."

1. *The Use Scale.* The use scale consisted of four multiple choice items. These items were as follows: (1) "How frequently have you had problems with the MIS since implementation?" (2) "If you could do away with the MIS and go back to the old way of doing things, would you?" (3) "How frequently do you find it necessary to bypass the MIS and use the old way of doing things?" (4) "How frequently do you feel like hitting the MIS terminal or breaking a light pen?" There was considerable variation in answers to each of these questions. Responses to these questions are described in more detail elsewhere (Kjerulff et al., 1983).
2. *The Change Scale.* The change scale asked the question "How has the MIS changed your job?" Then, the cue "This MIS has made my job" was given, and subjects rated changes in their jobs using five seven-point semantic differential style items: "more difficult/easier," "more interesting/less interesting," "less stressful/more stressful," "more fun/less fun," and "more pleasant/less pleasant."
3. *The Behavioral Scale.* Each person in the study was also rated by his or her supervisor concerning observable adaptation behaviors. There were six positive behaviors, such as "praising the MIS," and six negative behaviors, such as "increased absenteeism or tardiness." Negative items in each of the three scales were reversed, and total scores computed. Cronbach's alpha, a standard measure of reliability, was computed for each scale. The alpha coefficient for the use scale was 0.79; for the change scale, 0.82; and for the behavioral scale, 0.80. These coefficients are quite acceptable and indicate good internal consistency for these scales.

Table 1 indicates the minimum and maximum possible for each scale, as well as the means for the employees at six months and one year postimplementation. Each of the scales was scored such that the higher the score, the more positive one is toward the MIS. One can see from the table that for the use scale, the employees reported relatively few problems. For the change scale, the results indicated that the MIS had not changed people's jobs a great deal. The mean on the behavioral scale indicated that in general,

TABLE 1 Adaptation Scale Scores

Adaptation scale	Possible minimum	Possible maximum	Six-month mean	One-year mean
Use scale	4	21	16.68	17.16
Change scale	5	35	22.01	23.55
Behavioral scale	12	48	39.25	40.23

there had been some problems among employees learning to use the MIS, but not an extreme number of problems. It was somewhat surprising that there was almost no change on the adaptation scores from six months to one year postimplementation. Presumably, individuals have reached a level of adaptation at six months after implementation that does not change to any great degree. It is also possible that a significant increase in level of adaptation does not occur until after one year postimplementation.

2. Prediction of Adaptation

By the first postimplementation data collection stage (six months postimplementation), there were 53 of the original 68 subjects left. Adaptation was measured at that point, using the three adaptation scales described above. Stepwise multiple regression with hierarchical inclusion was then used to examine the effects of several predictors and their combined explanatory power. The predictors used were as follows:

a. Predictors of Adaptation

1. *Attitude Toward Computers in General.* A 20-item semantic differential inventory was developed by the authors to measure general or stereotypic attitudes toward computers. At the time of the first data collection stage (prior to implementation), none of the employees had received any training on the MIS. This inventory is described in more detail elsewhere (Kjerulff and Counte, 1984).
2. *Attitude Toward the MIS.* After training, but prior to implementation, the employees in the study were given a questionnaire designed to measure their attitudes toward the specific MIS that they had just been trained on. This inventory was developed by the authors (Kjerulff and Counte, 1984) and consists of 20 attitude statements. These items express positive or negative opinions of the MIS or potential reactions to the MIS. Sample items are "I plan to avoid using the MIS as much as possible" and "the MIS will increase the quality of care given to patients at the hospital." Subjects could agree or disagree with each statement using a five-point Likert scale ranging from "strongly agree" to "strongly disagree."
3. *Personality.* Two personality scales from the Jackson Personality Research Form (Jackson, 1967) were chosen. The first scale, called change orientation, measures the extent to which an individual seeks and enjoys new things in life. The second scale, called cognitive structure, measures the extent to which an individual is perfectionistic and meticulous, and seeks order in the way that he or she thinks about the world. Each scale consisted of 12 true-false items.
4. *Job Perceptions.* A 20-item job satisfaction inventory was used, as well as two scales designed to measure role ambiguity (the extent to which an individual's job

expectations are unclear) and role conflict (the extent to which an individual is met with conflicting demands on the job). These inventories were earlier described in more detail.

5. *Personal Characteristics.* Several basic background characteristics were also entered into the multiple regression equation, including age, educational level, number of hospitals worked at prior to the current one, and shift the individual worked on. Most of the employees were assigned to only one shift, with very little shift rotation.

There were 14 predictors in each of the multiple regression equations.

b. Results

The 14 predictors were entered into three stepwise multiple regression equations, one for each of the measures of adaptation. The results indicated that there was a different pattern of significant predictors for each of the measures of adaptation. For the use scale, there were three significant predictors—cognitive structure, change orientation, and job mobility (number of hospitals worked at previously). These results indicated that employees who were meticulous and perfectionistic, enjoyed change in their lives, and had previously worked at fewer hospitals experienced fewer problems using the computer system. For the change scale, there were also three significant predictors—attitudes toward computers in general, role ambiguity, and shift. These results indicated that individuals were positive toward the changes the MIS created in their jobs to the extent that they were positive toward computers in general, experienced less role ambiguity on their jobs, and were not on the day shift. There was only one significant predictor of the behavioral scale, and that was shift. These results again indicated that individuals working on the day shift received lower ratings of adaptation by their supervisors. The results are described in more detail elsewhere (Counte et al., 1983, Kjerulff et al., 1982).

As previously described, adaptation was also measured one year postimplementation. Stepwise hierarchical inclusion was again used to examine the effect of each of the predictors on the three measures of adaptation (Counte et al., 1986). The results were as follows: For the use scale, there were three significant predictors—cognitive structure, change orientation, and educational level. These results showed that employees who were meticulous and perfectionistic, enjoyed changes in their lives, and better educated experienced fewer problems using the computer system. For the change scale, there were two significant predictors—attitudes toward the MIS and job mobility. These results indicated that to the extent that the employees were positive toward the computer system itself and had worked at fewer hospitals previously, they were more positive toward the changes the MIS created in their jobs. There were two significant predictors of ratings received on the Behavioral Scale. These were age and shift, indicating that the younger employees received higher ratings from their supervisors and employees on the night or evening shift received higher ratings. Table 2 summarizes the significant predictors of adaptation at six months and one year postimplementation.

c. Discussion

Comparison of the statistical results six months and one year postimplementation shows that some variables persisted in having an impact on adaptation and others did not. The two personality scales, cognitive structure and change orientation, persisted as relevant factors in adaptation as measured by the use scale, despite the fact that they had

TABLE 2 Significant Predictors of Adaptation

Use scale	Change scale	Behavioral scale
Six months postimplementation		
Cognitive structure	Attitude toward computers in general	Shift
Change orientation	Role ambiguity	
Job mobility (–)	Shift	
One year postimplementation		
Cognitive structure	Attitudes toward MIS	Shift
Change orientation	Job mobility (–)	Age (–)
Education level		

been administered prior to implementation. For the change scale, attitude toward computers in general was no longer a significant predictor, but attitude toward the MIS became a significant predictor at a year postimplementation. This finding indicates that stereotypic attitudes workers held prior to implementation played a less significant part in predicting satisfaction with the changes the MIS made in their jobs, and attitudes specific to the MIS itself began to play a stronger role over time.

Job mobility was a significantly negative factor in predicting responses to the use scale at six months postimplementation. At one year postimplementation, job mobility was a significant negative predictor of responses to the change scale. This result indicates that employees with higher levels of previous job mobility initially report more problems with using the system and that they are, over time, less content with the changes the system has made in their jobs.

The employees' shift continued to play a significant role as concerns supervisor ratings on the behavioral scale, with lower scores continuing on the day shift. These results are easily understood, since the majority of the downtime, slow response time, and other systems problems occurred on the day shift, during the mid-afternoon, peak demand hours. These problems caused considerable discontentment among the employees on the day shift.

There were two variables which became significant predictors of adaptation at a year postimplementation, which had not appeared relevant at six months postimplementation. These were age and educational level, suggesting that in this sample, those employees who were younger and better-educated had adapted somewhat better than their older, less-educated peers.

d. Conclusions

Several conclusions can be drawn from this line of research. These are as follows:

1. Adaptation to computers is multidimensional. There are many different facets to adaptation. The research described in this section focused on three aspects of adaptation:

perceived problems using the system, satisfaction with the changes the system created in jobs, and overt behaviors toward the system. Another measure of adaptation, which Anderson and Jay (1984) and other researchers have used, is actual level of use of the system (as measured by the system). If it is possible to measure actual use, a very clear picture can be derived as to who is using the computer and to what extent. However, in some hospitals, there is a great deal of exchanging of passwords. Individuals simply leave the terminal logged on to one person's password, and many people use the terminal. It appears, therefore, that one person has been using the terminal for many hours, when, in fact, many people may have used it. In that case, it is difficult to get an accurate measure of individual use of the system.

2. Several factors persisted as significant predictors of adaptation from six months through a year postimplementation. The two personality scales, orientation toward change and cognitive structure, continue to be significant predictors of the use scale. The employees on the day shift continued to receive lower evaluations from their supervisors on the behavioral scale. At six months postimplementation, stereotypic attitudes toward computers was a significant predictor of responses to the change scale. At one year postimplementation, they were no longer significant predictors, but were replaced by attitudes specific to the MIS. Job mobility persisted in being a negative influence as concerns adaptation, but changed from being a significant predictor of responses to the use scale, to being a significant predictor of responses to the change scale.

3. Several new factors emerged at one year postimplementation that had not been significant predictors at six months postimplementation. These new factors were age and educational level, with better-educated employees reporting fewer problems with the system, and older individuals receiving lower ratings from their supervisors.

In summary, it appears that a variety of factors are relevant to the process of adaptation to a new computer system. These factors are both individual (such as personality and attitudes) and environmental (such as shift). Suggestions for fostering acceptance of a new system will be discussed in the following section.

VII. SUMMARY AND DISCUSSION

A. Technological and Human Issues in MIS Planning

This chapter has focused on three goals. The first has been to increase the reader's appreciation of the growth of the medical information system industry. Second, we have discussed current and potential applications of MIS in health care organizations. Finally, we have noted the importance of understanding the factors that affect the effective implementation of such systems to organizational researchers and managers.

From this, we have reached a number of conclusions. Our review of research and expert opinion suggests that the introduction of the MIS has changed the very basic organization and functions of health care systems. It has increased access to data in ways that not only provide more information, but provide integrated information. This has led to improved inventory control, cost capture, cost control, billing, financial planning, and policy-making, to say nothing of simply improving the quality of patient records.

In many ways, these systems have changed the nature of work for employees in the hospital. In so doing, they have changed the skills and even the temperments required of workers. These changes show up in attitudes toward computers, job satisfaction, and attitudes toward the specific MIS. The nature of the workplace has been changed. We can expect, then, that those whose skills and attitudes make them most adept at the new forms of work implemented with the MIS will remain on the job, while those intimidated by computers and unable to adapt will eventually leave.

An additional change is in the nature of interaction between employees. Interaction frequency, mode of interaction, and content of interaction all may be changed by the MIS. In some cases, the MIS replaces the interaction itself, replaces contact via the telephone or the mail tube, and changes interaction from the search for information to verification of information that is already in hand. Of most interest is the change in the frequency of interaction between levels of the organization. As clerks become gatekeepers to the system for nurses and physicians, they accrue power and self-esteem. This finding may explain the reason that job satisfaction appears to increase among employees after implementation, despite negative attitudes toward the MIS itself.

Given the extensiveness of these changes, it appears that successful implementation of an MIS requires several steps: (1) It is imperative that prior to implementation, both technological and human dimensions be carefully planned. (2) Once a system is introduced, affected employees must be carefully monitored. (3) Accurate appraisals of the impact of the system need to be made from both a systems perspective and the perspective of individual employees. These issues are especially important when one realizes that the implementation of an MIS is probably a first step in the successive implementation of a number of new systems over the life of a hospital. Employee acceptance and effective use of new generations of MIS technology may be molded by the first experience.

B. User Expectations and MIS Planning

Many hospitals throughout the United States are currently at one stage or another of implementation of a medical information system. Generally, these systems take two to five years to be fully implemented. Quite frequently, implementation is behind schedule (often several years behind schedule). There are several reasons for this. Many of the current vendors in the MIS field are new companies that are developing and modifying software as they go along. Software development is very labor-intensive and tends to take much longer than people expect it to. New software must also undergo extensive modification until it is ready for use. A second reason implementation is often behind schedule is that a medical information system is very complex, involving the coordination of many subsystems. Decisions about the design and coordination of each of these subsystems must be made to the satisfaction of each hospital department. The pattern of political clout in a hospital often influences the type of system chosen and the order of implementation of each component of the system.

The MIS market is very competitive, with a handful of vendors competing for dominance in the field. A hospital's decision about which of several vendors to choose from much depends upon which vendor can make the biggest promises. The discrepancies between what has been promised and what can be delivered do not usually become obvious until one vendor has been chosen and the implementation process is well under way. By that time, much time and money have been invested in the chosen vendor, and a decision to switch to another vendor is unlikely.

Ultimately, implementation generally takes much longer than anticipated and the system implemented is generally not as sophisticated as the hospital had been led to expect. The MIS field is currently one of high potential and expectations, and there is an enormous underestimation of the complexities involved with the design and implementation of these types of systems.

From the users' perspective, this creates a situation beginning with high expectations. As time passes and the implementation schedule becomes more and more drawn out, the users can begin to become cynical and disappointed. Once the system is implemented, if it does not do what the users expected it to do as readily and as easily as expected, the users will again be disappointed.

The market for choice of an MIS vendor is so competitive, though, that if a vendor chooses to be honest as to what can be promised and by when it can be promised, that vendor may not get the contract.

It is, therefore, up to the hospital or medical center administration to lay the groundwork for realistic expectations among the hospital staff who will be working with the new MIS. This is difficult, because it is very rarely clear what one can realistically expect in terms of when implementation is to take place. There may be a time in the future when implementation of a full-scale MIS is a quick and easy process, but currently it is not. We would suggest, therefore, that administration make it clear to the hospital staff that (1) development, modification, customization, and implementation of the MIS will take several years; (2) it will most likely be characterized by unanticipated delays and problems; and (3) most likely, it will not do everything that they would like it to do. If the staff are truly realistic in terms of their expectations of the MIS, they may, in fact, be pleasantly surprised when it is finally implemented, rather than disappointed.

C. Monitoring the Impacts of a Medical Information System

In addition to carefully planning the implementation of a medical information system, it is very important to systematically evaluate the effects of the system after it has been fully implemented. There are several reasons why such evaluation is important. First, when a system is being purchased from a vendor, a number of potential benefits of the system are visualized and are weighed against anticipated costs. Postimplementation evaluation or monitoring allows for a more precise determination of actual costs and benefits to the host organization. Second, close attention to the effects of an information system allows for early surveillance of problems that may be occurring (such as lower morale among employees because of system breakdowns). This, in turn, should enhance resolution of the problem and prevention of its reoccurrence.

The authors conducted several studies concerning adaptation to an MIS which was implemented at a large medical center in the Midwest. Prior to data collection for this study, the hospital administrators felt that by and large, the staff were quite discontented with the system and were having a great deal of trouble adapting to the system. Our research indicated that only about eight percent of the staff were discontented with the system and were having difficulty adapting to it. This minority, however, was quite vocal and centrally located in the medical center. Only after a systematic study was conducted did it become clear that the vast majority of the staff were quite pleased with the MIS.

On the other hand, a systematic study of the same information system implemented in the pharmacy department indicated that there was, during the first six months of implementation, an unusually high rate of employee turnover. Further analyses indicated that the strongest predictor of who was leaving the hospital was attitudes toward computers, with those who were less positive toward computers significantly more likely to seek employment elsewhere.

Unless systematic research is conducted to assess employee responses to a new system, one cannot obtain a clear and accurate picture of what is occurring with the new system. There are too many individuals and variables involved to allow administrators a quick and easy analysis of what is occurring during implementation of an MIS.

A systematic study is a study conducted in such a way as to decrease the extent to which the results will be biased. There are several characteristics of systematic research which can help a researcher to avoid biased results. These are as follows:

1. If participants in the study are chosen using a random sampling technique spanning the departments involved, this will help to assure that those providing their opinions of the system have not been hand-picked.
2. If the data are collected by researchers who are not associated with the vendor or with the hospital and have no particular stake in which way the results turn out, this will help to avoid results that are biased.
3. If confidentiality is promised to those who are participating in the study, they will be more likely to feel that they can present their honest opinions than if they can be personally identified.
4. If the questions asked of the participants are phrased in such a way that they will allow participants to express the full range of potential opinions toward the system, then participants will not be limited as to what they can say about the system.
5. If unobtrusive and relatively objective data can also be collected—such as frequency of use data collected by the computer system itself, or employee turnover rate during implementation—this will provide an independent source of information as to how the employees are adapting to the new computer system.

D. Global versus Parochial Perspectives on Technology Assessment

Technology assessment as a field or group of evaluative methods has been on the scene for many years. Different types of researchers have contributed to the growth of the field, including management scientists, industrial engineers, sociologists, and economists. As might be suspected by the reader, each of these professional groups has developed its own particular set of major questions of interest and analytic techniques. For example, in the case of medical information systems, management scientists are most interested in effects upon the structure and functional operations of the host organization; industrial engineers are concerned with issues such as improved information flow, effective utilization, and the modifications of work operations; sociologists focus upon the effects of a system on work-related employee attitudes, behavior, and interpersonal relations; and economists are interested in cost savings that might be attributed to the system. The major problem with such "parochialism" is that such restrictions may well lead to a very limited understanding of the actual range of impacts of an information system, and they will likely prevent researchers from understanding the relations between different types of outcomes (for example, perhaps changes in social interaction affect the efficiency of operational procedures). Much more of an emphasis needs to be placed upon multidisciplinary evaluation projects that allow for the determination of a bigger picture than that provided by current strategies.

E. Future Changes in Technology and People

Future attempts to implement medical information systems in health care organizations, especially 10 years from now and beyond, will likely be affected by two significant developments. First, there unquestionably will continue to be improvements in the technology itself that will radically improve access to a system and employee utilization. There is already substantial evidence that systems are becoming increasingly easy to use because of the advent of user-friendly programming and voice-recognition input devices. Second, the amount of computer literacy in the general population is increasing due to the wider prevalence of information systems and frequent exposure at every level of the educational system to computer utilization. Thus, in the future, it is quite conceivable that given the computerization experience that people will be acquiring, there will be a lower likelihood of resistance because of personal unfamiliarity. On the other hand, a computer-sophisticated populace may well be much more demanding due to their computer expertise and skills. This may pose a different type of problem to health care organizations of the future.

In the future, implementation of a new medical information system will not involve switching from manual to computerized procedures, but switching from one type of computer system to another. Research on the impacts of computerization will focus less on the people impacts of computerization and more on the pros and cons of one type of computer system versus another. Nearly everyone employed in a hospital or medical center will be computer-literate, and adaptation will concern the ease with which individuals can switch from one type of computer system to another.

Regardless, there is every reason to predict that computerized information systems will become an increasingly common part of health care organizations. It is hoped that future studies of the implementation of such systems will lead to an improved understanding of the dynamics of planned technological change and what steps can be undertaken by health care organizations to maximize the benefits that they and their employees receive from implementing information systems.

REFERENCES

Allen, B. (1982). An unmanaged computer system can stop you dead, *Harvard Business Review, 60*: 77.

Anderson, J. G., and Jay, S. J. (1985). Computers and clinical judgement: The role of physician networks, *Social Science and Medicine, 20*: 969.

Anderson, J. G., and Jay, S. J. (1984). Physician utilization of computers: A network analysis of the diffusion process, *Journal of Organizational Behavior Management, 6*: 21.

Austin, C. J. (1983). *Information Systems for Hospital Administration*, Health Administration Press, Ann Arbor, Michigan.

Austin, C. J., and Greene, B. R. (1978). Hospital information systems: A current perspective, *Inquiry, 15*: 95.

Barrett, J. P. (1975). *Evaluation of the Implementation of a Medical Information System in a General Community Hospital: Final Report,* Battelle Laboratories, Columbus, Ohio.

Brady, N. A., and Bergstein, M. E. (1978). Hospital information systems: A management perspective, *Topics in Health Care Financing, 4*: 93.

Brewer, G. D. (1980). On the theory and practice of innovation, *Technology in Society, 2*: 337.

Campbell, D. T., and Stanley, J. C. (1963). *Experimental and Quasi-Experimental Designs for Research*, Rand McNally, Chicago.

Champion, D. J. (1975). *The Sociology of Organizations*, McGraw-Hill, New York.

Christman, L. P., and Counte, M. A. (1981). *Hospital Organization and Health Care Delivery*, Westview, Boulder, Colorado.

Counte, M. A., Kjerulff, K. H., Salloway, J. C., and Campbell, B. C. (1983). Implementation of a medical information system: Evaluation of adaptation, *Health Care Management Review, 8*: 25.

Counte, M. A., Kjerulff, K. H., Salloway, J. C., and Campbell, B. C. (1985). Implementing computerization in hospitals: A case study of the behavioral and attitudinal impacts of a medical information system, *Journal of Organizational Behavior Management, 6*: 109.

Counte, M. A., Kjerulff, K. H., Salloway, J. C., and Campbell, B. C. (1986). Adapting to the implementation of a medical information system: A comparison of short term vs. long term findings, *Journal of Medical Systems, 11*: 11.

Dowling, A. F. (1980). Do hospital staff interfere with computer system implementation? *Health Care Management Review, 5*: 23.

Farlee, C. (1978). The computer as a focus of organizational change in the hospital, *Journal of Nursing Administration, 8*: 20.

Farlee, C., and Goldstein, B. (1972). *Hospital Organization and Computer Technology: The Challenge of Change*, Health Care Systems Research, New Brunswick, New Jersey.

Fisher, J. H. (1984). "Innovation in Medical Systems Design: The Computer-Human Interface," Proceedings of the Eighth Annual Symposium on Computer Applications in Medical Care, pp. 561-563.

Fleischer, M., and Morell, J. A. (1985). The organizational and managerial consequences of computer technology, *Computers in Human Behavior, 1*: 83.

Frederiksen, L. W., and Riley, A. W., and Myers, J. B. (1984). Matching technology and organizational structure: A case study in white collar productivity improvement, *Journal of Organizational Behavior Management, 6*: 59.

Goldstein, B., and Farlee, C. (1973). How hospital information systems change the organization of hospitals, *How to Select a Computerized Hospital Information System* (M. Ball, ed.), Karger, Basel, Switzerland, p. 56.

Grams, R. (1984). *National Survey of Hospital Data Processing: 1983*, University of Florida, Gainesville, Florida.

Grams, R. R., Peck, G. C., Massey, J. K., and Austin, J. J. (1985). Review of hospital data processing in the United States (1982-1984), *Journal of Medical Systems, 9*: 175.

Greer, A. L. (1981). Medical technology: Assessment, adoption and utilization, *Journal of Medical Systems, 5*: 129.

Gutek, B. A., Bikson, T. K., and Mankin, D. (1984). Individual and organizational consequences of computer-based office information technology, *Applied Social Psychology Annual* (S. Oskamp, ed.), Sage Publications, Beverly Hills, California, p. 231.

Hage, J., and Aiken, M. (1965). An axiomatic theory of organizations, *Administrative Science Quarterly, 10*: 289.

Hancock, W. M., Macy, B. A., and Peterson, S. (1983). Assessment of technologies and their utilization, *Assessing Organizational Change* (S. Seashore, E. E. Lawler III, P. Morvos, and C. Cammann, eds.), John Wiley and Sons, New York, p. 257.

Herner, and Company (1970). *The Use of Computers in Hospitals*, National Technical Information Service, U.S. Department of Commerce, Springfield, Virginia.

Hodgdon, J. D. (1979). "ADP Management Problems and Implementation Strategies Relating to User Resistance to Change," Proceedings of the Third Annual Symposium on Computer Applications in Medical Care, pp. 843-849.

Hodge, M. H. (1977). *Medical Information Systems: A Resource for Hospitals*, Aspen Systems, Germantown, Maryland.

Jackson, D. N. (1967). *Personality Research Form Manual*, Research Psychologists Press, Goshen, New York.

Jay, S. J., and Anderson, J. G. (1982). Computerized hospital information systems: Their future role in medicine, *Journal of the Royal Society of Medicine, 75*: 303.

Jenkin, M. (1982). Computerized health information systems in the 1980s, *Medical Informatics, 7*: 1.

Kaluzny, A. D., Barhyte, D. Y., and Reader, G. G. (1978). Health systems, *The Diffusion of Medical Technology* (G. Gordon and G. L. Fisher, eds.), Ballinger, Cambridge, p. 29.

Kjerulff, K. H., and Counte, M. A. (1984). "Measuring Attitudes Toward Computers: Two Approaches," Proceedings of the Eighth Annual Symposium on Computer Applications in Medical Care, pp. 529-535.

Kjerulff, K. H., and Counte, M. A. (1986). A look at the relation between employee attitudes and adaptation to computerization. Unpublished manuscript.

Kjerulff, K. H., Counte, M. A., Salloway, J. C., and Campbell, B. C. (1982). "Predicting Employee Adaptation to the Implementation of a Medical Information System," Proceedings of the Sixth Annual Symposium on Computer Applications in Medical Care, pp. 392-397.

Kjerulff, K. H., Counte, M. A., Salloway, J. C., and Campbell, B. C. (1983). Measuring adaptation to medical technology, *Hospital and Health Services Administration, 28*: 30.

Kjerulff, K. H., Counte, M. A., Salloway, J. C., Campbell, B. C., and Noskin, D. E. (1984). Medical information system training: An analysis of the reactions of hospital employees, *Computers and Biomedical Research, 17*: 303.

Klinger, C. A. (1985). Information systems technology: Coming of age, *Health Care Strategic Management, 3*: 14.

Krobock, J. R. (1984). A taxonomy: Hospital information systems evaluation methodologies, *Journal of Medical Systems, 8*: 419.

Kwon, I. W., Vogler, T. K., and Kim, J. H. (1983). "Computer Utilization in Health Care," American Association for Medical Systems and Informatics Congress Proceedings 1983, Bethesda, Maryland, pp. 538-542.

Lindberg, D. A. B. (1979). *The Growth of Medical Information Systems in the United States*, D. C. Heath, Lexington, Massachusetts.

MacFarlane, S. J. (1982). Computers: The focus is on the patient, *Health Care, 24*: 14.

Melhorn, J. M., Legler, W. K., and Clark, G. M. (1979). Current attitudes of medical personnel toward computers, *Computers and Biomedical Research, 12*: 327.

Moos, R. H., and Insel, P. M. (1974). *Issues in Social Ecology: Human Milieus*, National Press Books, Palo Alto, California.

Morris, D. C. (1986). Information systems: The direction of things to come, *Healthcare Financial Management, 40*: 31.

Ochs, L. J. (1984). "A Case Sudy of a User/Vendor Dispute," Proceedings of the Eighth Annual Symposium on Computer Applications in Medical Care, pp. 567-570.

Office of Technology Assessment, U.S. Congress (1977). *Policy Implications of Medical Information Systems*, U.S. Government Printing Office, Washington, D.C.

Olson, M. H., and Lucas, H. C. (1982). The impact of office automation on the organization: Some implications for research and practice, *Communications of the Association for Computing Machinery, 25*: 838.

Pasmore, W., Francis, C., Haldeman, J., and Shani, A. (1982). Sociotechnical systems: A North American reflection on empirical studies of the seventies, *Human Relations, 35*: 1179.

Randall, A. (1985). Preparing for the '80s and beyond, *Computers in Healthcare, 6*: 38.

Rayman, R. (1981). Manager involvement needed in computer selection, *Harvard Business Review, 59*: 54.

Remsberg, J. S., and Anderson, J. G. (1984). Minnesota hospital manages microcomputer technology, *Hospitals, 58*: 102.

Rizzo, J., House, R., and Litzman, S. (1970). Role conflict and ambiguity in complex organizations, *American Sociological Quarterly, 15*: 150.

Robbins, S. R. (1983). *Organization Theory: The Structure and Design of Organizations*, Prentice-Hall, Englewood Cliffs, New Jersey.

Rousseau, D. M. (1983). Technology in organizations: A constructive review and analytic framework, *Assessing Organizational Change* (S. Seashore, E. E. Lawler III, P. Mirvos, and C. Cammann, eds.), John Wiley and Sons, New York, p. 229.

Salloway, J. C., and Dillon, P. B. (1972). A comparison of family networks and friend networks in health care utilization, *Journal of Comparative Family Studies, 6*: 131.

Salloway, J. C., Counte, M., and Kjerulff, K. (1985a). The effects of a computerized information system in a hospital, *Computers and the Social Sciences, 1*: 167.

Salloway, J. C., Counte, M., and Kjerulff, K. (1985b). Proceedings of the Second Annual Symposium on Computers and Society, pp. 60–71.

Sandrick, K. (1985). Information needs change, *MULTIS, 3*: 10.

Schmitz, H. H., Ellerbrake, R. P., and Williams, T. M. (1976). Study evaluated effects of new communication system, *Hospitals, 50*: 129.

Shaffert, T. K., and McDowell, C. E. (1978). Hospital information systems: An overview, *Topics in Health Care Financing, 4*: 1.

Smith, P., Kendall, L., and Hulin, C. (1969). *The Measurement of Satisfaction in Work and Retirement*, Rand McNally, Chicago.

Startsman, T. S., and Robinson, R. E. (1972). The attitudes of medical and paramedical personnel toward computers, *Computers and Biomedical Research, 5*: 218.

Suchman, E. A. (1967). *Evaluative Research: Principles and Practice in Public Service and Social Action Programs*, Russell Sage Foundation, New York.

Symposium on Computer Applications in Medical Care (1977–1986). Annual Proceedings.

Weaver, C. G., and Johnson, J. E. (1983). "Nursing Participation in Computer Vendor Selection," Proceedings of the Seventh Annual Symposium on Computer Applications in Medical Care, pp. 472–474.

Whitehead, J. J. (1985). Information systems revolutionizing health care, company's new chief says, *Federation of American Hospitals Review, 18*: 48, 50.

Worthley, J. A. (1982). *Managing Computers in Health Care*, AUPHA Press, Ann Arbor, Michigan.

Zaltman, G., Duncan, R., and Holbek, J. (1973). *Innovations and Organizations: Resistance to Innovation*, John Wiley and Sons, New York.

Index